# Atlantic Communications

Germany and the United States of America
The **Krefeld Historical Symposia**

Previous titles published in this series by Berg include:

German and American Constitutional Thought: Contexts, Interaction
and Historical Realities
Edited by *Hermann Wellenreuther*

Confrontation and Cooperation: Germany and the United States in the
Era of World War I, 1900–1924
Edited by *Hans Jürgen Schröder*

German and American Nationalism:
A Comparative Perspective
Edited by *Hartmut Lehmann and Hermann Wellenreuther*

Visions of the Future in Germany and America
Edited by *Norbert Finzsch and Hermann Wellenreuther*

# Atlantic Communications

## The Media in American and German History from the Seventeenth to the Twentieth Century

*Edited by*
**Norbert Finzsch**
*and*
**Ursula Lehmkuhl**

**BERG**

*The Krefeld Historical Symposia*
Oxford • New York

First published in 2004 by
**Berg**
Editorial offices:
1st Floor, Angel Court, 81 St Celements St, Oxford, OX4 1AW, UK
175 Fifth Avenue, New York, NY 10010, USA

Berg is the imprint of Oxford International Publishers Ltd.

**Library of Congress Cataloging-in-Publication Data**
A catalogue record for this book is available from the
Library of Congress.


**British Library Cataloguing-in-Publication Data**

A catalogue record for this book is available from the British Library.


ISBN 1 85973 679 3 (Cloth)


Typeset by JS Typesetting Ltd, Wellingborough, Northants.
Printed in the United Kingdom by Biddles Ltd, King's Lynn.


**www.bergpublishers.com**

# Contents

## Contents

Comment

**Part III Journalism and the Problem of Modernity**

Comment

**Part IV Producing and Consuming Radio: Political and
Social Dimensions**

Comment

# Contents

vii

# Notes on Contributors

*Markus Behmer* is lecturer at the Institut für Kommunikationswissenschaft und Medienforschung of the Ludwig-Maximilians University of Munich. He specializes in communications and media history, culture communication, current developments in the press and media landscape and international communications policies. He has published *Medienentwicklung und gesellschaftlicher Wandel: Beiträge zu einer theoretischen und empirischen Herausforderung* (2003), as well as articles about critical journalism such as "Gerechtigkeit für Jakubowsky. Oder: Was kann engagierte Publizistik bewirken?" in Bernhard Debatin and Arnulf Kutsch (eds) (2002), *Großbothener Vorträge II*.

*Rosalind J. Beiler* is Associate Professor of History at the University of Central Florida. Her research focuses on Early American History, European Migration to the British American Colonies, and the History of the Atlantic World. She wrote a dissertation on *The Transatlantic World of Caspar Wistar: From Germany to America in the Eighteenth Century* (1998). Her publications include studies on the legal status of German-speaking immigrants in the first British Empire and on Caspar Wistar as a German-American entrepreneur and cultural Broker.

*Menahem Blondheim* teaches at the Department of American Studies and the Department of Communication and Journalism, Hebrew University of Jerusalem. His research and teaching focuses on the nature of social communication systems and their historical development. He is author of *News Over the Wires: The Telegraph and the Flow of Public Information in America, 1844–1897* (1994) and of *The News Frontier: Control and Management of American News in the Age of Telegraph* (1989).

*Volker Depkat* is Assistant Professor of Contemporary History at the University of Greifswald. He has just finished a book on historic caesura and biographical crises of the twentieth century. His research interests include the Mühlenberg Correspondence and German images of America between 1750 and 1850. He is author of *Amerikabilder in politischen Diskursen: Deutsche Zeitschriften von 1789 bis 1830* (1998).

*Thomas Doherty* is Associate Professor of American Studies and Chair of the Film Studies Program at Brandeis University. Among his numerous publications are *Teenagers and Teenpics: The Juvenilization of American Movies in the 1950s* (1988); *Projections of War: Hollywood, American Culture, and World War II* (1993), and *Pre-Code Hollywood: Sex, Immorality, and Insurrection in American Cinema, 1930–1934* (1999).

*Lewis Erenberg* is Professor of History at Loyola University, Chicago. His research focuses on US cultural and social history, the history of American music, culture, and entertainment and the history of gender. He is author of *Swingin' The Dream: Big Band Jazz and The Rebirth of American Culture* (1998), and *Steppin' Out: New York City Nightlife and the Transformation of American Culture, 1890–1930* (1981).

*Norbert Finzsch* is Professor of North American History and Director of the Anglo-Amerikanische Abteilung des Historischen Seminars der Universität zu Köln. He teaches American history of the nineteenth and twentieth centuries, African American history, the history of sexuality, and history and theory. He is author of several books, among them *Von Benin nach Baltimore: Die Geschichte der African Americans*, with James and Lois Horton (1999), and *Die Goldgräber Kaliforniens: Arbeitsbedingungen, Lebensstandard und politisches System um die Mitte des 19. Jahrhunderts* (1982). He is member of the Academic Advisory Council of the City of Krefeld.

*Jessica C. E. Gienow-Hecht* is a member of the Committee on Degrees in History and Literature at Harvard University. As a member of the editorial board of *Diplomatic History* she specializes in the cultural approach to diplomatic history. She teaches American History and Culture of the Nineteenth and Twentieth Centuries. She is author of *Transmission Impossible: American Journalism as Cultural Diplomacy in Postwar Germany, 1945–1955* (1999). She has just finished a book on *Sound Diplomacy: Music, Emotions, and Politics in Transatlantic Relations since 1850.* She received the Krefeld Young Scholars Award of the year 2002.

*M. Michaela Hampf* is member of the Anglo-Amerikanische Abteilung des Historischen Seminars der Universität zu Köln. She is author of *Freies Radio in den USA: Die Pacifica-Foundation, 1946–1965* (2000). She received the Krefeld Young Scholars Award of the year 2002.

*Michele Hilmes* is Professor of Media and Cultural Studies and Director of the Wisconsin Center of Film and Theater Research at the University of Wisconsin-Madison. Her research interests include the history of American broadcasting and issues of race, ethnicity, and gender in the media. She is author of several books among them *Connections: A Reader in US Broadcasting History* (2002); *Only Connect: A Cultural History of US Broadcasting* (2001), and *Radio Voices: American Broadcasting, 1922–1952* (1997).

*Wulf Kansteiner* is Assistant Professor at the History Department of the State University of New York at Binghamton. His academic interests include the representation and collective memory of World War II and the Holocaust in Germany, theory and practice of historiography, historical culture as well as comparative genocide studies. He is author of *Television and the Historicization of National Socialism in the Federal Republic of Germany: The programs of the Zweite Deutsche Fernsehen between 1963 and 1993* (1997).

*Olaf Kistenmacher* is research assistant and Ph.D. student at the Institut für Sozialforschung of the University of Hamburg.

*Kenneth L. Kusmer* is Professor of History at Temple University, Pennsylvania. He teaches American social history since 1870, history of ethnic and racial minorities in America, and recent American history. He recently published *Down and Out, On the Road: The Homeless in American History* (2002), and is editor of a volume on *Black Communities and Urban Development in America, 1712–1990* (1991).

*Sebastian Küster* is a high school teacher. He passed his Ph.D. at the Seminar für Mittlere und Neuere Geschichte of the Universität Göttingen with a thesis on *Dettingen: Eine Schlacht im Licht der Öffentlichkeit*, which will be published in 2004.

*Franklin T. Lambert* is Professor of History at Purdue University, West Lafayette, Indiana. His academic focus is on American colonial and revolutionary era history. He is author of *The Founding Fathers and the Place of Religion in America* (2003), *Inventing the "Great Awakening"* (1999), and *"Pedlar in Divinity": George Whitefield and the Transatlantic Revivals, 1737–1770* (1993).

*Ursula Lehmkuhl* is Professor of North American History and Head of the History Department of the John F. Kennedy Institute for North American Studies, Free University of Berlin. She teaches nineteenth century

American cultural and social history and twentieth century American diplomatic history, and the history of American foreign relations. She is currently working on the social construction of the Anglo-American "special relationship" during the second half of the nineteenth century. She published several books, among them *Theorien der internationalen Politik*, 3rd edition, 2000, and *Pax Anglo-Americana: Machtstrukturelle Grundlagen anglo-amerikanischer Asien- und Fernostpolitik in den 1950er Jahren* (1999). She is a member of the Academic Advisory Council of the City of Krefeld.

*Inge Marszolek* is Professor of History at the Department of Cultural Studies, University of Bremen. She teaches German social and cultural history. Her recent research focuses on the history of denunciation. She is the author of *Die Denunziantin: Helene Schwärzel 1944–47* (1993), and edited a volume on *Radio im Nationalsozialismus: Zwischen Lenkung und Ablenkung* (1998).

*David Paull Nickles* is currently working at the Historian's Office of the US Department of State in Washington DC. His academic interests focus on US diplomatic history, and the history of international relations. He is author of *Under the Wire: How the Telegraph Changed Diplomacy* (2003). He received the Krefeld Young Scholars Award of the year 2002.

*Regina Mühlhäuser* is research assistant and Ph.D. student at the Institut für Sozialforschung of the University of Hamburg. Her academic interests focus on the national discourse on victimization and the individual recollections of affected women in post-war Germany. She is author of *"Das will erzählt werden, genau wie die Kriegserlebnisse der Männer, aber er wollte es nicht hören . . .": Die Massenvergewaltigungen am Kriegsende in Berlin und ihre Widerspiegelung in zeitgenössischen Zeugnissen 1945/46 und lebensgeschichtlichen Interviews 1994–1999* (2000).

*Jörg Requate* is a lecturer in History at the Department of History of the University of Bielefeld. His research focuses on the history of journalism and the social and political role of public opinion in Europe. He is author of *Journalismus als Beruf: Entstehung und Entwicklung des Journalisten-berufes im 19. Jahrhundert: Deutschland im internationalen Vergleich* (1995), and edited a volume on *Europäische Öffentlichkeit: Transnationale Kommunikation seit dem 18. Jahrhundert* (2002).

## Notes on Contributors

*Hermann Wellenreuther* is Professor of History at the Seminar für Mittlere und Neuere Geschichte of the Georg-August-Universität Göttingen. His research interests include early American and colonial history, and American social and economic history of the eighteenth and nineteenth centuries as well as early modern English history. He is the author of numerous books, among them *Ausbildung und Neubildung: Die Geschichte Nordamerikas vom Ausgang des 17. Jahrhunderts bis zum Ausbruch der Amerikanischen Revolution 1775* (2002), and *Niedergang und Aufstieg: Geschichte Nordamerikas vom Beginn der Besiedlung bis zum Ausgang des 17. Jahrhunderts* (2000), for which he received the prestigious Schurmann Prize. He is Executive Director of the Academic Advisory Council of the City of Krefeld.

*Carola Wessel* is a research assistant at the Niedersächsische Staats- und Universitätsbibliothek Göttingen, where she is editing early printings (*Einblattdrucke*) as well as part-time librarian at the university library at Bielefeld. Her research focuses on early American and colonial history. She is author of *Delaware-Indianer und Herrnhuter Missionare im Upper Ohio Valley 1772–1781* (1999), and co-edited a volume on *Herrnhuter Indianermission in der Amerikanischen Revolution: Die Tagebücher von David Zeisberger 1772 bis 1781* (1995) with Hermann Wellenreuther.

*Jürgen Wilke* is Professor of Media Studies at the University of Mainz. His academic interests include nineteenth-century journalism and the history of the developing news market, as well as the history of telegraphy and international postal services. He has published numerous books and articles, among them *Grundzüge der Medien- und Kommunikationsgeschichte: Von den Anfängen bis ins 20. Jahrhundert* (2000). He co-authored *Kanzlerkandidaten in der Wahlkampfberichterstattung: Eine vergleichende Studie zu den Bundestagswahlen 1949–1998* (2000), and *Holocaust und NS-Prozesse: Die Presseberichterstattung in Israel und Deutschland zwischen Aneignung und Abwehr* (1995).

# Introduction

## *Ursula Lehmkuhl*

Communication and communication technology are historical phenomena that more than many others shaped the common history of Europe and America during the last three centuries, and both will have an important impact on the cultural, social, economic and political developments of the future. Hence, when the Academic Advisory Council of the City of Krefeld began to think about an appropriate topic for the first Krefeld Historical Symposium of the new millennium, it did not take long until the idea of organizing a conference addressing the role of the media and communication in the history of the Atlantic World was brought forward and gained momentum. Numerous arguments in favor of this topic were presented. Catchwords such as medialization and Americanization came to the fore, and although everybody tried to avoid the G-word we finally also came up with pointing out the historical importance of the simultaneity of globalization and localization as a trend intimately connected with the history of communication in the Atlantic World.

Communication technology was a crucial catalyst of the historical emergence of structures and interaction patterns that we categorize today as global interdependencies. Mass communication technologies developing since the mid-nineteenth century are part of the process of techno-globalization that historians are just beginning to reconstruct and analyse with regard to its historical foundations. It is not by serendipity that the postmodern theorist David Harvey, in order to describe what globalization means, uses a phrase that he could have borrowed from James Carey or Marshall McLuhan [1] Harvey argues that globalization suppresses time and space. He talks about the "annihilation of space through time" to the extent that politics, diplomacy, society, institutions, and ideas of the nation-state have been transformed into an internationalized, market-oriented, fluctuating, and malleable system.[2]

Almost everything connected to the globalization process and the way it expresses itself relies on mass communication and modern communication technology: the organization of production involving transnational networks, the international financial system, the convergence of ideas, systems, and ways of life (such as democracy, individual rights, customs and habits). Moreover, as Thomas Zeiler argues, the transformations and

1

developments taking place during the "American Century" are rooted in the "technological leaps of transportation improvements . . . Transatlantic cables, then direct telegraph links to Latin America and connections through British cable to Asia, allowed American investors and merchants to communicate faster abroad, thus expanding their markets."[3]

Research on the political, social, and cultural dimensions of communication and the development of media technology is well established.[4] News agencies, mass journalism, radio, film and television have attracted the attention of historians on both sides of the Atlantic. How these media were used as political instruments and how they changed social life are questions dealt with by historical subfields like diplomatic history, social history, economic history, and the history of mentalities. However, the questions how progress in the field of communication technology and the process of techno-globalization influenced the history of transatlantic relations and how it shaped global developments and policies during the "American Century" will be a subject for future research, which we hope that this book will help to stimulate.

The articles published in this volume start from historical insights into national, above all German and American, developments of communication technology, their use and function; these developments are put into the context of Atlantic history from the seventeenth to the twentieth century. What was the influence of period-specific media on the structure and development of the Atlantic World? How did the structure and process of Atlantic communication change? How did common social spheres emerge? How were these media used or abused politically? And how was the history of the Atlantic World influenced by the development of media and communication technology and its use in a transatlantic setting?

The issues raised by the role of the media in history are quite numerous, of course. As a first step it was therefore necessary to narrow down the scope of historical analysis and define specific issue areas and corresponding communication tools that were of particular importance to historical developments in the Atlantic World. We identified five means of communication or media that from a historian's point of view are of particular importance: "speech" or "voice" for the seventeenth and eighteenth centuries, the telegraph for the nineteenth century, mass journalism for the turn of the twentieth century, radio for the 1930s and 1940s and television for the last third of the twentieth century. Accordingly, the book is organized in five parts, each covering a certain time span, period-specific means of communication and specific systematic topics that demonstrate the interplay of communication technology and crucial socioeconomic and sociopolitical developments during the period under scrutiny. Apart

2

from the overarching comparative perspective, the analysis provided by the articles in this book is organized according to a tripartite heuristic concept: chronology, specific historical phenomena central to the period, and the major period-specific means of communication.

The complexity of the research design produced some methodological complications or at least challenges. A minor one was bringing together specialists of different periods in German and American history who have a special interest in both media and communication history. Far more challenging was the problem that we needed specific methodologies and theoretical approaches from communication sciences or cultural studies in order to solve the complex hermeneutic problems involved in the analysis of media other than texts, especially the voice and the image and the interplay of both. Visual literacy is a competence that historians trained in a traditional text-oriented way usually do not have. Hence we needed a disciplinary mix of participants in order to fill this gap and to avoid interpretive and analytical pitfalls. We think that we have been successful in recruiting methodological, theoretical and empirical competencies that complemented one another and even more that developed certain syner-getic effects, the results of which are published in this volume.

In consonance with our preliminary discussions during the planning period, we decided that "speech" in the form of sermons and religious fairs during the seventeenth and eighteenth centuries had to be at the very beginning of our comparative reflections on communication and media in the Atlantic World. "Speech" was a dominant medium of the seventeenth and eighteenth centuries, when priests and preachers as mediators or cultural brokers played a significant role in producing and spreading knowledge about "America". This knowledge and the images of America it transported were of special significance for the settlement of the colonies and the development of specific political and social structures within them. The Pietists, especially, had established networks that could be used for the dissemination of information. The aim of these cultural brokers was above all to spread *"good tidings" at home and abroad*. Starting from this observation we asked the authors contributing to the first part of this volume to focus on the following questions: Were representatives of religious, economic and political elites functionalized in order to transport certain well-defined contents? Was religion used for the construction of a public sphere? If so, what were the constitutive elements of such a public? And what were the differences between the colonial public and the European concept of a representative public? Going beyond our prelimi-nary discussion during the planning period we learned from Sebastian Küster that not only sermons and religious ceremonies but also gun salutes

3

and church bells had a significant communicative function during the seventeenth and eighteenth centuries. The comments from Hermann Wellenreuther and Carola Wessel integrate this exceptional means of communication eloquently and persuasively into a consistent narrative about the way official messages where communicated and spread in America and on German territory during the early days.

The second part of the book is dedicated to "communication in the age of the telegraph", covering a crucial period in the history of our communication system. Within the span of a single lifetime, virtually all of the basic communication technologies still in use a century later came into being: photography and telegraph (1830s), rotary power printing (1840s), the typewriter (1860s), transatlantic cable (1866), telephone (1876), motion pictures (1894), wireless telegraphy (1895), magnetic recording (1899), radio (1906), and television (1923).[5] At the same time the technological competition between the Old and the New World became a driving force for the history of transatlantic relations and to a certain extent signifies the beginning of the techno-globalization process.[6]

Competition and cooperation developed new dimensions with the invention of the telegraph and the concomitant emergence of news agencies. The spreading of telegraph technology was a prerequisite for the commercialization of information. Knowledge and information sold by news agencies, which very soon developed trust-like structures, became more and more standardized. This facilitated those fundamental socioeconomic and sociopolitical changes that James Beniger characterized as the "control revolution",[7] a historical process representing the beginning of the restoration of "the economic and political control that was lost . . . during the Industrial Revolution." Beniger argues that

> before this time, control of government and markets had depended on personal relationships and face-to-face interactions; now control came to be reestablished by means of bureaucratic organization, the new infrastructures of transportation and telecommunications, and system-wide communication via the new mass media . . . [N]ew societal transformations – rapid innovation in information and control technology, to regain control of functions once contained at much lower and more diffuse levels of society – constituted a true revolution in societal control.[8]

Telegraphy, as is shown in the papers presented in Part 2, enhanced the control capabilities of the political and economic centers and reduced the importance of economic or political brokers on the spot, like diplomats and economic agents. The telegraph not only helped to centralize decision-making processes and thus enabled political and economic control of the centers over the distant periphery, the telegraph also narrowed Atlantic distances and furthered the development of economic and political interdependencies in the Atlantic World. The papers presented in Part 2 discuss the following aspects and problems: How were the political and economic decision-making processes during the nineteenth century influenced by the progress in communication technology, above all by the invention of the telegraph? How did diplomatic style change as a result of a growing flow of information and communication via the telegraph? What was the result of the fact that Europe dominated the production and distribution of information during the second half of the nineteenth century? Did the production and distribution system as well as the quality of information change with the foundation of Associated Press or were European styles and structures adapted?

Regaining and centralizing control became a crucial functional element of the technological development of new media and communication systems during the twentieth century. The political control of public opinion by instrumentalizing new media like the yellow press and radio for political purposes is another aspect of the control revolution, which according to Beniger encompasses mainly two essential elements, both of them are at the center of the analyses presented in part three and four: "Influence of one agent over another, meaning that the former causes changes in the behavior of the latter; and purpose, in the sense that influence is directed toward some prior goal of the controlling agent."[9]

With the turn of the century the mass production of print media became possible because of technological innovations in the context of paper production and the printing process. Print media, daily journals and especially weekly magazines became the medium of a critical style of journalism.[10] The Muckrakers, representatives of the political and intellectual elite, criticized the social and cultural consequences of technological progress, thereby highlighting the negative effects of modernization and modernity. Severe criticism and the search for a solution of the social and cultural problems accompanying the industrialization process also characterized the political and intellectual discussions in Germany. On both sides of the Atlantic the process of modernization and the icons of modernity lost their unequivocally positive connotation. The new critical perspectives were transmitted to a broad public via the widely circulated new print media. Journalism, especially muckraking journalism, was the way to discuss problems of modernity critically. Taking these premises into account, part three focuses on the following questions: Which elements of "modernity" and "modernism" were actually criticized and how? What was the relation between social and political criticism?

How did governments react to the new style of journalism? What is the connection between "muckraking journalism" and "muckraking style"? Which functionalities of "muckraking journalism" were adopted in Europe? Was there a "unique" tradition of muckraking journalism in Germany?

During the 1920s and 1930s radio was popularized. Like mass journalism and the muckraking press it served different purposes in the functional sense mentioned above.[11] Education and entertainment were the first among them, but during the 1930s politics became more and more important. The radio very soon became instrumentalized and politically abused. Not only Josef Goebbels recognized the political importance and effects of reaching the people directly via radio; Franklin D. Roosevelt also used the radio to transmit his political messages in the form of "fireside chats" and thus, to a certain extent, became the first media president of the United States. The political instrumentalization of radio became possible also because the attitude of the consumer towards the mass media and media technology changed. Aspects that need to be scrutinized are the relation between "fact and fiction" (one could mention, for example, the reactions provoked by Orson Welles' *The Invasion from Mars*, 1940), and between information and propaganda, which became more opaque. The radio offered also a possibility to articulate political resistance. Atlantic cooperation, for example in form of British and American support for German exile radio, is of special importance in this context. The articles presented in part three cover these two sides of the new mass medium, the aspect of production and of consumption and its respective political and social dimensions by applying Foucault's concept of the *dispositif* adapted by Hickethier for the analysis of the interplay of technology, content and reception patterns.[12] The following questions are addressed: What were the political and social conditions for the production and reception of broadcasts? What was the function and goal of propaganda? Were there competing propaganda ideologies in the context of transatlantic warfare? When and why did an event become newsworthy? How did radio affect social life?

Like the telegraph, radio developed important transnational dimensions. Radio from the very beginning was a hyper-national medium overcoming national borders and cultural constraints.[13] Hence not only radio's effect on social life has to be pinpointed but also its transnational impact. The transnational effects of radio in times of crisis are analysed by Lewis Erenberg who focuses on the role of radio and swing music during World War II, while Inge Marszolek tries to discover the comparative dimensions of the way radio shaped social life in the United States and Germany.

*Introduction*

Looking at radio as a transnational medium involves methodological consideration going beyond a mere comparative approach and tackling the difficult question of what transnational history is and how a transnational approach to the study of broadcasting should look like. How can a transnational approach help us to understand the way non-national influences are operating in times of international crises? What is the function of transnational developments in each nation's domestic setting?

Although television became a mass medium at least in the United States as early as the 1950s, we did not go back that far in television history, but decided to focus on the 1980s and 1990s, when film and television were discovered as a means to communicate the past, especially the historical experience of the Holocaust. To focus on the function of the TV as history educator or the producer of historical knowledge is a fruitful undertaking because of the well-known effect of television as a modernized form of the ancient Greek agora. Television is an arena for debate on public affairs, society, and history. The mass effect of these debates has a deep impact on "public opinion" and the public sphere.[14]

The public and political demand to tackle the psychological and social problems in German society stemming from the experiences during the Third Reich, put forward especially by the student movement, was taken up with far greater effect by the American mini series 'Holocaust', which was shown on German television in 1978, than by high school teachers, history professors or the institutions for political education that were officially in charge of *Vergangenheitsbewältigung* (coping with the past). Television became (among other things) the prime medium to produce public memory and to communicate problems of the past, especially the Holocaust, to a broad audience. Although the medium as well as the topic were the same, Germany and the United States developed specific ways and means to represent the Holocaust on the screen, thereby perpetuating differences in the existing cultures of memory. It was therefore necessary to address certain perspectives dealing with the intricate interplay of television and the visual representation of the Holocaust and public memory: What are German and American specificities of using and presenting history in film and television? How are these specificities connected to the respective national "culture of memory"? How does the representation of history as "fiction" (film) or "document" influence the content of public memory? What are the differences between the United States and Germany with regard to the content of remembering National Socialism and the Holocaust? Is the German way to deal with questions of guilt and expiation Americanized by the reception and the massive impact of the Hollywood way of remembering the Holocaust?

7

The control revolution is certainly one of the most important secular trends accompanying techno-globalization processes induced and led by the media discussed in this volume. It encompasses not only control over the agents and information producers on the political and economic level but also control of demand and consumption. The communication of information about goods and services to a mass audience demanded mass communication technology, like the radio and television but also journals or for example mail-order catalogues, "to communicate information about goods and services to national audiences in order to stimulate or reinforce demand for these products; at the same time, it requires a means to gather information on the preferences and behavior of this audience – reciprocal feedback to the controller from the controlled."[15] One major result of the control revolution had been the emergence of the so-called Information Society. The concept dates from the late 1950s and the pioneering work of an economist, Fritz Machlup, who first measured that sector of the United States' economy associated with what he called "the production and distribution of knowledge."[16] The research presented in this book shows that certain characteristics of the Information Society already existed in the seventeenth and eighteenth centuries. As Carola Wessel summarizes in her commentary: "Most people introduced to us by the articles [in part one, U. L.] were secular leaders or leaders of religious groups. They were used to dealing with the word, be it the word of God or other words, and to communicate messages to other people. In addition, especially the Pietists had established networks that could be used for the dissemination of information. It helped to have commercial ties that could also be used for religious purposes."[17]

Other important media could have been discussed. The telephone and the Internet are just two that immediately come to mind; another one is the Gutenberg press.[18] Although the invention of printing from movable types had a critical effect upon our civilization, we did not deal with the so-called "print revolution" of the late fifteenth century, because a comparative analysis of these effects in Europe and America would not have been feasible for obvious reasons. (In 1492, when Columbus arrived at a tiny subtropical island about 370 statute miles southeast of present-day Florida, Europe was undergoing severe religious, linguistic, and socioeconomic changes, while America was still populated by Indians.) Although there exists some research about Indian traditions of communication,[19] the comparative base and a common topic fitting the tripartite heuristic model of analysis were lacking.

We also deliberately left out the problem of the Internet and cyberspace. As historians, we are aware that the Internet and especially the way it

8

interacts with other more traditional modes of communication will be a central focus of research on the development of the communication system of the twenty-first century. Especially the blending and dual use of different media like video games and the Internet, printed journals and electronic journals, email, instant messaging and telephone, mobile phone and short message service (SMS) will have a deep and critical impact on the communication structures of the future. However, the Internet and the phenomenon of cyberspace did also not really fit the tripartite structure of analysis that we developed for this book. We wanted to combine the analysis of a medium with a certain message it transported, and in this regard television as a medium, which among other things transported the immediate German past into German and American living rooms, was our first choice.

Since this is a book on ways and means of communication and communication technologies, it might be appropriate to consider it as akin to a user's manual. How is one to read or use this book? The answer to this question has to begin with the character and scope of the Krefeld Symposia. These are organized as workshops with about thirty participants who are all actively involved in the conference as paper givers, commentators or chairs. The conference focuses on discussion. All papers are distributed to all participants well ahead of the conference itself. All participants have read the papers before the beginning of the symposium; none of the papers is actually presented. Instead the speakers have 10 minutes to present only major theses of their paper and each commentator has 15 minutes for an opening statement. The general discussion, which is tape-recorded, usually lasts 2 hours per session. After the symposium the authors are encouraged to revise their papers for publication on the basis of the discussion. Tapes are provided for this purpose. Hence the comments and the discussion are at least as important for the final version of the papers – the articles presented in this book – as the authors' research and ingenuity. All participants have shared with us their knowledge and have made substantial contributions, without which this volume would not exist. We therefore suggest the following way of reading this result of scholarly cooperation. Since the commentators have of course summarized key points of the papers, we suggest that those readers who are interested in quick information start with the comments. We hope, however, that they will very soon develop a deeper interest in the papers themselves and finally will get involved in reading them. Those readers who are interested in a particular period or a specific medium or topic presented and analysed might start with that part of the book covering his or her specific interests and go ahead with the other parts later on. The bibliography gives an idea of the scholarship on which papers, comments and interventions by participants in the sessions are based. We hope that this information is useful for those who, while reading the papers and comments, develop an interest of their own in tackling one of the many open questions mentioned in the papers and comments and envisage embarking on a research project of their own. The bibliography will provide a survey of the relevant literature. However, it is also meant for readers who wish to teach a course on aspects of Atlantic communication. The information provided facilitates the preparation of course material and reading lists.

It has been mentioned in previous volumes, but I think that it is worthwhile reiterating: the City of Krefeld generously participated in and financially supported this conference. It is a singular and remarkable effort by an urban community to contribute to national and international scholarship and understanding. Krefeld was and is the only city in Germany and the United States undertaking such an effort, devoting time and energy as well as funds to this scholarly enterprise. This is why special thanks are due to those who are politically responsible and those who are academically involved in preparing the conferences. We also wish to express our gratitude to the Deutsche Forschungsgemeinschaft (German Research Council) who financed the travel expenses of our American participants.

Many hands helped to make the conference and the volume possible. It would be impossible to name them all. Some, however, deserve to be mentioned; first among them Friedhelm Kutz, head of the marketing office of the City of Krefeld. He made us feel not only welcome but at home during our four days in Krefeld. He prepared the necessary ambiance to make fruitful discussions and scholarly interchange possible. Thanks are also due to Stefanie Schneider, who was responsible for the Web presentation of the conference, and who managed the tape recording, copying and distribution of the taped discussions, so that the ideas that were voiced during the intense communication process did not get lost and could be used for the revision of the papers. We also have to thank Stephen Aranha, who helped us prepare the manuscript for the publisher, looking for inconsistencies in footnotes, in spelling and in formatting. He never lost his good sense of humor – even in times when his boss (one of the editors) was torturing him with emails and telephone calls sometimes very early in the morning, because time was running short and the publisher was growing impatient about receiving the manuscript. Last but not least we have to thank Berg Publishers and especially Kathleen May and Felicity Howlett for their amiable way of putting pressure on us, as well as the copy editors of Berg Publishers for their meticulous work on the manuscript. Everybody mentioned here contributed to the final product in a particular way. This book is evidence of successful scholarly teamwork. Thanks to all members of the Krefeld Team 2002.

# Notes

1. Marshall McLuhan, *Understanding Media*, New York, 1964; J. Carey, *Communication as Culture* (Boston, 1989); see also M. Poster, *The Mode of Information*, Chicago, 1990.

2. David Harvey, *The Condition of Postmodernity* (Oxford, 1990), 299, quoted in: Thomas W. Zeiler, "Just Do It! Globalization for Diplomatic Historians", *Diplomatic History* 25 (2001), 530.

3. Zeiler, "Just Do It!", p. 534f.

4. See select bibliography in this volume.

5. James Beniger, "The Control Revolution", in D. Crowley and P. Heyer (eds), *Communication in History: Technology, Culture, Society*, New York, 1999, p. 305.

6. For an overview see Wilbur Schramm, *The Story of Communication*, New York, 1988.

7. James Beniger, *The Control Revolution: Technological and Economic Origins of the Information Society*, Cambridge MA, 1986.

8. Beniger, *The Control Revolution*, p. 305f.

9. Ibid., p. 306.

10. See Michael Schudson, *Discovering the News: A Social History of American Newspapers*, New York, 1978.

11. For an overview over the history of radio see: Asa Briggs, *The History of Broadcasting in the United Kingdom*, London, 1966; Andrew Crisell, *Understanding Radio*, New York, 1986; Susan Douglas, *Inventing American Broadcasting: 1899–1922*, Baltimore, 1987; Tom Lewis, *Empire of the Air: The Men Who Made Radio*, New York, 1991.

12. See Part 3 especially the comment by Michaela Hampf and the article by Inge Marszolek.

13. See the comment by Michele Hilmes.

14. Mark Poster, "The Net as a Public Sphere", in David Crowley and Paul Heyer, *Communication in History: Technology, Culture, Society*, New York, 1999, p. 335.

15. Ibid., p. 309.

16. Fritz Machlup, *The Production and Distribution of Knowledge in the United States*, Princeton, NJ, 1962.

17. See Carola Wessel in this volume.

18. Robert Darnton and Daniel Roche, *Revolution in Print: The Press in France, 1775–1800*, Berkeley CA, 1989; Elizabeth Eisenstein, *The Printing Revolution in Early Modern Europe*, New York, 1983; William L. Joyce et al., (eds), *Printing and Society in Early America*, Worcester, 1983.

19. See Amanda Wood, *Knowledge Before Printing and After: The Indian Tradition in Changing Kerala*, Oxford, 1985.

# Part I
## Spreading "Good Tidings" at Home and Abroad: Media and Mediators during the Seventeenth and Eighteenth Centuries

# 1
# Evangelical Revivals as Communicative Spheres in the Colonial Era

## Frank Lambert

The nature of settlement in British North America encouraged religious pluralism, thus assuring that the Word of God for America would have multiple meanings. Relying on trading companies and individuals to finance and organize individual colonies, the English Crown granted charters that permitted the colonizers to determine religious matters. In addition, some of the adventurers offered extensive religious toleration to attract settlers. Despite the diversity of religious opinion, the colonial period provides three Words that have had wide appeal and lasting influence in the American collective memory. The first, stated most explicitly in the Puritan settlement in New England, is the idea of America as a Christian Nation, expressed by Governor John Winthrop as establishing a "City upon the Hill." The second, voiced by many groups seeking refuge from persecution, particularly in the Middle Colonies, is the notion of America as a Haven of Religious Liberty. And, the third, coming from a number of evangelical groups with rich revival traditions such as German Pietists and Scottish Presbyterians, is the expectation of periodic "Great Awakenings," or extraordinary outpourings of God's grace just as faith seems to be at its weakest.

To explore how various transplanted Europeans interpreted the Word of God as America's Word, this chapter examines three communicative spheres in the colonial period. The first is the private or semi-private sphere of seventeenth-century Puritan New England where the religious faith and practice occurred largely within the confines and under the direction of local congregations. Upon arrival in Massachusetts Bay in 1629, Puritans declared that they had entered into a covenant with God, and as a chosen people they would organize their society as a Christian Commonwealth. That meant establishing ecclesiastical and political institutions that bound their constituents to each other and to God through a series of sacred covenants. At the center was the local congregation, whose members consisted solely of "visible saints," or those who could demonstrate that they were of the Elect. Educated, ordained ministers had the task of ensuring that all local beliefs and practices conformed to Scripture and reason. Moreover, only Church members could participate in political affairs within towns, which functioned as "Christian Utopian Closed Corporate" communities.[1] One of the main responsibilities of ministers and magistrates was to defend religious purity and religious freedom, which to Puritans were the same. Indeed, they defined the latter as freedom from error. One Massachusetts minister, Nathaniel Ward, made clear that those of a different mind should go elsewhere, writing, "all Familists, Antinomians, Anabaptists, and other Enthusiasts shall have free Liberty to keep away from us, and such as will come to be gone as fast as they can, the sooner the better."[2]

The second sphere is that created by the Great Awakening, an ecumenical revival whose inclusive, global perspective challenged exclusive, parochial views and began to move religion into the public realm. While revival services occurred within churches, they also spilled out into the public sphere, into marketplaces, taverns, coffee houses, and public parks. Ordained ministers played an important role, but the laity joined the debate over theological issues and sought to change public policy governing the practice of religion in colonies with establishment laws. Inspired by German Pietists who sought to deepen their own personal faith while also spreading the gospel throughout the world, the revival arrived in America from England as an "imported Divinity" that confronted local ministers with competition while offering the laity choice.[3] The dynamic Anglican itinerant preacher, George Whitefield, was the instrument that brought Americans into the transatlantic revival, and he arrived with two notions that turned the colonial religious world upside down. First, he directed his message at the individual, proclaiming that the "One Thing Needful" was a personal conversion, or, a New Birth experience. By making individual experience authoritative, rather than theological creed or Church covenant, the revivalists strengthened the laity and weakened the clergy. Second, Whitefield proclaimed that the "whole world [was his] parish," thereby ignoring geographical and denominational boundaries within which churches and sects had exercised discipline over their members.[4]

The third sphere was the free marketplace of religion that emerged gradually from the ecumenical revival and found fuller expression during the American Revolution. Dissenters resisted the control of both the clergy of established churches and the political leaders who supported them and insisted that churches should be voluntary organizations with no government support or control and that individuals should be free to choose among competing faiths. Americans were on the move in the eighteenth century with a rapidly growing population expanding westward and spilling over the Appalachian Mountains. Doubling every twenty-five years, the population rose from both a favorable birth rate and from immigration. Most of those arriving voluntarily came from Germany and Scotland, including many evangelicals. Ten of the colonies had some form of religious establishment, but the state-supported Churches lacked the institutional machinery to incorporate and control the growing, more diversified population. Especially along the frontier where the established Churches were weakest, men and women chose among competing sects in a *de facto* free religious market long before the Founders recognized religious freedom as a natural right. The South Carolina Anglican minister, Charles Woodmason, provided a first-hand description of the religious competition he faced in the backcountry as invaders from northern colonies overran his remote parish: "Itinerant Teachers, Preachers, and Imposters from New England and Pennsylvania – Baptists, New Lights, Presbyterians, Independents, and an hundred other Sects – so that one day you might hear this System of Doctrine – the next day another."[5]

In each of the spheres considered, Americans represented themselves in particular ways to Europeans. New England Puritans judged European Protestantism to have become so corrupt by abandoning Reformation principles that "true" Christians should remove themselves from such influence. Cotton Mather made the case in his *Magnalia Christi Americana* (1702) interpreting the Puritan migration as bringing "the WONDERS of the CHRISTIAN RELIGION" from East to West, from the Old World to the New, "flying from the depravations of Europe, to the American Strand."[6] Jonathan Edwards, pastor at Northampton, Massachusetts, considered it noteworthy "that *America* was discover'd about the Time of the Reformation . . . which Reformation was the first Thing that God did towards the glorious Renovation of the World, after it had sunk into the Depths of Darkened Ruin, under the great Antichristian Apostacy." Now with the "new World . . . (as it were) created . . . God presently goes about doing some great Thing to make Way for the Introduction of the Churches Latter-Day Glory."[7] Given that perspective, the best New England Puritans could do for Europe was to offer an example of the possibilities of a Commonwealth based firmly on the Word of God and Reformation principles.

But, when the faith of second- and third-generation Puritans weakened, they found hope for revival of "true piety" in "the Midst of Europe." In a typical jeremiad or warning, Boston divine, John Higginson, called on his parishioners to remember their origins: "New England is originally a plantation of Religion, not a plantation of Trade."[8] While Cotton Mather reminded readers that they had failed to live up to the lofty mission of their forefathers, he also directed them to look back to Europe, specifically to Halle in Lower Saxony where a group of German Pietists had dedicated themselves to "advance *True, Real, Vital Piety*, and such a *Knowledge* of a Glorious Christ, as will bring the Children of Man, into the *Service* of their only Saviour." Mather noted that the small band of dedicated Pietists had developed a global reach through establishing schools, colleges, orphan-houses, pharmacies, printing presses, and mission posts stretching from Europe to Africa and Asia. In language that would conjure images of New England's shining "City on a Hill," Mather wrote that the work emanating from Halle "begins to feel a Warmth from the *Fire of God*, which thus flames the Heart of Germany, [and begins] to extend into many Regions." He concluded by hoping that this *"Good News from a Far Country"* would promote *"Right Christianity* and a Glorious Revival of the *Primitive"* or Scripture faith.[9]

It was the third sphere that was most distinctive for America. Britain and Europe had experienced the evangelical revival as well, but, for the most part, strong state Church traditions channeled the movement into existing structures or checked it at the margins. With much closer Church-state relations and more fully developed ecclesiastical institutions, with few exceptions state Churches exercised effective discipline over wayward members. On the other hand, when America's founders sought to create a "more perfect union" in 1787, they viewed the sectarian, pluralistic, and contentious character of American religion as a threat to unity. Their solution was to give the proposed consolidated government no voice in religious affairs. Then, the First Amendment gave constitutional weight to the free market of religion where individuals would have "free exercise" in choosing among competing, voluntary Churches. That meant all claims, including that of America as a "Christian" nation, would be contested through persuasive argument rather than state or church fiat.

## Closed, Covenanted Communities

The preached Word of God stood at the center of Puritan worship. After an opening prayer, scripture reading, and Psalm singing, the pastor would deliver his sermon according to the "Plain Style" that characterized Puritan preaching. He would first read a biblical text, and then explain or "open" it in its context. Then he would proceed to make a "few and profitable points of doctrine out of the natural sense," and, finally, apply "the doctrines rightly collected, to the life and manners of men in a simple, plain speech."[10] It would be difficult to overestimate the place of the sermon in Congregational worship. As one scholar observed, "Puritan life, in the New England theory, was centered upon a corporate and communal ceremony, upon the oral delivery of a lecture."[11] While individuals engaged in daily private devotion centered on Bible-reading, they gathered as a covenanted community to hear the Word of God preached by one educated and called for that sacred task.[12] Though a literate people, New England Puritans believed that "the voice of Christ was made known . . . by the Bible, and then by the Bible as preached from the pulpit."[13]

New England Puritans believed that preaching was the primary means of conveying the Word of God and that sound preaching required sound theological education. Scripture contained truth, but its messages were often hidden or obscure, and someone with a divine calling must "open" the Bible's proper meaning. Thus, a central goal of Harvard was to instruct students intended for the ministry in biblical interpretation. But biblical study involved more than a close reading of biblical texts; it also meant mastering the doctrinal teachings of the giants of Reformation faith who had systematically set forth the Bible's great truths. As one Puritan exclaimed, "What worthy Ministers did that first age of the Reformed Churches yeeld? as *Luther, Calvin, Martin Bucer, Cranmer, Hooper, Ridley, Latymer, &c.* What a wonderfull measure of heavenly light did they of a sudden bring into the Church? and that out of the middest of darknesse and Popery."[14] However indebted the Puritans were to sixteenth-century reformers for ideas and inspiration, they maintained that it was not those mortals, but God's Word itself, that was the "same schoolmaster" of true Christians of all ages. Their primary task as ministers then was that of expounding the Word, and how to do that properly was the heart of the curriculum at Harvard and Yale in their formative years.[15]

To serve the truth, theological education was devoted to honing an intellectual sword that would slay all opposing claims, especially those advanced by papists. While Calvin's thought on such doctrines as the sovereignty of God, predestination, and limited atonement provided raw material for Puritan learning, it was insufficient. What was lacking was what English Puritan Richard Baxter called "method." He believed that "truth should be long studied and diligently elaborated, 'till it be con-cocted into a clear methodical understanding, and the Scheme or Analysis of it have left upon the soul its proper image, by an orderly and deep impression."'" Harvard and Yale students pored over Samuel Willard's *A Compleat Body*, New England's greatest effort in "method," in order to "organize and classify all doctrines methodically before they endeavored to write sermons." Other texts at Harvard and Yale that offered systematic, methodical exposition of all knowledge included William Ames' *Medulla Sacrae Theologiae* and John Wollebius' *The Abridgement of Christian Divinity*. Early in the eighteenth century Cotton Mather recommended a new systematic work, Petro van Mastricht's *Theoretico-Practica Theologia*; within its 1,300 pages "the whole of Christian theology and morality, theory and practice, is laid out with a minuteness and precision that bring a hundred years of methodizing to a stupendous fulfillment."[16]

Armed with a sound biblical education, a graduate was prepared to accept a "call" from a local congregation to become its teacher or pastor. In Puritan New England, churches were local, autonomous communities resting on the Word of God as expressed in two solemn covenants, and it was the minister's primary responsibility to uphold those holy compacts through preaching. The first was the Covenant of Grace wherein God granted his grace to individuals, not because they merited his favor, but because of his own goodness. As Calvinists, Puritans embraced the doctrine of predestination by which God foreordained some to salvation and some to damnation. Because it was to the Elect alone that the Almighty extended the Covenant of Grace, the place of evangelistic preaching within a Calvinist tradition is puzzling for many. Why preach the good news of Christ's sacrificial death to all if God, before human existence, had already decided the ultimate fate of each man and woman? Calvin's answer was that the gospel must be preached to all persons everywhere because the visible Church could not distinguish between saint and sinner. Moreover, while the Church could not guarantee salvation for anyone, it was, in Calvin's theology, "the only route to grace." Unlike some of the eighteenth-century revivalists, Calvin taught that regeneration was a lifelong process rather than a sudden, wrenching "new birth." Growth in grace rested on "a rational understanding of [God's] word as well as on illumination by the Spirit". And the Christian in his or her daily behavior was to strive always for the elusive goal of moral perfection, believing that a life of disciplined faith was a clear indication that he or she was numbered among the elect.[17] It was evangelical preaching then that informed men and women of the possibilities of divine election and convinced them of the insufficiency of their own good works.

The second covenant central to Puritan life was the Church covenant that all members of a local congregation signed. The purpose of this compact was to "knit saints into one visible body." According to a leading Puritan divine, Richard Mather, "Some union or band there must be amongst them, whereby they come to stand in a new relation to God, and one towards another, other then they were in before: or else they are not yet a Church." New Englanders believed that the Church covenant rested on "the Word" and was essential for keeping their faith pure. Puritan minister, John Cotton, declared, "Our principall care and desire is to administer and partake *in all*, and *no more then all*, the ordinances of Christ himselfe, and in all those (so farre as the Lord hath lent us light) in their *native puritie and simplicitie*, without any dressing or painting of humane inventions."[18] Thus, the church covenant served as a constant reminder that the saints subscribed to the authority of God's Word, especially as preached by those called especially for that sacred task.

Church covenants did not, however, protect Puritans from spiritual indifference or even decline within their own ranks. As early as the 1660s, most New Englanders could not meet the exacting requirements for full membership in local Churches, leading a synod of pastors to contrive a "Half-Way Covenant" to tie inhabitants to the local congregation, albeit in a non-voting capacity.[19] Any number of factors contributed to the decline: the lack of an adequate supply of orthodox ministers to serve the rapidly expanding population, especially along the frontier; increased "worldliness" occasioned by growing affluence and the "Baubles of Britain" arriving daily from London; the rationalist teachings of the Enlightenment that elevated human reason at the expense of divine revelation.[20] To some Puritans, the Church was in a deep sleep and needed to be awakened.

While Puritans believed that most of the time God dispensed his grace through ordinary means, such as preaching, prayer, Bible-reading, and public worship, they also held that upon occasion God chose to pour out His mercy through the extraordinary means of revivals. Pastor Samuel Torrey explained in a 1695 election sermon delivered in Boston when and how God attempted to save his people when ordinary means failed:

> At some times, and in some cases God doth in Sovereign Mercy, Save his Churches and People, both from Sin and Judgment, in a more immediate and extraordinary way of working by himself . . . There are certain times and extraordinary cases wherein God thus Saves his People by himself . . . when their Condition . . . is altogether hopeless and helpless.[21]

In the preface to Torrey's sermon, Samuel Willard, pastor at Boston's Old South Church, explained that "when Good men in all Orders find all attempts to recover a Backslidden People awfully to be frustrated," they need not despair because God often intervened to save a people though times are "so black."[22]

Solomon Stoddard, pastor at Northampton, Massachusetts from 1670 to 1725, explained that revival came in two distinct expressions: "sometimes more General and sometimes more Particular." "It is more General," he observed, "when it is throughout a Country, when all Parts of a Land there is turning to God." The only historical example of a general awakening that he cited was "about Luther's time, when some Nations broke off from Popery, and imbraced the Gospel." However, just as an entire nation can experience revival, "sometimes the Country doth generally Decline." Writing early in the eighteenth-century, Stoddard lamented that the American colonies were currently in such a state. Not all revivals were extensive; in fact, most were not. "Sometimes this reviving is more Particular," he stated, "when in some particular Towns Religion doth revive and flourish." The New Testament described local awakenings at Sardis and Laodicea. And, referring to the revival then underway in Northampton as he wrote, Stoddard added, "So it is in this Case."[23]

Revivals became a regular feature of Puritan experience among New England congregations, none more so than that at Stoddard's congregation in western Massachusetts. Under his leadership and that of his successor, his grandson, Jonathan Edwards, parishioners witnessed eight "harvests" or revivals over the period 1689 to 1735. Each followed the same pattern. First, the minister recognized that the congregation had lapsed into an "extraordinary Dullness in religion," and that the youth of the upcoming generation was filled with "*Pride, Scornfulness and Ungovernableness.*" Second, the pastor organized special prayer meetings where men and women offered "Extraordinary Prayer for the Revival of Religion and the Advancement of Christ's kingdom on earth." Third, in addition to "*praying them down,*" Stoddard and Edwards promoted revivals by "*preaching them up.*" For Stoddard the beginning point in good preaching was to scare the hell out of people – that is, to convince men and women that their sins would result in eternal damnation, and that they were powerless to save themselves. Sinners must understand that they were totally dependent upon a merciful God for their salvation. Fourth, God did the rest, pouring out his grace during an "extraordinary" season, a "Time where there were no small appearances of a divine Work . . . and a considerable Ingathering of Souls."[24]

Thus, when yet another revival began in 1733, it had all the appearance of those that preceded it: a local awakening that had become part of the congregation's rich evangelical tradition. However, this time what began with all the appearance of a particular revival, was but one of several awakenings in the Atlantic World that would merge into a general revival and reshape New England's religious communicative sphere. Ironically, what made the 1733 revival different from early awakenings at Northampton was not Edwards' powerful preaching but printed reports of the revival that circulated far beyond the Connecticut Valley. When Boston pastor, Benjamin Colman, received Edwards' letter describing the local revival, he sent copies to London Dissenters, Isaac Watts and John Guyse, who replied with a plea that Edwards write a more extensive account of the revival. Colman and his London correspondents were part of an active transatlantic letter-writing network through which evangelicals exchanged reports on local revivals and made suggestions for promoting similar awakenings elsewhere.[25] Upon reading Edwards' expanded revision, Watts and Guyse published it in London in 1737 as *The Faithful Narrative.* In a preface, they wrote, "never did we hear or read, since the first ages of Christianity, any event of this kind so surprising as the present narrative hath set before us." They declared that the work deserved wide circulation, arguing that "certainly it becomes us to take notice of such astonishing exercises of [God's] power and mercy . . . and it gives us further encouragement to pray, and wait, and hope for the like display of his power in the midst of us."[26] Edwards' *Narrative*, especially as it converged with John Wesley's visit to the German Pietists at Halle, inspired the Oxford Methodists, a group of evangelical students dedicated to the practice of piety and the global spread of the gospel. Wesley recorded in his diary: "I read the truly surprising narrative of the conversions lately wrought in and about the town of Northampton, in New England. Surely this is the Lord's doing, and it is marvelous in our eyes." And when George Whitefield arrived in New England in 1740, he desired especially to visit Northampton, "having read in England, an account of a remarkable work of conversion there, published by their Pastor the Rev. Mr. Jonathan Edwards."[27]

# The "Whole World is My Parish"

New Englanders were accustomed to revivals but they were ill prepared for the "great and general awakening" that descended upon them in 1740, arriving like the mighty rush of wind associated with the first Day of Pentecost. All their previous revivals had been "particular" or local affairs under the direction of the settled ministry; this one was "general" or global and inspired by an outsider. When George Whitefield in 1739 attracted crowds of 20,000, 40,000, and even 60,000 in London's public parks with thousands professing a New Birth or conversion experience, evangelicals believed that a mighty Work of God was underfoot, one as extensive as that of the Reformation. With its growing popularity, the revival became a newsworthy event that garnered front-page coverage in newspapers throughout England and America. A group of New England laymen attested to the effectiveness of the advance publicity in Boston, noting that Whitefield's "Name and Character were very great among us before his Arrival. He had made such a Noise and Bustle in Europe and America, that the Expectations of the People and their Curiosity were very much rais'd both to see him, and hear him preach."[28]

Whitefield lived up to the advance billing. His inaugural sermon in Boston was to an overflow crowd of 4,000 at Benjamin Colman's meeting house. One admirer described his performance in delivering the message of regeneration or New Birth: "he uses much gesture, but with great propriety: every accent of his voice, every motion of his Body, speaks, and both are natural and unaffected. If his delivery is the product of art, 'tis certainly the perfection of it, for it is entirely unconcealed."[29] Crowds continued to grow: 6,000 the next day at South Church and 8,000 at Old Brick Church, with many people at both places unable to enter the overcrowded buildings. As many as could pressed up against the windows to catch a glimpse of the celebrated preacher while others spilled out into the church yard to hear his booming voice. New England's religious structures were inadequate for the popular revival. At one service, as Whitefield prepared to preach, someone in the balcony broke a board to make a seat, and the sound "triggered a panic." Thinking that the gallery was falling, several people jumped onto the crowd below, and before the panic subsided, five people were killed in the crush. Whitefield "remained bent on preaching" and moved the service to Boston Common where he preached in a driving rainstorm. Remarkably, no one in the audience left as the evangelist "drew from the event powerful applications" about death, sin, and the necessity of the New Birth.[30]

Historians have offered many explanations for why thousands thronged to hear Whitefield. Two seem particularly noteworthy for analysing changes in America's religious communicative sphere. First, he enabled men and women to participate in a much larger evangelical community than that afforded by their local parishes. Clearly something grand and rare was occurring in salvation history, and Whitefield invited Americans to become part of it. Through hearing the same sermons that the evangelist had delivered in London in similar settings and by reading of similar

responses by audiences throughout the Atlantic World, colonial evangelicals joined an "imaginary" evangelical community of far-flung
members, most of whom would never meet each other but were aware of
their shared experiences.[31] Global in scope and ecumenical in nature, this
awakening could be the long-hoped-for and prophesized Work of God that
would complete the Reformation. Second, while enlarging their vision and
religious community, Whitefield empowered individuals by making the
necessity of the New Birth the single emphasis in his sermons. Moreover,
he dismissed the importance of denominational distinctions and doctrinal
debates. To him, regeneration took place through a divine infusion of
grace within the individual, and thus, that experience, not subscribing to
a church covenant or agreeing with dogma, was authoritative in the crucial
matter of salvation.

The Puritan clergy were divided in their response to Whitefield and the
Work of God that he proclaimed. For one thing, Whitefield introduced a
new popular communicative style, "a rhetoric of persuasion that was
strange to the American ear." Through his extemporaneous sermons
delivered in everyday language, the itinerant "sought to transcend both the
rational manner of polite Liberal preaching and the plain style of orthodox
preaching in order to speak directly to the people-at-large." And, his mass
outdoor services ignored the social conventions deemed central to good
order by New England's Standing Order who "believed traditionally with
Samuel Willard that God did 'Ordain Orders of Superiority and Inferiority
among men.'" That hierarchical view of society was reinforced every time
congregations met, manifested in "forms of attire, the seating of public
meetings, and patterns of speech." Pre-revival worship services served to
sustain the prevailing social organization, and in that context, speaker and
audience assumed socially constructed positions, "constantly reminded of
their places in the community." To many local ministers, the revival's
revolutionary setting undercut their authority as their parishioners joined
those of other churches and even those outside any church in one undiffer-
entiated audience to hear the gospel preached by an outsider and a
stranger. What defined them as pastors "was not simply the preaching of
the Word but also a direct, authoritarian identification with a specific
flock."[32] Now a "Wandering Levite" came between them and their
parishioners.

The presence of itinerants gave the laity choice, a power that threatened
to turn the Standing Order on its head. Before the revival, the local pastor,
supported by ecclesiastical laws, addressed a captive audience that
gathered once or twice each week for public worship and instruction.
Now, parishioners decided which of competing services they would attend

and whose authority they would recognize in religious matters. With the arrival of itinerants such as Whitefield and Gilbert Tennent, a Presbyterian preacher from New Jersey, local pastors faced competition for the first time, and their parishioners now had a choice: whether to follow the outsiders with their powerful message of personal liberation or remain obedient to the traditions of their parish ministers. To the dismay of their pastors, thousands began to substitute their personal experience or "secret Impulses" for the "written Word" of God as the rule of faith and conduct. Unlicensed itinerants roamed from "Place to Place" without receiving permission from "the stated Pastors in such Places," and these intruders "assemble[d] their People to hear themselves preach," thus, providing parishioners with a choice. Individuals without education and with no "regular Call" engaged in exhorting men and women to follow the Word of God, a practice deemed by many ministers to be a "heinous Invasion of the ministerial Office . . . [and] contrary to Scripture." Groups of New Lights, as revival devotees were called, separated from their congregations "to join themselves with and support, lay Exhorters or Itinerants," again a practice "opposite to the Rule of the Gospel." And, finally, New Lights in the throes of conversion experiences disrupted worship services with emotional outbursts, manifested by shouting and fainting.[33]

While some pro-revival ministers invited Whitefield to preach in their churches, much of his preaching and exhorting occurred outside New England's churches.[34] It seemed that people everywhere wanted to see and hear him, and church buildings were often inadequate for the huge crowds. A Connecticut farmer and carpenter, Nathan Cole, has given us one of the most colorful accounts of a gathering crowd rushing to hear him. Throughout 1740, Cole had read or heard frequent accounts of Whitefield's preaching in Pennsylvania, New Jersey, and New York. Then on 23 October, a messenger rode through Cole's town of Kensington informing residents that Whitefield had preached at Hartford and Wethersfield the previous day and was en route to Middletown for a ten o'clock service that morning. Thereupon, Cole ran from his field to tell his wife the good news. He and his wife mounted their horse and raced toward Middletown. As he approached the town, he rode along a ridge and saw an incredible sight on the road below. At first he thought that it was a cloud of fog rolling in along the river, but then, as he came nearer to the road, he could see that

> . . . this cloud was a cloud of dust made by the horses' feet. It arose some rods into the air over the tops of hills and trees; and when I came within about 20 rods of the road, I could see men and horses slipping along in the cloud like

26

shadows, and as I drew nearer it seemed like a steady stream of horses and their riders, scarcely a horse more than his length behind another, all of a lather and foam with sweat, their breath rolling out of their nostrils every jump . . . We went down in the stream but heard no man speak a word all the way for 3 miles but every one pressing forward in great haste; and when we got to Middletown old meeting house, there was a great multitude, it was said to be 3 or 4,000 of people, assembled together.

The crowd was too large for the structure, so Whitefield preached from a scaffold erected in the churchyard.[35]

Whitefield and the itinerants that succeeded him after he departed New England operated outside the settled Churches in ways other than preaching outdoors. They refused to submit to any denomination's authority. Evangelical Scottish Presbyterians, for instance, implored Whitefield to become an ordained minister of their persuasion, but he refused, declaring that the "whole World was his Parish." Though he remained nominally an Anglican, he was one of the Church's severest critics. Even when a group of "Calvinist" Methodists organized themselves into a denomination in England and Wales, Whitefield declined to assume leadership. As outsiders, evangelical itinerants defined their audience in the broadest possible terms, directing their message to church members as well as those affiliated with no church. Indeed, itinerants warned that subscribing to a covenant or creed or confession of faith was insufficient for salvation. And, to the dismay of many New England pastors who supported them, the itinerants charged the settled ministry with failing to preach the "One Thing Needed."

Shortly after leaving New England, Whitefield attacked the settled ministry's authority by publishing a scathing indictment of Harvard College, the institution that had prepared them for ministry. As graduates of Harvard, the ministers found the attack unwarranted and mean spirited, and they argued that the institution did indeed prepare young men to preach the Word of God in a sound, orthodox manner. Whitefield's accusations included the following: that discipline was "at a low Ebb;" that tutors neglected to "examine the Hearts of their Pupils," that "bad Books are read, *Tillotson* and *Clark*, instead of *Shepard* and *Stoddard*."[36] Whitefield extended his criticism to Harvard graduates as well, claiming, "the generality of Preachers talk of an unknown unfelt Christ." Harvard's president and faculty fired back a response that charged Whitefield with "enthusiasm," suggesting that the itinerant based his sermons on claims of direct revelation rather than squarely on the canonical Word of God. Further, they denounced his "going about in an Itinerant Way," a practice that was "very much to the Detriment of Religion, and the entire Destruction of the Order of these Churches of Christ, which our Fathers have taken such Care and Pains to settle." Clearly, the Establishment considered Whitefield not only an outsider, but also a dangerous threat to the "Discipline of the Churches of New England."[37]

When the Presbyterian itinerant Gilbert Tennent arrived from New Jersey in early 1741 to succeed Whitefield, he too attracted large crowds with an evangelical preaching style aimed at those in a "Slumber of carnal Security." Tennent's father had been instrumental in transplanting the Scottish Presbyterian tradition of "Communion Seasons" or "Religious Fairs" to the Middle Colonies.[38] Well before Whitefield perfected his pulpit oratory, Tennent had earned a reputation as a "searching" and "awakening" preacher. Indeed, when Whitefield first heard the Presbyterian deliver a sermon, he called him a true "Son of Thunder," one who delivered the Word of God as a warning for those who did not repent. He called on men and women, those within as well as without the church, to search their hearts for the sin of pride that gave them a false sense of security in their salvation. He reminded them that God alone was the dispenser of Grace. Most of all, he warned, "it is high Time to awake out of Sleep." In a 1735 sermon published in Boston, Tennent made clear the message that he continued to preach throughout the Great Awakening:

> Awake, Awake Sinners, stand up and look where you are hastning, least you drink of the Hand of the Lord, the Dregs of the cup of his Fury . . . Awake, ye secure Moralists, and lifeless, sapless Formalists, who are Strangers to the Power of experimental Religion . . . Awake every of you that are yet in a Christless unconvinced State!"[39]

While his New England audiences found his message of repentance to be familiar, having heard similar warnings from their own pastors, they were hardly prepared for Tennent's attacks on their ministers.

After Whitefield and Tennent left New England, the laity maintained contact with the transatlantic revival through print. Just as itinerant preachers extended the communicative sphere in which New Englanders heard the Word of God, printed reports of the transatlantic revival informed men and women of a genuine "Work of God" beyond the boundaries of their parish churches. As they read how thousands throughout the Atlantic World underwent a life-changing spiritual New Birth, they too wanted to partake of the experience. Some wondered why their pastor either did not embrace the revival or, like some, opposed it. And, they found in the news reports a new reference point for religious experience, one that sometimes was at odds with that offered by their pastors. Before the revival, parishioners tended to take their cues primarily from their minister, looking to him for interpretation in spiritual matters. They judged the crucial question of their own salvation or election against the minister's standards and his understanding of scripture. But, a flood of printed matter, especially newspapers and revival magazines, brought news to individuals of an awakening from beyond their parish lines and influenced the way they experienced and interpreted the Word in their local settings.

Throughout America's colonial period, the preached word had been the principal means of conveying the Word of God, although the printed word had been an important means as well. In Puritan New England, printed sermons served to reinforce the calling of ministers to interpret scripture and to extend the reach of the spoken word through time and space. The Great Awakening introduced a new kind of print and a new role for the printed word. While printed sermons continued to be popular, newspaper reports of the revival reinforced the revivalists' message that a mighty Work of God was afoot and its progress could be recorded in newsprint throughout the Atlantic World. Print took the Awakening into the public sphere as men and women in taverns and coffeehouses read revival reports in the weeklies. Dr Alexander Hamilton, a Maryland doctor and *bon vivant*, traveled through the colonies during the Great Awakening and was surprised to hear religious discussions in public places among ordinary people. At inns and taverns, he frequently heard uneducated people debating the finer points of theology. On a ferry crossing the Connecticut River he listened to a group of "lower class" people "talk so pointedly about justification, sanctification, adoption, regeneration, repentance, free grace, reprobation, original sin, and a thousand other such pritty, chimerical knick knacks as if they had done nothing but studied divinity all their life time and perused all the lumber of the scholastic divines, and yet the fellows look . . . like clowns."[40]

In 1742, Jonathan Edwards saw first-hand how printed reports of revival elsewhere challenged his pastoral authority. Though a staunch support of the awakening, Edwards was concerned about some interpretations of the New Birth. Noting that some converts reduced salvation to a single emotional outburst, he warned his congregation that genuine conversion involved the understanding as well as the affections and that it also translated into changed behavior. He reported that the revival at Northampton avoided excessive emotionalism "till we were infected from abroad." He explained, "Our people, hearing and some of them seeing the work in other places where there was a greater visible commotion than here . . . were ready to think that the work in those places far excelled what was among us."[41] In other words, Edwards' congregation accepted as their standard for judging the New Birth what outsiders reported rather than what their pastor prescribed.

As the transatlantic revival grew, it became big news, and its progress filled British and American newspapers. Only war between England and France rivaled it for front-page coverage when the awakening was at its peak in the early 1740s. Enamored by the huge crowds that followed Whitefield and by unusual circumstances surrounding his meetings, editors found the revival to be an irresistible story. A hill outside Bristol covered with black-faced miners emerging from the coal pits and confrontations in pulpits between Whitefield and London clergymen made good copy. To revival believers, however, news represented more than colorful accounts; they provided evidence of an extraordinary "Work of God." While a saddler in Dedham, Massachusetts, Samuel Belcher, testified that he was "first stirred by Whitefield" at a revival meeting, he added that his faith was reinforced by "news of a revival" occurring elsewhere.[42] Newspaper coverage also publicized upcoming revival meetings, thus preparing future audiences for hearing the preached Word of God. Boston minister and revival opponent, Charles Chauncy, wrote about Whitefield's advance publicity and its impact on the services that followed. "The Minds of People in this Part of the World," he remarked, "had been greatly prepossest in Favour of Mr. Whitefield, from the Accounts transmitted of him . . . Accordingly, when he came to Town, about two Years since, he was received as though he had been an *Angel of God; yea, a God come down in the Likeness of Man*."[43] The disadvantage of the public prints for revivalists was their sensationalism and, in some cases, opposition. Opponents soon learned that one of the most effective ways to counter the revivalists' claims that they were mere participants in a Work of God was to suggest that the revival was more the result of enthusiasm and manipulation.

Growing dissatisfaction with newspaper coverage led evangelicals in Britain and America to establish revival magazines. One London revivalist suggested the publication of a magazine devoted entirely to revival news, a specialty periodical similar to others that began to appear in England catering to such interests as gardening, literature, and art. In a letter to John Lewis, a pro-Whitefield printer, he noted that the "polite world have their Spectators, Tatler's Guardian's, and Comedies," adding that "the Children of God also [should have] their proper entertainment, their weekly amusement, their divine miscellany, and the historical progress of their Lord's kingdom."[44] By printing their own accounts of the awakening, revival editors could ensure a steady flow of good news that charted the successes and progress of the Work of God. By 1743, revival magazines were being published in Scotland, England, and New England. The title of the Boston publication speaks to its purpose: *The Christian History, Containing Accounts of the Revival and Propagation of Religion in Great-Britain and America.* Editor Thomas Prince explained that the magazine was a response to evangelicals' thirst for news. "Our pious People were, last Summer," he wrote in the first issue, "greatly refresh'd with the glad Tidings arrived and reprinted here, of a remarkable Revival of Religion at Cambuslang [Scotland]. He proceeded to fill the first twelve issues with news from Scotland that tracked "the further Progress of that blessed Work" in other parts of Scotland."[45] By publishing news of the revival in Scotland as well as in New England, Prince connected the "Holy Fair" tradition of the former with the "great awakening" of the latter. And in subsequent issues, he reprinted revival narratives from even more far-flung revival centers, thus portraying the revival as a global event.

Editorial transitions from one narrative to the next transported readers to remote places where men and women responded in similar ways to the same message. After completing the report from Scotland, Prince wrote, "having given our pious Readers some entertaining Accounts from Scotland, we now Return to the Christian History of New-England." He divided his "Account of the more surprising and more extensive Revivals . . . in the present Day" into two parts. The first described the "remarkable Revival in this Country before Mr. Whitefield's Arrival hither," what Stoddard would have classified as a "particular" revival. Then he wrote about the "further Progress of the Revival since," depicting what had become a "general" awakening.[46]

Prince took readers back and forth across the Atlantic through his coverage, always showing how local events were part of a single Work of God. After returning to Scotland for additional evidence of the revival's spreading, he wrote, "having at present closed our religious Accounts from Scotland, as transmitted by the last Ship from there, we now return to America, and Begin at the Westernmost End of the British Empire, (about four Thousand miles to the Westward of Glasgow)."[47] His next transition represented his greatest geographical reach. Prince wrote:

From viewing the joyful Progress of Christianity among the Aboriginal Natives in the West-Indies, it may be a suitable Transition to pass over the Atlantick Ocean thro' the Continents of Europe and Asia, in a strait Course about ten Thousand Miles, to view the happy Progress of the same Religion among the Aboriginals at Bengal, Cormandel, Malabar, and the Islands of Ceylon, and Batavia in the East-Indies.[48]

With that breathless sweep, the editor made the revival coextensive with the British Empire.

Prince also extended the revival's temporal reach by interpreting it as an extension of German Pietism, an evangelical movement begun in the late seventeenth century. He first noted that Pietists in Rotterdam had recognized the Scottish revival as a genuine Work of God and had translated the Scottish revival narrative into Dutch. Then Prince discussed the Great Awakening in Pennsylvania where tens of thousands of German Protestants had immigrated over the previous forty years. From an account of the revival in Pennsylvania, the editor then presented a "History of the Revival of Religion in Germany in the last century," by way of reprinting portions of Hermann Auguste Francke's *Pietas Hallensis*.[49] The book was an inspiring narrative of how a small group of Lutherans sought to deepen their faith by adhering to rigorous standards of practical piety in their community at Halle and at the same time supporting world evangelism through translating the gospel in many different languages as well as sending missionaries to places in Africa and Asia. Anglo-American evangelicals regarded the book as the handbook of practical piety. John Wesley visited Halle and came away with organizational ideas that would shape the way he framed the Methodist Church, and George Whitefield found *Pietas Hallensis* to be a blueprint for joining works of charity with evangelism. He ordered his orphanage at Bethesda outside Savannah, Georgia along the lines Francke described.

Prince published his last edition of the *Christian History* in 1745. While the revival would continue in parts of America, particularly in Virginia, by the end of the 1740s even its most ardent supporters in New England referred to the awakening in the past tense. Some opponents compared the revival to a comet that burns brightly for a short time and then is extinguished. They pointed out that all the evangelical fuss had left little changed: no new denominations or institutions belong to the revival's legacy. However, the Great Awakening would have profound and lasting influence by altering the communicative sphere in which Americans proclaimed and experienced the Word of God. Though the parish system would remain intact, its boundaries would become much more permeable, and local ministers would face greater competition.

# A Free Marketplace of Religion

Just as Whitefield had attacked Harvard upon his departure from New England, Tennent leveled a broadside at the Congregational clergy. In a reversal of the jeremiads that pastors frequently directed toward their parishioners, Tennent aimed his best-known sermon at the pastors and their shortcomings. In his discourse *The Danger of an Unconverted Ministry*, he made the condition of the pastor's soul, not educational attainment or even orthodoxy, the sole criterion for his worthiness to lead his congregation. Differentiating between "Natural" and "New-born" men, Tennent declared, "Natural Men, not having true Love to Christ and the Souls of their Fellow-Creatures, hence their Discourses are cold and sapless, and as it were freeze between their Lips." While some ministers had picked up the language of conversion during the Great Awakening, and thus could "prate a little more orthodoxly about the New Birth," nevertheless they remained "great Strangers to the feeling Experience of it." An unconverted ministry is, he averred, a "*dead Ministry*, [and] have not in them the Temper of that Saviour they profess. It's an awful Sign, that they are as blind as Moles, and as dead as Stones, without any spiritual Taste and Relish." He concluded by suggesting that such was the "Case of Multitudes" of ministers. Without having undergone a conversion experience themselves, little wonder that they go about their ministerial duties "so coldly, and *insuccessfully*."[50]

Tennent and other itinerants assured men and women that they had a choice, that they did not have to remain within a congregation led by an unconverted minister or by one who did not preach the New Birth. It was at this point that the itinerants lost some of their erstwhile ministerial supporters who came to see these wandering preachers as driving a wedge between pastor and parishioner. Before the Great Awakening, even in Pennsylvania and Rhode Island where the absence of religious establishments promoted pluralism, persons exercised little choice in religion. Most people attended the local parish church and ethnic groups tended to settle together. While Pennsylvania numbered many different sects, their members lived together in communities and supported their own congregations. But, in the eighteenth century, a rapidly growing population meant that people of different faiths were more likely to live in close proximity with each other. Gilbert Tennent thought that the old private religious sphere was too rigid and limited the options available to seekers after the "true" gospel. Specifically, he encouraged people to ignore parish boundaries in the "Getting of Grace and Growing in it." While pointing out the scriptural admonition to hear the Word preached, Tennent asked, "why we should be under a fatal Necessity of hearing . . . our Parish-Minister." He added that he had "known Persons to get saving Good in their Souls, by Hearing over their Parish-line." He urged evangelicals to choose from among the growing variety of printed and preached sermons, "seeing at one time we cannot hear all, neither doth the Explication and Application of all, equally suit such a Person, in such a Time, or Condition, or equally quicken, and subserve the Encrease of knowledge."[51] While the Word of God was unchangeable and timeless, how it was proclaimed was not. Clearly Tennent rejected the notion that one sermonic style – that of the parish minister – fit all.

By urging men and women to choose among competing ministers, Tennent advocated what Adam Smith described as a free market of religion. In his *Wealth of Nations* published in 1776, the Scottish political economist analysed systems of exchange, comparing state-regulated commerce and free trade. But his far-reaching study went beyond economics and included a section on religious teaching, suggesting that religion operated in patterns analogous to trade. "The clergy of every established church," he wrote, "constitute a great incorporation." Supported by the state and protected from competition, "they can act in concert, and pursue their interest upon one plan and with one spirit, as much as if they were under the direction of one man."[52] Before 1740, New England's settled ministers operated within a regulated religious sphere known as the Standing Order, which gave them a virtual monopoly within their own parishes. By contrast, Smith continued, if a society had no established religion, it would likely have "a great multitude of religious sects." Faced with competition on all sides, "each teacher would no doubt [feel] himself under the necessity of making the utmost exertion and of using every art both to preserve and to increase the number of his disciples." Moreover, a competitive religious market would offer inhabitants choice. "If politics had never called in the aid of religion," Smith reasoned, "it would probably have dealt equally and impartially with all the different sects, and have allowed every man to choose his own priest and his own religion as he thought proper."[53] New Lights subscribed to the notion of choice and defied ecclesiastical laws to make certain that men and women heard the message of the "one Thing needful."

Upon occasion the choice was made in dramatic confrontations between parish minister and revival itinerant. On Sunday, 26 July 1741, parishioners at Stonington, Connecticut walked toward the meeting-house for morning worship as they and their ancestors had on each Sabbath since the town's founding in 1649. Their minister for the past thirty-seven years, Nathaniel Eells, was an orthodox, Harvard-educated pastor whose stated goal was "to promote the true Religion of the Holy Jesus, and hand it uncorrupt to succeeding Generations."[54] But as they approached the church on this particular Lord's Day, the townspeople divided; some filed into the meetinghouse as usual while others veered off toward a spot on the village green "under the Trees" where an itinerant evangelist, John Davenport, was about to preach. A farmer, Joshua Hempstead, described what happened next in his diary. Out of curiosity aroused by extensive newspaper coverage, Hempstead had ridden from his nearby home in New London and joined the "great Number of hearers" standing expectantly around Davenport.[55] What struck him more than anything else about the unusual proceedings was that on that this Sunday the people of Stonington had a choice between two different versions of the Word of God.

While we do not have a record of Eells' sermon that day, we do know from his writings how he regarded the spiritual empiricism by which New Lights made one's conversion experience authoritative. He feared that "some in our Land look upon what are called *secret Impulses* upon their Minds, without due Regard to the *written Word*, [as] the Rule of their Conduct." He thought that the revival was in fact reviving the heresy of Antinomianism that had threatened the Puritan community a hundred years earlier. In a dramatic courtroom confrontation in 1636, Anne Hutchinson had claimed an immediate revelation as sufficient authority for disregarding certain biblical dictates.[56] Eells, as John Winthrop had before him, insisted that personal experiences must conform "to the pure Doctrines of the Gospel" and withstand "Arguments fetched from *Scripture* and *Reason*."[57]

We do know from Hempstead what Davenport preached that day. Directing his sermon at Eells' parishioners, Davenport assumed that most of the members had never undergone a spiritual conversion, thereby suggesting that the pastor's preaching had been misdirected and ineffective. Like other New Light preachers, Davenport first tried to shake the sense of security that church members had developed by virtue of being part of a covenanted community. He warned them that only the indwelling Spirit could save them through a divine act of regeneration, a New Birth. Having made them aware of their spiritual peril, Davenport then proceeded to provide assurance that conversion could come instantaneously and that the convert could know for certain that he or she had been redeemed. The itinerant did not blame his audience for their lost condition; rather, he blamed Eells. While New Englanders were familiar with jeremiads, they were unaccustomed to attacks on their ministers. For an outsider to criticize an ordained minister that had been called by a gathered congregation to preach the Word of God was to question the authority and integrity of the Congregational polity that had prevailed since the Puritan fathers had settled the region. Nonetheless, Davenport pressed his case, and was in Hempstead's opinion, "Severe in Judging & Condemning Mr. Eells." The itinerant's message and manner appealed to some while repelling others, thus presenting the people of Stonington with a clear choice that Sunday. Hempstead witnessed the choices exercised: "many of the People in [Davenport's] Assembly withdrew into the meetinghouse where Mr. Eells preacht to them as he was wont to do & ye Rest Stayed by Mr. Davenport until ye Exercise was over."[58]

New Englanders based their choices on their own assessments of the itinerant's message and performance as illustrated by the responses of two Connecticut farmers. After listening to Davenport and other itinerants on several occasions, Joshua Hempstead decided to remain within his New London congregation as an Old Light, as anti-revivalists were called. In addition to hearing Davenport preach that day in Stonington, Hempstead continued to attend the itinerant's preaching services in and around New London, probably at the urging of one of his sons. However, his assessment of the evangelist's message and methods grew more negative. On Sunday, 27 February 1743, he attended one of Davenport's meetings and commented on the sermon: "it was Scarcely worth the hearing," and he complained, "the praying was without form or Comelyness. It was difficult to distinguish between his praying & preaching for it was all Confused Medley." Hempstead dismissed the sermon: "he had no Text nor Bible visable, no Doctrine, uses, nor Improvement nor anything else that was Regular."[59] In other words, when judged against the Plain Style sermons that Hempstead was accustomed to and preferred, Davenport's sermon fell short. Hempstead also disapproved of New Light exhorters after hearing a number at a meeting at New London in late 1742. Before the minister arrived for services, two young men, "Newlight Exhorters begun their meeting and 2 or 3 Women followed both at once and there was such medley that no one could understand Either part."[60] Preferring order to enthusiasm, Hempstead remained an Old Light although at least one of his sons was a New Light.

Farmer and carpenter, Nathan Cole, from Kensington, Connecticut had a very different assessment of the New Lights and became one of their most zealous followers. His response to George Whitefield's preaching at Middletown stands in stark contrast to Hempstead's reaction to Davenport, and the difference has more to do with the individuals than with the itinerants. Hempstead listened with a critical ear that weighed Davenport's performance against a traditional standard and found Davenport wanting. Cole, on the other hand, described a powerful emotional, almost mystical experience in hearing Whitefield. Upon looking up at Whitefield standing above him on the scaffold built for the occasion, Cole said the evangelist "looked as if he was Cloathed with Authority from the Great God." Then when he preached, his words gave the farmer "a heart wound," because he began to think that he was not one of God's Elect. Indeed, when he went home that day, Cole was miserable. He wrote, "I was loaded with the guilt of Sin, I saw I was undone for ever; I carried Such a weight of Sin in my breast or mind, that it seemed to me as if I should sink into the ground every step." But later, "in the twinkling of an Eye, as quick as A flash of lightning" God appeared to him offering grace and forgiveness, and Cole said, "my burden was fallen off my mind; I was set free."[61] As a result of his conversion, Cole separated from the Congregational Church, became a lay exhorter who helped organize a Separatist Church in Kensington, and eventually joined the Baptist Church.

Hempstead's and Cole's choices represent two possibilities along a range of options prompted by the Great Awakening. In communities and congregations across New England and throughout America, the revival confronted individuals with questions of how and where they wished to worship. Many looked at events surrounding the revival and, like Hempstead, were skeptical that they constituted a "Work of God" as claimed by revivalists. These Old Lights remained within their congregations, preferring the doctrinal clarity and liturgical order to the evangelicals' "errors and disorders." Some of these Old Lights sought even more order and left their Congregational or Presbyterian churches to join the Church of England with its episcopal hierarchy and liturgical worship. New Lights also exercised a range of choices. Some, who embraced the revival's message but rejected its excesses, remained within their congregations and gave their local churches more of an evangelical emphasis. Fearing that their pastor or a majority of their co-worshippers were "unconverted", others separated from their congregations and formed new churches altogether. Still others, like Cole, became seekers, first joining one or more Separatist bodies and then gravitating toward the Baptists who became the fastest-growing group in the colonies.

From the perspective of settled ministers, the Great Awakening turned an orderly communicative sphere into an unregulated free-for-all.[62] New Lights questioned their authority, and indeed, their spiritual state. Itinerants trampled on their parish boundaries. Unlearned lay exhorters deigned to expound upon such doctrines as regeneration and sanctification. New Lights organized their own schools for training ministers, and one, the Shepherd's Tent at New London, attracted more students in 1742 than did Yale.[63] And, large numbers of parishioners separated from local churches, claiming that their covenants did not bind them to unconverted ministers.

Ministers and magistrates worked together to reassert the authority of the Standing Order and constrain the New Lights. Moderate New Light leaders, such as Jonathan Edwards, lectured the more enthusiastic revivalists on the necessity of weighing experience against reason and scripture. The ubiquitous Joshua Hempstead heard Edwards preach against extremist teachings and practices, bearing witness "agst ye prevailing disorders & distractions yt are subsisting in the Country by means of Enthusiasm."[64] Old Lights took stronger steps. One congregation at Kingston, Massachusetts appointed a committee in 1745 "to see that there be hooks and staples put to the casements in the meeting-house, that nobody may get in at unseasonable times to do damage in the meeting-house." The church gave the committee explicit power to deal with the "insolence" of "itinerant ministers" and lay exhorters.[65]

However, ministers needed help in reinforcing the Standing Order, and they sought it from the legislature. The Connecticut Assembly responded in 1742 with the Act for Regulating Abuses and Correcting Disorders in Ecclesiastical Affairs. The law banned itinerants from entering a parish to "preach or exhort" without the pastor's "express invitation." When New Lights set up their own school to train ministers, the lawmakers "legislated it out of business" at the insistence of its opponents. When Massachusetts Separatists in large numbers left the Congregational churches and joined Baptist congregations, the legislature stepped in to preserve the *status quo ante* revival. Prior to the Great Awakening, the Assembly had granted exemptions to Baptists and other sects outside Establishment from paying the ministerial rates. That is, orderly, legally constituted Dissenting sects could apply their parish tax funds toward the support of their own ministers. In 1753, the General Court set up a formidable roadblock for newly organized Baptist congregations to secure exemptions. The legislature enacted a law requiring a petitioning church to qualify for an exemption by securing certificates from three other Baptist churches certifying that the petitioners are indeed "one of their denomination."[66] New Light Separatists and Baptists found the law particularly offensive because the state gave power to persons outside the congregation to judge the beliefs of the members, a clear violation of liberty of conscience.

Despite opposition from the ministers and magistrates, New Light Churches flourished during the years between the Great Awakening and the American Revolution. Almost three hundred Separatist or Separate Baptist congregations sprang up in New England alone. And, by 1776, the legally established Congregational and Episcopal Churches constituted only about one-third of the total number of congregations in the newly declared United States, a percentage matched by the fast-growing Presbyterians and Baptists.[67] Several factors explain the evangelicals" success. First, American religious establishments were relatively weak when compared with European state Churches. For instance, Anglicans lacked the institutional machinery necessary to counter aggressive Dissenters who threatened uniformity. There was no resident bishop to ensure that parishes were filled with qualified, orthodox priests and to supervise the clergy. And there were no ecclesiastical courts to maintain discipline among ministers and parishioners. Both Congregationalists in New England and Anglicans in the southern colonies were wed to the parish system, which tended to confine preaching and worship to fixed positions, not a scheme particularly well suited for a rapidly expanding population on the move. The number of European inhabitants in British North America grew an astounding ten fold from 1700 to 1775, from 250,000 to 2,500,000. And much of the population was on the move, pushing westward in search of arable land.

Second, most of the Irish and German immigrants who flooded into the colonies in the eighteenth century joined the growing number of Dissenters. Many were evangelicals who were sympathetic with the New Lights. Ulster Presbyterians brought with them their tradition of "Communion Seasons" and tended to identify with the revivalist New Side Presbyterians of Pennsylvania and New Jersey. Many of the Germans were evangelicals, identifying either with the Halle or the Herrnhut Pietists. Settling primarily along the frontier in a great arc from Pennsylvania to the Carolina Backcountry, the newcomers dissented from the Anglican Establishments.[68] Both Germans and Scots sent itinerants to preach on the frontier.[69]

The state churches were ineffective in competing with evangelicals in winning new members, especially along the rapidly expanding frontier. Trying to beat the itinerant preachers in the Carolina backcountry at their own game, Charles Woodmason reported failure. He wrote that whenever he gave notice "to be at such a place at such a Time [for preaching services], three or four of these Fellows [New Lights] are constantly at my Heels – They either get there before me, and hold forth – or after I have finish'd, or the next Day, or for days together." Given the choice between Woodmason's Anglican liturgy as set forth in the *Book of Common Prayer* and the evangelicals' extemporaneous sermons, Backcountry men and women in overwhelming numbers chose the latter. Woodmason noted that "twelve months past most of these People were very zealous Members of our Church and many of them Communicants," but, he added, the New Lights have had "Success" and have made "rapid Progress."[70] Fired by their evangelical mission of preaching the gospel to people everywhere, inside or outside churches with no regard for parish boundaries, the New Light itinerants had a competitive advantage over the Anglican clergymen.

Woodmason explained that within the Anglican polity, "ev'ry Minister has a Particular and distinct Charge. He has a Circle assigned Him, in which He is to move and not stir out of. He cannot leave his Church for one Sunday without leave of the Vestry . . . under Pain of a Fine."[71]

Southern Anglicans were no more effective in containing the spread of New Lights than were northern establishments. The invaders simply ignored parish boundaries and preached where they wished, while the weak ecclesiastical establishment protested but did little to stop them. Defenders of the old parish system would not admit it, a *de facto* free marketplace of religion had emerged. The American Revolution would begin the process of making religious choice and freedom of conscience a constitutional right. Thomas Jefferson and James Madison are usually credited with securing the passage of the Virginia Statute for Religious Freedom, which became the model for the constitutional recognition of religious liberty as a natural right, but they recognized that they prevailed only because a majority of Virginians were dissenters who demanded choice. Reflecting on the triumph of religious liberty, Madison explained how the measure passed in a legislature dominated by Episcopalians favoring establishment. "It is well known," he wrote in 1788, "that a religious establishment would have taken place in that State, if the legislative majority had found as they expected, a majority of the people in favor of the measure."[72] But they did not, and, now, as then, politicians pronounce what the Word of God means for America at their own peril.

# Notes

1. See Lockridge, K. *A New England Town The First Hundred Years: Dedham, Massachusetts, 1636–1736*, New York, 1970, p. 17.

2. Nathaniel Ward, *The Simple Cobler of Aggawam in America*, (Boston, 1713), p. 6.

3. The identification of Whitefield's itinerancy as "imported Divinity" is found in Thomas Foxcroft's preface to Jonathan Dickinson, *The True Scripture-Doctrine Concerning Some Important Points of Christian Faith* (Boston, 1741), pp. I–IV.

4. John Gillies, ed., *The Works of the Rev. George Whitefield*, 6 vols, London, 1771, vol. 1, p. 105.

5. Richard Hooker, ed., *The Carolina Backcountry on the Eve of the Revolution: The Journal and Other Writings of Charles Woodmason, Anglican Itinerant*, Chapel Hill NC, 1953, p. 13.

6. Cotton Mather, *Magnalia Christi Americana, or the Ecclesiastical History of New-England, From the First Planting, in the Year 1620, Unto the Year of Our Lord, 1698*, 2 vols, 1702; reprint, Hartford CT, 1853, vol. 1, p. 25.

7. Jonathan Edwards, *Some Thoughts Concerning the Present Revival of Religion in New England*; cited in Alan Heimert and Perry Miller (eds), *The Great Awakening: Documents Illustrating the Crisis and its Consequences*, Indianapolis IN, 1967, p. 271f.

8. John Higginson, *The Cause of God and His People in New England*, Cambridge MA, 1663, p. 11. For more on jeremiads and their place in New England history, see Michael Crawford, *Seasons of Grace: Colonial New England's Revival Tradition in Its British Context*, New York, 1991, p. 28ff.

9. C. Mather, *Nuncia Bona E Terra Longingua: A Brief Account of Some Good and Great Things a Doing For the Kingdom of God, in the Midst of Europe*, Boston MA, 1715, 1f., 9.

10. For plain-style preaching, see William Haller, *The Rise of Puritanism; Or, the Way to the New Jerusalem as set Forth in Pulpit and Press from Thomas Cartwright to John Lilburne and John Milton*, 1938; repr. New York, 1957, p. 134.

11. Perry Miller, *The New England Mind: The Seventeenth Century*, Cambridge MA, 1939, p. 298.

12. For relation between private and public worship among Puritans, see Charles E. Hambrick-Stowe, *The Practice of Piety: Puritan Devotional Disciplines in Seventeenth-Century New England*, Chapel Hill NC, 1982, p. 117.

13. Miller, *The New England Mind*, p. 297.

14. Ibid., p. 92f.

15. Ibid., p. 93.

16. Ibid., p. 95f.

17. David D. Hall, *The Faithful Shepherd: A History of the New England Ministry in the Seventeenth Century*, Chapel Hill NC, 1972, p. 15f.

18. Cited in Miller, *The New England Mind*, p. 436f.

19. A synod in 1662 adopted the Half-Way Covenant which enabled the children of parents who had confessed no personal conversion experience to become members of the Church with all privileges except that of participating in the Lord's Supper. Implementation was left to individual congregations.

20. A "consumer revolution" in the eighteenth century flooded America with merchandise that ministers feared diverted attention from the things of God to the things of the world. See, in particular, Timothy

H. Breen, ""Baubles of Britain": The American and Consumer Revolutions of the Eighteenth Century," *Past and Present* 119 (May 1980), 73–104.

21. Samuel Torrey, *Man's Extremity, God's Opportunity* Boston MA, 1695, p. 9f.

22. Ibid.

23. Solomon Stoddard, *The Efficacy of the Fear of Hell to Restrain Men from Sin*, Boston MA, 1713, p. 190.

24. Ibid., p. 185f.

25. Susan O'Brien, "The Transatlantic Community of Saints: The Great Awakening and the First Evangelical Network, 1735–1755," *American Historical Review* 91 (1986), 811–32.

26. Cited in C.C. Goen, (ed.), *Jonathan Edwards: The Great Awakening (The Works of Jonathan Edwards 4)*, New Haven CT, 1972, 130–2.

27. J. Gillies, *Memoirs of Reverend Mr. George Whitefield*, New York, 1774, p. 73.

28. Clifford K. Shipton (ed.), *Early American Imprints, 1639–1800*, Worcester MA, 1963, micro-card p. 3, doc. 5300.

29. Cited in Harry Stout, *The Divine Dramatist: George Whitefield and the Rise of Modern Evangelicalism*, Grand Rapids MI, 1991, p. 118f.

30. Ibid., p. 119f.

31. Benedict Anderson, *The Imagined Community: Reflections on the Origins and Spread of Nationalism*, London, 1983.

32. Harry Stout, "Religion, Communications, and the Ideological Origins of the American Revolution," *William and Mary Quarterly* 34 (October 1977), 525–7.

33. Though differing over their assessments of the revival, both pro- and anti-revival ministers condemned practices that undermined their authority. See their concerns listed in separate testimonials in Richard L. Bushman, *The Great Awakening: Documents on the Revival of Religion, 1740–1745*, New York, 1970, pp. 127–32.

34. In addition to the best-known itinerants, including Whitefield, Gilbert Tennent, and James Davenport, many others traveled about New England preaching the necessity of the New Birth. Most of these were pastors who preached at the invitation of other pro-revival ministers.

35. M. Crawford, "The Spiritual Travels of Nathan Cole," *William and Mary Quarterly* 33 (January 1976), p. 92f.

36. *Boston Gazette*, 20 April 1741.

37. *The Testimony of the President, Professors, Tutors, and Hebrew Instructor of Harvard College, against George Whitefield*, Boston MA, 1744, cited in Heimert and Miller (eds), *The Great Awakening*, pp. 342 and 353.

38. See Marilyn Westerkamp, *Triumph of the Laity: Scots-Irish Piety and the Great Awakening, 1625–1760*, New York, 1988, p. 24f. For a fuller discussion of the holy fairs, see Leigh H. Schmidt, *Holy Fairs: Scottish Communions and American Revivals in the Early Modern Period*, Princeton NJ, 1989.

39. Cited in Bushman, *The Great Awakening*, p. 17.

40. Carl Bridenbaugh, *Gentleman's Progress: The Itinerarium of Dr. Alexander Hamilton, 1744*, Chapel Hill NC, 1948, p. 162f.

41. [Boston] *Christian History*, 14, 21, 28 January 1744.

42. See Kenneth Minkema, "A Great Awakening Conversion: The Relation of Samuel Belcher," *William and Mary Quarterly* 44 (January 1987), 123.

43. Charles Chauncy, *A Letter from a Gentleman in Boston, to Mr. George Wishart, One of the Ministers of Edinburgh, Concerning the State of Religion in New-England*, Edinburgh, 1742, p. 5f.

44. [London] *Weekly History*, 4 July 1741.

45. Thomas Prince, *The Christian History, Containing Accounts of the Revival and Propagation of Religion in Great-Britain and America, For the Year 1743*, Boston MA, 1744, pp. 1–4.

46. Ibid., pp. 93 and 113.

47. Ibid., p. 364.

48. Thomas Prince, *The Christian History, Containing Accounts of the Revival and Propagation of Religion in Great-Britain and America, For the Year 1744*, Boston, 1745, p. 28.

49. Ibid., 260–2.

50. Gilbert Tennent, *The Danger of an Unconverted Ministry, Considered in a Sermon on Mark VI.34* . . . Boston MA, 1742, pp. 6–8, 11–13.

51. Ibid., p. 14.

52. Roy Hutcheson Campbell and Andrew S. Skinner (eds), *An Inquiry into the Nature and Causes of the Wealth of Nations by Adam Smith*, 2 vols, Indianapolis IN, 1981, vol 2, p. 797.

53. Ibid., vol 2, p. 792f.

54. See Convention of Pastors of Churches in Massachusetts-Bay, *The Testimony of the Pastors of the Churches in the Province of the Massachusetts-Bay in New-England, at their Annual Convention in Boston, May 25, 1743. Against several Errors in Doctrine, and Disorders in Practice* . . . Boston MA, 1743, p. 13. Eells was moderator of the convention and drafted the orthodox opposition to innovations introduced by the evangelical revival that swept New England in the early 1740s.

55. *Diary of Joshua Hempstead: A Record of Life in Colonial New London, Connecticut, 1711–1758*, New London CT, 1998, p. 375.

56. For the so-called Antinomian Controversy, see Winship, M., *Making Heretics: Militant Protestantism and Free Grace in Massachusetts, 1636–1641*, Princeton NJ, 2002.

57. *The Testimony of the Pastors of the Churches.*

58. *Diary of Joshua Hempstead*, p. 375.

59. Ibid., p. 401.

60. Ibid., p. 396f.

61. Cited from "The Spiritual Travels of Nathan Cole" in Richard L. Bushman (ed.), *The Great Awakening: Documents on the Revival of Religion, 1740–1745*, New York, 1970, pp. 67–70.

62. Although he sees the transformation occurring later, during the Second Great Awakening of the early nineteenth century, Richard Brown describes the erosion of New England ministers' authority as "interpreters of events". Increasingly they faced parishioners who, through alternative sources of knowledge, began "to think and act for themselves." In many parishes, that process was well under way during the first Great Awakening. See Richard Brown, *Knowledge is Power: The Diffusion of Information in Early America, 1700–1865*, New York, 1989, p. 80f.

63. See Richard Warch, "The Shepherd's Tent: Education and Enthusiasm in the Great Awakening," *American Quarterly* 30 (Summer 1978), p. 184.

64. *Diary of Joshua Hemstead*, p. 401.

65. C. C. Goen, *Revivalism and Separatism, in New England, 1740–1800*, New Haven CT, 1962, p. 56.

66. Ibid., pp. 59, 63, and 268.

67. See Roger Finke and Rodney Stark, *The Churching of America, 1776–1990: Winners and Losers in Our Religious Economy*, New Brunswick NJ, 1992, p. 25.

68. Hooker, *The Carolina Backcountry*, p. 13.

69. For German itinerants, see John Frantz, "The Awakening of Religion among the German Settlers in the Middle Colonies," *William and Mary Quarterly* 33 (April 1976), 266–88; for Scots, see Milton Coalter, *Gilbert Tennent, Son of Thunder: A Case Study of Continental Pietism's Impact on the First Great Awakening in the Middle Colones*, New York, 1986.

70. Hooker, *Carolina Backcountry*, p. 13.

71. Ibid., p. 90.

72. Cited in Michael Kammen (ed.), *The Origins of the American Constitution: A Documentary History*, New York, 1986, p. 369.

# 2
# Bridging the Gap: Cultural Mediators and the Structure of Transatlantic Communication

## Rosalind J. Beiler

On 5 August 1677, a large crowd gathered at Gertrud Dirck's house in Amsterdam. The audience included people from different parts of the Netherlands and was made up of "presbiterians, socinians, baptists, seekers etc."[1] They had come to hear for themselves the traveling English and Scottish Quakers debate with local clergy. Among the retinue of ministers were the Society of Friends' most prominent leaders: George Fox, William Penn, Robert Barclay and George Keith. Each of these men had suffered imprisonment for preaching their religious views. Indeed, Barclay and Keith had been released shortly before setting off on their journey. The Friends had traveled to Holland to help heal schisms within the fledgling Quaker meetings there and to establish formal relationships with them. They also went as missionaries, intent on spreading their message of "truth" to anyone who would listen.

One of the key figures at the gathering that day was Benjamin Furly, an English Quaker living in Rotterdam. Born in Colchester, England, in 1636, Furly joined the Society of Friends around 1655. By the time he moved to Rotterdam in 1659, he had received an excellent education and established himself as a merchant connected to his family's business. Furly quickly became a prominent leader in the small Dutch Friends' community. Meetings for worship were held in his home throughout the second half of the seventeenth century and he offered his hospitality and aid to traveling Quakers who came through the city on business or missionary journeys. He helped them by changing money, providing visas or passports, advising them about travel routes, or writing letters of introduction.[2] On that particular day in August 1677, Furly, along with Johann Klaus, offered his language skills by interpreting for Fox, Penn, Barclay and Keith as they "declared the Everlasting truth opening many things Concerning ye Estate of man in ye fall."[3] The meeting lasted five hours and included lively exchanges between clergy in Latin, which Furly translated into Dutch for the audience. He then conveyed audience questions into English for the missionaries.[4]

Furly's employment of his language skills and the various backgrounds of those who gathered at Gertrud Dirck's house that day suggest the extent to which religious beliefs were critical elements of early modern identity. For the Quaker missionaries and many among their audience, religious ideas and practice took precedent over national, political, ethnic or linguistic affiliations. Those who were dissenters or did not belong to officially sanctioned churches, perceived themselves as separated from the rest of the population. Indeed, at times, very real discrimination kept them from enjoying the economic and political privileges of their neighbors. In response to intolerance, imprisonment and exile, they established their own communication and commercial networks. This was certainly the case with the Society of Friends in seventeenth-century England, Scotland and Ireland as well as with Anabaptists spread from the Netherlands to Switzerland and with various Pietist groups throughout the German principalities.

The English and Scottish missionaries who traveled to Amsterdam in 1677 carefully sought out others they thought would be receptive to their message. They did not shy away from preaching the "truth" to the Reformed, Lutheran or Catholic clergy and lay people they met along the way but they were especially interested in meeting with Mennonites, Labadists and the Pietist followers of Spener. While the Quakers did not necessarily hold the same theological beliefs as these groups, they shared a similar approach to their spiritual lives. Above all, they sought to meet with others who shared their emphasis on a personal, unmediated relationship with God and their desire for simple, pious living.[5]

Like the members of their own Society, those the Quaker missionaries sought to convert had suffered from discrimination and persecution. Fox, Penn, Barclay and Keith had all been arrested and imprisoned for preaching their views. Penn had been arrested in Ireland in 1667, incarcerated in the Tower of London for blasphemy in 1668 and 1669, arrested again for preaching in 1670, and imprisoned in Newgate in 1671.[6] While Dutch Mennonites had achieved religious toleration by the end of the sixteenth century, Anabaptists in Switzerland and several principalities along the Rhine River were forced into exile or imprisoned throughout the seventeenth century.[7] At the same time, Pietist groups throughout the German states were also suffering from banishment.[8] In response, members of each group established regular communication channels to funnel information, assistance, money and household goods to those in need.

One of the critical means for curtailing religious persecution and discrimination was convincing heads of state to establish official policies of toleration. As an English gentleman of means, Penn used all of his social connections to free Quakers from imprisonment and foster freedom of conscience. He frequently petitioned and visited local authorities to pressure them into releasing Quakers. After renewing his connections to the court of the Stuart monarchy, he sought relief from the King and from Parliament for his co-religionists.[9] Dutch Mennonites also negotiated with heads of state for religious toleration when Swiss Anabaptists were banished from Zurich and Bern.[10] In a world where heads of state determined the religion of the land, the first step in winning freedom of conscience was to lobby those in power.

Those suffering from discrimination also needed the practical knowledge and connections of the commercial world. Bailing people out of prison required access to funds. Helping those who were banished set up new homes demanded the ability to obtain transportation and passports. Furthermore, religious exiles frequently needed to be supplied with household implements and tools. Religious leaders relied on the economic networks of merchants to assist fellow believers in need and to carry out missionary work.

Thus, when Furly acted as translator on that warm August day, he was positioned at the nexus of several extensive communication networks. Throughout the second half of the seventeenth century he was actively involved in shipping, intellectual pursuits, and missionary activities for the Society of Friends. His commercial connections, language skills and acquaintances among the English and European nobility and their courts enabled him to provide advice, translation and interpretation services, and information to a wide variety of travelers. In his capacity as a mediator and advisor, Furly facilitated communication between a surprising spread of people who participated in larger Protestant international networks. He acted as an interpreter for English, Dutch and European Quakers, promoted William Penn's colony to Mennonite and sectarian emigrants from the Rhine Valley and Switzerland, and advised traveling teachers and missionaries from the Pietist institutions at Halle. In the process, Furly and other mediators like him helped to create a complex web of communication that enabled far-flung religious, commercial and colonial schemes to succeed.

# Furly as Quaker Missionary

Perhaps the most important service Furly offered to the Quakers was his work as a translator and interpreter. His knowledge of languages was extensive and impressive. When he was in his mid-twenties, he assisted Fox and John Stubbs in compiling *The Battle-Door for Teachers and Professors to learn Singular and Plural*, an explanation and defense of the Quakers' use of "thee" and "thou" which used thirty-five different languages. Furly supposedly contributed segments in Chaldean, Syrian, Welch and French.[11] In addition, he translated numerous English and Latin publications into Dutch, German and French. In 1675 and 1684 he participated in publishing two Dutch compilations of Quaker treatises and he translated numerous religious tracts by Penn. Furly also published his own treatises throughout the 1660s and 1670s. As a publisher of Quaker literature, he often added prefaces or postscripts to pamphlets, supervised the printing process, and distributed the final products.[12]

Furly's translation services went beyond print culture, however. He frequently acted as interpreter when traveling Friends visited Rotterdam or Amsterdam. As we have already seen, when Fox, Penn, Keith and Barclay traveled to the Netherlands in 1677, Furly hosted them and interpreted their sermons.[13] Edward Haistwell, Fox's secretary, noted that on 29 July, the missionaries held two meetings at Furly's house, where the Friends preached in English and Furly and Klaus acted as translators. The two men were kept quite busy. They offered their language skills again on 2, 3 and 5 August before Furly left with Penn, Barclay and Keith for their trip through Germany.[14] In 1684 and again in 1686 he acted as an interpreter for Fox and Penn.[15]

Furly not only used his language skills for visiting missionaries, he himself traveled as a ministering Friend. In 1671, he accompanied Penn and Thomas Rudyard to Herford in an attempt to convert Labadists there.[16] The Labadists were followers of Jean Labadie, who had spent some time in Amsterdam before Princess Elizabeth of the Palatinate, granddaughter of James I, invited them to Herford. Elizabeth had become acquainted with Anna Maria van Schurman and the Dutch Countess Anna Maria van Hoorn, two of Labadie's followers, during the time she lived in the Netherlands. They moved to Herford after they faced growing discrimination in Amsterdam. Since the Labadists shared some common beliefs with the Quakers, Penn and other Friends thought they might be more receptive to conversion. The missionaries' visit in 1671 marked the beginning of a correspondence between the Quakers and the Princess that continued throughout the 1670s. Furly delivered her letters to the English

Friends and periodically translated letters from other Labadists at Herford on their behalf.[17]

Furly and the Quaker missionaries were especially interested in establishing friendships with the Protestant European nobility and elites who were sympathetic to the Quakers or Pietism in general. In German states where individual leaders determined the religion of the realm, finding sympathetic princes or members of their courts enhanced the possibilities of toleration for fledgling Quaker meetings. In 1676 Furly traveled with Barclay a second time to visit the Princess and Countess van Hoorn.[18] The following year, when he went with Penn and Keith on a month-long tour of western Germany and eastern Holland, Furly and his companions visited their friends at Herford twice.[19] In August 1677 they also tried unsuccessfully to visit the court of Carl Ludwig, Elector Palatine in Mannheim to secure religious toleration for Quakers living in the Palatinate. The Elector had gone to Heidelberg and the missionaries had already promised to meet with Quakers in Kriegsheim the next day. No doubt their friendship with Elizabeth, a sister of the Elector Palatine, would have opened the doors for their visit to his court, had he been there.[20]

Another friend who connected Furly and his fellow Quaker missionaries to the European nobility was Francis Mercurius von Helmont. Von Helmont was the son of a chemist, physician and Baron from Belgium. Deeply interested in mystical religion, von Helmont spent much of his life traveling around Europe and England studying philosophy and religion. He was on friendly terms with many of the heads of state along the Rhine and first came into contact with the Quakers in 1660 when William Ames was visiting the court of Carl Ludwig in Heidelberg. From 1670 to 1679 he lived in England, where he served as the personal physician to Anne, Viscountess Conway. With Conway's conversion to Quakerism, von Helmont began regular correspondence with Keith, Fox, Penn, Barclay and Furly.[21] Elizabeth wrote to her brother, the Elector Palatine, in May 1677 noting her visit with the English Friends and commenting that "our Helmont greatly loves these people and says that their life is just like that of the Apostles, and that the nobility of England desire to have them in their service because of their honesty and Faithfulness."[22]

Furly gained important connections to the continental nobility and members of their court when he acted as interpreter on Quaker missionary journeys. Von Helmont, Princess Elisabeth and the Countess van Hoorn all participated in a larger network of European intellectuals seeking to reform society through individual Piety. One of their correspondents was Philip Jacob Spener, the founder of the Pietist movement, who was in

Frankfurt during the 1670s.[23] Spener and his friend, Johann Jakob Schütz, began weekly meetings in their homes to read and discuss devotional literature. The focus of their *collegium* was to promote personal piety. Spener and his followers were deeply influenced by Labadie's ideas of a Philadelphian community in which members demonstrated an experience of rebirth and lived in close fellowship with one another. Schütz, in particular, had corresponded with Anna Maria von Schurmann, one of Labadie's followers who had moved to Herford at Princess Elizabeth's invitation. He also was heavily influenced by the ideas of Christian Knorr von Rosenroth, a Lutheran minister from Bavaria, who was closely associated with von Helmont. Sometime after 1675 differences over these Philadelphian ideas led to a split between Spener and Schütz and the latter formed a group that became known as the Saalhof Pietists.[24]

On their 1677 journey throughout the Netherlands and Germany, Furly, Penn, and Keith solidified their connections with this network of religious seekers. In addition to their visits at Herford, they met with the Saalhof Pietists in Frankfurt. Among this group was Johanna Eleonora von Merlau, Juliane Baur van Eysseneck, Johann Wilhelm Petersen, and Jacob Vandewalle, the merchant with whom they lodged.[25] While their goal in visiting these elites was to participate in conversations about their religious beliefs, the missionaries also established relationships that would have a profound influence on later colonizing schemes.

Furly's and Penn's ties to the nobility and their missionary journeys led directly to lobbying on behalf of European Quakers suffering from persecution. In Kriegsheim, members of the Society of Friends were fined and imprisoned as early as 1658 for refusing to perform military service or pay war taxes. Several English Quaker women who preached publicly also created animosity toward Kriegsheim Friends when they visited the city in 1678. A lively pamphlet exchange ensued between Johann Reinhard Hermann, the Reformed pastor of a neighboring village, and Peter Hendricks, a Quaker button maker in Amsterdam. Although the Elector Palatine officially encouraged religious toleration, local clergy, magistrates, and citizens were openly hostile toward Quakers. English missionaries, including Penn, repeatedly petitioned the Elector on behalf of the persecuted Friends.[26]

Further down the Rhine, Quakers in Krefeld experienced similar episodes of discrimination beginning in 1679. Hendricks reported to English Friends that "Concerning ye Crevelt friends, they have been banished and sent away twice with a threatning from ye deputie of Crevelt the last time if they come in againe, they should be whipt and burnt on theire backs, sweareing by his soules salvation he should do it." He continued by noting: "but they have been theire again peacably a prettie while, about 6 or 7 weekes; only ye husbandman Johannes, was beaten greiveously of late, by 2 of his neighbors, when he was passing by them."[27] As they had done for the Kriegsheim Quakers, English and Dutch leaders wrote petitions to government officials on behalf of the Krefeld Friends. Furly, Hendricks, and Arent Sonnemans wrote from Holland to local officials while Penn wrote to the Prince of Orange requesting toleration for fellow Friends.[28]

Many of the Kriegsheim and Krefeld Quakers whose suffering Furly worked to alleviate had been Mennonites prior to joining the Society of Friends.[29] They participated in another series of communication channels that was evolving during the second half of the seventeenth century. Consequently, while Furly's missionary work and his services as translator and interpreter greatly expanded his network of contacts among Europe's religious leaders and nobility, they also provided the Quakers entry into another web of information that had emerged as another group of dissenters sought religious toleration.

## Caring for their own: Anabaptist/Mennonite Communication Channels

By the end of the 1670s, Mennonites in Kriegsheim and Krefeld were communicating with Dutch Mennonites; Anabaptists living in Alsace, the Palatinate and the Rhine Valley; and Swiss Brethren in Bern and Zürich. Each of these groups traced their origins to the radical Reformation and shared a common belief in adult or "believer's" baptism. Consequently, they became known as *Wiedertäufer* or Anabaptists (re-baptizers). From the mid-sixteenth century on, Anabaptists throughout the Rhine Valley and the Netherlands called themselves Mennonites (*Mennoniten, Menisten*) in reference to Menno Simons, a former Catholic priest who worked to unite Anabaptists in Holland and Northern Germany. In the Netherlands, Dutch Mennonites achieved religious toleration by 1580. Within a century, university-educated ministers led the Church with the aid of lay leaders who were well established doctors and merchants.[30]

The wealth and religious toleration Dutch Mennonites enjoyed laid the foundation for the communication channels they developed in the seventeenth century. In the late 1630s, Swiss authorities passed measures banishing Anabaptists in Zürich. When news reached Holland, Dutch Mennonites responded by sending food, money and supplies up the Rhine

River to aid in resettling religious exiles. They worked together with small Anabaptist congregations settled throughout the Palatinate to provide new homes for Swiss refugees. In addition, they successfully lobbied state and Church authorities in Zürich to halt persecution.[31]

Beginning in 1670, however, new measures sent another wave of Swiss Brethren into Alsace and the Palatinate. Once again, Dutch Mennonites collected money, food, clothing and tools to distribute among the exiles. Clergy in the Palatinate reported that 643 refugees had settled in areas on the east and west banks of the Rhine where Anabaptist congregations were helping them establish new homes. The exiles posed a heavy financial burden on their benefactors because they had brought little property or money with them. According to the report of Valentine Huetwohl, a Mennonite minister at Kriegsheim, the total value of their goods amounted to only 1654 *Reichstaler* and a few household goods. Thus the refugees relied heavily on the financial assistance of the Dutch Mennonites.[32]

The financial aid system that Mennonites living in the Rhine Valley established was headed by a handful of church leaders who collected and redistributed information, goods, and money to their congregants. In the Netherlands, Hans Vlamingh, a wealthy merchant from Amsterdam and a deacon in "the Sun" congregation began the initial efforts to aid Swiss exiles. By the end of the seventeenth century, church and lay leaders from congregations in Rotterdam, Haarlem, and other Dutch cities were also soliciting goods and money on behalf of religious refugees. Assigned committees traveled up the Rhine to deliver items and money to those who needed help.[33]

While Dutch urban areas functioned as collection points, several cities and towns along the Rhine became important distribution and communication centers. In the Palatinate, congregations in Kriegsheim and Mannheim provided shelter for refugees fleeing Switzerland. Church and lay leaders in these cities helped the exiles find homes in the surrounding areas. In 1671, Jacob Everling in Obersülzen noted that they had housed sixty of the exiles, many of whom were very old or very young. Fifty others had gone to Mannheim. The following year a church council met at Kriegsheim to determine how to assist the influx of recent arrivals.[34] Huetwohl and Georg Liechti, the leader of the Swiss refugees, spent four days traveling from village to village to construct a census of the 76 Swiss families scattered among the Palatine Anabaptists. Further down the Rhine, Mennonites in Krefeld also contributed money and supplies to aid the cause.[35]

In each place, those who joined the efforts to help religious refugees had been targets of religious discrimination. Anabaptists and Mennonites living in the Palatinate and along the Rhine enjoyed limited religious toleration but their situation always remained precarious. In 1660, Mennonites in Kriegsheim who petitioned the Elector claimed their neighbors were not allowing them to purchase property because of their religious identity.[36] In 1680 they petitioned again because the local inspector claimed that only 20 people could meet in one place for worship. They believed their congregations could include the members of 20 families.[37] Further down the Rhine, Mennonites in Gladbach had moved to Krefeld in search of religious toleration in 1654.[38] Forty years later, when thirty men, women and children from the Mennonite congregation in Rheydt were imprisoned, some of those same refugees collected 8,000 *Reichstaler* in bail money to purchase their release.[39]

Like leading Friends, Mennonite ministers and elders petitioned local officials and heads of states in their efforts to retain the privileges they had won and to extend them to the newly exiled members of their community. At times they directed their petitions to local and regional officials, as was the case in 1660 when Rotterdam Mennonites convinced city officials to write to the city of Bern on behalf of Swiss Anabaptists who had been banished.[40] In other cases, they appealed to heads of state, as the Kriegs heim Mennonite Church leaders had done in 1680.[41] They also recruited other Protestant kings and members of the nobility sympathetic to their cause to apply pressure on appropriate political leaders. In 1694 Krefeld Mennonites solicited the help of the Dutch States General and William, King of England, in their attempts to free imprisoned congregants from Rheydt. Both the States General and the English King sent letters to the Catholic Elector Palatine, Johann Wilhelm, pressuring him to change his policies concerning the Protestant dissenters.[42]

Thus, ministers and elders of congregations covering a wide swath between Amsterdam and Zürich corresponded regularly to aid religious exiles and achieve toleration. At the same time, Furly, Penn and Keith traveled up the Rhine to convince Mennonites in places like Kriegsheim, Worms and Frankenthal of the "truth." Although the two groups differed in some of their beliefs, they shared a common emphasis on an individual's direct relationship to God and an abhorrence of war. More significantly, members of both groups worked regularly to alleviate discrimination and intolerance based on their status as dissenters.

# Furly as Penn's Agent

In the midst of this concern for religious toleration, Penn received his charter for Pennsylvania. His intent for the colony, according to his own account, was "The service of God first, the honor and advantage of the king, with our own profit."[43] He hoped to establish a colony that would both provide a haven for those suffering from religious discrimination and supply him with an income to combat his growing debt. To recruit settlers for his colony, Penn commissioned a group of agents, including Furly. Furly was ideally suited to serve Penn's purposes. His language skills, religious connections, and commercial ties were indispensable assets in advertising Pennsylvania on the European continent.[44]

Furly's first task as Penn's agent was to translate and distribute promotional literature in France, the Netherlands and the German states. At least fifty-eight broadsides, books and pamphlets were published in English, Dutch, German, and French to promote Pennsylvania. Penn and Furly wasted no time in publishing information about the colony. In 1681, immediately after receiving his charter, Penn wrote *Some account of the Province of Pennsilvania in America; Lately Granted under the Great Seal of England to William Penn, &c*, which Furly translated into Dutch and German. To strengthen the appeal of the pamphlet, Furly appended a copy of Penn's "Liberty of Conscience" to the Dutch and German translations. He also included a postscript in which he gave specific instructions from Penn's agents in England and a note that "further information can be obtained in Amsterdam from Jan Roelofs van der Werf, in the Heere-Straat, at the Vergulde Vijfhoek, and in Rotterdam from Benjamin Furly, English merchant."[45] The following year Penn published *A brief Account of the Province of Pennsylvania, Lately Granted by the King Under the Great Seal of England, to William Penn and his Heirs and Assigns*. Furly also translated this tract into German, Dutch and French.[46] Throughout the early years of the colony's settlement, he extended the translation services he had offered the Quakers by using his language skills to promote Penn's colony.

As he had done with the Friends' literature, Furly distributed Penn's promotional pamphlets to his personal, religious and business correspondents. Through his efforts, literature about Pennsylvania circulated throughout the Netherlands and as far as Lübeck and Danzig to the east and Switzerland to the south.[47] Furly immediately advertised the new colony to the Quakers at Krefeld, on whose behalf he had lobbied local leaders just the previous year. Jacob Telner, Dirck Sipman, and Jan Streypers, of Krefeld and Kaldenkirchen, were the first purchasers from that area when they bought 15,000 acres on 10 March 1682.[48] Shortly after purchasing land from Penn, Sipman agreed with two Kriegsheim Quakers, Gerhardt Hendricks and Peter Schuhmacher, to become co-tenants on his land with Herman Isacks op den Graeff, another Krefeld Friend.[49] Quakers at Kriegsheim, like those at Krefeld, were interested in escaping the harassment of religious and local officials. Over the next decade, most of the Quaker community in Kriegsheim and many of their Mennonite neighbors and family members migrated to Pennsylvania. Furly's connections established during his missionary journeys provided an excellent outlet for recruiting Quaker and Mennonite settlers from the Rhine Valley and the Palatinate.[50]

The influence of Furly's Quaker missionary networks is also evident in the investments of the Frankfurt Company. He sent private letters to the Saalhof Pietists he had visited in Frankfurt in 1677 encouraging them to migrate to Pennsylvania. As a result of his efforts, Francis Daniel Pastorius purchased land on behalf of eight of the Pietists. When the Frankfurt Company formed in 1686, its investors included Van de Walle, Schutz, Johann Wilhelm Ueberfeld, von Merlau (wife of Petersen) and Gerhard von Mastricht, all people Furly had met on his missionary trip in 1677.[51] Pastorius was the only one of the original investors who emigrated to Pennsylvania. He consulted with Telner, the Krefeld settlers, and other Dutch Quakers at Rotterdam on his way to London and Philadelphia.[52]

In addition to distributing promotional literature and sending private letters to advertise Penn's colony, Furly hand-copied and translated letters emigrants sent home and passed them on to business partners. One example of this is a set of letters Furly sent to Jaspar Balthasar Könneken, a Pietist book-dealer in Lübeck. These letters were first-hand reports about what to expect in Pennsylvania and how to make arrangements to emigrate. As both a Pietist and merchant, Könneken had access to commercial markets and religious information networks. Another business connection Furly used for distributing information was Johann Jawert, also from Lübeck. Jawert was the son of Balthasar Jawert, one of the original members of the Frankfurt Company who communicated regularly with Pietists and other religious dissenters throughout Germany. He worked together with Könneken to spread information about Penn's colony to potential emigrants.[53]

Finally, in addition to selling them land, Furly used his resources as a merchant to help emigrants find transportation to the colony. In 1683, when the Krefeld Quakers emigrated, Telner accompanied them to Rotterdam, where Furly met them. He and Telner then arranged for their passage to Pennsylvania through James Claypoole, a Quaker merchant from London. Furly sent a list of names and money for the fare of thirty-three passengers who were to join Claypoole on board the "Concord."[54] He provided similar services to the Quaker emigrants from Kriegsheim and to the settlers who accompanied Johann Jacob Zimmerman from Württemberg in 1693.[55] Zimmerman, who died in Rotterdam before making the journey to Pennsylvania, was the original leader of a Philadelphian community established by Johannes Kelpius on the Wissahickon later that same year.[56]

## Furly's transatlantic networks

Furly's attempts to help the Krefeld emigrants and Zimmerman's followers secure transportation to Penn's colony reveal just how extensive his communication networks became by the early eighteenth century. His relationships with two participants in these migrations, Telner and Daniel Falckner, demonstrate the wide range of connections fostered by Protestants wishing to secure religious toleration and promote reform through individual Piety. For several decades at the end of the seventeenth and beginning of the eighteenth centuries, the concerns of religious leaders intersected with those of European heads of state, colonial proprietors, and governors. Men like Furly, Telner and Falckner participated in multiple conversations that cut across political and religious boundaries and they perceived the potential of colonization for achieving their goals.

Telner, who worked with Furly to find transportation for the Krefeld Quakers in 1683, was a Dutch Mennonite from Amsterdam who joined the Society of Friends by 1676. A wealthy merchant, he faced occasional difficulties with his fellow Quakers concerning his opulent lifestyle. Nevertheless, Telner traveled as a missionary to New York and the Delaware Valley between 1678 and 1681. Either before he left or shortly after he returned, he moved to Krefeld where he soon invested in Penn's colony. In 1683, Telner accompanied his neighbors on their way to Pennsylvania as far as Rotterdam, where he helped them make transportation arrangements and consulted with Pastorius, who was traveling to the colony on behalf of the Frankfurt Company. The following year, Telner moved to the British colonies with his wife and daughter. After a brief stay in New York, he settled in Germantown, from where he maintained contact with Quakers and Labadists in New York. Although he made several trips back to Europe, he remained in Germantown until either 1696 or 1698. Upon returning to Europe, Telner settled in London where he worked as a linendraper.[57]

Evidence of Telner's activities after his return to London is sketchy but glimpses of them indicate his ongoing connections to several colonization schemes involving issues of religious toleration. In 1706 Telner acted as a conduit for the Thuringia Company, an unsuccessful attempt to settle people from Saxony in South Carolina. He received letters from the company and helped to have them translated and then passed on to John Archdale, a prominent Quaker and proprietor of South Carolina. Others who played a role in the scheme were Johann Heinrich Sprögel, the son of a prominent Lutheran Pietist minister at Quedlinburg, and Daniel Falckner.[58] Both Sprögel and Falckner were involved with the Frankfurt Company's investments in Pennsylvania and both lived in Germantown either during or shortly following the period when Telner lived there.[59] It is not clear exactly who was behind the Thuringia Company's plans, but Sprögel's and Falckner's participation suggests that Pietists in Saxony may have been the primary promoters of the scheme.

Pietism had begun to take hold in Saxony after Spener moved to the city of Dresden in the late 1680s. August Hermann Francke, a student at the University of Leipzig, came under Spener's influence in 1687 and 1688. By the early 1690s, Francke had emerged as the leader of the movement in central and northern Germany. However, both Francke and Spener lost favor with the political and religious authorities and the Elector of Saxony prohibited Pietist "coventicles" from meeting in 1690. Francke was forced to leave Leipzig and take a position as the pastor at Glaucha and professor of oriental studies at the new university in Halle in 1692. Spener left the Elector of Saxony's court chapel in Dresden for the pastorate of St Nicholas Church in Berlin.[60] It is conceivable that Pietists seeking religious toleration were among those who were secretly plotting to migrate to Carolina.

Certainly Falckner was actively recruiting settlers for Penn's colony at the same time he was associated with the Thuringia Company's plotting. The son of a Lutheran minister in Saxony, Falckner had established ties to Spener and Francke by the 1690s. He had also come under the influence of Zimmerman and Kelpius. When they decided to migrate to Pennsylvania in 1694, Falckner joined them. After spending several years in the colony, he returned to Europe to recruit additional settlers.[61] Sometime late in 1698, Falckner arrived in London where he and Henrich Bernhard Koster were planning a trip to Sweden and Saxony to raise money for the Lutheran church in Pennsylvania and secure the services of a minister.[62] Upon his arrival in Halle later that year, Francke posed a series of questions to Falckner about Pennsylvania. His reply to the questions was published in *Curieuse Nachricht von Pensylvania in Norden Americas* in

1702 and was very influential in spurring migration to the colony.[63] On his return trip in 1699, Falckner visited members of the Frankfurt Company in Frankfurt, where he was commissioned to act as their agent. He also met with Furly in Rotterdam where he and his brother received a power of attorney to act as Furly's agent in Pennsylvania.[64]

Falckner was not Furly's only connection to the new Pietist center at Halle. On April 10, 1699, Jacob Bruno Wigers reported from Rotterdam that Furly had translated his "testimonial" into English and had promised to recommend Wigers and his traveling companion to an Earl in London.[65] In addition, he reported, Furly's advice had spared the two men from paying extra duties on their books and other goods when they arrived in England.[66] Wigers was a teacher trained in the newly minted pedagogical institutions at Halle who was on his way to England to spread Pietist ideas about reforming society through education. He was writing to Francke about the status of friends and acquaintances sympathetic to their mission and the conditions of his journey to the Netherlands. By pointing out who could provide help at each stop along the way, Wigers self-consciously laid the groundwork for others to follow in his footsteps to England.

Wigers' reliance on Furly's assistance confirms just how extensive the English Quaker merchant's connections had grown. Men like Furly, Falckner and Telner provided critical links in the transatlantic information networks that shaped migration to the British colonies. They were tied together by their interests in reforming society through individual piety, their attempts to unite divisions within the Christian Church, and their appeals for religious toleration. The correspondence they carried out on behalf of their religious interests provided ideal conduits for advertising Penn's colony, which they viewed as a haven for religious refugees. Their commercial knowledge furnished the practical information missionaries and immigrants needed to travel from one place to another. In short, Furly, and others like him, were mediators who linked together a broad range of religious, economic and political interests and allowed a wide variety of colonial and religious schemes to succeed.

# Notes

1. Mary Maples Dunn and Richard S. Dunn (eds), *The Papers of William Penn, 1644–1679*, Philadelphia, 1981, vol. 1, p. 439 (hereafter *Penn Papers*); Norman Penney, (ed.), *The Short Journal and Itinerary*

*Journals of George Fox*, New York, 1925, p. 239 (hereafter, *Haistwell Diary*).

2. William I. Hull, *Benjamin Furly and Quakerism in Rotterdam*, Lancaster PA, 1941, pp. 3–50.

3. *Haistwell Diary*, p. 239.

4. Hull, *Benjamin Furly*, 46; Ethyn Kirby, *George Keith, 1638–1716*, New York, 1942, p. 37.

5. D. Elton Trueblood, *Robert Barclay*, New York, 1968, pp. 84–7; Kirby, *George Keith*, pp. 36–9; *Penn Papers*, vol. 1, p. 425f.

6. *Penn Papers*, vol. 1, pp. 24–6; Trueblood, *Robert Barclay*, 61–77; Kirby, *George Keith*, pp. 19–34.

7. Cornelius J. Dyck, (ed.), *An Introduction to Mennonite History*, Scottdale PA, 1967; Cornelius Krahn, *Dutch Anabaptism*, Scottdale PA, 1981; Richard K. MacMaster, *Land, Piety, Peoplehood: The Establishment of Mennonite Communities in America, 1683–1790*, Scottdale PA, 1985, pp. 19–34.

8. F. Ernest Stoeffler, *The Rise of Evangelical Pietism*, Leiden, 1971; Durnbaugh, D. *European Origins of the Brethren*, Elgin IL, 1958, pp. 19–36.

9. See, for example, *Penn Papers*, vol. 1, pp. 205–8, 211f., 259–61, 276–84.

10. See documents #1746–1783 (section entitled "Voorspraak bij de Overheid") in the papers of the Dutch Mennonites' *Commissie voor de Buitenlandsche Nooden* (Commission for Foreign Needs), Archives of the Dutch Mennonite Church, Amsterdam Municipal Archives, Amsterdam, Netherlands (hereafter CFN).

11. Hull, *Benjamin Furly*, pp. 8, 68f.

12. Ibid., pp. 32f., 43f., pp. 69–76.

13. Ibid., pp. 45–47.

14. *Haistwell Diary*, p. 238f.

15. Hull, *Benjamin Furly*, p. 51f.

16. Ibid., p. 31.

17. William I. Hull, *William Penn and the Dutch Quaker Migration to Pennsylvania*, Philadelphia, 1935, pp. 21–31; Stoeffler, *The Rise of Evangelical Pietism*, 162–9; Trueblood, *Robert Barclay*, 85–91. For Penn's correspondence with Labadie's followers, see *Penn Papers*, vol. 1, pp. 215–19.

18. Trueblood, *Robert Barclay*, p. 84f.

19. Penn's journal of this journey is in *Penn Papers*, vol. 1, pp. 425–508. See also Hull, *William Penn*, 64–106.

20. Paul Michel, "Täufer, Mennoniten und Quäker in Kriegsheim bei Worms," *Der Wormsgau* 7 (1965/66), 46; *Penn Papers*, vol. 1, pp. 451–4.

21. Hull, *Benjamin Furly*, 105–12. For Conway's life, see Marjorie H. Nicolson, ed., *Conway Letters: The Correspondence of Anne, Viscountess Conway, Henry More, and their Friends, 1642–1684*, New Haven CT, 1930. See Ibid., 359–451, for her correspondence concerning Von Helmont and Quakerism.

22. Hull, *Benjamin Furly*, p. 110.

23. Stoeffler, *The Rise of Evangelical Pietism*, p. 229.

24. Elizabeth Fisher, "'Prophesies and Revelations': German Cabbalists in Early Pennsylvania," *Pennsylvania Magazine of History and Biography* 109 (1985), 302–06.

25. Fisher, "'Prophesies and Revelations'," p. 316f.; for a description of the missionaries' visit, see *Penn Papers*, vol. 1, pp. 447f., 454–6; Hull, W., *William Penn*, 132–9.

26. Documents concerning the Quakers in Kriegsheim are in the Badisches Generallandesarchiv Karlsruhe (hereafter GLA), 77/4337. See also reports about Quaker missionary trips to the area in Roger Longworth, Amsterdam, to Phineas Pemberton, n.d., Pemberton Papers, vol. 1, p. 117; Roger Longworth, Rotterdam, to James Harrison, 24 August 1679, Pemberton Papers, vol. 1, p. 119, Historical Society of Pennsylvania, Philadelphia, PA (hereafter HSP). For general background, see Michel, "Täufer, Mennoniten und Quäker," p. 43f.; Hull, *William Penn*, pp. 266–91.

27. Petter Hendriks, Amsterdam, to Roger Longworth, 4 June 1680, Etting Collection, Misc. Mss., 4:9, HSP.

28. Hull, *William Penn*, pp. 196–204.

29. Michel, "Täufer, Mennoniten und Quäker," p., 50.

30. Rosalind J. Beiler, "Distributing Aid to Believers in Need: The Religious Foundations of Transatlantic Migration," *Pennsylvania History: Special Supplemental Issue* 64 (1997), 73–6.

31. Beiler, "Distributing Aid," p. 76. The communication channels of European Anabaptist groups are outlined in CFN, Archives of the Dutch Mennonite Church, Amsterdam Municipal Archives, Amsterdam, Netherlands. The collection consists of more than one thousand documents which are abstracted in J. G. de Hoop Scheffer, *Inventar der Archiefstukken Berustende bij de Vereenigde Doopsgezinde Gemeente te Amsterdaam*, Amsterdam, 1883. A selection of these papers is available on microfilm at the Lancaster Mennonite Historical Society, Lancaster, PA. An additional selection of transcripts is at the HSP in a collection identified as "Dutch Papers." I have identified all of the original documents with the numbers from de Hoop Scheffer's inventory.

32. CFN #1248 lists the heads of households, family members and the property they brought with them.

33. CFN #s 1248, 1400–1406; Nanne van der Zijpp, "The Dutch Aid the Swiss Mennonites," in Cornelius J. Dyck (ed.), *A Legacy of Faith*, Newton KS, 1962, 139f.; R. MacMaster, *Land, Piety, Peoplehood*, p. 27.

34. CFN #1405. The ministers who signed a letter from the council included Valentin Huetwohl, Kriegsheim, Christian Peters, Gundersheim, Jacob Everlingh, Obersülzen, Jacob Gut, Hilsbach (Kraichgau), Hans Luscher, Schimbsheim, and Ulli Seyler, leader of the Swiss refugees. CFN #1248. For locations of the ministers, see Harold S. Bender, (ed.), "Palatine Mennonite Census Lists, 1664–1774," *Mennonite Quarterly Review* 14 (1940), 5–40.

35. CFN #1248. Many of the Mennonites in Krefeld originally came from the surrounding areas of Gladbach (1654) and Rheydt (1694). Those from Gladbach and Rheydt were linen weavers who were instrumental in making Krefeld the regional center for the textile industry. Peter Kriedte, *Proto-Industrialisierung und großes Kapital. Das Seidengewerbe in Krefeld und seinem Umland bis zum Ende des Ancien Regime*, Bonn, 1983, pp. 221–224.

36. GLA 77/4336a, p. 63f.

37. November 26, 1680, GLA 77/4337.

38. Ralf Klötzer, "Verfolgt, geduldet, anerkannt: Von Täufern zu Mennoniten am Niederrhein und die Geschichte der Mennoniten in Krefeld bis zum Ende der oranischen Zeit (ca. 1530–1702)" in: *Sie kamen als Fremde: Die Mennoniten in Krefeld von den Anfängen bis zur Gegenwart*, ed. by Wolfgang Froese, Krefeld, 1995, pp. 34–6.

39. Ibid., p. 48f.; CFN #1427, 1759, 1760, 1761, 1752, 1753; see also documents in 80/4/5, 30/4/6, 80/4/7, 80/4/8, 80/4/12, 80/4/14, 80/4/15, 80/4/16, Archiv der Mennonitengemeinde Krefeld, Stadtarchiv, Krefeld, Germany.

40. CFN #1746.

41. 26 November 1680, GLA 77/4337.

42. CFN #1749, 1750, 1751, 1752, 1753, 1755; 80/4/7, 80/4/10, 80/4/11, Archiv der Mennonitengemeinde Krefeld.

43. William Penn, New York, to William Blathwayt and Francis Gwyn, 21 November 1682, in Jean R. Soderlund (ed.), *William Penn and the Founding of Pennsylvania, 1680–1684: A Documentary History*, Philadelphia, 1983, p. 190.

44. Between 1681 and 1700, Furly sold almost 50,000 acres of land in Penn's colony. Hull, *William Penn*, p. 253.

45. Julius Sachse, "Daniel Falckner's Curieuse Nachricht from Pennsylvania," in: *Pennsylvania: The German Influence in its Settlement and Development. A Narrative and Critical History* (*The Pennsylvania-German Society Proceedings and Addresses* 14), Lancaster PA, 1905, p. 10; Hull, *William Penn*, 311f. Quote is from Hull, *William Penn*, p. 312.

46. Sachse, "Daniel Falckner's Curieuse Nachricht," 9–12; "Address of Julius F. Sachse," *The Pennsylvania-German Society Proceedings and Addresses* 7 (1897), 157–64.

47. Sachse, "Daniel Falckner's Curieuse Nachricht," p. 10.

48. Ibid., p. 10f.; Samuel Pennypacker, "The Settlement of Germantown, PA and the Causes which Led to It", *Pennsylvania Magazine of History and Biography* 4 (1880); reprinted in: *Historical and Biographical Sketches*, Philadelphia PA, 1883, 11f.

49. Hull, *William Penn*, p. 290f.

50. Beiler, "Distributing Aid," pp. 73–87.

51. Pennypacker, "The Settlement of Germantown," pp. 12–14; Hull, *William Penn*, pp. 243, 336–9; *Penn Papers*, vol. 1, p. 447f.

52. Hull, *William Penn*, p. 243; Pennypacker, "The Settlement of Germantown," p. 16f.

53. Hull, *William Penn*, pp. 329–36; Sachse, "Daniel Falckner's Curieuse Nachricht," pp. 14–21. For facsimiles of the hand-copied letters Furly sent, see Julius Friedrich Sachse, ed., *Letters Relating to the Settlement of Germantown in Pennsylvania, 1683–4, from the Könneken Manuscript in the Ministerial-Archiv of Lübeck*, Philadelphia, 1903.

54. Hull, *William Penn*, p. 254f.; Marion Balderston, *James Claypoole's Letter Book: London and Philadelphia, 1681–1684*, San Marino CA, 1967. See letters from Claypoole to Furly, 5 June 1683, p. 215f.; and Claypoole to Furly, 10 July 1683, p. 221f.

55. Hull, *William Penn*, 337–9.

56. Fisher, "'Prophesies and Revelations'," pp. 299–302, 318–25.

57. Hull, *William Penn*, 239–53; J. G. de Hoop Scheffer, "Mennonite Emigration to Pennsylvania," *Pennsylvania Magazine of History and Biography* 2 (1878), 122f.; Pennypacker, *Historical and Biographical Sketches*, 32–4.

58. Polycarpus Michael Richenbach to John Archdale, 22 September 1705; German Thuringian Company to the Lords [Proprietors], 22 September 1705; German Company in Thuringia to the [Lords Proprietors], 23 May 1706; John Archdale to the [German Company in Thuringia], [n.d.]; Archdale Manuscripts, copies in the Library of Congress. For Archdale's attempts to recruit German-speaking settlers, see Henry G. Hood, *The Public Career of John Archdale, 1642–1717*,

Greensboro, NC, 1976, pp. 31–3. Several years later Telner also worked as an advocate on behalf of several Palatine Mennonite families on their way to Pennsylvania. In a letter to the Mennonite congregation "the Lamb" in Amsterdam, he requested financial assistance for six families who were destitute. He noted that London Quakers had already given money to eight families for their ship fare to Pennsylvania and these also needed aid. The migrating families were Swiss refugees who had settled in the Palatinate but had never succeeded in earning a living. They were seeking better living conditions in the British colonies. CFN #2250. For context, see John Ruth, *Maintaining the Right Fellowship: A Narrative Account of Life in the Oldest Mennonite Community in North America*, Scottdale PA, 1984, p. 88f.

59. For information about Sprögel, see Julius Friedrich Sachse, *The German Pietists of Provincial Pennsylvania*, Philadelphia: printed for the author, 1895, repr. New York, 1970, p. 313; and Craig W. Horle et al., (eds), *Lawmaking and Legislators in Pennsylvania: A Biographical Dictionary, 1710–1756*, Philadelphia, 1997, vol. 2, p. 937f. For a brief biography of Falckner, see Sachse, "Daniel Falckner's Curieuse Nachricht," pp. 31–8 and Sachse, *The German Pietists of Provincial Pennsylvania*, pp. 167–75.

60. Stoeffler, *The Rise of Evangelical Pietism*, p. 229f.; Fred Ernest Stoeffler, *German Pietism during the Eighteenth Century*, Leiden, 1973, pp. 1–7; Markus Matthias, (ed.), *Lebensläufe August Hermann Franckes*, Leipzig, 1999, pp. 33–47; Richard L. Gawthrop, *Pietism and the Making of Eighteenth-Century Prussia*, Cambridge, 1993, p. 118f.

61. Sachse, *German Pietists*, pp. 167–75; Sachse, "Daniel Falckner's Curieuse Nachricht," pp. 31–8; Daniel Falckner, Lübeck, to A. H. Francke, 26 August 1691, Falckner, Lüneburg, to A. H. Francke, 8 February 1692, Falckner, Hamburg, to A. H. Francke, 27 January 1693, Francke-Nachlass, Amerika Fasc. XII, pp. 1106–11, Archiv der Franckeschen Stiftung, Halle, Germany (hereafter Halle Archives).

62. Jacob Bruno Wigers, London, to Henry July Elers, Halle, 3 May 1699, Hauptarchiv, B71a, pp. 69–74, Halle Archives. Fisher traces the connections between Kelpius and Zimmerman's followers who went with him to Pennsylvania and Jane Leade's Philadelphians in London as well as those on the Continent. Eleanora von Merlau and her husband Johann Wilhelm Peterson, investors in the Frankfurt Company, were both leaders of the movement in Germany. They also corresponded regularly with Francke. E. Fisher, "'Prophesies and Revelations'," p. 320. Falckner's involvement in the Thuringia Company's schemes is illusive. However, he had been seen in London in 1699 together with several deputies the

company sent to America. See microfilmed documents from the Säch-sisches Hauptstaatsarchiv, Dresden for the year 1706, #2249, pp. 7–9, Library of Congress, Washington DC.

63. Sachse, "Daniel Falckner's Curieuse Nachricht," 39f., pp. 45–63.

64. Sachse, "Benjamin Furly," *Pennsylvania Magazine of History and Biography* 19 (1895), 287. See also Sachse, *German Pietists*, 144f., 167–71.

65. Jacob Bruno Wigers, Rotterdam, to August Hermann Francke, Halle, 10 April 1699, Hauptarchiv B71a, pp. 57–62, Halle Archives.

66. Jacob Bruno Wigers, London, to Henry July Elers, Halle, 3 May 1699, Hauptarchiv B71a, pp. 69–74, Halle Archives.

# 3
# Te Deum for Victory: Communicating Victories through Sermons, Illuminations and Gun Salute

*Sebastian Küster*

Rumors, songs, spoken words, oral and written proclamations, hand-written newsletters, printed pamphlets, newspapers, medals, processions and theatre-plays – during the first half of the eighteenth century all kind of media served to establish communication between people, between governments and subjects and to secure the exchange of information. Not everybody in the hierarchy of the social structure of a state had access to all these media. Were there, nevertheless, media accessible to everyone, to the whole population of a state? And if so, what kind of information could people get via these media?

In the following, communication processes in Austria, the Electorate of Hanover, France and Great Britain in the 1740s will be analyzed to see how the inhabitants of these states came in contact with information about the current affairs of their country. The focus of interest will not be the well-informed minister of state or a small social elite but the wider public of the subjects. What kind of information about the current political and military affairs could they obtain? Which media served them for their information and who used these media to distribute news? In the four countries examined, the Church with its *Te Deum Laudamus* plays a role in these communication processes. But what kind of message was sent via this at first glance purely clerical communication channel? Who was the sender, for which purpose was the message sent, and who was intended to receive it? It will be shown, that the role of the *Te Deum Laudamus* and of other media inside the Austrian, Hanoverian, French and English communication network varied from state to state.

Austria, Vienna, Sunday, 7 July 1743. The bells of all the churches in Vienna were ringing; Maria Theresa, the young archduchess of Austria, having arrived with her carriage from the Palace of Schönbrunn, entered the Cathedral of Saint Stephan. While the nobility and the clergy of state and town were assembled in the cathedral to sing the *Te Deum Laudamus* with all solemnity and to listen to a special thanksgiving-prayer of the suffragan bishop, a regiment of soldiers gathered outside the church. In the midst of the bell ringing they fired a three-gun salute that was answered from the city walls by a salute of the heavy artillery.[1] What had happened? What was the reason for these celebrations?

Ten days earlier, on 27 June, Austrian troops, who together with English and Hanoverian troops formed the so-called "Pragmatic Army", had been led into battle by George II, King of Great-Britain and Elector of Hanover. They had fought against a French army under the command of the experienced Maréchal de Noailles. In this combat, which took place near a little village called Dettingen on the Main River in the south-west of the Holy Roman Empire, the combined army was fighting to secure the Pragmatic Sanction and to settle Maria Theresa's husband safely on the Empire's throne. George II finally won this battle at Dettingen more from chance than to military skills after several hours of combat.[2] Even though the victory on the Main was not an entirely Austrian one, it still brought new hope that times were changing. Therefore, four days after the news had reached the city, the air in Vienna was filled with bell ringing and shooting. The victory of Dettingen was celebrated by a special thanksgiving service in the Cathedral of Saint Stephan.

It was not only in Vienna that Austrian people took notice of the battle on the Main River. When the good news came to Brussels on 30 June the bells of all the churches in that city, too, were ringing, the cannons on the walls were fired and in the evening the houses of the wealthy inhabitants of the city were illuminated.[3] Three weeks later Prague was filled with the noise of bells, canons and military marching.[4] To other towns of the Austrian territory the news of the victory came with less noise and celebrations. In the month of July until mid-August it was spread through all parts of Austria. In every church the Catholic community sang a *Te Deum Laudamus* on behalf of the victory. Mostly the praising of the good Lord was combined with thanks to the "weapons of our most gracious mother of the people and sovereign Maria Theresa."[5]

Bell ringing, gun salute and – all over the Austrian territory – singing of the *Te Deum Laudamus*: this was how the information of the victory at Dettingen made its way through the Austrian dominions. To be able to put this manner of spreading the news in a greater context of communication practice in Austria, it will be necessary to answer the following four questions: Who was responsible for the spreading of the news through the vast Austrian state? What was the content of the *Te Deum* and the prayers held in their context? Who could take notice of the news of the victory?

And finally, what were the alternatives to get in touch with the news; what other media helped to spread the information?

The bell ringing and other celebrations in the Austrian Netherlands were initiated by the local Austrian authorities in Brussels. The thanksgiving service in the Cathedral of Saint Stephan was due to orders of the archduchess herself. The spreading of the news throughout the Austrian state that followed later on, was then organized by the central military board in Vienna, the "Hofkriegsrat", who sent written orders to the bishops in the country to sing *Te Deum* for the victory of Dettingen.[6] In every case it was the secular authority that took the initiative and who used the network and the voice of the Church to execute its orders and to spread the arranged message.

In fact, the message distributed by the government to dioceses and parishes was a short one. It contained barely more than the order to pray for a victory gained on 27 June at Dettingen near the Main River against a French army for the good cause of the Archduchess Maria Theresa. No details of the battle itself, no lists of the wounded and dead were transmitted. Not even the heroic conduct of the Austrian troops was mentioned, not a word was said about the political context. Though the information given to the clergy was very limited, the audience addressed by the message was a very large one: Almost 100 per cent of the Austrian population was Catholic. Due to the social structure of villages and towns nobody could dare not to go to the weekly or even daily services without a serious reason. Therefore it was guaranteed that nearly every Austrian from the youngest child to the oldest man, from the poorest day-laborer to the wealthiest landlord would hear the good news of the victory through the voice of the local priest.

The system of public relations in which both Church and state were involved was very efficient and brought the most essential news to everyone in the vast Austrian territory. Nevertheless, a very important question still needs to be answered: how could people in Austria get further information about what had happened on 27 June near the Main? How could they satisfy their curiosity to learn which regiment had suffered most and which part of the troops had fewer casualties in order to know whether their beloved relatives in the army had been in danger or not? What were the alternatives to the information system of state and Church? For the majority of the Austrian population there was none! Surprisingly, there appeared no pamphlet with a description of what had happened during the battle, no list of the wounded and dead and only two engravings with a picture of a battle scene were published.[7] Only in Vienna, where the state-run newspaper *Wiennerisches Diarium* appeared twice a week, people were able to read more details about the development of the battle and its victims. But it was only a small part of the Viennese population that had enough money to buy the newspaper,[8] and even those who had access to the newspaper were only roughly informed about the military events and were left ignorant of the diplomatic and political background of the war and its coalitions and oppositions. The paper contained barely more than superficial information about what actually had happened. Outside the Habsburg Empire there obviously existed other, well-informed newspapers. However, they were expensive and censorship made it difficult and even more expensive to subscribe to one of these papers.[9]

No prints, no pamphlets, no newspapers except the *Wiennerisches Diarium* with its trivial choice of information – if we take into consideration this non-existence of media and mediators in the Austrian press and information landscape concerning the victory of Dettingen, the nationwide celebration of thanksgiving services gains importance: The *Te Deum*, ordered by the state and celebrated by the Church was the only medium to inform all the inhabitants of the Habsburg Empire. There were almost no other reactions to the victory a wider public could have noticed outside the capital of Vienna and outside the conference rooms at court or some aristocratic drawing rooms. This kind of reaction to Dettingen was by no means exceptional.

Looking at other "good tidings" we find that they were celebrated, noted and communicated in the same way. In 1743 alone four other events besides Dettingen caused similar public reactions: In January and February the news of the recapture of Prague after several months of French occupation in December 1742 made its way through the Austrian dominions with bell ringing, canon shooting and – in every little village – the singing of the *Te Deum Laudamus*. In February and March 1743 this good news was immediately followed by the *Te Deum* for the Austrian victory at Campo Santo. Then, in May and June, the Catholic community praised God for the Austrian victory at Braunau. In these latest thanksgiving services the *Te Deum* for the military victory was often combined with thanks to God for the coronation of their beloved sovereign Maria Theresa as Queen of Hungary that had taken place in May 1743 in the Bohemian capital of Prague.[10] As in July and August 1743 the *Te Deum Laudamus*, ordered by the secular authorities and sung in the churches of the Austrian dominions was the only medium that reached nearly the entire population of the state regardless of the social and intellectual background of the individual. Only in Vienna and Prague, which represented at the same time the "scene of the action" for the recapture and the coronation, was the situation different: The central thanksgiving service in the cathedral, accompanied by bell-ringing and cannon shooting (as performed also at the services for the victory of Dettingen), was surpassed by other, more glamorous celebrations. For several days, scenes of joy and happiness were staged in both cities, but apart from the situation in these two cities there was just one medium used to inform the entire population of the whole state: the *Te Deum Laudamus*.

*Te Deum* for victory – was the predominance of the religious voice for the distribution of good tidings, was this collaboration between state and Church unique in Europe at least in Catholic states? It is obviously not possible to generalize on the characteristics of the public or on the relation between the government and the public and the reality of communication processes in the various states within the Empire,[11] but there is at least one other example where we can find a similar close relationship between Church and state: the Electorate of Hanover. The victory of Dettingen, which we have so far looked at from the Austrian point of view, acquires a different meaning if studied from the perspective of Hanover in northern Germany.[12] Hanoverians were confronted with the news of the victory via the voice of the Church three times: The first time it was a spontaneous reaction when the good news came to Hanover on the morning of Sunday, 30 June. The church bells in the small town were ringing and from the steeples trumpets and kettledrums were announcing the news to the ignorant people. From the pulpit the parsons were praising God who had brought the victory and preserved the life of their beloved Elector George August.[13] As in Vienna, the good news was spread through the voice of the Church in Hanover, too, but unlike the Austrians, Hanover celebrated its thanksgiving services only in the capital. In the weeks following the victory on the Main River there was no clerical celebration in the entire territory. It was not until October, when finally – this was the second time that the voice of the Church could be heard – thanksgiving services were held all over the state: on Sunday, 20 October a *Te Deum Laudamus* was sung in every Lutheran church of the Electorate to praise God and the victorious George August.[14] It is very likely that the initiative for these services came from the Elector himself who shortly after his return from the Pragmatic Army to the city of Hanover had given corresponding orders to his Council of State.[15] This governmental body then forwarded an appropriate order to the central Lutheran governing board for the Electorate of Hanover, the "Konsistorium", which, accordingly, sent a printed circular with the order to sing the thanksgiving liturgy as well as a short text of a prayer to the parish clergy in the cities and villages of the Hanoverian dominion.

The voice of the Church proclaiming the victory of Dettingen to Hanoverian citizens for the third time was not heard in the capital but in the camp of the Pragmatic Army on the Main. Already on 7 July 1743, ten days after the victory, the whole army was assembled for an open field thanksgiving service: about 60,000 men sang the *Te Deum Laudamus* and for every regiment the responsible army chaplains held a prayer to commemorate the glorious victory and to thank God for divine help and George II for good guidance in the midst of battle.[16] It was the sovereign himself who had given orders – and money – for the services and it was he who had chosen the biblical text for the sermons.

*Te Deum Laudamus* in the city of Hanover, *Te Deum* in the whole Electorate and *Te Deum* in the army camp – this was the way the news of the victory, strongly combined with a glorification of the sovereign, was spread throughout the dominions of Hanover. In order to be able to judge the importance of the clerical voice – as in the Austrian example – we have to look at the other media and mediators in Hanover who communicated the news to a wider public. However – just like in Austria – for the majority of the Hanoverian population there was none! In an aristocratic inner circle at the court of Hanover and in some local elites in other towns of the Electorate and finally at the University of Göttingen some poems were published that praised and glorified the Elector and his victory. Yet there was no pamphlet, no description of the military action and not even a list of the dead and wounded that circulated in the whole Electorate. No woodcut or engraving was made to give an impression of the battle scenes to interested spectators. Nowhere in the whole state, not even in the capital, was a newspaper published – thus, not even this medium could furnish information to the people. No doubt, in other states surrounding the Electorate, newspapers offered more information on what had happened in Dettingen, and broadsides and pamphlets about the battle were published in various cities of the Holy Roman Empire.[17] However, these foreign press products did not come to the Electorate. They were not imported into Hanoverian territory.[18] In addition to this lack of media it is surprising that there were not even spontaneous parties of singing and drinking in the streets of Hanover or in other towns of the Electorate. Except the bell ringing on 30 June and the very hesitant prayer on 20 October, the victory passed almost unnoticed by the wider Hanoverian public.[19] Looking at this astonishing absence of media for communicating the victory of Dettingen in the Electorate of Hanover, the nationwide *Te Deum* late in October 1743, ordered by the secular and realized by the clerical powers, acquires importance in the way communication was practiced in this German state.

It was not only in the context of Dettingen that this kind of collaboration between Church and state proved to be important as the only medium that regardless of social position or education reached nearly the whole population of the state: between April and December 1743 every subject in the Electoral territory was informed from the pulpits about the visit of the sovereign to his German dominions. At the end of April all the parsons in the Electorate started praying in their parishes for a good and safe journey of their beloved George August. Then, at the end of June – although the Christian community still had not heard a word about the safe arrival of the Elector on 17 May in Hanover – the whole state prayed for the health of its King and Elector who went on the campaign for the good cause of Maria Theresa and the common peace in Europe. Prayers were continued throughout the whole summer – without even mentioning the victory of 27 June. On 20 October the Hanoverians finally thanked God for the safe return of George II and for his successful campaign. One month later the people of Hanover were informed about the departure of their Elector when their parsons prayed for the sovereign's safe journey back to England. The last news of George's visit to his German dominions echoed through the churches when on 8 December a thanksgiving song was sung everywhere for the safe arrival of his Majesty in his British kingdom. Five times during 1743 the Electoral subjects were informed from the pulpits about the current doings of their sovereign. Each time the initiative to this practice of communication came either from George II himself or from his Council of State in Hanover who then transmitted the order to the clerical administration. That body distributed the printed forms of prayer to all Lutheran parsons in the state.[20] Yet this mixed secular-clerical policy of information by no means kept the inhabitants of the state well informed; they did not learn any details about the background of their sovereign's visits nor even of the current affairs of politics or diplomacy – but at least they received a minimum of information.

The way information was disseminated in 1743 in the Electorate was characteristic. Not only were the *Te Deum* and the means of informing of the entire population via the pulpit practised at other times too, but the contents of the messages themselves were very similar. In 1743 all five messages communicated through the voice of the Church were devoted to the person of the sovereign. Messages spread in other years in the same way contained information about the death of the former Elector (1727) and the coronation of George II (1727); in 1739, 1741, 1743, 1745 and 1749 the pastors were praising God for the Princess of Wales having given birth to a healthy child. In short: all information brought to the Hanoverian population was dynastic information. During Sunday morning services people did not learn anything about current diplomatic affairs in Europe, the coalitions or wars their country was engaged in, the dangers their soldiers would have to face – instead the only things they learned about were the most important events in the ruling family.

Austria and Hanover – two states in the German Empire in the beginning of the 1740s. In both states public communication and discourse were characterized by surprising silences and a lack of reactions on the part of the people concerning all good or bad tidings about domestic or foreign affairs of state. These results of my analysis of the Austrian and Hanoverian public acquire even more significance when compared with the situation in England and France. For these states participated at Dettingen, too – the latter lost the battle.

In Vienna and even more significantly in the city of Hanover the inhabitants stayed mostly quiet after the good news of the battle arrived, but the reactions in Paris were quite different: there was joy and happiness on the streets. For two days, on 3 and 4 July, the inhabitants were convinced of a French victory. They were singing and drinking, praising the victorious army and the glorious military leader, the Maréchal de Noailles, for his strategic masterpiece. But the joy about the pretended victory did not last long. On 5 July, the first rumors came up that French troops suffered severe losses and that even the battle as a whole was lost. People realized that the mail from the army was being intercepted and opened by officials and anger against the government grew. Simultaneously, all kinds of mockeries in form of songs and ballads poked fun of the elite troops of the "Maison du Roy" whose behavior at Dettingen had not been royal at all. Uneasiness engulfed the city; for some days it remained uncertain if the action of 27 June had ended in victory or defeat for France. As contradicting pieces of news arrived, all kind of rumors circulated in the streets of Paris and at the court of Versailles. Finally, about two weeks after the battle everybody who wanted to know the truth had to realize that the troops under the Maréchal de Noailles had lost the battle of Dettingen. Where did these differing news come from? It was a whole variety of news media that emerged in France, mostly in Paris. Many of them came from outside the country into the city.[21] The most influential of them were the different types of handwritten and printed newspapers. In the first days the official, state-run *Gazette* kept completely quiet and then published meaningless and indecisive reports about what had happened at the Main, but other papers were much quicker and more accurate in informing their readers. Only some hours after the first messenger from the battlefield had arrived in Paris and Versailles did some clandestine handwritten newsletters circulate that distributed the fresh –

but still imprecise – news.[22] In the following days more and more printed newspapers arrived from the Netherlands. They were generally well informed and the interested readers in the French capital knew very well that their news were more reliable than the articles published in the official *Gazette*. Even though the government intercepted letters from the army, even though the court did not publish any comment on the battle and even though the *Gazette* provided only superficial information, these hand-written and printed newspapers served the public as reliable channels of information about what was going on outside the country.

At first glance it seems as if in France only the private, the non-official and non-governmental part of the society reacted to news of the battle, but a closer analysis of official pronouncements emanating from court and government in the first days and weeks allows us to discern a whole chain of official reactions, as well. Already the first outbursts of joy about a French victory most likely had its origin in false information spread systematically by high court officials from Versailles. During the first week of July 1743 in several towns at the Dutch border this policy even lead to the celebration of a glorious *Te Deum* for the French "victory" at Dettingen.[23] The propaganda initiative started by the court in the first hours after the news arrived at Versailles was paralleled by the interception and reading of incoming mail. Then, realizing that the spreading of the truth could not be stopped, the government remained quieter: Even though the *Gazette* published an account of the battle there was no statement about who had won. Some days later, when oral, written and printed critique had grown loud and louder and was uttered with less and less caution, the court reached for different weapons: for having spread critical information several people were sent to the Bastille. During the summer, however, the government did not try to contradict the news of the defeat and the fury and anger about it circulating in the streets of Paris with its own, false or manipulated publications. As late as the end of November, the court propagated an engraving depicting the action in a remarkably impertinent manner as a French victory. Five months after the battle, the government once again tried to manipulate the public with its propaganda.

Rumors, information and misinformation, news spread in oral, hand-written and printed form, originating from governmental and non-governmental sources. People were acting and reacting with publications to one another. It was a network of communication that emerged in Paris and Versailles in the context of the battle of Dettingen. But it was not only in France that different parts of the society developed such a variety of public activities. Across the Channel, in England, public reactions on behalf of the battle reflected a similar range and variety.

London, 23 June 1743 (old style). The bells of several churches were ringing, the canons in the park and the Tower were fired and at night there were bonfires and illuminations everywhere. Shortly after the first royal messenger had arrived, a wave of joy and happiness spread over the whole country and even in Ireland loyal toasts to the Protestant succession and the House of Hanover were offered. But it was not only through bonfires and bells that people learned about the victory. Even though the bell ringing still played an important role as a communication medium on the British Isles, the main media for the distribution of news in London and in other cities in the kingdom were newspapers and pamphlets.[24] Already on 23 June, the date the messenger arrived, an *Extraordinary Gazette* published the official account of the battle and still the same day the first non-official copies of the text appeared and were sold in the streets. During the next days the daily and weekly newspapers were full of various accounts of the action; a number of pamphlets published "original" letters from members of the army. According to the well-developed business of producing, distributing and selling news it was every printer's interest to attract his clients and readers with fresh information. Printers outside London very often simply reproduced what their colleagues had already printed. Sometimes, however, using letters just arrived from the army, they also published their own reports.

While the private printers with their network of shops, newsmen and hawkers[25] actively distributed a broad variety of information about what had happened on the Main River, the English government for the most part remained quiet. After the Lords of the Regency had given orders on 23 June to fire canons and light some bonfires, and after having published the first account "by authority" in the semi-official newspaper *London Gazette*, they stayed passive for several days. About one week later the government published a second account. Then, more than three weeks after the good news had reached London, the officials addressed their subjects through a different medium: on Sunday, 17 July, during the morning prayer a *Te Deum Laudamus* was sung to praise God for the victory. Instead of a nationwide thanksgiving, a prayer was held only within the region encompassed by the Bills of Mortality, the greater area of London and Westminster.

During July 1743, all over Britain people of different social rank and education could hear the message of the victory. Especially in London nearly everybody had access to the news: those who could not afford to buy a newspaper or a pamphlet could go to one of the 550 coffee houses of the city where, for the price of a cup of coffee, they would always find an up to date variety of printed news. Those who were illiterate would find someone who would read the interesting articles for them,[26] and even those who did not frequent coffee houses heard the most essential news during the public rejoicing on the street where the hawkers, too, were advertising their prints, papers and broadsides. For several weeks the newspapers and pamphlets published all kind of details about the military event. Then, gradually, the battle lost its appeal as recent information and disappeared further and further from the top of the news agenda.

At the end of September, however, after a period of silence, the topic of Dettingen reappeared. This time it was neither the battle nor the military event that was the main point of interest, but the entire strategy of the actual foreign policy, the question of an English military engagement on the continent and the person of the Secretary for the Northern Department, Lord Carteret. Suddenly, in preparing the new parliamentary session, Dettingen became a weapon for the political opposition in Parliament. "Dettingen" became the keyword, a *pars pro toto* for the "ill" and "wrong" policy of the government. Suddenly, newspapers and pamphlets were not used any more to inform the people "neutrally" but became powerful tools for systematic political propaganda in a purely English battle over domestic affairs. Prints had changed their function: from a medium of pure information in the weeks after the battle they had become a medium of political propaganda.[27]

Austria, the Electorate of Hanover, France and Britain – these four countries had been involved in the battle of Dettingen, and in all of them the battle had produced a noticeable public echo. Regardless of the quality and intensity of this echo we could always distinguish these two groups: the official, the governmental side and the private, the non-governmental side of the subjects. However, in the four countries these groups played different roles in the process of communication: Sometimes, they communicated actively, sometimes passively, sometimes they took on the role of the receiver sometimes that of the sender of messages.

In the two member states of the German Empire both subjects as well as the governments surprised with a lack of reactions. Neither in Austria, nor in Hanover did any medium exist that could report a victory or a coronation as good news and spread it in the entire territory – if there was any, a printed text or an engraving, it was created only for a small group of recipients as an exclusive part of the "public". The only medium designed especially for nationwide communication was the *Te Deum Laudamus*, which was ordered by the state and executed by the Church. In both states, the one mainly Catholic, the other mainly Lutheran, governments used the voice of the Church to spread information that was supposed to reach the whole population of their country. In doing this, the governments, well aware of their almost complete monopoly of information, in collaboration with the Church created a specific form of "public", the "public of the people". The fact that in Austria and Hanover it was the governmental power that created this "public of the people" gains even more importance when we look at the states' constitution: Hanover and Austria were ruled by "absolutist" monarchs. Theoretically, Maria Theresa and George August, the two sovereigns had no need to explain or justify their politics to anyone; they had only to answer to God for their decisions. But why did these two absolutist monarchs spread information to their subjects? Could they not act as completely independent sovereigns?

At first glance it seems as if Hanover and Austria used the Church in the same manner as their mouthpiece, but at a closer look at the *Te Deum* and the news spread from the pulpits in the two states, one important difference becomes apparent: The voice of the Church communicated different messages. In Hanover, the news focused on dynastic information and especially on the person of the ruling sovereign George August, while Austrian churches' news covered a greater variety. This – at first glance irrelevant – difference in the spectrum of information published by the two governments reveals a different attitude of the government to its subjects. In Hanover the government considered all information concerning the state and its domestic and foreign affairs as part of the *arcana imperii*. There was only a small, mainly aristocratic group of people that had access to details about current affairs of state. All Hanoverians outside this limited circle were regarded as politically immature citizens and, according to the idea of absolutist government, they were not mature enough to receive information about what was going on in and outside the Electorate. But – and this is important – even these people were not left completely ignorant. Even in Hanover "absolutism" did not mean a complete silence between the government and its subjects. As the communication practices of the 1740s had shown, they were at least informed about the important dynastic changes in the ruling family. Apparently this dynastic information was so important that it was spread through the medium that was certain to reach nearly the entire population: the *Te Deum Laudamus* in the churches. Even though Hanoverian subjects were left ignorant about political and diplomatic affaires, the government nevertheless realized this public's existence and felt the need to communicate with it.

In Austria, too, dynastic information was important. It also belonged to the repertoire of governmental news spread through the voice of the Church, but in Austria the absolutist government went one step further still: it used the clerical media systematically to distribute political information, notably military victories to the entire population, to the "public of the people". Unlike in Hanover, in Austria these victories did not belong to the *arcana imperii*. They were used to show the people that a good and successful sovereign, strongly supported by the divine God, was governing them. Apparently the absolutist Austrian government saw the need to justify its doings. It had discovered its subjects as an important communication partner, as a "public" it had to talk to. The choice of the information published to this "public of the people" was very limited, but it nevertheless demonstrated the need felt by the government to inform its people at least on a minimum basis about the current affairs of the state.

In contrast to this careful information policy of the Austrian government it is surprising to note that not only the choice of the published information was restricted. The media used for the distribution were equally limited – there was no other medium than the *Te Deum Laudamus*, sometimes intermixed with cannon shooting and soldier parades. But if the government wanted to communicate with its subjects and thus legitimate and propagate its doings, why did it not use other media too? Almost no pamphlet, no engraving and no woodcut appeared to glorify a victory, a birthday or a coronation. Why? Especially at the beginning of the 1740s, the political situation in Austria was tense: Bavarian and French troops were menacing the Austrian dominions and, in 1742, even the capital of Vienna. Maria Theresa was far from being safely settled on her throne. In this situation all means available had to be marshaled for the support for the young archduchess. Why did the government not expand its repertoire of media in order to improve its "self-promotion"? The same question can be asked for Hanover. Even if, for various reasons, the Elector and his council wanted to inform the "public of the people" about nothing else but the monarch and his dynasty, and if therefore the choice of information was even more restricted than in Austria, this does still not explain why they refrained from using other media. Why were no pamphlets or engravings published that would have propagated even more efficiently the image of a good, righteous and successful ruling family? In contrast to Austria, Hanover could not even boast of a state-run newspaper that would have helped the government to spread selected news. This total neglect of the printed word as a medium of propaganda cannot be explained by ignorance of the techniques of printing and of spreading information through this medium. In other situations, for example the distribution of new laws, the Hanoverian government knew very well how to use publications as an appropriate medium for its purpose. But why did it not use them to cultivate its image?

Let me begin by raising a question that will sound rather strange to us today: Were the subjects in Hanover and Austria even interested in looking at engravings and reading printed texts? As mentioned above, it was an astonishing fact that no media owned by subjects existed in both countries. Almost no author, no printer and no engraver in Hanover or Austria had been inspired by the various occasions, the victories, the birthdays or the coronations to produce something that could be sold in the bookshops or on the streets. Only a part of this passiveness can be explained by the system of censorship. Even if the publishing situation in the two countries was far from being liberal, there were still legal possibilities for printing and engraving. Not even a censor could find fault with a glorifying poem about the young Archduchess or with an engraving of a picture of the heroic Elector in the midst of a dangerous battle. Even if the censors would have been so severe and so efficient that not a single pamphlet could have been produced and sold legally in the open market, there always existed possibilities to sell products illegally.[28] Yet nobody took the opportunity of profiting by selling legal or illegal press products. Why? The only explanation is that there was no market for these products. Apparently there was no customer for pamphlets or engravings; there was nobody who was interested in such press products. In both countries we have to notice an astonishing lack of interest in information about what happened within as well as outside the state. Not even the worries about their beloved relatives fighting in the army could overcome the subjects' passiveness. It seems that the curiosity of the majority of the people was satisfied by the restricted information spread from the pulpits.

This contrasts starkly with the situation in France. At first glance the French kingdom under Louis XV was an absolutist state like Austria and Hanover. But looking at the strongly varying actions and reactions of the two counterparts, the governmental and the private group in the public communication process, the relationship between government and subjects was manifestly different from that in Austria and Hanover. Whereas the Austrian and Hanoverian governments conveyed their carefully chosen information only through one particular means of communication, the French court was more active. It used a greater variety of media; the mere fact that it tried systematically to manipulate the people with false information – probably even twice – shows that the government considered its subjects as an important communication partner. Much more than in Austria and Hanover the French government saw the need to justify its doings to its people. The recipients of these communications, however, did not content themselves with the tailor-made or even manipulated information published by the government. They had realized that they could not rely on official information; they thirsted for more and better news. Obviously in France, and especially in Paris, there was also a whole system of censorship at work – it was probably even more efficient than those in Hanover and Austria. However, the curiosity, the sometimes even criminal energy and the financial interest of the people were strong enough to surmount official barriers and build up a legal and illegal system of collecting, producing, distributing and selling news in oral, handwritten and printed forms. Moreover this unofficial information system was not restricted to the small social elite. Whereas in Hanover and Vienna the few existing prints and the accessible newspapers circulated only between some dozen men, the circle in Paris was much broader and less restricted by the borders of social classes. In the Tuilleries where the *nouvellistes de bouche* gathered together, the nobleman met other aristocrats as well as day-laborers and the people gathering the news for the next number of a handwritten newsletter were nobles as well as non-aristocratic people. In Paris and Versailles there still existed restricted circles, well-defined exclusive publics. But much more so than in Vienna and Hanover, the French public represented a broader, more homogeneous group that included several social classes.

What about "absolutism" in France, then? Was Louis XV still an absolutist king? Yes, he was. But taking into consideration the situation of the public and the situation of communication practice, the French version of absolutism was different from that in Hanover and Austria. Manifestly, the French government saw the need to justify its doings and to "prove" to its subjects – even by false information – that they were governed by a good and victorious king. It even seems as if this official information policy, so different from the Hanoverian one, was due to the more "self-conscious" French subjects demanding information with more vehemence. Despite the prevalence of absolutism and censorship, in Paris and Versailles at least, these subjects had installed a system of self-information. Step by step, over several decades, they had taken from the government the monopoly of information and had gained access to part of the *arcana imperii* of the French state. But – and this is important – it was only a small part of the *arcana*. Looking at the information available in the capital, it can be seen clearly that, despite the variety of media and information, the news as a whole was quite restricted. It was the military event with its details that dominated the media. Almost nothing could be heard or read about the political and diplomatic background of the current situation and there was not a word said about the domestic affairs of France. There were people criticizing the French elite troops as well as Maréchal de Noailles and other officers, but neither the French nor the

Dutch papers dared to criticize Louis XV himself or the French policy. Both remained untouched by the "freedom" of the non-official information system and the insight into the *arcana imperii*. It seems as if there existed an unspoken rule that the topic of all politics was taboo to the private publishers. But why? Why did the French, so keen on all kinds of information about the battle, not demand details about the political context? If they took the liberty to criticize the military leaders – who, as part of the French nobility and as representatives of the state were at least part of the ruling political system – why did they not do the same with the king and the government?

This was precisely what the people, the publishers and newsagents did in England, the only one of the four states involved in the battle of Dettingen that was not an absolutist monarchy. Here, especially in the greater London area, the public of the people had even fewer social barriers than in Paris. Nearly everybody in the city – and also outside of London – had access to a huge variety of media that were published daily. Contrary to the situation in Vienna or Hanover, printed news was not just the preserve of a small social elite. The accessibility of the media and the content published were subject to almost no restrictions. As long as an author did not affect somebody's personal rights he could treat nearly every imaginable topic, and, as the example of Dettingen had shown, that was what the authors and printers did. Serving the demands of their readers and customers, they first published all available details about the military action at the Main. Worrying about their relatives, the people wanted to know precisely what had happened and which part of the army had suffered the most. After a variety of articles, letters and lists of the dead and wounded had been published in July, the content of the publications changed. Neither foreign nor domestic politics were taboo (as they were in France). More and more, the battle was discussed in the context of the current political and especially the English domestic affairs, and politicians of the opposition turned it into a weapon of propaganda. In moving the topic of Dettingen to the area of national politics, an enormous exchange of ideas and opinions and a real press debate took place between these publications: Quite often one author published a text in answer to another tract; his counterpart would respond in turn, referring to a third print and even citing a part of a fourth one. Such debates were not confined to theoretical issues and did not only serve the purely economic purpose of expressing an opinion and selling it. While on the other side of the Channel newspapers were scrambling to catch up with what had happened in the past, the English papers and pamphlets looked to the future and systematically tried to influence their readers. Authors of several pamphlets addressed themselves not only to the broad public but also to the specific public of the Members of Parliament and urged them to change politics. Obviously, this propaganda machine worked quite successfully: When Parliament met in December, "Dettingen" was no longer an innocent name for a glorious victory but a polemical term the opposition used skillfully against the government and Minister Carteret.[29] The debate, first held outside Parliament, had been carried by the newspapers, broadsides and prints into the Houses of Parliament. In London the people as the public had the possibility to participate not only passively but also actively in current politics.

While London's all encompassing public, with its publications, actively took part in politics, the English government stayed strangely quiet. Except for the two official publications and the *Te Deum Laudamus*, celebrated weeks after the victory and then only in a restricted area, the government surprisingly did not use other media for promoting its own image. When George II came back to London on 15 November 1743, he was received by a cheerful populace and acclaimed as a victorious king. But the court itself did not use the high spirits of the subjects and did not systematically stress the image of a good and righteous ruler.[30] Even in late autumn, when the representatives of the state, especially Minister Carteret, were openly attacked in public, they did not respond with other publications. Did the government simply underestimate the impact of the press and the necessity to justify its politics? Certainly not – other ministers had demonstrated on other occasions how skillfully English governments could manipulate the press and the people as public.[31] It seems, as if the government considered the voice of the people so strong and powerful that it did not even dare to answer the critique with its own texts for fear that this might only provoke further critical pamphlets and articles.[32] What a difference to the situation in France and even more to Hanover or Austria! In England the people as public had not only gained at least partially access to the *arcana imperii* but were also able to oppose the government and to influence its politics successfully.

Four countries – four public spheres. In the states I have discussed in this chapter, governments and subjects had very different ways of communicating with each other. This communication culture reflected different national political constituencies and their individual realities. In Hanover, the Elector George August judged his subjects as politically not mature enough to understand more than dynastic information; but even he had to realize that as an "absolutist" sovereign he could not govern his country without communicating at all with his people. In Austria, Maria Theresa took her subjects more serious as partners in a communication process, but Hanoverians and Austrians alike were still satisfied at that time with the little information they got from their sovereign through the voice of the Church and they did not yet develop any activities on their own to procure for themselves information from other non-governmental sources. One wonders whether they had internalized so much of the role as loyal, blindly obedient subjects to an absolutist ruler that not even their curiosity could change this situation, and that, perhaps, they were not even curious? If so, what had caused the remarkably radical changes in France, an equally "absolutist" state? French subjects had succeeded in shaping a completely different communication practice between government and people. They had succeeded in creating a different reality of an absolutist state. At least for some *arcana imperii* the state had lost its monopoly of information. The government had to realize that in certain areas of the communication process the people as public had developed their own network. In England the situation was again dramatically different: the people as public had not only access to most of the *arcana imperii* but even enjoyed some power to influence politics. What had shaped and created these different publics? Had the French been more curious than the Hanoverians or the Austrians? Where did the developments leading to the English communication network of the 1740s on the British Isles have their roots? In the second half of the eighteenth century, even in Austria and Hanover sermons and gun salutes lost their importance. A growing number of people began to ask for more information. They imported foreign newspapers to satisfy their increasing hunger for information. They asked to print their own, privately run newspapers and began to want even more – legal or illegal – information. Future research will have to focus on what became the transforming power that caused all these changes.

# Notes

1. *Wiennerisches Diarium* 54 (6 July 1743) and 55 (10 July 1743); and Johann Josef Khevenhüller-Metsch et al., (eds), *Aus der Zeit Maria Theresias: Tagebuch des Fürsten Johann Josef Khevenhüller-Metsch, Kaiserlichen Obersthofmeisters 1742–1776*, vol. 1, Vienna and Leipzig, 1907, pp. 165–7.
2. The most detailed description of the battle and its military and diplomatic context can be found in Wolfgang Handrick, *Die Pragmatische*

*Armee 1741 bis 1743: Eine alliierte Armee im Kalkül des Österreichischen Erbfolgekrieges*, Munich, 1991. For the context of the war of the Austrian Succession see Reed Browning, *The War of the Austrian Succession*, New York, 1993 and Matthew Smith Anderson, *The War of the Austrian Succession, 1740–48*, London and New York, 1995.

3. Details about the celebrations in Brussels can be found in *Wiennerisches Diarium* 57 (17 July 1743); and Henri de Calenberg, *Le Journal du Comte Henri de Calenberg pour l'année 1743*, Brussels, 1913, vol. 1, pp. 130–40.

4. *Wiennerisches Diarium* 61 (31 July 1743).

5. See *Wiennerisches Diarium* 60 (27 July 1743) to 65 (14 August 1743).

6. Vienna, Military Archives: Kriegsarchiv, Hofkriegsrat, Protokoll Exp. Index 1743, vol. 756; Protokoll Exp. 1743 pro Jul. et Aug., A Folio 1944–2440, vol. 758; Protokoll Exp. 1743 pro Sept. et Oct., A Folio 2441–2915 vol. 759. Kriegsarchiv, Hofkriegsrat, Protokoll Regist. Index 1743, vol. 761; Protokoll Regist. 1743 pro Jul. et Aug., A Folio 1437–1840.

7. For details about all kinds of information published as a reaction to the victory of Dettingen see Sebastian Küster, *Dettingen: Eine Schlacht im Licht der Öffentlichkeit* (unpublished Ph.D. diss., Göttingen, 2001).

8. Not much research has been done about this Viennese newspaper, but it is safe to estimate that the total circulation of each issue did not exceed 300 to 500 copies and that the price was too high for the average inhabitant of Vienna to afford it. There were some subscribers to the newspaper outside the capital city, but their number was very limited.

9. Even though we have some vague information that the thirty or forty existing Viennese coffee houses were places of conversation and leisure and even though some coffee house owners made the effort to lay out some officially approved newspapers in order to attract more clients, we have no evidence that these establishments – well observed by the local censors – were places of dense political discussions or even politically motivated anti-governmental meetings. More research has to be done about the people frequenting the coffee houses and about the papers that could be read there.

10. The singing of the *Te Deum Laudamus* in all parts of the Austrian territory could be read in the corresponding issues of the *Wiennerisches Diarium* of 1743.

11. Very often the research done on the subjects of "the public", the press and communication procedures generalizes the different developments in the various territories of the German Reich. It is not possible to look at the Reich as one equally organized political and social system. In

order to obtain precise information about "the public" and all kinds of communication processes, more research must be done on the local level of the political territories inside the Reich.

12. As mentioned above, George II, King of Great Britain and Elector of Hanover, led not only Austrian and English but also Hanoverian troops into battle when he fought on 27 June 1743 at the Main River.

13. Two days later, on Tuesday, 2 July 1743, the Catholic and the Jewish parishes in the new part of the city of Hanover also celebrated splendid thanksgiving services. Apparently these two communities, directly under the protection of the protestant Elector, wanted to use the event of the victory to demonstrate their loyalty to the sovereign.

14. Surprisingly, the text of the prayer that had to be read with the *Te Deum* did not include the name of the place of victory – Dettingen – and did not even mention the heroic behavior of the Elector during the battle. Neither the battle nor the victory were the main point of interest, but the return of the beloved sovereign.

15. This council, the Geheime Rat, was in charge of the Hanoverian government when the sovereign George II was not in Hanover but in London. It had the authority to take all decisions concerning the state's day-to-day business, whereas all important decisions had to be transferred to the king himself in London to be decided there.

16. This solemn Sunday morning service was just the beginning of a whole day of clerical and secular celebrations that ended with a parade and a banquet for the whole army.

17. A few exceptions apart, the contents of these prints were all in favor of Hanover and the Elector George August and would have been worth reading by good and loyal subjects of the Electorate.

18. Like the inner-Hanoverian prints these foreign newspapers and pamphlets also reached only a tiny group of the social elite of Hanover. Outside this elite Hanoverians hardly had a chance to experience these media. The reading culture in coffee houses (where they existed), pubs or private reading circles was not at all developed in the Hanover of the 1740s. Once again it has to be stated that the well developed culture of producing, distributing, selling and consuming news in other German territories like Hamburg, Altona or some states in the Rhineland must not be generalized for the whole Holy Roman Empire. The existence of some "international", in some cases even European newspapers does not mean that their distribution network did not have huge blanks on the map of the Reich. For details about the Hanoverian press and reading culture see Küster, *Dettingen*, pp. 157–181.

19. For details about media published as a reaction on the victory of Dettingen inside the Hanoverian territory see Küster, *Dettingen*, pp. 183–201.

20. The occasions celebrated with a thanksgiving and the hierarchy of the orders can be studied in the documents in the ecclesiastical archives of Hanover: Landeskirchenarchiv Hannover, Ephoralarchiv Sievershausen, D14, Gen. 185, Staatsoberhaupt I, 1724–1796, Fürbitten und Danksagungen für den König.

21. For the different kinds of media see Küster, *Dettingen*, pp. 285–313.

22. The publishing of these handwritten *nouvelles à la main* was always linked with an efficient oral information network of the *nouvellistes de bouche* who had their places of news exchange on public squares and in public gardens. For further information see Küster, *Dettingen*, p. 279f.

23. In times of well-justified victories the nationwide *Te Deum* belonged to the French repertoire of public celebrations, but the contemporaries all over Europe knew very well that the French did not start back to use a "false" thanksgiving for the purpose of manipulation. It is uncertain if these *Te Deum* of July 1743 were the result of the initiative of a local bishop in the northeast of France or if they were part of a large propaganda campaign. There remains no official order of the King to hold a nationwide thanksgiving. Küster, *Dettingen*, pp. 296, 326f.; and Michèle Fogel, "Le Système d'information ritualisée de l'Absolutisme français: lettres royales et mandements épiscopaux ordonnant le Te Deum pour les victoires et la paix (XVII<sup>e</sup>–XVIII<sup>e</sup> siècles)." in: *Le Journalisme d'Ancien Régime, Centre d'études du XVIII<sup>e</sup> siècle de l'Université de Lyon II*, Lyon, 1981, pp. 141–9.

24. For the number of existing newspapers and the whole variety of media reflecting the battle of Dettingen see Küster, *Dettingen*, 371–376, 391–468.

25. For further information about the system of producing and distributing prints see Karl Tilman Winkler, *Handwerk und Markt: Druckerhandwerk, Vertriebswesen und Tagesschrifttum in London 1695–1750*, Stuttgart, 1993.

26. The English and especially London coffee houses were meeting places for everybody. Regardless of all social barriers, the Lord met the day-laborer reading the papers. Even those who could not afford a cup of coffee could stay there for reading if they did not take up a chair and a table. Some of these establishments actually had small libraries growing every day and for *Tom's Coffee House* it is even possible to trace an –

incomplete – list of pamphlets that could be read there. See Küster, *Dettingen*, p. 506.

27. The domestic fight for Carteret was a fierce one and his position in the government suffered severely in the aftermath of "Dettingen". But that time, in December 1743/January 1744, he could still defend his office. He finally resigned on 24 November 1744.

28. It is likely that, in Vienna, clandestine handwritten newspapers also existed in the 1740s, but the fact that not a single copy of these newspapers survived and that there are no traces of their existence in official reports or private correspondences seems to indicate that their number and their influence on the public was not very great. Furthermore it should be noticed that the few remaining newsletters from the 1730s do not contain mainly critical political information. Even though these papers were not approved by the official censors and appeared clandestine they are by no means "opposition" papers. See Doris Tautscher-Gerstmeyer, *Die geschriebenen Zeitungen des 18. Jahrhunderts in Wien*, Vienna, 1982, p. 355; Küster, *Dettingen*, p. 63f. Unlike the situation in Vienna there are no traces at all that there existed handwritten newspapers in the Electorate of Hanover.

29. The same arguments already published in pamphlets and newspaper articles in October and November were repeated in the first session of Parliament when the Houses had to decide whether the Hanoverian soldiers should continue to be paid by the English or not. Therefore – contrary to Winkler's theory – it can be stated that the English press could influence future politics. See Karl Tilman Winkler, *Wörterkrieg: Politische Debattenkultur in Walpoles England 1720–1742*, Stuttgart, 1995, pp. 91, 319f., *et passim*.

30. It is astonishing that there was no solemn thanksgiving service held in Saint Paul's Cathedral as contemporaries had expected. The "Dettingen Te Deum" composed by famous George Friedrich Händel in honor of the victory was only played in the Royal Chapel at court.

31. Already Robert Harley at the beginning of the century and, later on, also Robert Walpole paid a lot of attention – and money – to the production and distribution of pamphlets and state-run newspapers serving the purposes of their governments.

32. In this context, it has to be taken into account that in 1743 there were no such tactical politicians like Harley or Walpole in power, being able to start a successful press campaign. Furthermore even inside the actual government there were several politicians opposing Carteret and hoping for a more powerful position. It was not in their interest to defend their attacked "colleague".

# 4
# On Forms of Communications: A Commentary

## Hermann Wellenreuther

The three papers in Part I introduce us to three different forms of communication, to three different kinds of communication networks, to three different functions and uses of communication. Frank Lambert's paper focuses on the "word of God" spreading through North America. In doing so he focuses on "three communicative spheres" of which the first focuses on Puritan New England, the second on the Great Awakening and the third on the "free marketplace of religion" in British North America. Lambert's "public" focuses first on the parish, then on believers who transgress confessional parish boundaries, and finally on believers who conscientiously exploit the variety of confessions by making choices between them. From a different perspective Lambert's first communicative network is defined by elite pronouncements on the spiritual state of the believers in published tracts and sermons, by mass meetings that unite huge crowds – only the army in Dettingen singing the *Te Deum* seems a parallel in Old Europe! – listening to the good word of the Lord and then disperse as multipliers of the sermons of George Whitefield, Gilbert Tennent or James Davenport, that had brought them together.

A third perspective would be to describe the three communicative systems as a progression from a semi-private, parish focused sphere to the public sphere.[1] All that is needed now, is to link the insights of this fine paper to the overall theme of the conference: communication. In doing so, I hope that I can convince Mr Lambert to outline for us the connection between elite theological products in the seventeenth and early eighteenth century to the imagined or potential readers – lay readers or professional co-authors. Could it be that there was a division of labor with tracts acting as communicative links with the clergy who within their parishes in their sermons and lectures would use the insights of the printed word to shape the spoken word?

Similar questions could be raised with greater urgency about the Great Awakening: Aside from the fact that the paper focuses exclusively on the English Great Awakening and ignores the equally important German Great

Awakening, the relationship between prints and spoken word seems to me to be much more complex; for it was the spoken word that the listeners carried back into their parishes, which caused trouble that provoked the angry responses to Whitefield, Tennent and other awakening traveling preachers. If, in the seventeenth century the printed word traveled, in the eighteenth it seems the other way around: the spoken word traveled and the printed word seems to have remained local – at least initially.[2] Mr. Lambert has analysed extensively the inter-colonial nature of the public debate during the Great Awakening. What we would now like to know is how this inter-colonial nature affected the individual colonist on the one hand, the institutional structure of the Churches on the other. And finally: does the possibility of choosing between confessions really emerge only after 1750? I suspect that this is true only for Connecticut and Massachusetts, but not for Rhode Island and certainly not for the middle colonies where choices were possible much earlier.

\*

Professor Beiler returns to the Old World in her analysis of communication networks in the second half of the seventeenth century within dissenting Churches. I can detect at least three different forms of communication. The first systematically relates communication to traveling and missionary activities and is exemplified by early members of the Society of Friends; it would be fun to compare this preaching with the activities of the traveling preachers during the Great Awakening. The second type of communication combines the exchange of information with relief work, an aspect that has been studied in depth for the Huguenot communities;[3] the third builds on the first two: communicative links established through missionary activities and relief work for persecuted Dissenters are now refocused through letters, word of mouth and printed media on the newly founded colony Pennsylvania.

Viewed from the point of view of the "public", Beiler's communicative systems are largely "private spheres" – not by choice but because she describes communicative structures within groups of persecuted people that survived because of their illegitimate links to co-believers in other territories. The communication enters the public sphere in two precisely defined areas: first, as public missives addressed to the religious "other" as well as to authorities defined as persecutors of "true believers", and secondly as communication between territories beyond the Atlantic and the persecuted of Europe. The paper does not give an answer to the question of whether these propaganda tracts on Pennsylvania were really openly circulated.

Regrettably, both, Beiler's as well as Lambert's paper remain largely silent on the role of authorities in shaping these communicative networks. I would like the authors to comment on my impression that the communication Beiler describes is secretive, written in coded language, and belongs to the underworld hidden from the authorities while Lambert's communicative spheres are open, accessible by all and couched in language understandable by all.

\*

In Sebastian Küster's paper the authorities hold center stage: Empress Maria Theresia of Austria and Georg August as Elector of Hanover shape the communicative networks in ways that are hard to imagine in North American contexts yet fundamental to any understanding of monarchical regimes in Europe. In his splendidly focused paper praising the Lord acquires an entirely new meaning: Transporting dynastic news and victories to all subjects. While we learn in this paper a lot about the function of the authorities' communication, about the different publics it addressed – questions that I think should equally be asked within the contexts of Beiler's and Lambert's papers – we feel challenged by Küster's provocative answer to his final question: Why was there so little public discourse, hardly any newspapers, no pamphlets, no prints of the battle – only bell ringing, praying, singing: *no interest*, we are told, is the answer and we feel grieved. It is hard for us to relate to populations without curiosity. Faced with constant hard-disk information overloads, with a surfeit of curiosity by the press, which claims to do this because the public wants, must, will want to know what they write about, this answer is profoundly startling and unsettling. Yet if we put the results of Küster's inquiries into a transatlantic perspective, they may loose some of their startling qualities. German settlers in the British middle colonies were faced with no censorship, no ruler's crafty interference in what they wanted to print or read. They could print, say and sing what they wanted as long as it broadly conformed to decency and loosely conceived Christian morals. Did they then use this new freedom to branch out into politics? Between 1747 and 1774 I count (without broadsides) 302 German publications in the colonies. Of these only twenty-seven (8.94 per cent) related to politics, and of these twenty-seven prints sixteen were published between 1763 and 1766: optimal conditions produced about the same result as censorship and rulers' strict control of the public sphere.[4] Put differently: Küster's result may point to something extremely important: People in the early modern world under normal conditions probably really considered politics *arcana imperii* about which they only cared if they *directly* affected their own life. Beiler's and Lambert's papers on the other side indicate, as does the bulk of the German publications in North America, that this lack of curiosity was strictly confined to politics, not to the religious world, to which the bulk of German and English publications in the eighteenth century belonged.[5]

In the revised version of his paper, Dr Küster has taken up the challenges to his major thesis and has expanded his paper by offering concise descriptions of the French and English reactions to the battle of Dettingen to his paper. This is most welcome indeed, for both the French as well as the English reactions differ sharply from the Austrian and the Hanoverian ones. The latter are strictly focused on the rulers and guided as well as initiated by the rulers' councils and ministers, but the French and English reactions very quickly developed a life apart from that of government and courts. Indeed, more than that, both were rather critical of the role rulers and their governments played, queried the veracity of news spread by the courts, presented information in ways that generally helped readers interpret the events at Dettingen in their wider political and military contexts while at the same time suggesting alternative behaviors.

These valuable extensions still, of course, leave us without an answer to why there were so sharply divergent reactions in countries that essentially shared the same constitutional set-up. And indeed we still do not know whether indeed people in France and England were more curious about political processes than those in the electorate and in Austria. One possible answer might be that the reactions might have been part of a public discourse mainly between members of the political elite – although Dr Küster does indeed mention that the readership of these newspapers and pamphlets did reach wider. His paper suggests, too, a most important question that deserves much further study: Why did rulers within one monarchy feel that they have to inform a public, communicate with it and engage in critical dialogue with the subjects while rulers in other monarchies strictly discouraged such dialogues, restricted their information policy to particular ritualistic forms like prayers and the singing of the *Te Deum*? These stark differences suggest structural divergences between eighteenth-century monarchies that deserve to be explored at greater depths by future historians.

*

If it is true that there is a direct relationship between the accessibility to politics *and* people's curiosity in politics – and I formulate this thesis on the flimsiest of evidence just presented – then focusing on the word of God as the primary area for public debate and communicative networks seems more than justified. But this will only hold if we define communication only as meaning "exchanges of words" within the public sphere. Communication, however, comes in many more shapes and sizes, too. Within the religious world we have the world of devotional objects from the rosary to images of the cross; equally significant is the world of what Timothy H. Breen called the "baubles of Britain", the world of goods with the many meanings they carried – from the special *habit* of the clergy to the sweet delights of West Indian sugar.[6] And of course hidden from the public we have the tons of reports, instructions, letters and missives exchanged between merchants in the Atlantic World[7] and rulers and their underlings; these were efforts to keep up with developments in other parts of the world and structure them within the possibilities technology provided: Time and distance shaped these efforts – factors largely unimportant within the religious world – and in doing so colored the nature of political and mercantile decision making. In this context Geoffrey Parker used the terms "micro-management" and "macro-management" to describe the nature of decision making: Time and distance constricted the ruler and the merchant to macro-management; when he failed to abide by these rules and indulged in micromanagement he was bound to mess up as Philip II did repeatedly.[8]

One other thing we learn from the example of Philip II: In the early modern period (as may even be true today) the problem often was not a lack of information but an information overload that led to indecision and confusion – an insight that points to the important links between institutions, organizations, and the management of communications. And that brings me back to the religious world. The rulers' overload of information meant choosing between conflicting information without clear criteria; the believer on the other hand had clear criteria that guided him in choosing between right and wrong, between the true believers and the sycophants, between the heretics and the saints. Poor and devout Catholic Philip II lacked this sure perspective – and probably we historians do, too.

# Notes

1. On the distinction and its importance for eighteenth-century North America cf. Michael Warner, *The Letters of the Republic: Publication and the Public Sphere in Eighteenth-Century America*, Cambridge MA, 1990.

2. Drawing on statistics on the publication of pro- and anti-religious tracts relating to Whitefield and Tennent that I published in Hermann Wellenreuther, *Ausbildung und Neubildung: Die Geschichte Nordamerikas vom Ausgang des 17. Jahrhunderts bis zum Ausbruch der Amerikanischen Revolution 1775*, Münster, 2002, p. 327; it seems to me that the inter-colonial discourse was limited to George Whitefield; pamphlets against him were published between 1738 and 1746 in Boston (34), Newport, RI (1), New York (1), Philadelphia (8) and Charleston (5). These figures indicate that the oral message of Whitefield may have been spread much wider than the printed word for or against him.

3. For a splendid summary of what we know cf. Thomas Klingebiel, "Huguenot Settlements in Central Europe," in Hartmut Lehmann et al. (ed.), *In Search of Peace and Prosperity: New German Settlements in Eighteenth-Century Europe and America*, University Park PA, 2000, pp. 39–67.

4. I have used figures I published in Wellenreuther, *Ausbildung und Neubildung*, p. 644f.

5. Ibid., pp. 641–5.

6. Timothy H. Breen, ""Baubles of Britain": The American Consumer Revolutions of the Eighteenth Century," *Past and Present* 119 (1988), 73–104; Breen, "An Empire of Goods: The Anglicization of Colonial America, 1690–1776," *Journal of British Studies* 25 (1986), 467–499; John Brewer and Roy Porter, (eds), *Consumption and the World of Goods*, London, 1994; Carole Shammas, "Changes in English and Anglo-American Consumption from 1550 to 1800," in J. Brewer and R. Porter (eds), *Consumption and the World of Goods*, London, 1994, pp. 177–205; C. Shammas, *The Pre-Industrial Consumer in England and America*, Oxford, 1990.

7. The communicative structures and networks of the Atlantic World are the subject of Claudia Schnurmann, *Atlantische Welten: Engländer und Niederländer im amerikanisch-atlantischen Raum 1648–1713*, Cologne, 1998; Schnurmann, *Europa trifft Amerika: Atlantische Wirtschaft in der Frühen Neuzeit, 1492–1783*, Frankfurt a. M., 1998.

8. Geoffrey Parker, *The Grand Strategy of Philippe II*, New Haven CT, 1998; I have discussed the relation between time, information and mercantile decision making in Wellenreuther, *Ausbildung und Neubildung*, pp. 452–6.

# 5
# Spreading "Good Tidings" in Various Ways: How Sovereigns, Furly, and Whitefield used the Media that Suited their Messages Best

*Carola Wessel*

Communication consists of a number of elements: A message, somebody who sends this message, somebody else who receives it, and a medium to transport the message. The articles by Rose Beiler, Sebastian Küster and Frank Lambert tell different stories, spanning almost 100 years and two continents. However, in comparing the elements of communication named in each article, it is possible to see striking differences as well as surprising agreements that tell us a lot about the development of communication in the seventeenth and eighteenth centuries. The *messages* referred to in each article are quite different. In Sebastian Küster's contribution, one event is the content of all communication: The battle at Dettingen. A very different message is that of George Whitefield and other preachers dealt with by Frank Lambert: They preach the gospel as they understand it in promoting the "New Birth." Rose Beiler does not concentrate on one topic, but analyses the various theological and economic messages included in the communication of Benjamin Furly and his friends. To compose and distribute such a message, it needs a *sender* or a *mediator*. It is helpful if the people who want to send a message dispose of the influence and relations to spread it as far as possible. Most people introduced to us by the articles were secular leaders or leaders of religious groups. They were used to dealing with the word, be it the word of God or other words, and to communicate messages to other people. In addition, especially the Pietists had established networks that could be used for the dissemination of information. It helped to have commercial ties that could also be used for religious purposes.

Küster names a number of senders: the empress of Austria, the elector of Hanover, the government of France, and the government of England. In Austria and Hanover, the sovereigns of the states were the only source of information, and they used the churches (Catholic as well as Lutheran) as their mouthpiece, also in a one-dimensional way. In this case religion, in the form of a liturgical hymn, was utilized, and this can be interpreted as a recognition of the efficiency of the clerical modes of communication, better than those the state had at its own disposal. Although the rulers of France and England also conveyed information, other voices were added to theirs in these countries. People send particular information in private letters. More important, however, were the printers and publishers of pamphlets and newspapers: They added information not necessarily available through the head of state, and they did not hold back with their own opinions, especially in England where they used the battle of Dettingen to criticize the politics of Parliament.

The sovereign of the state as the single source of information, distributed through the single Church – this way of communication would not work in North America as presented to us by Lambert in lack of a single government as well as a single Church.[1] Although Whitefield acted in a religious realm, he was not confined to one Church, which is nicely illustrated by the fact that he did not let himself be constrained to a specific church building, but addressed all people in an open field. Without wanting to take this image too far, it can be interpreted as a symbol for the new way of freedom of information that was possible in North America. In the absence of a single government and single Church, the field to reach as many and as various people as possible was open, and what Furly had done in his private circle of friends was transferred to a higher level: building a network of communication that stretched to a previously unknown size. Since the colonies were mostly settled by people who favored freedom of religion, no laws or censors would hinder Whitefield or other preachers to do this. Therefore, many voices were heard in North America, including various preachers who existed next to each other and in this way offered people a choice: everybody could make his or her own decision about whom to listen to, something people in Austria or Hanover could not even imagine.

Beiler concentrates on the communication network of one person, Benjamin Furly, who mostly distributed information instead of being a sender himself. In fact, he was a prototype of a mediator with wide-ranging connections and broad language skills. He translated the religious messages of other Pietists, and he also distributed Penn's pamphlets on Pennsylvania or copied the letters of people who reported on this new colony. Here we do not have a one-dimensional way of the distribution of information, but a number of senders who would also be recipients. Many of their messages, however, went through the mouth or the hands of Furly.

In this way, Beiler's contributions ask us to pay attention to the mediators, here Furly, in the case of Dettingen the church in Austria and Hanover, or the publishers of newspapers in the case of Whitefield. One person was very seldom in the position to get his or her message across on his or her own; even monarchs relied on multipliers, and it would be very interesting to follow the ways of the messages and analyse if they were changed on the way.

This important role of communication networks is obvious in the papers of Beiler and Lambert, and Beiler also points us to other networks that existed next to the religious network of people like Whitefield: economic networks. In the case of Furly, both religious and economic partners were used similarly; he applied his commercial connections to reach religious goals.[2] However, there also existed purely economic networks, and it would be very interesting to compare their communication networks. In addition, these papers concentrate on connections between Protestants – Catholic networks also existed.[3]

Concerning the *recipients* of the messages, we are presented with various types of audiences. In Austria and Hanover, the people who sang the *Te Deum* seem to be an undistinguishable mass. Almost all of the subjects could be reached via the Catholic or the Lutheran Church respectively. It seems that they were only concerned about their own small world; they accepted whatever information they received from the rulers through the Church as sufficient, and they did not ask for additional facts or other opinions. In France and England, however, the addressees of the message did not just accept it, but asked further questions and voiced their own opinions, and in turn they found an audience that was interested in learning more and listened to them or bought their papers. Here, at least the writers and publishers emerge as people with their own voices, and they offered their audience several opinions to choose from.

The participants in Beiler's as well as in Lambert's stories differ very much from the inhabitants of Austria and Hanover. Their horizon was much wider. Most of them had traveled themselves; they were aware of a world outside of their own town, and they were interested in the events in other areas of the world.[4] However, in both cases their audience does not include the whole public, but only those interested in religious topics. Furly and his friends exchanged news about pietistic movements in a number of countries, and here senders and recipients enjoyed similar respect and came from the same group of people. When he conveyed information on the newly available land in Pennsylvania, Furly also addressed this message to members of pietistic groups and offered them a land of refuge. That the addressees of Furly's messages belonged to a more specific group of people instead of a general public was caused by their specific situation: since persecution was threatening, they did not want to arouse too much attention. Although Whitefield's audience did not suffer persecution, they were similar to that of Furly in their open-mindedness. Lambert tells us how the news of Whitefield's sermons was distributed through newspapers, broadsides, and printed sermons, and how people eagerly read about the awakening and longed to be part of a inter-colonial and even trans-Atlantic movement. Whitefield did not address a congregation as a whole, but each individual, and each listener was asked to make his or her personal decision. Other than the masses addressed in Austria and Hanover, Whitefield wanted to reach each person individually, and he succeeded; individuality was discovered in mass meetings. It was no contradiction that, at the same time, he tried to reach as many people as possible.

Lambert has shown the development of a marketplace of religion: There was more than one source of information, more than one message to listen to, and people had to make a choice.[5] People were interested in listening to somebody else in addition to their own pastor and his well-known message; they came to hear Whitefield and the other itinerant preachers. This willingness of an audience to listen to new messages was a requirement, and obviously there were more people in North America than in Austria or Hanover who wanted to be such an audience (and for some of them, this may have been a reason to emigrate to the colonies). Would people in Hanover or Austria have come to meetings like this, in case the Church would have allowed it? On the other hand, had the battle of Dettingen concerned North America as much as the four countries analysed by Küster, it can be assumed that the reactions in the news would have been even more numerable and diverse than in England.

In looking at the audience, we can see how both elements depend on one another: People can only develop a sense of alternatives when there is a market that offers choices. On the other hand, such a market can only develop when people are willing to try something new and to make choices. We can see such a marketplace of opinions already in England in looking at the reactions to the battle of Dettingen; however, the marketplace of religion described by Lambert for New England is a very striking example for this development.

The *medium* that was used to convey the message also differs in the stories told by Beiler, Küster, and Lambert. To inform the people of the battle of Dettingen, the *Te Deum* seemed to be the medium of choice across borders. Using just this one medium of oral communication was obviously considered sufficient in Austria and Hanover. Gun salutes and ringing bells did not carry a message in itself, they were just used to alert the listeners that something had happened.

Other forms of media were added in France and England. In addition to private letters,[6] printed media were very important. Newsletters, pamphlets, and newspapers contributed information about the battle or the names of the wounded, and they were also used as a way to spread personal opinions on this event. Whitefield and the other itinerant preachers used, according to Lambert, mainly two media: speech and print. As in traditional churches, the word of God was preached in sermons. Whitefield spoke to his audience, as other preachers did too. His success, however, was supported by his use of printed media: his sermons were published, so that people could read his message even in places he did not visit. Newspapers, in addition to the oral reports of participants, distributed information on his meetings. In this way they did not only inform people about these events but raised their curiosity and kindled the wish to listen to this preacher in person. In announcing the dates and places of Whitefield's next appearances, they also assured that their readers would know when and where their curiosity would be answered. As Lambert has aptly shown, Whitefield knew how to use the press for his purposes, and the press was happy to have something to report on, so both profited from their collaboration. Even specific revival magazines were printed. This use of the press distinguished this revival from previous awakenings, enlarged its impact and enabled its big success.[7]

On the other hand, the use of this medium was a result of the absence of a single church that could be used to convey information to almost everybody, as Maria Theresa and George August had done: Whitefield had to look for other media because he could not reach everybody through announcements made by a priest or pastor. He could (and would) not count on the help of an official Church to get his message heard, and so he enlisted another force, the press. In this case, Whitefield used the press to distribute his religious message. It would be interesting to see how secular messages were announced. How, for example, would the news of a victory in a battle as in Dettingen be made known to the American public?

The differing use of media among Furly and his friends was caused by the specific composition of their group. They did not want to inform as many people as possible, but just a few other people, and handwritten correspondence was the medium of choice. Therefore, an extensive network of letter writing was established, which was quite common in pietistic circles.[8] Whenever possible, oral communication was added, and therefore visits and travels played an important role to communicate information. When it came to propagate the land in Pennsylvania, however, Furly and his friends used printed pamphlets to reach a wider audience. Among their circle of friends, Whitefield and the other preachers also used such a letter-writing network. Letters were written to inform congregations about the advent of Whitefield and about his successes.[9] In publishing his journals and some of his letters, Whitefield transgressed the boundaries between handwritten and printed media.

As can be seen in these examples, speech was one of the main forms of communication used in the eighteenth century, but it was not the only one. In addition to oral forms of communication, various forms of handwritten and printed media conveyed information. The right use of the right medium at the right time enabled the success of the sender – a simple truth that has not changed until today. We still know so much about the people portrayed in these papers because they used the various forms of media well and were successful, otherwise we would not have any records of their messages. On the other hand, governments may deliberately decide to keep their subjects uninformed by not using media, and as long as the people did accept this and did not look for additional ways to gain information, on a battle or on other topics, the governments also were successful.

Although various media have been named in the contributions of Beiler, Küster and Lambert, I would like to add some more to enlarge the picture. So far, we have focused on forms of communication that consist mainly of words, either spoken or written. Speeches, sermons, newspapers, even *Te Dea* mostly apply to the mind of the listener or reader. There were, however, possibilities to reach the other senses and thereby raise the attention of the audience and influence the emotions of the addressee.

Whitefield is a very good example for somebody who used other media than those appealing to the mind of a person. For him and his colleagues, religion was a matter of the heart. To be saved was not an intellectual experience but an emotional one. Although Lambert mentions the fact that Whitefield tried to provoke an emotional response from his audience, he does not elaborate on Whitefield's use of dramatic elements to reach this goal. This element seemed so important to Whitefield's biographer Stout that he titled his book *The Divine Dramatist*, and in this biography we find a large number of references to drama and the stage that very convincingly explain why Whitefield was so successful. He would not preach in churches but outdoors and use the surroundings to illustrate his message: when he was standing on a hill, he would talk about Jesus' sermon on the mound; when the crowd assembled in the areas where executions took place, he would stand on the scaffold and remind his audience of torments and death. He possessed a strong, "lion-like" voice and made sure that he was standing in the right direction so that the wind would carry it; in this way he reached thousands of people. When preaching, he would take on various roles and impersonate the biblical figures he talked about. Body language and gestures were important ways to underline his message, and his listeners were captivated by this theatrical performance, especially in North America where stage plays were less common than in England. In addition, he used music to transform his audience into participants through the singing of hymns. And Whitefield succeeded in moving his audience, as was obvious when tears were flowing.[10]

A medium that became increasingly popular in the eighteenth century was the broadside. Since it consisted of only one page, it could be printed quickly and therefore carry up-to-date information. It was also quite cheap and could be bought by people who were not able to subscribe to newspapers or buy books of sermons or other topics. Often, a woodcut would raise the attention of the potential buyer. The text was frequently printed in verse and was therefore easy to memorize and pleasant to listen to in case the broadside was read to a public. Unfortunately, broadsides were often thrown away when, for example, the preacher whose arrival it had announced had left town or the interest in the topic had dwindled.[11]

A good example for the use of such broadsides is the death of White-field in 1770. Looking at a sample of ten broadsides printed on this occasion, we can see that all of them are surrounded by a thick black border, signaling the sad content of their message. Four broadsides show a woodcut of Whitefield lying on a bench next to his coffin, demonstrating how Whitefield's corpse was placed at the foot of the pulpit during the funeral service at "Old South" Presbyterian Church in Newburyport on 31 September 1770, where he was also buried. Another woodcut shows Whitefield when he was still alive, preaching from a pulpit and surrounded by men and women eagerly listening to him. Others only display small ornaments of an angel or a scull. Whitefield's name and death are always mentioned in a pre-eminent way in the title. The texts are also similar. Most of them are in verse, and the poem composed by Whitefield himself for his death is printed in three of these broadsides. One even adds the tune to the ode printed. All mourn the death of this pious person, and most of them do this in words that could easily be remembered and told to others: "Still is that voice which once with music rung, on whose soft accent crowds enchanting hung! Conceal'd those eyes whose light'nings could control, perswade, inflame, or sooth th' extatic soul!"[12]

This example illustrates the use of another medium, namely broadsides, to inform the public of an event, here the death of a famous person, to convey additional information on the circumstances of the event and to use this opportunity to appeal to the readers, in this case to lead a more pious life themselves.

Another broadside announces the use of yet another medium: "Just arrived from London, For the Entertainment of the Curious and Others . . . The Solar or Camera Obscura Microscope . . . For the Evening Diversion, The Clock and Camera Obscura, with the Battle of Dettingen, and several Italian Landscapes . . ."[13] This broadside was printed in 1744, only one year after the battle of Dettingen. It can be assumed that the image of the Battle of Dettingen had already toured in Great Britain for a while before coming to North America. Whether it was indeed the topic of this battle or rather the Camera Obscura that attracted viewers to this show is hard to tell, however, this was a way of bringing more information about the events of Dettingen to people on another continent. In appealing to the eyes of the audience, the battle scenes could be portrayed much more lively than by just using words. It would be interesting to know how many people saw it in England and whether this image also traveled through Germany.

These are just a few examples for the use of additional media. One could also imagine songs celebrating the victory in the battle of Dettingen or hymns composed about the Great Awakening, as well as illustrations portraying the wonderful land of Pennsylvania or depicting Whitefield preaching to a crowd of people. These would have been means to reach an even wider audience, especially people who could not read and had no opportunities to travel and see Whitefield or Pennsylvania themselves.

All of the three cases presented here deal with examples where national borders are crossed. Concerning the content of the message, it would be interesting to see if and how this message was changed when directed to another audience. Did Furly write differently when addressing his correspondents in Europe or in North America? Did Whitefield try to adapt his message to the varying circumstances in England or in North America? How did the *Te Deum* and the announcement combined with it differ in Austria from that in Hanover? Another aspect not dealt with in the articles are the requirements for these forms of communication, such as the availability of paper, ink, and a press or the access to channels of distribution like mail riders and ships. Especially in times of war, such resources were often limited and led to breakdowns of communication. Also, the influence of the technology on the content of the message would need further investigation.

In comparing the three stories told in the articles by Beiler, Küster, and Lambert, we can see that the use of some media did not depend on time, place or topic: Both Furly and Whitefield exchanged letters with their friends, English newspapers reported on the battle of Dettingen as well as on the Great Awakening. More striking than these similarities, however, are the differences: while Austrian and Hanoverian citizens seemed content with the information they received from their rulers, at the same time people in England and North America were able to choose from a number of opinions and decided themselves what they wanted to believe concerning Dettingen or the way to salvation. The ways of communication that were available to them formed the demands of the audience and in return the expectations of the people influenced the content and form of the information they received. The success of the sender depended on his correct assessment of his audience and the optimal use of the media available to him. These contributions show us some steps on the road to communication as we know it today: worldwide and diverse in form as well as in content. In general, the message, the recipients and the circumstances influenced the choice of the medium. Obviously, oral communication can only be successful with a relatively small group of people and over short distances. As soon as news needed to be transferred over a longer distance or even the Atlantic Ocean, it became necessary to write or print it. Spreading good tidings at home could be done by speeches; spreading them abroad needed other media.

# Notes

1. However, his first sphere of closed Puritan communities as named by Lambert can be compared to Austria and Hanover as described by Küster in the way that it did not offer choices. Here a further distinction between New England and the middle colonies would be necessary.

2. Many Pietists cared for the spiritual as well as the material needs of their fellow Christians. Halle, for example, exported Bibles as well as medicine.

3. See, for example, the trading network of the Augsburg firm of Obwexer to the Caribbean as described in Michaela Schmölz-Häberlein, *Connecting Worlds: Communications and Commerce in Consumer Goods between Latin America, the Caribbean and Central Europe in the 18th Century*, Paper presented at the Annual Meeting of the DGfA, Wittenberg, 23 May 2002). Also, compare the studies of English-Dutch relations in the North Atlantic by Claudia Schnurmann.

4. This is at least true concerning religious topics, see the comment by Hermann Wellenreuther.

5. Although this marketplace is very obvious in the Great Awakening, it was not invented by it. Especially in the middle colonies, the inhabitants were already used to a number of different denominations.

6. Küster does not mention private communication for Austria or Hanover, although one could imagine that such letters existed there as well as in France. However, it is difficult to find evidence for this.

7. It was not unique, though: in Germany, the Pietists in Halle, for example, knew very well how to use printed media to spread information on the orphanage or their mission activities.

8. August Hermann Francke in Halle, for example, spent a good deal of his time reading and writing letters to his fellow Pietists, as can be seen from his diaries, preserved in the Archives of the Francke Foundation in Halle.

9. Harry S. Stout, *The Divine Dramatist: George Whitefield and the Rise of Modern Evangelism*, Grand Rapids MI, 1991, XXII and 101.

10. Stout, *Divine Dramatist*. Stout gives a number of examples throughout his book, just a few references: Voice: 40, 90, body language: 40, 94, 118, taking on of roles: 106, drawing on the physical landscape to enliven his message: 78, use of music: 79, tears: 81 et passim.

11. I am convinced that a large number of broadsides announced visits of Whitefield and reported on the masses that listened to his sermons. Küster only mentions broadsides in passing because he thinks that they did not reach a large public audience. I assume, however, that broadsides on the battle of Dettingen made their way to Hanover and added information to what was heard in church. In addition to poems praising the King, there is, for example, an "Aufrichtiges Send-Schreiben Eines guten Freundes aus Hanau An Einem seiner Bekandten in Franckfurt am Mayn, Von der ohnlängst Zwischen der Alliirten und Frantzösis. Armeen Bey Dettingen und Klein-Ostein vorgefallenen Action: In welchem Einige Merckwürdig-keiten, so sich sowohl vor als nach dem Treffen zugetragen, welche dieser gute Freund theils selbst mit angesehen, und theils von wahrhaftigen Persohnen mündlich benachrichtiget worden; enthalten sind." "Zuver-läßige Nachricht, Von Dem am 27. Junii 1743. zwischen denen Herrn Alliirten und den Franzosen bey Dettingen vorgefallenen Treffen: Nebst einem Verzeichniß Der vornehmsten Französischen Gefangenen Todten und Verwundeten; Wie auch Der Oesterreichischen und Hannöverischen Todten und Bleßirten." "Vollkommene Beschreibung, Von der am 27. Junii 1743 zwischen denen Hohen Alliirten und Denen Frantzosen, bey Dettingen vorgefallenen Action: Wie nicht weniger eine Summarische

Specification Der Frantzösischen Gefangenen und beyderseits gebliebenen Toden und Bleßirten; Nach dem zum Vorschein gekommenen Englischen Original. [Hannover]: Zu bekommen bey J. L. Heynen, [1743]." Even a list of casualties was printed: "Liste Derer am 27sten Junii 1743. in der bey Dettingen vorgefallenen Action gebliebenen Mannschafft von Sr. Königl. Majest. von Groß-Britannien und Chur-Fürstl. Durchl. zu Braunschweig-Lüneburg Teutschen Regimentern zu Fuß, wie auch von der Artillerie." See also: Sebastian Küster, *Dettingen: Eine Schlacht im Lichte der Öffentlichkeit*, passim.

12. Unfortunately, none of these broadsides includes an imprint. It is therefore hard to tell if, for example the woodcut was used by just one printer who published several broadsides on this occasion or by various printers. Phillis Wheatley, "An elegiac poem, on the death of that celebrated divine, and eminent servant of Jesus Christ, the late Reverend, and pious George Whitefield . . .," *Historical Society of Pennsylvania AbG 1770–8*; "A hymn, composed by the Reverend Dr. Whitefield, to be sung over his own corpse, taken from the original, May 1, 1764", *Historical Society of Pennsylvania*, p. 9, "Two funeral hymns, composed by that eminent servant of the most high God, the late Reverend and learned George Whitefield . . .", *Historical Society of Pennsylvania*, p. 10; "An elegy on the death of the Rev. Mr. George Whitefield . . .", *Historical Society of Pennsylvania*, p. 11 (quote from this text); "A true copy of the last will and testament of the late Rev. George Whitefield.", *Historical Society of Pennsylvania*, p. 12; "A short poem, on the death of the Rev'd Mr. George Whitefield . . .", *Historical Society of Pennsylvania*, p. 13; "A funeral elegy, on the Revd. and renowned George Whitefield . . .", *Historical Society of Pennsylvania*, p 14; "A funeral elegy, on the Revd. and renowned George Whitefield . . .", *Historical Society of Pennsylvania*, p. 15; "An ode set to music, consecrated to the memory of the Rev. George Whitefield, A. M., who left this transitory life in full assurance of one more glorious . . . by one of his friends in Boston . . ." *Historical Society of Pennsylvania*, p. 16; "Phillis's Poem on the death of Mr. Whitefield.", *American Antiquarian Society BDSDS 1770*.

13. Library Company of Philadelphia, sm#Am 1744 Jus 177.F. The Camera Obscura was a dark box or room with a hole in one end. If the hole was small enough, an inverted image would be seen on the opposite wall. Lenses improved the picture shown, and the cameras became quite popular. Even more popular was the Laterna Magica, where images were projected onto a wall from a small painting on a piece of glass by using lenses and a source of light. Possibly the image of Dettingen was shown through such a Laterna Magica.

# Part II
## Narrowing Atlantic Distances: Communication in the Age of the Telegraph

# 6
# The Telegraph and Transatlantic Communication Relations

*Jürgen Wilke*

## Introduction

The "communication revolution" of the nineteenth century was a result of various factors.[1] The Gutenberg press had been in use since the middle of the fifteenth century, yet it had not undergone any noteworthy changes. In 1811 though, the construction of the high-speed printing machine led to a considerable increase in printing capacities. Thus, newspapers could be produced in higher numbers and in less time than before. The invention of the rotary press in the second half of the nineteenth century led to yet another increase in circulations. These innovations and inventions did not only change the means of production, but also the means of communication. The telegraph should be mentioned foremost in this respect, followed by the telephone.

The invention of the electric telegraph was an important breakthrough in human communication. Since antiquity, man had sought for ways to accelerate communication,[2] yet all attempts to solve this problem remained insufficient or unrealistic. For millennia, messages had to be delivered by messengers, whose speed could (at best) be increased by using horses or establishing a relay system. The use of messengers, however, imposed limits on the speed of communication – limits that only the immaterial transmission of signals through electricity could surpass. The telegraph made time irrelevant to communication because the transmission and the reception of a message occurred (almost) simultaneously. Space, too, was also virtually irrelevant. No longer did geographical distance determine the time it took to deliver a message. The telegraph did – as some experts claim – "annihilate" time and space; distance "disappeared".[3] The telegraph not only speeded up communication and made distance an unimportant factor; it also caused an integration of communication relations and networks, both on the national and the international level. The telegraph signaled the beginning of the age of globalization at least in the field of communication. Of course, messages had been relayed over great distances before the invention of the telegraph, but the impediments to transportation, such as road quality or weather conditions, made delivery quite difficult. In comparison, the telegraph offered clear economic advantages, which made it a prominent and dynamic factor in trade and commerce. Moreover, the mass media profited from the telegraph, particularly the organizations that evolved into today's news agencies.

The topic of this article is the role the telegraph played in transatlantic communication relations, particularly between Germany and the United States. My main focus will be the period from 1875 until World War I, but I will also provide some additional remarks about the postwar period. First, I will explain how the telegraph developed, following with a description of the dimensions and preconditions of transatlantic telegraphic communication. Next, I will deal with the forms and content of telegraphic communication and the importance of the telegraph in developing a transatlantic news exchange. The question I will address is: how did technology and its implementation by various organizations change the ways of information?

# The Evolution of the Telegraph

The telegraph is the result of a long chain of discoveries, ideas and scientific experiments conceived and carried out by numerous scientists and inventors (today called "engineers").[4] At the beginning of the nineteenth century, some of these inventors were looking for a conventional solution to the problem of long-distance communication. In France for example, Claude Chappe experimented at the beginning of the 1790s with a system of optical telegraphy.[5] Yet, it was not until scientists experimented with and learned to manage electricity in the nineteenth century that the telegraph became a realistic option. Not only were significant improvements in conducting technology necessary for the construction of the telegraph, inventors also had to solve problems regarding encryption and recording. As a consequence, many different types of telegraphs emerged in the early decades of the nineteenth century. These "prototypes", however, still suffered from several technical and practical flaws. Eventually, Samuel F. B. Morse – an American – found a satisfying solution to these problems. On 4 September 1837, he demonstrated his telegraph in a public experiment in New York City. For several years, Morse continued to improve his telegraph until it was ready for a large-scale experiment in 1844. On 1 May, the Morse telegraph transmitted the nomination of the presidential candidate from the Whig (now Republican) party convention in Baltimore to Washington DC. This proved that telegraphing was much faster than sending a message by train.[6] Later that month, the complete line was opened for public use.

It took much longer to implement the telegraph in Germany; because the German Federation was not a strong centralized state but rather a conglomerate of many autonomous states, the development of the telegraph varied regionally.[7] Traditionally, private entrepreneurship had not played an important role in building an infrastructure, and therefore – in contrast to the US – German governments took on the task of constructing the necessary networks themselves, which were mostly designed to suit the needs of the railroad companies. This does not mean though, that private interest did not count at all. In fact, Prussia was the first country in continental Europe to open its telegraph lines to the public on 1 October 1849, first the lines from Berlin to Hamburg and Aachen, then from Düsseldorf to Elberfeld.[8] In the decades following 1849, the Prussian telegraph network gradually became more extensive; until 1871, the year the German Empire was founded, it remained the most far-reaching network of all the German states, followed by Bavaria and Saxony. Before the founding of the North German Confederation in 1865–6, 653 telegraph stations existed in Prussia connected to a network with a total line length of 12,148 km.[9] In contrast, US telegraph lines had already reached a total length of 16,735 miles by 1852.[10]

## The Extent and Intensity of Telegraphic Communication

We have statistics on the number of telegraph stations and the length of telegraph lines in several German states, beginning in the 1850s.[11] Yet, there are no statistical data regarding the degree to which the telegraph was used. This was not recorded before the foundation of the German Empire and the establishment of the Deutsche Reichs-Post- und Telegraphen-verwaltung (German Post and Telegraph Administration). The annual statistics issued by this administration enable us today to describe the extent and the intensity of telegraphic communication from 1875 until 1913, the year prior to World War I. Certainly, these are basic statistics that lack the specific details today's historians desire. Therefore, although these statistics do not provide an answer to all our questions, we can still use them to describe in detail some developments of importance.

Looking at Figure 6.1, one notices immediately how fast telegraphic communication grew in the German Empire. In 1875, 11,044,426 telegrams were transmitted, by 1913 there were 61,217,520. Within four decades, there had been an increase in telegraphic communication of more than 500 per cent. In 1888, for the first time the total number of telegrams exceeded 20 million, 30 million in 1893, 40 million in 1899 and 50 million in 1907. Figure 6.1 shows clearly a steadily rising graph. Yet, a closer examination of the available data shows that the reality behind this large growth is more complex (Figure 6.2), because the growth of telegram traffic varies from one year to another, but only twice did the number diminish, in 1876 and – to a lesser degree – in 1908. Otherwise, the years between 1875 and 1913 saw a continuous, albeit varying, increase in telegraphic communication. There were high rates of growth in 1879, 1880 and 1888 (an increase of more than 10 per cent) compared to low rates in 1885 (+ 1.51 per cent), 1896 (+ 0.73 per cent), 1901 (+ 1.17 per cent), and 1902 (+ 0.01 per cent). A sharp increase in 1879–80 was followed by a decline that lasted a few years. In the middle of the 1880s, this downward trend was reversed and from then on growth fluctuated until the middle of the 1890s. Until 1905, the average rates of growth remained much lower than before. From then on, telegraphic communication seems to have grown again by a large percentage, in comparison to the previous year (+ 9.6 per cent in 1913). During the entire period under investigation the average increase of telegram traffic was 5.1 per cent, while the average increase of foreign trade was four per cent.[12]

The statistics of the Deutsche Reichs-Post- und Telegraphenverwaltung also indicate the origin and the destination of all transmitted telegrams. Using these statistics, we can roughly describe the national and international scope of German telegraphic communication. As expected, telegram traffic took place mostly within the German Empire. Of all the telegrams transmitted in 1875, 67 per cent had a destination in Germany, compared to 16 per cent that were sent to other countries, 14 per cent that came from abroad, and three per cent that only passed through Germany. These proportions remained constant for the following years. Two thirds (or slightly less) of all telegrams had domestic destinations. International telegrams accounted for only a sixth of Germany's telegram traffic – a fraction that remained quite stable, too. In the beginning, the number of telegrams that were sent *to* other countries slightly exceeded the number of telegrams coming *from* other countries. From 1883 on, telegrams from other countries prevailed. However the scale of Figure 6.1 is too small to clearly show this. In 1908, for example, the "inflow" exceeded the "outflow" by nearly 1.8 million telegrams. One might compare this to the

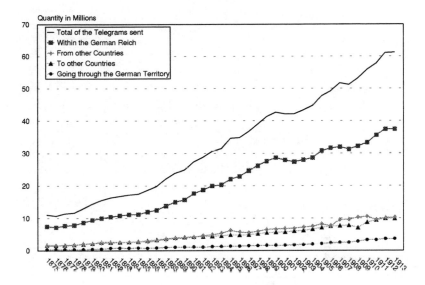

*Note:* As there were no data available for 1909, 1911, and 1912, averages of earlier and later years were calculated.

*Source:* Statistik der Deutschen Reichs-Post- und Telegraphenverwaltung.

**Figure 6.1** *Telegram Traffic in the German Reich (1875–1913).*

fact "that the German balance of trade was negative during most of the nineteenth century."[13] In addition, the statistics of the telegraph administration classified telegrams according to their country of origin (since 1875) and their country of destination (since 1881). In the beginning, this classification listed twenty-six countries; it later increased to thirty countries. The records included mainly most European countries and all other continents of the world, and for legal reasons (because they had retained their own postal administration) the kingdoms of Bavaria and Württemberg were listed separately. Listing the data for every country would be redundant, but I will select some points from these statistics that are quite instructive in the larger context of this article.

Telegrams from Austria-Hungary accounted for a considerable proportion of the telegraphic communication in Germany in the early years. Since 1883, however, most telegrams to Germany originated from Great Britain and Ireland. Beginning in this year, this connection remained predominant, with one out of five or one out of six telegrams being British (or Irish). As in general, telegram traffic with and via Great Britain and

*Jürgen Wilke*

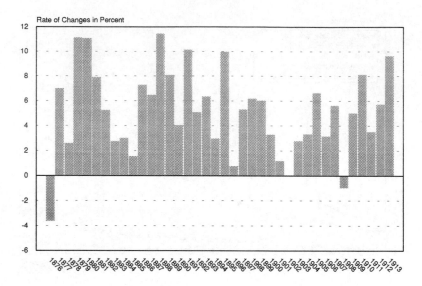

*Note:* As there were no data available for 1909, 1911, and 1912, averages of earlier and later years were calculated.

*Source:* Statistik der Deutschen Reichs-Post- und Telegraphenverwaltung.

**Figure 6.2** *Rate of Changes in the Telegram Traffic in the German Reich (1875–1913).*

Ireland grew during the following decades (Figure 6.3). The first peak was reached in 1895 with a total number of 1,306,214 telegrams. After a small decline, the number rose again until it reached 1,944,965 telegrams in 1908. In the prewar years, numbers sharply declined. During the entire period under examination, there were more telegrams transmitted from Great Britain and Ireland than telegrams transmitted to these countries – a veritable imbalance in the flow of communication.

Another country I will focus on is France. Communication relations were extensive but – as Figure 6.3 shows – telegraphic communication between France and Germany could not equal British-German communication. The same applies to the growth rate over a long period of time. My central point of interest, however, is telegraphic communication with the Americas. Official records contain information about this; yet, this information is not broken down into data for different countries, so it is not possible to tell from which countries the telegrams originated. For various reasons, mostly historical, the United States is likely to have had

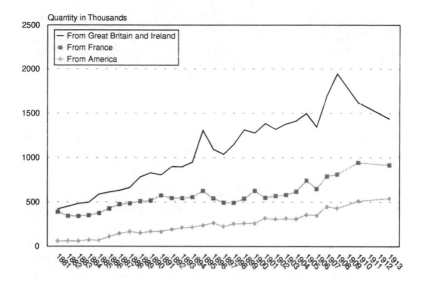

*Note:* As there were no data available for 1909, 1911, and 1912, averages of earlier and later years were calculated.
*Source:* Statistik der Deutschen Reichs-Post- und Telegraphenverwaltung.

**Figure 6.3** *Telegrams from other Countries to the German Reich (1881–1913).*

the predominant position in transatlantic communication. It is impossible to estimate if – and to what degree – telegrams from and to "America" included telegrams from Canada and Southern America as well. Although, judging from the route of the transatlantic wires, it is safe to assume their share was minute.

Figure 6.3 shows the number of telegrams coming from America in relation to those from Great Britain, and France. This figure highlights the gap that existed in the communication to these countries. Fewer telegrams were sent from America (and fewer had this destination) than from the big European nations. Compared with telegrams from Great Britain and Ireland (which accounted for 14 to 20 per cent of all international telegrams in Germany) and telegrams from France (their share declined from 15 per cent in 1881 to eight per cent around the turn of the century), for 30 years telegrams from America accounted for only 2 to 5 per cent of all international telegrams in Germany. Telegram traffic with America peaked in 1913 with 5.28 per cent. Its share had been higher than 4 per

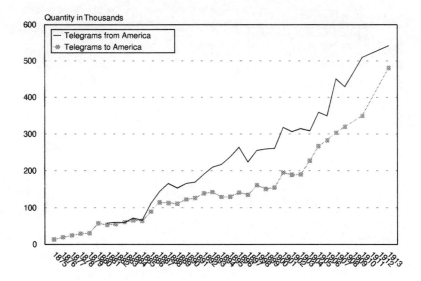

*Note:* As there were no data available for 1909, 1911, and 1912, averages of earlier and later years were calculated.

*Source:* Statistik der Deutschen Reichs-Post- und Telegraphenverwaltung.

**Figure 6.4** *German–American Telegram Traffic (1875–1913).*

cent in the previous years; yet, this still meant that in Germany only one out of 25 international telegrams came from America.

In regard to quantity, telegraphic communication between Germany and America was not of paramount significance. Still, in absolute numbers, the amount of telegrams was quite considerable and rapidly increased over the years (Figure 6.4). In 1881, only 58,186 telegrams came from America. By 1913, their number had jumped to 541,640 – an increase of nearly 1,000 per cent, compared to the average increase of 500 per cent. Several reasons may have been responsible for this, including the growing immigration to the United States and the intensifying relations in trade and commerce. It follows, then, that German-American telegram traffic also boomed. The graph illustrates this: in the early 1880s, as many telegrams were transmitted from America as were sent there. This situation had changed by the end of the decade. At this point in time, the number of telegrams coming from America exceeded those sent to America by 120,000 in 1896.

Certainly the development of telegraphy seems to draw connections to the growth of the German economy:[14] Imports and exports increased from three billion Marks in 1880 to 10 billion Marks in 1913. Britain was the most important market for German goods, although its share decreased from 20 per cent to 14 per cent between 1890 and 1913. Germany's trade was heavily financed through London. The imports from Britain were lower than the exports to Britain, and their share in 1913 was cut to nearly half the level from 1890. Nevertheless, German exports to Britain doubled between 1890 and 1913, and those to the United States increased by about 50 per cent. The American imports to Germany grew even more (whereas those from Europe fell) so the United States became Germany's biggest single supplier (28 per cent of all imports in 1913). Although the majority of all German foreign investments were in Europe before the World War I, 20 per cent were in America, particularly in prospering industries and especially in American (and Canadian) railways.

## Preconditions of Transatlantic Telegram Traffic

There can be no communication by telegraph unless there are wires that carry electric signals over great distances. These wires can be above or below ground. A transatlantic line posed specific problems; in both the distance that had to be crossed and the fact that the cable had to be laid on the bottom of the sea. This demanded powerful, trouble-free wires with appropriate isolation. Since a sea conduit had been successfully laid between Calais and Dover in 1851, the idea became more prominent that America and Europe should be connected by a cable, too. Private companies tried to realize this plan in the late 1850s but failed initially.[15] A new endeavor, carried out with the help of the cable steamer *Great Eastern*, the biggest sea ship at the time, succeeded. On 5 August 1866, the first transatlantic line leading from Valentia, Ireland, to Heart's Corner, Newfoundland, was opened. That same day, the line was used to transmit the Prussian King William I's entire speech to the Prussian Parliament after his victory over Austria. The transmission is said to have cost 29,000 Marks.[16]

By the second half of the nineteenth century, extending the global telegraph network became a primary goal of governments and telegraph companies. The United Kingdom, with its vast empire, had a particularly strong motivation, and also the necessary financial resources to do so.[17] Telegraph companies were founded for the purpose of enlarging and improving telegraph networks. The Anglo-American Telegraph Company was one of them. It was responsible for laying further transatlantic wires in 1873, 1874, and 1880.[18] The introduction of the "duplex technology" in 1875 permitted the use of copper wires simultaneously in both directions, which increased transmission capacities. In 1869, a French company (in which Paul Julius Reuter, the "father" of the British news agency, had a share) laid a wire between Brest and Duxbury, Massachusetts.

In the early years of transatlantic telegraphic communications, the German Empire depended on using British lines. In 1871, Germany built a line to Lowestoft on the east coast of England. The line continued on to London and from there to Valentia, the starting point of the transatlantic wire of the Anglo-American Telegraph Company. The British maintained a wire that connected Lowestoft and Emden via Norden. A German line (with a length of 1,654 km) leading directly from Greetsiel to Valentia is listed in the official telegraph records after 1881. We can assume that its construction was necessary because of the increased German-American telegram traffic. The Deutsche Reichs-Post- und Telegraphenverwaltung was the owner of these wires, which also controlled the lines to Lowestoft.

German dependence on British wires did not change until 1895. This meant that British cable lines had to be used, and therefore had to be paid for, giving their owners not only financial profit but also the possibility to control the flow of contents. To avoid this, coding patterns were introduced in telegraphy. Officially, the Anglo-American Telegraph Company's line from Valentia to Sydney, Cap Breton (situated on the Canadian peninsula Nova Scotia), was simply seen as a part of the German telegraph network. This perception started to change, though, when Germany began to make plans for a transatlantic connection of its own. In 1898 a new wire connected Borkum and Vigo on the Spanish west coast. The new line acted as a junction for a German transatlantic wire. On 1 September 1900, a new wire connecting Borkum and New York City via Horta (Azores) was opened for telegraphic communication. It was 7,670 km long and was maintained by the Deutsch-Atlantische Telegraphengesellschaft. Another line of the Horta-New York cable began operation in 1904. From this year until the outbreak of World War I, the German Empire used these two transatlantic lines in German possession.

The global telegraph network reached far by the end of the nineteenth century. Consequently, international communication had become increasingly interconnected.[19] Figure 6.5 illustrates this. As is seen in Figure 6.6, the United Kingdom dominated the existing network. By 1898, two thirds of the world's telegraph lines were owned by the Crown or English companies. The US ranked second with a sixth of the market share. In comparison, Germany owned only two per cent of all telegraph lines. Even though the British share decreased to 54.3 per cent by World War I,

*Source:* Lenschau (1903)

**Figure 6.5** *Trans-Atlantic Cable Network at the Beginning of the Twentieth Century.*

it did not lose its prominent position. The German share, in contrast, grew to 8.3 per cent, a development that particularly after 1900 would have been impossible without the creation of a German transatlantic cable (compare with Figure 6.4). It seems that this cable benefited primarily because the number of telegrams sent to America rapidly increased between 1903 and 1913.

## The Forms and Content of Telegraphic Communication

Official telegraph records contain additional information on telegram traffic, yet they list the information along purely formal categories.

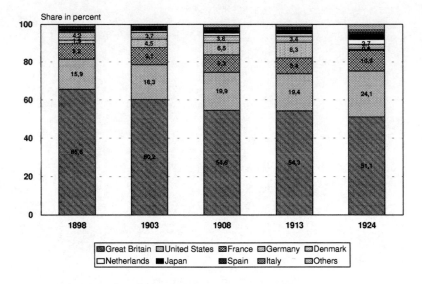

*Sources:* Roscher (1914) and Tenfelde (1926).

**Figure 6.6** *Share of World Cable Network Owned by Countries.*

Unfortunately, this is quite insufficient for a further description of the forms and content of telegraphic communication. Of course, to record more information in this field would have been a violation of the privacy policy of mail and telecommunications. Therefore, the records only make distinctions between telegrams free of charge and chargeable telegrams (including sub-categories for urgency, delivery, and so forth.). Telegrams free of charge include the so-called "Reichsdienst-Telegramme", telegrams sent by public service authorities, including the post offices themselves. These accounted only for a very small fraction of overall telegram traffic. In the years preceding World War I, this fraction rarely exceeded 3 per cent. In 1876, for example, this meant a total number of 233,094 telegrams (3.25 per cent). The number of Reichsdienst-Telegramme increased with the general growth of telegram traffic. In 1913, it reached 1,157,770 telegrams (2.45 per cent). The majority of these telegrams were sent to destinations within Germany; only a small proportion left the country – 4,970 (0.33 per cent) in 1876, 31.440 (0.32 per cent) in 1913. Official records at this time do not contain any categories concerning the destination of a telegram, which is why we cannot tell to what extent German authorities communicated with America.

We do, however, have disposal of official statistics concerning the length of telegrams. This is an essential indicator when it comes to determining the intensity of and the information provided by telegraphic communication. Usually, the length of a telegram was measured in words. This was important because the charge for a telegram was determined by the number of words and its destination – the "wordier" a message and the greater the distance, the higher the charge (unless discounts were given). Consequently, telegrams within Germany were, on average, much longer than telegrams to a foreign destination. Since the late 1870s, 10 per cent of all telegrams transmitted within Germany contained less than five words (this decreased to one or two per cent in the 1890s). Regarding the telegram traffic to countries outside Europe (again, there are no sub-categories), up to a third of all telegrams did not contain more than five words. Presumably such telegrams transmitted either figures or other short conventional messages. Whereas telegrams with a length of up to twenty words accounted for almost 50 per cent of all telegrams in Germany, they were 66 to 75 per cent of all telegrams with a destination outside Europe. Only about one out of ten telegrams in Germany was longer than twenty words. The same was true for 4 to 6 per cent of all telegrams sent to non-European countries. The number of words in telegrams sent to European countries was somewhere in between those sent to Germany or the United States. Transatlantic communication relations were under considerable pressure to be cost-efficient, which limited their volume. A telegram from Europe to America with a length of twenty words cost 400 Marks in 1866 with a charge of 20 Marks for each additional word. In 1872, the charge per word had sunk to 4 Marks, then to 1.50 Marks in 1888.[20] The pressure to be cost efficient resulted in the evolution of a "Telegrammstil", a text style that used standardized expressions and abbreviations and left out anything that was redundant or not essential to the message. Codebooks, prepared not least for the needs of different industries, were used to replace often-used terms, entire phrases and figures of expression.

As we have seen, state telegrams did not play a primary role in overall telegraphic communication. The telegraph was mainly used for business purposes. We do know that telegrams with commercial or stock market information were the primary motivating force behind the creation of a global telegraph network. To a much lesser degree, the telegraph was used for personal reasons. News agencies benefited from the new technology in their own way, because they used it to procure and spread news for the press more rapidly.

*Jürgen Wilke*

# Early News Agencies and Transatlantic News Traffic

From the early days of the telegraph, newspapers (in addition to other commercial enterprises) were among the main users in the United States. Soon, reporters replaced the telegraphers. They provided news for various newspapers, the content of which (to the detriment of competition) became consequently more alike. The Harbour News Association played a major role in intensifying the use of telegraphy. The Association was a cooperative venture of six New York newspapers, aimed at gathering news. It was later renamed Associated Press,[21] but even in the United States, the gathering of news by mail did not cease in the age of the telegraph.[22]

A similar development in Germany was considerably less dynamic than in the United States, although use of telegraphic news dispatches by the press was possible after Prussia had opened the wires to the public. On 28 November 1849, the *National Zeitung*, a Berlin newspaper founded in the previous revolutionary year as a liberal party paper, announced that it would feature news dispatches from Paris, London, Amsterdam, and Frankfurt. Further dispatches would come from Hamburg and Stettin in a few days. The day of this announcement is seen as the "birthday" of the Wolff'sches Telegraphisches Bureau (WTB), which was to become the first – and until 1933 – the most important German news agency. It was named after Bernhard Wolff, manager of the *National Zeitung* and the driving force behind the enterprise.[23] Soon, Wolff had the idea of selling his news dispatches to other newspapers – an idea that necessitated the creation of a separate institution.

The first three telegraphic news dispatches, which the *National Zeitung* published on 28 November 1849, contained nothing but quotations from the stock markets in Frankfurt, London, and Amsterdam. Therefore, stock quotes thus became the first telegraphic news to be noticed by the public and they were a major factor in creating and enlarging the business section of daily newspapers. Soon, other news appeared, too. Already on 29 November 1849, the quotations in the *National Zeitung* featured a report from Paris, which had been transmitted from Rome. For some time, though, such reports remained the exception. Even if newspapers had access to the telegraphic news dispatches of the WTB since the 1850s, these dispatches did not figure prominently in the papers. Usually, the editors ran them in special columns and highlighted them by using bold letters ("Telegraphische Depeschen"). Because of high transmission charges, the reports were usually very short. Gradually, the number of published news dispatches grew, which also increased to be several lines long, yet they still occupied only a small proportion of the newspaper.

If one looks for telegraphic news from the United States, it can be found only rarely in newspapers dating as late as the 1860s. In general, German newspapers seldom covered the continent on the other side of the Atlantic – a situation that had existed for a long time.[24] In the 1770s, however, the American Revolution had figured prominently in the *Hamburgischer Unpartheyischer Correspondent* and remained the most talked about subject for some time.[25] Later, interest in America once again subsided. Even in 1856, only 4 per cent of all foreign news in this newspaper referred to the United States. The use of the telegraph did not change this amount quickly. Wire news was transmitted more rapidly from New York City – and this was important in regards to the stock exchange. Taking the *National Zeitung* as an example, every Monday the readers got the weekly closing prices from New York, including trade reports on cotton from New Orleans, petroleum from Philadelphia and other goods. Until the end of the nineteenth century, political news dispatches from the United States remained rare, although some came from Washington DC, the capital. A provisional content analysis shows that 5 per cent of the stock market news in the *National Zeitung* originated from New York, giving the city the eighth in the rank order (Paris was first with 18 per cent). Within the factual news, only one per cent was submitted from New York (rank twenty), somewhat less than from Washington DC (barely 2 per cent, rank thirteen). The *National Zeitung* still used other sources, including British or American newspapers for more detailed reports about the United States, if such reports appeared at all.

The WTB progressed slowly. In 1865, the business was transformed into a joint-stock company ("Continental Telegraphen Agentur"), which provided fresh capital. Moreover, the German government began subsidizing the WTB. This caused financial dependency and gave the WTB a semi-official status.[26] The WTB's new status was made evident by the agency's move into a wing of the main telegraph office of the Reichspost in 1869, which was an advantage in terms of getting the dispatches as quickly as possible. In the midst of the 1870s about 15,000 telegrams a day were received and sent at the "Haupt-Telegraphenamt" on average. The WTB remained in this building until 1877. It organized its news gathering in cooperation with smaller news services in other parts of the country.[27] This cooperation was impaired, however, by the telegraph charges being graded according to several time zones until 1877.[28] In 1893, the WTB opened its first branch office in Cologne.

Due to high charges, this strategy of cooperation was also applied to international news gathering. An agreement concluded by WTB, the French Agence Havas, and the British Reuters agency in the 1860s was joined by contract in 1870, which divided the world into "reserved areas". According to the contract, each agency was allowed to gather and spread news only in one region of the world (some regions were assigned to two agencies) and obliged to share their news with its partners. The agreement established a triangular "news cartel" that dominated news coverage worldwide. Even though the monopoly had many adversaries (which became competitors), the contract, which was often modified, remained formally valid until 1934. According to this contract, Reuters covered the countries of the British Empire, the Agence Havas covered Southern Europe and Latin America, and the WTB was responsible for Northern and Eastern Europe. Thus, the WTB's own news research was limited to the European continent, something that an increasing number of Germans criticized and even complained about. With respect to America, WTB received most of its telegraphic news from Reuters, which, in turn, depended on the Associated Press of Illinois until 1900 for its American news reporting.[29] Consequently, there can be no talk of news coverage that considered German interests. In 1893, the Associated Press became an equal partner of the news monopoly, and it was responsible for the coverage of Northern and Central America.

We cannot actually speak of a transatlantic "news market" in the late nineteenth century because the existence of the news cartel excluded competition. Furthermore, we would be mistaken if we imagined the transatlantic news service as being very extensive. In no way can the situation be compared to today's situation. According to the WTB's records of 1880, the news dispatches of the agency that were published by Berlin newspapers amounted to between 500 and 600 lines daily. This number rose to 1,500 to 2,000 lines in 1904–5. At the same time, the amount of telegraph charges increased from 425,000 Marks to 1,090,000 Marks.[30] Since 1890, the WTB had also placed its own correspondents in various European capitals. With regard to the United States, even modest progress could not be achieved until the turn of the century: "The opening of the German-American wire in 1900 resulted in the Associated Press's news coverage being controlled by a representative of the WTB in New York City. This precluded the possibility that foreign news material for the German press was arranged according to foreign interests."[31]

The improved flow of information between the United States and the German Empire at the beginning of the twentieth century had consequences for reporting in newspapers, too. As early as 1906, 11 per cent of all foreign news in the *Hamburgischer Correspondent* was of American origin. The wire news became more detailed, particularly where important events were concerned, such as the election of a new Congress and many governors in 1906. Yet, the WTB still lacked the means to spread news about events in Germany through the United States. The other news agencies continued to filter this information for the American public. In Germany, the Associated Press could not market news about America. An agreement with WTB in 1903 gave the AP permission to have a representative in Wolff's Berlin office, who would sort the news material for the United States public according to its value.[32] Soon, this developed into a branch agency that supplied AP's first European office in Paris with information. Yet, the first American news agency to establish a news service for Europe was United Press, an agency that had evolved from the E. W. Scripps publishing house. As an independent company, United Press was not subject to the cartel and could therefore send its own representatives to London, Paris, Rome, and Berlin.[33] Another news agency founded by Richard Schenkel also remained an exception. Schenkel was a correspondent for the *Berliner Börsen-Courier* in New York, and this commercial newspaper was his main customer. In 1913, Schenkel's agency was bought by another German news service.[34]

## Telegram Traffic during and after World War I

World War I caused a tremendous change in international communications relations, particularly in transatlantic telegram traffic between Germany and the United States.[35] A British ship cut all four German transatlantic wires on the evening of 4 August and the morning of 5 August 1914. This was one of the first British acts of war and it had significant consequences. It immediately halted German communication with America since it literally cut off the German Empire's most rapid connection with the United States. The result was, despite its efforts to the contrary, that Germany was plunged into isolation. The other transatlantic wires led through Great Britain, and could therefore be controlled quite easily by the British. The destruction of the transatlantic wires to America (and later to the German colonies) not only affected the German economy and news coverage by the German press – it also prevented German authorities from influencing the United States and impaired the work of social organizations which maintained strong ties to America.[36]

Consequently the German Empire had to look for alternatives. Efforts were made to develop and utilize wireless communication. The facilities necessary had been prepared for a long time.[37] In 1906, a transmitting aerial had already been erected on the premises of the station at Nauen in the northwest section of Berlin. The corresponding station at Sayville,

Long Island, went into operation in February 1914. Further receiving stations were added in other areas, so the German Empire could switch to wireless transmission after the outbreak of the war. The transmitter at Nauen had considerable power. In 1915, 50,000 words were transmitted to Sayville, twice as many were transmitted the following year. Until 1918, the range of the frequencies could be extended to 20,000 km. The sender could transmit seventy-five words per minute, 20 hours per day.[38] Until 1918, the sender was mainly used for military purposes. Just as Nauen served transatlantic communication, so too did other stations for wireless communication with friendly or neutral European nations. When the United States entered World War I in 1917, the station at Sayville went out of service.

Because of the war, statistic data on telegram traffic is incomplete. No statistics exist for 1914 and 1915. From 1916 to 1918, they were written down as notes "for official use only", but even when the Reichspost started measuring telegram traffic again in 1919 – after 1924 these statistics were called "Geschäftbericht" (business report) – it did not classify international telegrams according to their destination or country of origin, as had been done previously. Nevertheless, the basic data as shown in Figure 6.1 shall be continued in Figure 6.7.

In 1919, the first postwar year, telegram traffic in Germany reached its peak. There were 90,277,610 telegrams transmitted, an increase of 47 per cent compared to 1913, the last prewar year. In 1920, telegram traffic began to decline (Figure 6.8). Apart from 1921, 1925, and 1927, when telegram traffic grew again, the number of telegrams sank, particularly in 1922, 1924, and 1931. In 1934, 22,783,000 telegrams were transmitted, which is a quarter of the total amount of telegrams sent in 1919 or roughly equal to the amount sent in 1895. The reasons for this decline will be discussed in the following section.

The impact of the war on the international telegraph network of the German Empire was disastrous. In 1919, little more than four million telegrams were sent to or received from other countries, less than half of the amount transmitted in 1913. Although telegram traffic generally declined, the number of telegrams to other countries increased slightly in the following years. It remained constant for most of the 1920s and then declined again by more than two million cable telegrams annually until 1932. Unfortunately, statistical data that classify international telegrams according to origin and destination are not available. Therefore, it is not possible to say which countries were affected by this trend and to what degree. It is quite certain that telegram traffic with America was affected, because our statistics concern electric telegraphy. In 1924, the German

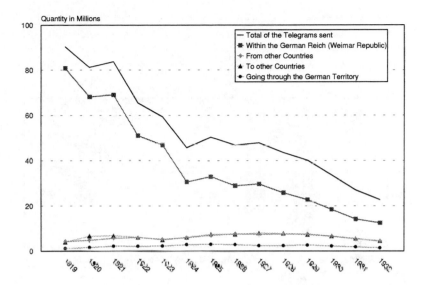

Quantity in Millions

Legend:
— Total of the Telegrams sent
✱ Within the German Reich (Weimar Republic)
✦ From other Countries
▲ To other Countries
● Going through the German Territory

*Source:* Statistik der Deutschen Reichs-Post- und Telegraphenverwaltung (until 1923), Geschäftsberichte der Deutschen Reichspost (since 1924).

**Figure 6.7** *Telegram Traffic in the Weimar Republic (1919–32).*

Empire owned only 0.57 per cent of the global cable network – a consequence of the war (Figure 6.6). A cable from Emden to the Azores, which was intended to repair the line between Germany and North America, could not be put into operation until March 1927.[39] In early 1929, a direct line to New York was completed, which made the recoding of telegrams at Emden unnecessary.[40]

The decline of wired communication in the 1920s resulted from many causes. Some of these were economic, such as the inflation at the beginning of the decade and the Great Depression at the end. Yet, the introduction of new communication technology played a more decisive role in bringing down the telegraph. The telephone, invented in the 1870s, gained ground by offering the advantage of direct communication between people and made personal access to the technology easier than the telegraphs which were often only placed at the post office. While in 1885 there were only 15,000 telephone connections in Germany, by 1900 there were around 290,000, by 1913 1.4 million, and by 1919 1.9 million connections (a ratio of 30.7 per 1,000 inhabitants).[41] Until 1930, the

## Jürgen Wilke

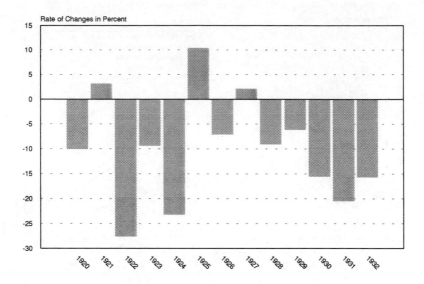

Rate of Changes in Percent

*Source:* Statistik der Deutschen Reichs-Post- und Telegraphenverwaltung (until 1923), Geschäftsberichte der Deutschen Reichspost (since 1924).

**Figure 6.8** *Rate of Changes in the Telegram Traffic in the Weimar Republic (1919–32).*

number of telephone connections increased even more in Germany, to 3.21 million. This however did not contribute much to long distance, or transatlantic, communication (the first phone call between Europe and America by submarine cable was made no earlier than 1956). In 1924, the Reichspost stated that the use of the telegraph was "limited mainly to communication with places that cannot be reached by phone (overseas destinations) and in general to commercial correspondence – such as stock market information – which does not allow for ambiguity; moreover, the telegraph is partially used by the press and for the exchange of personal messages like congratulations, family news, and so on. The portion of these personal telegrams is relatively small (25 per cent)".[42] In 1925, the statistics make an exception and include information on the originators respectively the target groups and their share in the telegram traffic. Trade and commerce accounted for the main portion (47 per cent). The self-employed and private parties ranked second (28 per cent), and industrial enterprises ranked third (17 per cent). Of all telegrams seven per cent were addressed to enterprises in the information or transportation industry. The

126

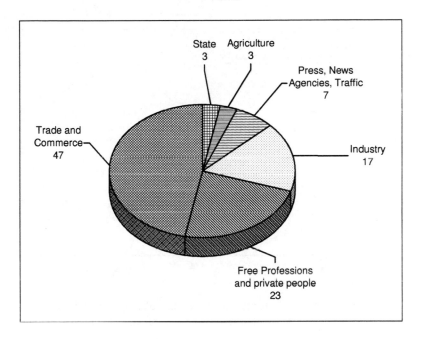

*Source:* Geschäftsbericht der Deutschen Reichspost 1925, 51.

**Figure 6.9** *Share of Different Groups of Addresses of the Telegrams to Germany (1924).*

public authorities and agricultural businesses each received 3 per cent (Figure 6.9).

At the same time, wireless telegraphy had become more reliable and was being increasingly used. In fact, the number of telegrams transmitted and received by radio stations grew tremendously in the period examined (Figure 6.10). With only 288,751 in 1920, their number rose to 646,159 in the following year and to one million by 1923. Figures peaked at 2.5 million telegrams in 1929, when the quantity of wireless telegrams began to decline, a process also observed with regard to wire telegrams. Of course, the number of wireless telegrams never equaled that of wire telegrams. Yet wireless telegrams were a supplement to wire telegrams and, to a certain degree, they compensated for the others' loses, particularly where international telegraphic communication was concerned. In the beginning, the amount of wireless telegrams sent abroad was more than twice as large as the amount of telegrams coming from abroad. The

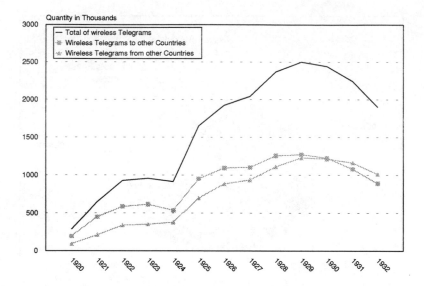

*Source:* Statistik der Deutschen Reichs-Post- und Telegraphenverwaltung (until 1923), Geschäftsberichte der Deutschen Reichspost (since 1924).

**Figure 6.10** *Wireless Telegram Traffic in the Weimar Republic (1920–32).*

number of incoming ones increased, however, until it surpassed the outbound in 1931–2.

As statistics for the second half of the 1920s show, communication relations between Germany and overseas countries started to intensify again. The number of wire telegrams, as well as that of wireless telegrams, increased. There were 15.5 million words telegraphed across the Atlantic in 1926. This number grew to 29.7 million in 1930 and decreased to 27.9 million in 1931. Wireless communication grew particularly with New York City, the important junction in international communication. In 1925, about six million words were wirelessly transmitted to New York. 3.5 million were received from there. In 1929, 7.8 million words were transmitted to and 4.6 million words received from New York City, a total of 12.4 million words, but then numbers plummeted: in 1932, only about seven million words were exchanged by the wireless stations at Nauen and in New York, 3.5 million in each direction. The Great Depression, following the "Black Friday" at the New York Stock Exchange on 29 October 1929, is a likely cause of this.

Aside from the data mentioned, official statistics do not help much when it comes to classifying the telegrams according to form or content. There is, however, documentation of the dimension of overseas news services for the years since 1925. One of them was Transocean (TO). The Syndikat Deutscher Überseedienst, a syndicate initiated by the government and financed by industry and commerce, founded this news agency in 1915. Its aim was to supply foreign audiences with more and better information about Germany than the WTB, the work of which was thought to be insufficient.[43] During World War I, the foreign ministry used the TO to propagate the German cause. In fact, the TO was able to market its news overseas because agencies like AP, UP, and INS included official German war reports for the purpose of providing neutral coverage. Apart from that, the TO's successes were small because Germans lacked an understanding of what information was important to the American press. Transocean intensified its international activities in the postwar era and started a daily news service in English in 1924. This service was accepted mostly by German language US newspapers, but rarely by newspapers that printed in English. The main focus of news distribution was, again, South America and Asia.

Due to the news monopoly, the WTB continued to depend on Associated Press for news coverage of the United States throughout the 1920s. The WTB lost its monopoly when a competing agency was founded in 1913. The name of this agency was Telegraphen-Union (TU).[44] It was largely influenced by the heavy industry and belonged to the conservative, right-wing Hugenberg holding. During the years following the inflation in Germany, the TU worked to improve its foreign news gathering. For this purpose, it employed its own staff of correspondents and created contracts with other agencies. One of these contracts was made with United Press[45] in order to get news from the United States, but the TU failed to establish an independent network of correspondents in the United States, not because of technological reasons – the telegraph and the wireless transmission had existed for some time by then – but because of a lack of financial resources.

## Conclusion

From its beginning in the nineteenth century, telegraphy meant more to people than just another way of communicating.[46] They hoped that telegraphy would result in progress, not only in an economic way but also a moral one. In regards to politics, the telegraph had a considerable impact on international relations. Governments could not ignore the new technology, which required specific provisions in bilateral and multilateral contracts. Of course, like every modern communication technology, telegraphy also created fears, too.

The telegraph affected life tremendously. Not only did it influence transatlantic relations, but its introduction also sent reverberations through the economy, politics, society, and the media.[47] The economy was the greatest benefactor of the new technology, which integrated markets and had a huge effect on prices and competition. The network of the international market was spreading. Together along with better means of transportation, the telegraph created interest in foreign price movements and had "scale effects", like favoring equal prices.[48] Disparities between goods were no longer as common as before. On the other hand commercial messages could be laden with false information, possibly causing financial panics. In the political sphere, the effects of the telegraph are particularly clear in the field of diplomacy. It changed the relations between the center and the periphery. With regard to society, telegraphy influenced social relations, language, knowledge, and conscience.

The telegraph revolutionized journalism and press information not just because it increased the speed of communication. In the United States, the idea is widely accepted that the telegraph contributed, if not caused, the transition from a political party press to a press with objective news coverage. News had to be short, focus on the "hard facts", and was required to be as neutral as possible so it could be offered to various newspapers.[49] As a matter of fact, news became a "commodity" in the actual sense of the word. In Germany, the telegraph did not have the same impact because the political party press continued to predominate (unless impartial newspapers like the *Generalanzeiger* are taken into account). Telegraphic news dispatches were available as a new commodity, but they did not account for much more than a small fraction of the entire news coverage. In the first decades of its existence, it can hardly be said that the agencies' news – although they contributed to newspaper content – already had an "agenda setting" effect in the German press. The role of the new mediators remained relatively small, probably as consequence of the limitations set by the news cartel. Through the electric telegraph, new channels of exchange were established, but the peculiarities of the technology, and especially the financial pressures, still left limitations that long distance communication would need to overcome in the future.

# Notes

1. Jürgen Wilke, *Grundzüge der Medien- und Kommunikationsgeschichte: Von den Anfängen bis ins 20. Jahrhundert*, Cologne, 2000, p. 155ff.

2. Volker Aschoff, *Geschichte der Nachrichtentechnik I: Beiträge zur Geschichte der Nachrichtentechnik von ihren Anfängen bis zum Ende des 18. Jahrhunderts*, Berlin, 1984.

3. Peter Weibel, "Vom Verschwinden der Ferne: Telekommunikation und Kunst," in Edith Decker and Peter Weibel (eds), *Vom Verschwinden der Ferne: Telekommunikation und Kunst*, Cologne, 1990, pp. 19–77.

4. Artur Kunert, *Die Entwicklung des Fernmeldewesens für öffentlichen Verkehr (Ein geschichtlicher Überblick) I: Telegraphie*, Berlin, 1931; Wilhelm T. Runge, "Geschichte der Funkentelegraphie," *Technikgeschichte* 37 (1970), 146–166; Volker Aschoff, *Geschichte der Nachrichtentechnik II: Nachrichtentechnische Entwicklungen in der ersten Hälfte des 19. Jahrhunderts*, Berlin, 1987; Franz Pichler, "Telegrafie- und Telefonsysteme des 19. Jahrhunderts," in Decker and Weibel (eds), *Vom Verschwinden der Ferne: Telekommunikation und Kunst*, Cologne, 1990, pp. 253–86.

5. Klaus Beyrer and Birgit-Susann Mathis (eds), *So weit das Auge reicht: Die Geschichte der optischen Telegrafie*, Karlsruhe, 1995, pp. 29–54.

6. Menahem Blondheim, *News over the Wires: The Telegraph and the Flow of Public Information in America, 1844–1897*, Cambridge MA and London, 1994, p. 32f.

7. Horst A. Wessel, *Die Entwicklung des elektrischen Nachrichtenwesens in Deutschland und die rheinische Industrie: Von den Anfängen bis zum Ausbruch des Ersten Weltkrieges*, Wiesbaden, 1983.

8. Ibid., p. 169f.

9. Ibid., p. 161.

10. Blondheim, *News over the Wires*, p. 65.

11. Wessel, *Die Entwicklung des elektrischen Nachrichtenwesens*.

12. Wolfram Fischer, *Germany in the World Economy during the Nineteenth Century*, London, 1984.

13. Ibid., p. 19.

14. Ibid.

15. Thomas Lenschau, *Das Weltkabelnetz*, Halle a. S., 1903; Max Roscher, *Die Kabel des Weltverkehrs hauptsächlich in volkswirtschaftlicher Hinsicht*, Berlin, 1911; Fritz Thole, "Das erste Seekabel Europa-

Amerika 1858," *Archiv für deutsche Postgeschichte* 1 (1959), 3–17; Daniel R. Headrick, *The Invisible Weapon: Telecommunications and International Politics*, New York and Oxford, 1991; Tom Standage, *The Victorian Internet: The Remarkable Story of the Telegraph in the Nineteenth Century*, London, 1998.

16. Roscher, *Die Kabel des Weltverkehrs*, p. 88f.

17. Gerald Reginald Mansel Garratt, *One Hundred Years of Submarine Cable*, London, 1950; Paul M. Kennedy, "Imperial Cable Communications and Strategy, 1840–1914," *English Historical Review* 86 (1971), 728–52.

18. Headrick, *The Invisible Weapon*, 33.

19. Lenschau, *Das Weltkabelnetz*; Max Roscher, "Das Weltkabelnetz," *Archiv für Post und Telegraphie* 12 (1914) 373–89; Eduard Tenfelde, *Die Welttelegraphie als zuverlässiges Verkehrsmittel vor und nach dem Weltkriege* (Ph.D. dissertation, Cologne, 1926); Cornelius Neutsch, "Erste "Nervenstränge des Erdballs": Interkontinentale Seekabelverbindungen vor dem Ersten Weltkrieg," in Hans-Jürgen Teuteberg and Cornelius Neutsch (eds), *Vom Flügeltelegrafen zum Internet: Geschichte der modernen Telekommunikation*, Stuttgart, 1998, pp. 47–66.

20. Neutsch, "Erste 'Nervenstränge des Erdballs'," p. 58.

21. Richard A. Schwarzlose, *The Nation's Newsbrokers I: The Formative Years, From Pretelegraph to 1865* (Evanston IL, 1989), p. 89 ff; Blondheim, *News over the Wires*, p. 47ff.

22. Richard B. Kielbowicz, "News Gathering by Mail in the Age of the Telegraph: Adapting a New Technology," *Technology and Culture* 21 (1984), 26–41.

23. Dieter Basse, *Wolff's Telegraphisches Bureau 1849 bis 1933: Agenturpublizistik zwischen Politik und Wirtschaft*, Munich, 1991.

24. Jürgen Wilke, "Foreign News Coverage and International News Flow over Three Centuries," *Gazette* 39 (1987), 147–80.

25. Jürgen Wilke, "Agenda Setting in an Historical Perspective: The Coverage of the American Revolution in the German Press," *European Journal of Communication* 10 (1995), 63–86.

26. Basse, *Wolff's Telegraphisches Bureau*, p. 28ff.

27. Christine Wunderlich, "Telegraphische Nachrichtenbüros in Deutschland bis zum Ersten Weltkrieg," in Jürgen Wilke (ed.), *Telegraphenbüros und Nachrichtenagenturen in Deutschland: Untersuchungen zu ihrer Geschichte bis 1949*, Munich, 1991, p. 41ff.

28. WTB, *Vom 75. Geburtstag des W. T. B. 27. November 1924*, Berlin, 1924.

29. Donald Read, *The Power of News: History of Reuters 1849–1989*, Oxford and New York, 1992, p. 81.

30. WTB, *Vom 75. Geburtstag des W. T. B.*, 7.

31. Ibid.

32. Friedrich Fuchs, *Telegraphische Nachrichtenbüros: Eine Untersuchung über Probleme des internationalen Nachrichtenwesens*, Berlin, 1919, p. 107.

33. Ibid., 143; Martina Schumacher, *Ausländische Nachrichtenagenturen in Deutschland vor und nach 1933*, Cologne, 1998, p. 21f.

34. Wunderlich, "Telegraphische Nachrichtenbüros in Deutschland," p. 82f.

35. Tenfelde, *Die Welttelegraphie als zuverlässiges Verkehrsmittel*, p. 48ff.

36. Jürgen Wilke, "German Foreign Propaganda During World War I: The Central Office for Foreign Services," in J. Wilke (ed.), *Propaganda in the Twentieth Century: Contributions to its History*, Cresskill NJ, 1998, pp. 7–23; Michael Kunczik, "British and German Propaganda in the United States from 1914 to 1917," in J. Wilke (ed.), *Propaganda in the Twentieth Century*, Cresskill NJ, 1998, pp. 25–55.

37. Michael Bollé, *Die Großfunkstation Nauen und ihre Bauten von Hermann Muthesius: Mit einem Beitrag von Georg Frank*, Berlin, 1996; Margot Fuchs, "Anfänge der drahtlosen Telegraphie im Deutschen Reich 1897–1918," in H.-J. Teuteberg and C. Neutsch (eds), *Vom Flügeltelegrafen zum Internet*, Stuttgart, 1998, pp. 113–131.

38. Bollé, *Die Großfunkstation Nauen*, p.19.

39. *Geschäftsbericht der Deutschen Reichspost für das Wirtschaftsjahr 1926*, Berlin, 1926, p. 51.

40. *Geschäftsbericht der Deutschen Reichspost für das Wirtschaftsjahr 1928*, Berlin, 1928, p. 63.

41. Werner Rammert, "Telefon und Kommunikationskultur: Akzeptanz und Diffusion einer Technik im Vier-Länder-Vergleich," *Kölner Zeitschrift für Soziologie und Sozialpsychologie* 42 (1990), 20–40.

42. *Geschäftsbericht der Deutschen Reichspost für das Wirtschaftsjahr 1924*, Berlin, 1924, p. 31ff.

43. Cornelius Klee, "Die Transocean GmbH," in Jürgen Wilke (ed.), *Telegraphenbüros und Nachrichtenagenturen in Deutschland*, Munich, 1991, pp. 135–211.

44. Martin Neitemeier, "Die Telegraphen-Union," in Jürgen Wilke (ed.), *Telegraphenbüros und Nachrichtenagenturen in Deutschland*, pp. 87–134.

45. Ibid., p. 124.

46. Karl Knies, *Der Telegraph als Verkehrsmittel: Mit Erläuterungen über den Nachrichtenverkehr überhaupt*, Tübingen, 1857.

47. James W. Carey, "Technology and Ideology: The Case of the Telegraph," in J. W. Carey, *Communication as Culture: Essays on Media and Society*, London, 1992, pp. 201–30.

48. Richard B. du Boff, "The Rise of Communications Regulation: The Telegraph Industry, 1844–1880," *Journal of Communication* 34 (1984), 52–66; R. B. du Boff, "The Telegraph in Nineteenth-Century America: Technology and Monopoly," *Comparative Studies in Society and History* 26 (1984), 571–86; Jorma Ahvenainen, "Telegraphs, Trade and Policy: The Role of the International Telegraph in the Years 1870–1914," in W. Fischer et al., *The Emergence of a World Economy 1500–1914: Papers of the IX. International Congress of Economic History*, Wiesbaden, 1986, vol. 2, pp. 505–518; Museum für Kommunikation, (ed.), *In 28 Minuten von London nach Kalkutta: Aufsätze zur Telegrafiegeschichte aus der Sammlung Hans Pieper*, Bern, 2000.

49. Donald L. Shaw, "News Bias and the Telegraph: A Study of Historical Change," *Journalism Quarterly* 44 (1967) 3–12, 31.

# 7
# Diplomatic Telegraphy in American and German History[1]

*David Paull Nickles*

## Introduction

Both the United States and Germany became world powers over the course of the nineteenth century. In 1800, the United States was a sparsely populated federation of states huddled along the Atlantic seaboard. France and Britain preyed upon American commerce, often with impunity. By 1914, slightly more than a century later, the United States possessed the largest and most productive economy in the world, a large navy, and a military potential unmatched by any other country. Germany's trajectory over the same period shows many similarities. At the dawn of the nineteenth century, what was called Germany was mainly a collection of small and vulnerable states. Even the largest among them proved to be no match for Napoleon's armies. By 1914, however, a Prussian-dominated Germany possessed the largest economy in Europe and the most powerful military in the world. By this year, both the United States and Germany governed global empires.

The transformation in the international position of these two countries owed much to technological change. The electric telegraph was among the most important of these new technologies. Economically, the telegraph facilitated the development of the large, multi unit, geographically dispersed businesses that helped spearhead the nineteenth-century industrial revolution in both countries.[2] Politically, the telegraph helped solve seemingly insurmountable obstacles to US and Prussian growth. In the United States, it allowed geographical expansion to be combined with the maintenance of existing political institutions. From the earliest days of the United States, many Americans, especially the Antifederalists (a group that opposed the adoption of the United States constitution because it created a stronger central government), believed that republican government could only function over a small area.[3] The existing state of communication supported their position. During the 1840s, a journey

135

from Oregon to Washington DC required 25 weeks. Without improvements in communication and transportation, it would have been impossible for a congressman to stay in touch with his constituents while fulfilling his legislative duties in the nation's capital. New communication technologies changed this. The railroad, telegraph, and steamboat allowed the United States to expand its territory across a vast continent while keeping its system of representative, elected politicians intact.[4] Lewis Cass, a US senator from the state of Michigan, proclaimed, "The telegraph has come . . . to bind still closer the portions of this empire, as they recede from its capital."[5]

Prussia faced different problems. Surrounded by powerful neighbors, its main arena for expansion was the smaller German states. Yet, the prospect of Prussian enlargement in this direction was not generally popular with either the people or regimes of the rich mosaic of polities that comprised Germany.[6] More decisively, it appeared doubtful that Austria and France, two of Prussia's formidable neighbors, would permit the Prussian conquest of Germany. Despite these obstacles, the Prussian-led unification of Germany occurred. Military events played a determinative role in this outcome. Prussia's assimilation of new technologies – most notably, the railroad, the telegraph, and the breech-loading rifle – created a highly mobile army with impressive firepower.[7] The speed of the Prussian army allowed it to defeat Austria and France in two quick wars, presenting the opponents of Prussian imperialism with a *fait accompli*.

By helping to transform the economy, international position, and military power of the United States and Germany, telegraphy shaped the context within which diplomacy occurred. Yet, change went further than that. Telegraphy also influenced the actual conduct of diplomacy in both countries. This essay focuses upon three areas in which the influence of the telegraph was pronounced: first, writing style; second, the extent of centralization in the process of foreign policy decision-making; third, the unevenness of international information flows.

## Diplomatic Style

Foreign ministries found that sending telegrams was expensive.[8] The necessity of protecting the wires required either suspending them in the air or burying them underground for long distances. Submarine cables were even more costly due to the exacting standards required to build a telegraph line capable of resisting the effects of salt water, underwater currents, and marine life. In addition, one needed to buy, rent, or build an enormous ship with specialized equipment for laying cable. Whether telegraph wires operated on land or in the water, highly skilled operators helped transform words and numbers into electric impulses and then back again. The transatlantic cable initially cost $10 per word in 1866.[9] Telegrams between London and the western coast of South America cost nine shillings (about $2.18) a word during the 1880s.[10] Over time, increased competition and technical improvements helped lower prices in most parts of the world. But despite these reductions, unacceptably high costs discouraged many businesses from routinely using telegraphy.[11]

From the telegraph's early days, social commentators wondered how the price of telegrams would affect the way people wrote.[12] In the United States, many believed that international relations would benefit from a change in writing style. Following the completion of a short-lived transatlantic cable in 1858, an American clergyman sermonized that this invention would "compel statesmen [toward] greater simplicity of expression." Diplomatic intercourse would move toward "plain and frank speech."[13] Likewise, an article in an American publication rapturously proclaimed that telegraphy produced a simplification and homogenization of language: "our Great Maker is preparing the world in His own good time to become one nation, speaking, one language, and when armies and navies will no longer be required."[14] Others took a more skeptical view. They believed that the telegraph undermined gentility. A British observer remarked, "the telegraphic style banishes all the forms of politeness."[15]

The high cost of telegrams affected diplomacy. The US State Department, faced with notoriously stringent financial constraints, generally prohibited diplomats from using the telegraph except in cases of emergency.[16] In 1870, the United States' legation in France was so concerned about saving money that Hamilton Fish, the US Secretary of State, only learned of impending hostilities between France and Prussia when foreign diplomats inquired as to the United States' stance.[17] The German Auswärtiges Amt (the Foreign Ministry) was better funded than its American counterpart, but it nonetheless faced an increasingly skeptical Reichstag bent on curbing the excesses of playboy diplomats.[18] Admonitions in favor of frugality had an effect. A German envoy in Latin America wrote his superiors that he was often unsure as to when an event was important enough to justify sending an expensive trans-Atlantic cablegram.[19] Such pressures became more intense during and after World War I. At that time, exasperated German officials obsessed over the need to slash expenditures, and threatened diplomats who sent "useless and unnecessary" telegrams.[20]

Demands for concision conflicted with the cultural ideals of diplomats. By birth and training, diplomats were conservative and loathe to abandon established notions of epistolary etiquette. Ever since the origin of resident envoys in renaissance Italy, diplomats have generally possessed a humanistic education. Not surprisingly, many have themselves aspired to be men of letters.[21] Some succeeded. Although German diplomat Otto von Bismarck was often dismissive of intellectuals, historians have sometimes compared him to "Luther and Goethe as a supreme master of German prose."[22] Diplomats who had not risen through the ranks in the standard fashion sometimes owed their appointment to their literary renown. An American humorist, Finley Peter Dunne (who wrote with an Irish-American brogue), poked fun at this phenomenon when he noted that nowadays, an ambassadorial candidate caught the eye of the President on the basis of having "just sint a pome on spring to th' Atlantic Monthly." The President then considered whether the candidate had "saved anything an' can affoord a vacation." If so, he would become the new ambassador to Britain.[23]

Given these literary pretensions, it is striking to see how the cost of telegrams forced diplomats to strip their telegrams of ornamentation. Germany's Auswärtiges Amt remonstrated against diplomats who sent long telegrams dwelling on detail remote from immediate policy concerns.[24] A Habsburg diplomat lamented the decline in the literary quality of messages, which he attributed to the adoption of the telegraph.[25] In one famous example from 1881, a US diplomat in Russia sent a two-word telegram to the State Department reporting the news of Czar Alexander II's assassination: "Emperor dead."[26] During the Paris Peace Conference, the German Auswärtiges Amt reminded diplomats to employ "the terse telegraph style."[27] Envoys could gain notice by artfully violating the rules about official cablegrams. United States Chargé d'Affaires George F. Kennan's "Long Telegram," arguably the most influential telegram in American diplomatic history (it helped persuade the United States to adopt a policy of "containing" the Soviet Union), gained so much attention in part because he flouted the conventions concerning telegram length.[28]

# The Decision-making Process: Centralization

From the standpoint of diplomats, telegraphy's most important influence upon the decision-making process was its tendency to centralize the conduct of foreign policy. This was part of a larger trend that affected many organizations. Historians of business and labor have argued that during the late nineteenth and early twentieth centuries, corporations acted to expand their control.[29] Businessmen hoped to gain greater leverage *vis-à-vis* the marketplace via mergers and horizontal integration.[30] They sought control over their inputs through vertical integration and techniques for regulating the activities of workers, such as automation and time/motion studies.[31] Telegraphy, by promoting time synchronization[32] and the precise coordination of activity over large distances, provided an important tool for corporations in their quest for centralized command, and facilitated the erection of gigantic, multi-unit firms. The same trend was apparent in the military, where telegraphy contributed to closer oversight by political authorities over military subordinates.[33] In all of these domains, those subjected to such oversight frequently perceived it as unwelcome interference.

In an analogous fashion, the telegraph served politicians and foreign policy bureaucracies seeking to centralize their control over far-flung diplomats. German Chancellor Otto von Bismarck, always keen to increase his power, believed that railroads and telegraph lines strengthened the authority of Foreign Ministers over diplomats.[34] Lord Salisbury, Britain's Prime Minister, echoed this opinion. Salisbury asserted in 1889 that overactive agents were the source of a conflict over Samoa between Germany, the United States, and Britain. In order to resolve the situation, he recommended, "The greatest reform of all would be to lay a cable from Auckland to Apia. So, and so only, we should get rid of the *furor consularis.*"[35]

Telegraphy frequently isolated diplomatic missions from information flows. For example, the Austro-Hungarian Foreign Ministry tended to keep its envoys ignorant about the overall international situation, and therefore less able to participate actively in the policy-making process. It used telegraphy to centralize foreign policy by forbidding its missions from sending telegrams to one another. Instead, all such messages were to be sent to Vienna, from whence the necessary information would be doled out on a need-to-know basis.[36] Security concerns – resulting from the vulnerability of telegrams to interception – increased the compartmentalization of information and kept individual posts ill informed about the general direction of policy. In order to preserve secrecy, the Auswärtiges Amt required that "every mission have a particular cipher that it uses only for correspondence with the Foreign Ministry." This practice resulted in complaints from German diplomats unable to read messages that they forwarded to other posts.[37] In the light of such restrictions, it is fortunate that diplomats did not require the same grasp of their government's foreign policy that they had once typically possessed. Individual initiative on the part of diplomats became less prized, due to the increased ability of foreign ministries to instruct them in the age of the telegraph.

At the other end of the wire, many diplomats believed that telegraphy diminished their autonomy and importance. One British Foreign Ministry official wrote that in the days before the electric telegraph, a diplomat could make an agreement with a foreign government in "the expectation that what he promises will be ratified by his sovereign." Such license, when used prudently, was defensible as long as communication times were lengthy and the matter at hand urgent. "But," as this official continued, "in these days, when telegraphic communication is possible between capitals even the most distant from each other, a prudent diplomatist will take care not to commit his Government by a provisional acceptance of what is not warranted by his previous instructions."[38] An American diplomat observed, "the office of ambassador or minister is in most cases not so important as it once was; in these days of rapid communication a large part of the relations of two governments may be conducted practically direct between the two foreign offices."[39] This reduced liberty was not always unwelcome; it frequently reduced the pressures of a diplomatic post. Edwin O. Reischauer, who served as United States ambassador in Tokyo during the 1960s, remarked, "as communications have speeded up . . . Ambassadors need no longer agonize alone over crucial decisions."[40]

In the eyes of many, the advent of telegraphy was a significant blow to the status of ambassadors. French observers suggested that railroads and telegraph lines had rendered diplomats "useless".[41] Reischauer acknowledged that some commentators went so far as to consider an ambassador as "little more than a postal clerk" or, to update the analogy, "a telegraph operator" who did nothing more than convey messages.[42] If ambassadors, who frequently prided themselves on being wide-ranging generalists, did not adjust to their new and less exalted role, they could lose power to subordinates possessing specialist knowledge of telegraphy and codes. For example, in 1917, the US ambassador to Vienna did not know how to operate the telegraph code. As a result, he was compelled to hand over for processing an extremely sensitive telegram – which he had been told was for his eyes only – to one of his subordinates in the embassy.[43] In such cases, use of the telegraph caused influence to gravitate toward technically skilled individuals who, despite their relatively humble status, played a crucial role in the communication process.

Even when ambassadors did adapt to telegraphy, they tended by so doing to yield power to their own Foreign Ministries. Within Foreign Ministries, the bureaucrats, who had once acted as little more than scribes, gained decision-making powers and even a degree of authority over ambassadors.[44] In this way, telegraphy weakened one group of intermediaries – ambassadors – who were at the periphery, and empowered another – Foreign Ministry clerks – located closer to home. Some ambassadors rebelled against this loss of power and status. Count Khevenhüller, the Habsburg ambassador to Paris, took umbrage when he received criticism from a Viennese bureaucrat. At one point, he admonished "a simple section chief from writing to His Majesty's ambassador in such a tone."[45] Many diplomats considered themselves great men and bridled at efforts to impose bureaucratic strictures upon their conduct.

Part of the conflict in this last case may have arisen because the telegraph exacerbated a disjuncture between the social hierarchy and the bureaucratic hierarchy. Diplomats were often of higher social standing than Foreign Ministry bureaucrats.[46] To the extent that telegraphy subordinated ambassadors to Foreign Ministries, it tended also to subjugate them to officials descended from families that, according to their own increasingly anachronistic standards, were undistinguished. One of Bismarck's confidants discussed the employment of a diplomatic corps drawn from the social elite: "High birth is . . . a qualification; and it is of considerable advantage to employ members of princely families in the diplomatic service, on condition, of course, that these exalted personages are willing to observe discipline and submit under all circumstances to the will of their chief, the Minister."[47]

Such submission did not always occur. Bismarck found himself engaged in a vicious struggle with Harry von Arnim, Germany's well born ambassador to France, who infuriated the Iron Chancellor by jumping rank and appealing directly to the Kaiser. Indeed, Bismarck himself, who often pursued his own policies rather than those of the sovereigns he supposedly served, once noted that the Hohenzollerns were "a Suabian family no better than mine."[48] In a similar manner, German diplomats from ancient families ridiculed Wilhelm von Schoen, their nominal chief, who had been ennobled during his own lifetime and became the German Foreign Secretary in 1907.[49] Likewise, Baron Hermann Speck von Sternburg, the German ambassador to the United States from 1903 until 1908, saw his career blighted by his recent aristocratic title. Sternburg possessed wealth, the right religious background, and military experience – all useful for a successful career in the German diplomatic corps. But he was also descended from a shepherd who had amassed a fortune by developing a superior breed of sheep. This was hardly the sort of ancestry that earned respect from his peers and assistants.[50] US Secretary of State John Hay noted that Sternburg, as ambassador to Washington, and his wife were socially ostracized by his own subordinates (the counselor and second secretary at the embassy) due to "his inferior social standing."[51] Telegraphy exacerbated such conflicts by subjecting pompous diplomats to commands from less exalted bureaucrats. Moreover, the brusque "telegraphic style" discouraged the sending of flowery niceties that might have smoothed ruffled feathers.

# International Inequalities in the Production and Distribution of Information

Scholars who examine international information flows have devoted considerable attention to the disparate abilities of states to project cultural influence. Joseph Nye, a political scientist and former government official, has argued that the United States' success in marketing its culture provides a "soft power" that strengthens its ability to achieve its own international ends and, indeed, serves the wider goals of all nations.[52] Others have viewed this phenomenon with less enthusiasm. Concern over the possibility of American cultural hegemony, although just one among many factors, has provided some impetus to the project to create a community of European states able to provide an alternative locus of cultural power. Such fears also contributed to Third World demands for a "New International Information Order," an attempt by governments to gain greater control over information flows into and out of their countries.[53]

Like many important phenomena, the recent debate concerning United States' influence over electronic media has historical antecedents. During the nineteenth century, the United States and Germany expressed some of the same concerns over British cultural power that are now directed against the West in general and the United States in particular. At that time, Americans complained that European wire services emphasized news – such as stories of lynchings and other lurid crimes – that cast the United States in a bad light.[54] Likewise, some Germans contended that the British wire service Reuters and its French counterpart Havas possessed a bias against their country. In 1888, Chancellor Bismarck embraced this critique, denounced what he termed the lies of these two news sources, and attempted to form a wire service alliance with Italy and Austria-Hungary.[55] The resulting media battle did little to achieve Bismarck's ostensible objectives. Reuters and Havas maintained, or even increased, their powerful international positions.[56] Multi-lateral diplomacy, in the form of the International Telegraph Union (one of the earliest modern international organizations), ultimately provided a somewhat more productive means of managing Britain's influence over international communications, while also ameliorating the problems of interdependence created by the recently erected transnational telegraph network.[57]

By 1900, the United States and Germany possessed great economic and military strength. Both had begun acquiring overseas empires during the late nineteenth century. Statesmen in Washington and Berlin realized the importance of the communication links that connected them to their colonial possessions and their overseas economic interests. They also understood that these links were vulnerable. In 1898, during the Spanish-American War, the United States had discovered that it depended on British telegraph lines in order to communicate between Washington and its forces fighting in East Asia.[58] After the war, the United States acquired the Pacific Islands of Midway, Wake Island, and Guam, which were well suited to become cable stations for an anticipated American telegraph line to the Philippines. The United States completed this cable in 1903.[59] For Germans, a realization of telecommunications vulnerability appears to have occurred at the time of the Boer War. During this conflict, Britain stopped allowing foreign governments to converse in code over British cables. Germany's sudden inability to communicate in code with its own colonies starkly revealed its dependence upon Britain.[60] Within the German government, the Algeciras conference (which convened on the southern coast of Spain in early 1906 following the first Moroccan Crisis of 1905–1906) reinforced a sense that their country's international communications were insecure. During the conference planning, German officials struggled to find ways of communicating with their diplomats; they sought to avoid the use of Spanish land lines – deemed "slow and unreliable" – while also circumventing the cables and territory of Germany's political rivals, who might conceivably obstruct communication between the German delegates and Berlin at a crucial moment during the conference.[61]

Germany, like the United States, responded by developing its own networks of cables independent of Britain. In 1900, the Deutsch-Atlantische Telegraphengesellschaft (German Atlantic Telegraph Company) in Cologne completed a cable from Emden to New York via the Azores.[62] United States President McKinley commemorated the event by sending Kaiser Wilhelm II a cablegram declaring, "In this age of progress every tie that brings nations nearer in their commercial relations and friendly interest works [to] their common good and can not fail to strengthen their cordiality and promote their mutual advancement in their paths of peace."[63] More significantly, this cable allowed Germany to circumvent

Britain when communicating with the Americas. A second German cable reached New York in 1904. Germany's network also gradually extended to include some locations in the Pacific (centered on the island of Yap) and West Africa (centered on Liberia).[64]

Despite these expensive efforts, the American and German networks remained incomplete and lacked redundancy. Both countries would continue to depend upon British sufferance for access to their own international telecommunications grid during a crisis.[65] Britain, in addition to an extensive cable network (which comprised 56.2 per cent of the world's submarine cables in 1908), possessed a cable hegemony based upon naval superiority, mastery of the techniques of laying and cutting cables, and control over the sources of gutta-percha, a Malayan product used to insulate cables against seawater.[66] The commencement of World War I in August 1914 made obvious the susceptibility of cable systems to attack or disruption. Britain and, to a lesser extent, France irritated the United States government and public by interfering with American telecommunications during the two-and-a-half years of the United States' neutrality. The Entente powers read, delayed, and censored American telegrams, causing American businessmen to protest loudly.[67] In addition, France and Britain damaged United States economic interests by cutting and seizing German telegraph cables that landed in the Western hemisphere. Although a serious source of friction between the United States and the Entente, this "cable war" did not produce enough damage to prevent a boom in the American economy brought on by the war.[68]

The vulnerability of Germany's international communications proved to be a matter of greater consequence. On 5 August 1914, shortly after declaring war on Germany, the British government snipped the telegraph cables connecting Germany to the international telegraph grid.[69] This effort to destroy Germany's system of intercontinental communication was not completely successful. Some neutral countries, most notably Sweden, covertly carried German messages. In addition, wireless telegraphy (radio), then in its infancy, provided an erratic and insecure but nonetheless important means of breaching the Entente's information blockade.[70] Yet, Britain and France increasingly intercepted or interfered with these alternative means of communication. Over the course of the war, Germany found itself largely unable to communicate with its overseas colonies, cut off from its considerable economic interests beyond Europe, and ineffective in its efforts to compete in the propaganda war. During the war's first year, the *New York Times* received only 4 per cent of its front-page war news from Germany, whereas 70 per cent came from the Entente powers, statistics that seem to have been representative of other newspapers.[71] Many factors contributed to this situation. Even if Germany's transatlantic cables had remained intact during the course of the conflict, the country's propagandists would have been severely tested by the challenge of making the invasion of Belgium and unrestricted submarine warfare palatable to world opinion. Nonetheless, Britain's hegemony over the international cable network does provide part of the explanation to the mystery of how Imperial Germany, with the world's most powerful military in 1914, managed to lose World War I. The Entente won the information war in the United States, a country that Germany could not afford to estrange.

# Conclusion

How have the three themes of this paper evolved since World War I? First, the problem of expense declined over time as technology improved and telegraphy became more cost efficient. Nonetheless, diplomatic telegrams are less literary than they were before electric telegraphy. Many factors account for this. Foreign Ministries are more bureaucratic than they once were, and this affects the way their employees write. The social composition of foreign services in the Western world has changed: Aristocratic dilettantism – the outlook that typified many diplomats and animated their literary forays – is less admired within Foreign Ministries than it was formerly. Writing styles within the wider society have perhaps become simpler and less ornamented. Despite the complex variety of factors involved, the telegraph does seem to have contributed to this shift. Second, the trend toward centralization has continued, at least until recently.[72] Again, while one can point to other factors – such as bureaucratization and novel information technologies (such as secure phones) to explain this phenomenon – telegraphy seems to have furthered it. Third, information inequalities have persisted. As the Enlightenment tract gave way to the cabled journalistic story, and then the televised news feature, cultural power moved westward from France, to Britain, to the United States. Meanwhile, the size of the communication grid, across which information flowed, expanded and became more global. In all three of these cases, electric telegraphy contributed to trends that have been powerful and seem long-lived.

# Notes

1. The opinions presented in this paper are those of the author and do not necessarily reflect the views of the United States government and the Department of State. The author wishes to thank Alexis Albion, Akira Iriye, and those involved in the 2002 Krefeld Conference.

2. Alfred D. Chandler, Jr., *The Visible Hand: The Managerial Revolution in American Business* pt. II, Cambridge MA, 1977; Ronald H. Coase, "The Nature of the Firm (1937)," in Oliver E. Williamson and Sidney G. Winter (eds), *The Nature of the Firm: Origins, Evolution, and Development*, New York, 1991, p. 25.

3. Drew R. McCoy, *The Elusive Republic: Political Economy in Jeffersonian America*, New York, 1980, pp. 200, 204.

4. Walter LaFeber, *The American Age: United States Foreign Policy at Home and Abroad since 1750*, New York, 1989, p. 105f.; Thomas R. Hietala, *Manifest Design: Anxious Aggrandizement in Late Jacksonian America*, Ithaca, 1985, pp. 195–8; Daniel J. Czitrom, *Media and the American Mind: From Morse to McLuhan*, Chapel Hill NC, 1982, p. 12.

5. Hietala, *Manifest Design*, p. 197.

6. James J. Sheehan, *German History, 1770–1866*, Oxford, 1989, pp. 868, 900f., 906–8.

7. Sheehan, p. 903. Telegraphy greatly facilitated the coordination of large armies in transit. On this point, see Michael Eliot Howard, *The Franco-Prussian War: The German Invasion of France, 1870–1871*, London, 1967, p. 23f.; Vary T. Coates et al., *A Retrospective Technology Assessment: Submarine Telegraphy – The Transatlantic Cable of 1866*, San Francisco, 1979, p. 98. For an analysis contending that the Prussian Army showed considerable skepticism toward electric telegraphy, see Dennis Showalter, "Soldiers into Postmasters: The Electric Telegraph as an Instrument of Command in the Prussian Army," *Military Affairs* 37 (April 1973), 48–52.

8. For a listing of the telegraph rates charged to American embassies in 1912, see 119.21/73, RG 59, 1910–29, the National Archives and Records Administration, College Park, Maryland (hereafter NARA). Information on German telegraph tariffs is available in Artur Kunert, *Die Entwicklung des Fernmeldewesens für den öffentlichen Verkehr I: Telegraphie*, Berlin, 1931, pp. 179–87.

9. Coates et al., *A Retrospective Technology*, pp. 87, 89.

10. The figure in shillings is from Raymond A. Jones, *The British Diplomatic Service, 1815–1914*, Waterloo, Canada, 1983, p. 125. I

converted it into dollars using the exchange rates at http://eh.net/hmit/exchangerates/pounda.php.

11. JoAnnne Yates, *Control through Communication: The Rise of System in American Management*, Baltimore, 1989, pp. 23–5; Richard B. du Boff, "Business Demand and the Development of the Telegraph in the United States, 1844–1860," *Business History Review* 54 (Winter 1980), 478. On the other hand, some companies operated in sectors, such as finance or journalism, in which the value of information derived largely from its timeliness. Such businesses made heavy use of the telegraph.

12. "Influence of the Telegraph upon Literature," *The United States Magazine and Democratic Review* 22 (May 1848), 412.

13. Ezra Stiles Gannett, *The Atlantic Telegraph: A Discourse Delivered in the First Church, August 8, 1858*, Boston, 1858, p. 12.

14. Annteresa Lubrano, *The Telegraph: How Technology Innovation Caused Social Change*, New York, 1997, p. 126.

15. "The Electric Telegraph," *Quarterly Review* 95 (1854), 133.

16. *Instructions to the Diplomatic Officers of the United States*, Washington DC, 1896, p. 100f., E729, RG 59, NARA.

17. David Paull Nickles, "Telegraph Diplomats: The United States' Relations with France in 1848 and 1870," *Technology and Culture* 40 (January 1999), 14–18.

18. At one point, the Reichstag's Budget Commission reduced the appropriation for diplomatic telegrams by 15,000 Marks. Extract from the *Kölnische Zeitung* of 3 February 1903, R138277, Auswärtiges Amt, Politisches Archiv, formerly Bonn and now Berlin (hereafter AA-PA).

19. Dispatch to Bülow, #67, 29 April 1907, R138279, AA-PA.

20. Zimmermann to the Germany Embassy in Constantinople, 3 February 1915, R138730, AA-PA.

21. For a list of "distinguished writers who have held diplomatic, consular, or senior State Department posts," see http://www.state.gov/r/pa/ho/faq/#ambassadors (consulted 29 September 2003).

22. A. J. P. Taylor, "Bismarck: The Man of German Destiny," in: *Europe: Grandeur and Decline*, New York, 1979, p. 87.

23. Finley Peter Dunne, "Mr. Dooley on Diplomatic Indiscretions," *New York Times*, 22 March 1914, section 5.

24. Schoen circular, 24 December 1908, R139521, AA-PA.

25. Freiherr von Musulin, *Das Haus am Ballplatz: Erinnerungen eines österreich-ungarischen Diplomaten*, München, 1924, p. 141.

26. Peter D. Eicher (ed.), *"Emperor Dead" and Other Historic American Diplomatic Dispatches*, Washington DC, 1997, pp. 18–19, 237.

27. Haniel to Baron Langwerth, Versailles, 3 May 1919, R2589, AA-PA.

28. For Kennan's account of this episode, see George F. Kennan, *Memoirs, 1925–1950*, Boston, 1967, pp. 292–5.

29. David Montgomery, *Workers' Control in America: Studies in the History of Work, Technology, and Labor Struggles*, Cambridge, 1979, p. 113.

30. Glenn Porter, *The Rise of Big Business: 1860–1920*, Arlington Heights IL, 1992, pp. 58–90.

31. Susan Douglas, "The Navy Adopts the Radio, 1899–1919," in Merritt Roe Smith (ed.), *Military Enterprise and Technological Change: Perspectives on the American Experience*, Cambridge MA, 1985, p. 171; Porter, *The Rise of Big Business*, pp. 45–58, 100–7; Charles S. Maier, *Recasting Bourgeois Europe: Stabilization in France, Germany, and Italy in the Decade after World War I*, Princeton NJ, 1975, pp. 576, 583.

32. Peter Galison, "Einstein's Clocks: The Place of Time," *Critical Inquiry* 26 (Winter 2000), 360–67.

33. Rebecca Robbins Raines, *Getting the Message Through: A Branch History of the US Army Signal Corps*, Washington DC, 1996, p. 4; Jeffrey Kieve, *The Electric Telegraph: A Social and Economic History*, Newton Abbot, 1974, p. 240; Maurice Pearton, *Diplomacy, War and Technology Since 1830*, Lawrence KS, 1984, p. 59; Martin van Creveld, *Technology and War: From 2000 B.C. to the Present*, New York, 1989, p. 41f., 170.

34. George O. Kent, *Arnim and Bismarck*, Oxford, 1968, p. 65.

35. Salisbury to Malet, 24 April 1889, in: Lady Gwendolen Cecil, *Life of Robert, Marquis of Salisbury* IV, London, 1932, p. 128. This proposal was probably not entirely disinterested. Salisbury's solution would have served British aims by telegraphically connecting Samoa to a British colony.

36. William D. Godsey, Jr., *Aristocratic Redoubt: The Austro-Hungarian Foreign Office on the Eve of the First World War*, West Lafayette IN, 1999, p. 197f.

37. Memo by Emil Propp, 20 November 1915, R2589, AA-PA.

38. Ernest Satow, *A Guide to Diplomatic Practice I*, London, 1917, p. 158f.

39. William Fenwick Harris, "The Consular Service as a Profession," *Harvard Advocate* (1911), 67–71 (available at Harvard University's Widener Library at OW:Int 6080.1). This is presumably the William Harris who was a Vice and Deputy Consul for the United States at Cardiff, Wales.

40. Edwin O. Reischauer, "Foreword," in Armin H. Meyer, *Assignment: Tokyo. An Ambassador's Journal*, Indianapolis, 1974, p. IXf.

41. B. D'Agreval, *Les diplomates français sous Napoléon III*, Paris, 1872, p. 4.

42. Reischauer foreword to Meyer's *Assignment: Tokyo*, IX.

43. Joseph C. Grew, *Turbulent Era: A Diplomatic Record of Forty Years, 1904–1945*, Boston, 1952, p. 317. The telegram concerned American efforts to negotiate an end to Austria-Hungary's participation in World War I.

44. Brian Layton Blakeley, *The Colonial Office: 1870–1890*, Ph.D. diss., Duke University, 1966, pp. 102, 109, 302; describes how telegraphy empowered clerks by centralizing policy, increasing workloads, and heightening the desire for rapid decision-making.

45. William D. Godsey, Jr., *Aristocratic Redoubt: The Austro-Hungarian Foreign Office on the Eve of the First World War*, West Lafayette IN, 1999, p. 198.

46. Diplomats were representatives of the sovereign, and needed to possess the "dignity" to defend his or her rights of precedence while moving among the ruling elite of the societies to which they were accredited. High social standing was generally an advantage to this mission. Foreign Ministry officials were more closely akin to clerks, although the status of these officials rose over the course of the nineteenth century.

47. Moritz Busch, *Our Chancellor: Sketches for a Historical Picture I*, New York, 1884, p. 223.

48. A. J. P. Taylor, *Bismarck: The Man and the Statesman*, New York, 1967, p. 10.

49. Lamar Cecil, *The German Diplomatic Service, 1871–1914*, Princeton, 1976, p. 300.

50. Stefan H. Rinke, *Zwischen Weltpolitik und Monroe Doktrin: Botschafter Speck von Sternburg und die deutsch-amerikanischen Beziehungen, 1898–1908*, Stuttgart, 1992, p. XIV; Cecil, *The German Diplomatic Service*, p. 63; John C. G. Röhl, *The Kaiser and his Court: Wilhelm II and the Government of Germany*, Cambridge, 1987, p. 156f.

51. Hay to White, 5 March 1903, in Allan Nevins, *Henry White: Thirty Years of American Diplomacy*, New York, 1930, p. 214; Rinke, *Zwischen Weltpolitik und Monroe Doktrin*, p. 94f.

52. Joseph Nye, *Bound to Lead: The Changing Nature of American Power*, New York, 1990, pp. 190–5.

53. Anthony Smith, *The Geopolitics of Information: How Western Culture Dominates the World*, New York, 1980.

54. Coates et al., p. 82. Such criticism of media bias, although not entirely without merit, was and continues to be a tactic used by those who wish to obscure serious human rights abuses.

55. Rosteinburg memo, Friedrichsruh, 24 November 1888, R532, AA-PA. Bismarck's proposal may well have been part of the broader geo-political maneuverings of which he was so fond. In any case, although Italian Prime Minister Crispi welcomed the opportunity to reduce his country's dependence upon Havas, Austro-Hungarian Foreign Minister Count Kálnoky claimed that challenging Reuters would be too expensive. The diplomacy surrounding these negotiations is available at R532, AA-PA.

56. Graham Storey, *Reuters' Century, 1851–1951*, London, 1951, pp. 112–15.

57. The International Telegraph Union originated in 1865, one year after the establishment of the International Red Cross. On the origins of modern international organizations see Akira Iriye, *Global Community: The Role of International Organizations in the Making of the Contemporary World*, Berkeley, 2002, Chapter 1; Francis Stewart Leland Lyons, *Internationalism in Europe: 1815–1914*, Leyden, 1963, pp. 39–42.

58. Daniel R. Headrick, *The Invisible Weapon: Telecommunications and International Politics, 1851–1945*, New York, 1991, p. 84; James A. Field, Jr., "American Imperialism: The Worst Chapter in Almost Any Book," *American Historical Review* 83 (1978), 665f.

59. P. M. Kennedy, "Imperial cable communications and strategy, 1870–1914", *English Historical Review* 86 (1971), 748; Field, "American Imperialism," 667. In fact, most of the capital for this venture came from covert British sources. See Headrick, *The Invisible Weapon*, p. 101.

60. "Memorandum on the Censorship of Telegrams to and from South Africa on the Outbreak of Hostilities with the Transvaal and Orange Free State," November 1900, FO 83/2196, British Public Record Office, London (hereafter PRO); Headrick, *The Invisible Weapon*, pp. 87–9, 106; R. Hennig, "Die deutsche Seekabelpolitik zur Befreiung vom englischen Weltmonopol," *Meereskunde* 6 (1912), 9f., 24, 31; Paul David Fischer, "Der Krieg und die internationalen Verkehrseinrichtungen," *Internationale Monatsschrift für Wissenschaft Kunst und Technik* 9 (November 1914), p. 227.

61. Sydow of Reichs Postamt to Staatssekretär des Auswärtigen Amts, 14 December 1905, R901, Akt. 834, 1f., Bundesarchiv (formerly Koblenz, since moved to Berlin).

62. Artur Kunert, *Geschichte der deutschen Fernmeldekabel: Telegraphen-Seekabel*, Cologne, 1962, vol. 2, pp. 240–59.

63. Telegram from President William McKinley to Kaiser Wilhelm II, 30 August 1900, M336, reel #126, NARA.

64. Headrick, *The Invisible Weapon*, pp. 105–10; Kunert, *Geschichte der deutschen Fernmeldekabel*, vol. 2, pp. 317–48.

65. Given Britain's later dominance, it is ironic to note that until the development of long-distance submarine telegraph cables, no European country depended upon Britain for telegraphic communication, whereas Britain depended on nearby European countries for all of its international electric communication. Long-distance submarine cables, by freeing telegraphy from dependence upon land, allowed Britain to become the dominant force in international communication. Coates et al., p. 100.

66. Field, "American Imperialism," p. 661. The statistic on cable ownership is from Headrick, *The Invisible Weapon*, p. 94. For complaints about the English "cable monopoly", see Hennig, "Die deutsche Seekabelpolitik zur Befreiung vom englischen Weltmonopol," pp. 9f., 24, 31.

67. In response to complaints, the US State Department declared that it had "continuously" made "urgent representations" to the governments of Britain and France regarding the transmission of neutral cablegrams. In the meantime, the State Department professed a willingness to use its facilities to "forward, in its discretion, messages in plain language that have actually been held up by the censors." Robert Lansing to Beer, Sondheimer & Company, 6 March 1915, R901, Akt. 856, s. 93–95, Bundesarchiv (formerly Koblenz, since moved to Berlin).

68. For State Department concern over British telegraphic espionage during World War I, see F. M. Gunther to W. Phillips, 11 June 1915, 119.2/147, 1910–29, RG 59, NARA; US embassy in London to secretary of state, 15 February 1916, M367, reel 25 (763.72/2408), NARA.

69. The most thorough examination of German cables during World War I is by Kunert, *Geschichte der deutschen Fernmeldekabel*, vol. 2, pp. 349–59. See also Headrick, *The Invisible Weapon*, p. 140f.; Paul David Fischer, "Der Krieg und die internationalen Verkehrseinrichtungen," *Internationale Monatsschrift für Wissenschaft Kunst und Technik*, 9 (1914), 227. The British plan for attacking Germany's cable system was articulated in the "Report of the Standing Sub-Committee of the Committee of Imperial Defence: Submarine Cable Communications in Time of War," December 1911, p. 14, no. 50, CAB 38/19/56, PRO, London.

70. Pascal Griset, *Entreprise, technologie et souveraineté: Les télécommunications transatlantiques de la France (XIXe–XX siécles)*, Paris, 1996, p. 284. For an early comment upon the unreliability of, and restrictions upon, Germany's wartime wireless communication with the United States,

see Haniel to the Reichskanzler, Newport, 16 August 1914, Bestands-signature 901, Aktenbandes 754, 96f.

71. Headrick, *The Invisible Weapon*, p. 148; Coates et al., p. 81; Michael Kunczik, "British and German Propaganda in the United States from 1914 to 1917," in Jürgen Wilke (ed.) *Propaganda in the 20th Century: Contributions to its History*, Cresskill NJ, 1998, p. 27f. As the war continued, Germany's increasing use of wireless amplified its ability to disseminate its message, but it remained at a decided disadvantage relative to Britain and France.

72. Email is said to have flattened corporate hierarchies and decentralized decision-making within the business world. Whether this is also happening within foreign ministries deserves further study.

# 8
# "Slender Bridges" of Misunderstanding: The Social Legacy of Transatlantic Cable Communications

*Menahem Blondheim*

In June 1745, the Board of Trade in London sent Governor Johnston of North Carolina a chastising letter. It scolded him for not having written the Board a single letter in the previous three years. Immediately upon receipt of the reprimand, Johnson hastened to reply, apologetically, to the Board of Trade. That was one full year after their letter had been sent. Scholar Daniel Boorstin, who recounted this gem of communication history, used it to illustrate his argument that the great time distance between the Old World and the New was an important wedge of separation between mother country and its North American colonies. The dearth of communication and contact between Englishmen on either side of the Atlantic was the seed of their estrangement, and ultimately of their separation.[1] Such a notion is reasonable enough. After all, do not industrial relations consultants, child psychologists, and even parents-in-law universally recommend "talking about it" – to strengthen relationships by enhancing communication? Relations between nations and societies are intuitively presumed to follow a similar dynamism: From the advent of the steamship and telegraph to the rise of the Internet, relations were thought to improve as communication improved.[2]

The rhetoric greeting the transatlantic telegraph demonstrated how pervasive the notion was that better communications fostered harmony and understanding. Politicians and clergymen, journalists and business leaders, vied for the most ringing statement of the inevitable improvement of international relations to be wrought by cable communications. The notion permeated even the highest echelons of national leadership. The establishment of the first purported trans-Atlantic telegraph link, in 1858, was considered a significant enough occasion for the Queen of England and the President of the United States to exchange inaugural messages welcoming the new and rapid conduit between their nations. Both

153

believed that the slender wire connecting their countries would strengthen their friendship, as Queen Victoria "fervently" hoped, and prove "a bond of perpetual peace and friendship between the kindred nations," as President Buchanan expected. Further, the President saw the cable as an agent of globalization, a divine instrument for diffusing "religion, civilization, liberty and law throughout the world."[3] It took more than two weeks to complete the exchange of these inaugural messages. This may suggest that they were conveyed across the Atlantic by ship rather than by cable, or in other words, that the cable of 1858 was a hoax.[4] But far more troubling, the political history of subsequent decades may suggest that the contentual gist of the inaugural messages was also a chimera.

The masterful essays on transatlantic telegraphy in this volume by David Nickles and Jürgen Wilke, focusing on the German-American cable nexus, represent state-of-the-art launching pads for contemplating this troubling aspect of human communications. Wilke shows us with authority, and on the basis of a close and creative reading of complex nineteenth century records, that message traffic between the United States and Germany increased dramatically in the latter nineteenth-century. At the turn of the twentieth century the volume of messages further exploded until 1914, when hostilities began in Europe. Between 1881 and 1913 the throughput of cable messages between Germany and America increased by an astounding 1,000 per cent. Two years later, however, Americans and Germans would be fighting each other in a terrible, protracted war. Whatever forces led to the war, the supposed binding power of real time communicative access and of upwardly spiraling message traffic, was far from enough to offset them.[5]

But further, these two studies of transatlantic message flow and its institutional underpinnings appear to delineate aspects of international telegraphy that could underlie a dynamic of distancing rather than of binding through communications. Jürgen Wilke's findings concerning the economic and institutional constraints of cable communications, together with David Nickles' discussion of language and diplomacy, and their common focus on news transmission, can serve to chart a plausible course through which instantaneity and continuous accessibility came at the expense of harmony and understanding.

## II.

By the time a fully functional cable was laid across the Atlantic, in 1866, observers did have a conspicuous and troubling precedent for evaluating the nexus of telegraphic communications and social relations. Inaugurated in 1844, American telegraphy took off in the latter 1840s, followed by the severe deterioration of sectional relations. In the early 1850s the country's fragmented telegraph system moved decisively in the direction of integration, just as its party system was breaking down. Eastern seaboard telegraphy from Maine to New Orleans was finally consolidated into the smooth operating system of the American Telegraph Company in the late 1850s. But within just a few years, the company's well-integrated system would be divided between two warring sections. News transmission, too, was nationalizing prior to the disintegration of the American nation. The New York Associated Press, established in 1846 as a telegraphic news service providing New York's leading newspapers with telegraphic news, expanded into a national system of news distribution in the 1850s. It had linked the entire country by a single, comprehensive news report just prior to the nation dividing itself into two warring entities. Communicative unification thus preceded national disruption.

Historian David Herbert Donald has proposed a causal relation between communicative unity and national division, underpinned by the mediating variable of the political process. In the second quarter of the nineteenth century the second party system featured two competing cross-sectional national parties. Sectional differences were negotiated within each party, and neither had an interest in having sectionalism become the focus of national political debate. Such controversy would have the potential of breaking up the national parties along geographical lines. Each party could contain the sectional issue by muffling it – the party line was left open to divergent interpretation in either section. With the advent of instantaneous national news media, focused on the telegraph and wire service, national parties could no longer speak to each section in a different voice. Political statements were now received by "all America . . . immediately, and literally with the emphasis of lightning;" they no longer had "time to work in the region for which they were especially designed."[6] Parties, having to speak with a single unambiguous voice could no longer contain the sectional tension. The consequence was the breakdown of the second party system, and the emergence of sectional parties. Now inter-party and inter-sectional tensions compounded rather than offset each other, bringing on political impasse, then war. Thus, in the particular circumstances of antebellum America, improvement in communication could entail conflict and crisis rather than "the glorious tale of brotherhood and peace," told by the telegraph.[7]

This case of disintegrative communications may illustrate a more general dynamic, which sociologist Lewis Mumford appropriately called "the paradox of communications." He found "nothing to indicate, as earlier exponents of instantaneous communication seem pretty uniformly to have thought, that the results [of neotechnic communications] will automatically be favorable to the community." Far from it: People, Mumford found, "often tend to be more socialized at a distance," and that their "intercourse sometimes proceeds best . . . when neither group is visible to the other." In fact, the "lifting of restrictions upon close human intercourse" could be dangerous, by foregrounding "areas of friction" and hastening "mass reactions, like those which occur on the eve of a war," together bringing about the specter of international conflict.[8]

Should this indeed be the general case – counter-intuitive as it may be – it still remains necessary to try and understand how trans-Atlantic telegraphy could actually operate to increase friction rather than concord. Nickles and Wilke's articles direct us to three relevant aspects of cable communications, which bear on the "paradox of communication." The first of these, and one of the most fundamental, concerns language features characteristic of cable messages as constrained by economic and operational circumstances. A second approach emerges from zooming in on veteran institutional arrangements for regulating relations between transatlantic entities and observing how instantaneous communications affected their performance. In this thrust, David Nickles cogently points us to the key institution of diplomacy. Finally, public information flows, reaching the masses through the newspaper press, brought the cable to bear on the sensibilities of the public at large, at either side of the Atlantic. As both Jürgen Wilke and David Nickles show us, news communication by cable radically altered the nature of public information flows between the continents, and had the potential of shaping and transforming public attitudes and opinions.

# III.

In *The Portrait of a Lady*, Henry James' globetrotting Mrs Touchett communicates with her husband and son in England mainly by means of telegrams. Upon a prolonged visit to the United States, Mrs Touchett, "who has thoroughly mastered the art of condensation," cables home that she "Changed Hotel, very bad, impudent clerk, address here. Taken sister's girl, died last year, go to Europe, two sisters, quite 'independent'." The receipt of the polysemic cablegram, which "seems to admit of so many interpretations," signalled the commencement of a torturous exegetical process by father and son thus described to a friend:

We thought at first that the sister mentioned might be the sister of the clerk; but the subsequent mention of a niece seems to prove that the allusion is to one of my aunts. Then there was a question as to whose the two other sisters were; they are probably two of my late aunt's daughters. But who's "quite independent," and in what sense is the term used? – that point is not yet settled. Does the expression apply more particularly to the young lady my mother has adopted, or does it characterize her sisters equally? – and is it used in a moral or in a financial sense?[9]

"You'll see for yourself," responded the friend, clinching the impossibility of the virtual "cablese" to properly represent, let alone replace, social co-presence.

The Touchetts and their friend serve James – himself for many years an expatriate – to use the ambiguity of cablegrams as a leading metaphor for the cultural distance between people on either side of the Atlantic, and the impossibility of their fully understanding each other. The cryptic nature of cablegrams, for James, is emblematic for the limits of cross-cultural understanding and empathy, ultimately of the impenetrability of humans to one another.

Indeed, an obvious cause of misunderstanding via cable was the characteristic brevity of messages, owing to the high cost of every single word. Upon its opening to commercial traffic in 1866, cable charges were as high as $5 in gold per word (about $7.50 in greenbacks), and although prices declined dramatically over subsequent decades, following the proliferation of transatlantic cables, they remained high nonetheless. Not surprisingly, communicators saved money by sparing words. Wilke reports the remarkable finding that up to a third of all telegrams transmitted from Germany to non-European countries in the late 1870s included less than five words, and between 66 and 75 per cent contained less than twenty words. Considering the implications of the cable-packing business, which combined messages as a way of saving fees, the share of brief messages must have been considerably higher.[10] While much information conveyed by these short messages was apparently unambiguous – comprised of commercial quotations or referring to set phrases in code books – the imperative of condensation affected more expressive and stylized messages as well. As Nickles finds, even diplomats conveying messages in which detail and nuance might be crucial, worked under strict limitations on scope.

The specter of misunderstandings due to brevity, on matters which communicators considered important enough to pay for dearly, was only one aspect of the problem. Nickles shows us, clearly and crisply, the systemic shortcomings of the medium in conveying complex messages.

When an American diplomat's report on the assassination of Czar Alexander II consists of two words – "Emperor dead" – rather than providing a thick description of the political and military constellation, the "langue" of diplomatic discourse is disrupted and sacrificed by an inapt "parole" – to use de Saussure's classic distinction. Moreover, as communications scholar James Carey has pointed out, the "stretching of language in space" – the lingo Hemingway called "Cablese" –

> changed the forms of social relations mediated by language. Just as the long lines displaced a personal relation mediated by speech and correspondence in the conduct of trade and substituted the mechanical coordination of buyer and seller, so the language of the telegraph displaced a fiduciary relationship between writer and reader with a coordinated one.

While diplomacy is an outstanding setting for observing this process at work, it clearly underscored most other cable-mediated relationships as well, promoting efficiency at the cost of fraternity.[11]

Information theorists would consider this kind of distancing a combination of semantic, and then semiotic, noise. But the language of cablegrams appears to have affected something deeper. As Carey implies, the first element to be omitted from messages out of considerations of cost and timeliness was the social, the personal, and the emotive. Yet the distancing of communicators went even further: telegraphy had ever been a "cold" and unfriendly medium. Its messages were transparent to clerks and operators. Transcribed on impersonal corporate forms, they left no trace of the author's own hand and individuality, promoting aloofness and distance. But at the same time telegraphy implied unprecedented closeness between communicators at a distance. By bringing parties separated by great distances together in near real-time, it enabled a deep sense of co-presence. The inevitable dissonance between the intimacy of sharing time and the telegram's linguistic, bureaucratic, and spatial distance, bred a consistent notion of frustration and estrangement – of dealing with parties that "seem so near but are indeed so far away."[12]

Most generally, media philosophers suggest that communication is an intrinsically paradoxical pursuit. Its essence is an attempt to diminish the separateness of communicators, a project ultimately frustrated by the fundamental distinctiveness of the communicating entities. The more successful a communication process is in bringing the parties closer, the more apparent their separateness becomes – the challenge that had launched the communicative circuit in the first place.[13] Telegraph and cable, by providing the technical means for making "one neighborhood of the whole country," and then a "global village," inevitably showed that in reality neither was really the case. The imagined closeness affected by the temporal proximity cable communications implied, actually contradicted genuine, deep going differences that separated nations at the time. Accordingly, communicative proximity tended to underscore that which remained foreign and separate. Thus, as Louis Mumford proposed, connectedness via real-time technologies could foreground differences and increase areas of friction, leading to antagonism and conflict, rather than promoting "a communion of the Old World the New."[14]

# IV.

Charles Bright, a nineteenth-century cable telegraphy expert, was a firm believer in the ultimate improvement of international relations that cable communications was bound to bring about. Yet his *fin de siècle* analysis of submarine telegraphy was more cautious than the characteristic utopian rhetoric launched by the less informed. Writing a generation after trans-Atlantic cables were first put into operation, his retrospective technology assessment could hardly point to any noticeable improvement in the relations between the UK and other world powers.

Perceptively enough, Bright pointed out that instantaneous communications, while bound to improve international relations in the long run, had a regressive potential as well. Although relations between nations ultimately reflected the confluence of individual and institutional interactions, their formal shaping and management was entrusted to national leadership through the institution of diplomacy. Diplomacy, Bright suggested, could be ill served by the speed of electric communications. It fostered a sense of urgency and called for immediate action, leaving authorities with little time to consult, contemplate, and ultimately to defuse emergencies. It could have the effect of "producing ruptures which 'a little more time to think' would have avoided."[15] Thus, United States Congressman John Blound complained of "the confusion provoked by instantaneous discussion" in the wake of the Baltimore affair, in which a series of brisk exchanges of acrimonious cable dispatches between United States and Chilean leaders brought their nations to the brink of war.[16]

David Nickles convincingly establishes less obvious, but at least as significant, disturbances to the international process that cable communications presented. He focuses on the ways in which cable communications affected traditional decision making in the field of international relations. Most importantly, he charts the process by which decision making gradually shifted from foreign missions – who had the best grasp of conditions on the ground – to foreign affairs headquarters at each nation's center, notwithstanding the distance of these centers from the unfolding events.

The dysfunction of diplomacy, resulting from the temporal constraints of telegraphy, as pointed out by Bright, and the spatial and structural dysfunctions analysed by Nickles, may be aspects of a much broader pattern of change accompanying the emergence of new communication technologies. This pattern, tagged "disintermediation" by communication scholar Elihu Katz, is "the cutting out of the middleman" through the application of new technologies to the communicative process. To illustrate the disintermediation pattern: in premodern Europe God's message to humanity, assumed to be contained in the Bible, was conveyed to the public by the Catholic Church as middleman. Its personnel, versed in scripture and theology, served as mediator between the divine message and the Christian masses. But the printing press made possible the short-circuiting of the Church establishment as mediator. Piggy-backing on the printing press, Protestantism suggested that individuals could verse themselves in the godly message of the scriptures – mass-printed in the vernacular – disintermediating the Catholic Church in the process. Similarly, using mass broadcast media, charismatic leaders could sway the public, addressing it over the heads of its elected representatives, not to mention the local apparatus and activists of political parties. In the same way, mass advertising allowed manufacturers to "cut out" the influence of retailers, by appealing directly to the end-customer with their brands.[17]

Describing this general pattern, Katz points out its two important consequences. One is structural and the other functional. In structure, he argues, it is not that institutional mediation vanishes with the rise of the new medium. Rather, the former mediating institution is replaced by the new medium as an institution. Thus, printing, radio, satellites – their technique, business arrangements, regulation, and such like (what Thomas Hughes calls the system surrounding every technology) – become a new institution mediating between source and its target audience.[18] Moreover, the prevalent use of a medium may have in itself deep-going cognitive effects on its users (as McLuhan suggested) and a transforming effect on social organization and the distribution of power in the societies that adopt it (as Innis suggested). Functionally, Katz proposes, cutting out the middle man can inject irrationality into the relational process, subordinating the delicate negotiation of needs and interests and their adjustment to a blind, distant, technological imperative. In the process, instability and even irrationality are injected into formerly well-adjusted relationships.

The fate of diplomacy in the cable age, as rendered by Nickles, represents a prime example of the disintermediation model at work. What print had done to the Church, television to political bosses, computer trading to stockbrokers, and Kazaa to the music industry, was done by cable to foreign missions. Their role as policy adjusters and decision makers was undercut by direct home-office intervention. Displacing the diplomat-on-the-spot as middleman there emerged Foreign Ministry desks and experts, code makers and code breakers, clerks with technical know-how and shallow and short telegraphic lingo that had emerged with the new technology.

And indeed, as Katz cautions and as Nickles demonstrates, this process of disintermediation could have its costs in terms of relations between nations. Cutting out the middlemen of international relations was the disposing of the intimacy and acumen bred of unmediated personal contact that diplomats had cultivated with policy makers on the other side. Those diplomats, who were best acquainted with delicate bilateral situations, became institutionally marginalized. They were displaced by the powers that be at a great physical and mental, although not communicative, distance. The decline in the influence of the diplomatic corps with the advent of cables could inject misapprehension, insensitivity, and even irrationality into the system of international relations, to the detriment of understanding, adjustment and ultimately of peace and harmony. The woeful record of world peace in the cable age makes this proposed dysfunction plausible enough, and presumably quite consequential.

## V.

Public opinion has ever been an important determinant of foreign policy, and information from overseas fed the process of shaping such opinion. While only a tiny minority of Germans or Americans ever communicated by cable, most were exposed to a significant share of its message flow. These were messages cabled to the press, intended for the newspaper-reading public. Such news that could shape perceptions of other nations and mold opinion attracted considerable public interest in the nineteenth century. Early-century sources describe thousands of New Yorkers congregating around newspaper offices waiting for the most recent news from Europe as conveyed by news-bearing vessels that just arrived from overseas.[19] The new order of timeliness brought about by submarine telegraphy may well have further increased the public's interest in foreign news at both ends of international cables. Yet with the cable the nature of that news and the modes of its supply were radically transformed.

Here too, the structural features of change followed the logic of disintermediation. Cable, the new communication technology, signalled the decline of traditional journalism as mediator between foreign affairs and the newspaper reading public. In its stead, wire service dispatches, conveyed directly by cable and printed uniformly and simultaneously in most local newspapers, disintermediated the individual newspaper's foreign news arrangements. As we shall see, the most important aspect of this process concerned the new sources of the foreign news reports that the wire services distributed, an aspect of cable telegraphy addressed by both Nickles and Wilke.

To be sure, individual newspapers did retain foreign correspondents into the telegraphic age and well beyond it. However, once the cable provided breaking foreign news, the role of newspaper representatives abroad was attenuated. They remained correspondents, in the literal sense of writing letters and essays that provided in-depth coverage of foreign affairs, but they no longer filled the function of news reporters. News agencies' cable dispatches now provided that service.[20] Plentiful evidence suggests that the public's interest focused on the "fast news" conveyed by telegraph, its interest in the "slow news" of publicists' essays conveyed by mail declined.[21]

The process of cutting the individual newspaper out of the international news reporting process followed a different temporal pattern in Germany and America. Whereas in Europe the major news services – Agence Havas, Reuters, and the Wolff'sches Telegraphisches Bureau – had dominated the supply of foreign news by telegraph from early on, in America the NYAP received European news by ships that could cheaply convey competing reports for individual newspapers. The NYAP's advantage was in its rapid and cost effective access to the national loop when news-bearing steamers reached the New World. But once cables enabled the extension of landlines to Newfoundland, then to Ireland, the NYAP's advantage was extended from hours to days, effectively disintermediating the newspaper in the provision of foreign news reports.[22]

Early on, the NYAP's new cable-based power was hotly contested. Shortly after the laying of the cable the *New York Herald* – the city's most affluent daily – attempted to supplant the NYAP in providing America's foreign news. It did so by establishing a dense network of reporters in Europe, at the annual cost of $40,000, then inaugurating an extremely expensive traffic of foreign news by cable.[23] However, the *Herald*'s autonomous service cost far too much, and other newspapers were not prepared to pay the price it charged. NYAP's other members closed ranks behind its low-cost system and crushed the *Herald*'s ambitious attempt to substitute the wire service system of international news by independent, unilateral, and expensive news gathering. The *Herald*'s failure seemed to prove that the process of disintermediation was irreversible. A newspaper could not extend its traditional modus operandi into the cable age. New institutions bred of the novel technology would inevitably carry the day.[24]

Thus, with cable, the technological, economic, and systemic constraints that had shaped the European pattern of foreign news gathering became applicable to America, and so did its consequences. A major consequence of the European system was that the wire service distributing the foreign news was not its source; rather, each national agency reported the news of its own country (and of its international hinterland) to foreign newspaper readers. A series of agreements between the leading agencies structured this arrangement, which became firmly institutionalized. Shortly after the Atlantic cable was laid, Havas, Wolff, and Reuter had in place a formal agreement for a multilateral exchange of the news that each gathered exclusively in its own sphere of influence.[25]

The NYAP was not an independent party to the world-sharing agreement of the three European wire services in the nineteenth century. It effectively was, however, a player in the tripartite news exchange through a bilateral arrangement with Reuters. Indeed, the two services had worked together for years before the Atlantic cable, on a straight-exchange basis. Thus, the NYAP was in practice, if not formally, a party to the international news exchange. Via Reuters it provided the news of America that Europeans read, and distributed the European agencies' dispatches received from Reuters to the United States' press.[26]

The meaning of the telegraph and cable mode of international news reporting was far reaching. It implied the invasion of the national press by foreign organizations that foisted their self-serving messages on a distant public. Jürgen Wilke authoritatively illustrates this process in the case of German and American news flow, and finds that only by the turn of the century did wire services begin to actively select and adjust the news provided by foreign national agencies to their own indigenous needs. In the case of German and American reciprocal news supply, this arrangement, problematic to begin with, was further complicated by the mediating role of a third, self-serving, party – the Reuters agency.

The role of politics in shaping the news of each of the national wire services underscored the shortcomings of this system. As Wilke finds, Bismarck had a stranglehold on the operations of the Wolff'sche Bureau. Historian Fritz Stern had previously delineated the political and financial process through which the propaganda-minded Chancellor managed to gradually achieve political control over the agency's news reporting.[27] Donald Read has traced a comparable dynamism in Reuters' case, which led to the agency's reports coalescing with Crown policies and interests.[28] I have recently demonstrated how Reuters, through its arrangement with the NYAP, served the publicity interests of the Union administration in the Civil War years. The NYAP was the war administration's loyal mouthpiece, and through the straight-exchange arrangement between it and Reuters, the Union administration had the first chance to make a first impression on European public opinion.[29]

Attempts to rig and manipulate world opinion via the news of a subservient wire service must have served governments' immediate, unilateral, political interests. For precisely that reason, they could not possibly have worked to improve bilateral relations. More generally, the global arrangement for transnational news flow, viewed as an overall system, was founded on efficiencies and economies on the supply side. It was the one-sided, self-serving perspective of the news provider that dominated news flow. Economies of scale and scope came at the expense of the receiving end, where the particular requirements and needs of diverse audiences were neither consulted nor accommodated. After all, wire service news distributed globally could not be tailored to the particular sensibilities of any given national audience. Such a plan of communications was hardly conducive to the increase of mutual understanding and the strengthening of bilateral bonds. It could alienate distant recipients at the same time it was informing them and propagandizing to them. Thus, however efficient and economical, this entire system could carry the seeds of alienation through advanced communications.[30]

This potential unleashing of the "paradox of communication", may be seen to follow from the disintermediation of the newspaper in foreign news reporting. As James Carey has suggested, the rise of modern media in the industrial age signalled the emergence of the "professional communicator" as a distinct type of vocation and social function. The facile interface of people at a distance, inevitably of different sensibilities and mind-sets, called for a mediating function, one that would make either side explicable to the other. This was the function of the professional communicator. If the translator was its archetype, the journalist represented its ideal type. The professional communicator's role was to translate meaning from one environment to another, on the basis of an understanding of both.[31]

The reporting of foreign news was a prime site for the performance of the professional communicator's function. The journalist in the German-

American news nexus was to make developments in Germany plausible to Americans, and to make the American way and the mind of its people penetrable to Germans. Such a process of mediation could plausibly increase mutual understanding, just as the mere fact of communicating increased mutual awareness.

But as both Wilke and Nickles demonstrate, this was not the way news communication between Germany and the United States developed in the cable age. Submarine telegraphy as a technological system disinter-mediated the professional communicators who had served the German and American publics. In their stead the national wire services, influenced as they were by the powers that be on either side, did the talking. Although faster, cheaper and more accessible, this system of news reporting by cable was audience-blind and mediation insensitive, it could heighten awareness without improving understanding. As theory suggests and history seems to bear out, this could be a lethal combination.

## VI.

The foregoing represents a mere exploratory, perhaps even speculative, extension of Jürgen Wilke's and David Nickles' sound and responsible studies, from a communication theory perspective. Nevertheless, it underscores the great potential of wholesome and innovative historical research, such as theirs, to address theoretical – and practical – issues of the highest significance to the concerns of other disciplines. But moreover, these studies and their foregoing spin-offs suggest a more general historiographical moral, or morals. Primarily, and most patently, these studies show how wide-open the field of communication history really is – how little has been done and how much needs doing in documenting and interpreting communications as an aspect of history and life.

The fundamental reason for the relative neglect of communication themes in traditional historical enquiry is simple enough: Communication has only recently taken its place, alongside the likes of economics, politics, or religion, as an aspect of the human experience that can and should be investigated historically. After all, communication is a surprisingly young concept, let alone a category of analysis. An ingredient of social life that is as elusive as it is ubiquitous, "communications" as a conceptual cluster lacked a usable defining framework or even a definitive terminology throughout most of history. It was, in fact, the telegraph that by separating communication from the physical process of transportation gave rise to thinking about communication as a category unto itself, generating, in the process, "an entirely new class of ideas, a new species of consciousness," as the *New York Herald* surmised in 1844.

This formative process of shaping notions and crystallizing ideas about communications, traceable to the discourse of the telegraph, was effectively elaborated and formalized in social-scientific investigation only in the second half of the twentieth century. Historical research thus has a considerable catching-up job to do with regard to this aspect of the historical experience. As the preceding pages may suggest, such a project can profitably be informed by theory developed in the social-scientific research of communication. But the link between the disciplines could and should be a two-way bridge. Ideally, history would serve as the ultimate database for verifying – but also for generating – ideas about communications. Communication research, in turn, might provide theoretical insight that could inform historical investigation.

Such a joint project would appear to be a worthy one. After all, communications, from the Tower of Babel to our own era of globalization, is really much more than what Marshall McLuhan considered to be the "social hormone." It is, in fact, the confluence of the slender communicative bridges charting human relations and human society. Communications may thus be thought of as the DNA of history.

# Notes

1.  "Slender bridges" in the title is from the *New York Express*, 29 May 1844. Daniel J. Boorstin, *The Americans: The National Experience*, New York, 1965, p. 394.

2.  A thorough historical analysis of this notion is provided in John D. Peters, *Speaking into the Air: A History of the Idea of Communication*, Chicago, 1999; it is also a major aspect in Armand Mattelert, *The Invention of Communication*, Minneapolis, 1996.

3.  From the compilation of messages passed over the cable in George Prescott, *History, Theory and Practice of the Electric Telegraph*, Boston, 1860, pp. 187, 189. The best summary of public responses to the laying of the cable is provided in Philip B. McDonald, *A Saga of the Seas: The Story of Cyrus W. Field and the Laying of the First Atlantic Cable*, New York, 1937, pp. 59–81.

4.  This iconoclastic proposition is discussed in Menahem Blondheim, *News over the Wires: The Telegraph and the Flow of Public Communica-*

*tion in America, 1844–97*, Cambridge, 1994, pp. 110–17; and developed in an essay on "The Enigma of the First Atlantic Cable and the Problem of Cross-Ownership," *Historia*, 12 (2003): 12–32.

5. Jürgen Wilke, "The Telegraph and Transatlantic Communication Relations," p. 10.

6. *New York Times*, 9 September 1858. Donald's argument is presented and developed in Blondheim, *News over the Wires*, 191–5. Standard accounts of the breakdown of the second party system are David M. Potter, *The Impending Crisis, 1848–1861*, New York, 1976, and Michael F. Holt, *The Political Crisis of the 1850s*, New York, 1978.

7. O'Reilly quoted in Prescott, *History Theory and Practice*, p. 183.

8. Lewis Mumford, *Technics and Civilization*, New York, 1963, pp. 239–41.

9. Henry James, *The Portrait of a Lady*, New York, 1951, pp. 13–14.

10. Wilke, "The Telegraph and Transatlantic Communication Relations," p. 10. I am currently investigating the cable-packing business as performed by the personnel of the New York Associated Press, apparently as a private rather than an association enterprise.

11. "Emperor dead" quoted in David P. Nickles, "Diplomatic Telegraphy," p. 5; Ferdinand de Saussure, *Course in General Linguistics*, London, 1960; and see Patrick Baert, *Social Theory in the Twentieth Century*, New York, 1998, p. 17ff.; James W. Carey, "Technology and Ideology: The Case of the Telegraph," in James W. Carey, *Communication as Culture: Essays on Media and Society*, New York, 1992, p. 210f.

12. The impersonal nature of telegraphy is discussed in Blondheim, "When Bad Things Happen to Good Technologies: Three Phases in the Diffusion and Perception of American Telegraphy," in Yaron Ezrahi et al., *Technology, Pessimism and Postmodernism*, Amsterdam, 1994, pp. 77–92. Quotation is from the *Philadelphia Pennsylvanian*, 30 December 1846.

13. Peters, *Speaking into the Air*; Amit Pinchevski, *Interruption and Alterity: Dislocating the Ethical Possibilities in Communication*, Ph.D. dissertation, McGill University Montreal, 2003.

14. The quotation is from a statement made by Henry Ward Beecher, recorded in the *New York Times*, 18 August 1858, quoted also in Charles F. Briggs and Augustus Maverick, *The Story of the Telegraph and the History of the Great Atlantic Cable*, New York, 1858, p. 246f.

15. Charles Bright was the son of Charles T. Bright, the prominent pioneer of English submarine telegraphy. Charles Bright, *Submarine Telegraphs: Their History, Construction and Working*, London, 1898, p. 171. See also Vary T. Coates and Bernard Finn, *A Retrospective*

*Technology Assessment: Submarine Telegraphy – The Transatlantic Cable of 1866*, San Francisco, 1979, p. 83.

16. The Baltimore affair is discussed in John Britten, "Cables, Commerce, and Conflict: International Communications in the Americas, 1867–1898," unpublished paper.

17. Elihu Katz, "Disintermediation: Cutting Out the Middle Man," *Intermedia* 16 (1988), 30f.

18. Katz proposes an analysis of these effects in terms of Innisian and McLuhanite theory: Katz, "Disintermediation", 31. On the system approach to technology see Thomas P. Hughes, *Networks of Power: Electrification in Western Society, 1880–1930*, Baltimore, 1983; and see also Th. Hughes, "The Evolution of Large Technical Systems," in Wiebe E. Bijker et al. (eds), *The Social Construction of Technological Systems*, Cambridge, 1989, pp. 51–82.

19. For the 1830s see, for example, Frederic Hudson, *Journalism in the United States: From 1690 to 1872*, New York, 1873, pp. 364f., 391; and for the 1840s see, for example, *New York Herald*, 26 January 1847.

20. On the distinction that had emerged by mid-century between reporting and correspondence see Blondheim, *News over the Wires*, p. 226, n.66. It should be noted that before the cable much of the foreign news was not gathered by the representatives of individual newspapers but by special newspapers published in England and intended for an American audience: Richard A. Schwarzlose, "The Foreign Connection: Transatlantic Newspapers in the 1840s," *Journalism History* 10 (Autumn/Winter 1983), pp. 44–9, 67.

21. The *London Times'* Mowbray Morris thus averred that "the telegraph has superseded the newsletter, and has rendered necessary a different style and treatment of public subjects." Graham Storey, *Reuters' Century, 1851–1951*, London, 1951, p. 54. The increase of interest in news due to its rapid transmission emerges from numerous sources. Thus, Horace Greeley testified to a British Parliamentary Committee that "the quickest news is the one looked to," and that the "the telegraphic dispatch is the great point" with newspaper readers. Quoted in Hudson, *Journalism in the United States*, p. 548; and see James D. Reid, "The Western Press and the Telegraph," *National Telegraph Review* 1 (October 1853), 233.

22. Menahem Blondheim, "The Click: Telegraphic Technology, Journalism, and the Transformations of the New York Associated Press," *American Journalism*, 17 (Fall 2000), 27–52.

23. *New York Herald*, 25 December 1866. Not only were the *Herald*'s outlays for its news gathering infrastructure staggering, its early use of the

cable indicated its outlays for actual use of the wires would be lavish. Thus, on 8 August 1866 the *Herald* transmitted the full text of a very long speech by the King of Prussia at the expense of $4,000 (!) *The Telegrapher*, 1 September 1866.

24. The story of the *Herald*'s abortive attempt to take control of foreign news by cable emerges from the correspondence of Manton Marble, editor of the *New York World*, located in the Manton Marble papers, Manuscript Division, Library of Congress. See, for example, Nathaniel D. Bangs to Marble, 11, 13, 22, 25 August 1866; William Henry Hurlbert to Marble, 17 August 1866 and two other undated letters of August 1866. For a summary see "The New York Press Gang," quoted in the *New York World*, 11 December 1866.

25. Robert W. Desmond, *The Information Process: World News Reporting to the Twentieth Century*, Iowa City, 1978, pp. 158–68; Donald Read, *The Power of News: The History of Reuters, 1849–1989*, New York, 1992, pp. 53–9; Storey, *Reuters' Century*, pp. 46–53.

26. Desmond, *The Information Process*, p. 143; Storey, *Reuters' Century*, pp. 32–9; Peter R. Knights, "The Press Association War of 1866 1867," *Journalism Monographs* 6 (1967).

27. Fritz R. Stern, *Gold and Iron: Bismarck, Bleichroder, and the Building of the German Empire*, New York, 1979, pp. 262–79, *passim*.

28. Read, *Power of News*, pp. 63–6; cf. Storey, *Reuters' Century*, p. 19f., n.35, 47.

29. Menahem Blondheim, "'Public Sentiment is Everything': The Union's Public Communications Strategy and the Bogus Proclamation of 1864," *Journal of American History* 89 (December 2002), 880.

30. This fundamental problem prefigures, in many ways, our contemporary debate on post-colonial transnational news and media flow. See, for example, E. Katz and Eberhard George Wedell, *Broadcasting in the Third World: Promise and Performance*, Cambridge MA, 1977; Oliver Boyd-Barrett and D. Kishan Thussu, *Contra Flows in Global News*, London, 1992; Eli M. Noam and Anjali Singhal, "Supra-National Regulation for Supra-National Telecommunications Carriers?" *Telecommunications Policy* 20 (1996), 768–80; Hamid Mowlana, "International Flows of Information: A Framework for Analysis," in Hamid Mowlana, *Global Information and World Communication*, London, 1997.

31. James Carey, "The Communications Revolution and the Professional Communicator," *The Sociological Review Monograph* 13, 23–38.

# 9
# Producing and Consuming Knowledge: Comparative Perspectives on the Development and Usage of the Telegraph in Nineteenth-century Germany and America

*Ursula Lehmkuhl*

The previous chapter of this book addressed the history of Atlantic Communication in terms of media that physically carried certain kinds of information. To move the information, one moved the medium. With the advent of harnessable electricity, a major shift occurred. To paraphrase Marshall McLuhan, beginning with the telegraph, messages could travel faster than messengers. Communication over distance was no longer tied to the available means of transportation.[1] James Carey described the telegraph as *the* medium that "provided the decisive and cumulative break of the identity of communication and transportation."[2] The telegraph, like most innovations in the field of communication throughout time as far as the computer, had its first and most profound impact on the conduct of commerce, government, and the military. Early research on the telegraph had a special focus on commerce. Studies like *Wiring a Continent* by Robert Thompson, published in 1947, or Richard Du Boff's work are examples. The topics addressed by the papers on the telegraph published in this volume, however, go beyond the traditional focus on economics. The two papers under scrutiny here cover two aspects that will help to complement our knowledge about the historical impact of the telegraph by analysing its influence on the development of an international news market and on international diplomacy.

I will comment on the findings of the two papers on the basis of a two fold comparative perspective: First, by addressing national differences and similarities and by comparing the case studies on news agencies and international diplomacy with the published findings on the impact of the telegraph on business and commerce. With the second perspective I would like to introduce a more topical comparative approach. In a third step I will go beyond mere comparison by addressing processes of cultural transfer in the Atlantic World induced and carried by the telegraph.

*

The analyses provided by David Nickles and Jürgen Wilke point out three commonalities between Prussia and the United States with regard to the usage and function of the telegraph: In both cases the telegraph had a strong centralizing effect on the political system. The new communication technology reduced the importance of regional political sub-centers and strengthened the decision-making power of the political center. In the United States this had a positive effect on nation-building processes after the Civil War. Centralization also furthered the development of a national market economy. In Germany the telegraph together with the railroad facilitated the unification process pushed forward by Prussia and the Prussian army.

Both papers show that the telegraph offered new ways of governmental control over information flows, with repercussions not only on the developing print media but also regarding foreign policy decision making. The telegraph was an instrument of securing and strengthening political power. It was also used as an instrument of power projection as in the case of the Prussian King William II, who – as Jürgen Wilke mentions in his paper – spent an unbelievably huge amount of money, no less than 29,000 Marks, to transmit the entire speech he had made at the opening of the Prussian Parliament after his victory over Austria on 5 August 1866 across the ocean to the United States. The amount of money spent for this telegram would have bought approximately 160 tons of wheat or 1,343 tons of potatoes.[3] Telegraphing was expensive in the early days. Hence, the telegram was a means of communication almost exclusively used by the political and economic elite.

At the end of the nineteenth century both the German Empire and the United States developed a special interest in globalizing the telegraph network in the context of their colonial policies. In both cases the telegraph was an important strategic device for Empire-building.[4] It furthered economic growth by facilitating export and import trade. The communication links that connected the imperial centers to their colonial possessions and their overseas markets strengthened the centers' political and economic control capacities. Thus, the telegraph had an important impact on the international power position of the major international actors at the end of the nineteenth century. Possession and control of telegraph lines was a new instrument of securing and enhancing one's position in the international power hierarchy. However, despite these imperial interests, the telegraph was first and foremost used on a national or continental basis. Transoceanic cable technology was introduced on a larger scale only in the 1870s. Only toward the end of the nineteenth century did it become the primary technological device for a globalized communication system.

Beside these similarities, the papers pinpoint two major differences: whereas the telegraph emerged as a powerful instrument of continental communication in the United States as early as in the 1840s, the German telegraphic network only came into being more than a decade later. Wilke argues that this time lag of about thirteen to fifteen years was mainly the result of the decentralized political situation on German territory. Already in 1852 more than 16,700 miles of telegraph lines existed in the United States, which was more than twice as much as in Prussia thirteen years later (1865–6: 7,556 miles).[5] If we compare the numbers more synchronically the following picture emerges. In 1850, when the Deutsch-Österreichische Telegraphenverein was founded, 4,266 miles of telegraph lines existed in the four member countries: 2,217 miles in Austria (52 per cent), 1,515 miles in Prussia (35 per cent), 422 miles in Bavaria (10 per cent), and 112 miles in Saxony.[6]

But measuring miles of telegraph lines alone does not necessarily tell us much about the usage and function of the telegraph as a communicative means, because the geographical dimensions of both countries, Prussia and the United States, were so different. Whereas in the mid-nineteenth century the United States was about nineteen times as large as the Norddeutscher Bund (4,863,945 square miles and 257,873 square miles respectively), the Norddeutscher Bund was more densely populated than the United States, with at least as many economically and politically important urban centers.[7] Moreover, to get a realistic picture about the density of the telegraph network one has to take into account not only the miles of wire in use, but more so the number of cities that were connected and the number of telegraph offices as well as the number of lines that could be used simultaneously between each station. In most cases only one line existed, hence only one customer at a time could transmit a message.

In 1850 Berlin was connected via telegraph with most of the important larger cities in Prussia as well as with Frankfurt (Main) and Hamburg; in 1852 Vienna could communicate with every capital of the Kronländer by means of cable technology. In Austria-Hungary the total length of telegraph lines quadrupled within four years after the foundation of the Deutsch-Österreichische Telegraphenverein. Between 1858 and 1860 it increased again by another 30 per cent. In Prussia an extraordinary increase in the length of telegraph lines can be observed for the years 1851–2, 1859 and between 1863 and 1865.[8] Hence I do not claim that the backwardness of Prussia is a myth, but that a far more sophisticated study taking into account far more factors than cable length would be required to find out who was ahead of whom and by how much and most of all why. The picture is clearer, however, if one considers the trans-Atlantic cable system. In the early years the German Empire depended on British lines. It was the Anglo-American Telegraph Company that laid transatlantic wires in the course of the 1870s. The first German-controlled wire connecting the North Sea island of Borkum and New York City was installed as late as 1900; another German line operated by the Deutsch-Atlantische Telegraphengesellschaft went into service in 1904.

The second major difference refers to the ownership of the telegraph companies. Whereas in the United States the government chose not to own and operate the telegraph, the opposite occurred in Europe. And this decision was crucial for the different directions the media industry took in Europe on the one hand and the United States and Canada on the other. As James Carey and Richard Du Boff pointed out: "The decision against public ownership and governmental control gave rise to one of the first corporate monopolies in the United States, namely Western Union, and set the stage for a future of private media ownership".[9] And only in the United States and Canada did the telegraph remain under private control after 1868, when Great Britain nationalized all inland telegraph companies.[10]

The historical evidence and analyses presented by the two papers in this section demonstrate that telegraphy helped to transform the national and international economic system; it improved the efficiency of the military, had an impact on the international power hierarchy, and last but not least shaped the context and the way of diplomatic interaction and decision-making in America and Europe. As statistical data are lacking, we have no information about the extent to which the telegraph was used prior to 1875; we also cannot tell to what extent German political authorities communicated with American ones via telegraph because postal statistics for that period do not contain any categories concerning the destinations and the character of telegrams. For a quantitative and qualitative analysis and evaluation of the usage of the telegraph as a means of transatlantic communication on the political level, for example, we need to search the official papers of the United States and the German governments of that time for telegrams that were sent to or received from the United States and vice versa. A large enough sample of telegrams sent back and forth would allow a content analysis, which would help to clarify the picture of the political function of the telegraph for the developing German-American relationship.

*

Postal statistics tell us that the telegraph was used mainly for economic purposes. The interest in commercial or stock-market information was the primary motivating force behind the creation of a global telegraph network. Regarding the structural or systemic influence of the new technology, its impact on the development and functioning of an Atlantic – or in a sense global – economic system was obviously most important. As Richard du Boff points out: "In the world of business and finance, the telegraph was widely regarded as an agent for expediting competition and perfecting markets over space and time: Intermarket price disparities would be diminished, and information on prices of goods and quantities available was henceforth to be available to everyone on an equal basis. Sources of monopoly power would be weakened." [11] Some specific monopolies, however, were strengthened. The telegraph is one reason why big business emerged so swiftly in the last third of the nineteenth century in the leading capitalist economies. The telegraph industry became the first industrial monopoly in the United States when Western Union Telegraph Company swallowed up its last two rivals in 1866 and then in the 1870s established a strategic alliance with Associated Press, the monopolized news agency that, next to big business companies, was the second major user of the telegraph.[12] The advantages arising for each other by the Associated Press and Western Union hardened monopoly control in both industries. Dallas Smythe in *Dependency Road* explains: ". . . Western Union protected the Associated Press and its affiliated local newspapers from competition by refusing wire service to others . . . In return, the Associated Press . . . took its policy on news, and hence political matters, such as the issue of public ownership of telegraphy and railroads, from Western Union."[13] Jürgen Wilke shows that these monopolizing or centralizing tendencies could be found not only in the United States but were spread across national borders within the Atlantic system.

Due to high charges, this strategy of cooperation was also applied to inter-national news gathering. An agreement concluded by WTB, the French Agence Havas, and the British Reuters agency in the 1860s was joined by contract in 1870, which divided the world into "reserved areas". According to the contract, each agency was allowed to gather and spread news only in one region of the world (some regions were assigned to two agencies) and obliged to share their news with its partners. The agreement established a triangular "news cartel" that dominated news coverage worldwide.[14]

In the end, news became more alike because reporters provided news for various newspapers, and the telegraph companies controlled how and when news were distributed. News agencies also had an impact on political agenda setting.

But these were not the only centralizing or standardizing effects of the telegraph. Jürgen Wilke and David Nickles point out five additional processes of standardization induced by the telegraph: the telegraph brought diverse regional centers of buying and selling under a unified price and market system; the telegraph helped create standard time zones; the telegraph helped to establish democratic or republican political systems; the telegraph furthered the simplification and homogenization of language; and with the telegraph cultural power moved westward from France, to Britain, to the United States. These processes of standardization are an interesting field for the analysis of cultural transfer within the Atlantic World or even on a global scale. Moreover, they are important topics of "global history".

Considering intercultural transfer the analytical focus shifts towards the reconstruction of ways and means of productive appropriation of foreign ideas and institutions accompanying processes of collective identity building. It is assumed that these processes are steered not by the will to export ideas but by the willingness to import new and/or foreign ideas. The intrinsically motivated interest in the other is one of the premises for cultural transfers. Research on transfer processes is based on the assumption that national cultures do not constitute closed but rather open systems and develop only in permanent exchange with new or foreign cultural patterns in the shape of appropriation and rejection or disappropriation.[15]

The mechanism of cultural transfer is skillfully analysed in studies like *Atlantic Crossings* by Daniel Rodgers or *Spreading the American Dream* by Emily Rosenberg.[16] However, I think we have to go beyond the analysis of travel literature or the work of missionaries and take into account, for example, the potential of the news cartels and telegraph monopolies in deciding what information is important and which ideas are imported or exported. A number of questions and research topics come to mind: How did news agencies use their function as transmitter of knowledge to transfer elements of cultural knowledge from one culture to the other? Which elements of the cultural knowledge system were transferred in one or the other direction? What was the domestic function of the importation of cultural knowledge? Is it used to legitimize existing social, economic or political conditions or to undermine a certain social and political order or even to improve a certain condition?[17] In order to answer these and similar questions we first and foremost need a deeper knowledge of what was really communicated. That is why I argue for a content analysis of the telegrams that were actually sent. Only by analysing the content of the telegram can we discover how national cultures interacted and how this influenced the political, social and economic developments of the respective societies. It would be important to know, for example, whether and how the telegraph helped to spread ideas of democracy and republicanism in the Atlantic World, especially in the German Empire after 1871. At least some early observers saw the telegraph as a means to achieve a peaceful international order, civilization and moral progress. For the *Daily Chronicle* in 1847, the telegraph was "facilitating Human Intercourse and producing Harmony among Men and Nations". Twenty-one years later, *Hunt's Merchants' Magazine* characterized the telegraph as "the portent of all means of civilization, and the most effective in breaking down the barriers of evil prejudice and custom that interfere with the universal exchange of commodities."[18] I am skeptical.

Eventually, if we try to get a closer understanding of processes of cultural convergence or adaptation the focus on language or style may be important. Both papers mention the development of a new language – the "telegram style". Although this sort of research may be more appropriate for a linguist than for a historian I would nevertheless like to point out some questions that have to be addressed. Was the new language, the telegram style, composed of international semantics indicating the development of a sort of "lingua franca telegrafica" or did it develop national specificities thus strengthening and accentuating the cultural and language borders of the nation-state? The social and cultural consequences of the new language style for international diplomacy and for the identity, self-definition and role ascription of the diplomatic corps also have to be scrutinized.

\*

The papers of this session are weaving culture, economy/business, politics/diplomacy and technology into a new analytical perspective on the evolving Atlantic communication system. The thesis that the introduction of new communication technologies like the telegraph or the telephone annihilated the dimensions of time and space in the communication process, resulting in *The Death of Distance* as Frances Cairncross entitled one of her books[19] is clearly put into question by the findings of

Jürgen Wilke and David Nickles. We do need more case studies about the communicative aspects of the usage of the telegraph in order to be able to answer the question whether this new technology "annihilated time and distance" on the cultural and social level. Future research needs to analyse the cultural and communicative foundations of the Atlantic System by addressing question such as the following: What created (communicative) distance in politics, in economics, in culture/aesthetics? Were mental barriers between the Old and the New World abolished with the usage of the telegraph or the introduction of telegraphy, or did these barriers just change their cultural representation? Was the discourse on the telegraph able to introduce a new imagined landscape or mental map overcoming the idea of being "oceans apart"? How can we characterize the overall relationship between Europe and the United States during the second half of the nineteenth century? Is it more to be expressed in the language of "distance, difference and distinction" or is it one of "similarity, identity and affinity"? How do we evaluate the ambiguous historical function of the telegraph regarding the structure of the international system during the second half of the nineteenth century? Did it create transnational economic, political, cultural and social systems or did it promote more centralized political entities, the nation-states, by enabling the centralization of decision-making power and reducing regional or peripheral decision-making autonomy? Or did it enhance both tendencies simultaneously and to what effect? Even if not all of these suggestions for further research prove feasible or fruitful, I believe I have shown that there is plenty of useful work ahead of us.

# Notes

1. Marshall McLuhan, *Understanding Media*, New York, 1964; Marshall McLuhan, *The Gutenberg Galaxy*, New York, 1969.

2. James Carey, *Communication as Culture*, Boston, 1989.

3. Gerd Hohorst et al., *Sozialgeschichtliches Arbeitsbuch: Materialien zur Statistik des Kaiserreichs 1870–1914*, Munich, 1978, vol. 2, p. 22.

4. See Harold Innis, *Empire and Communications*, Toronto, 1986.

5. Jürgen Wilke in this volume.

6. Josef Reindl, *Der deutsch-österreichische Telegraphenverein und die Entwicklung des deutschen Telegraphenwesens 1850–1871*, Frankfurt a. M., 1993, p. 124.

7. See Gustav Neumann, *Das Deutsche Reich in geographischer, statistischer und topographischer Beziehung I*, Berlin, 1874; G. Hohorst et al., *Sozialgeschichtliches Arbeitsbuch*; Bureau of the Census with the Cooperation of the Social Research Council, *Historical Statistics of the United States: Colonial Times to 1957*, Washington DC, 1960.

8. Ibid., p. 125.

9. James Carey, "Time Space and the Telegraph," in David Crowley and Paul Heyer (eds), *Communication in History: Technology, Culture, Society*, New York et al., 1999, p. 137.

10. Richard B. du Boff, "The Telegraph in Nineteenth-Century America: Technology and Monopoly," *Comparative Studies in Society and History* 26 (1984), 571–86, at: 572.

11. Ibid.

12. Ibid.

13. Dallas Smythe, *Dependency Road: Communications, Capitalism, Consciousness, and Canada*, Norwood NJ, 1981, p. 59.

14. Wilke, in this volume.

15. Johannes Paulmann, "Interkultureller Transfer zwischen Deutschland und Großbritannien: Einführung in ein Forschungskonzept," in Rudolf Muhs et al. (eds), *Aneignung und Abwehr: Interkultureller Transfer zwischen Deutschland und Großbritannien im 19. Jahrhundert*, Bodenheim, 1998, pp. 21–43.

16. Daniel T. Rodgers, *Atlantic Crossings: Social Politics in a Progressive Age*, Cambridge MA, 1998; Emily Rosenberg, *Spreading the American Dream: American Economic and Cultural Expansion 1890–1945*, New York, 1982.

17. Matthias Middell, "Kulturtransfer und Historische Komparatistik," *Comparativ* (2000), 18; J. Paulmann, "Interkultureller Transfer," pp. 28f., 32.

18. "The Electric Telegraph," *Daily Chronicle* (Cincinnati), 16 November 1847 and "Influence of the Telegraph on Commerce," *Hunt's Merchants' Magazine* 59 (August 1868), 106f, both quoted in R. du Boff, "The Telegraph in Nineteenth-century America," p. 571.

19. Frances Cairncross, *The Death of Distance: How the Communications Revolution will Change our Lives*, Boston, 1997; see also Stephen Kern, *The Culture of Time and Space: 1880–1918*, Cambridge, 1983.

# Part III
## Journalism and the Problem of Modernity

# 10
# Modernization and its Discontents: Homelessness and Middle-class Media in the United States, 1850–1930

## Kenneth L. Kusmer

During the nineteenth and early twentieth centuries the United States evolved from an agriculturally based social order to one dominated by large cities and huge industrial enterprises. Many of the changes associated with modernization in the United States had their roots in the early nineteenth century or even before,[1] but the process of social and economic change accelerated dramatically in the last half of the nineteenth century. By 1900, New York's population had reached five million, and a half dozen other cities exceeded one million. A massive reorganization of urban life accompanied this growth in numbers. The "walking city" of the first half of the nineteenth century, with its haphazard arrangement of stores, small factories, and residences, was replaced by a much more tightly organized urban structure. The introduction of the electric streetcar and, in some cases, subway or elevated lines after 1890 led to the exodus of the middle class to outlying sections of cities while the poor, the foreign-born, and (after 1915) African Americans became concentrated in inner-city slums.[2] During these decades the American class structure was also in flux. Mechanization of industrial processes led to violent labor conflict and the usually successful drive by management in basic industries to gain control over its now largely immigrant work force. At the same time, the "old" middle class of farmers and small businessmen was declining, while a new group of white-collar workers and professionals, their skills more closely connected to the needs of urban industrial society, were increasing in number. The line of demarcation between the middle class and the working class was never very clear, however, because some highly skilled manual laborers saw themselves as "aristocrats of labor" and identified with traditional aspects of middle-class culture.[3]

These changes were accompanied by important innovations in the technology of communication, which created the basis for mass culture while speeding up and diversifying the means by which people gained information about the society in which they lived. The last half of the nineteenth century witnessed a rapid growth in the circulation of newspapers, magazines, and inexpensive books. These changes were closely connected to the development of consumerism and advertising, which played a major role in financing the growth of print media during these decades.[4] This expansion of print culture was by no means limited to the bourgeoisie, but it grew most rapidly among the educated middle and upper class, whose tastes and ideological predilections influenced the tone and content of many journals, even those that appealed to a broader, cross-class audience. Although literacy, at least in the North, was already widespread as early as 1800, manual laborers had less time and money to spend on reading, especially books and magazines.[5]

One unforeseen negative consequence of the economic and social transformation associated with industrialism in the decades following the Civil War – one that would attract increasing attention in the media – was a vastly increased homeless population. Today as in the past, measuring the numbers of homeless with any exactitude is almost impossible.[6] It is clear, however, that the size of the "down-and-out" population was much greater during the era of industrialization than at any time before or since. Especially for the manual working class that made up the majority of the population, it was common at the beginning of the twentieth century for young men to enter the ranks of the homeless at some point in their lives. (It was far less typical of women to become homeless, but at the beginning of the twentieth century perhaps 10–15 per cent was female.) Manual laborers who did not become homeless themselves usually knew someone who had been "down and out." Initially, homelessness itself was fairly uncommon among the middle class, and throughout the industrial era it remained primarily a working-class experience. There is evidence, however, that by the early twentieth century some members of the middle class were falling into the ranks of the homeless. Regardless of their social class, however, most Americans of the time had some contact with this destitute group. Urban beggars proliferated during the industrial era, and it was quite common for train-riding tramps, looking for handouts, to appear at the back doors of residences. It should come as no surprise, then, that homelessness became a major cultural concern during the industrial era.[7]

Negative stereotypes of the homeless were already well established in the print media by the time of the Civil War. Labeled as "sturdy beggars," "the wandering poor," or simply as vagrants, the homeless of the mid-nineteenth century invariably earned the enmity of newspaper editors and popular writers commenting on the urban scene. The first urban "guide-books" expressed consternation over the increase in the number of street beggars during downturns in the economy. In the 1840s and 1850s, editorials in newspaper regularly bemoaned the large number of "loafers" who wandered the streets, "infest[ing] the doors and dwellings of our citizens." Such hostile views, common among middle-class citizens as well as many skilled manual laborers, echoed the perspective of the founders of the first large urban charities established to assist the poor. Organizations such as the Association for Improving the Condition of the Poor (AICP) condemned the practice of giving money to beggars and urged a "scientific" approach to poverty that would separate the "worthy" from the "unworthy" poor. Commentators on poverty consistently ignored the economic causes of homelessness and urged a punitive policy toward the homeless, whom they saw as lazy and immoral – one of the groups that reformer Charles Loring Brace labeled "the dangerous classes" of urban America. In 1857 the *New York Times*, in one of its first editorials, argued that the police should arrest "every person, man, woman, or child who may be found begging in the streets." Others, like Brace, made an exception for vagrant children, who artists and illustrators of the day sometimes portrayed sympathetically as Dickensian figures. Brace believed such "street Arabs" could be reformed, but only if they were physically removed from the corrupting environment of the city streets. The adult vagrant, he maintained, was usually incorrigible.[8]

Such views, popular throughout the nineteenth century, represented the dominant image of the homeless in print media directed at the middle class. While often casually disparaged as a negative feature of urban life, however, homelessness was rarely discussed or debated to any degree in the American press prior to the 1870s. This situation changed decisively with the collapse of the economy in 1873. The subsequent six years of unemployment and unprecedented labor conflict brought with it a dramatic change in the nature of homelessness. The number of homeless people reached an all-time high, and this destitute group became much more mobile than they had been in the past. Prior to the Civil War, the "wandering poor" who traveled from town to town did so on foot. In many parts of the country, the distance between communities limited the mobility of vagabonds. Beginning in the 1870s, however, the homeless began to ride the railroad illegally, stowing themselves away in empty boxcars or riding between, on top of, or even underneath freight cars. The rapid increase in the number of homeless persons, coupled with the easy movement of tramps (as they now came to be called) over long distances, meant that no part of the country was now immune from the intrusion of homeless wanderers. Homelessness became a national issue, and it would remain so throughout the industrial era.

With the rise of the tramp phenomenon in the 1870s, homelessness began to attract the attention of journalists and social commentators. Short articles on tramps, published in local papers that appealed to a general audience, became a staple of reporting in the late nineteenth century. Seldom did such stories critically examine this issue; instead, the often anonymous reporters played upon the readers" fears about this strange new class of homeless men (there were few women who rode the freights) called tramps. Their accounts focused on the relatively small number of men on the road who engaged in violence. A particularly popular news item in the 1870s and 1880s described the attack of one or more tramps on a family farm – especially when the husband was away in the fields and the wife was left alone with the children. Headlines announcing, "Tramp Brutality to a Woman" and "A Foul and Fiendish Crime" had something in common with contemporaneous, sensational stories about blacks accused of assaulting white females in the South. This kind of copy made tramps seem more dangerous than they actually were in most instances; it also led to vagabonds being blamed for crimes they did not commit. A *New York Times* article of 1879, for example, entitled "A Tramp's Ingratitude," was really about a crime of violence resulting from a rather ordinary lover's quarrel. The assailant is referred as a tramp for no other reason than because he had been unemployed for several months prior to the incident. As one vagabond explained to investigator John J. McCook, "There are lots of crimes committed by people that are residents of the community that [are] laid at the feet of the unfortunate tramp." The tendency to see the homeless as criminals was not new. Since the colonial era, the line between paupers, vagrants, and hardened criminals had been a hazy one; in its first reference to vagrancy, in 1837, the United States Supreme Court had lumped all three together in the same category. The assertiveness of the men riding the trains, however, led to a greater emphasis in newspapers and magazines on the alleged criminality of the homeless.[9]

The initial reaction by editorialists and critics to the new homeless population was fiercely hostile. "They are like the barbarians who came down like wolves upon Rome!" exclaimed the *New York Tribune* in 1876. The editors of *Scribners*, one of the nation's leading opinion journals, likened them to lepers. The *New York Times* ominously declared tramps to be "the most dangerous class in society," and a number of writers, including the young John Hay in his pseudonymous novel, *The Bread-Winners* (1883), portrayed them as potentially violent radicals, often of immigrant background. The most common criticism of the tramps, however, emphasized their incorrigible laziness. As the popular writer Elizabeth Oakes Smith put it, the homeless man "hates work. He has no respect and no shame." Numerous writers demanded a punitive approach to these destitute wanderers, including incarceration in workhouses, and some even urged a return to the eighteenth-century method of dealing with vagrants – the whipping post.[10]

With very few exceptions, prior to about 1895 journalists and social commentators had little interest in exploring the diverse causes of homelessness. The growing inequality of the new urban order, with its wretched poverty, chronic unemployment, and unsafe working conditions, obviously contributed to the increase in the number of destitute people; but commentators instead focused almost entirely on the perceived "moral failings" of tramps and beggars. This lack of sympathy for the homeless was part of a broader condemnation of the dependent poor, commonly labeled with the pejorative term "paupers" in the late nineteenth century. The homeless, however, were singled out for special condemnation. Nowhere is this more apparent than in Jacob Riis' landmark 1890 study of the slums of New York, *How the Other Half Lives*.

Riis' book is particularly important because it was the first significant example of a new, personalized style of journalism that would become increasingly popular in the early twentieth century. Riis (who began his career as a newspaper reporter) wandered the tired streets of the Lower East Side, sometimes accompanying a policemen on his beat, exploring the crowded tenements that harbored the urban poor, many of them recently-arrived immigrants. As reflected in the book's title, he explicitly acted as a mediator between the increasingly suburbanized middle class and the poor. Riis saw himself as "a kind of war correspondent," bringing back reports to the middle class about the strange world of the inner city.[11] Unlike later examples of muckraking literature, *How the Other Half Lives* rarely excoriates the powerful, and the book is filled with stereotypes and half-truths about ethnic groups, a biased perspective that native-born Americans would have felt comfortable with. Nevertheless, Riis enlightened his audience about conditions in the slums and balanced moralistic statements about immigrant drinking habits and lack of cleanliness with positive comments about their work habits.

Significantly, Riis' vivid portrayal of the homeless and their lodgings contains none of the balanced treatment he accorded most immigrant groups. Like the rest of the book, his report on urban tramps and beggars is filled with fascinating stories, delivered by the author in the jocular style of one insider talking to another, but in this case the vignettes are primarily designed to reinforce the customary negative image of the homeless. The homeless individuals introduced to the reader are not hungry men walking the streets in search of work; they are the denizens of the "stale beer dives," thieves, and people who are paid by political bosses to vote for one or the other candidate. The down-and-out in the Bowery, according to Riis, are drawn from the ranks of "the lazy, the shiftless, and the unfortunate." "[H]omeless and hopeless in their utter wretchedness," they are irreclaimable. This sardonic commentary demonstrates that it was quite possible for someone to use a strikingly innovative journalistic method, combined with a flamboyant style, to deliver a traditional, socially conservative message. In the end, there was little difference between Riis' pessimistic conclusion and that of his celebrated contemporary, social Darwinist William Graham Sumner, who once emphatically stated, "a drunkard in the gutter is just where he ought to be."[12]

In reality, the homeless were connected in myriad ways to the development of industrial society, which brought with it devastating economic disruptions and social dislocations for some at the same time it enhanced the standard of living for others. In the hands of Riis and many other lesser writers, however, the image of the homeless in the mainstream press functioned as a kind of negative reference group, a counter-symbol to the dominant mythology of the United States as a land where hard work and perseverance yielded just rewards and fostered upward mobility. Conceptualizing tramps in this way calmed middle-class fears during a particularly disruptive stage of modernization of the American economy. If in a nation that honored productive labor some individuals seemed to prefer idleness, these writers implied, this was not evidence of a weakness in the economic system. Instead, it was a sign of flawed character in the men who rode the rails and begged for handouts on city street corners. The fault lay with the homeless themselves.

This moralistic view of the homeless remained influential throughout the industrial era – and beyond, but it did not go completely unchallenged. Henry George's best-selling volume, *Progress and Poverty*, published in 1879, expressed the not-unfounded fear that a nation of small producers was being replaced by a sharply drawn system of class divisions. Tramps and millionaires, he argued, were both products of this dangerous trend. George avoided direct appeals to class consciousness by placing the blame on the "idle rich" (financiers and landlords), rather than on industrial capitalists, and he argued that a "single tax" on land would solve this problem of growing economic inequality. His theory was particularly appealing to farmers and shopkeepers, and skilled artisans – groups that felt financially squeezed by the forces of industrial capitalism, yet were still unwilling to abandon the traditional creed that identified America with the opportunity for upward mobility. George's view of the homeless man conformed well to this mentality. He injected a new viewpoint into the debate over homelessness by suggesting that the tramp was a product of forces outside his control. He did not, however, fundamentally challenge the conventional negative stereotypes of the homeless man, who he referred to as a "poisonous pariah" who had "lost all that animates and elevates and stimulates a man to struggle and to labor."[13]

During the decade after the publication of *Progress and Poverty*, a few popular writers – notably Mark Twain in his satirical novel, *A Connecticut Yankee in King Arthur's Court* – picked up on the themes stressed by George. Most middle-class commentators, however, firmly rejected George's view that tramps and millionaires should be discussed in the same sentence. In 1887, the *New York Tribune* editorialized that the two had nothing in common, because the typical millionaire was a man of "character, temperament and capacity" while the tramp was "born lazy" and had "neither ambition [n]or self-respect." Mainstream journals of opinion viewed George as a dangerous radical, a view that was only confirmed when the Populist Party platform of 1892 echoed his rhetoric by proclaiming that "governmental injustice" had bred "two great classes – paupers and millionaires."[14]

The severe depression of the 1890s, however, led to a more serious questioning of traditional views of homelessness. William Dean Howells, a sensitive observer of American life in the late nineteenth century, set the tone for a new approach to the "Tramp Problem" in his widely discussed article, "Are We a Plutocracy?" which appeared in the *North American Review* in 1895. By then, the depression that had begun in 1893 had deepened, labor conflict had returned, and the nation had witnessed the march on Washington by Coxey's Army, demanding government aid for the unemployed. In his 1894 novel, *A Traveler from Altruria*, Howells had made the inequities of work and leisure among different classes a major theme, but he had used thinly veiled satire to make his point. Now, he forthrightly stated that the surge in homelessness signaled a coming crisis in American civilization. America's vast wealth, he stated, "is like witch's gold in its malign and mocking effects . . . The tramps walk the land like the squalid spectres of the laborers who once tilled it."[15]

Howells was no ordinary critic. Well known as a novelist and the editor of *Atlantic Monthly*, a prestigious literary journal, his opinion carried with it the authority of the Boston Brahmin intellectual class from which he had sprung. During the next two decades, many writers would follow Howells' lead and use the rise of mass homelessness as a foil to critique the inequalities and injustices of the new social order. This view went hand-in-hand with the rise of Progressivism, a political reform movement that found its strongest base of support in the middle class. Samuel M. Jones, the reform mayor of Toledo, Ohio, stated in 1899 that if the nation continued to permit "a system of industry and trade that makes million-aires and billionaires on the one hand, we must have paupers and tramps on the other." In the years ahead, reformers as diverse as Robert Hunter and Theodore Roosevelt would draw upon similar rhetoric to attack the failings of the "idle rich."[16]

The crisis of the 1890s led to a break with the tradition that dictated a harshly moralistic condemnation of the homeless. In 1895, *Outlook* magazine published a mildly sympathetic essay, "Tramps As Human Beings." The title was significant, because it was common at the time for editorialists to speak of the homeless as subhuman or animalistic. Three years later, when a writer in *Forum* reiterated the oft-expressed notion that "the vast majority of beggars on the streets are idle, lazy vagabonds and quasi-criminals," the magazine published a sharp rejoinder in the next issue. The tramp, said E. L. Bailey, is "harmless" and "bears the world no ill-will." He added, "Many hoboes are merely men out of work who were forced to the road by circumstances which they could not control . . . [N]either tramps nor hoboes are criminals." The fact that the tramp "begs for food without offering recompense," he concluded, "does not argue necessarily that he is lazy. It may indicate that he is suffering intensely from hunger, or that the offer of his services has been so constantly met with contempt or suspicion that he has not the courage to offer them again . . ."[17]

Commentators like Howells and Bailey broadened the middle-class reader's understanding of homelessness, but their perspective remained that of the outside observer, trying to assess the meaning of an experience that he had not made his own. The first writer to provide a personal account of what it meant to be "down and out" was Josiah Flynt, whose articles on tramps appeared in several well-known journals in the 1890s and were collected together in his popular book, *Tramping With Tramps* (1899). He would later publish three other books dealing with this subject. Flynt had himself tramped for eight months in 1889 and intermittently thereafter, and this enabled him to provide readers with vivid descriptions of the day-to-day existence of vagabonds. Flynt was ambiguous, even contradictory at times in his discussion of tramps, and virtually every image of the homeless man that had ever appeared or would appear can be found in *Tramping With Tramps*. His narrative retained elements of the traditional conservative view. Flynt often concluded discussions of interesting or attractive aspects of life on the road by tacking on a moralistic disclaimer, and hypocritically (in light of his own activities) urged the railroads to crack down on illegal train riding. The final pages of the book are filled with contradictory messages. Flynt first speaks nostalgically about the potential disappearance of the tramp as an authentic part of the American experience, and then promises the reader that the tramp would always exist to some extent and would always deserve his contempt. The same glaring inconsistencies are evident in Flynt's novel, *The Rise of Ruderick Clowd* (1903), in which he extols the outcast life of a tramp as exhilarating, only to end the story with the aging protagonist settling down to a safe existence as a night watchman. Nevertheless, despite glaring inconsistencies – or perhaps because of them – Flynt's writings promoted a more sympathetic image of the homeless man. Unlike Jacob Riis, another author with a vivid, personal style of writing, Flynt soundly rejected the notion that all tramps were drunkards, potentially violent, or prone to criminal behavior (other than petty theft on occasion), and he graphically described the dangers and hardships of tramping. *Tramping with Tramps* attracted attention because the author's experiences were authentic. Flynt's "insider" status allowed him to provide a view of homelessness that was based on something other than conjecture or paranoia. His narrative of life on the road helped to humanize an aspect of American life that had too often been perceived in abstract terms as a "problem."[18]

Another author who broadened middle-class views of the homeless was Walter Wyckoff, a Princeton University theology student who traveled about the country in the late 1890s, working as an unskilled laborer, and described his exploits in a two-volume memoir, *The Workers: A Study in Reality*. "This account is strictly accurate to the details," Wyckoff stated on the opening page of the first volume. Except for the use of pseudonyms, he claimed that "no element of fiction has intentionally been allowed to intrude." Perhaps so, but Wyckoff, like Flynt, was not able to entirely break free from older preconceptions. He believe that "the professionally idle" made up the majority of the homeless and in one contradictory breath could speak of the existence of a "vagrant type . . . draped in the mystery of inherited tendencies, and cloaked in the stern facts of a hard environment."[19] The first part of this description reinforced the notion, put forward by early eugenicists, that the predisposition to pauperism was hereditary. The second half offered a quite different judgment by suggesting that the homeless were victims of socio-economic conditions, not unchanging biological laws. The reader was left to choose whichever view accorded most with his own prejudices. The impact of

Wyckoff's memoir, however, did not come from the author's casual generalizations about the causes of homelessness but from his vivid factual account of life among the unemployed. Wyckoff realistically described vagabond life, the camaraderie of men on the road as well as the hardships they faced. Regardless of their prejudices, few readers were likely to come away from Wyckoff's chronicle without feeling some sympathy for the homeless.

To middle-class readers, one theme that must have struck a responsive chord was the anxiety Wyckoff experienced in searching for employment. The fact that Wyckoff was not a genuine member of the underclass of homeless men may actually have enhanced the impact of his descriptions of the terrors of being unemployed. After all, he was writing not as a person who had always known the modest material standards and uncertain employment that were often the lot of the working class, but as someone who had taken a measure of status and financial security for granted. The contrast between the lifestyle of the substantial citizen and the penniless unemployed was all the more dramatic; the vicarious experience of sliding into the vagrant class all the more frightening. Wyckoff communicated to his readers what it was like "to look for work and fail to find it; to renew the search under the spur of hunger and cold" until one was willing to accept any job, "no matter how low in the scale of work." Something more than physical deprivation accompanied such a fall. If Flynt had been somewhat exhilarated by taking on his new persona, for Wyckoff the effect was one of alienation. A few days after he began tramping, Wyckoff accidentally encountered a friend at a railroad station; but in his new garb, he "passed unnoticed in the crowd." Later, while walking down a road with a gang of day laborers, he passed a group of well-dressed young women in a carriage. He recognized one of them, but "she did not see us, or rather saw through us, as through something transparent . . ." Stephen Crane, while researching his own brilliant essay on homelessness, "An Experiment in Misery," had a similar experience. To the middle class, to be homeless and unemployed was to be almost nonexistent. Wyckoff's explanation was starkly existential: "[Y]ou are thrust back upon yourself and held down remorselessly to the cold, naked fact that you, who in all the universe are of supremest importance to yourself, are yet of no importance to the universe."[20]

There is evidence that, after 1900, some elements of the middle class became more susceptible to unemployment and hence to slipping into homelessness. Studies of destitute men staying at municipal lodging houses in New York and Chicago found that between 7 and 10 per cent were former clerical workers or salesmen, and there were even some lawyers and teachers. Skilled workers – many of whom undoubtedly considered themselves middle class – made up between 15 and 20 per cent of the homeless.[21] Some middle-class Americans might have had good reason to be sensitive to the fearful possibility of "falling from grace." It is not surprising, then, that this theme began to show up in literary works. The most famous of these by far was Theodore Dreiser's *Sister Carrie* (1900), which described the gradual, excruciating decline of George Hurstwood, the affluent manager of an opulent restaurant, into penury, beggary, and eventual suicide. More popular writers, such as Elizabeth Stuart Phelps, also wrote about the slide of white-collar workers into destitution, although in one of her stories, "Unemployed," she allowed her protagonist to escape a life of mendicancy through the fortuitous intervention of a friend.[22]

The image of the tramp as victim was part of a larger shift in mainstream attitudes toward poverty in general at the end of the nineteenth century. As historian Robert Bremner noted, "it was increasingly apparent that individuals suffered as often from the misdeeds and miscalculations of others as from their own failings."[23] The writings of Howells, Wyckoff, Dreiser and others raised doubts about the traditional view that condemned homelessness as the product of laziness or weakness of character. Still, the image of the tramp and the experience of homelessness that these writers presented remained largely negative. The tramp characters in Howells' novels are generally unsavory characters. For critics of the economic system like Howells, the tramp functioned as a convenient symbol of capitalist oppression, but he was not ennobled as a result. Coincidentally at the turn of the century, however, another image of the homeless man was emerging. Sometimes picturing the man on the road as heroic, sometimes as humorous or picturesque, the new image often resonated with positive connotations.

If invidious comparison of tramps and millionaires indicated doubts about the fairness of the new economic order, the portrayal of the vagabond as a heroic or picturesque figure revealed a latent hostility to the nature of work itself under the new industrial/bureaucratic regime. The origins of the heroic theme can be traced, ironically, to conservative critics who were generally antagonistic to the homeless. John J. McCook, one of the most prolific writers on tramps in the 1890s, compared the men on the road to undomesticated animals in which "nature is triumphant." How, McCook mused in another article, was the vagabond able to retain his good health? "This in spite of alcohol, in spite of licentiousness, in spite of scant clothing . . . Can the explanation possibly be in this – that their life, as compared with the average [person], is free from worry and responsibility?" Another writer even more hostile to the homeless than McCook claimed that beggars, "inured to the open air," were "much healthier than the pent-up factory hand or shop-girl." He added humorously, "They have little care or anxiety, except the fun of dodging the policeman."[24] To be sure, an element of rebelliousness was evident among many younger tramps, who sometimes voluntarily left their jobs in factories to go on the road in search of better work elsewhere; and while traveling they shared the communal camaraderie of the hobo "jungles," where homeless men shared food and could find a place to sleep while waiting for the next freight train. To present tramps as healthy, robust, and carefree, however, was a considerable misrepresentation. This view of tramping was far removed from the attempt at realism provided by Walter Wyckoff. Instead, these writers projected middle-class anxieties about the new social order onto the figure of the homeless man. It represented a dream of what it would be like to escape from what one writer, in 1894, called "the American disease" – excessive nervousness brought on by technological innovations, the increased regimen of urban life, and the incipient bureaucratic organization required of many of the new white-collar jobs in corporations.[25]

As first-person narratives of tramping began to displace the authority of the outside observer, the behavior that McCook saw as irresponsible began to be lauded by others as a virtue. Josiah Flynt was among the first to forthrightly praise aspects of life on the road. Throughout *Tramping With Tramps*, he expressed admiration for the courage and endurance of men on the road. A man riding the freights "encounters numerous dangers and hardships, and it is months before he knows how to meet them heroically." To be successful, Flynt said, the tramp had to practice for these activities, "just as a pugilist trains for a fight, and it is only when he is a real artist that he can enjoy it." What for Flynt was only part of the story for Jack London was virtually the whole point. In *The Road* (1907), London effectively integrated the figure of the tramp into the primitivist genre, a literary form that London had helped develop with novels like *The Call of the Wild*. In one chapter, "Holding Her Down," London provides an exciting description of his successful effort to evade capture by a determined train crew, using superior knowledge and endurance to outwit his opponents. It is a fast-paced tale of tramp against train, of a man who adapts modern technology to his own uses against the paid agents of one of the nation's largest enterprises. In London's exciting narrative, the courageous individual faces down the soulless corporation.[26]

*The Road* contains some useful insights into the lifestyle of tramps, but they are often expressed in exaggerated form. At times the trials and tribulations of life in the boxcars and hobo jungles acquire an almost mythic aura. The book's success demonstrated that, to a growing number of readers, the more mundane aspects of tramping were no longer very interesting. *The Road* appealed strongly to those who feared that, with the passing of the frontier and the growth of a more sedentary lifestyle, American civilization was drifting into soft middle age. There is a repeated emphasis in the book on youthfulness, with all the rugged strength that London associated with that term. London spoke of the "youth, delight in life, zest for experience" that led him to become a tramp and claimed that "barring accidents, a good hobo, with youth and agility, can hold a train down despite all the effects of a train crew to 'ditch' him." In *The People of the Abyss* (1903), he had argued that savagery was preferable to the degraded conditions under which some workers toiled in the industrial world. "Far better," said London, "to be a people of the wilderness and desert, of the cave and the squatting place, than to be a people of the machine and the Abyss."[27] Some critics complained that *The Road* "glorified the morally disintegrating influence of tramp life" and was "far from the best kind of reading for American youth." Others reviewers, however, found the book attractive for that very reason – its lack of sympathy for the placid, bourgeois life: "The reading world is richer because the author had both wander-lust and the power of making his experiences live again before staid people who have nothing but vaguely remembered cravings for 'the road.'" London's book was useful precisely because it did *not* purport to be scientific. The author had created a "hobo epic . . . because it is the result of a phase of his own nature rather than the record of carefully compiled sociological notes."[28]

*The New York Times* reviewer argued that a "genuine realist" would never confuse London's heroic vagabond with "the shifty-eyed, lazy, dirty tramp of common experience." London astutely recognized that the more Americans became ensnared in the disciplines and order of technological society, the more they needed to believe that there still were individuals who embodied the nineteenth-century ideal of freedom in its most primitive form. Lennox Kerr, an Englishman who tramped in the United States in the 1920s, recalled how he had often heard "decent men with banking accounts and desks, say enviously, 'Gee, Kerr, I wish I could knock around as you do.'" Another observer added: "Everybody now and then has a desire to forsake his job, 'chuck the whole works,' and either see the country or change his surroundings." Some individuals did follow such impulses and take to the road for varying periods of time. Most of London's readers, however, did not become vagabonds, and undoubtedly they were thankful if economic conditions did not force them to try the experiment.[29]

Most of the approximately two dozen memoirs of tramping published prior to 1935 were more realistic than London's "hobo epic" and did not try to present the tramp as a heroic figure. Elements of London's narrative, however, did become an established part of the genre. It became *de rigueur*, for example, to include vignettes of tramp endurance or hardship and to contrast this mode of life with what one writer called "the soft security and comfort of a dull-spaced city existence." Such views also found expression in the intense interest the press accorded individuals who traveled long distances on foot. Between 1906 and 1913, the *New York Times* published about thirty articles about the expeditions of one Edward Payson Weston, dubbed "The Leather Man" because of his ability to hike for miles without resting.[30]

*The Road* helped shape a new image of the homeless man, but ultimately it was less influential than the view of the tramp as a picturesque or humorous figure. If London's "hobo epic" appealed to those who feared an urbanizing America was undermining the nation's frontier virtues, the image of the vagabond as a quaint "character" was attractive to those disturbed by the homogenizing sameness that modernization seemed to entail in a democratic society – what Henry James called "that property of the America air that reduces so many aspects to a common denominator."[31] Both images were spawned by a nebulous anxiety about the effects of industrialism and technology. There was a major difference between the two, however. Although his actions were purely individualistic in nature, London's heroic tramp nevertheless exemplified a spirit of rebellion that echoed earlier stereotypes about men on the road. The picturesque vagabond, on the other hand, seemed to drift about aimlessly. Far from being rebellious, he seemed not very troubled by his lot in life. His inherent laziness was more a source of humor than a threat to dominant values.

The first significant author to develop aspects of this new image of the homeless was William Dean Howells. The novelist's writings often contained scenes involving tramps and beggars. Unlike many writers, however, Howells did not conflate these two types but instead assigned them quite different symbolic meanings. Howells always used tramps to illustrate injustice, and his depiction of them was invariably unflattering, as for example in his novel *The Minister's Charge*, where he describes a group of tramps, "clad in their filthy rags," as "a hideous gang." Howells' urban beggars, on the other hand, were quaint, even likable figures which the novelist often used as a foil to criticize the mobile, aggressive, increasingly technologized nature of American society. Howell's travel writings about Italy, where he served in a diplomatic post as a young man during the American Civil War, provided an opportunity to contrast the American tramp with his Italian counterpart. Italian beggars, in their "picturesque and desultory costume" may have been an annoyance, but they were harmless. It was true, Howells stated, that the *lasagnone* was an idler. Unlike the "loafers of [the] northern race," however, he had no "admixture of ruffianism . . . He may be quite worthless, and even impertinent, but he cannot be a rowdy," as was too often the case with the homeless of "our fast, high-fed, thick-blooded civilization." Howells described the alleyways of Toledo as filled with "idlers of every age and sex," yet there was "nothing so full of local color, unless it be the little up-and-down-hill streets of Genoa." Subsequently, when he turned his attention to social conditions in his native land, Howells livened up his narrative about "dull" America by introducing a lengthy discussion of the charming Italian beggars and organ grinders whom he encountered during his walks through Charlessbridge. "The truth is," Howells explained, "we Northern and New World folk cannot help but cast a little romance about whoever comes to us from Italy, whether we have actually known the beauty and charm of that land or not." In a curious way, these beggars seemed representative of a European civilization that had learned to value leisure, use it creatively, and resist "the ruthless hand of Progress" that dominated American life.[32]

The ambiguity about the homeless population inherent in these statements, written between 1866 and 1872, seemed out of place in the crisis-ridden 1870s and 1880s, when a harshly negative image of the railroad-riding tramp emerged and became dominant in middle-class literature. By the turn of the century, however, a growing awareness of the stressful nature of life and work in the new industrial system created a basis for a different attitude toward the "professional idler." In 1911 one writer was bold enough to question the work ethic directly, claiming that "it takes no great penetration to discover that all useless toil is a social crime, and that in economic leisure we have the possibilities of all that makes a nation happy and prosperous and great." "The American soul," he concluded, "is amazingly meagre. We have been frightfully industrious." At a time when steel workers still labored twelve hours a day, such views were designed strictly for the middle and upper classes, who were now more involved in consumer culture and looking for ways to increase their leisure time. Ambivalence about work and idleness was increasingly evident in articles and leading magazines, which argued that laziness could be both "positive and negative." Calvin Coolidge's statement that "the business of America is business" notwithstanding, by the 1920s even such staid middle-class journals as *The Saturday Evening Post* and *Harpers* were admonishing readers about "tapering off on work" and "our need for wasting more time."[33]

Articles in newspapers and magazines designed for a middle-class audience now stressed the endearing or idiosyncratic traits, which allegedly set the homeless apart from the rest of the population. Some of these characteristics were exaggerations; others were close to being complete fabrications. Stories about the crowning of a "hobo king," for example, became popular in the press, even though these incongruous "coronations" were little more than stunts initiated by publicity seekers or, as in the case of the famous Britt, Iowa, "hobo convention," by local businessmen trying to promote their town.[34] Tramps' alleged use of markings on trees, fences or buildings, in a secret code, which only they understood, also fascinated readers. The best evidence, however, indicates that the use of coded signs was, at most, quite limited and that the variety of such marks was certainly not as elaborate as many people believed.[35] Another aspect of tramp life that became exaggerated was the jargon that the homeless used when talking among themselves. To be sure, tramps did use slang terms when discussing some aspects of life on the road (derogatory terms for authority figures were especially popular), and they commonly referred to cities by nicknames. Tramp memoirists who overemphasized the "rich vein of hobo vernacular . . . in the picturesque drollery of the original," however, were caricaturing this aspect of life on the road. Writers like Floyd Dell and Harry Kemp, who became known as the "tramp poet" despite his very limited real life experience on the road, self-consciously identified tramp life with an artistic or bohemian sensibility that, they believed, was too often missing from the lives of ordinary Americans.[36]

While there were many variations on the theme of the picturesque tramp, most of them to some extent presented the homeless man as an object of humor. The down-and-out "bum," impoverished but content, as there to entertain, to amuse, to be the butt of someone else's joke. The quaint vagabond had no goals of his own. He served as a charming antidote to the perceived monotony of American life, an entertaining reminder that the work ethic had its limitations. This image simultaneously encouraged the audience to entertain the nostalgic fantasy of escape from the workaday world of modern America while reinforcing a mild sense of superiority in the reader. The carefree hobo might be enjoying himself, but who would want to trade places with him? It was an image that was easily adapted to cartoons, including the popular newspaper comics "Happy Hooligan" and "Weary Willy," and to the vaudeville stage, where performers like Lew Bloom and Nat Wills became famous as "tramp comics" in the early twentieth century.[37]

By the 1920s, the figure of the nostalgic or romanticized tramp had largely replaced the traditional negative stereotype. Some authors, while discussing "the gentle art of tramping," even explicitly repudiated the older view.[38] But the innocuous caricature they presented was in its own way as false as the earlier image of the vicious, criminal vagabond. The fact that both images were exclusively that of white men sidestepped the fact that perhaps 20 to 25 per cent of homeless Americans were African Americans or women. The nostalgic view, however, also emptied the image of the tramp of any element of class conflict or inequality. Most importantly, by excluding most negative aspects of homelessness, the picturesque image provided a rationalization for neglecting the real problems of the homeless. In a way, this had almost always been the case. Whether the homeless were portrayed as dependent or defiant, as immoral or victimized, there was a striking continuity in the inability of writers to acknowledge their basic humanity as ordinary human beings facing extraordinary problems. To be sure, anthropological studies like Alice W. Solenberger's *One Thousand Homeless Men* (1911) and Nels Anderson's *The Hobo* (1923) were available and conceivably could have provided the middle class with a more realistic understanding of the nature and causes of homelessness.[39] Outside of a fairly select academic audience, however, few people were reading them, and it was relatively rare for mainstream magazines or newspapers to publish articles that reflected their broadly humanistic approach. Regrettably, the most popular examples of writings about the homeless all too often functioned to divert attention from structural socio-economic issues that were the prime causes of much real-life homelessness.

# Notes

1. For the origins of modernization in the decades between the Revolution and the Civil War, see Richard D. Brown, *Modernization: The Transformation of American Life, 1600–1865*, New York, 1976.

2. An excellent survey of many of these changes is Thomas J. Schlereth, *Victorian America: Transformations in Everyday Life*, New York, 1991. For an overview that focuses more on labor, see Alan Dawley, *Struggles*

*for Justice: Social Responsibility and the Liberal State*, Cambridge MA, 1991.

3. The classic work on the shift from the old to the new middle class, C. Wright Mills, *White Collar: The American Middle Classes*, New York, 1951; should be supplemented by William Leach, *Land of Desire: Merchants, Power, and the Rise of a New American Culture*, New York, 1993. An excellent case study of the urban lower middle class, a group that has not received the attention it deserves, is Jerome Bjelopera, *City of Clerks: The Lower Middle Class in Philadelphia, 1870–1920*, Urbana IL, forthcoming 2004.

4. On the importance of magazines to establishing new patterns of consumption, especially for the middle class, see Jackson Lears, *Fables of Abundance: A Cultural History of Advertising in America*, New York, 1994, pp. 138–195, 210–234; and Richard Ohmann, *Selling Culture: Magazines, Markets, and Class at the Turn of the Century*, London, 1996.

5. On variations in availability or interest in reading matter in the first half of the nineteenth century, see Richard Brown, *Knowledge Is Power: The Diffusion of Information in Early America, 1800–1865*, New York, 1989, p. 282f.

6. For an excellent analysis of methodological problems of measuring homelessness, see Kim Hopper, "Counting the New York Homeless: An Ethnographic Perspective," *New England Journal of Public Policy* 8 (1992), 771–91.

7. For a quantitative assessment of homelessness during the industrial era, see Kenneth L. Kusmer, *Down and Out, On the Road: The Homeless in American History*, New York, 2002, pp. 99–122.

8. *Cleveland Leader*, 12 January 1855, in Works Projects Administration, *The Annals of Cleveland*, Washington, 1937–8, vol. 38, p. 24; Paul Boyer, *Urban Masses and Moral Order in America, 1820–1920*, Cambridge MA, 1978, pp. 86–93; Michael B. Katz, *In the Shadow of the Poorhouse: A Social History of Welfare in America*, New York, 1986, pp. 58–66; *New York Times*, 26 November 1857; Charles Loring Brace, *The Dangerous Classes of New York City*, New York, 1972, pp. 115–17. The romantic image of homeless children in American art, see Lisa Peters, "Images of the Homeless in American Art, 1860–1910," in Rick Beard (ed.), *On Being Homeless: Historical Perspectives*, New York, 1987, pp. 43–53.

9. "Tramp Brutality to a Woman," *New York Tribune*, 22 June 1877; "Tramp Frightens Woman to Death," *New York Times*, 6 June 1879; "A Foul and Fiendish Crime," *Chicago Tribune*, 3 June 1886; "A Tramp's Ingratitude," *New York Times*, 26 April 1879; John J. McCook, "Leaves

from a Diary of a Tramp, Part IV," *Independent* 54 (1902), 24; City of New York v. Miln 36 US 102, 142 (1837).

10. "Tramps in Regiments," *New York Tribune*, 28 November 1877; "Topics of the Times," *Scribner's Monthly* 13 (1877), 4; Kenneth Allsop, *Hard Travelin': The Hobo and His History*, New York, 1967, pp. 110–13; "Playing with Fire," *New York Times*, 28 November 1877; [John Hay], *The Bread-Winners*, New York, 1883; Elizabeth Oakes Smith, *The Newsboy*, New York, 1884, p. 33.

11. Jacob Riis, *How the Other Half Lives: Studies Among the Tenements of New York*, New York, 1957 [1890], p. 52.

12. Riis, *How the Other Half Lives*, p. 57; William Graham Sumner, "The Forgotten Man," in Stow Persons (ed.), *Social Darwinism: Selected Essays of William Graham Sumner*, New York, 1963, p. 122.

13. Henry George, *Poverty and Progress: An Inquiry into the Causes of Industrial Depressions, and of Increase of Want with Increase of Wealth*, San Francisco, 1879, pp. 6–9; Henry George, *Social Problems*, New York, 1883, p. 129.

14. Mark Twain, *A Connecticut Yankee in King Arthur's Court*, New York, 1889, p. 159; "Tramps and Millionaires," *New York Tribune*, 26 July 1887; John D. Hicks, *The Populist Revolt*, Lincoln NE, 1961, p. 436.

15. William Dean Howells, *A Traveler from Altruria*, New York, 1957 [1894]; William Dean Howells, "Are We a Plutocracy?" *North American Review* 158 (1894), 194.

16. Samuel M. Jones, "Charity or Justice – Which?" National Conference of Charities and Correction, *Proceedings, 1895*, 291f.; Robert Hunter, *Poverty*, New York, 1904, pp. 69–71; "Roosevelt to Stop Big Man Rascality," *New York Times*, 27 August 1908. The best study of Howells is Kenneth Lynn, *William Dean Howells: An American Life*, New York, 1971.

17. Morrison I. Swift, "Tramps As Human Beings," *Outlook* 52 (1895), 342f.; Henry E. Rood, "The Tramp Problem: A Remedy," *Forum* 26 (1898), 90–4; E. L. Bailey, "Tramps and Hoboes," *Forum* 26. (1898), 217–21.

18. Josiah Flynt, *Tramping With Tramps: Studies and Sketches of Vagabond Life*, New York, 1899; Josiah Flynt, *The Rise of Ruderick Clowd*, New York, 1903, pp. 349, 370; Josiah Flynt, "Railroad Police and the Tramp," *Railroad Gazette* 32 (1900), 579f.

19. Walter Wyckoff, *The Workers: A Study in Reality, The East*, New York, 1897, pp. VII–IX; Walter Wyckoff, *The Workers: A Study in Reality, The West*, New York, 1899, pp. 88f., 120; Walter Wyckoff, *A Day With a Tramp and Other Days*, New York, 1901, p. 5.

20. Wyckoff, *The Workers: . . . The West*, p. 1f.; Wyckoff, *The Workers: . . . The East*, p. 23f.; Linda H. Davis, *Badge of Courage: The Life of Stephen Crane*, New York, 1998, pp. 79–81.

21. Kusmer, *Down and Out, On the Road*, p. 118f.

22. Theodore Dreiser, *Sister Carrie*, New York, 1900; Elizabeth Stuart Phelps, "Unemployed," *Harper's Monthly* 113 (1906), 904–12.

23. Robert H. Bremner, *From the Depths: The Discovery of Poverty in the United States*, New York, 1956, p. 21.

24. J. McCook, "Leaves from the Diary of a Tramp: Part I," *Independent* 53 (1901), 2765; K. K. Bentwick, "Street Begging as a Fine Art," *North American Review* 158 (1894), 126f.

25. Edward Wakefield, "Nervousness: The National Disease of America," *McClure's* 2 (1894), 302–7; George Beard, *American Nervousness: Its Causes and Consequences*, New York, 1881; Joseph Kett, *Rites of Passage: Adolescence in America, 1790 to the Present*, New York, 1977, p. 160f.

26. Flynt, *Tramping With Tramps*, p. 355; Jack London, *The Road*, New York, 1907, pp. 24–52.

27. London, *The Road*, pp. 21, 24, 32, 47f.; London, *The People of the Abyss*, New York, 1903, quoted in Andrew Sinclair, *Jack: The Biography of Jack London*, New York, 1978, p. 89.

28. Book reviews quoted in King Hendricks, "Introduction," J. London, *The Road*, Santa Barbara CA, 1970, p. XVf.; Frederick Feied, *No Pie in the Sky: The Hobo as American Cultural Hero in the Works of Jack London, John Dos Passos, and Jack Kerouac*, New York, 1964, p. 53.

29. Anonymous review in *New York Times Book Review*, 28 December 1907, p. 861; Lennox Kerr, *Back Door Guest*, New York, 1927, p. 179.

30. Charles Ashleigh, *Rambling Kid*, New York, 1930; quoted in K. Allsop, *Hard Travelin'*, p. 245; Glen Mullin, *Adventures of a Scholar Tramp* New York, 1925, p. 8f.; Jim Tully, *Beggars of Life*, New York, 1925, p. 203f. The *New York Times* published numerous articles about Weston's hiking tours between 1906 and 1913.

31. Henry James, *The American Scene*, Bloomington IN, 1966, p. 203. For examples of such comments from contemporary British and German visitors, respectively, see James F. Muirhead, *The Land of Contrasts*, Boston MA, 1898, p. 38; and Wilhelm von Polenz, *Das Land der Zukunft* (Berlin, 1904), 79; in which von Polenz exclaims: "Fuer ein Land, in dem immerfort so viel Sensationelles passiert, ist die Monotonie des eigentlichen Daseins erstaunlich."

32. W. D. Howells, *The Minister's Charge*, Boston MA, 1887, p. 104; W. D. Howells, *Venetian Life*, Boston MA, 1866, pp. 27, 342, 347; W. D.

Howells, *Italian Journeys*, Boston MA, 1867, pp. 23, 77; W. D. Howells, *Suburban Sketches*, Boston MA, 1871, pp. 45, 35–51 passim; and the discussion of W. D. Howells, *Their Wedding Journey*, Boston MA, 1871 in K. Lynn, *William Dean Howells*, p. 212.

33. C. Hanford Henderson, *Pay-Day*, Boston MA, 1911, pp. 85, 88; "Laziness: Positive and Negative," *Independent* 91 (1917), 241; S. G. Blyth, "Tapering Off on Work," *Saturday Evening Post* 198 (8 August 1925), 3f.; F. C. Kelly, "Our Need for Wasting More Time," *Harper's Monthly* 150 (1925), 659–62. See also Daniel T. Rodgers, *The Work Ethic in Industrial America, 1850–1920*, Chicago, 1978. I believe, however, that the rise of mass consumption during these years promoted a more ambivalent attitude toward work than Rodgers indicates.

34. The first reference to the crowning of a "hobo king" that I have found is "The King of Tramps," *New York Times*, 17 October 1892; there are numerous articles dealing with this between 1900 and 1920. On the Britt, Iowa, hobo convention, see Gretchen Carlson, "The Hobo Convention," *The Palimpsest* 12 (1931), 257–72.

35. For journalistic examples of the fascination with tramps' marks or signs, see "Believe in Signs," *New York Tribune*, 23 August 1903, part II, 14; and Towne Nylander, "Tramps and Hoboes," *Forum* 71 (1925), 233–5. Thomas Page, *Bohemian Life: Or, the Autobiography of a Tramp*, San Francisco, 1884, p. 182; stated that only a "crude and meager system of wayside signs" existed. Nels Anderson, writing as Dean Stiff, *The Milk and Honey Route*, New York, 1931, p. 84f.; doubted their existence altogether.

36. "Review of Mullin, *Adventures*," *The Bookman* 41 (1925), 484; William Edge, *The Main Stem*, New York, 1927, p. 81; "Do You Give the Tramp a Ride?" *Sunset* 54 (1925), 79; William Brevda, *Harry Kemp: The Last Bohemian*, Lewisburg PA, 1986, pp. 111–29.

37. On the Happy Hooligan character (there were also several early films made about him), see Stephen Becker, *Comic Art in America*, New York, 1959, p. 18; Maurice Horn, *The World Encyclopedia of Comics*, New York, 1976, p. 302f. On Vaudeville, see Marion Spitzer, *The Palace*, New York, 1969, pp. 26, 40, 47.

38. On the importance of nostalgia to American culture in the 1920s generally, see Lawrence W. Levine, *The Unpredictable Past: Explorations in American Cultural History*, New York, 1993, pp. 189–205.

39. Alice W. Solenberger, *One Thousand Homeless Men*; N. Anderson, *The Hobo*, Chicago, 1923.

# 11
# Protesting against "America" as the Icon of Modernity: The Reception of Muckraking in Germany

## Jörg Requate*

In Europe, talking about the future of the media, almost automatically entails talking about Americanization. Not only is this true for today – it was true in the late nineteenth century. Usually, however, this Americanization discourse is little concerned with the actual similarities and differences in the media and the various types of journalism in either continent. In the media discourse, Americanization has rather been a synonym for "commercialization" on the one hand, and certain ideas about "modernity", especially regarding methods of research and of getting news, on the other.[1] The ambivalence of fascination and rejection already known to be prominent in other aspects of the image of America can thus also be found in the press.[2] It was clearly in the press discourse of the late nineteenth and early twentieth centuries that the rejection of an "American state of affairs" and a defense against it predominated, for ideas about the "American state of affairs" were inseparably linked with the term "commercialization". It was not only in the first half of the twentieth century that the entire German literature on newspapers was united in its rejection of this commercialization. At least in the German Empire, this often also had an anti-Semitic component, as it was seen in the context of a supposed supremacy of the Jewish press.[3]

This verdict of commercialization was acknowledged in Habermas' influential book *The Structural Transformation of the Public Sphere* (*Strukturwandel der Öffentlichkeit*).[4] In short, one of his central arguments was that the commercialization of the press contributed substantially to the gradual falling apart of the bourgeois public. As a result, the press changed its character from a platform usually open for debate to a potential instrument of power of manipulative interests. Admittedly, Habermas did not use the term "Americanization". His main argument about the press,

*Translated by Veronika Huesmann

205

however, draws on exactly the kind of literature liking to contrast a press based on political principles (*Gesinnungspresse*) with one based on business interests (*Geschäftspresse*) in order to play off political principles against business interests.

There can hardly be any doubt, however, that the bourgeois public has not fallen apart. The opposite is true: the development of new structures of the public was closely connected with this and other social and political processes aiming at the "masses". There is much to say for the argument that the emerging mass journalism of the nineteenth century laid the foundation for a development of the media, the main features of which have basically remained the same until today. As a result of decreasing restrictions on the press, there have been attempts to take political influence both through and on the media. Moreover, the many parameters constituting economic structure and its resulting influences as well as the role definitions and dynamics of the media and the journalists alike have formed the cornerstones of the media's room to maneuver ever since.[5] Since the end of the nineteenth century at the latest, the development of both the American press and the American media has played a leading role for all developments in this area. It cannot be contested that the American press could only produce such an enormous dynamism during the nineteenth century because more and more clever publishers wanted to profit from the expanding market for newspapers. As much as this was obviously linked to an increase in tabloid journalism and rather brutal journalistic methods, the entire development cannot be reduced to this.[6]

Admittedly, the American press needed time to develop what have since become known as "American" journalistic methods in the course of the nineteenth century. However, in order to explain the differences between America and Germany both in their journalistic methods and in their journalistic code of ethics (*journalistisches Selbstverständnis*), in short, to explain the rejection of "American" journalism in Germany, it is necessary to go further back in time. This is why this essay will first go into the development of the American press and its specific features. The focus will be on the emergence of certain journalistic methods and the code of ethics lying behind. After sketching the development of the German press from the same point of view, the conclusion will point out the reasons for the differences between the two countries.

# From Revolutionaries to Muckrakers: Changes in the Journalistic Code of Ethics of American Journalists in the Nineteenth Century

Whoever thought of himself as a political journalist at the time of the American or French Revolutions, and whoever took up his pen as such, did not do so conscious of a "journalistic independence" so crucial to the ethos of every journalist today, but he was partisan. With some exceptions, the political and publishing protagonists in the period of rapid change in the United States of America and in France at the end of the eighteenth century were identical.[7] This is not only true for the period when American society organized itself against its colonial ruler, but also for the following very quick formation of the political parties.[8] In the period when the political elite, which had still been in general agreement during the Revolution, began to split up over questions concerning the inner formation of American society, the newspapers started acting as mouthpieces of the different opinions that were to lay the foundation of the emerging parties.

Of course, there were also newspapers claiming not to be leaning towards any party. This declaration of impartiality, however, did not mean anything but that the newspapers were made "with scissors and glue", as the Germans would later say. Thus political journalism as such did not exist in these newspapers. Whoever made a political newspaper at the time took sides and did not claim to be impartial. "Professions of impartiality I shall make none", the editor of *The Porcupine's Gazette* William Cobbett wrote in his newspaper in March 1797 and continued to say that he would not like to belong to those "who look on the conflict with perfect indifference, and whose only anxiety is the strongest side." An editor not able to arrive at an opinion of his own he called "a poor passive fool and not an editor."[9]

Whoever wanted to be taken seriously either as a journalist or as an editor of a newspaper could not afford impartiality. Generally speaking, as the political debate was dominated and structured by the two opposing parties, the Federalists and the Republicans, this usually meant a decision about which of the two parties to support. Accordingly, within a relatively short period of time, the majority of the newspapers took the side of one of the two parties. What had begun as a politicization of the debate and had brought life into the media, however, gradually petrified during the first decades of the nineteenth century. In 1825, an American journalist stated: "The press is now so conditioned in the United States that nearly every publisher is compelled to take a side in personal electioneering."[10]

In times of low circulation numbers, the publishers regarded the close connection of their papers with political parties as the most secure support for the survival of their papers. Not only did the parties provide them with information, in times of difficulty, they could also hope for financial support. In his groundbreaking work on American journalism, Frank L. Mott called the years between 1801 and 1833 "The dark ages of Partisan Journalism".[11] This judgment resulted mainly from the petrifaction of the press and the resulting tone in the newspapers. Once the bipolar party system had established itself, the newspapers lost their party-building function and were reduced to mere mouthpieces of the parties. It is telling of those times that the arguments between the two parties were more often than not accompanied by sharp polemics, personal smear campaigns, and so forth. The success of the Penny-Press emerging in the 1830s can only be understood against this background of the immobility of a press shaped by stereotypical partisanship and tiring polemics.

When James Gordon Bennett founded the *New York Herald* in 1835, he was neither the first nor the only one trying to make and, even more importantly, sell newspapers with a totally different concept. He was, however, the most successful. Indeed, the importance of the *Herald* can hardly be exaggerated. It is probably not wrong to argue that the paper founded by James Gordon Bennett basically gave birth to the features that have ever since been essential for the modern (mass) press in very different ways depending on the newspaper. This is true for Bennett's *Herald* to a far greater extent than for any other comparable English or French newspaper that may have appeared in the 1830s. Two aspects are most important in this respect: firstly, the paper's shift of focus on the spreading of news and the fact that the news was researched and not only unquestioningly copied by the journalists. It is precisely the example of the further development of the American press that makes clear how closely detailed and well-founded research was connected with demands of reform on the one hand and tabloid journalism on the other. Bennett's *Herald* drove on the development in both directions. In any case, for decades the *Herald* was regarded as the newspaper with the most and the most reliable information. Secondly, the claim of party-political impartiality. Bennett wrote in a special edition of the *Herald* on 6 May 1835:[12] "We shall support no party – be the organ of no faction or coterie, and care nothing for any election or any candidate from President down to a constable". Admittedly, the claim of party political impartiality did not mean that it was really present. It was of fundamental importance for the development of the press, however, that the newspapers began to attempt being something other than the mouthpiece of political parties or groups.

Despite the milestone that the foundation of the *Herald* was without a doubt, the American press did not immediately go in the direction of a total predominance of the kind of journalism based on news and reports, the kind of journalism Europeans would later call "Americanism". Of course, in America there were also still a great number of newspapers closely linked to the parties. After the foundation of the Republican Party in the mid-1850s, however, the party system as we know it today gradually emerged. With the end of the Civil War on the one hand, and the confrontation between Republicans and Democrats that has been continuing ever since on the other hand, it organized society in such a way as to provide – with almost no changes up until today – a political framework for all following arguments and debates. The press, which had been an integral part of all arguments about the state and being (*Verfasstheit*) of society before, could now stop its direct involvement in party political disputes, and instead focus on increasingly developing its inner dynamism.

This inner dynamism became noticeable predominantly on the papers' news pages. Even though it was certainly the commercial aspects that mattered most to the publishers, it was in this context that American journalists developed the tradition of investigative journalism. The report in its various forms became a synonym for American journalism as such. Both publishers and journalists soon realized that reports based on well-researched facts had a much greater and, even more importantly, a much more direct effect than editorials. As early as 1866, an observer wrote:

> The prestige of the editorial is gone . . . There are journalists who think the time is at hand for the abolition of editorials, and the concentration of the whole force of journalism upon presenting to the public the history and picture of the day. The time for this has not come, and may never come; but our journalists already know that editorials neither make nor mar a daily paper, that they do not much influence the public mind, nor change many votes, and that the power and success of a newspaper depend wholly and absolutely upon its success in getting, and its skill in exhibiting the news . . . The news is the point of rivalry; it is that which constitutes the power and value of the daily press; it is that which determines the rank of every newspaper in every free country.[13]

Admittedly, especially with regards to the 1860s, this statement is exaggerated and did not remain unchallenged. On the whole, however, the observation was accurate.[14] It is particularly remarkable that not only a paper's success but also its power was regarded as dependent on the paper's ability to research and to present news. The American Civil War had increased the significance of fast and reliable information, but it was only in the following years that a number of American journalists could prove in a very impressive way that a report's potential could not be reduced to merely getting the most spectacular news possible.[15] Thus, one of the best known police reporters of the time, Jacob A. Riis, also used "murder, fire and sudden death" as raw material for his features. He did not stop there, however, but used his material to emphasize the social background of a crime or events other than the sensational story.[16] Riis was born in Denmark in 1849. Since 1877, he worked as a police reporter in New York for various newspapers and magazines, amongst them the *Tribune*, the *World* and the *Sun*. Like some of his colleagues, Riis had something resembling an office straight opposite the police headquarters on Mulberry Street, which ran through the city as a kind of social dividing line. On its other side, the slums of the Lower East Side began. In his reports, Riis digested the insights he gained during his research into housing, living and working conditions of the inhabitants of the slums. These experiences finally turned him into an enthusiastic social reformer. "How the other half lives: Studies among the tenements", was the title of an article published in *Scribner's Magazine*. It caused such uproar mainly because Riis was the first to add photographs to his report thus founding social documentary photography. That this kind of journalism also paid economically for the publishers can be concluded from the fact that Scribner offered Riis to print an extended version of the article as a book, which was published in 1890.[17]

As a special form of report, the role report was developed in the 1890s. Either in disguise, using faked documents or under false pretences, so-called "stunt reporters" gained entry to public institutions to report, from an insider's perspective, about the dealings of this institution and to uncover its abuses. The most famous of these investigative journalists was Elizabeth Cochrane, born in 1867, who started working as a journalist in Pittsburgh in 1885. She became known very quickly under the pseudonym Nellie Bly.[18] Only two years later she went to the *New York World*, founded by Joseph Pulitzer. Pulitzer's name is closely linked to the so-called "new journalism", which is characterized not least by the role report. Pulitzer and his star reporter Elizabeth Cochrane are another example of how intimately bound up sensational journalism and well-researched features were with a social reform approach while trying to achieve as high a circulation as possible. Elizabeth Cochrane alias Nellie Bly's outwardly most spectacular "stunts" were her travels around the world in Jules Verne's style, for which she needed eight days less than her literary model. What was important here was to keep the reader's attention on the event the newspaper had staged itself for the entire length of her journey. In this, as in other stunt reports, the newspaper makers were certainly most interested in the spectacular and the commercial success it brought, but at the same time they created a genre, which is remarkable from a sociological and a social reform point of view. Pretending to be mentally deranged, for instance, Elizabeth Cochrane let herself be checked into the infamous madhouse on Blackwell's Island. Another example of her many stunts was her provoking her own arrest in order to write about the state of women's prisons. Her great success meant that she soon found many imitators, and within a short period of time this kind of report became most fashionable. With the readers' interest decreasing, however, it also disappeared again. Soon after, a new variation of the investigative report developed: so-called "muckraking".

The "classical era of muckraking" was between 1902 and 1912/17, and it was both, the most successful form of report journalism and the one with the most consequences. It had a decisive influence not only on the understanding of the press but also of democracy.[19] The impact of muckraking was mainly so great, because the kind of report thus labeled was not published in the daily papers but in the new "ten cent magazines" such as *McClure's*, *Everybody's*, *Collier's*, and *Cosmopolitan* to name but the most important. Thus, they were not limited to a specific region but were read nationwide. The methods of the muckrakers essentially remained those of other investigative journalists. In contrast to their colleagues in the daily papers, however, they had more time and space for their report. This not only created the possibility for much more profound research but also for a more detailed presentation, which could go much further into the social complexities of a topic. Both, the most influential and most work-intensive report of this kind was probably Ida M. Tarbell's article on the history of the Standard Oil Company, into which she put four years of research. Her expenditure of roughly 50,000 dollars was paid by the publisher McClure, in whose magazine the story was published as a series in 1903 and 1904.[20] The example of the Standard Oil Company was meant to make public the corrupt economic practices of large industrial trusts. "The reports mainly aim to uncover what Flynt [Josiah Flynt Willard, one of the most influential muckrakers; J.R.] using a term from underworld slang called "graft" . . . Graft signals a back-stage point of view, it promises insider knowledge and thus forms a metaphor for the detective character of journalistic work, which – independent of its goal and purpose – gains news value from its investigative nature."[21]

Even though the impact of the muckrakers is difficult to assess in individual cases, there can be no doubt that their articles contributed essentially to a climate that underlined American society's need for reform. Directly or indirectly they thus initiated reforms. It is important in this context, however, that these "Crusaders for American Liberalism" (Filler) originated from the dynamism of American journalism that had begun with the emergence of the Penny Press in the 1830s. The magazines did not serve as a platform for social reformers; rather it was the journalists who, motivated by their research, gave impetus to social reforms. As Rolf Lindner has shown recently, the way a report is researched can be understood as an early form of the sociology of great cities. In the person of Robert Ezra Parks, one of the most important muckrakers, who had been a police reporter on Mulberry Street together with Jacob A. Riis and Lincoln Stefens, and who later became the head of the Chicago School of Sociology, there even exists a direct personal connection between the report and scientific sociology.

In its excessive form, muckraking, too, was a kind of fashion that disappeared with the decreasing interest of the readers. To a certain extent, muckraking thus fell victim to the same dynamism that had brought it about. Even though some of the magazines, to which the wave of muckraking had brought quick success, went bankrupt between 1910 and 1915, it was in the muckraking era at the latest that the press had established itself as a publicly feared and respected control institution. Investigative journalism thus also became a purpose in itself. On the one hand it made the control function of the press independent of the political attitudes of the journalists, at least to a certain extent. On the other hand it meant that the boundaries between investigative and sensational journalism became increasingly blurred. At the latest since the last third of the nineteenth century, both tendencies can be clearly recognized in the strongly news-oriented American journalism. In the end, they are two sides of the same coin.

# Standing by One's Principles as a Question of Professional Honor: The Journalistic Code of Ethics in Germany

Whereas in the United States of America as well as in France and England, the development of the commercial mass press took place in two waves – the first one in the 1830s, the second between the 1860s and the 1880s – in Germany the breakthrough was achieved in one go in the last third of the nineteenth century. Besides the relative "delay", there are three points in particular, which have to be emphasized in comparison to the Western pioneering countries, as they shaped the press and thus the structure of the public in Germany decisively.

Firstly, the long tradition of censorship and press control had a significant impact on German journalism and the structure of public communication in general long after the end of the nineteenth century. Journalistic practices of the American kind would have been totally unthinkable in Germany at the turn of the century. Not the least important reason for their failure would have been a jurisdiction that denied the right of the daily press "to publicly reprimand supposed abuses, and to make public every occurrence, even if it injures the honor of others."[22] As not only persons but also institutions were allowed to feel insulted in a legal sense, every form of criticism of "supposed abuses" could lead to a charge of libel or slander. In such a case, the reporter either had to prove in court that his claims were correct – this was usually impossible to do, as the informants, who had provided the journalist with the insider information, were hardly willing to give up their anonymity to give evidence in court – or, alternatively, the journalist had to prove that the matter he had criticized touched upon his own interests. Only then his "reprimanding judgements" could be interpreted as a "taking up of justified interests", thus offering an escape from a sentence for libel or slander. Until far into the twentieth century, German law thus prevented journalists from standing up as defenders of public interests.[23]

A second central point important for the development of both the German press and the German public is closely connected with the tradition of press control. A highly restrictive information policy existed in many ways. The Journalist Max Reiner, who was born in Vienna and worked in Berlin since 1906, described in his autobiography how unthinkable it was in the Ministries to receive a journalist. Only the Ministry of Foreign Affairs passed on "information" to two or three selected journalists. Reiner writes that in all other ministries "the appearance of a journalist created almost a panic." After all, the worst that could happen to a higher ranked German civil servant was "to be suspected to have said something to a journalist."[24] As a result, interviewing politicians or other public persons, became common only very late and quite hesitantly; rather almost all areas of society "blocked" the press. The work of a reporter, which, in England and the United States, had long formed the basis of all journalistic activities, was regarded as undignified snooping around in Germany. Certainly, this did not contribute to the emergence of a self-confident and powerful press. This is why there are only so few examples of a well-researched piece of journalism following the American model.

Admittedly, the emergence of the social report could be used to prove this argument wrong. Leaving aside the fact that this genre was much more prominent in Austria, it is when analysing this kind of report that differences can clearly be pointed out despite some similarities that without a doubt existed. Paul Göhre's attention-catching social report "A factory worker and an apprentice in the crafts for three months" ("Drei Monate Fabrikarbeiter und Handwerksbursche") could indeed at first sight be counted as a role report imitating the American model.[25] A closer look, however, reveals that precisely this example shows typical features of German journalism. Göhre was a Protestant clergyman and at the same time a journalist working for the *Christliche Welt* (*Christian World*). The report, for which Göhre worked as a factory worker for three months, was first published in this paper, but in contrast to comparable American reports, it was not created by the dynamism of the press. It was Göhre's personal social and political involvement inspiring him with this idea, which at the time was unique. Probably unlike an American journalist, he also sought the factory owner's permission for his plan. Even though Göhre wrote a couple of other reports, he could not set further journalistic hallmarks. Instead, the experiences he had gained in the factory gave rise to his support for the social democrats.

Friedrich Kürbisch, who collected a number of reports in German and published them again, stresses the implicit difference of the development of the American press, stating that it was not the hunger of the press for new stories that was responsible for the development of the genre but the desire for enlightenment.[26] Kürbisch aimed to underline that idealism and not the wish for easy money was the driving force behind the articles. He thus stands in the long tradition of a criticism of journalism that emphasizes standing by one's principles as a central value. It is indeed remarkable that at the turn of the century in the cases of both German and Austrian authors of social reports their journalistic work was often closely linked to a party-political involvement in the Social Democratic Party. This is not at least true for the Austrian journalists Victor Adler and Max Winter, called "k. and k. Muckrakers" by the press historian and scientist of communication Hannes Haas.[27] This is not to belittle the value of these reports. It could be argued that it was decisive that such reports were written at all, and that the motivation to write them was of secondary importance. However, one cannot neglect that the majority of the social reports were either published in the social democratic press or in magazines with a relatively modest circulation. Even though the content and the style of the reports thus showed clear similarities with their American counterparts, the addressees and thus the importance of the reports in the sphere of public communication differed. The German-speaking social reporters mainly aimed at their own, social democratic environment and wanted to strengthen the social democratic consciousness. In the public, these reports thus were a part of a communication dominated by the parties. They were not part of a journalism stressing its independence and claiming its own importance vis-à-vis the political parties. It is thus no accident that the German reporter, Egon Erwin Kisch, translated his journalistic experiences into an involvement in party politics, without, however, ever losing his instincts as a reporter. It appears that in Germany, journalists, too, regarded the parties as having the decisive potential to criticize and influence society. Until far into the Weimar Republic, direct or "independent" support for a party seemed much more obvious to German journalists than the strengthening of the press itself as a self-reliant institution or a "fourth power".

This leads directly to the third point, namely the strength and longevity of the German party or party-partisan press (*Partei- oder Parteirichtungs-presse*),[28] which was in turn bound up with both, the long and intensive press control and the restrictive passing on of information. After the grip on the press was slightly loosened in the "New Era" at the end of the 1850s and journalists were given the opportunity to express their political principles (*politische Gesinnung*) more freely, for many there was no doubt but to support the emerging Liberal Party. Instead of hiding behind a pretended "impartiality", as journalists had long done in order to survive, journalists now defined the decided declaration of their political principles as a question of professional honor (*Standesehre*). Against this background, impartiality could not serve as a value upon which to build a journalistic code of ethics. On the contrary: since the end of the 1850s, a great part of the journalists expressed their political principles mainly by declaring their support for one of the emerging parties. Journalists regarded openly siding with a party as standing by their principles (*Gesinnungsfestigkeit*). This became a kind of ethos of the profession. In 1872, a journalist wrote in a letter to one of his colleagues that "in a circle of decent journalists" in Paris, he had recently made the claim "that there was no capital in the world where so many members of the political press stood by their principles" as Berlin.[29] Thirty years later, the editor of the journalists' magazine *Die Redaktion* asked the question: "Is the journalist a mercenary, who does not care about the flag he fights under?" He answered it at once: "No, his political convictions are an inseparable part of himself, the loyalty towards his convictions is his honour."[30] Facing the rise of the commercial mass press, the former journalist Albert Schäffle wrote that the impact of "capital" on the press must be pushed back, in order to make journalism again "a matter of parties and societies and of scientific, political and religious propaganda."[31] The Publishers' Society founded in 1894 as a defense against the new successful "business press"

(*Geschäftspresse*), in 1901 used their magazine to declare their incapability to see an advantage in impartiality: "A newspaper dedicated to entertainment and instruction, obviously does not need to declare its support for one party. A daily newspaper, however, which must devote considerable space to political issues, cannot be independent of a party without being unprincipled ('gesinnungslos')"[32]

All those, who fought so devotedly for standing by one's principles at the end of the nineteenth century shared a concept of an enemy: the supposed Americanization of the German press, the rise of the commercial mass press, the so-called *Generalanzeiger*. As in Germany in the 1870s, conditions arose favoring the emergence of newspapers addressing more than the rather limited circle of bourgeois dignitaries. These newspapers underlined their claim of impartiality: "Amongst the papers published daily in Leipzig, there is none that can rejoice in a significant circulation and none that, based on this circulation, could serve the interests of both the readers and the advertisers in their full extent", the *Generalanzeiger für Leipzig und Umgebung* ("Generalanzeiger for Leipzig and Surroundings") wrote in its program in its first issue of 7 October 1886:

> There is a lack of an evening paper, which is distributed evenly in all strata of the populations and which is read by everybody . . . Our newspaper can thus be found in almost every family in Leipzig and its surroundings. It is read by members working in all kinds of jobs and belonging to all classes of society. It is a platform of all. Showing consideration to this, the Generalanzeiger will always aim at the greatest possible objectivity and impartiality. Especially with regards to politics, the point of view of this paper will be strictly neutral and independent of any influence of party doctrines."

This claim of impartiality does not enable us to draw any conclusions as to the actual work practices. Looking at precisely these practices, however, two things become noticeable. Firstly, the attempts of many a *Generalanzeiger* to translate their program into reality can clearly be seen in the first period after their foundation. This concerns their claim of impartiality as well as their eagerness to acquire their information themselves. Even though this still cannot be compared to the practices of the English, and especially of the American press, it is unmistakable that the *Generalanzeiger* pursued a new direction. Secondly, it is noticeable that the *Generalanzeiger* gradually gave up its claim of impartiality. Under massive attack because of its supposed lack of principles (*Gesinnungslosigkeit*), it increasingly declared its leaning towards certain parties rather than self-confidently strengthening its impartiality as Anglo-American papers had done. In this context, it is interesting that, in some ways, it was the journalists and not the publishers who had their way. Contrary to the widespread opinion that the publishers of the *Generalanzeiger* kept their journalists under the yoke of a political colorlessness, in many cases, it were indeed the journalists who, if the circulation was right, steered their papers back into party politics.[33] When new commercial papers were founded, the massive criticism by journalists, other press critics and not least by the publishers of the traditional newspapers trying to defend themselves against the new competitors, quickly stopped such direct claims of impartiality as the one of the *Leipziger Generalanzeiger*. As the *Berliner Morgenpost* founded by the Ullstein publishing house remarked in its program in 1898: it wanted to be "somebody who took sides – not a partisan mouthpiece" ("Parteinehmer – nicht Parteigänger"). This was a reaction to the criticism of the supposedly colorless and unprincipled *Generalanzeiger* without, however, declaring support for a party.[34] Leopold Ullstein, however, who had founded the *Berliner Zeitung* in 1878 thus laying the foundation for the success of his publishing house, was, at the time, a member the Fortschrittspartei (Progress Party). Moreover, in the 1870s he was also a member of the Berlin town council (*Stadtverordnetenversammlung*). Publishing papers as successful as the *Berliner Zeitung* and later the *Berliner Morgenpost* and the *Berliner Illustrirte Zeitung*, it was, however, out of the question to have too close connections to any party. Still, the essentially left-liberal stamp of the Ullstein newspapers remained recognizable until the end of the Weimar Republic. Something similar can be said about the Mosse publishing house, the home of the *Berliner Tageblatt*. It is indeed remarkable that no German publisher followed the English model and tried to make money out of the claim of impartiality after the Generalanzeiger had been labeled as "unprincipled" (*gesinnungslos*). Even the publishing house of the Generalanzeiger magnate Huck, basically the home of the supposed "lack of principles", did not follow its own program in all consequences. Like the other *Generalanzeiger*, the Huck newspapers, too, increasingly took political sides and presented various liberal standpoints, without, however, adopting one single point of view. The new ordering of the political parties at the beginning of the Weimar Republic meant that the newspapers of the Huck-combine moved into the area of the DDP (German Democratic Party). This development was particularly fostered by the Berlin correspondent of the Huck papers, Richard Bahr, who took up a key-position in the combine. He had close connections to the right wing of the DDP, especially to Hermann Dietrich, and he regarded himself as a link between the DDP and the press, feeling close to the Party.[35] The publishing house does not seem to have prohibited these party-political advances. Rather the new head of the combine, the son of its founder August Huck, was himself in close contact with the head of the DDP and of the Deutsche Staatspartei (German State Party). Against this background, the Hugenberg combine does not seem so extraordinary. In 1916 it bought up the Scherl publishing house and then many other newspapers and shares in newspapers to push its goal of a collective movement of the right under the leadership of the DNVP (German National People's Party). With regards to its size, its complexity and its enormous structure, branching out into all areas of the media in Weimar, there can be no doubt as to the extraordinary position of the combine. However, in trying to combine in his newspapers the primacy of political attitudes with commercial success, Hugenberg did not differ fundamentally from other press combines, even though he had special financial means and with special success. Thus it needs to be underlined that it was not simply the commercialization and the American-ization of the press that made possible a combine such as that of Hugen-berg. Rather, the problem of the development of the German press was that the press did not use the opportunities commercialization offered in a way that would have provided the press with a greater weight in relation to the political parties.

# Conclusion

For reasons of clarity, the differences between the development of the German and the American press were analysed quite trenchantly. An important argument was that the early commercialization of the American press formed a central element in the dynamic development of American journalism. On the other hand, the strict discouragement of this kind of commercialization was an important part of the German journalistic code of ethics, the main feature of which lies in the great significance it attached to the value of standing by one's principles. Despite the importance attributed to the commercialization with regards to the development of journalism and of the press, this should not merely be regarded as an economic argument. For the resistance to "commercialization" that can be observed in Germany in the late nineteenth and early twentieth centuries certainly did not mean that German publishers did not want to make money with their newspapers. The fight against the so-called *Generalan-zeiger*, the German form of a commercialized mass press, was also a fight of the traditional publishers for their market position, which was based on addressing a fairly pre-defined group of people. In their opposition to the newspapers aiming at a mass-readership the interests of the independent yet clearly liberal newspapers met with those of the Catholic and Social Democratic Party press with each of them aiming at their own clientele. On the other hand, it has to be said that despite the rise of the mass-press in the United States, plenty of politically partisan papers continued to exist, mainly at the regional level. Their impact on the development of a journalistic code of ethics, however, was far from being as decisive as that of the comparable German press. The second reason for arguing that the emphasis on the significance of commercialization cannot merely be reduced to economic factors lies in the context of the commercialization. It was not an isolated phenomenon but it was only against the background of other processes that it gained the importance stressed previously.

In conclusion, it is necessary to recall the four aspects responsible for the different development of the German and the American press. Firstly, the shaping influence of the restriction of the freedom of the press and of information could be demonstrated with various examples. Although the extent of the freedom of the press cannot be used as a monocausal explanation for the differences between both countries, it nevertheless played an important role. Censorship and other measures employed to restrict the freedom of the press, however, did not only delay the development of the press. Censorship in particular also contributed to the fact that the press as such remained a political matter for such a long time. In this context, it is important that the gradual success of the freedom of the press in Germany since the 1860s offered more opportunities to make use of the freedom of opinion than of the freedom of information. This, in return, was the reason why journalists became much more involved with providing opinions rather than information. Correspondingly, the willingness to pass on information to journalists was reduced considerably. At the beginning of the twentieth century, Germany was thus a long way away from a freedom of information.

The freedom to associate in societies and parties was closely connected with the development of the freedom of the press. While the different processes of the formation of political parties in Germany and in the United States of America can be regarded as the second factor influencing the development of journalism and the press, again this argument is not exclusively about the delayed development of Germany in comparison to the United States. Fundamentally, it is true for both countries that the newspapers and journalism had a central role in the period of party building. In the terms of systems theory, it could thus be said that, at first, journalism emerged as a part of the system politics. In times of a great politicization of society, be it in the context of the American Revolution or of the German Revolution of 1848 or be it against the background of the gradual success of the citizens' rights since the 1860s, the development of the press was not only pushed ahead considerably, but the press also became the mouthpiece of various social groups and parties. The potential of social self-organization, which characterized the press in those periods of politicization, however, was transferred to the political parties to the same extent to which they formed organizations and stabilized them. In Germany and in the United States, this process not only took place at different times, but also in different ways. Thus in the United States during the Revolution, a comparatively stable, bipolar party system emerged. While it changed only very little in the course of the nineteenth century and remained essentially bipolar, in Germany a multifaceted party system often with very strong organizations emerged. Without wanting to offer a detailed discussion, it must still be mentioned that these two systems of parties also reflected two very different societies. For our purpose, however, it is important that a press more or less closely connected with the parties emerged. The bipolar, American party system meant that, in the United States, this process resulted in a petrifaction of the press earlier than in the broader and more differentiated, German party system. It was, therefore, not a lack of pluralism that the German public suffered from at the turn of the century. An impartial coverage possibly based upon extensive, independent research, however, emerged in Germany, compared to the United States, only at its beginning. The impact the press could achieve on its own account was thus much lower in Germany than in the United States. To express it once more in the terms of system theory: the German press and German journalism remained intimately connected with the political system long after the turn of the century. The inner dynamism of the media, which cause scientists of communication and the media today to talk about the media in system theoretical categories, were developed to a much greater extent in America than in Germany at the turn of the century.

Against this background, the commercialization of the press must be regarded as a third aspect. Both the greater freedom, which the American press enjoyed from early on when researching information, and the relative petrifaction of a party spectrum reduced essentially to two parties offered comparatively advantageous conditions for the development of a commercialized mass press with the consequences described above. The fourth aspect, the journalistic code of ethics worked as a kind of link between the conditions shaped by the structures described on the one hand and the different journalistic practices on the other. This code of ethics was not unchanging, but it was closely bound up with the entire development of journalism and the press. The argument is that the emergence of a specific code of journalistic ethics was, on the one hand, influenced by the various aspects mentioned above. On the other hand, however, it developed a shaping influence itself, not only on the press, but especially also on the structure of public communication in general. For the way German journalists regarded their profession and practiced it did not contribute to building a potentially independent counter-weight to the parties and other societies. They rather saw to it that the positions particularly of the parties but also of some lobby groups were especially well represented in the process of public communication. Admittedly, the journalistic code of ethics must not be the same as their journalistic practice. The connection between the two, however, cannot be overlooked. It cannot be without consequences for journalistic practice if the work of a reporter is regarded as the basis of all journalistic work or if it is looked at as a lowly esteemed supply work. Equally, the ethos of standing by one's principles has different consequences from the ethos of independence, even though – and this cannot be emphasized enough – there might be huge gaps between people's ideals and claims and the reality. It goes without saying that, with the various waves of commercialization and the emergence of new newspaper combines, the press became dependent not only on potential advertisers, but also on supposed and actual interests of the readers. The discussion of these aspects belongs to the central topics of a history of the media in the twentieth century. The United States and the supposed Americanization of the media remain a central point of reference for the writing of this history.

# Notes

1. As a first detailed discussion of American journalism regarded from a clearly German point of view: Emil Dovifat, *Der Amerikanische Journalismus*, Berlin, 1927.

2. For the view of America in the ending nineteenth and early twentieth centuries see: Alexander Schmidt, *Reisen in die Moderne: Der Amerika-Diskurs des deutschen Bürgertums vor dem ersten Weltkrieg im europäischen Vergleich*, Berlin, 1997.

3. See, for example, Emil Löbl, *Kultur und Presse*, Leipzig, 1903; Walter Hammer, *Die Generalanzeiger Presse kritisch beurteilt als ein Herd der Korruption*, Leipzig, 1912; Karl Bücher, *Gesammelte Aufsätze zur Zeitungskunde*, Tübingen, 1926; Emil Dovifat, "Generalanzeiger," in

W. Heide (ed.), *Handbuch der Zeitungswissenschaft*, Leipzig, 1940/41, pp. 1217–32.

4. Jürgen Habermas, *Strukturwandel der Öffentlichkeit*, Frankfurt a. M., 1990, originally published: Neuwied, 1962.

5. For a full discussion see Jörg Requate, *Journalismus als Beruf: Entstehung und Entwicklung des Journalistenberufes im 19. Jahrhundert – Deutschland im internationalen Vergleich*, Göttingen, 1995.

6. For basic orientation toward the history of American journalism and of the American press see Frank Luther Mott, *American Journalism: A History of Newspapers in the United States through 260 Years, 1690 to 1950*, New York, 1950; Edwin Emery, *The Press and America*, Englewood Cliffs NJ, 1972; Sydney Kobre, *Development of American Journalism*, Dubuque IA, 1969.

7. See, for example, Donald Stewart, *The Opposition Press of the Federalist Period*, Albany NY, 1969; Jerry Knudson, *The Jefferson Years: Response by the Press, 1801–1809*, Ph.D. dissertation, University of Virginia, 1974.

8. David Sloane, "The Early Party Press: The Newspaper Role in American Politics, 1788–1812," *Journalism History* 9 (1982), 18–24.

9. Ibid., p. 18.

10. Niles' Register, 19. February 1825 (XXVII, 286), quoted from Mott, *American Journalism*, p. 168.

11. Mott, *American Journalism*, p. 167.

12. Quoted from Kobre, *Development of American Journalism*, p. 233.

13. *North American Review* 102 (April 1866), 375f.; quoted from Mott, *American Journalism*, p. 385.

14. For contradictions, see *Nations*, 8 May 1866, 584–6.

15. Beside the standard works on the history of the American press see Leonard on the general development of the report in the United States. For a very good survey over various aspects of the feature and its development in German see Rolf Lindner, *Die Entdeckung der Stadtkultur: Soziologie aus der Erfahrung der Reportage*, Frankfurt a. M., 1990, especially 17–49.

16. See Riis, *The Last*, pp. 119–121. On Riis see Lane; on the significance of the feature for the emerging modern urban culture see Gunther Barth, *City People. The Rise of the Modern City Culture in Nineteenth-Century America*, New York, 1980, pp. 58–109.

17. Jacob A. Riis, *How the Other Half Lives. Studies among the Tenements of New York*, New York, 1890; see also Susan Henry, "Reporting 'Deeply and at First Hand': Helen Campbell in the 19th Century Slums," *Journalism History* 11 (1984), 18–25.

18. See Isabel Ross, *Ladies of the Press*, New York, 1974, 48–59.

19. The term "muckraker" was first used by Theodore Roosevelt in a speech in 1906, to mark journalists, who, in his opinion, only wrote about corruption and scandals, and did not have anything good to say about their country. Opinions about the time of end of the "muckraking-era" vary between 1912 and 1917. From the broad literature on muckraking see especially Louis Filler, *The Muckraker: New and Enlarged Edition of "Crusaders for American Liberalism"*, Chicago, 1968; John M. Harrison and Harry H. Stein, *Muckraking: Past, Present and Future*, University Park, 1973; Robert Miraldi, *Muckraking and Objectivity*, New York, 1990.

20. The report was published as a book soon afterwards. On Ida Tarbell see K. Brady, *Ida Tarbell: Portrait of a Muckraker*, New York, 1984; Mary Tomkins, *Ida E. Tarbell*, Boston, 1974.

21. Lindner, *Die Entdeckung der Stadtkultur*, p. 42.

22. Decision of the central court (*Reichsgerichtsentscheidung*), 16 December 1881, court decision 5, 239, quoted from K. Ulrich, *Die Wahrnehmung berechtigter Interessen bei der Beleidigung in § 193 StGB*, Ph.D. dissertation, Göttingen, 1908, p 34; see also E. P. Obenholtzer, *Die Beziehungen zwischen dem Staat und der Zeitungspresse im Deutschen Reich*, Berlin, 1895; for a summary of the laws and of the jurisdictional framework of the German press see Requate, *Journalismus*, pp. 244–64.

23. See Ulrich Klug, *Presseschutz im Strafprozeß: Ein Rechtsgutachten im "Spiegel"-Verfahren*, Berlin, 1965.

24. M. Reiner, *My Life in Germany: Before and After January 30, 1933*, 8ff., Houghton Library, Harvard University, Manuscript Collection bMS Ger 91 (182).

25. See Paul Göhre, *Drei Monate Fabrikarbeiter und Handwerksbursche*, Leipzig, 1891.

26. Friedrich G. Kürbisch (ed.), *Dieses Land schläft einen unruhigen Schlaf: Sozialreportagen 1918–1945*, Berlin and Bonn, 1981, p. 9ff.; see also F. G. Kürbisch (ed.), *Der Arbeitsmann, er stirbt, verdirbt, wann steht er auf? Sozialreportagen 1880–1918*, Berlin and Bonn, 1982.

27. Hannes Haas, *Empirischer Journalismus: Verfahren zur Erkundung gesellschaftlicher Wirklichkeit*, Vienna, 1999, p. 246; see also Haas, "Die hohe Kunst der Reportage: Wechselbeziehungen zwischen Literatur, Journalismus und Sozialwissenschaft," in: *Publizistik* 32 (1987), 277–94.

28. The terms "party" and "partisan press" refers not only to the press directly owned by a party but also to newspapers that openly declare their support for a party, while often, especially in the case of liberal newspapers, stressing their independence from the party at the same time. For further information see Requate, *Journalismus*, p. 290ff.

29. J. Amter to Wilhem Wehrenpfennig, undated (1872), Geheimes Staatsarchiv Berlin-Dahlen, NL Wehrenpfennig, C IV 3 (uncounted sheets).

30. "Im Anfang war die Tat", *Die Redaktion*, 15 October 1902.

31. Albert Schäffle, *Bau und Leben des sozialen Körpers*, 4 vols, Tübingen, 1875–8, vol. 3, p. 521.

32. *Der Zeitungsverlag*, 23 February 1901, p. 66 (Hvhb.i.O.).

33. See Requate, *Journalismus*, p. 374ff.

34. *Berliner Morgenpost*, 20 September 1898; also see Peter de Mendelssohn, *Zeitungsstadt Berlin*, Berlin, 1982, new edition with additional material, first edition 1959.

35. See Kurt Koszyk, *Deutsche Presse im 19. Jahrhundert II: Geschichte der deutschen Presse*, Berlin, 1966, p. 259ff.

# 12
# Who is Afraid of Modernity? Germany and the United States in the Era of the Penny Press

## *Jessica C. E. Gienow-Hecht*

European travelers to the United States around the turn of the century consistently commented on the power and efficiency of the American print media. In an interview with a Boston newspaper, in 1893, musical artist Arthur Nikisch from Berlin lamented the slowness of the German press while commending United States' newspapers on their breadth, entrepreneurship and speed. Nikisch related the story of a Leipzig resident whose father lived in Connecticut. The father in America typically received groundbreaking news from Berlin half a day earlier than the daughter in Leipzig, even though Leipzig was less than three hours by railway away from Berlin, while the trip to the United States consumed several days. Nikisch did not attribute the local delay to press censorship but to the sloppiness of German journalists. They were "too sleepy-headed to get out a special edition" and, instead, chose to report the news in the next regular edition on the following day. In contrast, Nikisch commended the *Boston Herald*, which had enabled him to read an article pertaining to the recent great fire just minutes after he himself had observed the firemen rushing to the site.[1]

Transatlantic perceptions on the role of the media have long constituted a source of fascination for international travelers, critics, and long-term visitors alike. The papers by Kusmer and Requate address this issue in the context of modernity, even though, at first sight, their essays do not seem to overlap theoretically or factually. One talks about poverty, the strains of modernization, and the uneasiness on the part of those who have with those who have not. The other explains, on both the comparative as well as the interactive level, how our ideas and perceptions about the media (and what they should do) are very much shaped by the culture that produces them.[2]

As Kenneth Kusmer explains, nineteenth-century editors typically labeled vagabonds as lepers and as lazy slugs, addicted to crime and to

225

booze. Until the end of the century, media observers invested little time in examining the causes for widespread homelessness but stereotypically attributed poverty to individual "moral failure," caused by the poor themselves. As a result, critics typically demanded harsh punishment of those who seemed to aimlessly roam the American landscape. Only at the end of the nineteenth century did writers become aware of the complex social transformation ushered in by the nation's urbanization, industrialization, and the massive influx of immigrants, a transformation that was beyond the control of the individual. Progressive turn-of-the-century writers such as Theodore Dreiser and Jack London reattributed a sense of dignity to the vagabond whom they often portrayed as a victim of his or her environment rather than an agent of moral decay. Still, most middle-class observers reacted to this realization with a sense of disturbance if not escapism that led many to view homelessness as an exciting alternative form of existence far away from the nervous pace of modern city life. By 1920, the vagabond had become a romantic incarnation of all those values and qualities that American business men (and with them most of the American people) seemed to lack most: time, leisure, contemplation, and adventure in the wilderness. In doing so, Kusmer concludes, authors and the public at large did not only deprive the homeless of their human dignity but also conveniently sidestepped the reality of widespread poverty as a result of the growing income gap throughout the nation.

Kusmer's paper sheds new light on a topic well familiar to historians of transatlantic tourism. Specifically, his account underlines the ignorance of many European observers vis-à-vis the economic pitfalls of the American dream. European observers commented incessantly on the fact that there seemed to be less poverty in the United States than in Europe (particularly in big cities) and that Americans seemed to work harder, even if they were already well off. The above mentioned Arthur Nikisch, for example, stated that

> The average people of this country are much better off than the common people of Europe. I was much surprised at the number of people in this country who possess property. This state of well being, which prevails all through the United States, is an element of great importance in the creation and maintenance of musical taste. All moderately well to do people in this country can afford to attend concerts and thus encourage musical enterprise.[3]

Victorian Americans loved to read such accounts poured out by pro-American foreigners.[4] In the eyes of most nineteenth-century Americans, social problems, particular urban destitution, represented a European phenomenon. Jefferson's ideal of a country predominantly organized in rural communities, deliberately distanced itself from the slums of Europe, and the slums associated with big cities. Hence, industrial poverty was regarded in many ways as an "imported problem," accelerated by foreign immigration, urbanization, and industrialization, and spurred by an individual's failure to comply with the requirements of the American Dream, however vaguely defined.

Kusmer's tale is squarely located in the Gilded Age and the era of Progressivism. These decades saw the emergence of mass media on an unprecedented scale. It is true that newspapers and journals became affordable as mass production, technological innovations, and new forms of paper manufacturing and printing opened the way to a vastly expanded press market. Papers and magazines underwent a transformation similar to the radio, the television, and perhaps eventually the Internet. No more accessible (and of interest) to a chosen few, mass print grew into the standard form of information dissemination. Even more important (and often overlooked) in the process of modernization was the simple fact that more people than ever before learned to read in the second half of the nineteenth century. They did so not necessarily because they were smarter but because print became one of the dominant forms of communication in areas that expanded beyond the locale of the township. Commercialism represented the most important cause of growing literacy rates. In this context, commercialism did not necessarily mean studying newspapers but the acquisition of reading ability to peruse commercial documents.

In the United States, the American Revolution played a significant role in the development of a mass press. The year 1776 represented, among other things, a revolution of print, led by lawyers and intellectuals whose very legalistic arguments with Britain were published in pamphlets designed for average people. As a result, national bureaucrats grew increasingly concerned with people's ability to familiarize themselves with the laws of the new republic. One such indication was the census act for 1840, which authorized an inquiry into school attendance and illiteracy. Of course, these developments need to be considered with caution. From a historical point of view, schooling did not guarantee widespread literacy, because the schooled came from literate families. Moreover, the question on the 1840 census was ambiguous; it asked how many members of a household could not "read or write", although of course some people could read but not write. Illiteracy rates in states without public schools, such as antebellum North Carolina, was chronically high. In the American South, many farmers were self-sufficient, and to them, reading represented an unnecessary skill. Historians therefore agree that it was only with the enforcement of compulsory education in the late nineteenth and early twentieth centuries, that schools actually began to make an effort to slay illiteracy.[5] Generally speaking, then, wherever an efficient system of public schools was established, illiteracy declined.

The decline of illiteracy and the widespread establishment of a public school system were among the most important side effects in the process of modernization because both reflected a fundamental change of ideology, more so than financial ability. To put it differently, it was not just the presence or absence of public institutions of education that mattered but the motives, cultural and economic, to effect schooling. Before the Civil War, for example, the South clearly had the money to establish a public education system, and some Whigs supported this cause. Yet very few voters and congressional delegates seem to have paid attention to school education at large. Part of the reason for this was that the Old South had a slave labor force, which it was determined to keep uneducated. In contrast, seventeenth-century Puritans in New England founded a college in 1636, in the wilderness, later to become Harvard University. Massachusetts even passed a compulsory education law in the early 1850s, although compulsory education laws were famous for not being enforced and the states that passed them were already states with high literacy. States with low literacy did not get into the act until the twentieth century. That included most of the South, where the school system was not modernized till after 1910 or so, and then only for whites.[6]

In a cybersociety where we are confronted with print wherever we turn, it is hard to understand the radicalism embedded in this transformation. Just like even retirees today (who throughout their lives may never have touched a typewriter) feel they have to purchase a computer in order to function in a world beyond their immediate environment, people increasingly understood that in an urban environment they could not find a job, rent an apartment, go to the doctor and buy medicine, or just find out what happened if they did not know how to read. Kusmer correctly points to the rapid disappearance of the "walking city" and it is important to bear in mind that the census of 1910 reported that for the first time more people lived in cities than in rural areas. If there was one characteristic about the new urban centers throughout the industrialized world, it was that there seemed to be print everywhere, on price tags, in shop windows, on advertising pillars, in stores, saloons and everywhere else in public life. Print promised the ability to advertise yourself and to interact with others in a world where people did not know each other any more and where things changed all the time. As a result, as David Tyack and others have shown, the modern American school system with its insistence on a standardized rudimentary form of education for every citizen (though still a far cry from the Jeffersonian ideal of an informed citizenry) emerged during precisely those years.[7]

There is no discounting about the fact that this transformation to a mass print society formed one of the pillars of modernization throughout the Western world as it enabled communication (and consumption) on a supra-local level. This is the background for the two essays presented on journalism and the problem of modernity. Without readers, a mass press, however biased it may have been in Germany or the United States, is unthinkable. As more and more people learned how to read for information purposes, a broad public now received news and with them, critical assessments of news, through the medium of a mass press. Without this development, there might have been a debate on poverty and vagrancy as Kusmer describes it, but this debate would have been limited to the middle classes. In line with a rigorous behavioral code that emphasized seriousness, self-righteousness, didacticism, and competition, Victorian American writers restricted their analysis to judgmental morality and authoritarianism; hence the debate would have been far narrower.[8] It would not have included a broad public (what Kusmer calls "the average citizens"); two generations earlier, many of these "average people" participating in the debate would not have been able to read a paper.

The same is true for the object of Jörg Requate's essay. Comparing the development of the press in Germany and the United States since 1800, Requate reviews peculiarities evolving in both countries. During the nineteenth century, he explains, the press gradually distanced itself from an openly partisan coverage of politics in favor of "fact" and objective reporting, much of which was tied to sensational feature reports. This transformation culminated, after 1900, in a generation of muckrakers who exposed the evils of party machines, power politics and business moguls, thereby establishing themselves as a "fourth power," an agency of non-partisan control and exposition. Requate elaborates on the reception of muckraking in Germany and the protests against "America" as the icon of modernity. Censorship, we learn, was not simply enforced by authoritarian civil servants who feared confrontations with the press. Even more so, it was pushed by journalists who believed in partial reporting as an ethos and proudly distanced themselves from the commercially driven sensationalism marking the United States press market around the turn of the century. The extent of press freedom, the commercialization of the press, and the distinct nature of the party systems in both countries, Requate concludes, account for a different development of the press in

Germany and the United States. Ironically, even in Germany the very commercialism local journalists worried about responded to a new demand coined by people's ability and eagerness to read the printed word. In consequence, the influence of the press as a "fourth power" (be it outside the governmental structure or at the service of a political party) could only materialize because of the rapid development in education.

On a footnote, it is ironic that the differences portrayed by Requate even prevailed in the face of the United States' massive democratization program in Germany after World War II. As Norbert Frei and others have shown, the reorganization of the media figured as one of the key ingredients in Germany's imposed "democratization" in and after 1945. "Democratization" (later "reeducation" and still later "reorientation") meant the attempt to turn every individual German into a responsible citizen who would have an independent political and critical opinion while subscribing to the principal pillars of a democracy.[9] American officials sketched the application of the German press as an essential component of re-education – one of the very few points upon which all four Allies agreed. First, the entire Nazi press and propaganda system was to be completely dismantled. Each power would then distribute press licenses to German anti-Nazis. When German editors seemed to be "democratic enough" the press market would finally be opened to free competition.[10] More than the other occupation powers, United States' press officers opposed the revival of German local newspapers (Heimatzeitungen) and party publications – the very kind of journalism that Requate identifies as the core of the German media system – and, instead, they insisted on the separation of news and opinion.[11] Even though historians continue to disagree over the success and failure of these efforts, there is no denying that German newspapers both from a structural as well as a design-oriented point of view continue to differ from the American model.[12]

Despite their different areas of concentration, the essays by Kusmer and Requate complement each other in important ways. First, while Requate insists on the increasingly independent and fact-oriented nature of journalism in the United States, Kusmer gently points to the limitations of this development and, implicitly, warns us not to rush to hasty conclusions about progress and improvement. For all the muckraking and feature reporting exhibited by authors such as Mencken, Flynt, Cochrane and countless others, books, essays and news reports exposing poverty managed to preserve the status quo and the peace of mind on the part of the more affluent classes by portraying homelessness in either romantic or despicable terms. Independence from political parties, that is, did not entail independence of the mind. Second, and more importantly for the purposes of this volume, both papers share a common interest in the public discourse on the downside of modernization. By 1900, on both sides of the Atlantic Ocean, the fascination with "things modern" increasingly gave way to a rather skeptical and, as in the case of the German journalists, negative assessment. The concern with social problems resulting from rapid industrialization with all the sensationalism and reluctant partiality exposed in both papers, thus formed one of the principal topics of interest for a socially mixed mass society. To put it more bluntly, the first issues addressed by a medium open to different social groups, were pain, sorrow, and corruption.

Both papers alert us to the subjectivism exhibited in the debate. When commenting on the pitfalls of modernization, German observers unfailingly referred to the United States, and, as the nineteenth century came to a close, less and less as a model and increasingly as a scenario to avoid. Connotations of "modernity" and "American" became virtually synonymous. This criticism could not only be found in the field of journalism and public opinion but in virtually every aspect of life, economics, social reform, demographics, industrialization, and consumer culture. Volker Depkat's research on the image of America between the two French revolutions as well as Alexander Schmidt-Gernig's study on "travels into modernity" in the late nineteenth century have alerted us to the crucial aspect of subjective references in these assessments.[13] These analyses show how images of America were interwoven with already prevailing discourses on local concerns such as the future of the family, freedom, progress, tradition, and cultural identity, an observation that can easily be applied to the specific case laid out by Requate.

In a way, then, the German reception of muckraking said at least as much about Germany as about the United States. For one thing, the debate mostly underscored the need to preserve the status quo. For another, the German journalists' response to muckrakers like Mencken and others reflected the tremendous anxiety contemporary observers exhibited in the face of the unrestrained power of capitalism, an anxiety they shared with their great grandchildren, notably the revisionists of the New Left who likewise were ready to limit the market along with the power of the press.[14] Requate cites Habermas as one of the principal critics of a commercialized press. It is open to speculation whether there is much of a difference between the commercialism and sensationalism of the United States muckrakers rejected by turn-of-the-century German journalists in favor of political outspokenness (note that they are not in favor of censorship), and the commercialism and sensationalism of the post-World War II German tabloid press attacked by the generation of 1968. I do think it is ironic, though, that we tend to see the former as arch-reactionaries who did not value freedom of speech (which they didn't) while hailing the latter as progressive thinkers at the dawn of a new age.

When viewed in tandem, both authors (unknowingly) point to one of the fundamental paradoxes in the international discourse on moderniza- tion, and one in which to my knowledge historians have not been particu- larly interested. Modernization meant many things to many people. Besides economic and industrial developments, it also encompassed intellectual thought, artistic expression, and the power to kick the old masters off their pedestal.[15] Around the turn of the century, European conservatives did not only reject the mass press and the terror of commer- cially driven public media. They began to resent on a very general level everything that they perceived as the menace of American culture. European critics such as William Stead, D. H. Lawrence, and Adolf Halfeld were among the first to give a voice to all those fears that have since become so commonplace around the world.[16] Fears that United States culture, standards and way of life would overrun everyone else's. Fears that American consumer products would erase other countries' cultural independence. Fears that American culture would extinguish local identities. To many observers, American civilization was not just different but formed a subversive threat to European culture at large.[17]

Curiously, and this is where the paradox begins, at precisely the time when people everywhere began worrying about the "Americanization" of the world, no one worried so much about cultural identity and modernity as Americans themselves.[18] Daniel Rodgers and Axel Schäfer have shown how in their search for the most pressing social questions marring American cities, United States intellectuals and reformers looked to Europe to examine social programs developed abroad.[19] Yet for all their interest in European strategies, American reformers realized preciously little of their newly acquired knowledge once they returned to the United States. In every great economic crisis moment during the twentieth century, notably during the Great Depression of the 1930s, the Great Society of the late 1960s, and the recession of the 1990s, Americans retreated to the recognition that the peculiarity of their culture and their country prevented them from adopting the European model.

More importantly, critics did not just focus on the obvious downside of modernization such as seasonal poverty as described by Kusmer. Instead, just like Europeans began to dread the massive influx of US artifacts and its presumably annihilating impact on their national cultures, Americans felt threatened by the preponderance of foreign cultures and foreign ways of life.[20] Middle-class Americans were profoundly disturbed not just by foreign-looking lower-class immigrants but by the influx of European culture at large, including secessionist expressionism, French naturalism à la Emile Zola, and the tunes of Gustav Mahler. Their anxiety did not so much reflect profound disgust as a fundamental frustration with the fact that despite their military and industrial power, the United States was unable to knit an independent brand of modern artistic production. European cultural agents, so the argument went, suffocated the emergence of a genuine American culture. And as a result, American critics increasingly rejected modern art, modern music and modern poetry.

Nowhere was this rejection more obvious than on the musical scene where since the 1850s, European, notably German, artists and compositions had ruled supreme. Decades before the Great War, American musicologists cited the "Teutonization" of the American music scene and deplored the fact that the country had fallen prey to the sounds of Wagner, Brahms, and Richard Strauss while ignoring the works of Henry Fry, George Chadwick and Edward Macdowell. A nation without music was a nation without soul. That was a troubling scenario in an age obsessed with the image of the nation state as an organic body. A soulless nation did not simply lack culture but it was no nation to begin with, let alone one that could compete with other hegemonic powers.[21] And as the century came to a close, United States art critics stirred up their complaints about the American love affair with foreign cultural artifacts. "We always import – especially in music," observed the *Musical Courier*, in 1909. "It sounds so much better when it is imported, just as imported Frankfurter tastes so much better because it is imported than our healthy, succulent American sausage . . . We yell and hurrah for America and then we rehearse our orchestras in German because we import them, instead of educating our own bright and dashing and joyous American boys to play in them."[22]

When World War I broke out in Europe in August 1914, American cultural critics' first reaction was a profound joy over the fact that European artists were less likely to travel across the Atlantic and "impose" their craft on Americans; finally, indigenous art – however bad – would enjoy the chance to prove itself. "The path is clear for the first true *practical* demonstration of our latent powers in the country's artistic annals," *Musical America* announced in August 1914. "Competition of the sort that stifled and paralyzed is ruthlessly shattered and crushed." United States concert halls, art museums, and theater stages suddenly seemed within reach for an armada of American artists. No longer could young artists travel abroad in order to finish their creative education. No longer could collectors look for expensive paintings abroad. And no longer could conductors peruse European novelties. All talent had to be found at home.[23]

The interesting story, then, about the attack on modernity in Europe and the United States, and its interplay via the mass media emerges when we examine in tandem the debates exhibited in both Kusmer's and Requate's essays. Even among journalists, modernization meant different things to different people. A composite evaluation as proposed above reveals that fears of corruption or a different way of life represented mere side-effects of a phenomenon that, at its core, focused very much on national culture and national identity. Such fears did not just cause sleepless nights to European observers (where historians consistently refer to Germany as the most anti-modernist and anti-Western camp) but throughout the Western world, including the one country that was most identified as the incarnation of modernity at large.

In the end, such fears even affected Arthur Nikisch whose enthusiastic comments on the United States press we encountered at the beginning of this essay. Surrounded by the modern celebrity cult that later generations would associate with twentieth-century music directors like Arturo Toscanini and Leonard Bernstein, throughout the musical world, Nikisch was known for his mesmerizing style of conducting and his eclectic music programs. When he was hired as the musical director of the Boston Symphony Orchestra, in 1889, the *American Musician* scolded that the Boston Symphony Orchestra had failed to solicit American names and American conductors to compete with Nikisch for the position. Four years later, the departure of Nikisch caused wild speculations as to his successor and one Boston paper noted that "it is a singular and humiliating fact that no American has been mentioned or apparently thought of as successor to Mr. Nikisch."[24] What looked like a mere labor dispute over nationality on first sight reflected, in reality, a profound trepidation on the part of many Americans to be culturally suffocated by Europe's current stars and latest productions. Modernization and the resulting anxiety was a two-way street and we are well advised to understand this complexity rather than stereotypically ascribing tradition to Europe and the future to the United States.

# Notes

1. "Arthur Nikisch," n.d. (approx. 23 April 1893), n.p., BSO scrapbooks MF 125.5/4, Boston Symphony Archives (hereafter cited as BSO).

2. In this essay, I employ the terms "modernity" and "modernization" but I do not wish to imply that they are synonymous. Following Madan Sarup's explication, modernity connotes "the progressive economic and administrative rationalization and differentiation of the social world." The idea of modernity is closely connected to the evolution of the capitalist state. In contrast, modernization "is often used to refer to the stages of social development which are based upon industrialization. Modernization is a diverse unity of socio-economic changes generated by scientific and technological discoveries and innovations." Madan Sarup, *An Introductory Guide to Post-Structuralism and Postmodernism*, Atlanta GA, 1993.

3. "Arthur Nikisch," n.d. (approx. 23 April 1893), n.p., BSO scrapbooks MF 125.5/4, BSO.

4. "Victorian" is a term commonly used in the Anglo-American (and even English-speaking) world to describe the middle-class generation both in the United States and Great Britain living through the life and reign of Queen Victoria of England (1837–1901). On the Victorian American weltanschauung see Daniel Walker Howe, *Victorian America*, Philadelphia 1976; and T. Jackson Lears, *No Place of Grace: Antimodernism and the Transformation of American Culture, 1880–1920*, New York, 1981.

5. I am indebted to Joseph Kett for these hints.

6. For further reading on literacy's history, see Lee Soltow, *The Rise of Literacy and the Common Schools in the United States: A Socioeconomic Analysis to 1870*, Chicago, 1981; Harvey J. Graff, *The Literacy Myth: Cultural Integration and Social Structure in the Nineteenth Century*, New Brunswick NJ, 1991; Carl F. Kaestle, *Literacy in the United States: Readers and Reading since 1880*, New Haven CT, 1991; and William J. Gilmore, *Reading Becomes a Necessity of Life: Material and Cultural Life in Rural New England, 1780–1830*, Knoxville TN, 1989. Gilmore investigates the motives to acquire a sufficient amount of literacy to read. Soltow examines the role of schools in this process. Kaestle focuses his account on the spread of reading, though not the spread of literacy.

7. On the development of the public school system in the United States, see David B. Tyack, *The One Best System: A History of American Urban Education*, Cambridge MA, 1974. For adult education, see Joseph F. Kett, *The Pursuit of Knowledge under Difficulties: From Self-Improvement to Adult-Education in America, 1770–1990*, Stanford CA, 1994.

8. Daniel Walker Howe, "Victorian Culture in America," in Howe, *Victorian America*, pp. 3–28.

9. "Report of a Conference on Germany after the War," called by the Joint Committee on Post-War Planning, April, May, June, 1944, reprinted in Helmuth Mosberg, *Reeducation: Umerziehung und Lizenzpresse im Nachkriegsdeutschland*, Munich, 1991, pp. 171–81; Richard Brickner, "Is Germany Incurable?" *Atlantic Monthly* 171 (1943), 84–93.

10. Harold J. Hurwitz, *Die Stunde Null der deutschen Presse: Die amerikanische Pressepolitik in Deutschland*, Cologne, 1972, pp. 36, 41, passim; Michael Balfour, "Reforming the German Press, 1945–49," *Journal of European Studies* 3 (1973), 268–275.

11. Norbert Frei and Johannes Schmitz, *Journalismus im Dritten Reich*, Munich, 1989, pp. 186, 280ff., 291; Heinz-Dietrich Fischer, *Parteien und Presse in Deutschland seit 1945*, Mainz, 1971, pp. 49–51; Frei, "Die Presse," p. 276; Kenneth-Raymond Nelson, *United States Occupation Policy and the Establishment of a Democratic Newspaper Press in Bavaria, 1945–1949*, Ph.D. dissertation, University of Virginia, 1966.

12. For a review of the debate, see Jessica C. E. Gienow-Hecht, *Transmission Impossible: American Journalism as Cultural Diplomacy in Postwar Germany, 1945–1955*, Baton Rouge LA, 1999, pp. 2–8.

13. Alexander Schmidt, *Reisen in die Moderne: Der Amerika-Diskurs des deutschen Bürgertums vor dem Ersten Weltkrieg im europäischen Vergleich*, Berlin, 1997; Volker Depkat, *Amerikabilder in politischen Diskursen: Deutsche Zeitschriften von 1789 bis 1830*, Stuttgart, 1998.

14. Herbert Marcuse, *Der eindimensionale Mensch: Studien zur Ideologie der fortgeschrittenen Industriegesellschaft*, Neuwied, 1970, p. 19; Daniel J. Czitrom, *Media and the American Mind: From Morse to McLuhan*, Chapel Hill NC, 1982.

15. William B. Scott and Peter M. Rutkoff (eds), *New York Modern: The Arts and the City*, Baltimore, 1999; Christine Stansell, *American Moderns: Bohemian New York and the Creation of a New Century*, New York, 2000.

16. Jessica C. E. Gienow-Hecht, "Shame on US? Cultural Transfer, Academics, and the Cold War – A Critical Review," *Diplomatic History* 24 (Summer 2000), 466–79.

17. D. H. Lawrence, *Studies in Classic American Literature*, New York, 1950, pp. 9–21; Adolf Halfeld, *Amerika und der Amerikanismus: Kritische Betrachtungen eines Deutschen und Europäers*, Jena, 1927; Mary Nolan, *Visions of Modernity: American Business and the Modernization of Germany*, New York, 1994, pp. 26, 113–14; Frank Costigliola, *Awkward Dominion: American Political, Economic, and Cultural Relations with Europe, 1919–1933*, Ithaca NY, 1984, pp. 19ff., 167–83, 264ff.

18. The most comprehensive account of Progressive reform remains Robert M. Crunden, *Ministers of Reform: The Progressives' Achievement in American Civilization, 1889–1920*, New York, 1982.

19. Axel Schäfer, *American Progressives and German Social Reform: Social Ethics, Moral Control, and the Regulatory State in a Transatlantic Context*, Stuttgart, 2000; Daniel T. Rodgers, *Atlantic Crossings: Social Politics in a Progressive Age*, Cambridge MA, 1998.

20. John Higham, "The Reorientation of American Culture in the 1890s," in John Weiss (ed.), *The Origins of Modern Consciousness*, Detroit MI, 1965.

21. Jessica C. E. Gienow-Hecht, "Music and Emotion in German-American Relations since 1850," Habilitationsschrift, Martin-Luther-Universität Halle-Wittenberg, 2003.

22. Blumenberg [*sic*], "By the Editor," *Musical Courier*, 15 December 1909, p. 22, NYP press excerpts, 1909–10, Gustav Mahler/*Musical Courier*, New York Philharmonic Archives.

23. "European Musical Life Paralyzed by War," *Musical America*, 8 August 1914, Fritz Kreisler collection, 17/17, Music Division, Library of Congress, Washington DC.

24. Newsclip, n.d., n.p., BSO scrapbooks, M.125.5/3, BSO. The list of candidates included Edouard Colonne, Hans Richter and Felix Mottl with Richter in the lead. "Arthur Nikisch," n.d. (March 1893), n.p., BSO scrapbooks M.125.5/4, BSO; "About Hans Richter," n.d. (approx. 14 April 1893), n.p. (*Journal*?), BSO scrapbooks, M.125.5/4, BSO; "The Nikisch Matter, *American Musician*, 29 September 1889, BSO scrapbooks, M.125.5/3, BSO; Marc A. De Wolfe Howe, *The Boston Symphony Orchestra, 1881–1931*, Boston MA, 1931, p. 90.

# 13
# "Muckraking" in Germany and Austria: A Unique Tradition?

## *Markus Behmer**

Kenneth Kusmer gives a comprehensive report about how homelessness developed in the United States between 1850 and 1930 and how the American public perceived this problem. He also writes about the reservations that existed towards the common tramp, in society as well as in the media. Giving numerous impressive examples, he points out some stereotypes that were dominant in literature, newspapers and magazines in particular, and he shows how the perception of the type of a tramp changed at least gradually (along with the general change of the social circumstances) and that there were some differentiating descriptions of the social problems, even if they were not at all predominant.

Jörg Requate presents a brief and vivid abstract of the development of media and journalism in Germany and the United States during these stirring decades, and he precisely points out essential differences. These were, for example, the ongoing partiality in German journalism, and the rise of the tabloid press in America, but also the development of investigative journalism claiming to support social reforms. Homelessness existed in Germany, too – at every time, and especially during the period of time between 1880 and the beginning of World War I that we will focus on here – even if the number of tramps was much lower than in the United States. Tramping, "Landstreicherei", was even liable to prosecution, according to Article 361, Paragraph 3 of the Criminal Code, which was released in 1871.[1] The public image of the tramps was mixed. While they were despised as outlaws and scum, they were at the same time also perceived as a romantically heroic type, above all in numerous novels after the turn of the century.[2]

Homelessness is and has always been a symptom of extreme social hardship, in America as well as in Germany. Since the end of the eighteenth century the increasing misery of the lower classes has been a serious

*Translated by Franz Ertl and Lucia Bauer-Ertl

topic in Germany. Poverty, says the famous German historian Thomas Nipperdey, "became a mass phenomenon around 1830. It stopped being an individual problem and became a collective one".[3] The term "pauperism" was coined for this phenomenon. New jobs were created in the era of industrialization, which started rather late in Germany, but the pay was even below the living wage. Yet with the population steadily increasing and more people moving into the cities and areas of industrial concentration, the social problems became more and more urgent. These problems were the starting point of the socialist movement in the middle of the nineteenth century – a development that can be discussed in only a few words here.

It was in the newspapers of this socialist movement, in the workers' press, where investigative journalism and social reporting in the German language region developed – a long time before Egon Erwin Kisch, the famous "running reporter" (*rasender Reporter*), who brought (together with others) the news report to quite some reputation during the Weimar Republic. In my opinion, Paul Göhre, who was mentioned by Jörg Requate, is not the unique exception as he was described. It is largely undisputable that reporters like him had much better working conditions and better platforms in Austria than in Germany.

Max Winter, who was also mentioned by Requate, is a good example. He is generally considered a "genius of the social report"[4] and quite rightly so (but he had been forgotten for a long time and he's still largely unknown). Here is the introduction to one of his articles:

> To be homeless, jobless and hungry like the others . . . I wanted to have that same experience. So once again I put on my shabby coat and strolled out to the 10th district. Wandering slowly and languidly like someone who is coming home after having looked for a job without success or feeling like a homeless person who returns to the district where his last dwelling had been – I drag myself to the market square. There's "Puchsbaumgasse", a lane that promises me something, me and all the others who are forced by their misery to wander in the same street – a bowl of soup and slice of bread.[5]

It is the beginning of a rather typical piece of investigative journalism, written in 1901 at the peak of the American muckraking movement. Disguised as a homeless person, Winter moved into a hostel for homeless people in Vienna. By playing this role he was able to investigate the conditions in the hostel, and he included a lot of background information; this approach was quite similar to an investigative reporter's approach of the muckraking era in the United States. Winter published this story – and hundreds of others like it – in the *Arbeiter-Zeitung* (*Workers Newspaper*) in Vienna. And he was not at all the only one.

Thus it can be confirmed that there was something like muckraking, there was investigative reporting in Central Europe, too, in Austria and (although to a lesser extent) in Germany. However, it cannot be denied that the importance of social reporting in America was very different from that of (at first sight) similar phenomena in the German speaking countries in Central Europe. In his rough outline Requate demonstrates why this type of journalism had no real chance of developing in Germany. First – in short – because the long tradition of strict press control had a permanently restraining effect; second, there was a highly restrictive information policy in all aspects of public life and reporters suffered from an extremely bad reputation; and third, the party press and partisan or party-orientated press had such a strong impact that the expression of certain political views became dominant in journalism and completely suppressed the journalists' code of ethics. Investigative journalism based on objective facts could hardly develop.

Basically, I agree with that. As early as 1927 Emil Dovifat, one of the most influential German communication scholars, pointed out the significant difference between both press systems in one of the first German scientific studies about American journalism. The German press, he says:

> has always been a press based on political views that commits itself to a certain program, tries to fight and win over people and gain support for this program, thus dropping the American business principle of attracting as many readers as possible . . . That has an effect on the editors. On average they are not business-men selling news or hunters of news, their job ideal is not "der rasende Reporter", the reporter who hunts the news, as the Americans say, but the publicist in charge.[6]

All the reservations that were expressed towards this type of reporter were concisely summed up at approximately the same time (1928) by Otto Groth, one of Dovifat's colleagues. According to him, reporters are often people who "are not inclined to a regular job, who have little education and are not socially trained, sometimes social misfits with a dubious past, careless and unreliable, even corrupt and without a conscience."[7] It is exactly what Requate describes by saying that in Germany the work of a reporter was "regarded as undignified snooping around." Nevertheless there were good reporters, investigative journalists with a social con-science who, like Winter, were forgotten for a long time and were hardly noticed by communication science. That has changed to some extent. There are a few anthologies that deal with – mainly Austrian – journalism, for example the impressive collection of reports published by Friedrich G. Kürbisch[8] (as mentioned by Requate) and the volume *Sensationen des Alltags: Meisterwerke des österreichischen Journalismus* (*Sensations of Every Day Life: Masterpieces of Austrian Journalism*), edited by Wolfgang R. Langenbucher.[9] There are also some scientific studies about social reporting in Germany before the Weimar Republic; apart from the recently published profound work by Hannes Haas[10] (see Requate) there is Michael Geisler's 1982 publication *Die literarische Reportage in Deutschland* (*The Literary Report in Germany*), which is also worth mentioning.[11]

Haas meticulously examines the development of the social report, its roots and its effects – even on sociology, which, especially in America (as Jörg Requate mentioned, too) vastly gained from the muckraking movement. Elsewhere Haas explicitly deals with the question whether there were relations between or a mutual influence on American and German social reporters, concluding that at least they knew of each other. Egon Erwin Kisch (but rather late in the era of the Weimar Republic) was familiar with the works of John Reed and Upton Sinclair and wrote prefaces for some of their books, which reached a high circulation in the 1920s. Arthur Hollitscher, a social reporter from Berlin (born in Hungary), was in touch with several American muckrakers when he stayed in America before the World War. He was introduced with the sentence: "He is a good muckraker."[12] "But," as Haas continues, "the fact that they knew about the others' existence didn't influence the contents of their reports and their ways of working, because the German social reporters could rely on a long tradition in their home country."[13] This tradition can be followed back to Georg Forster, Heinrich Heine, Bettina von Arnim or Friedrich Engels. One author is repeatedly mentioned as the "raw version (Rohguss) of the report":[14] Georg Weerth (who later was in charge of the feature pages of the *Neue Rheinische Zeitung* edited by Karl Marx). In 1843/44 Georg Weerth published a number of letters containing "Sketches of the Social and Political Life of the British" ("Skizzen aus dem sozialen und politischen Leben der Briten") in the *Kölnische Zeitung*. In these letters he used those very methods – role plays, on the spot investigation, background information – that later became characteristics of the muckraking reports. However, he was still an exception. This form of the social report was more or less institutionalized in the above-mentioned *Arbeiter-Zeitung* (*Workers' Newspaper*) in Vienna, which was founded in 1899 by the leader of the Austrian Social Democrats, Victor Adler, who was also its editor. In this paper Adler himself wrote quite a number of social reports, just as the above-mentioned Max Winter in particular. So did a lot of other reporters.

There were however significant differences between the German (and Austrian) and the American muckrakers. In fact, the German-speaking authors of social reports were normally connected to the Socialist or Social Democratic Party; consequently partiality was an important feature of many of their texts. Their content was nonetheless thoroughly investigated. The media were different, too. In Europe, it was the workers' press, often newspapers and magazines with a small circulation, in America it was magazines such as *Collier's* and *McClure's* that were read nationwide and had a high circulation. These different papers and magazines were aimed at different audiences, too. In Germany it was the working class that was to be mobilized by these texts, in America it was basically the middle class whose attention was to be drawn to social problems in their immediate environment. Yet the approach of social reform that was characteristic of the American muckrakers was also typical of their German-speaking counterparts. They may have contributed very little to the development of German social science, but some of them became politically active themselves. There were above all Victor Adler, who – shortly before he died – became the first Secretary of State of Austria, and Max Winter, who participated in a number of social projects, became a member of the Reichsrat (Parliament) and in 1919 vice mayor of Vienna. With the Nazis taking over in Germany and the development of Austro-Fascism, followed by the *Anschluss*, the annexation by the Third Reich, many of the reform-orientated journalists were exiled and investigative journalism in their own country was made impossible. Totally impoverished, Max Winter died in Hollywood in 1937; Arthur Hollitscher died in a home of the Salvation Army in Geneva in 1941. However indirect, it is a rather sad connection between the German "muckrakers" and one of their themes – homelessness.

In conclusion I would like to sum up my thesis: there were in fact significant differences between American journalism and German journalism at the end of the nineteenth and the beginning of the twentieth century when "Americanization" conjured up the image of an unscrupulous business and sensational American press in Germany (but people were fascinated by it at the same time), but there was also investigative journalism with a social reformatory impetus in Germany and – and this is even more important – in Austria. There were obvious differences in detail, but this phenomenon was similar to the muckrakers' journalism in the United States. Yet they developed independently from each other and showed different characteristics; it cannot be said that journalists in Germany and Austria closely followed the American example.

# Notes

1. This regulation remained valid for more than a hundred years and through all the different political systems in Germany. In the Federal Republic of Germany, it was not abrogated before 1974.

2. See, for example, Hermann Bahr's *O Mensch* (1910), Hermann Hesse's *Knulp* (1915) and many others with less literary importance.

3. Thomas Nipperdey, *Deutsche Geschichte 1800–1866: Bürgerwelt und starker Staat*, Munich, 1983, p. 220. For more information on the social problems in the nineteenth century see pp. 219–48.

4. Hannes Haas, "Die hohe Kunst der Reportage: Wechselbeziehungen zwischen Literatur, Journalismus und Sozialwissenschaft," *Publizistik* 32 (3/1987), 277–94, 289.

5. Max Winter, "Vor und in der Wärmestube," *Arbeiter-Zeitung* 17 December 1901; reprinted in Friedrich G. Kürbisch (ed.), *Der Arbeitsmann, er stirbt, verdirbt, wann steht er auf? Sozialreportagen 1880 bis 1918*, Berlin and Bonn 1982, pp. 81–90.

6. Emil Dovifat, *Der amerikanische Journalismus*, Berlin, 1927, newly edited by Stephan Ruß-Mohl, Berlin, 1990, pp. 212–213.

7. Otto Groth, *Die Zeitung: Ein System der Zeitungskunde (Journalistik)*, Berlin, 1928, vol. 1, p. 418.

8. Kürbisch (ed.), *Der Arbeitsmann, er stirb, verdirbt, wann steht er auf?*

9. Wolfgang R. Langenbucher (ed.), *Sensationen des Alltags: Meisterwerke des österreichischen Journalismus*, Vienna, 1992.

10. Hannes Haas, *Empirischer Journalismus: Verfahren zur Erkundung gesellschaftlicher Wirklichkeit*, Vienna, 1999.

11. Michael Geisler, *Die literarische Reportage in Deutschland: Möglichkeiten und Grenzen eines operativen Genres*, Königstein im Taunus, 1982.

12. Quoted by Haas, *Die hohe Kunst der Reportage*, p. 288.

13. Ibid.

14. Geisler, *Die literarische Reportage in Deutschland*, p. 220.

# Part IV
**Producing and Consuming Radio:**
**Political and Social Dimensions**

# 14
# Radio Days: Did Radio Change Social Life in Germany and the United States?

*Inge Marszolek*

Back in the 1970s, Freddy Mercury wrote his radio reminiscence that became one of Queen's Classics, titled *Radio Ga Ga*. It was aired and listened to on both sides of the Atlantic. In this song, Mercury describes himself as a lonesome boy, watching the device's light and listening to the radio tunes during the nights, the radio being his only friend and only connection to the outer world. At that time radio was, on one hand, a nostalgic medium being superseded by television as the new leading mass medium. On the other hand, it played a central role in propagating the music that was so important for the shaping of the rebellious youth cultures of this period.[1]

Already at this point it is clear that the question above is a rhetorical one. The answer is obvious. Yes, radio did shape everyday life in both societies. The image of the lonely listener, sitting in front of the apparatus, perhaps staring at the light controls of the receiver, may suggest a wrong way of how radio penetrated into social life, hiding the complex net of politics, economy and technology. Here we need some more investigative work. As Freddy Mercury's song shows, radio users often produce a different narrative. To refer to Michel de Certeau, we have to understand the process of appropriation as social practice: "Diese ist listenreich und verstreut, aber sie breitet sich überall aus, lautlos und fast unsichtbar, denn sie äußert sich nicht durch eigene Produkte, sondern in der Umgangsweise mit den Produkten, die von einer herrschenden ökonomischen Ordnung aufgezwungen werden."[2]

A history of the radio must do more than merely describe the adaptations of the media to the ongoing changes in culture and politics. The political situation after World War I with its dramatic social and political disruptions was crucial for the emergence of the radio as a hyper-national media, as Michele Hilmes points out.[3] Thus the potential of the radio as an instrument in the nation-building process was very much welcome by all governments. We have to write the history of the radio by focusing on the frame behind the medium itself, understanding the medium in its complexity, seeing the apparatus as well as the user, the discourses shaping and shaped by the power structure as well as the grammar of the public and the private spheres.

## How to Establish a Comparative Design in Media History

First of all I would like to share some methodological reflections concerning historical media studies in general and the comparative design in my paper. Looking just at political history, the differences between the German and the American case are overwhelming. In Germany from 1920 to the 1950s we are dealing with two democratic and two dictatorial systems, one short period of Allied occupation, not to mention World War II and the Holocaust as well as the Cold War and its impact on both Germanies after the war. In the United States we are speaking about different presidents, different policies, but of course of one democratic system. Even from the perspective of the organization of broadcasting in Germany and in the Unites States again the differences come to mind. From its beginnings, radio in Germany was a public medium, although in the 1920s, very much embedded in governmental policies, it became a propaganda tool for both dictatorships and a public radio again in the Federal Republic. In the United States, broadcasting became central in establishing the consumerist society and was thus organized along the demands of the market. Of course the history of the radio in Germany has to tell the story of catching up with the technology as well as the distribution and the programming of broadcasting in the Unites States and Great Britain. The gap became very significant after World War II, as in the Unites States television had already taken over, whereas in Germany this was only the case at the end of the 1950s (West) and in the beginning of the 1960s (East), but at a closer look, similarities emerge and the political disruptions seem to have had less of an effect on the media itself and the ways in which radio was consumed.

Being a global player, radio was always discussed in its potential to cross all borders, (this is true as well for the telegraph as for the television). Despite this, media history still remains caught in national contexts. I think that the time has come to open the fields for cross-national media history.[4] However, seeing the thrilling aspects of this new field of media history, one has to cope with many difficulties. Comparative history has up to now limited itself to comparing what I call the solid facts, for example, the different institutions, the power structures, the decision-making processes in two or more systems. For a comparative analysis in the media field, this would mean restricting the analysis to the building of the institutions, the impact of the government on radio, the dissemination of the radio sets, and so forth. Even though this sort of comparison would have to cope, in the German and American cases, with difficulties concerning the differences described above, not to mention the different levels of research, I suggest an approach which concentrates on the complexity of the media itself, focusing on the organization, the technology, the programming as well as on the consumer practices and routines.[5] In doing so, I would like to draw on two different methodological streams in media studies.

Anglo-American cultural studies and media ethnologists have enhanced the role of the consumer: Media messages can be decoded only if the consumers are familiar with their central symbols and patterns from their own experiences in their everyday life. Decoding these messages happens in an individual, sometimes even subversive way.[6] The German media historian, Knut Hickethier, has suggested we understand the radio as a *dispositif*, following the French film theoreticians with their descriptions focusing on the relations between subjects and devices.[7] Hickethier emphasizes the importance of the listeners' experiences in interaction with radio technology and programming, referring to the understanding of the idea of a *dispositif* as developed by Foucault, which allowed Foucault to link the discourses to social practices and the power structures. This is the way in which he describes the anatomy of power. Hickethier underlines that the socialization of the electronic mass media is written into the apparatus. French film theoreticians, namely Jean Louis Baudry,[8] have developed the triangle apparatus – spectator – program, establishing the subject as part of the *dispositif*, thus allowing us, as Michaela Hampf describes in her comment, to improve our knowledge of the often neglected consumer practices: because the content of the program depends on the apparatus as well as on the context of its use, regarding the *dispositif* may empower us to understand the approbation logics of the media consumer. Foucault himself defines the *dispositif* as a heterogeneous ensemble containing discourses, institutions, buildings, controlling decisions, laws, scientific statements and so forth.[9] Focusing on the *dispositif* genealogy of technology, program and listener/spectator, we can analyse the perception of the media as well as its societal configurations.[10]

Based on these preliminary remarks I suggest the following framework. Whereas Cultural Studies were sometimes prone to underestimate the impacts of the industry and the state, or neglected the importance of social or cultural capital for the consumer practices, preferring a model of soft hegemony, Foucault thinks of the *dispositif* as an integral part of the power system. Stressing the radio as a producer and distributor of discourses, the perceptions, imageries and the ways in which they define cultural production, come into view. Thus the practices of politics become central to the analysis. The emergence of radio was accompanied by debates about the mass subject and the blurring of the borders between private and public spheres. These debates are going on and lead us to rethink our understanding of private and public which includes our recurrence to a liberal bourgeois notion of the public sphere by neglecting the inherent contradiction to the mass-mediated public. Focusing on the discursive fields in which the radio fuels, produces and transmits discourses, and thus plays an active part in the structure of the microphysics of power, we might gain some clues, which may shed new light on these debates.

A discursive approach to the audiences might bridge the gap between the audiences invented by the media, by the politicians, and so forth, and the interactions between the listeners and the media. By decoding the media messages, new meanings are produced. These may be integrated into partial discourses or even create new ones, which shape the hegemonic discourses as well as the social practices. So again, the power structures come into view. The notion of the *dispositif* as an ensemble, mapping the technology, the device, the programming, and the listening in a discursive field, opens up the comparative frame and makes the coordinates flexible.[11] In this understanding, the comparison may even contain discursive fields for one case, which do not exist or are less dominant in the other case. In the following I will try to unfold my comparative analysis along these methodological remarks. Considering the many blind spots on the map of radio history in Germany[12] – the situation in the States seems much better – the risks of a cross-national analysis, and the limitations of an article, I see myself on a very slippery slope.

# The Emergence of the New Media: The Organization of the Broadcasting System

Wireless communication was developed before World War I and achieved its technological perfection through the research and development efforts of the military industry: in both countries radio broadcasting started after the war and has to be clearly distinguished as a new medium. The first radio transmissions – in the United States in November 1920, in Germany in October 1923, were only three years apart, but the differences in the development of broadcasting were significant.

First of all, although further research still has to be done for the German side, the linkages between the wireless technology and early broadcasting in the Unites States are much stronger than in Germany.[13] Early wireless technology was widely spread in the Unites States, where all over the nation thousands of amateurs, mostly schoolboys, were experimenting with the new technology. Unlike in all other countries, regulations came only as a reaction to the collision of two ships, in which wireless communication played a central role in saving lives, and was enforced after the catastrophe of the *Titanic*, when Congress passed the Radio Act in 1912. During the war it became crucial for the navy to gain control of the airwaves. Yet after the war, Congress was eager to roll back the wartime federal powers, but at the same time gain an important role for America in the development of radio communication technology. Thus the Radio Corporation of America (RCA) was founded, and it was the RCA that saw the potential of the radio becoming a "household utility" like the piano and the phonograph. Other companies joined in order to explore the future of the "radio music boxes". Thus the model for organizing the radio was the wireless telegraph, with free access to the airwaves, orientated along both the needs of the amateurs as well as the interests of the highly competitive selling industries.

The first transmission was on 4 November 1920, reporting on the Harding-Cox presidential election by the Westinghouse Company. Yet this transmission did not seem very spectacular: it was not even mentioned by the *New York Times*. This is significant for the early perception of radio, which was not perceived as a new medium. Only when at the end of 1921 the industry could supply the customers with sufficient radio sets, the number of radio stations exploded. In the period between 1922 and 1936, many of the fledgling radio stations were ill equipped and undercapitalized. The market was swamped by the demand for radio devices.

As with the telegraph, listeners demanded some sort of regulation because of interference from stations, which was hampering the quality of reception and the programs. This made the need to establish a certain control of the airwaves obvious. Again, although the debates circled around government controlled radio to paid broadcasting – which would be achieved by granting temporary licenses through the government to gain public control – commercial broadcasting was already so deeply entrenched, that the Radio Act of 1927 provided only for weak state interference. The state granted the licenses but left the stations free to choose the channels. Again the necessary regulations were made by the market. This period saw the stabilization of the national networks. During the Depression, due to a lot of the smaller companies collapsing, there was a shift toward larger corporations becoming involved in the program production of the national network. At the same time non-commercial broadcasting was badly undermined. The Federal Communications Commission had neither the power nor the inclination to interfere in commercial broadcasting.[14]

Thus, at the end of the 1930s all elements that were to characterize American broadcasting could be found: ". . . the alliance of advertizers and commercial broadcasters, who dominated programming over national networks, an oligopoly of manufacturers making radio equipment, a weak, administrative type of federal regulation, and the widespread diffusion of receivers in American homes, where they served increasingly as centers for family life."[15] As in the United States, Germany also utilized the model of wireless communication for the organization of the radio, and again it was the experience of World War I that pushed the radio. The British and American models also influenced Germany.[16] The Reichspost, which had already been responsible for the wireless, seemed the appropriate institution to organize a public radio from which the industry was excluded and which distanced itself from direct political influence.[17] The broadcasting system was financed through fees paid by the listeners. This system largely excluded working families from the audiences. Although the scope of the radio quickly increased (compared to the Unites States, the difference is not that great) it remained an upper class medium until 1933.[18]

The hegemonic political discourse in the Weimar Republic was organized around a clear distinction between the state and (party) politics. Though the influence of the state – the Reichspost had the majority of votes in all transmission corporations – was clear, the state was considered as "neutral", beyond all "egoistic party interests". One might say that with the first broadcasting regulation Act from 1926 the idealist state philosophy had triumphed again.[19] Broadcasting committees in which the societal groups were represented decided on the contents of programming. Practically, this construction left aside all left-wing parties as well as the trade unions. In contrast to the situation in the United States, German radio was organized and implemented from top to bottom, with clear state regulation and supervision from the beginning. Despite its claimed distance from party politics, the political programming propagated the official governmental positions, while critical voices were excluded by censorship. Only after 1928, with the great coalition, the radio opened itself to the social democrats, but four years later, Reichskanzler von Papen centralized and nationalized the broadcasting system, turning it overtly into a tool of the government. Six months later the Nazis found a medium most suited to their needs. With the *Gleichschaltung* some of the journalists were dismissed, partly for racial reasons, partly for political ones. The directors of the regional stations were replaced by dedicated members of the NSDAP. Reichspropagandaminister Goebbels made clear from the beginning that he regarded the radio as the "most modern and most important instrument to influence the masses, a true servant of the *Volk* working to unite the German people in a common vision."[20]

Besides the complete control over a centralized broadcasting system, the most important step was the introduction of the *Volksempfänger* (people's radio set) by the Nazis. Already in the beginning of the decade German broadcasting industries had had plans for a serially produced, cheap device. Goebbels himself supported the big companies in their plans, and in April of 1933 twenty-eight companies signed an agreement to share the market in producing an inexpensive radio set. The government decided to exempt those buyers with low income from radio license fees and to induce them to purchase radio sets by implementing an installment regime. Without going further into details, the success of these combined actions was that the radio found its way into workers' households as well as into the rural regions.[21] At the same time, the *Volksempfänger* was imbedded in the Aryan discourse in shaping the Volksgemeinschaft and became one of the icons of modernity for the regime.

After the defeat of the Nazi regime and the end of World War II, German broadcasting was under the control of the Allied Forces. In the first months after the war, radio became the most important instrument of communication between the Allies and German society as newspapers did not exist. It was seen as a central tool in the process of reeducation and denazification.[22] In the Western zones the rebuilding of public broadcasting mirrored the public service model of the United Kingdom, taking into consideration the parallels to the Weimar Republic and the knowledge of the entanglement of industry and Nazi regime and the economic situation in postwar Germany. This system was effective even though Adenauer's government struggled to control the medium. In Eastern Germany, the SMAD (Soviet Military Government) and the German communists favored a centralist broadcasting model based upon the principles of party lines and shaping of socialist society. Thus the organization of radio was central to the communists' attempts to create the socialist society and was affected by the cleansing waves in 1949/50 and 1952.[23]

# Linking Hegemonic and Media Discourses: Inventing Citizenship, Community and Nation

Since the founding of the United States, Americans have worried about their social and ethnic cohesion. In the early 1920s, two generations of rapid immigration, industrialization, urbanization, and technological changes had widened the ethnic, social and cultural differences as well as the gap between huge cities and rural regions. The Depression at the end of the decade fueled these anxieties. The idea of the radio (and before radio, that of wireless communication) and later on television, contained the utopian imagery of a tool for social unification,[24] and was perceived as a remedy against the threat of an opening of the social and cultural divides, not only by the intellectual elite but also by many listeners.

Central keywords in the intellectual discourses were the concept of community in an industrialized society where old bonds of personal relationship were transformed into rational impersonal interactions, and linked to it the imagined dichotomy between "crowd mentality" and citizenship, the latter being based on the competence of independent thinking.[25] Whereas the intellectual discourses were underlined by a profound pessimistic attitude, the broadcasting unfolded these views in a different, more optimistic way. Again different partial discourses emerged:

1. The radio as educator of the citizens.
2. The radio as unifier of the classes and of blue- and white-collar workers.
3. Inventing the nation by the politics of good taste.
4. The radio as the ethnic unifier or a means of re-assessing white hegemony.
5. Unifying the society by the transformation into a consumer-community.

This was very different from the German situation, as I will show below, in that the broadcasters were dependent on their audiences and the industry. There was broad consent about the pedagogical potential of the radio, but the educational broadcasting stations, mostly run by universities and other tertiary organizations, vanished from the airwaves at the end of the decade. The national networks had to combine educational value with commercial interests, and as some of the programs became successful, the presumption that educational programs were unpopular was challenged in the late 1930s. Nevertheless Craig comes to the conclusion that the radio educators were unable to influence programming significantly.[26] Instead the stations chose to inform listeners: The onset of the Depression and the New Deal gradually established the news as part of the programming, the worsening crisis in Europe and the threat by the Nazis demanded a bigger share (10 per cent in 1938–9).

In 1930, Merlin Aylesworth, head of NBC, declared that the radio presented an ideal way "to preserve our vast population from disintegrating into classes . . . We must know and honor the same heroes, love the same songs, enjoy the same sports, and realize our common interest in our national problems . . ."[27] It is significant that Aylesworth chose the imagery of popular culture to re-create social cohesion as a common frame of reference. As Michele Hilmes argues, the self-imagery presented by the commercial stations as the "nation's voice" was so successful that this became part of the hegemonic discourse.[28] Between 1932 and 1948 the serial show *Vox Pop*, incorporated by NBC in 1935, traveled along in search of the "voice of the people".[29] Thus network radio explored the new mass-mediated national public, helping to reshape national identity along with constructing the average American in a consumer society based on consensus. By doing so, the broadcasters explored the borderlines, and produced and readapted codes of exclusion and inclusion. Being on the show and the listeners' ability to identify themselves with the performing voices became pivotal in the process of shaping the audience and the nation.

In the early radio days racial issues did not seem to concern American radio – until the war the broadcasting programming relied heavily upon traditional cultural forms, thus reaffirming white hegemony. The first truly national hit, *The Amos'n'Andy Show*, which swept the country in 1928, was transported from minstrel characters into the radio and created a new world eagerly shared by most listeners.[30] Partially because of the positive impact of the show, it triggered a sometimes-turbulent debate among Afro-Americans, exploring the representations of black from a white perspective. Despite the fact that one of the pleasures of the show for whites came from its racial voyeurism, the perception was multifaceted; as Susan Douglas shows, there was a renewed fascination with black English and many catch-phrases of the show found their way into the everyday language of the listeners.[31] Ironically, when the serialization of *Amos'n'Andy* became a model, a lot of the black bands and orchestras as well as actors were replaced by white musicians and performers. These were the years when Swing got white, and when the representation of the negro as a "simpleton" and so forth became the stereotype in the media until World War II.[32]

Only with the onset of the war did anxieties about national cohesiveness lead federal officials to foster a broader notion of inclusiveness for the sake of national unity. One of the results was the production of a national broadcast series *Americans All, Immigrants All*, which was based on a narrative construction of success of immigration of African-Americans and Jews in an Anglo-Saxon nation. For the African-Americans, this series opened the possibility to pursue their political issues of inclusion and freedom on radio. During the war the race question became crucial for the War Department – but attempts to construct radio programming around the discourse of racial unity were thwarted by Southern conservatives in Congress. At the end of World War II and the beginning of the Cold War Afro-Americans took advantage of the international spotlight on the country's policies of segregation and racial discrimination: programs that tackled racial issues were transmitted by national broadcasting although they simultaneously promoted white voices on racial questions. Only two local stations – one in New York City and the other one in Chicago – redefined the dreams of freedom and equality of the Afro-Americans, by using black voices on the airwaves. Thus it was in and by the radio that the construction of race relations was reassessed, introducing equality and freedom as the crucial issues. Here the intertwining relations between mass media and the political discourses come into view.

Any discussions on the close relationship between politics and mass media must include the "fireside chats" of Franklin D. Roosevelt. Roosevelt not only became the first political star of the radio age, but the New Deal's publicity campaign used the radio as an important instrument in promoting the President's policies. The range of Federal Agencies Network Programs was wide and combined educative, entertainment and political functions. But the best propagator was the President himself. Roosevelt not only possessed a radio voice but became a radio persona. In his chats he created a sense of intimacy, referring to himself in first person and addressing his audiences familiarly as "you". Thus he made use of the essence of the radio, which blurred the borders between private and public, transporting the outside world into the domestic sphere and creating a broadcast intimacy even between the President and the listener(s).

As already mentioned above, broadcasting in Germany was invented along the dominant lines of a culturally conservative discourse in which the needs of national cohesiveness were used as a defense against the threat by political parties' impacts. The cultural anxieties in Germany – seen against total defeat in World War I, revolution that swept away the Emperor, and inflation, reflected the deep moral, cultural, economic and political crisis, and were much more traumatizing to Germany than to the United States. At the core of the culturally conservative discourse in Germany was the fear of masses and of modernity, both identified with Americanization and democracy. Referring to German-ness as a cultural nation with its classical heritage and to the German *Geist*, seemed a remedy against the threats of mass-culture and Anglo-American civilization. These debates were written into the early history of the radio.[33] With the approval of many politicians and broadcasters, the German pioneer of broadcasting and state secretary for the radio, Hans Bredow, praised the new media as an educational tool, which "helped to keep the adolescent children in the house and away from the ruinous impacts of the streets and the pubs".[34] Unlike the American case, educational programs such as lectures, as well as classical music and literature played a large role in the programming, especially in the evenings. The common understanding was that the radio should promote the education in citizenry (*Staatsbürger*) by imparting high culture to the listeners. In the view of Carsten Lenk, listening to a radio-concert, was similar to going to the opera: families got dressed up, and listened to the concert from home, inviting friends over.[35] Popular music radio entertainment was mostly banned from the waves; classical music as well as lectures were dominant until the late 1920s. Thus the radio in Germany reaffirmed the ideals of the *Bildungsbürgertum* (educated classes).[36]

To shape the new *Volksgemeinschaft*, a term that was widespread in the cultural conservative discourse and by no means an invention of the Nazis, radio programming was made relevant to the different regions, thus mirroring the basic principle of its structure. Fostering the dialects, folklore music and various representations of regional culture meant not only a rejection of the urban mass culture – only sports were an exception – but a return to an organic prehistoric cultural unity of German-ness, shaped by the Germanic tribes.[37] At the end of the decade, with the great economic crisis, radio programming enforced this imagery of the *Volksgemeinschaft*, so when the Nazis took over, they underlined the concept of *Volksgemeinschaft* by their racial anti-Semitic discourse.

The Nazis, however, especially Reichspropagandaminister Goebbels, not only understood the radio as the most powerful instrument of propaganda, but were also fully aware of the potential and character of the medium. Thus, Nazi broadcasting not only kept jazz – in the smoothened tunes of white swing – in its programming until 1937,[38] but developed genres of entertainment programs that took over American and British models in combining music and comical sketches, and so forth. Older forms of comical imagery, mostly gendered jokes, were adapted in these programs. As far as we know, they were mostly designed along the lines of regional differences, unifying the German tribes into the organic Aryan *Volksgemeinschaft* beyond and above class and citizenship.

Radio played a very active role in constructing and representing the *Volksgemeinschaft*. The simulation of being present and taking part in the emotional setting on stage of the Nazi community, was enforced by the role the broadcasting played within the central events by which the regime celebrated itself; for example on the occasion of the first Nazi May Day celebrations in Berlin, the radio covered the event with a 24-hour broadcast, and the speeches of Goebbels and Hitler on the Tempelhofer Feld in Berlin were transmitted by public loudspeakers to the marching masses in all towns and villages.[39]

The discourses of racial exclusion and anti-Semitism were marginalized in the programming: focusing on the setting of the Nazi *Volksgemeinschaft* those who were excluded, did not have a voice. Anti-Semitism was dealt with in lectures, but Jews were not represented on stage, were excluded as listeners (from 1940 onwards) and as existing persons. Unlike the print media, which dealt regularly with racial politics, not only against the Jews but, during the war, also against the Russian *Untermensch*, thus reinforcing the racial measures, the radio refrained from presenting the enemies of the *Volksgemeinschaft*.[40] A good example is the request concert (*Wunschkonzert*), which became the most popular program during the war. The issue was to unify the home front with the warfront. Combining classical and popular music, anecdotes from the front, with announcements of the donations made by the women at home and transmitting the names of the new-born children to their soldier-fathers and thus to the nationalized community, it reconfirmed the *Volksgemeinschaft* from inside, without mentioning the racial enemies.[41]

In contrast to Franklin D. Roosevelt, Hitler had a lot of trouble presenting himself on radio.[42] His radio speeches were not as charismatic as his public speeches; therefore most of his speeches on radio were recorded public speeches. The Führer never tried to explore the potential of the medium in creating an intimacy between the audience and himself.

The transmitted speeches, both the recorded ones and the few he gave in the studio, mirrored the ideal of the National Socialist public as presented in an advertisement for the Volksempfänger: the Führer's voice coming out of a huge device overwhelmed a mass of shapeless listeners.[43]

Shaping new identities was on the political agenda of both postwar German states, where the radio took an active part in the discourses about the position in the Cold War. Whereas in the Unites States programming the Cold War was more or less the task of The Voice of America, all stations in both Germanies perceived the "other" as an enemy. Recurring themes in Western radio stations were the discourses on shaping a new identity between West Germans and refugees from Eastern parts by re-adapting the Weimar imagery of folklore of the German regions, re-defining Europe and the idea of the Occident by struggling against American pop-culture.[44] The broadcasting of the German Democratic Republic was seen as a tool in building a socialist new society in direct contrast to Western decadence. The programming concentrated on the concept of ennoblement of the workers, which had been central for the workers movement in Germany from its beginnings in the nineteenth century. The unsolvable problem for the broadcasters in East Germany was to define "socialist entertainment" and to convince an audience whose listening routines had been shaped by the "Volksempfänger".[45] Those who were born during the war were now tuning in to the airwaves, which were crossing borders: There is a striking resemblance in the discourse on rock 'n' roll in East and West Germany and in the cultural conservative discourse of the 1920s.

## Inventing the Audiences

In both cases the early audiences of radio were predominantly male. In the United States there were 15,000 amateurs who regarded the listening consumers condescendingly: "After you got tired of the broadcasting stuff – Com in with us and enjoy the real radio" was an advertisement in one of their periodicals.[46] A new series of juvenile books "The Radio Boys" flourished in the 1920s. A whole series of magazines, instructing the radio fans, swamped the market. DXing, trying to get the most distant station, became a new sport to the young, white, male radio audience. Their vision of the radio as linking people (male) from one place in the Unites States to another in an interactive way was ended by business, but still marked a potential and a dream of every new medium. This was accompanied by changes in the technology that enabled the radio to become a center for family entertainment.

Like the German discourse, broadcasters and manufacturers argued that radio listening would provide domestic harmony, reinforcing family life. Some insisted that housework and motherhood would again become attractive for women, for radio would make the housework into a "fascinating endeavor". Of course the advertisers became aware of the housewife consumer. NBC told its advertisers that because 70 per cent of women were not in paid employment, they were the purchasing agents of the nation. During the day the audiences were female. "Radio mindedness" became equated with femininity, but again the opinions about these female listeners were divided. Housewives used the radio more as an "occasionally apprehended background to the noise", than as a medium of information.[47] Michele Hilmes describes how female audiences were desired and feared at the same time: "Desired because their participation was central to the basic functioning of the institution, especially as it was colonized by the program production departments of major advertising agencies, yet feared because they occupied a discursive space linked to threatening concepts of the irrational, passive, emotional and culturally suspect 'masses'."[48]

In the radio programming women were addressed within the confines of their domestic sphere. Obviously, the commercial interests of women as consumers and buyers went hand in hand with the traditional pedagogical perspective on women. Another part of programming for the female audiences was the soap operas, which became very popular in the second half of the 1930s. The soaps contained traditional female images and representations and thus legitimated and reinforced these domestic values, but they also were subversive in presenting patriarchy. Albeit offering mostly romanticizing limited way-outs, they nevertheless opened the cultural shut-ins. Radio advertisers concentrated on white women as having the greatest purchase power, the programming focused on domesticity. Broadcasters and advertisers argued that women were not interested in news, politics or economics. With very similar arguments women were excluded from most areas in the radio itself. The female voice seemed not to be apt for the airwaves. Despite the intervention of Eleanor Roosevelt, who suggested hiring female news commentators, to make women listen to the news, the national networks virtually banned women from the airwaves.

After the war, with the need for radio to redefine itself against competition from television, the stations rediscovered the "radioactive housewife". Radio stations used advertising agencies to persuade sponsors, that radio still was the better medium to catch the attention of housewives: "Among all advertising media, radio and only radio reaches people while they are at work . . . daytime radio reaches the housewife, the purchasing agent of America, during her business hours, and in her office. She is unusually alone, not distracted by other persons in the household. She hears one voice, her radio, while she works."[49] Obviously one of the great attractions of radio was the ability to bridge the divide between rural and urban life. But the rural radio market lagged far behind the urban regions until the end of the 1930s: in 1938 only 35 per cent of rural American families had a radio compared to 73 per cent of urban ones. The national networks therefore put farm programming quite low on their priorities, and the farmers often rejected this sort of program. More successful were farmers' stations with a regional program thus helping to fortify a sense of community in facing their economic crisis.[50] The local stations' programming did everything to make radio a viable and successful medium in farm households in addressing rural women.[51]

The strong coalition between broadcasters and advertisers had to convince their audiences to tune in. The programming coming from the outside world had to be translated into infinitely varied private spaces. Thus the audience seemed to be the arbiter of the new culture of listening. Networks referred to the democratic culture of America constructing their audience around good taste, improving cultural standards by mediating between the middlebrow and high culture. Trying to maximize their audience, broadcasters embedded their programming in what they thought was the mainstream of good taste, political consent and shared values. Thus the radio enforced the discourses of cultural hegemony by inventing an audience that was offered some choices within the "American System". Other voices, politically radical parties and marginalized groups were excluded. Towards the African-American audience, radio presented an imagery that insisted largely on segregation and inequality. Even jazz, which introduced black culture to the white majority, was programmed only at the request of listeners. Nevertheless it was the radio that made jazz popular.

Programming "good taste" in times in which anxieties about shattered masculinity were underlining the popular culture and public debates, did not prove easy. The confusion on the gendered order based on hetero-sexuality threatened the fragile relationship between the broadcaster, the advertiser and their construction of the audience. This was the reason why the sketch of Mae West on Adam and Eve triggered such uproar in 1937. Obviously, whereas the "lavender gentleman" was part of many a comical gag,[52] the "unruly loose woman" was a danger for the consent between radio and its invented audience, and as this audience was partly imagined as female, she had to be banished from the airwaves.

Discourses about gendered audiences in Germany were very similar to those in the Unites States. Obviously there was not such a widespread wireless movement in the early years of the radio as in the Unites States, because of state regulations, but with the appearance of radio, a much smaller movement started, which was already closely linked with it. The so called *Radiobastler* (radio amateurs) were not only attracted by the new technology and had gained their knowledge during the war, but at the same time they avoided paying the fees, charged by the German postal service. These *Radiobastler* finally became an important part of the cultural workers' movement, seeing themselves in clear opposition to the bourgeois broadcasting that excluded communists and social democratic voices from the radio.[53] Though the communist wing of the workers' radio movement in particular was highly critical of public broadcasting, propagating the utopian ideas of Bertolt Brecht in his Radio Theory,[54] it obviously never became real competition. Thus toward the end of the Weimar Republic the communist newspapers published the programming of the stations and referred to it in many articles.

With the transformation from the detector to valves, radio entered the domestic sphere. Broadcasters and manufacturers discovered the female audience; the radio was advertised as a piece of furniture, easy to handle even for women. Located in the pedagogical and moral cultural conservative discourse, the housewife again comes into view. Radio was declared the domestic friend (*der Hausfreund*), but given the ambivalent meaning of *Hausfreund* (the lover) in German, radio was also perceived as a danger for women.

Male critics emphasized the importance of correct listening, which was described as concentrated listening, as male attitude, whereas women were listening in a distracted way, doing their domestic work. As a result "radiotisme", a sort of female illness, was discovered, which meant excessive, distracted listening.[55] Special programming for female audiences was developed, mainly educational programs, addressing the housewives and adolescent girls. The conservative women's movement had a big impact on the contents of the *Frauenfunk*. Nevertheless these niches offered potential careers for females in the broadcasting system as demonstrated by the example of Carola Hersel, who invented a special program for working girls.[56] Beside these exceptions, female voices were excluded from the airwaves with very similar arguments to those used in the Unites States. Unlike the programming there, and unlike the movies,[57] the radio in the Weimar Republic did not perform the anxieties caused by the crisis of masculinity and by troubled gender roles, but restricted itself to present women in their traditional domestic spheres.

The Nazi's broadcasting followed this line: Regarding the request concert, even in war-time, women were confined to the domestic sphere – conflicting with war needs, which required women to work in heavy industry. Only in popular songs, like the song in which the female tram conductor was praised, and in movies, were other images of women propagated. Especially in the rural regions, even in times of war, the central message of Nazi broadcasting was to reconcile modernity and mass-culture with the rural communities and their bonding to the families.[58] In 1940 the painter Paul Mathias Padua presented a painting "Der Führer spricht". This painting served as an advertisement for radio salesmen as well as a poster to decorate shop windows. Padua showed a farmer's family, several generations, sitting inside a Bavarian house in front of the radio set, listening to Hitler's voice, which was placed above their heads, thus replacing the traditional statue of Jesus Christ (*Herrgottswinkel*). As in the request concert, radio enhanced the meaning of the *Volksgemeinschaft* as a family that the Führer took care of in times of war.[59]

In the broadcasting programming in the early German Democratic Republic the imagery for women's roles became more sophisticated.[60] Despite the propagated equality of both sexes, the gender roles were complementary: men were responsible for building the socialist society, while women were to shape the socialist society in nice ways, for example women should accept their responsibility for moral values, and take care of the little things that make life comfortable, such as baking cake on May Day (*Hörfolge aus unseren Tagen*). In the early Federal Republic, the ideal of the family was re-formulated by the conservative Christian Adenauer regime as a refuge after the war and the Nazi damage to the morality of the German people, and a bulwark against communism during the onset of the Cold War. The daily programming addressed a female audience, housewives and working women in their role as mothers and housekeepers. The redefining of the family as the core of the postwar and post-Nazi society was also represented in the very successful quiz shows[61] adapted from American broadcasting as well as in soap operas such as *Family Hesselbach*, where a middlebrow patriarchal family was set on stage. In both postwar societies the recurrence to traditional gender relations obviously served to calm anxieties about the future.

# Conclusions

This very rough outline offers similarities as well as differences: The similarities exist in the discursive fields covering the medium, the responses to societal conflicts, gendering the audiences and the interaction between politics and the media. Obviously, radio became a hyper-national media on both sides of the Atlantic, as Michele Hilmes points out. The differences – besides the very obvious ones, which are rooted in different organization, different political systems, and different technological development – are sometimes hidden if we look much deeper and closer into the discursive strategies. But at this juncture I would like to concentrate on two issues:

1. The discourses on the new media.
2. Radio and entertainment.

The emergence of every new medium triggers debates about its potential. These discursive narratives can be divided very clearly into those underlining the utopian effects and those stressing dangerous influence on society. In the climate of cultural anxieties, politicians, broadcasters and intellectuals on either side of the Atlantic were both optimistic and pessimistic about the new media. So, in many ways, the partial discourses were quite analogous. But referring to the broader cultural, political and economic context, the hegemonic discourses and their impact on programming itself differed a lot.

Speaking of the radio as a virtual unifier of society, the commercial radio constructed its audience as a unified consumerist society, in which different agents were discovered, along with their competence and power in purchasing. Thus national networks tried to shape their representations along the lines of the imagined audience, excluding Afro-Americans as citizens as well as radical left-wing organizations. In Weimar Germany the public radio, being embedded in culturally conservative discourse, excluded left-wing culture and parties as well as Jews (there were Jews working in the stations, but not represented in the programming). This was done because they were seen as a threat to the hegemony of the *Bildungsbürgertum* as well as to German culture: Germany should be unified as an idealized organic community. At the same time, broadcasting was perceived as a pedagogical tool – which was rejected by commercial radio. It may be regarded as an ironic turn in history that in 1945 German radio again became a pedagogical tool, now in the hands of the Allies, an instrument for re-education and denazification.

In both countries, despite the differences, radio put itself beyond the reach of the radio utopians as well as of overwhelming political or economical influence. The medium aired its messages into the private rooms, so tuning in or out became a choice. Inventing the audiences was a risky enterprise and broadcasters, politicians, advertisers and consumers were all very well aware of this. Although the mass media transport hegemonic discourses and imageries, these narratives have to be negotiated anew. Radio in the Unites States was part of discursive strategies dealing with "good taste". That means stabilizing the hegemony of middlebrow white culture. In Germany the notion of culture and Kulturnation had to be redefined after World War I. The German *Geist* had to be defended against Americanization and mass culture – from the 1920s to the 1950s. Thus broadcasters in Germany tried to re-enhance high culture using the radio. Only with the Nazis did these borderlines become blurry.

Goebbels, who certainly was well aware of the ambivalence of the radio as a propaganda tool – he emphasized the need for intelligent propaganda – attempted to provide good entertainment as well as to reconcile high and popular culture. Thus, popular music was aired into the domestic sphere as well as Beethoven, serving as virtual realms in the view and memories of many Germans against the impositions of the regime. Whereas the political speeches were transported into the public sphere, being visible parts of the settings of the Nazi propaganda, Goebbels used the mass media for acquiescence. In both postwar Germanies, broadcasters had to cope with the listening routines shaped by the Nazi regime, with their high standards in entertainment programming. At the same time, it was American popular music, jazz and later rock 'n' roll, which became synonymous with the American way of life, with freedom and a consumerist democracy. German stations did not play this popular music: West German youths were listening to AFN and later to Radio Luxemburg. Again, this challenges our view on the democratic potentials of the media as well as its being part of the microphysics of power. Tuning in or out can become a crucial question. Decoding the messages of entertainment programming like soaps or *Amos 'n'Andy*, the request concert or listening to rock 'n' roll becomes an individual and collective agenda. The ear of the listener is not innocent – he or she is part of the microphysics of power.

# Notes

1. Susan J. Douglas, *Listening In: Radio and the American Introduction, from Amos'n'Andy and Edward R. Murrow to Wolfman Jack and Howard Stern*, New York, 1999, p. 3f.

2. Michel de Certeau, *Kunst des Handelns*, Berlin, 1988, p. 13.

3. See the commentary by Michele Hilmes.

4. Kate Lacey, "Radio in the Great Depression: Promotional Culture, Public Service, and Propaganda", in Michele Hilmes and Jason Loviglio (eds), *Radio Reader: Essays in the Cultural History of Radio*, New York and London, 2002, pp. 21–40.

5. My approach is based on many discussions with Adelheid von Saldern, Daniela Münkel, Monika Pater and Uta C. Schmidt during our research project. Inge Marszolek and Adelheid von Saldern (eds), *Hören und Gehörtwerden: Radio zwischen Lenkung und Ablenkung*, 2 vols, Tübingen, 1998. A short sketch of our methodological framework is published in Inge Marszolek and Adelheid von Saldern, "Massenmedien im Kontext von Herrschaft, Alltag und Gesellschaft: Eine Herausforderung an die Geschichtsschreibung," in Inge Marszolek and Adelheid von Saldern (eds), *Radiozeiten: Herrschaft, Alltag, Gesellschaft (1924–1960)*, Potsdam, 1999.

6. See Stuart Hall (ed.), *Culture, Media, Language*, London, 1980; Peter Dahlgren, "Cultural Studies as a Research Perspective: Themes and Tensions," in John Corner et al. (eds), *International Media Research: A Critical Survey*, London and New York, 1997, pp. 48–64.

7. Knut Hickethier, "Kommunikationsgeschichte: Geschichte der Mediendispositiv. Ein Beitrag zur Rundfrage 'Neue Positionen zur Kommunikationsgeschichte'," *Medien and Zeit* 2 (1992), 27; Carsten Lenk, "Das Dispositiv als theoretisches Paradigma der Medienforschung: Überlegungen zu einer integrativen Nutzungsgeschichte des Rundfunks," *Mitteilungen des Studienkreises Rundfunk und Geschichte* 22 (1996), 5–17. In combining the focus of the research project on German radio with a discoursive understanding of mass-media I hope to establish a flexible comparative framework.

8. See Jean-Louis Baudry, "The Apparatus: Metapsychological Approaches to the Impression of Reality in Cinema," in Philip Rosen (ed.), *Narrative, Apparatus, Ideology*, New York, 1986, pp. 299–318.

9. Michel Foucault, *Dispositive der Macht: Über Sexualität, Wissen und Wahrheit*, Berlin, 1978, p. 128; see Gilles Deleuze, "Was ist ein Dispositiv?", in François Ewald and Bernhard Waldenfels (eds), *Spiele der Wahrheit: Michel Foucaults Denken*, Frankfurt a. M., 1991, pp. 153–62.

10. Some studies that refer to this concept neglect the importance of the power structure, for example Carsten Lenk, "Das Dispositiv als theoretisches Paradigma der Medienforschung. Überlegungen zu einer integrativen Nutzungsgeschichte des Rundfunks," *Mitteilungen des Studienkreises Rundfunk und Geschichte* 22 (1996), 5–17; especially Friedrich Kittler, *Grammophon, Film, Typewriter*, Berlin, 1986.

11. I agree with Michaela Hampf's objection that, in Foucault, society and media cannot be separated, but I do insist on a pragmatic level to speak of the media as transmitter between society and power. See the commentary by Michaela Hampf.

12. From a German perspective it is fascinating that American scholars are continuously tackling the field of perception of the media without any need to legitimize their approach – and with fascinating results. This is very different from German scholars. For a good example see Konrad Dussel, *Hörfunk in Deutschland: Politik, Programm, Publikum (1923–1960)*, Potsdam, 2002. In his introduction (p. 23) Dussel speaks of the difficulties to cope with the challenge of the Cultural Studies to fit the cultural practices of encoding and decoding in a media history

13. Susan J. Douglas, *Inventing American Broadcasting 1899–1922*, Baltimore and London, 1987.

14. Douglas B. Craig, *Fireside Politics: Radio and Political Culture in the United States, 1920–1940*, Baltimore and London, 2000. Craig argues that the Communications Act of 1934 neither gave more power to the Federal Communication Commission (1927) nor encouraged the critics. Thus, besides state interventions were implemented during the New Deal, the American broadcasting industries triumphed with their concept of a commercial advertising radio.

15. Daniel J. Czitrom, *Media and the American Mind: From Morse to McLuhan*, Chapel Hill, NC, 1982, p. 79.

16. Research should be done into whether and how the German broadcaster discussed Anglo-American systems.

17. Dussel points out that the revolutionary soldiers' councils established for some weeks a "central directory for wireless transmissions (*Zentralfunkleitung*), and intended to build up an independent broadcasting system," Dussel, *Hörfunk in Deutschland*, p. 37f.

18. Karl Chr. Führer, "Auf dem Weg zur 'Massenkultur': Kino und Rundfunk in der Weimarer Republik", *Historische Zeitschrift* 262 (1996), 739–81; Dussel, *Hörfunk in Deutschland*, 137–75.

19. Adelheid von Saldern, "Rundfunkpolitik, Nationalidee und Volkskultur (1926–1932)," in Marszolek and von Saldern (eds), *Radiozeiten*, 59–82, 61.

20. Quoted in Ansgar Diller, *Rundfunkpolitik im Dritten Reich*, Munich, 1984, p. 109.

21. Uta C. Schmidt, "Der Volksempfänger: Tabernakel moderner Massenkultur", in Marszolek and von Saldern (eds), *Radiozeiten*, pp. 136–59.

22. Christof Schneider, *Nationalsozialismus als Thema im Programm des Norddeutschen Rundfunks (1945–1948)*, Potsdam, 1999, pp. 31–41. The reports on the Nuremberg trials played an important role. See Ansgar Diller and Wolfgang Mühl-Benninghaus (eds), *Berichterstattung über den Nürnberger Prozeß gegen die Hauptkriegsverbrecher 1945/46: Edition und Dokumentation ausgewählter Rundfunkquellen*, Potsdam, 1998.

23. Dussel, *Hörfunk in Deutschland*, p. 244ff.

24. In the multi-layered processes of imagining communities and inventing identities, the mass media play an important role. It is quite disturbing that up to now scholars have more or less neglected this part. See Benedict Anderson, *Imagined Communities*, London and New York, 1991; see also Eric Hobsbawm, *The Inventions of Tradition*, Cambridge, 1992.

25. Craig, *Fireside Politics*, p. 207ff.

26. Ibid., p. 216.

27. Quoted in Lacey, *Radio in the Great Depression*, p. 29.

28. Michele Hilmes, *Radio Voices: American Broadcasting, 1922–1952*, Minneapolis MN, 1997.

29. Jason Loviglio, "VOX POP: Network Radio and the Voice of the People," in Hilmes and Loviglio (eds), *Radio Reader*, pp. 89–112.

30. Melvin P. Ely, *The Adventures of Amos'n'Andy: A Social History of an American Phenomenon*, New York and Toronto, 1991.

31. Douglas, *Listening In*, p. 107ff.

32. Barbara D. Savage, *Broadcasting Freedom: Radio, War, and the Politics of Race, 1938–1948*, Chapel Hill NC, and London, 1999, p. 11; Hilmes, *Radio Voices*, pp. 77–8.

33. Research has been done thoroughly for one station: Thomas Penka, *Geistzerstäuber Rundfunk: Sozialgeschichte des Südfunkprogramms in der Weimarer Republik*, Potsdam, 1999; See also Carsten Lenk, *Die Erscheinung des Rundfunks: Einführung und Nutzung eines neuen Mediums 1923–1932*, Opladen, 1997.

34. Quoted in H. O. Halefeldt, "Das erste Medium für alle? Erwartungen an den Hörfunk bei seiner Einführung in Deutschland Anfang der zwanziger Jahre," *Rundfunk und Fernsehen* 3 (1986), 30.

35. Lenk, *Das Dispositiv als theoretisches Paradigma der Medienforschung*, p. 57ff.

36. Dussel makes this a crucial point. He entitles his chapter on the radio programming in the Weimar Republic: "Broadcasting for the educated classes," *Hörfunk in Deutschland*, p. 145ff.

37. Von Saldern, *Rundfunkpolitik*, p. 71ff.

38. In the Weimar Republic, jazz was marginalized in the programming. The question is whether there was more jazz and swing on the Nazi airwaves than before. See Michael H. Kater, *Different Drummers: Jazz in the Culture of Nazi Germany*, Oxford, 1992.

39. Inge Marszolek, "'Aus dem Volke, für das Volk': Die Inszenierung der 'Volksgemeinschaft' um und durch das Radio," in Marszolek and von Saldern (eds), *Radiozeiten*, pp. 121–35. The transcript of the record is published by Eberhard Heuel, *Der umworbene Stand: Die ideologische Integration der Arbeiter im Nationalsozialismus 1933–1935*, Frankfurt a. M. 1989), pp. 583–93.

40. David Bankier has pointed out in a paper, that this is the same for the weekly newsreel. Up to now, the interpretation whether these findings prove the thesis that anti-Semitism was not deeply rooted in the society and the regime preferred not to deal openly with it, or whether the reason are differences in the media themselves, is still an open question.

41. Monika Pater, "Rundfunkangebote," in Marszolek and von Saldern (eds), *Zuhören und gehört werden*, Tübingen, 1998, volume 1, pp. 129–242.

42. Marszolek, "'Der Führer spricht.' Hitler im Radio," in Josef Kopperschmidt (ed.), *Hitler der Redner*, München, 2003, pp. 205–216. .

43. A comparison between the radio performances of Father Coughlin and Adolf Hitler might be an interesting project

44. Inge Marszolek, "'. . . täglich zu Dir kommt das Radio': Zur Repräsentation der NS-Vergangenheit in Sendungen von Radio Bremen 1946–1952," *Tel Aviver Jahrbuch für deutsche Geschichte*, XXXI (2003), 162–86; Axel Schildt, *Moderne Zeiten: Freizeit, Massenmedien und "Zeitgeist" in der Bundesrepublik der 50er Jahre*, Hamburg, 1995, p. 254 ff.

45. Monika Pater, "Jawohl, der Deutsche Demokratische Rundfunk kann sich hören lassen: Radio in der DDR, eine Einführung," in Marszolek and von Saldern (eds), *Zuhören und gehört werden*, Tübingen, 1998, vol. 2, p. 182ff; Dussel, *Hörfunk in Deutschland*, p. 271ff.

46. Quoted in Czitrom, *Media and the American Mind*, p. 73.

47. Quoted after Craig, *Fireside Politics*, p. 244.

48. Michele Hilmes, "Desired and Feared: Women's Voices in Radio History," in Mary B. Haralovich and Laureen Rabinovitz (eds), *Television, History and American Culture: Feminist Critical Essays*, Durham NC, 1999, pp. 17–35.

49. Quoted after Jennifer Hyland Wang, "The Case of the Radio-Active Housewife: Relocating Radio in the Age of Television," in Hilmes and Loviglio (eds), *Radio Reader*, pp. 343–66.

50. Craig, *Fireside Politics*, p. 240ff.

51. J. Steven Smethers and Lee Jolliffe, "Homemaking Programs: The Recipe for Reaching Women Listeners on the Midwest's Local Radio," *Journalism History* 24 (1998/99), 138–47.

52. Matthew Murray, "The Tendency to deprave and corrupt Morals: Regulation and Irregular Sexuality in Golden Age Radio Comedy," in Hilmes and Loviglio (eds), *Radio Reader*, pp. 135–56.

53. Peter Dahl, *Arbeitersender und Volksempfänger: Proletarische Radio-Bewegung und bürgerlicher Rundfunk bis 1945*, Frankfurt a. M., 1978.

54. Bertolt Brecht, "Der Rundfunk als Kommunikationsapparat," *Blätter des Hessischen Landestheaters* 16 (July 1932).

55. Eve Rosenhaft, "Lesewut, Kinosucht, Radiotismus: Zur (geschlechter-)politischen Relevanz neuer Massenmedien in den 1920er Jahren," in Alf Lüdtke et al. (eds), *Amerikanisierung: Traum und Alptraum im Deutschland des 20. Jahrhunderts*, Stuttgart, 1996, pp. 119–43; Kate Lacey, "Zerstreuung, Langeweile und Kitsch: Der Weimarer Rundfunk und die Modernisierung des Hörens," in Marszolek and von Saldern (eds), *Radiozeiten*, pp. 218–30.

56. Angela Dinghaus, "Hersels Jungmädchenstunde: Identifikationsangebote für junge Frauen," in Marszolek and von Saldern (eds), *Radiozeiten*, pp. 233–50.

57. Sabine Hake, *Popular Cinema of the Third Reich*, Austin TX, 2001.

58. Daniela Münkel, "'Der Rundfunk geht auf die Dörfer': Der Einzug der Massenmedien auf dem Lande von den zwanziger bis zu den sechziger Jahren," in Münkel, *Der lange Abschied vom Agrarland: Agrarpolitik, Landwirtschaft und ländliche Gesellschaft zwischen Weimar und Bonn*, Göttingen, 2000, pp. 177–98.

59. Uta C. Schmidt, "Der Volksempfänger," in Marszolek and von Saldern (eds), *Radiozeiten*, p. 150.

60. Monika Pater, "Chiffre für geordnete Verhältnisse: Die Konstruktion des Geschlechterverhältnisses in den Radioangeboten der früheren DDR," in Marszolek and von Saldern (eds), *Radiozeiten*, pp. 101–20; Monika Pater, "Rundfunkangebote," in Marszolek and von Saldern (eds), *Zuhören und gehört werden*, vol. 2, pp. 171–258.

61. Schildt, *Moderne Zeiten*, p. 255ff.

# 15
# Broadcasting Freedom: Radio, Big Band Swing and the Popular Music of World War II

## Lewis Erenberg

In September 1942, thirty-eight-year-old Glenn Miller told his national following of listeners that he was disbanding his successful swing orchestra to enlist in the United States Army. "I, like every patriotic American," he declared, "have an obligation to fulfill. That obligation is to lend as much support as I can to winning the war." He would use his music, he said, to defend "the freedom and democratic way of life we have." In doing so, Miller embodied a wartime ideal of sacrifice. Besides lifting morale and encouraging military recruitment, he created a model of patriotic duty and a web of connections among military obligation, mass communications and an American way of life embodied in swing and understood by millions of young people. It was his ability to convey a particular version of the American way of life that made him a formidable radio presence before and during World War II.[1]

Miller's sacrifice was real: in giving up the nation's most lucrative swing band, he stood to lose millions. A key part of the band's success lay in radio. His orchestra broadcast three nights a week on CBS's prestigious *Chesterfield Hour*, appeared on many remote radio broadcasts from theaters, hotels, and ballrooms, starred in two movies and produced a string of hit recordings. Once he entered the service, however, his Army Air Force Orchestra (AAF) quickly surpassed its civilian predecessor. Under Captain (then Major) Miller's command, the AAF Orchestra's forty-two-man marching band, seventeen-piece dance unit, string ensemble, small jazz combo and special radio unit aided bond rallies, made Victory Discs for the troops and entertained soldiers – live and on radio – at home and abroad. Miller's mysterious disappearance in a small plane over the English Channel on 15 December 1944 proved his ultimate sacrifice and made him a national icon. His life highlights the powerful role that swing and radio played in World War II and helps explain the effects that the war had on American music and culture.[2]

271

In going to war, Miller infused the Depression's popular music with national purpose as part of a massive government attempt to create national unity around popular symbols of American culture. Swing's participation in the conflict signified that the war was being fought to defend popular values nurtured during the Depression and imbued with particular ideals of American life. Even more, the massive use of radio helped create what Benedict Anderson has called an "imagined community." Rather than print, this was an imagined community built on sound. With a nation at war across the world, soldiers and civilians could listen to popular music on the radio and imaginatively reconstruct a sound portrait of the nation while also connecting to family members and loved ones far from home. It should be no surprise that government propaganda agencies and broadcasting networks used the most widespread form of communication available at the time – radio. Not only could radio create an imagined community for Americans, it could also be used to broadcast symbols of American freedom to allies and enemy alike. Moreover, swing carried powerful associations for other nations as well. Because of its strong links to blacks and Jews and a culturally pluralist culture, for example, swing became a target for Nazi oppression and a tool for propaganda manipulation.[3]

Swing's role in the war effort did not come merely from the "top down." The music played by black and white bands proved the nation's "war" music, despite efforts by the Office of War Information and Tin Pan Alley to produce patriotic songs like those of World War I. The role of swing in part resulted from the use of civilian soldiers who wanted to return to their normal lives once their job was over. Miller recognized that GIs wanted "as narrow a chasm as possible between martial and civilian life." Radio, film, recordings, and live band appearances made popular music "a great new factor in the American way of life," as vital "as food and ammunition." A central ingredient in dating and personal freedom, swing also conveyed the virtues of ethnic and racial pluralism that could build a consensus of national support in a nation recently divided by class warfare during the Great Depression. For millions of young people at home, and a growing audience abroad, swing was firmly associated with the benefits and symbols of American life. Hence Miller's desire to streamline military music and lift morale met with moderate acceptance by officials bent on mobilizing society for total war. Yet Miller's version of swing brought to a head the musical and racial tensions that had long made the music and radio a contested sphere.[4]

Miller was not alone. As part of the effort to define national objectives and create national unity around familiar symbols of everyday life, popular music played an unprecedented role in the war. President Roosevelt declared that music could "inspire a fervor for the spiritual values in our way of life and thus strengthen democracy against those forces which subjugate and enthrall mankind." Fighting enemies who promoted racial supremacy as national ideology, FDR envisioned music helping to "promote tolerance of minority groups in our midst by showing their cultural contributions to our American life." His choice of Benny Goodman as the popular music chair of Russian War Relief acknowledged swing's importance as a symbol of American pluralism. Duke Ellington's role in war bond campaigns live and on radio, meanwhile, recognized the crucial role that blacks played in the creation of jazz as America's music and held out the hope of inclusion in a more tolerant society. Broadway impresario Billy Rose put it well. All forms of American entertainment, he said, had to "make us love what is good in America and hate what Hitler and the minor thugs around him stand for," such as the Nazi and Japanese suppression of American jazz, popular music and movies created by "inferior" black and Jewish races. Posed against Aryan supremacy, swing embodied an American way of life – democracy, pluralism, and personal freedom – under attack.[5]

As key figures in youth culture, Glenn Miller and other swing musicians helped make the music of the home front a vital part of the war. Radio magnified their role because for the first time worldwide broadcasting facilities were available for use in a military conflict. As a result, World War II was primarily a sound and radio war. Civilians saw newsreels and war films in movie theaters, but most of their war news, including the announcement of the bombing of Pearl Harbor, came from the expanded news departments of the radio networks. In addition, to boost morale the music industry worked with the government under the direction of radio executives and the army to bring popular music to the troops. Victory Discs united musicians, singers, recording and radio executives, the American Federation of Musicians, and army personnel to record and distribute popular music to soldiers wherever they were. The army also installed radios and phonographs in barracks and service centers so that servicemen could hear American music rather than the music of the country in which they were stationed as had occurred in World War I. "Wherever there are American soldiers with juke box and jazz tastes," noted jazz critic Barry Ulanov, "there are V Discs to entertain them."[6]

Similarly, the army created the Armed Forces Radio Service, which produced shows such as *Command Performance, Mail Call* and *Jubilee*. The top show, *Command Performance*, was intended to link the home front with the war front by encouraging GIs to "command" their favorite programs. Operated out of CBS Radio studios in Hollywood, the show featured major stars of stage, screen, radio and bands that donated their talent. Run by Tom Lewis, head of radio production for a prominent advertising agency, the show was recorded on vinyl disks and then shipped to the various theaters of war. Lewis was also effective at begging money from a reluctant army brass that during World War I had considered a few athletic events all that was necessary as morale builders. World War II, however, vastly expanded the extent of music and broadcasting available to the GIs. Because of the boredom of GIs with the BBC's class-based classical music and drama, General Eisenhower ordered the Armed Forces Network (AFN) to "be as much a duplication of American broadcasting at home as it was possible." In part, these popular music programs were intended to offset the swing-laced radio propaganda of Tokyo Rose and Axis Sally that competed for the allegiance of American GIs.[7]

Of all the popular bandleaders, Glenn Miller played an especially important role in the war effort. His achievement lay in taking the safest parts of swing youth culture to war against the Nazis. Miller's military career crowned his civilian accomplishments. He had codified swing, polished its jazz elements, and used it to create a rosy picture of American life. In his person and his art Miller blended swing with more traditional conceptions of national life to make it acceptable to the farthest reaches of American society. Miller's roots lay in the "typically American" farms and small towns of the West and Midwest. When his career took him east in 1928, he became an enthusiastic New Yorker, and he eventually fused disparate traditions to create a type of swing that became the epitome of an all-American music. The key to his success lay in merging the two strains of 1930s popular music – adventurous swing with its fluid beat, and romantic, more melodic "sweet" music – into a powerful amalgam: "Sweet swing." This clean-cut version of swing was suitable for expansion into the heartland and the South via jukebox and radio. By taking the edge off the hard-charging Goodman style, Miller made it clean cut and less dangerous sexually and racially for the majority of white dancers.[8]

Using his superb business skills, he mastered radio and jukebox play just as these media were peaking, which made him popular in small towns as well as in big cities. Of all the swing leaders, Miller led the pack in his mastery of radio. As his drummer Moe Purtill noted, "radio made Glenn Miller. Not records, not movies." His theory was "we go on the air as much as we can. He was paying for the lines, sometimes," to broadcast from the places the band played. "We'd shove the music down their throats," endlessly repeating their repertoire over the air. This attracted audiences to their live performances, who then requested songs they heard on radio. Miller then ranked the requests and made "records of the ones the public was responding to." All over the Northeast in 1939, they played *In the Mood* ten times a week on broadcasts. "We just did about 20 tunes at first, played those same 20 tunes over and over," noted Purtill. By the fall, they enjoyed national airtime at the Hotel Pennsylvania, and the national-broadcast *Chesterfield* show, which publicized the band three times a week. Radio had built the band a national following, and Miller cashed in with records and personal appearances.[9]

But it was more than radio that made Miller. "When we started out three years ago," he noted, "none of the big bands played pretty tunes . . . and the majority of people like to hear pretty tunes. We've tried to hit a happy balance between the two." On another occasion, he added that his band stressed harmony. At the same time, he built his band on a sound formula, based on everyone fitting into a tight arrangement. He demanded ensemble perfection rather than "one hot soloist jumping up after another to take hot choruses." As a result the band was stiff. As Woody Herman put it, "he was so intent on making a success, he lost all reasoning about anything else. You know, cleanliness, even the . . . uniforms of the musicians . . . He was building an erector set. And that's the way it sounded." Creating a uniform sound also required paternal authority and discipline. The image-conscious Miller demanded perfect deportment and perfect notes. This patriarchal air later enhanced his stature as an air force officer. Tall, "bespectacled and scholarly looking," he "was a commanding guy, youthful but mature," according to his press agent, who found that Miller "looked like security" unlike the usual jazz bandleader.[10]

Similarly, Miller's music combined big-city swing with the currents of a more stable and conservative Midwest into a broad-based music with truly national appeal. One critic noted that Miller's music had "a kind of inland sentiment that differed considerably from the big 'big town' aura that pulses in Ellington or Goodman." His best known swing tunes, *In the Mood* and *Tuxedo Junction*, broadcast big-city excitement and sophistication, while at the same time the band was known for songs about distinctively American regions and symbols: *Dreamsville, Ohio, Little Brown Jug, Kalamazoo*, and *Boulder Buff*. In 1942 *Chattanooga Choo-Choo* became the first song to sell a million records by combining a thrusting train imagery with a "carry me home" theme, while *Don't Sit Under the Apple Tree* conjured up a small-town couple hugging in a small town Eden. In Miller's music, the romantic context and small-town imagery made freedom less open-ended and more the product of typical American places and settings. During the war, American soldiers would be asked to defend this idealized vision of the American landscape.[11]

Besides merging sweet and swing, Miller built an All-American team that fused the ethnically varied big city and the Protestant heartland. With a Western face, glasses, and a folksy voice, this New Yorker recruited clean-cut musicians and singers Tex Beneke and Marion Hutton, whom he initially introduced as Sissy Jones, a name he felt connoted "apple pie, ice cream and hot dogs," and dressed her to feature her girl-next-door look. Yet Miller's orchestra was a religiously pluralist version of an all-American team. The Modernaires, his singing group, included a Jew, a Catholic, a Presbyterian, and a Christian Scientist. He also recruited ethnic musicians – especially Italians and Jews, whom he stereotyped. "You can't have a good band without at least one Jew," he said, while Italian trumpeters "seldom play good jazz" but made "great lead men." The Miller team, like his "sweet swing," included ethnic minorities, but in an idealized middle-class depiction of the nation. As part of that image, this was a whitened American team in which blacks played no visible role. The band used the energy of black jazz, but unlike the harder swinging outfits of Goodman, Shaw, Barnet or even Jimmy Dorsey, employed no black players. Miller engaged the services of black arranger Eddie Durham, so his racial timidity probably had less to do with prejudice than with his desire to attract the largest possible white audience. This could be achieved only by attracting radio sponsors and touring nationwide. His personal preferences fit well with government policy, which maintained strict segregation in service bands and in the armed forces at large.[12]

During the war Miller's AAF Orchestra expressed American values in music at home and abroad. Under the hand of a reassuring father figure who had sacrificed profit for duty, the band smoothly melded civilian values and military goals into a common team effort. Courtesy of Uncle Sam, the AAF Orchestra served as an "ethnic platoon" writ large because Miller now had at his disposal native Jewish, Italian and white Protestant and Catholic musicians from all the best white bands. This white version of ethnic pluralism underscored that the United States was a much broader nation than it had been in World War I when its image was an Anglo-Saxon country. Moreover, the orchestra's large size represented the heightened emphasis on the group required by war, while service musicians themselves kept alive civilian standards of personal freedom for men often at odds with military hierarchy. In Miller's hands, these civilian values entered into the rigidly old-fashioned marching band as he attempted to transform it into a modernized emblem of cosmopolitan American society. In a letter to army brass, he declared that "the interest of our boys lies definitely in modern, popular music, as played by an orchestra such as ours" rather than in their fathers' music. His conception became apparent when he unveiled a modernized super marching band for the Army Air Force Training Corps in July 1943 during a giant bond rally at the Yale Bowl. Instead of twelve marching snare and bass drums, the rhythm derived from two drummers and two bass players who rode atop two jeeps. When Sousa's *Stars and Stripes Forever* blared out "in jive tempo," charged *Time*, "sober listeners began to wonder what US brass-band music was coming to. Obviously, there was an Afro-Saxon in the woodpile." Other swing influences surfaced in numbers such as *St Louis Blues*, *Blues in the Night*, and the *Jersey Bounce*. One critic called this fusion "the loosest, most swinging marching band we'd ever heard. The horns played with zest and freedom, occasionally bending notes and anticipating others, the way true jazz musicians do well."[13]

When the army brass recoiled at the looseness and lack of discipline of a swinging marching band, Miller managed to make some jazzy march tunes a feature of the American military band. For the most part, though, he was forced to abandon his larger plans and instead devoted himself to raising troop morale at home and abroad. As long as they did not threaten military discipline, swing bands were permitted to play a variety of roles. One of the most important was as a strategic part of the radio effort in Britain to foster inter-allied cooperation and unity. The army not only wanted to boost the morale of the American troops – they also desired to create an Armed Forces Expeditionary Program on the BBC to foster unity among Great Britain, Canada and the United States, to go into operation immediately after D-Day. As a result, the Miller Orchestra appeared as the representative of American music and culture as one portion of the combined Allied effort on the BBC. In July 1944 Miller and his men arrived in Great Britain to promote the "all-allied team." As part of the policy of integration, British scriptwriters often contributed to the shows, while British singers and announcers periodically appeared on the band's broadcasts. Among the singers were Vera Lynne, Jimmy Miller, Anne Shelton, Beryl Davis and Paula Green. The band also made guest appearances on various radio shows produced by the BBC North American Service. *The American Eagle in Britain*, for example, featured servicemen's greetings via radio interviews with the wounded, and of course music and entertainment supplied by the Miller band. These were broadcast over 150 United States stations, mostly on the Mutual Network. In fact, so important were the broadcasts to the executives of the BBC, that they tried to discourage Miller from making live guest appearances. Despite initial resistance, the popularity of the programs eventually also forced the BBC to make the band's programs available on the Home Service so British civilians as well as allied troops could listen to the musical offerings.[14]

Whether at home or abroad, Miller's broadcasts also featured propaganda skits that dramatized the Four Freedoms and equated swing with free expression and American democracy. The orchestra's overt propaganda tunes, for example, hailed the United States as a cosmopolitan nation. *There are Yanks* (1944) praised the unity of diverse Americans, linking Yanks from "the banks of the Wabash" to "Okies, crackers," and "every color and creed/ And they talk the only language the Master race can read." Miller's six-week series of broadcasts for the Office of War Information, *The German Wehrmacht Hour*, beamed from England to Germany during fall 1944, also equated a pluralistic nation and its music. Coming after D-Day, these shows on the American Broadcasting Station in Europe (ABSIE), as part of the Voice of America, urged the German troops to surrender and attempted to give them a favorable impression of the United States. Using Miller in this way reflected a shift in American propaganda, as Holly Shulman has argued, from fomenting resistance and mass revolt to facilitating the acceptance of American power. Musical entertainment as symbols of a democratic American way of life would convince Germans to surrender and impress other Europeans with the beneficence of American motives – all without having to detail concrete American plans. To these ends, the program employed a German announcer, Ilse Weinberger, the singer Johnny Desmond doing popular American tunes in German, and German dialogue to trumpet the blessings of democracy in music. In one episode, for example, Ilse declared that an American could play any music he liked without "barriers . . . whether the music is American, German, Russian, Chinese or Jewish." Miller underlined the point. "You find all nationalities among," the orchestra. "There're even quite a number of boys whose parents came from Germany, Russia, Italy and many other countries. But today they are true Americans, sitting side by side with their buddies no matter who they are or where they came from. This is a true picture of the Great Melting Pot America, and a symbol of unity in the fight for freedom and peace." On another show he added that swing, with its "love of freedom and carefree life are two vital American characteristics." Dialogue was usually brief. The band's performances of popular tunes, such as *Body and Soul*, or a swing tune associated with Duke Ellington, Benny Goodman, or Miller himself usually said it all.[15]

Equally important, the orchestra served as the living embodiment of American culture abroad. In England, from July through December 1944, the band endured a grueling schedule to bring American music to GIs a long way from home. They broadcast thirteen times a week over AEFP, flew up and down the British Isles for live concerts and special events, and continued to record V Discs. Miller was committed to providing a variety of American jazz-based popular music. He divided the band into a group that played the *Swing Shift* radio program with Ray McKinley, another seventeen-piece orchestra that played many of Miller's civilian and military tunes, and *Uptown Hall*, a seven-piece traditional jazz group led by Mel Powell. In addition, singer Johnny Desmond appeared on the radio show, *Strings with Wings*. In England the band played seventy-one concerts for 247,500 listeners, often in huge airplane hangars on makeshift stages. Live shows ran to his familiar hits demanded by the soldiers and a series of army-related songs such as *Tail-End Charlie*, *Snafu Jump*, and *G.I. Jive*. The big band numbers humorously relieved the rigors of war and reminded the troops that they were defending the nation responsible for such personally liberating and hard-swinging big band music. As Miller put it, "We came here to bring a much-needed touch of home to some lads who have been here a couple of years" and were "starved for real, live American music." For lonely GIs, stranded on isolated bases in the British countryside, the live shows proved a major morale boost. As a member of the string unit put it, "It was a mad thing at the British bases . . . I never saw so much enthusiasm. It was incredible – it was really hysteria because they'd never heard a band like that." It also meant more since band members were part of the AAF.[16]

Enhanced by radio, Miller's band helped to personalize the war at home and abroad and create a web of connections between civilians and the fighting forces. As early as 1940 his civilian orchestra broadcast from army camps and dedicated songs to various units, a practice the AAF Orchestra continued abroad. On a Chesterfield show in 1940, for example, Marion Hutton sang *Five O'Clock Whistle* to the "boys" in the "New Fighting 69th," originally from "around New York way" but now stationed at Fort McClellan, Alabama. "They were among the first to leave in service for our country." In May 1942, Miller's dedicated his national CBS "Moonlight Serenade" to Fort Logan, Colorado. These shows featured a "top tune of the week" for soldiers at various bases, interspersed with references to home: Baseball, Ebbets Field and other bandleaders. Every week on *I Sustain the Wings* Miller urged families and girlfriends to "keep those V-Mail letters flying to the boys overseas. Mail from home is number one on their hit parade. They're doing the fighting. You do the writing." Other radio programs aimed at service personnel employed similar tactics. *Command Performance* featured GI song requests played by original artists. The "Sad Sacks in Africa," for example, asked for Marion Hutton to sing *I Have a Gal in Kalamazoo*. If they do not hear it, send "Marion Hutton, yea man!" One description called the show a "cross-section of America" so that "wherever Americans serve – some little part of their native land will be closely at hand." Enlisted men appreciated these efforts. "Your 'Sunset Serenade' is a fine tribute to all of us in the service," a letter in a California Army Base newspaper told Miller. "We all listen to it every Saturday." Even more, they painted the titles of Miller tunes on the fuselages of their bombers: *Moonlight Serenader, In the Mood, Jersey Bounce, Stardust, Sunrise Serenade*.[17]

What the troops wanted, and what policy makers stressed increasingly after late 1943 when the tide of battle appeared to have turned in Europe, was less talk of democracy and postwar planning, and more personal memories of home. Because of its ability to recreate familiar personal ties, Miller's twenty-piece concert unit became "the most popular band among the boys in the service." As a private noted of one concert, "the troops were a cheering mass of swing-hungry GIs. The Joes ate up everything the massive band dished out, most of them in a dream world." Yet he also criticized the steady diet of old tunes. Miller angrily replied, "We . . . didn't come here . . . to create any new swing styles." Rather, "we play only the old tunes" because the GIs, away from home and out of touch with current music, "know and appreciate only the tunes that were popular before they left the States." Most GIs agreed. One GI wrote that millions of us "want to hear things that remind them of home, that bring back something of those days when we were all happy and free and when we used to be able to put on a Miller record or listen to a Miller broadcast or even hear the band in person." A guy just "wants the songs he used to know played as he used to hear them played." Cut off from family, facing death, "your pent-up emotions run for . . . the thing you want most of all, *your home, and all your loved ones and all that they stood, stand and will stand for*." For 99.4 per cent of all GIs, "that's what Miller and his Men and their Music stand for too." The popularity of Miller's civilian hits reflected the desire of GIs to remain connected to personal memories of an idealized, secure home front that awaited them after the war. An AFN radio poll during the London Blitz bears this out. GI's invariably chose songs of home. *Long Ago and Far Away, I'll Be Seeing You, I Love You, I'll Get By, Amor*, and *I'll Walk Alone*, led the list.[18]

At the center of the homeward gaze lay the American woman, who embodied the virtues of American civilization and reminded soldiers of their personal obligation to defend her. Pinups, according to Robert Westbrook, reminded servicemen of their personal ties to the home front, occasioning emotions of love, lust, and longing. The Miller band acknowledged this in novelties such as *Paper Doll*, a Mills Brothers' hit, and *Peggy, the Pin-Up Girl*, which chronicles Peggy Jones, a girl "with a chassis that made Lassie come home," whose pictures in *Life* and *Look* were carried into battle "all over the world." Armed Forces Radio supplied servicemen with a living pin-up, the "fresh-faced blonde" DJ, GI Jill. After spinning records and reading listeners' letters, she whispered "in the sexiest voice imaginable, 'Good Niiight,' followed by sighs across the Pacific." The band also evoked memories of women and home. On one AEFP broadcast, Miller followed *Flying Home* with *Smoke Gets in Your Eyes.* "We'll supply the music," he said. "You supply the girl." An RAF pilot caught the band in a smoky English hangar crowded "to capacity with uniformed boys and girls swaying gently or 'jiving' wildly," the vocalist singing "of love not war." As the band played, "they were conscious of the music . . . the exhilarating rhythm and of course, the girl in our arms . . . she was Alice Faye, Betty Grable, Rita Hayworth or whoever our "pin up" of that particular week may have been." Perhaps it was Dinah Shore, on USO tour with the band or on *Command Performance,* who as a living pinup was the honey-voiced girl left behind. She cemented this image on AEFP by singing Cole Porter's *You'd Be So Nice to Come Home To,* because it brought her GI husband George Montgomery "closer to me."[19]

Under the force of separation, longing for home, and private dreams, popular music tastes began to change during the war away from swing and more toward ballads. The anguish of parting and declarations of faithfulness were the subject of "dialogue songs" between soldiers and women at home. Miller's *Don't Sit Under the Apple Tree,* for example, features a GI and his girl urging each other to remain true to each other. As he tells her not to go down "lover's lane with anyone else but me," she demands that he stay away from girls on foreign shores. Separation also produced vows by women singers to be true to their far-away lovers in *I'll Walk Alone* and *I Don't Want to Walk Without You,* both hits of 1944. On the male side, *Down Beat* columnist and GI Mike Levin noted that GIs dreamed of returning home, but it was only in the music that they heard live or on radio and records, however, that they could express these hopes. "That's why old songs and sentimental ballads as such have seen more interest than was ever thought possible in as desperately a bitter war as this; why war songs and patriotic marches by and large have fallen flat." Hearing *I'm a Little on the Lonely Side* on the radio, one woman wrote her fiancé, "It hits me right where it hurts. Me and a couple of million other lonely gals in this country. It's no wonder swing is on the decline and ballads are in again. It's the mood of the whole country with most of its lovers separated." After one girl's high school beau enlisted in 1943 she heard *I'll Walk Alone* on the radio with "tears streaming down my face."

At the prom there were "a lot of teary-eyed girls. It was really quite an emotional time for all of us." *Down Beat* noted that draft-age boys and their girls requested sentimental ballads: "They are not only more serious about it than others, but aren't so inclined to escape by means of *Sing, Sing, Sing* with added anvils." Instead, sweeter, more melodic bands with singers and string sections able to express the pain of separation rose in popularity on radio, especially with young women dominating the audience now that young men were away. For instance, Helen Forrest helped Harry James's band replace Miller's as the top orchestra on radio in 1942 with songs "aimed at wives and lovers separated by the war from their men in the service." In the ballads, women were the ideal of civilization for which men fought.[20]

Yet, songs of home front devotion also reveal anxieties that belied the war's master narrative of unity. *Don't Sit Under the Apple Tree* and *Everybody Loves My Baby* expressed fears over women's economic and sexual independence at home with men away and less patriarchal control. In 1943 Frank Sinatra brought the issue to a head as bobbysoxers swooned. "It was mass hysteria, all right," noted the narrator of *Shore Leave*. "Those kids were having a mass affair with Sinatra." In a lonely era he gave girls a vulnerable boy-next-door who expressed their desires in dreamy ballads. One fan declared, "The attraction was definitely sexual." At New York's Paramount Theater in 1943, noted Sinatra's friend Nick Sevano, "it was absolute pandemonium . . . they threw panties and . . . brassieres. They went . . . absolutely nuts." While giving vent to young girls' sexual and emotional longings, he also pricked male jealousy over women's home front temptations and the commitment of civilians to the war effort. "I think Frank Sinatra was the most hated man in World War II, much more than Hitler, " recalled William Manchester, because "we in the Pacific had seen no women at all for two years, and there were photographs of Sinatra being surrounded by all these enthusiastic girls." Irate sailors pelted his photo outside the Paramount with tomatoes, while GIs in the audience yelled, "Hey, wop, why aren't you in uniform?" The press noted that GIs wanted "to gang up on the guy who had "stolen" their sweethearts' affection." Skinny and frail, Sinatra's lure to women challenged wartime images of male toughness and deepened men's insecurities. One boyfriend in *Shore Leave* expressed male anxieties: "Us tall, dark and handsome guys ain't gotta chance, brother." Men feared that all women were susceptible. "It's hysteria, all right, but I can't explain it," one male in the novel muses. The Sinatra flap demonstrates male fears of women's independence and the fragility of their dreams of home.[21]

The war whipsawed women with opportunities for economic and sexual independence and increased demands for fidelity. After all, it was patriotic to work in defense plants and socialize with service personnel at USOs. Sexual tensions, however, could be resolved by the emphasis on women's independence as temporary. When Betty Grable, the war's most popular pinup and Harry James, the new star of CBS's *Chesterfield Show,* wed in 1943, they set a new model suburban dream. Men in and out of uniform sang *I Want a Girl Just Like the Girl That Married Harry James*. As war prosperity made marriage possible on a mass scale, James and Grable projected togetherness by going to movies and sports as a couple. She had been a free-spirited working girl and dancer at USO canteens, who now subordinated her sexuality and career to homemaking. One columnist said she had "the wholesome domestic habit of putting every-thing her husband does first." Enlisted men prized her photos because of her all-American blonde looks, which merged sexuality and the "model girlfriend, wife and finally mother." The marriage enhanced their popularity. As a GI wrote James, "we ought to be mad at you for marrying the sweetheart of our camp. But it couldn't have happened to a nicer guy." When Grable became a mother, GIs sent baby gifts, the Betty Grable Fan Club became the James Family Fan Club, and servicemen wrote her about their wives and babies. The sexy career woman became wife and mother, and the James-Grable marriage exemplified the dream of a suburban home to which a sexually attractive woman confined her energies. It was a dream that appealed to GIs yearning for a world that had not changed and to anxious women concerned that they might have changed too much.[22]

Although sexual conflicts remained an undercurrent in the music world, it was race that brought tensions to a height. Miller's orchestra served governmental and popular desires for national unity between home and war fronts, but for most of his listeners his idealized home front was white. As part of the goal of including blacks in a unified war effort, the orchestra incorporated elements of black swing and even particular songs – doses of Ellington, Basie, W. C. Handy, Fats Waller, and Lionel Hampton – in its repertoire. Yet Miller's commitment to cultural pluralism remained largely abstract when it came to African Americans. His preference for a clean-cut version of American jive and a sanitized conception of American culture fit the government's desire for a segregated military so as not to disturb racial values in a time of war. As a result, Miller's AAF Orchestra expanded the concept of the nation to include the sons of immigrants, but it remained all-white rather than all-American. By playing black music and emphasizing the pluralistic nature of American culture, however,

Miller demonstrated that racial issues were a critical part of national musical identity.

During the war, racial tensions increased in the music world over the meaning of America's home values. A segregated society fighting a white supremacist enemy heightened elements in popular music favorable to racial equality. Black and white radicals – and many swing players and fans – believed that swing carried a vision of democratic community rooted in ethnic and racial pluralism – the concepts that defined the war's purpose at home and abroad. The elevation of swing to national symbol allowed musical leftists and racial activists to link war and music to the fight for social democracy. They mounted benefits for Negro GIs and political causes, and many players identified with liberalism and supported FDR in 1944. For many, swing was the model of a more tolerant nation. *Pittsburgh Courier* music columnist, Frank Bolden, for example, declared that swing's inter-racialism made "this ole land really worth fighting for," noting that black and white swing bandleaders "are all brothers of the downbeat, and that's what makes America – America." The swing press also stepped up the fight against racism. As *Down Beat* put it, "Music Can Destroy Our Racial Bigotry." Black and white liberals in entertainment, for example, created racially integrated canteens in major cities in defiance of USO and government policy. Many Jewish liberals in the music press, aroused by a common Aryan supremacist foe, made common cause with civil rights groups and the black press in a wider attack on Jim Crow, especially in the AFM and the radio studios. At the same time, *Esquire Magazine* began to feature the interracial winners of its new jazz poll in All-American Concerts on ABC radio. The black press did the most to challenge the standard definition of the home front Americans were defending. The *Pittsburgh Courier* helped launch the Double V Campaign for victory against fascism abroad and racism at home, and part of their efforts focused on how the treatment of black entertainers compared to the goals of the war. When Ellington's orchestra was denied a hotel room, the *Courier* said, "It didn't happen in Tokio or Berlin, but right here in the good American city of Moline, Illinois, U.S.A."[23]

Amidst this upsurge, the federal government was forced to work extra hard to garner African American support for the national war effort and fend off potential enemy criticism without disturbing the present racial order. Radio played a key role. As Barbara Savage has shown, however timid, public affairs programs on CBS began to discuss the role of blacks in the United States after the race riots of 1943. In addition, the Treasury Department began to feature African American sportsmen and entertainers in special radio programs, concerts, and tours designed to sell bonds and the war to blacks. The Interracial Division of the campaign used Duke Ellington and Joe Louis to convey the notion that blacks had succeeded in the United States and thus owed the nation their loyalty. Carried out extensively through radio, film and live events, the bond campaigns inadvertently promoted the idea of the Double V – that African American loyalty would be rewarded in the postwar world.[24]

While many African American bandleaders and musicians played prominent roles in the government-sponsored effort, Ellington and his Orchestra were formidable parts of the war effort and achieved unprecedented radio time. In the first half of 1943 *Don't Get Around Much Anymore* became a hit through sheet music, radio and record, as did *Do Nothing 'Till You Hear From Me*. He also performed benefits for Russian War Relief and the Joint Anti-Fascist Refugee Committee, played bond rallies, and toured military camps across the nation. Moreover, he made transcription discs of more than seventy-nine half-hour programs for the Armed Forces Radio Service, cooperated with the V-Disc program, and in April 1945, began a series of fifty five-minute network radio programs entitled, *Your Saturday Date with the Duke*. The latter was sponsored by the Treasury Department to sell war bonds. Moreover, Ellington was part of the Interracial Section's Music Committee, which chose the best patriotic songs written by negroes to be played as bond-theme songs at rallies and on radio.[25]

Selling bonds in radio campaigns was more than a good career move for Ellington. He was eager to use his fame and talent to sell bonds and back the war. Ellington was particularly powerful in selling bonds to blacks, because he, like Joe Louis, seemed a visible symbol of the American dream of success. Elegantly attired, leader of the top black band, Ellington's presence testified to the opportunities blacks had in the United States without belaboring the existence of segregation and white supremacy. He rose to great heights in the Depression, and defied popular stereotypes of the "lazy" "inept" and "impotent" black male purveyed by Hollywood. Rather he was driven to great artistic success and financial gain. He not only led the most successful black band, he wrote high-toned compositions and popular hits, and never compromised his dignity. For ordinary black people as well as the black middle class, the Duke was a national symbol of pride. His stature and cooperation with the war effort opened hitherto closed doors on radio. He and other black bands appeared on Coca Cola's Spotlight Bands, and on ABC each week for the Sixth War Loan drive. Out of the necessity for wartime consensus, the Duke's presence on radio lent some truth to the notion of a democratic war while at the same not challenging racial oppression in the present. By stressing

Ellington's music, however, the government ensured that the black presence in the United States would be highlighted, but that their plight need not be discussed. For blacks and racial liberals, though, Ellington symbolized the hope that the war abroad would lead to the end of Jim Crow at home in the future.[26]

While Glenn Miller and other swing musicians were crucial parts of the radio campaign to broadcast the American Way of Life to the nation and to the enemy, the Nazis took over radio completely and attempted to impose rigid control of its contents. Their goal was to eliminate jazz and other forms of impurities from the German airwaves and the nation itself. From its inception in Germany, as Berndt Ostendorf has argued, jazz was enormously attractive and repulsive at the same time. With its rhythmic propulsion, individual improvisation, exciting dances, and black roots, jazz represented the high modernism of a world torn loose from the moorings of older hierarchical social and cultural forms. Coming from the United States after World War I the music seemed the harbinger of the new. In this light, the Charleston assumed tremendous importance for German youth – especially young women – and German musicians began experimenting with the form. That many of the best German jazz musicians were Jewish only added to the excitement and the ultimate horror of this symbol of a mongrel future at the same time that Germany became a democratic nation.[27]

The moral angst over jazz, which heightened as the Depression deepened in the early 1930s, fed into Nazi radio policy. The Nazis centralized radio, film, theater, the press and music under Party control to make the media a powerful instrument of their program. Because of its potential to reach into every home, radio was the most potent form of mass communications. According to Dr Josef Goebbels, "what the press was to the nineteenth century, radio will be to the twentieth." Organized hierarchically, German radio was the means to impose Nazi ideas on the citizenry to create a new character and political type. To get the message out, the Party promoted the "people's radio set," a cheap model for every home. In the attempt to eliminate the sources of weakness in the new state, Goebbels banned all *Neger-Musik* – jazz and swing – from the air in 1933 for its "musical decadence" and its violent abuse of melody. It took two years to remove swing from German radio. In 1937 he decreed that "the recording of music by Jewish composers and works presented and performed by Jews is forbidden." It took longer to cleanse the recording industry, but in 1938 it became harder to import jazz labels from abroad, especially those by Jewish artists, and local pressure was placed upon cabarets and bands to eliminate jazz from their offerings.[28]

For Goebbels and other commentators, the new music represented the decadence of modern life associated with American democratic society. As he put it, "Everyone knows, America's contribution to the music of the world consists merely of jazzified-up Nigger music, not worthy of a single mention." Black music with its sensual syncopation and modernistic dance steps threatened German women, while signifying the presence of blackness in German life linked to the French colonial troops in the Rhineland. Yet while the Nazis saw Negroes as animalistic, they considered them mentally and culturally naïve. Goebbels viewed the attraction of jazz and swing as the work of mentally craftier Jewish musicians, and recording and radio executives conspiring to destroy the strength and pride of German culture by consciously infecting German women with black sensual music and dance and rendering them vulnerable to Jewish sexual violation. As one music publisher put it, "Jazz music is a Jewish-American invention, which one could call Musical Bolshevism," and needs to be removed from the air. Instead of jazz, radio was to be a conduit of German music – stripped of its German-Jewish contributors.[29]

Yet the ban on jazz was less than absolute, in part because of the needs of the war. This proved especially true as regards radio propaganda aimed at allied forces. Axis Sally first appeared on the air as the Germans battled Britain and the Allies in North Africa and then continued as the conflict shifted to Italy and then the heart of Western and Central Europe itself. An American expatriate born Mildred Gillars, she read messages from British POWs to their families and played swing and sentimental ballads over the air. She was notorious among GIs as the girl next door who sympathized with "the boys" having to carry out orders of FDR, Churchill and the "Jewish gangsters". With a warm and intimate voice that recalled the girls left behind, she taunted the troops about their wives and girl friends back home. Her broadcasts fit the Guidelines for Propagandists at the Front, which viewed American troops as politically apathetic and primarily interested in their own fears of being killed, their sexual anxieties and their homesickness. On one 1943 broadcast, she asked, "What are your girls doing tonight fellows? – You really can't blame them for going out to have some fun, could you? It is all so empty back there now – better to go out for some drinks with that 4-F boy friend than to sit and wait forever, doing nothing." Then she reminded the boys that if they got wounded, "you'll have a pretty tough time with your girl. Any girl likes to have a man in one piece." The music and the voice proved the lure, but the propaganda proved heavy-handed. At the same time, German troops could also tune in the broadcasts to hear a heavy dose of swing and ballads of home.[30]

Despite complete control over German radio at home, the RKK still found that German civilians were drawn to foreign broadcasts, including those of the AEFP. Moreover, members of the Luftwaffe and Wehrmacht often wanted to hear the spirited music of swing. In a battle with stricter Party ideologues, Goebbels sought to work a compromise that would boost the morale of the citizenry and lure them away from foreign broadcasts by promoting lighter popular music on the air as a substitute for a steady diet of classics, folk music, and propaganda. Swing, however, remained unacceptable to the regime – "a form of music that totally ignores melody, indeed even makes fun of it, and is based on rhythm alone, rhythm which manifests itself principally in a cacophonous instrumental squawk that offends the ear." In this effort, he promoted the Deutsche Tanz- und Unterhaltungs-Orchester (DTU) made up of civilian jazz musicians, for domestic radio broadcasts. Composed of some of the best popular musicians available, the orchestra was restricted in what it could play for home consumption. Still fearful of swing, Goebbels demanded that the orchestra emphasize melody and that the strings, not the sensual saxophones or blaring trumpets carry that melody. At the same time, improvisation was frowned upon. At times the orchestra broke the rules only to find new directors in charge.[31]

Similarly, the demands of foreign propaganda during the war encouraged Goebbels to establish a swing band that would attract the Allies, especially the British, to German propaganda. Charlie and His Orchestra, featuring Charlie Schwedler's vocals and Lord Haw Haw's pronouncements on the same broadcasts, was a state-sponsored swing band broadcast over short wave radio. The orchestra copied an array of top American swing tunes and played them well. If nothing else, though, the lyrics seemed designed to turn off any British or American audience. With no confidence in the power of the music itself, the Orchestra covered Benny Goodman Orchestra's hit, *Goody Goody* of 1936 with lyrics filled with heavy-handed propaganda. In 1941 Schwedler sang, "Who is that guy who set you back on your heels?/ Winnie Churchill!/ Who never fought in France and doesn't know how it feels?" Accusing him of breaking up the British Empire, the song concludes with "Winnie – You had it coming to ya!/ You declared this war and you will be licked like never before!/ Now I hope you're satisfied, you rascal you!" This was mild compared to a 1942 rendition of *Alexander's Ragtime Band* which charged the Allies with fostering the Communist International. Even more offensive was a version of *I've Got a Pocketful of Dreams,* originally produced in 1938, which in 1941 had FDR sing, "Gonna save the world of Wall Street/ gonna fight for Russia, too/ I'm fightin' for democracy/ I'm fightin' for the Jew."

Perhaps nothing topped the new and improved lyrics to *Makin' Whoopee*: "Another war, another profit,/another Jewish business trick!/ Another season,/ another reason/ for makin' whoopee!" The last verse claims that "We throw our German names away, we are the kikes of USA."[32]

While the Nazis were fairly successful in confining jazz at home – with important exceptions – they found it much more difficult in occupied countries. Across Europe, swing bands continued to play despite the occupation. This depended on the protection of local officials, as occurred in Paris where jazz-loving Nazis allowed Gypsy guitarist Django Reinhardt and his Hot Five to play on a regular basis. Indeed, during the war the Germans exploited the cultural resources of Paris as a recreation center for the German army, which considered swing part of the amenities of the French capital. Theaters played to capacity, and nightclubs grew. According to John Pelzer, 125 of Paris's cabarets opened after 1940. In all of occupied Europe jazz achieved unprecedented popularity, but Paris was the capital of swing. Record sales rose, with many of them American style swing. "Jazz became the symbol of, or the last tie with, the outside free world," *Down Beat* claimed. "The French seized upon hot music as upon a floating straw in a sea of doom." The appeal was also political. "Jazz made an ideological statement. With its unrestrained style and African-American origins, it became the antithesis of everything for which fascism stood . . . It was an ideological challenge to fascism as well as an outlet for those forced to endure it."[33]

Cut off from American influences, moreover, swing became more indigenous during the war, and in this Django Reinhardt stood supreme. His popularity and Gypsy "outsider" status made him a hero to the Parisian "Zazous," home-grown swing youth who used nonconformity in dress and deportment to challenge the humiliation of German occupation and Nazi ideology. As the Parisian personification of swing, Django became the star of the most fashionable clubs in the city. The French avoided suppression because the Germans considered swing part of the amenities of Paris. The French retitled jazz standards in French or kept their origins hidden. American swing was banned but French jazz was permissible. Still, too overt a connection to the resistance could place jazz in jeopardy. This happened when the Gestapo raided the Hot Club of France's headquarters for serving as a Resistance meeting place. The officers, including Charles Delaunay, were jailed. While he survived after a month in jail, club secretary Madeleine Germaine and a Lieutenant in the underground went to the gas chamber.[34]

While the Nazis eliminated jazz on the air, they could not kill it entirely. Instead, they drove it underground – the tighter the restrictions, however, the greater the reaction at the local level. The equation of swing with the forbidden freedoms fostered "swing youth," clubs. While few of the swing clubs were overtly political, they still acted as forums for cultural resistance. Especially in Hamburg, Berlin and Frankfurt, swing clubs brought middle- to upper middle-class young men together with their working-class counterparts to listen to forbidden music. Child of an African father and German mother, Hans Massaquoi noted that "our unstated aims were to express our antiestablishment mind-set, short of getting into serious trouble with the Gestapo; to listen to whenever possible to jazz, which we had adopted as our favorite music because it was banned by the Nazis as *Neger-Musik*." Imported swing records were still available until 1938, private parties and gatherings were difficult to control, and until German occupation, foreign language stations in Belgium, Luxembourg, and France continued to broadcast swing. Moreover, not all local officials were as hostile toward jazz as the Party hierarchy and hence loopholes existed in the enforcement process. Until 1942 and the complete arrest and crackdown on swing youth as the war escalated, "swing boys" consciously tried to differentiate themselves from Nazi youths. According to Massaquoi, "this meant wearing our hair long and with sideburns in contrast to the short, military-style haircuts and clean-cut look" of the Hitler Youth. Even though most of his crowd were rough and ready workers, their "swingboy trademark was a dandylike façade" that was a putdown of the outdoors lifestyle advocated by the Hitler Youth. Various cafes, moreover, offered small bands that occasionally played swing, but the ban on dancing put a crimp in the activities. The prohibition of dance aimed at limiting the chances for hanky-panky by lonely wives on the home front and eager males. That a number of swing youth were Jewish also fostered the idea that swing represented religious and racial tolerance, and placed swing youth in the precarious position of looking to the United States as the source of their culture. By 1942, however, wartime austerities and the threat of losing led the authorities to throw conspicuous swing youth in jail.[35]

Both the Americans and the Germans played on the equation of jazz as the music of racial tolerance, freedom and democracy, but they evaluated it differently. By centralizing radio under strict government control, the Nazis were able to severely control its content. Yet they could never completely extinguish swing in the country, nor were they exempt from the demands of the military for rousing music. Their denunciations of jazz also made it "forbidden fruit." In the occupied areas, moreover, jazz blossomed as never before. For swing youth at home and jazz audiences abroad, swing represented the United States, the Allies and Freedom. Is it any wonder that Germans and the occupied countries listened to Allied broadcasts in order to hear the music. Nor is it surprising that variations of Glenn Miller's Orchestra from liberation to occupation and after assumed importance as symbols of American freedom. Because of its extended stay in Britain and its series of concerts and broadcasts over the BBC Home Service, the orchestra became the focal point of memories of inter-allied cooperation during World War II and the music of the war itself. To this day, there are Glenn Miller clubs in Great Britain and the orchestra has set the style for numerous nostalgic bands. Partly born on the wings of the United States' military presence and broadcasting over AFN, the Miller Orchestra's symbolic fame spread through all of Western Europe. Even today Miller-style bands exist throughout Germany and Austria and the Miller Orchestra itself is still a hot ticket when the band tours. Nor is it surprising that a number of German and Axis personnel chose to surrender to the country capable of producing the music they listened to on all fronts of the war.[36]

While racial and gender tensions filtered through dreams of national unity, Miller's music lived on at home and abroad, rooted in personal memories of wartime experiences and the collective memory of sacrifice and national unity. Conveying hopes for personal freedom, ethnic assimilation and security, Miller's band symbolized the American dream of freer private lives made possible by American culture. His mysterious death somewhere over the Atlantic, moreover, fueled his personal sacrifice to mythic status. His fate became a metaphor for lost lives and interrupted careers of GI's and all those affected by the war, including the many women, who like Mrs Miller, waited for husbands and boyfriends who would never return. In fact, a year after he disappeared, movie theaters across the nation observed "Glenn Miller Day," the first such tribute ever accorded a bandleader. For five hours, a number of swing bands broadcast live on a national radio network from New York's Paramount Theater as part of the Seventh War Loan Drive. Famous swing bandleaders, musicians and singers performed songs associated with the Miller Orchestra. Singers and musicians expressed hopes for Miller's safe return. Swing remained a symbol of the triumph of American ideals in World War II as well. After Miller died, the band performed a concert for 40,000 Allied troops in Nuremberg Stadium on 1 July 1945. This concert marked a victory over Hitler's belief that swing was a decadent example of a "mongrelized" society and highlighted an American personal and musical freedom rooted in cultural pluralism and religious and racial tolerance. At the National Press Club in Washington, moreover, the nation's highest political and military officials saluted Miller. After the opening bars of

*Moonlight Serenade*, President Truman and Generals Eisenhower and "Hap" Arnold led the assembled dignitaries in a standing ovation for a man who "felt an intense obligation to serve his country" and "made the supreme sacrifice." Abroad, *Melody Maker* mounted its own "Farewell to the Glenn Miller Band" in its 8 August 1945 issue. "The visit of the Miller Band, however, will never be forgotten here. Both as an inspiration to our own musicians and as a means of cementing a warm and lasting friendship, the visit of the American boys to these shores has become a treasured memory with us all."[37]

Listening to a pre-recorded broadcast of *Moonlight Serenade* over the radio in a GI recreation center in Britain shortly after Miller's death, Mike Levin noted that the music was "tied up with individual memories, girls, hopes, schools. It [was] a tangible tie to what we [were] fighting to get back to." In sum, "You owe these guys when they get back, not so much money or gadgets, but a shot at the way of life that many have been dreaming about." But many Americans at home were dreaming about re-creating their private lives – families, schools, and careers – if the shift to wartime ballads is to be believed. To an extent, the war helped tilt Americans away from civic culture and toward more conservative values. What about race? As *Down Beat* asked, "How can we hope for one world in peace, when we fail to check the spread of the same insidious poison within our own vaunted civilization?" For blacks, the war raised hopes of freedom, in part expressed by the turn of young blacks toward bebop. With a growing conservative tilt in the society at large, however, the stage was set for serious clashes at home in the postwar world. As American jazz spread through Western Europe after the war via personal appearances, Armed Forces Network and Voice of America broadcasts, its vaunted ideals and social failings were visibly on display for all to see and hear.[38]

# Notes

1. This article is an adaptation of material from my recent book, *Swingin' The Dream: Big Band Jazz and the Rebirth of American Culture*, Chicago, 1998, pp. 181–210. Miller is quoted in Frank Stacy, "Glenn Miller Day Boosts Bond Sale," *Down Beat*, 15 May 1945, p. 14.

2. On Miller's career, see George Simon, *Glenn Miller and His Orchestra*, New York, 1974; "Glenn Miller," *Current Biography* (1942),

597–9. For an earlier account of his mysterious death, see "Music World Waits Word about Miller," *Down Beat*, 15 January 1945, p. 1.

3. Benedict Anderson, *Imagined Communities*, London and New York, 1991; Michele Hilmes, *Radio Voices: American Broadcasting, 1922–1952*, Minneapolis, 1997, p. 22; Susan Douglas, *Listening In: Radio and the American Imagination*, New York, 1999, p. 23; Gerd Horten, *Radio Goes To War: The Cultural Politics of Propaganda during World War II*, Berkeley CA, 2002, all make use of the concept.

4. On the OWI and music, see John Costello, *Virtue under Fire* (Boston, 1985), 120. For "narrow chasm," see Glenn Miller, "Travel's Tough But the Jazzmen Hit the Road for Army Camps," *Daily Worker*, 3 July 1942, p. 7. On ethnic pluralism, see John Higham, "Ethnic Pluralism in Modern American Thought," in John Higham, *Send These To Me*, New York, 1975, pp. 196–230.

5. For Roosevelt, see *New York Times*, 19 June 1941, p. 23, and "May 2–8, National Music Week – Help Spread the Story!" *Down Beat*, 1 May 1943, 10. Billy Rose, "'Escapology' Not the Answer: Showmen Must Sell Americanism to Everybody," *Variety*, 7 November 1942, p. 28. The Germans and the Japanese officially banned jazz as a product of a decadent, racially mixed democracy. For the Japanese ban, see "Japs Can't Hear Jazz," *Down Beat*, 15 October 1940, p. 1; and E. Taylor Atkins, *Blue Nippon: Authenticating Jazz in Japan*, Durham and London, 2001, pp. 93–163. German jazz policy is discussed later in the essay.

6. Barry Ulanov, "V Discs," *Metronome*, May 1944, p. 20f. Gerd Horten, *Radio Goes To War*, emphasizes that World War II was a radio war. So too do Douglas, *Listening In*, p. 162; Holly Cowan Shulman, *The Voice of America: Propaganda and Democracy, 1941–45*, Madison, 1990; Edward M. Kirby and Jack W. Harris, *Star-Spangled Radio*, Chicago, 1948, foreword by David Sarnoff, V–VII.

7. Paul Gould, "The Armed Forces Networks," *Tune In*, September 1945, pp. 9–11. For Eisenhower's role, see Trent Christman, *Brass Button Broadcasters*, Paducah KY, 1992, p. 39.

8. For "typically American," see "Glenn Miller," *Current Biography*, 1942, p. 597.

9. Purtill is quoted in "Nostalgia Is a Very Dirty Word," in: Chip Deffaa, *Swing Legacy*, Metuchen NJ, 1989, p. 121.

10. "When we" is quoted in Clarissa Start, "Man of Musical World," *St. Louis Post-Dispatch*, 1 August 1940, n. p., Glenn Miller Archives, University of Colorado, Boulder. His preference for ensemble harmonies over individual soloing is in Dave Dexter Jr., "I Don't Want a Jazz Band," *Down Beat*, 1 February 1940, p. 8. Herman is in Chip Deffaa, *Swing*

*Legacy*, p. 354. Gunther Schuller, *The Swing Era: The Development of Jazz 1930–1945*, New York, 1989, pp. 671–673, points out that Miller created a total sound portrait. Miller's agent is quoted in Simon, *Glenn Miller*, p. 135.

11.  Irving Kolodin, "A Tonefile of Glenn Miller," *Saturday Review*, 1953, p. 63; Glenn Miller file, Institute for Jazz Studies, Rutgers University, Newark, notes Miller's "inland sentiment" "Choo Choo Chugs to Million Mark," *Metronome*, February 1942, p. 11. Norman Charles, "Social Values in American Popular Song", (Ph.D. dissertation, University of Pennsylvania, 1958), p. 77, notes the homeward direction in songs of the 1940s.

12.  Simon, *Glenn Miller*, p. 184. On the ethnic platoon, see Richard Slotkin, *Gunfighter Nation*, New York, 1992, pp. 318–26, and Lary May, "Making the American Consensus: The Narrative of Conversion and Subversion in World War II Films," in Lewis Erenberg and Susan Hirsch (eds), *The War in American Culture*, Chicago, 1996, pp. 71–102.

13.  Miller letter, 12 August 1942, in Simon, *Glenn Miller*, p. 311f. Miller's plans are in Mike Levin, "Miller to Build 30 TTC Bands," *Down Beat*, p. 1 February 1943, 1. For one reaction see Simon, *Glenn Miller*, pp. 337, 349–52. "Jive tempo" is in "Sousa with a Floy Floy," *Time*, 6 September 1943, p. 48.

14.  Geoffrey Butcher, *Next To a Letter From Home, Major Glenn Miller's Wartime Band*, New York, 1994, pp. 106–15.

15.  On ABSIE, see Butcher, *Next to a Letter from Home*, pp. 183–5. Musical material comes from *Major Glenn Miller and the Army Air Force Band, 1943–44*, RCA Victor, 63600-2-RB, 1987; and *Glenn Miller: The Lost Recordings*, RCA Victor, 09026-68320-2, 1996. Both Shulman, *The Voice of America*, pp. 10, 173–85, and Horten, *Radio Goes To War*, pp. 116–45, view war propaganda shifting from Popular Front themes to more conservative ones – to the acceptance of American power in Europe and of American business and corporate culture, symbolized by radio advertising, at home. In my view this same process was occurring in the music industry during the war.

16.  Simon, *Glenn Miller*, pp. 334, 361–71; Miller comments in Simon, 361. On the response to Miller, see Butcher, *Next to a Letter from Home*, p. 102.

17.  On broadcasts, see Edward Polic, *Glenn Miller Army Air Force Band: Sustineo Alas/I Sustain the Wings*, Metuchen NJ, 1985, vol. 1, p. 3; vol. 2, p. 714. *Salinas Army Base Observer*, 7 March 1942, p. 1, Glenn Miller Archives, University of Colorado, Boulder. "Sad Sacks from Africa," *Tune In*, March 1943, p. 11. For song titles on airplane fuselages, see Butcher, *Next to a Letter from Home*, p. 128.

18. Criticism of Miller is in Pfc. David Bittan, "Miller Over There," *Metronome*, September 1944, p. 26; Miller to Simon, 25 September 1944, in Simon, *Glenn Miller*, pp. 384–7; "Miller a Killer," *Metronome*, 15 November 1944, p. 15 (emphasis in original). Top hits on AFN listed in Christman, *Brass Button Broadcasters*, p. 52.

19. Robert Westbrook, "'I Want a Girl Just Like the Girl That Married Harry James': American Women and the Problem of Political Obligation in World War II," *American Quarterly* 42 (1990), 587–614, discusses the pin-up and the personal nature of American war aims. For GI Jill, see Christman, *Brass Button Broadcasters*, pp. 23, 29. The RAF pilot is quoted in Costello, *Virtue under Fire*, p. 130; Dinah Shore is quoted in "My Ten Favorite Songs," *Tune In*, July 1944, p. 9.

20. Mike Levin, "Since You Went Away," *Down Beat*, p. 1 November 1944, 1; Evelyn Marks, letter to author, 12 July 1944, p. 7. See also "Dancers Prefer Swing, Draft Age Groups Excluded," *Down Beat*, 1 June 1942, 3. Helen Forrest with Bill Libby, *I Had the Craziest Dream*, New York, 1982, pp. 128–37, for her songs of separation as performed with the Harry James band.

21. "Mass hysteria" is in Frederick Wakeman, *Shore Leave*, New York, 1944, 181. Nick Sevano is quoted in Kitty Kelley, *His Way*, New York, 1986, p. 80. Dana Polan, *Power and Paranoia*, New York, 1986, explores the sexual tensions surrounding Sinatra and informs my views. William Manchester is quoted in Kelley, *His Way*, p. 91. "Hey, wop," at p. 83. Other responses to Sinatra are from *Shore Leave*, pp. 181–5.

22. On Grable, see Westbrook, "I Want a Girl," pp. 587–614; Elaine May, "Rosie the Riveter Gets Married," in Erenberg and Hirsch, *The War in American Culture*, p. 139. Jane Gaines, *The Popular Icon as Commodity and Sign: The Circulation of Betty Grable, 1941–45*, Ph.D. dissertation, Northwestern University, Chicago, 1982, pp. 51, 291, 293, 297, is the source of these quotes.

23. For benefits, see "Noted Musicians Do Russian Relief Show," *Daily Worker*, 17 April 1943, p. 7; "Ace Jazzmen Produce 'Night of the Blues'," *Daily Worker*, 21 May 1942, p. 7; "Theatre Music World Honor [sic] Thomas "Fats' Waller," *Daily Worker*, 28 March 1944, p. 5. For swing and brotherhood, see Frank Bolden, "The Orchestra World," *Pittsburgh Courier*, 14 February 1942, p. 19; Editorial, "Music Can Destroy Racial Bigotry," *Down Beat*, 15 September 1945, p. 10. On canteens, see Margaret Halsey, *Color Blind: A White Woman Looks at the Negro*, New York, 1946. For more in-depth discussion of the canteens and the USO, see Bruce Tyler, *From Harlem to Hollywood: The Struggle for Racial Democracy, 1920–1943*, New York, 1992, pp. 137–70. Mike

Levin, "Jim Crow," *Down Beat*, 1 October 1944, pp. 1, 12; Levin, "Still Jim Crow," Levin, 15 October 1944, pp. 1, 12 are some of the many attacks by the swing press on Jim Crow and discrimination in the music business. For *Esquire*'s jazz poll and concert, see Leonard Feather, *The Jazz Years*, New York, 1987, pp. 81–9. For one of many examples of the black press, see "It Happened to the Duke," *Pittsburgh Courier*, 18 April 1942, p. 21. For a more extended discussion of race and swing during the war, see Erenberg, *Swingin' the Dream*, pp. 201–8, 211–13, 224–38.

24. Barbara Savage, *Broadcasting Freedom: Radio, War, and the Politics of Race, 1938–1948*, Chapel Hill NC, 1999; Lawrence Samuel, *Pledging Allegiance: American Identity and the Bond Drive of World War II*, Washington DC, 1996.

25. John Edward Hasse, *Beyond Category: The Life and Genius of Duke Ellington*, New York, 1993, pp. 276–8.

26. Samuel, *Pledging Allegiance*, pp. 171–204.

27. Berndt Ostendorf, "Subversive Reeducation? Jazz as a Liberating Force in Germany and Europe," in Bernard Vincent (ed.), *Revue Française d'Etudes Americaines*, Special Edition: "Play It Again Sim . . ." Hommages a Sim Copans (December 2001), pp. 54–72. See also, Michael Kater, *Different Drummers: Jazz in the Culture of Nazi Germany*, New York, 1992, pp. 3–28. For a concrete example of the attraction and repulsion, see Phyllis Rose, *Jazz Cleopatra: Josephine Baker in Her Time*, New York, 1991, pp. 81–134.

28. Kater, *Different Drummers*, pp. 46–52; Horst Bergmeier and Rainer Lotz, *Hitler's Airwaves: The Inside Story of Nazi Radio Broadcasting and Propaganda Swing*, New Haven, 1997, pp. 3–8.

29. Bergmeier and Lotz, *Hitler's Airwaves*, pp. 140–4.

30. Kater, *Different Drummers*, pp. 111–53, initially made the point that German propaganda kept jazz alive during the war. For an elaboration of this point and the quotes above, see Bergmeier and Lotz, *Hitler's Airwaves*, pp. 125–31, 129, 127.

31. Bergmeier and Lotz, *Hitler's Airwaves*, pp. 144–6; Kater, *Different Drummers*, pp. 125–35.

32. On Charlie and His Orchestra, see Bergmeier and Lotz, *Hitler's Airwaves*, pp. 148–73, (lyrics are from the Appendix); Kater, *Different Drummers*, pp. 130–35, 167.

33. See John Pelzer, "Django, Jazz and the Nazis in Paris," *History Today* 51 (October 2001), 33–39; see also Mike Zwerin, *La Tristesse de Saint Louis, Jazz Under the Nazis*, New York, 1985.

34. Pelzer, "Django, Jazz and the Nazis in Paris," pp. 33–9.

35. Hans J. Massaquoi, *Destined to Witness: Growing Up Black in Nazi Germany*, New York, 2001, pp. 159–63. For more on swing youth, see also Kater, *Different Drummers*, pp. 102–10, 152–62, 190–4, 210; Detlev J. K. Peukert, *Inside Nazi Germany: Conformity, Opposition and Racism in Everyday Life*, New York, 1989, pp. 78, 166–169, 172, 199–205.

36. On a recent plane ride in Europe, the historian Lary May had a conversation with his older Austrian seatmate who told him that after hearing American swing during World War II he was determined to surrender to the Americans rather than to the Russians. As told to the author, February 2002.

37. Simon, *Glenn Miller*, pp. 427–30, describes Glenn Miller Day and the tribute by the military. British jazz reaction is described in "Farewell to the Glenn Miller Band," *Melody Maker*, 4 August 1945, as quoted in Butcher, p. 254.

38. Mike Levin described the broadcast in "When Johnny Comes Marching Home," *Down Beat*, 15 June 1945, pp. 1, 4. He also raised the questions about race in "Only Superiority of Consequence is one of Intellect," *Down Beat*, 1 October 1943, p. 10.

# 16
# Radio Nations: The Importance of Transnational Media Study

## Michele Hilmes

A conference such as this one brings invaluable opportunities to explore the cross-cultural and transnational aspects of historical events that are too often confined within the borders of national knowledges and critical analyses. However, I want to point to the fact that some aspects of culture frequently experience the benefits of this sort of analysis, while others remain adamantly excluded. Primarily, the products and practices of high culture – literature, art, classical music, theater, dance, even (certain kinds of) film – frequently receive transnational critical attention, as they circulate through established cultural and educational circuits and reach a fairly elite strata of society: indeed, one marker of Western cultural capital is an ability to demonstrate familiarity and critical opinions on the products and meanings of pan-Western, if not global, arts, literature, and music, although, as recent studies have shown, such circulation of high-cultural knowledge has its political uses and applications,[1] for the most part critical study of the fine arts on a transnational basis takes place with a minimum of controversy and social disapproval – usually quite to the contrary. Every educated person, regardless of nationality, reads Tolstoy and Trollope, listens to Verdi and Beethoven, discusses Hitchcock and Fellini, studies Goya and Goethe alike, and may even read Hemingway. No social panic here, no fear of erosion of national cultures.

However, the same cannot be said of those cultural products and technologies that are associated with popular, or "mass," production and consumption. Here, international circulation is often construed as a "problem," competing with national cultures, spreading debased (usually American) forms indiscriminately, producing ill effects on youth, corroding standards of personal and social behavior and patterns of everyday life, and wreaking havoc on local cultural economies.[2] To a certain extent, all the technology-mediated means of communication discussed at this conference fall under this "problematic" category. From popular newspapers and magazines to telegraphic communications, radio, television, and film, they have tended to receive short critical shrift even within their own national settings, and what critical attention they receive often must contend with an overarching framework of social disapproval and disdain. The study of all of these mediated circuits of cultural production and consumption would benefit from increased integration within the traditional academic disciplines from which they have been too often excluded, and gain immensely when placed in a less negative transnational context.[3]

But I want to argue here that the historiography of radio, in particular, suffers more from national insularity than any other medium – also more from scholarly neglect in most national settings – and that the work at this conference demonstrates concretely what is lost in such insularity. So I wish to address three issues: why and how radio developed as such a hyper-national medium and what the consequences of this historical fact have been; what a truly transnational study of broadcasting might look like; and how such study helps us to understand that transnational influence does not just operate in times of international crisis or in marginal, interstitial spaces, but supplies a crucial function in each nation's domestic setting as well. Inge Marszolek's and Lewis Erenberg's papers demonstrate very persuasively what the benefits of a reconceptualized field of radio studies might be.

Radio emerged as a viable medium in an intensely nationalistic era. Coming immediately after World War I's disruptions of national boundaries and identities in Europe, a period that saw America's four-decade tidal wave of immigration rise to a crisis-ridden high point (to which it would not return until the 1990s), radio was seized upon by national governments after the war as a primary nation-building tool. Despite the fact that radio as a technology is ideally suited to just the opposite – breaking down barriers, crossing borders, defying physical boundaries, paying no attention to lines drawn on a map – radio was corralled, confined, brought under tighter control than any other medium before or since, chastised, disciplined, and often made the property and prerogative of the state. Its technological capacity for defying not only national borders and identities, but also internal ones – such as race, gender and class hierarchies, as well as public/private distinctions, as I have argued elsewhere[4] – was swiftly and with very little public debate transformed into methods for keeping radio waves *in house* and *in order*. National governments quickly asserted public ownership over the mysterious ether and moved to bring as much of it as possible under their own exclusive control. Radio became not an international but a national endeavor, except for a few tentative and barely tolerated anomalies, such as Mexican border radio in the US or the trans-channel commercial stations broadcasting from France and Luxembourg into Great Britain.

Radio, then, whether owned and operated by the state or held in private hands and operated commercially, or some combination of the two, found itself addressing a primarily *national* audience. It became the chosen medium of national identity formation in a troubled time, as the reconstruction of the 1920s gave way to political unrest and depression economics, and then again to wartime mobilization. Thus the construction of radio as a medium remains almost synonymous with the construction of twentieth-century national identities, not only in the US and Western Europe but across the globe. And its early status as a *live* medium, with recording difficult and technologically primitive, meant that radio was created in place, located firmly in a national space and time, with regulations to prevent its spread beyond national borders and limits on its ability to circulate in any other form. There are, of course, exceptions to this, such as US broadcasts into Canada; indeed the structure of Canadian broadcasting cannot be understood without taking this "excessive" phenomenon into account.[5]

Generally, efforts to expand radio broadcasting beyond national borders in the first part of the twentieth century mark explicitly propagandistic efforts to extend national hegemony into foreign spaces. The Soviet Union beamed communist messages into neighboring countries; imperialist nations such as Great Britain and France set up colonial broadcasting systems; Hitler's administration brought German radio under tight control as it extended its message into countries soon to come under attack. The United States attempted several radio ventures in Latin America in the 1930s[6] and initiated what would become the Voice of America in the midst of World War II, and Great Britain built the BBC World Service on the backbone of the old Imperial network. Yet, as opposed to these primarily national, state-sponsored efforts, the free flow of broadcasting as a popular, stateless, culturally hybrid medium has only begun to occur in the last twenty years, prompted by the increasingly international circulation of popular music and television, and now aided by technologies that bypass national controls: satellites and the Internet. And accordingly, the study of broadcasting (at least until recently, largely centered on television) has remained fixed within national boundaries, as Inge Marszolek argues. Aside from sweeping institutional surveys that take broadcasting's national compartmentalization for granted,[7] very little thought has gone into breaking out of this conceptual straightjacket based so closely on the institutional biases of the medium itself.

## Michele Hilmes

Just summarizing the absolutely essential, underlying *national-ness* of radio broadcasting helps us to begin to see through its arbitrary and historically determined limitations and to envision what a more transnational approach might look like. I would like to argue that a transnational study of broadcasting would need to consider three broad areas, all of which have been studiously neglected. First, studies of broadcasting institutions and structures, including regulation, economics, practices of production and circulation, and general social policy, must be extended out of their national frameworks to show how transnational debates and conflicts have influenced and, indeed, constructed national systems. This is the focus of Inge Marszolek's paper, and she theorizes a new way, based on post structuralist theory, to re-think comparative media study. Her argument that other kinds of power besides the national played crucial roles in the formation of broadcasting structures, practices, products and audience formations – power that cuts across national boundaries – gives us the necessary basis for bringing new modes of analysis into play, based on discursive analysis of power formations. However, as she acknowledges, this is a difficult task, especially because what limited scholarship exists in radio history tends to replicate the insistent, highly politically motivated nationalism of the process it describes. Where radio institutions are primarily concerned with building themselves up as national entities and fending off "foreign" interventions, their records and official histories will tend to minimize the effects of any influences outside the national. Often the most telling evidence is that which is most heavily and frequently *reviled and rejected* (or silenced) by traditional histories and official documents; as Foucault's principle of reversal reminds us, this is often a marker of discursive fixation and hidden centrality.[8] Transnational studies of broadcasting have the potential of allowing us a glimpse through the nationalistic veil, revealing those forces and aspects that are being actively silenced in the creation of national histories.

For example, many histories of national broadcasting systems mention the influence of the public service model of the BBC and the commercial model of the United States as formative poles between which their own national structures took shape, most adopting some variation of the BBC public service model.[9] Yet what is rarely considered is that these two models are not separate, distinct givens but were themselves constructed largely in opposition and as a result of various kinds of dialogue between the United States and Great Britain. The BBC public service system was dependent on the discursive construction of United States commercialism for many of its formative concepts and its continuing justifications, and the same was true of the United States system. Other nations adopted parts of this set of discursive oppositions as they fashioned their own broadcasting systems, thus exporting this historical dualism across the globe.

In Great Britain and in many other European countries, the American system and its essential commercialism became synonymous with a threatening, populist democratic "chaos" that needed to be brought under elite control: the familiar discursive construction of America as Europe's mass-modernized Other.[10] This created, especially in Britain, an environment in which the broadcast of indigenous popular culture became identified with foreign, "American" influences and thus justifiably banished from the airwaves – leaving Britain open to later foreign and pirate broadcasters who provided the popular entertainments that the BBC's high culture mission had shunned.[11] This tendency can be seen particularly well in the access of women and women's culture to the air. Kate Lacey and others have demonstrated how marginal most public service systems considered women's radio expression, since the same patriarchal hierarchies that dominated government and social life ruled state-run public systems.[12] In the United States, however, though the same patriarchal discourses dominated social life, the desire of advertisers to reach a feminine consuming audience supplied an alternative route to presence in the broadcast public sphere. American radio developed an extensive and lively tradition of women's expression on the air, though largely confined to the "daytime women's ghetto," hindered by commercial imperatives, and denounced by critics and educators. Women's power of consumption in the marketplace countered repressive social power and allowed women's voices to flourish on the air, discussing women's issues and experiences with a degree of freedom and entrepreneurial control not often seen elsewhere in the years before World War II.[13] The serial dramas, or soap operas, and "chat" shows that made up a large part of these daytime programs have, in the last few decades, proven popular with and meaningful to male and female audiences everywhere. The fact that they were discouraged and excluded from most public service broadcasting systems for most of the century points to an area of exclusion – and a set of cultural hierarchies that underlies the commercial vs. public service duality – that might not be noticed, or considered sufficiently significant, except through comparison.

Similarly, United States' broadcasting history resonates with policy decisions relying on definitions of what constitutes broadcasting "in the public interest" formulated essentially in Great Britain and Europe and imported to the United States, where "Britishness" in particular came to define "quality" to such an extent that early US public television (PBS) was sometimes known as the *"Primarily British Service."* This led to a dynamic similar to that described above, whereby attempts to reform United States broadcast policy or to strengthen public broadcasting were often met with rejection of their "foreign," "un-American" origins and placed on a slippery slope of "government control" leading through John Reith eventually to Goebbels and Stalin. Neither of these discursive strategies, used so effectively to protect existing political and institutional powers in both nations, can be understood without an examination of the cross-cultural and transnational flow of influence so vital to the construction not only of broadcasting in Great Britain and the United States, but in nations across the globe. There is every evidence to suggest that policy makers and practitioners in all nations were acutely aware of what was being done outside their own borders and used examples drawn from other countries to construct and defend their national systems and forms of expression – although frequently disavowing any such influence later. Analysts and historians, however, have been slow to pick up on this body of evidence and work it into their narratives, as it often upsets cherished foundational assumptions.

Second, a transnational analysis of broadcasting must include issues of content, looking at the spread of cultural forms and the creation of hybrids, as Lewis Erenberg does in his account of Glenn Miller's wartime career. This must include a more nuanced examination of the spread of popular culture as well as elite, bringing critical analysis to the development of such transnationally popular programs as the variety show, the situation comedy, the serial drama, the quiz or participation show, and the dramatic adaptation, as well as news, discussion, and public affairs formats. The formal study of radio aesthetic history is an almost completely forgotten area, and one in which transnational influence can most easily be seen. This extends to types of popular culture, notably music, in whose dissemination radio played a crucial role, such as Glenn Miller's swing and Duke Ellington's jazz. Erenberg's study reminds us that the equation of popular culture, especially American popular culture, with essential qualities of democracy, "classlessness," and freedom is itself a highly political construction, at home or abroad. The careful ethnic composition of Miller's popular orchestra – combining many varieties of European ethnic identities, yet carefully excluding African Americans inside a framework of white appropriation of black musical forms – shows how even the most commercial of popular culture has political roots and effects.

Yet there is an entire history of transnational broadcast genres waiting to be written, much of which will defy the commonly accepted, though unexamined, idea that *popular* culture innovation (as opposed to high) has largely flowed from America to Europe, corrupting European cultures and

bringing "forced commercialization" – sometimes known as "Dallasifica-
tion" – in its wake.[14] For instance, Germany's unique Lander system
produced a much more highly developed sense of the local or regional
within the national, when compared to the greater emphasis on the
national produced in most countries, including the United States. This
seemed to allow a greater blurring of the public and private, with more
attention to the specificity of local concerns and voices that sometimes
extended to permit a more personalized style of broadcasting. This may
partially account for the European origins of the present day "reality
show" genre, which plays not only on a renegotiation of the private/
personal within the public sphere, but also relies heavily on the cultural
priority accorded to "realism" or factuality in much public service, as
opposed to commercial, broadcasting forms.[15]

Finally, a transnational approach to broadcasting history must include
a re-consideration of the audience, keeping in mind what an artificial and
heavily ideological concept "the national public" has been, and the
significant power such a construction wields.[16] The national audience,
whether conceived as citizens or consumers, always exceeded in its
differences and its contradictions the often-invoked "public," including
many variations and distinctions that a totalizing national image of the
public had no interest in accommodating: immigrants, guest workers,
regional and local identities, the working class, women, and racial, ethnic,
and religious groups outside the mainstream, whose variety of experience
defied the unities of the nation. In other words, the project of *national
unity* worked to obscure *cultural and political differences* that radio might
either exacerbate or mitigate. Inge Marszolek describes a German national
public (or *volk*) addressed by Nazi radio in a manner that carefully
excluded Jews, gypsies, and other "undesirables", and which addressed
women as not fully participating members in the public sphere. Lewis
Erenberg's history of Glenn Miller shows how radio itself, in privileging
a type of jazz that catered to the white, middle-class mainstream, worked
to construct a sense of American identity, both at home and abroad, that
carefully preserved racial hierarchies while concealing that such inequities
and contradictions pervaded United States' democracy. A comparative
study of the construction of broadcasting's "publics" enables us to more
readily deconstruct the terms of inclusion and exclusion upon which such
a definition is based. It also allows us to see how important the distinction
between public and private spheres, and their appropriate inhabitants and
activities, has been in broadcasting history generally, and how radio
served powerful interests in preserving these key distinctions and
hierarchies, in both commercial and in public service systems.

Both Marszolek's and Erenberg's papers demonstrate the historical necessity of examining transnational cultural transfer, whether in the arena of institutions, cultural production, or reception. They both reveal hitherto unexplored moments of cross-cultural influence, and indicate the ways in which such under-analysed factors are necessary to a better understanding of cultural operations both within and without national boundaries. They also bump up against one of the pitfalls of doing such research: it is very difficult. Radio is hard enough to research, as an invisible, evanescent medium considered unimportant in many places and undeserving of preservation. Evidence of transnational influence is even harder to locate and reveal. But it is there: in newspaper accounts of concerts and programs, in overlooked corners of official archives, popping up in government debates, in obscure publications, in the memories of listeners old enough to recall former days. Radio historians must create the archive of transnational broadcasting history as they go along, making paths that other researchers can follow. The good news is that it is a wide-open scholarly frontier, and that conferences such as this one have had the prescience to recognize its value.

# Notes

1. Reinhold Wagnleitner and Elaine Tyler May (eds), *Here, There, and Everywhere: The Foreign Politics of American Popular Culture*, Hanover NH, 2000.

2. Richard Pells, *Not Like Us: How Europeans have Loved, Hated, and Transformed American Culture since World War II*, New York, 1997; Rob Kroes, *If You've Seen One, You've Seen the Mall: Europeans and American Mass Culture*, Urbana IL, 1996.

3. See, for instance, George Lipsitz, *Dangerous Crossroads: Popular Music, Postmodernism, and the Poetics of Place*, New York, 1994; Ien Ang, *Living Room Wars: Rethinking Media Audiences for a Postmodern World*, New York, 1996.

4. Michele Hilmes, *Radio Voices: American Broadcasting 1922 to 1952*, Minneapolis MN, 1997; see also Kate Lacey, *Feminine Frequencies: Gender, German Radio, and the Public Sphere*, Ann Arbor MI, 1996.

5. Richard Collins, *Culture, Communication, and National Identity: The Case of Canadian Television*, Toronto, 1990.

6. James Schwoch, *The American Radio Industry and Its Latin American Activities, 1900–1939*, Urbana IL, 1990.

7. Walter Byron Emery, *National and International Systems of Broadcasting: Their History, Operation, and Control*, East Lansing MI, 1969; Anthony Smith with Richard Paterson (eds), *Television: An International History*, New York, 1998.

8. Michel Foucault, *The Archaeology of Knowledge*, New York, 1972; see also Michel-Rolph Trouillot, *Silencing the Past: Power and the Production of History*, Boston MA, 1995.

9. See, for example, Rauno Enden (ed.), *Yleisradio 1926–1996: A History of Broadcasting in Finland*, Helsinki, 1996; T. Oren, *The Clenched Fist and the Open Palm: Israeli National Television, Media Policy, and the Struggle over Television*, Ph.D. dissertation, University of Wisconsin-Madison, 1999; Richard Collins, *Culture, Communication, and National Identity: The Case of Canadian Television*, Toronto, 1990.

10. Richard Pells, *Not Like Us: How Europeans have Loved, Hated, and Transformed American Culture since World War II*, New York, 1997; Rob Kroes, *If You've Seen One, You've Seen the Mall: Europeans and American Mass Culture*, Urbana IL, 1996.

11. Valeria Camporesi, *Mass Culture and National Traditions: The BBC and American Broadcasting, 1922–1954*, Florence, 1993; Stephen Barnard, *On the Radio: Music Radio in Britain*, Milton Keynes and Philadelphia, 1987; Michele Hilmes, *Only Connect: A Cultural History of Broadcasting in the United States*, Belmont CA, 2002.

12. Kate Lacey, *Feminine Frequencies: Gender, German Radio, and the Public Sphere*, Ann Arbor MI, 1996; Gill Branston, "Histories of British Television," in Christine Geraghty and David Lusted (eds), *The Television Studies Book*, London, 1998; June Root, *Open the Box: About Television*, London, 1986.

13. Michele Hilmes, *Radio Voices: American Broadcasting 1922 to 1952*, Minneapolis MN, 1997.

14. Dominic Strinati, "The Taste of America: Americanisation and Popular Culture in Britain," in Dominic Strinati and Stephen Wagg (eds), *Come on Down: Popular Media Culture in Britain*, London, 1992; Jeffrey S. Miller, *Something Completely Different: British Television and American Culture*, Minneapolis, 2000; Albert Moran, *Copycat Television: Globalisation, Program Formats, and Cultural Identity*, Luton, 2000.

15. R. Moseley, "Broadcasting in the Nineties: Quality or Dumbing Down?" in Michele Hilmes with J. Jacobs (eds), *The Television History Book*, London, 2003; John Ellis, *Seeing Things: Television in the Age of Uncertainty*, London, 2000.

16.  Ien Ang, *Desperately Seeking the Audience*, London, 1990; Paddy Scannell with David Cardiff, *A Social History of British Broadcasting, 1922–1939: Serving the Nation*, London, 1990; Jason Loviglio, *The Intimate Public: Network Radio and Mass-Mediated Democracy, 1927–1947*, Minneapolis MN, 2003; Susan Smulyan, "Now It Can Be Told: The Influence of the United States Occupation on Japanese Radio," in Michele Hilmes and Jason Loviglio (eds), *The Radio Reader*, New York, 2001.

# 17
# Radio as *Dispositif*: The History of the Yet-to-be-Written User Manuals[1]

## M. Michaela Hampf

When Roger Taylor wrote *Radio Ga Ga* for Queen in 1984, what he described was already a nostalgic, romanticizing way of using radio.[2] As much as we might be inclined to agree to the song's chorus: "You had your time – you had the power / You've yet to have your finest hour," I'm afraid this is not how radio works. What Inge Marszolek describes in her opening paragraph is an intimate, reciprocal relationship between an apparatus and a subject, illuminated by the dim control lights of the receiver. And yet the apparatus is being perceived as "my only friend through teenage nights": "Radio what's new? / Radio, someone still loves you."

Both papers in this section analyze certain aspects of the history of broadcasting in a comparative manner. The approach Inge Marszolek suggests is that of the *dispositif* developed by Michel Foucault and introduced to German media studies by Knut Hickethier following the French film theoretician Jean-Louis Baudry.[3] As Marszolek points out, the concept of the *dispositif* was originally developed by Foucault as a heterogeneous ensemble of discourses and practices. It consists of the elements Marszolek has quoted: "Discourses, institutions, buildings, regulatory decisions, laws, administrative measures, scientific statements and philosophical propositions."[4] What is crucial, though, is the following sentence: "Le dispositif lui-même, c'est le réseau qu'on peut établir entre ces éléments." ("The *dispositif* itself is the web that can be established between these elements.") Thus, the medium as an apparatus is not just an ensemble of distinct elements but rather a network that is in itself a power structure. If we follow Foucault, the "power structure" can neither be conceived outside of society nor as part of a mechanical model necessitating a "transmitter between society and power."

The history of media-*dispositifs*, according to Hickethier, can best be studied in periods that constitute "breaks, beginnings or endings" of linear historiographic narratives.[5] Inge Marszolek consequently looks at the emergence of the two quite different broadcasting systems in the United States and Germany. Although the technological development necessary for broadcasting was available on both sides of the Atlantic within a comparably short period of time, by the 1930s the two systems could hardly have been more different. Additionally, Marszolek analyses the discourses that surrounded (and preceded) radio and shows how national audiences were "invented", how network radio in the United States was thought to unite listeners into a classless society of consumers. Similarly, radio helped shape the German *Volksgemeinschaft* even before 1933.[6] Radio advertisers soon discovered women as consumption managers and courted the female audience while educators were worried about "radio-tism", another women's illness brought about by too much and too distracted listening to the radio.[7]

While Marszolek focuses on the institutional differences of the broad-casting systems, the technological implications of the apparatus and the surrounding discourses, Lewis Erenberg concentrates on the "wartime consensus" radio and popular music helped create during the Second World War. He acknowledges that this was not a monodirectional exertion of power but a function of various discourses and practices that neverthe-less reflected gendered and racial tensions of pre-war society. His analysis of the role of swing in the forging of "imagined communities" (Benedict Anderson) highlights the viability of the model of the *dispositif*. The program that was a function of various discourses of national identity in times of war as well as outright propaganda was "used" by white GIs to create and connect them to an idealized home front where "their" women stood for the same virtues they were fighting for. Erenberg shows convincingly how Glenn Miller and Duke Ellington came to be symbols for democracy, religious pluralism and personal freedom, albeit in a racially segregated way. While Americans, and to a lesser degree, their allies, negotiated racial issues, class struggles, and gender over swing music, it provided the German "swing youth" with means of cultural opposition to the totalitarian Nazi broadcasting politics.[8]

Both contributors compare the emergence of the commercial broad-casting system of the United States with that of the state-controlled system of the Weimar Republic from an institutional, cultural and societal perspective as well as the diverse attempts to exert some form of control over the media in times of war. The commentator is therefore free to concentrate on the model itself. In my comment I'm going to take up the model of the *dispositif* and show that it is not only valid to replace the classic approach of sender-message-receiver with an integrated means to describe media and communication technology in terms of their use.[9] The concept of the *dispositif* also enables us to analyse the interactions between technology, society and individuals in their historically specific discursive frameworks and, as Inge Marszolek points out, provides the flexibility needed to compare broadcasting systems of very different genealogies. It is thus extremely useful for a comparative analysis of greater scope.

The genealogy of everyday cultural practices such as listening to the radio has to integrate the history of technology, the history of organizations and institutions, various discourses on media and their use and a number of cultural practices relating to communications. If we treat these factors as distinct narratives and study the "effects" of media we run the risk of not taking into account the processes that occur between these strands and tend to overlook the junctions between discourses and practices that shape the use of media. In the American network broadcasting system the public "owns" what in the 1920s was called the "ether"; the government through the FCC allocates frequencies and issues licenses and the networks control the programming, which is being paid for by advertisers. The genealogy of this system cannot be understood by considering juridical, institutional or technological factors alone.[10] If we want to answer the question whether and how radio changed social life on both sides of the Atlantic, I suggest we employ a subject-oriented approach. A historiography of the "dispositiv" has to take into account the materiality of communication as well as the corporeality of the listeners, the social organization of reception, the surrounding discourses of education versus entertainment, regulating decisions by government agencies as well as the respective political and economic contexts. In other words, what has yet to be written would be a history of the diverse uses radio has been put to and the many yet-to-be-written user manuals.

When Jean-Louis Baudry developed his theory about thirty years ago, he spoke about cinema as the most theorized medium of European media philosophers at the time. Although this role has been taken over by television, the debates on how media influence people's actions, how the "effects" of its finished products shape people's belief systems are again widely publicized today. Baudry showed that the field of the signified, the content or program depends on its technological base as well as on the context of its use.[11] According to Baudry, the subject is part of the *dispositiv* in that the latter simulates not a *reality* but a *condition* of the subject. If the subject's senses are extended into the apparatus, we need not study the "effects" of a simulation but rather the modalities and framework of the subject's perception.[12]

By claiming that for a successful functioning of ideology it is necessary for the subjects to function by themselves, Louis Althusser introduced a dual structure of the subject.[13] The "subject of ideology" is as much an effect as a condition of ideology. Baudry conceptualized the subject of the cinematic *dispositiv* in much the same terms. One the one hand, the *dispositif* (through the apparatus of the camera) *constitutes* an imaginary subject position in that we all follow the camera's view in order to recognize representations as meaningful. It is this "subject to whom the projection is addressed" that is potentially unifying and totalizing.[14] On the other hand, the "dispositiv" also *includes* "real people", individual users who because of their desires and experiences have the potential of putting the technology to all kinds of uses, even misuses. The early history of radio is a classic example of the discursive and practical negotiations of what radio can be used for.

Hans Ulrich Gumbrecht and K. Ludwig Pfeiffer have pointed out the importance of the aspect of materiality of communication. Their theory sought to explain "the conditions, the place, the carriers and the modalities of communication as the creation of meaning."[15] This approach shifted the focus away from "the message" and included the modalities of communication, especially the technical apparatus without which there would be no message and no performing acts to study at all. Carsten Lenk, following Baudry and Hickethier, suggests a triadic model to analyse the use of media such as radio: at the center are the listening subject, the radio receiver and the program.[16] Listening is a communicative practice in which the subject is actively engaged in making sense out of what she or he perceives. The elements of the *dispositif* interact with each other but also with the societal context in which the situation occurs. Thus, historically specific discourses, institutions, knowledge, expectations, laws and norms can be inscribed in each of these relations. The elements of knowledge form a discursive sphere around the actual act of communication. They reflect for example what broadcasters believe they know about their audience or what listeners expect from the station or from the radio sets. In the United States as well as in Germany, the prospect of broadcasting was widely discussed before the technology was reasonably widely available, that is, before most people had access to a receiver and had developed a habitual use of the new medium. In the 1920s broadcasting in the United States was heralded as an extraordinary modern miracle. "Anyone could have the best seat in the Metropolitan Opera, for free!"[17] According to former RCA President James G. Harbord, radio was the greatest boon to democracy humankind had yet invented, freeing the citizen from the "contagion of the crowd." The solitary voter needed not be a slave to mob enthusiasm and meaningless rhetoric but now was free to make political judgments "solely to the logic of the issue."[18] In Germany after the First World War "entertainment broadcasting" was

## Radio as Dispositif

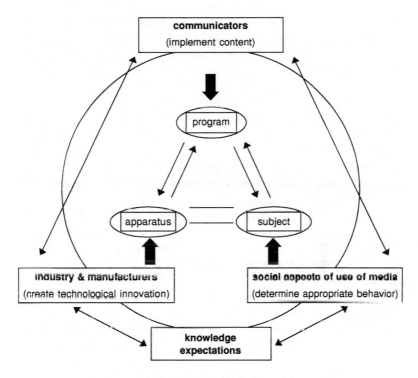

*Source:* Carsten Lenk, 'Das Dispositiv als theoretisches Paradigma der Medien-forschung.' *Rundfunk und Geschichte* 22 (1996).

**Figure 17.1** *Elements sof the "Dispositiv".*

debated in various special interest publications, rumors were widespread and, as with every new media since the alphabet was invented, fears and hopes were uttered concerning the effects on Western culture in general.[19]

If we take a more detailed look at the elements of the *dispositif*, it consists of close and reciprocal relationships between the subject and the apparatus, between the apparatus and the program and between the user and the program.

The interaction between the subject and the apparatus involves the user's body as well as a piece of technology, the radio set. The early receivers (1923–6) forced the listener into a crouched position in front of the huge apparatus, in fact an ensemble of tubes, heating and receiver, which required a significant amount of know-how to operate it. The frequency was adjusted with a tiny wire and every move in the room could mean one had to start over again. The earphones tied the listener to the set and isolated her or him from the environment. At the same time the apparatus is operated by the user, it forces what Carsten Lenk calls a "choreography" on him or her. (Best exemplified by the organization of the typical living room around the television set.)[20] This, however, does not mean that users haven't been quite creative in inventing other uses: earphones, for example, were taken apart and shared by passing around the halves or by amplifying the signal with a bucket. The introduction of speakers in the mid- to late 1920s made it possible to combine the experience of listening with pursuing one's work (*Nebenbeihören*). The transistor liberated teenagers from the confines of the family receiver and made the signal truly ubiquitous.[21]

Listening to the radio is foremost an interaction of the subject with the program, regardless of the fact that at a particular time thousands of individuals might be listening to the same show.[22] In the early days of the new medium the industry provided a number of models and images, (literally: photographs) as to how listening to the radio should look like, but the process of this becoming habitual occurred also along traditional lines of perception, shaped by older institutions of bourgeois or middle-class culture.[23] The aesthetics of the concert hall as well as the opera, including the appropriate dress or the contemplative, motionless listening posture, were imitated during the 1920s. Only later, when more broadcast-specific formats like reports from sports events were introduced, listening to the radio began to include other modes, like the attentive, upright listening posture as if one "was there".[24] Broadcasters, not only the advertising departments of the stations, have known or at least attempted to know about their listeners' expectations and experiences with their program.[25] In order for this communication to work, a certain amount of knowledge about the modalities and channels of representation (genres, program schedule) had to be acquired. The collective panic resulting from the broadcasting of Orson Welles' piece *War of the Worlds* is an example for the confusion that can arise when the modes of fictional representation are not communicated clearly.

The apparatus sets technical limits to the transmission of spoken words, sounds and music. Without a program, on the other hand, the receiver would only emit white noise, as was often the case in the early days of radio before most stations broadcast a program on a continuous basis. When Edwin Armstrong and the Radio Corporation of America (RCA) experimented with broadband frequency modulation (FM) between 1928 and 1933 it was soon found that this technology greatly improved the quality of the signal. There would be less interference between neighboring stations, the signal-to-noise ratio was greatly improved, less radiated power would be needed and the service areas for a given transmitter power would be easier to define and, unlike AM, would remain stable throughout day and night. The example of the newer standard of FM again illustrates the web of links between the quality and distribution of the apparatuses, the program and regulating decisions by a government agency. When the FCC in the 1940s declared FM to be commercially usable, applicants stood in line for new licenses. Although the manufacturers had been afraid of the high costs of conversion and feared they might lose both their advertising customers and their regular listeners, the conversion of stations turned out to be a smaller problem than the production of affordable and reliable radio sets. Between 1945 and 1949 the number of transmitters that were authorized almost doubled, but, contrary to what this initial enthusiasm suggested, FM had a hard time becoming accepted on the market and as early as 1950 the trend began to reverse. There were a number of reasons for this: to the general public neither the technical deficits of AM transmissions nor the broader bandwidth of the new standard mattered much. Listeners in urban areas, where the AM signals were strong enough, were hardly disadvantaged by static noise, while listeners in rural areas mostly lived outside the service areas of the new FM transmitters. The largest obstacle, however, were the programs themselves. The music that profited most from high-fidelity transmission was both classical music and music that exhibited many percussive elements and a broad dynamic spectrum. The bulk of the program in the 1940s and 1950s, however, news and sports reports, sit-coms and soap operas, had little to gain from the new reproduction quality.[26]

Programming decisions and economic factors such as "simulcasting", the transmission of the same signal on AM and FM, deterred the growth of FM.[27] For advertisement customers it turned out to be not lucrative to buy advertising time from pure FM stations as the old stations had a much larger audience. This downward trend ended only in 1957, again due to technical innovations, most notably the development of the transistor. Receivers could now be built and marketed that were much smaller and lighter than those based on tubes and new cars could be equipped with AM/FM receivers. High fidelity soon had its own market, not because the number of classical music lovers had risen dramatically, but because of a new phenomenon, known as rock 'n' roll, which spread explosively. After the introduction of television, radio, to which a substantial number of new channels had been added, now took to specialization. Harbingers of this development were programs for African Americans during the late 1940s, such as those of the first all-black station, WDIA in Memphis, Tennessee.[28] African Americans had previously not belonged to one of the economically interesting target groups for advertising on the radio. They had a lower median income and purchased fewer TV sets in the early 1950s. During the 1930s and 1940s they had been virtually excluded from being heard on national radio, with the notable exceptions of educational programs and the wartime programming Lewis Erenberg describes so eloquently. Only after the advent of television and its usurpation of radio's principal source of funding did the radio industry's network domination falter and radio was transformed into a medium that relied on more locally oriented, segmented appeals.[29] Advertisers now turned to the urban concentrations of recently migrated African Americans.[30] "Negro radio", which was still often owned by Whites and drew white audiences thus proved that a segmented radio market could be lucrative and that, with localization and specialization, radio could survive the direct competition with television.

As the user manuals of these media continue to be written, future research on other forms of broadcasting than those Inge Marszolek and Lewis Erenberg have so elaborately analyzed could especially profit from the model of the "dispositiv".[31] These could include community radio stations as well as listener-sponsored, non-commercial stations that exist in both countries in a number of different forms. If we broaden the analysis to include these and other decentralized media, radio's "finest hour" may well be yet to come.

# Notes

1. The second part of the title I owe to Melita Zajc, "The Concept of Dispositiv: Studying Technology in Terms of its Use Because of the All Yet-To-Be-Written User Manuals," in *A Decade of Transformation: IWM Junior Visiting Fellows Conferences* VIII, Vienna, 1999.

2. *Radio Ga Ga* was released in January 1984 and can be found on the album *Greatest Hits II*, Queen Music, Ltd/EMI Music Publishing, Ltd, 1991. According to press releases, the song was inspired by Roger Taylor's son, Felix. In the lyrics the narrator apparently switches between a child listener and an adult listener.

3. Jean-Louis Baudry, "Cinéma: Effets idéologiques produits par l'appareil de base," *Cinéthique* 7–8 (1970); Baudry "Le dispositif: Approches métapsychologiques de l'impression de réalité," in: *Communications XXIII: Psychanalyse et cinéma*, Paris, 1975.

4. "Un ensemble résolument hétérogène, comportant des discours, des institutions, des aménagements architecturaux, des décisions réglementaires, des lois, des mesures administratives, des énoncés scientifiques, des propositions philosophiques, morales, philanthropiques, bref : du dit, aussi bien que du non-dit. Le dispositif lui-même, c'est le réseau qu'on peut établir entre ces éléments." Le Jeu de Michel Foucault, in: Michel Foucault, *Dits et Écrits 1954–1988 III: 1976–1979*, Paris, 1994, p. 299.

5. Knut Hickethier, "Kommunikationsgeschichte: Geschichte der Mediendispositive," *Medien & Zeit* 7 (1992), 26–8.

6. For a history of radio during the Nazi years see Uta C. Schmidt, "Vom 'Spielzeug' über den 'Hausfreund' zur 'Goebbels-Schnauze': Das Radio als häusliches Kommunikationsmedium im Deutschen Reich (1923–1945)," *Technikgeschichte* 65 (1998), 313–27. That virtually no aspect of radio was without a political dimension is demonstrated in Michael P. Hensle, "'Rundfunkverbrechen' vor NS-Sondergerichten," *Rundfunk und Geschichte* 26 (2000), 111–26.

7. Eve Rosenhaft, "Lesewut, Kinosucht, Radiotismus: Zur (geschlechter-)politischen Relevanz neuer Massenmedien in den 1920er Jahren," in Alf Lüdtke (ed.), *Amerikanisierung: Traum und Alptraum im Deutschland des 20. Jahrhunderts*, Stuttgart, 1996, pp. 119–143.

8. On *Schwarzhören*, the forbidden reception of foreign stations Karl-Heinz Ruband, "'Schwarzhören' im Dritten Reich: Verbreitung, Erscheinungsformen und Kommunikationsmuster beim Umgang mit verbotenen Sendern," *Archiv für Sozialgeschichte* 41 (2001), 245–70.

9. Zajc, "The Concept of the Dispositiv," p. 6.

10. For a history of the regulatory function of the FCC see Hans J. Kleinsteuber, "Regulierung des Rundfunks in den USA: Zur Kontrolle wirtschaftlicher Macht am Beispiel der FCC," *Rundfunk und Fernsehen*, 44 (1996), 27–50.

11. This approach is similar to Marshall McLuhans, *Understanding Media: The Extensions of Man*, New York, 1994.

12. Jean-Louis Baudry, "Le dispositif: Approches métapsychologiques de l'impression de réalité, (1975)," *L'effet cinéma* (1978), p. 43.

13. Louis Althusser, *Ideologie und ideologische Staatsapparate* (Hamburg, 1969).

14. Jean-Louis Baudry, "The Apparatus: Metapsychological Approaches to the Impression of Reality in the Cinema [1975. Le dispositif: approches métapsychologiques de l'impression de réalité. Communications 23: Psychanalyse et cinéma. Paris.]" in Philip Rosen (ed.), *Narrative, Apparatus, Ideology: A Film Theory Reader*, New York, 1986, pp. 299–318, 317.

15. K. Ludwig Pfeiffer, "Materialität der Kommunikation?" in Hans Ulrich Gumbrecht and K. Ludwig Pfeiffer (eds.), *Materialität der Kommunikation*, Frankfurt a. M., 1988, pp. 15–30.

16. Carsten Lenk, "Das Dispositiv als theoretisches Paradigma der Medienforschung: Überlegungen zu einer integrativen Nutzungsgeschichte des Rundfunks," *Rundfunk und Geschichte* 22 (1996), 5–17.

17. Jeffrey Land, *Active Radio: Pacifica's "Brash Experiment"* Ph.D. dissertation, University of Oregon, 1994, p. 58.

18. James G. Harbord, "Radio and Democracy", *Forum* 81 (April 1929), 219; quoted from: J. Land, *Active Radio*, p. 59.

19. Horst Halefeldt analyzed the elements of the early German discourse in the press. Horst O. Halefeldt, "Das erste Medium für alle? Erwartungen an den Hörfunk bei seiner Einführung in Deutschland Anfang der 20er Jahre (1. Teil)," *Rundfunk und Fernsehen* 34 (1/1986), 23–43. See also: Inge Marszolek, "Radio in Deutschland 1923–1960: Zur Sozialgeschichte eines Mediums," *Geschichte und Gesellschaft,* 27 (2001), 207–39.

20. Lenk, "Das Dispositiv," 11.

21. For a technological history of early German broadcasting see Joachim Kniestedt, "75 Jahre Rundfunk in Deutschland," *Post- und Telekommunikationsgeschichte,* 4 (1998), 73–85; Sigfrid von Weiher, "Radiogrüsse aus Moskau: Erinnerungen an die Kindertage des Radios," *Kultur und Technik,* 4 (1998), 32f.

22. Different notions of the public are examined in: Axel Schildt, "Das Jahrhundert der Massenmedien: Ansichten zu einer künftigen Geschichte der Öffentlichkeit," *Geschichte und Gesellschaft* 27 (2001), 177–206; Edzard Schade, "Radio: Ein vielschichtiges Instrument für Massenkonsum," in: Jakob Tanner et al., *Geschichte der Konsumgesellschaft: Märkte, Kultur und Identität*, Zurich, 1998; Karl Christian Führer et al., "Öffentlichkeit – Medien – Geschichte: Konzepte der modernen Öffentlichkeit und Zugänge zu ihrer Erforschung," *Archiv für Sozialgeschichte* 41 (2001), 1–38.

23. Uta C. Schmidt, "Vom 'Spielzeug' über den 'Hausfreund' zur Goebbels-Schnauze'," p. 320f.

24. For Germany see also Axel Schildt, *Moderne Zeiten: Freizeit, Massenmedien und "Zeitgeist" in der BRD der 50er Jahre*, Hamburg, 1995, pp. 208–61.

25. Werner Hensel and Erich Keßler (eds.), *1000 Hörer antworten: Eine Marktstudie*, quoted from: Lenk, "Das Dispositiv als theoretisches Paradigma der Medienforschung," p. 12.

26. In 1990, only 44 out of 3,800 commercial FM radio stations in the United States stated that their programming consisted mainly of classical music. Nationwide broadcasting in hi-fi quality became possible with the

availability of satellites in 1980. Andrew F. Inglis, *Behind the Tube. A History of Broadcasting Technology and Business*, Boston, 1990, p. 141.

27. Ironically, in the 1990s this situation was reversed when stations again resorted to "simulcasting", this time to reduce the expenses generated by the unprofitable AM operations. Edward C. Pease and Everette E. Dennis (eds), *Radio: The Forgotten Medium*, New Brunswick NJ, and London, 1995.

28. Louis Cantor, *Wheelin' on Beale*, New York, 1992.

29. NBC's study "Urban Teen-Agers as Radio Listeners and Consumers" (1948) found that 64 per cent of adolescent listeners in four northern cities had their own radios. Their combined buying power was estimated at $6 billion and the favorite show among 18- and 19-year-old was "Your Hit Parade." Peter Fornatale and Joshua E. Mills, *Radio in the Television Age*, Woodstock NY, 1980, p. 15.

30. Barbara Dianne Savage, *Broadcasting Freedom: Radio, War, and the Politics of Race*, Chapel Hill NC, and London, 1999.

31. Even more distinct from the commercial or state governed broadcasting systems that have been discussed during this conference but certainly worth a systematic analysis are pirate stations, both overt (offshore stations, low-power FM) and covert (pirate stations of European cities some of which have historical ties to squatting, for example in Amsterdam.) For non-commercial stations see Hans Kleinsteuber (ed.), *Radio – das unterschätzte Medium: Erfahrungen mit nicht-kommerziellen Lokalstationen in 15 Staaten*, Berlin, 1991; Michaela Hampf, "Community, Control, Corporations: Zur Geschichte Freien Radios in den USA," in Andreas Stuhlmann (ed.), *Radio-Kultur und Hör-Kunst: Zwischen Avantgarde und Popularkultur 1923–2001*, Würzburg, 2001, pp. 135–62; Michaela Hampf, *Freies Radio in den USA: Die Pacifica Foundation 1946–1965*, Hamburg and London, 2000.

# Part V
**Television and Public Memory: Communicating the Past at the Beginning of the Twenty-first Century**

# 18
# The Holocaust on Screen: Speculations on an American Motion Picture Genre

## Thomas Doherty

If the assertion that the Holocaust is a motion picture genre risks blasphemy, then the notion that the genre is somehow peculiarly American amounts to a kind of warped chauvinism. Yet the popularity of Hollywood depictions of the Holocaust in a nation notoriously provincial in film tastes is as undeniable as it is anomalous. When it comes to the Holocaust, at least, Americans have been willing, even eager, to look beyond their own borders. Whether as a distinctly American or universally resonant phenomenon, the motion picture genre that has coalesced around the Holocaust calls for speculations equally informed by film smarts and historical awareness, an interdisciplinary outlook that keeps one eye on the screen and the other on the scholarship. Thus forewarned, the best way to proceed is to sketch out some basic definitions and critical categories and then to pose some questions that might guide an inquiry into Holocaust cinema. Some considerations are common to any study of the Holocaust, some are unique to film and television studies, and some are placed in heightened relief when the Holocaust is rendered in moving imagery. Not all, to be sure, speak only to an American perspective.

At the outset, even a confirmed cinephile must acknowledge the primacy of historical currents not film studies. To speak broadly, two main lines of interpretation shape the grimmest of academic disciplines, the field of Holocaust studies. The first line sees the Holocaust as unique and unprecedented in human history, the logical culmination of 2,000 years of anti-Semitism, the supreme expression of race hatred harnessed to the destructive power of the modern state. What happened to the Jews between 1933 and 1945 was an innovation. After all, the word "genocide" first entered the language during the Nuremberg Trials, a coinage made necessary by the postmortem tally from World War II. The second outlook sees the first as too optimistic and naive. Genocide has been a time-honored practice in human affairs since *homo sapiens* wiped out the neanderthals during the Pleistocene Age. What happened to the Jews – and the Slavs, Gypsies, and sundry other so-called *Untermenschen* – repeats the bloody rituals of a long tradition. The Armenians, Native Americans, Australian Aborigines, Cambodians, Rwandans, the untold millions exterminated in the USSR and in Communist China – all these peoples, whether targeted for reasons of race, class, ethnicity, or creed – were victims of genocidal campaigns no different in kind than that inflicted upon European Jewry by Nazi Germany. As Richard Rubenstein argues in *The Cunning of History: The Holocaust and the American Future*, "utterly mistaken is any view that would isolate Nazism and its supreme expression, bureaucratic mass murder and the bureaucratically administrated society of total domination, from the mainstream of Western culture."[1]

Yet in any litany of genocidal horrors, the Holocaust remains the classic case, the emblematic instance, the horror with the highest profile. In this, it is unmistakably unique and for a unique reason. As culture, if not history, the destruction of the European Jews achieved pre-eminence – at least in part – on the authority of the moving imagery that documents and dramatizes it. Just as World War II remains the twentieth century event most thoroughly chronicled by 35 mm film, so the Holocaust is the genocide most thoroughly recorded and portrayed by the motion picture camera. From the newsreels released to an astonished world in April and May 1945 – the *locus classicus* of Holocaust cinema – to the ongoing flood of archival documentaries, docu-dramas, and action-adventure fare – the sheer quantity and exceptional force of the film footage makes the Holocaust singular among genocides. Not to be glib, but the Holocaust has been a motion-picture-friendly event. A point of etymology is germane: the upper case designation "Holocaust" did not enter the language as a universal referent for the destruction of European Jewry until 1978, upon the telecast of the NBC miniseries of the same name.

In confronting an ever-proliferating body of Holocaust-themed films and television shows, the task of cataloging the material (a descriptive job of work) is a necessary first step before ruminating over the aesthetic, historical, technological, cultural, and, inevitably, moral questions (a speculative act of interpretation) raised by representations of the Holocaust on screen. The first question is self-evident: just what *is* a Holocaust film? Is it only a film that in documentary or dramatic form depicts the historical moment of the Holocaust? Or is the definition elastic enough to fit films that inquire into the causes, the details, the meaning, and the legacy of the Holocaust? To appreciate the divergence of styles and themes that fall under the rubric of Holocaust cinema, consider a pair of likely entries. Vittorio De Sica's *The Garden of the Finzi-Continis* (1971) is a serene period piece, more a dappled love story than a political tract, but as the Fascist background noise escalates into a cacophony that disrupts the quiet existence of a refined family of Italian Jews, history breaks up the garden party and the intra-religious class distinctions between aristocratic Jews and middle-class Jews collapse under the brand of the all-encompassing yellow star.

In blunt contrast to the elegant style and plush design of *The Garden of the Finzi-Continis* is the no-nonsense stance and low-tech resolution of Claude Lanzmann's epic documentary *Shoah* (1985). An investigation of the bureaucracy of mass death as clinical and systematic as its subject, the film fixes its gaze on the machinery of the Holocaust for every second of its nine-and-a-half-hour running time while unwinding not one single frame of archival newsreel footage.

A lush pageant and a blurry documentary: it would be difficult to imagine two films more dissimilar in sensibility and style. Yet each is – intuitively, indisputably – an exemplar of Holocaust cinema.

However, even with so common sense a notion of what fits the rough criteria, the definitional lines of Holocaust cinema, as with any motion picture genre, are bound to be hazy and porous. Inevitably, categories will blur into each other and critics should not to be too dogmatic about admission requirements. Just as the search for firm boundaries around motion picture genres such as the musical or the Western buckle around the edges, attempts to constrict the range of the Holocaust film are doomed to failure. Nonetheless, a working definition can offer some helpful guidance: Holocaust cinema embraces any motion picture or television show, documentary or fictional, that derives its narrative content or emotional core from the genocidal campaign waged by Nazi Germany, pre-eminently but not exclusively, against European Jewry. It need not be set during the Third Reich or depict Nazi depredations or concentration camps, but its interest in the means of discrimination and extermination, or the legacy of same, must be central not peripheral.

Again, to clarify the range of options while restricting the field, two examples might be useful. A landmark treatment of the Holocaust on film, Sidney Lumet's *The Pawnbroker* (1965) is a somber portrait of a concentration camp survivor trapped behind the bars of another kind of prison as a pawnshop proprietor in Harlem. Suffused with Christian imagery and climaxed with a Christ-like sacrifice, the film flashbacks from the Harlem present to the Nazi past – sometimes in jump-cut glimpses, sometimes in more extended reveries. Emotionally stunted, tormented by the "then" and the "now" alike, the pawnbroker shuffles like a sleepwalker through his own life, a survivor in name only. In a psychic sense, he has never been truly liberated from the concentration camp.

Seemingly light years away from the bleak milieu of *The Pawnbroker*, Bryan Singer's *X-Men* (2000) is a big budget fantasy awash in Computer Generated Imagery and wondrous FX. Against expectations, however, it opens with a striking prologue set in Poland in 1944. Evoking the *mise en scene* of *Schindler's List* (1993) more than the panels of Marvel Comics, the scene shows a parade of yellow-starred Jews and tattooed workers being led into a death camp. A young Jewish boy witnesses his family pass through the gates, to certain death. When the boy tries to follow, he is brutally beaten by Nazi guards. The trauma leaves him, a mutant with telekinetic powers over magnetism, with an abiding hatred of all humanity. Yet no matter how disturbing the introduction – and the prologue does send out an emotional and thematic energy for the reminder of the film – the Holocaust backstory in *X-Men*, unlike *The Pawnbroker*, is not central to the narrative. *X-Men* references the Holocaust, but does not confront it.

Scanning a sampling of likely films through this definitional filter can generate a modest taxonomy for Holocaust cinema. The conventional cinematic divide – between documentary and fiction – fixes the boundaries of the two main entries. Types of documentary include:

1.  *The archival originals*: documentary footage shot between 1933 and 1945 by any of the Axis or Allied powers, whether by commercial newsreel outfits or government agencies, whether professionally polished cinema or amateur home movies. Almost always in grainy black and white, the newsreels and kindred material comprise the privileged documentary record of the Holocaust, bequeathing a montage of indelible horrors and stark images: crematoria, corpses ("stacked like cordwood"), mass graves, tattooed forearms, the skeletal physiques and vacant eyes of survivors. So well known and incessantly unwound is this cinematic heritage, that the discovery of new archival originals can have an eerie and hypnotic impact, especially if shot in the rarer format of color. Exemplars include raw footage from the US Army Signal Corps and the newsreel issues.

2.  *The archival documentary*: far and away the most popular entry in the Holocaust genre, the postwar archival documentary sets footage from the past in relief against testimony from the present, drawing on the archival originals, supplemented and intercut with eyewitness and expert testimony, to uncover the horrors of 1933–45. All the standard techniques of documentary cinema are exploited for emotional impact (invisible editing, inquisitive camera movements, voiceover narration, commentating music), but the impulse is mainly historical, the theme an emphatic "Never Forget!" Exemplars include Alain Resnais' pioneering *Night and*

*Fog* (1955) and the "Genocide" episode from Thames Television's magisterial *The World at War* series (1975).

3. *The documentary meditation*: whereas the archival documentary tends to be single-mindedly historical in cast, the documentary meditation tends to be pensive and philosophical in temper. Rather than the emphatic declaration "Never Forget!" the plaintive query "How Did It Happen?" motivates the enterprise – though sometimes the tone may shift to the accusative ("How Could We Let It Happen?"). The inquiring expert – an historian or, increasingly, the filmmaker on a personal quest – is often granted equal screen time with survivors. Exemplars include Marcel Ophuls' *The Sorrow and the Pity* (1969) and Claude Lanzmann's *Shoah* (1985).

4. *The documentary biopic*: the intersection of wartime history and personal biography, the documentary biopic focuses on a single person, family unit, or informal cohort whose fate serves as synecdoche for the wider terror. Family photo albums and private home movies unwind as contrast to the Big Picture pageant of history; the testimony of relatives, not experts, tends to dominate the screen time. By turns a tribute to human endurance and a poignant eulogy for the dead, the documentary biopic seeks to give a single face to the mind-numbing statistics. Exemplars include *Kitty: A Return to Auschwitz* (1979) and Jon Blair's *Anne Frank Remembered* (1997). A variant of the form is *the documentary memoir*, in which the filmmaker undertakes a personal journey of discovery about his or her own family's Holocaust-torn past while exploring an intriguing tributary of Holocaust scholarship, such as Aviva Slesin's *Secret Lives: Hidden Children and Their Rescuers During WWII* (2002).

Types of drama include:

1. *The docu-drama*: set during the Third Reich, somber in tone and serious in purpose, the Holocaust docu drama recruits history in the service of melodrama – and vice versa. Almost always, Nazi depredations are depicted in realistic terms and the aesthetic stance purports to deny the pleasures of traditional Hollywood narrative while dutifully exploiting cinematic conventions to tug at emotions and quicken the pulse. Exemplars include the TV miniseries *Holocaust* (1978) and Steven Spielberg's *Schindler's List* (1993).

2. *The generic hybrid*: the grafting of the Holocaust either as foreground event or narrative backstory onto traditional film genres such as psychological portraits, thrillers, action adventures, and biopics. Though the Holocaust is the emotional hook and dramatic fulcrum for the

narrative, it may also be a kind of McGuffin, propelling a more-or-less conventional three-act dramaturgy. As the most open-ended and therefore most popular of the non-documentary variants, the generic hybrid or allegory drawing on the Holocaust tends to complicate matters of definition ("What is a Holocaust film?"). Exemplars include *The Pawnbroker* (1965), John Schlesinger and William Goldman's *Marathon Man* (1976), Franklin F. Schaffner and Ira Levin's *The Boys from Brazil* (1978), and Alan J. Pakula and William Styron's *Sophie's Choice* (1982).

3. *Artistic experiments and provocations*: a catch-all category for avowedly confrontational or controversial depictions of the Holocaust on screen. At one end, it encompasses works of high purpose and experimental nature whose treatment of the Holocaust is counter-intuitive and audacious but still manifestly earnest and sincere. Exemplars include Sean Mathias and Martin Sherman's *Bent* (1997) and Roberto Beningni's *Life Is Beautiful* (1998). At the other extreme, the films – sometimes dubbed "Nazi chic" or "concentration camp chic" – may revel in the ethos and iconography of the Third Reich and even the Holocaust to titillate spectators by eroticizing Nazi regalia and showcasing the nudity, sado-masochism, and bondage associated with the concentration camps. Where the generic hybrid foregrounds questions of definition, the artistic provocation highlights questions of decency ("Is this appropriation of the Holocaust beyond the pale?"). Exemplars include Liliana Cavani's *The Night Porter* (1974) and Lina Wertmuller's *Seven Beauties* (1976).

If the above categories may be accepted as a rough map to the terrain of Holocaust cinema, four frames of analysis suggest themselves: aesthetic, historical, technological, and cultural. As with the generic categories, each angle of inquiry trespasses freely into adjacent territory.

# The Aesthetic Bind

Aesthetics are always operative: Holocaust cinema is not a transcendent realm beyond artistic technique. Formal questions of beauty, tone, technique, and representation are crucial and unavoidable. Even in Holocaust cinema, the joy of creation inspires the filmmaker and the pleasure of the text lures the spectator. For many film critics, taking their cue from the literary tradition, the Holocaust is cheapened by too much flash and artifice: an austere, quiet, and understated tone is held to be more suitable than the ripe histrionics of sudsy melodrama or the bluster of vengeful action adventure. In Holocaust cinema, as in a Holocaust memoir, a blank, unblinking gaze packs more punch than a tear-stained wail to heaven. Compare, in *Schindler's List*, the crisp execution of a female engineer with the lachrymose soliloquy recited in the final reel. A telling instance of a bad aesthetic choice sabotaging Holocaust cinema occurs in the documentary *Anne Frank Remembered*, namely, the selection of the actress Glenn Close to play the voice of Anne Frank. The instantly recognizable tones of the strong-willed, middle-aged, full-boned Yankee woman reading the diary of the precocious, pubescent German-Dutch girl ring out only as a reminder of vocal miscasting. Close is mature, strong, and self possessed; Anne is young, vulnerable, and still a-borning.

The most important aesthetic choice comes at the very outset: tragedy or comedy, docu-drama or fantasy? When screening the Holocaust, entire motion picture genres are deemed off limits, none more so than comedy. Interestingly, the two most notable comic treatments of the Holocaust were produced in Italy not Hollywood: *Seven Beauties* and *Life Is Beautiful*, both of which generated heated controversy for farcical antics set in concentration camps.

If a live action depiction of the Holocaust must not be comically cartoonish, still less should actual cartoons be employed to caricature the most grotesque of realities. The prospect of a full-length animated cartoon portraying death camp existence may seem like a sick joke, but the high concept has circulated around Hollywood for years. In 1986, Art Spiegelman's comic book *Maus: A Survivor's Tale* took a conceit appalling on its face and created one of the most powerful depictions of the Holocaust in print – and indeed proved that the comic medium was especially well suited to the tragic meaning. The ultimate destiny of Spiegelman's brilliant, media-minded "tour de force" may well be on the motion picture screen, perhaps even under the corporate logo of Disney Pictures.

Finally, aesthetics shade the meaning of Holocaust cinema in another colorful if often unintended way. As in Milton's *Paradise Lost*, where Satan is the most magnetic character speaking the best lines, the full throated villainy of the Nazi oppressor limns a more charismatic screen character than the meek nobility of the Jewish victim. "The trouble with Eichmann," Hannah Arendt famously observed, "was precisely that there were so many like him, and that they were neither perverted not sadistic, that they were, and still are, terribly and terrifyingly normal."[2] By contrast, the trouble with Nazis in Holocaust cinema is that they are so terribly and terrifyingly attractive. Susan Sontag's phrase "fascinating fascism" well conjures the affinity of Nazi characters and costuming to celluloid. Michael Moriarty's performance as Dorf in *Holocaust* and Ralph Fiennes' performance as Goetz in *Schindler's List* are probably the two best known examples. Confess: how dreary would each film be were it not for its deliciously satanic Nazi villains?

## The Historical Baseline

In *Visions of the Past: The Challenge of Film to Our Idea of the Past*, historian Robert A. Rosenstone expressed something of an academic consensus when he declared that "film changes the rules of the historical game, insisting on its own sort of truths, truths which arise from a visual and aura realm that is difficult to capture in words."[3] Holocaust cinema defies the maxim: In this area, critics, historians, and most audiences insist on applying the old rules of the historical game. Of all the motion picture genres "inspired by actual events," none is held to sterner standards for historical accuracy than Holocaust cinema. A lighthearted costume drama or overblown biblical epic may with impunity ignore the historical record and narrative credibility: Holocaust cinema must adhere closely to known facts and plausible scenarios.

Normally so ready to sacrifice historical accuracy in the service of sure-fire entertainment, Hollywood has been more likely than not to embrace an ethos of somber realism to achieve dramatic impact and acquire moral ballast in depicting the Holocaust. Of course, many crucial details – the precise rendering of the concentration camp milieu and the physical condition of the inmates – cannot be conjured with utter fidelity to the source. Even the most megalomaniacal auteur cannot starve a cast into eighty-pound skeletons. As Lance Morrow ruefully observed after watching the execution scenes in the TV miniseries *Holocaust*: the victims will always look like "extras jumping on cue."[4]

Not incidentally, the relaxation of censorship constraints has encouraged the adoption of an aesthetic of brutal frankness in the depiction of the violence, torture, and gore of the death camps. In fact, the high seriousness of the Holocaust genre grants special dispensation from the normal censorship standards applied to motion pictures rated by the Motion Picture Association of America and television programming subject to oversight by network standards and practices departments. This was especially true in the case of the TV mini-series *Holocaust* and the first network telecast of *Schindler's List*, both of which, in their day, flaunted a shocking amount of explicit violence and nudity.

In terms of historical accuracy, Holocaust documentaries, even more than docu-dramas, are subject to a level of critical examination usually accorded only scholarly monographs. As a result, the credibility of two recurrent documentary characters has invited special scrutiny and due skepticism:

1. *The unimpeachable eyewitness*: either the warrior, the stalwart fighter who has endured the crucible of combat in the just cause of World War II, or the victim, the innocent sufferer and survivor of the Holocaust who has withstood torment beyond imagining. The moral statute of the warrior or the survivor grants an esteem to the speaker and a verification to the testimony that, when validated by the eye of the camera, seems above reproach. "The witness has the authority no one else has," declares Eli Wiesel, whose own unimpeachable presence has lent authority to more than one archival documentary.[5] The wary historian knows that the human memory recalling traumatic events from over half a century ago will tend to suppress, forget, embroider, and remember it all as actual fact. Clearly too, many eyewitnesses featured in archival documentaries have told their stories more than once; some speak with the pacing and eloquence of the practiced raconteur. Yet the apparatus of cinematic grammar invariably baths eyewitnesses in an aura of credence and respect – though, sometimes, surely, they do not deserve it.

2. *The star witness*: a subset of the unimpeachable witness, the star witness is the natural character actor, a mediagenic presence from the world of ordinary people whose articulate testimony, engaging personality, ready wit, and made-to-order visage dominates the screen space. In *Shoah*, the Polish resistance fighter Jan Karski fits this bill, as does past victim and present US Congressman Tom Lantos in James Moll's *The Last Days* (1998). A cautionary instance of star witness con artistry is Dr Leon Bass, the dynamic speaker from the notoriously duplicitous documentary by William Miles and Nina Rosenblum, *Liberators: Fighting on Two Fronts in World War II* (1992). In a riveting screen performance, Bass holds forth to wrenching effect – though much of what he says is in the opinion of this writer, patently fabricated.[6]

## The Technological Breakthroughs

Lately, a series of astonishing advances in make-up, special effects, and (especially) Computer Generated Imagery (CGI) have narrowed the distance between the apparently real and the obviously fabricated, even in the realm of Holocaust cinema. Tim Blake Nelson's *The Grey Zone* (2002), a searing depiction of a sonderkommando revolt in the Auschwitz death camp in 1944, may mark a kind of tipping point for cinematic representations of the Holocaust. The sonderkommandos were a unit of Jewish prisoners forced to perform the unimaginable tasks of corralling Nazi victims into the gas chambers, of hauling stacks of corpses onto carts, and of shoving the remains into the crematorium ovens. In *The Grey Zone*, that job of work is depicted with an unflinching eye to the graphic and the grotesque. Likewise, Episode #9 of HBO's miniseries *Band of Brothers* (2001) recreates the environs of a liberated concentration camp and the physical condition of the emaciated inmates with an unprecedented level of verisimilitude. All of the instruments of Hollywood magic have been orchestrated to make the unimaginable true-to-life.

Taken together, the profound technological innovations that have transformed computer-age motion pictures may one day alter the landscape of Holocaust cinema. When the technology of photofabrication, in videotape and cinema no less than the still picture, outpaces the ability of the spectator to detect it, the integrity and veracity of any moving image, perhaps the whole notion of documentary cinema, is called into question. The tell-tale indicators of tampering by which a discerning eye could once perceive alterations in the photographic image – the difference in film grain, the visible lines in airbrushing, the mismatch of lighting and background – have been wiped clean by seamless matching, "morphing," and digital editing techniques. Thus, though the computer revolution in motion picture art has allowed filmmakers to achieve unprecedented levels of verisimilitude in Holocaust cinema, it also has the potential to undercut the status of the archival originals. Once unimpeachable testimony of the reality of the Holocaust – 35 mm photography being the template of truth – film is now an infinitely malleable medium, no more a reliable reflection of reality than any other pictorial expression.

Iconic still images of the Holocaust have already been altered and exhibited as artworks, notably at the controversial show on the Holocaust and Art hosted by the Jewish Museum in New York in 2002. So far, on the theatrical screen, the Holocaust remains a sacred preserve. However, the rule of motion picture technology holds that if the FX means exists to achieve an effect, filmmakers will deploy them. In short, if Forrest Gump can appear in newsreel footage from the Kennedy administration, he can also pop up at Bergen-Belsen.

# The Cultural Angle

Hollywood has been a major player in a cultural usurpation that has been dubbed "the Americanization of the Holocaust," a movement that has shifted scholarly and dramatic attention away from the site of the event onto American shores.[7] The very title of Martin Ostrow's documentary *America and the Holocaust: Deceit and Indifference* (1994) signposts this trend – as does the billing in the hierarchy of importance. The focus *will* be America.

Of course, Hollywood is also the most prominent site for the success and influence of American Jews. Kinship networks and vicarious identifications have obviously heightened interest in, and eased the production path for, Holocaust-themed scenarios. As Steven Spielberg explained during the filming of *Schindler's List*, one of his animating motivations was to pay homage to his Jewish kinsmen and to repent for the frivolous depiction of Nazism in his Indiana Jones films. However, the box office returns, high ratings, and critical regard accrued by Holocaust-minded productions from Hollywood demonstrate an appeal beyond a niche market of American Jews. This is curious: whatever else the Holocaust is, it is a European event inflicted by Europeans on Europeans. Perhaps America – the city on the hill, the last best hope of mankind, the self-styled center of the universe – simply cannot abide the thought that the most dramatic event in twentieth century history happened on foreign shores and involves it only tangentially.

As guideposts for inquiry into the most discomforting of motion picture genres, the definitions, categories, and speculations proffered above are preliminary and tentative: meant to be suggestive not prescriptive. Speaking with calculated hyperbole, Eli Wiesel once declared that the only decent response to the Holocaust was silence, advice he never followed either on the page or on screen. In the age of the moving image, an historical event whose looming presence is so powerfully yoked to moving imagery, and whose raw material offers such fertile field for documentary, melodrama, and action-adventure, will continue to be drawn on, and exploited, for motion pictures and television shows. The best the critic can do is to look closely at the history and the cinema before presuming to break that silence.

# Notes

1. Richard L. Rubenstein, *The Cunning of History: The Holocaust and the American Future*, New York, 1974, p. 31.

2. Hannah Arendt, *Eichmann in Jerusalem*, New York, 1963, p. 276.

3. Robert A. Rosenstone, *Visions of the Past: The Challenge of Film To*

*Our Idea of History*, Cambridge MA, 1995, p. 15.

4. Lance Morrow, "Television and the Holocaust," *Time*, 1 May 1978, p. 53f.

5. Ron Wertheimer, "Challenging Humanity to Try to Do Better," *New York Times*, 24 October 2002, B8.

6. Of the many reports and scholarly articles debunking *Liberators*, see especially "Findings of the Review Team: *An Examination of Liberators: Fighting on Two Fronts in World War II*," prepared for Thirteen/WNET by Morton Silverstein, 19 August 1993, 13; Daniel J. Leab, "Clement Price, *Liberators*, and Truth in History: A Comment," *Historical Journal of Film, Radio, and Television* 14 (1994), 467–78.

7. See Hilene Flanzbaum (ed.), *The Americanization of the Holocaust*, Baltimore, 1999, and Peter Novick, *The Holocaust in American Life*, Boston, 1999.

# 19
# The Radicalization of German Memory in the Age of its Commercial Reproduction: Hitler and the Third Reich in the TV Documentaries of Guido Knopp

*Wulf Kansteiner*

Since the mid-1990s the historical documentaries of Guido Knopp have dominated the German airwaves and cable systems. No other type of historical programming, let alone any other type of historical representation, has reached as many citizens and consumers. No other vision of history had the same success in shaping Germany's collective memory of the Nazi era.[1] This outcome is the result of a complicated interaction between market forces, the evolution of modern communication technologies, and the generational dynamisms of Germany's historical culture. But at the heart of the Knopp phenomenon are the radical visual aesthetics of a new type of historical documentary that were crafted by Guido Knopp over the course of ten years and that have been effectively reproduced under his supervision by a small, cohesive, and privileged group of television makers in the Zweite Deutsche Fernsehen (ZDF).

The aesthetics of these programs are easily described and criticized. The numerous ZDF documentary mini-series about the Third Reich, which were released in the last ten years, rely on an attractive combination of fast cuts, iconic references, dialectics of color and black-and-white footage, dramatic music, an aura of authenticity, and a compelling narrative framework that is delivered in short, distinguished sound bites. On the visual level the programs combine eyewitness testimony, original photos and Nazi footage, blurry simulations of historical events, and short clips of historical sites, often with Knopp's reassuring presence in the foreground. Constant change keeps these different elements in motion and the viewers alert. The eyewitnesses, dramatically illuminated by spotlights, are never allowed to say more than a few sentences at a time; the photos are taped so that they appear like moving images; the original footage, featuring Nazi propaganda highlights, is digitally manipulated whenever the feed is not "up to speed" or when the images are already so familiar to the audience that some alienation devices seem appropriate; the staged historical events are shot with hand-held, subjective cameras that deliver unstable images with little informational value but lots of visual appeal. Each of these segments lasts less than a minute and often only seconds.[2]

The ZDF staff further accentuates the dynamic visual collages through carefully calibrated sound tracks that add sound effects to silent footage, introduce dramatic scores (with a particular partiality to Wagner and Klaus Doldinger), and rely on the sonorous voice of Christian Brückner (the German voice of Robert de Niro) to enact the script.[3] The voice-over as well as Knopp's remarks on the screen seem beyond reproach since they deliver only politically correct messages. The statements eloquently express the anti-anti-Nazi stance of their authors and impress upon the audience a general pacifist worldview and the need for international reconciliation. In addition, the commentary renders explicit one of the visual and conceptual construction principles of the programs and thus ties together the potentially dispersive images. In most cases the material unfolds along the conventional trajectory of the biography of Adolf Hitler. His actions, crimes, and neuroses, explicated in the commentary, integrate the Nazi footage, the eyewitness testimony, and the play scenes. The films feature two additional key subjects, the war and the Holocaust, but they are always visually and conceptually anchored in Hitler's objectives and obsessions. However, while the commentary links the different components of the programs and introduces one reading of the material, it never controls the semantic possibilities that Knopp's high-speed documentaries entail. In fact, as the new paradigm has taken shape the discursive level of interpretation has become increasingly detached from the visual text. A very appealing, provocative, and transgressive vision of Nazism has emerged that belies the politically correct messages and opens venues of identification that are engaging, revisionist, and, as some critics have charged, even fascist in nature.

It has to be appreciated that Knopp is really the first German television maker who has focused directly and extensively on Hitler. In the past, a few important documentary films have been made about the Führer, most important Erwin Leiser's *Mein Kampf* and Joachim Fest's *Hitler: Eine Karriere*,[4] but on television Hitler was both omni-present and marginal; he appeared in almost all programs about the Nazi past but was very rarely the primary subject of these shows.[5] Since the second half of the 1990s the Knopp school has explicitly restored Hitler to his position as a central historical agent for the benefit of generations of Germans who are quite unfamiliar with the historical record.

Even this superficial analysis illustrates that the specific achievements of the documentaries are visual in nature. The juxtaposition of very familiar material with novel and surprising images, for instance, color photographs from 1938 or simulated walks through Hitler's bunker, and the acceleration of this mix to neck-breaking speed represents an under-appreciated feast of television editing.[6] Unlike past productions, the films of the Knopp school are truly visual texts. Up until the 1980s German TV documentaries were primarily discursive constructs whose producers used visual material as illustrations or refractions of their intellectual concepts.[7] But even the best compilation, essay, or interview films produced in this tradition quickly became anachronisms with limited audience appeal as the medium evolved into a visually driven communication tool, especially in the context of the commercialization of German television after 1984. Knopp and his associates have taken the important step of bringing the genre of historical documentary up to date by relegating discourse to a secondary position in which it only assists the visual record but does not create its meaning. The resulting, complex weave of visual stimuli is clearly appreciated by the viewers. In fact, the films have been produced in collaboration with the audience since Knopp has developed the new paradigm partly in response to consumer feedback.

In contrast to the general audience, many professional and academic critics of Knopp's vision of history fail to understand his innovation. Reviewers have been too critical and too forgiving at the same time. They might appreciate the politically correct messages of the script or lash out against the intellectually insipid commentaries; either way they fail to understand that the script represents a marginal component in the overall design of the programs. In the same vein, critics have condemned the staged simulations of historical events and the digital manipulations of photographs and Nazi footage as superfluous technical frills and ridiculed Knopp's persistent search for new, unfamiliar visual material without realizing that these elements are at the core of the new language of history. As a result, the really important questions regarding the semantics of the new visual discourse and its relationship to Nazi culture have rarely been directly addressed. How did the new discourse evolve and how does the elaborate regimen of signs function on the primary, visual level? What interpretations of Nazism are suggested to the audience and how do these messages differ from the messages of Nazi visual culture on which the programs rely so heavily?

After Guido Knopp started working for the ZDF in 1978, he soon appeared on the screen as the moderator of a television discussion, a role he played frequently in the following decades.[8] In that capacity, he became involved in a high-profile project called *Narben*, whose production history illustrates what problems German television makers faced when they tried to respond to the media event *Holocaust* that had taken everybody by surprise in January 1979.[9] Broadcast by the ARD, the ZDF's only competitor in the age of the public television monopoly, the four parts of *Holocaust* had reached an average of 12 million viewers in 36 per cent of West Germany's television households.[10] This audience response to the US blockbuster made painfully clear that German television had neither recognized nor satisfied a popular demand for contemporary history. Not surprisingly, the media event caused hectic activity inside the public stations as television makers tried to get back in touch with their audience. The ZDF project *Narben*, developed in collaboration with Polish television, represents one of these attempts of making amends. The docudrama focused on the tumultuous history of Danzig/Gdansk in the twentieth century and approached the topic from the perspective of two actual individuals – one Polish, one German – who were born in the city before World War II.[11] Intended to advance the cause of German-Polish reconciliation and provide emotionally compelling everyday history, the production became the subject of intense internal politics. The budget spiraled out of control, one member of the production team entered contractual agreements with the Polish partners that had not been approved by the station's administration, and the director general of the ZDF, Günter von Hase, personally requested changes in the script, a highly unusual event as he himself acknowledged.[12] In the end, the program proved to be an awkward, slow combination of documentary and docu-play with little audience appeal. The three part series only reached a disappointing average of 2.2 million viewers.[13] Despite these shortcomings, *Narben* became a modest PR-success because reviewers applauded its political objectives.[14]

Knopp was not directly involved in the design or implementation of *Narben*, but he had approached his superiors with the idea to organize a live television discussion with prominent guests after the broadcast of the last episode because the docu-drama would raise all kinds of emotions that should be addressed in an open forum.[15] Von Hase welcomed the initiative with some "helpful" suggestions about the composition of the group of discussants and the program was broadcast at 10:30 pm on 17 May 1981.[16] The discussion like the preceding show caused a number of anti-Polish phone calls, but it is remarkable that none of the seventy callers personally attacked Knopp who moderated the exchange on the screen.[17] In addition, in the following days, several reviewers acknowledged Knopp's sensitive, intelligent performance as television host.[18] The participation in the project gave Knopp the opportunity to pass his first test in the public arena of memory politics and gave him valuable insights into the organization of international, high-profile memory events. If subsequent developments are any indication he made the most of that experience.

Knopp came to the ZDF at age 30 after a short career as a newspaper journalist with *Die Welt* and the *Frankfurter Allgemeine Zeitung*. In 1981 he was already the *de facto* leader of the small ZDF subdivision for programs on contemporary history.[19] In that capacity he administered a low profile weekly series that featured 15-minute-interviews with German academics about all kinds of topical concerns and helped produce programs about such diverse subjects as Hambach and nuclear power.[20] Knopp turned to Nazi history and memory only after the broadcast of *Narben* and after a couple of years of television experience.

Throughout the 1980s Knopp produced a string of fairly conventional documentaries that reflected his fundamental beliefs about the history of National Socialism and only occasionally foreshadowed the more radical formal innovations of the 1990s. From the very beginning, Hitler was the conceptual and visual center of these interventions. Even Knopp's first full-fledged television documentaries about the lack and failure of German resistance began with spectacular coverage of the Führer.[21] Subsequent programs went to great lengths to cast the German people in the role of seduced victims of Hitler and his propaganda minister, for instance the 1987 documentary about Goebbels entitled *Der Verführer*.[22] On that occasion Knopp and his colleagues paraded a string of associates of the propaganda minister, who enthusiastically attested to their former boss's exceptional intellectual powers and manipulative skills. Not surprisingly, the reviewers of the broadcast admonished the lack of critical distance and reproached Knopp for his refusal to explore the German people's willing participation in the dialectics of seduction.[23]

The programs of the 1980s already attested to Knopp's skill in delineating interpretations of Nazism that were acceptable to large segments of German society, even if that meant projecting an anachronistic, politically correct democratic consensus into the past. For instance, when exploring Hitler's rise to power the ZDF historians interviewed a range of contemporaries, from labor union activists and Communist Party members to industrialists and military officers.[24] This nicely balanced pool of eyewitnesses, which reflected the ZDF's permanent search for political equilibrium between Germany's political competitors, was asked about the reasons for their failure to resist Hitler's chancellorship. While the representatives of the left openly acknowledged their political and strategic mistakes, the more conservative interviewees seemed a little surprised by such inquiries since they had helped Hitler gain power in the first place and had harbored no intentions of resistance, at least not for many years.[25] In this case, fairly conservative interpretations of Nazism resulted from a sense of fairness, the ideal of *Ausgewogenheit* that is dear to any journalist who wants to keep his job in public television. On other occasions Knopp achieved the same effect by simply championing the perspective of the average eyewitness. For this purpose he even committed a modest taboo infraction when he included detailed testimony about rapes perpetrated by Soviet soldiers in a program on *Trümmerfrauen*.[26] But like other projects dedicated to the history of everyday life, the program proved severely flawed because Knopp highlighted the suffering of German civilians without providing the historical context of the German crimes in the Soviet Union. The pitfalls of *Alltagsgeschichte* had already been adamantly discussed by German historians and some reviewers rejected Knopp's highly selective representation of World War II history.[27]

By the end of the 1980s Knopp had established himself at the ZDF as a provider of well-researched historical documentaries for late night audiences. With few exceptions his programs were scheduled after 10 pm, and in that environment Knopp delivered respectable but not extraordinary audience shares between 7 and 17 per cent of television households. The public networks were not yet facing serious commercial competition and Knopp's ratings, which reflected audiences between 1.5 and 5.5 million West German viewers, placed him in the mainstream of late-night television information.[28]

Among more left leaning television critics, Knopp had gained a reputation for his routine anniversary productions featuring apologetic interpretations of the Third Reich that demonized Hitler and exculpated his followers.[29] From their perspective Knopp appeared as a staunch defender and popularizer of the politics of memory of Chancellor Kohl who launched an aggressive campaign of historical normalization and national revival through museums, memorials and public rituals after he came to power in 1982.[30] Because of these political predilections Knopp seemed a perfect match for the *Regierungssender* ZDF and it was not surprising that he became a central figure in the media festivities during the 40th anniversary of the Federal Republic in 1989 and the subsequent media celebrations of German unification in 1990.[31] His activism for the cause of German unity pleased his superiors and gained Knopp the

*Bundesverdienstkreuz* but the constitutional patriotism of the anniversary programs as well as the more conventional patriotism of the unification shows elicited little enthusiasm among West German viewers.[32] All programs, including Knopp's, produced mediocre ratings.[33] The lack of audience success might have encouraged Knopp to return to history and shape the popular memory of events that viewers found much more interesting than the "historic" liberation of their eastern brothers and sisters.

The large-scale visual exploration of the history of World War II, which Knopp launched in the 1990s, was already planned before unification and Knopp had already developed ties to Soviet television to gain access to new visual sources. But the disintegration of the Soviet Union made this long-term collaboration much more attractive to the Russian partners. Over the next decade the television historians of the ZDF pioneered the exploitation of Eastern European film archives that proved to be gold mines for Western media corporations. Opening this vault allowed Knopp to present his viewers with a seemingly endless supply of new footage of their favorite historical topic – Hitler and the Nazis, but he still faced one serious challenge. There is no indication that Knopp was particularly concerned about the critical reception of his work among intellectuals who regularly admonished that television in general and Knopp in particular failed to provide the type of accurate, analytically ambitious historical representations that they appreciated in the publications of their colleagues in academia.[34] But Knopp's public statements of the time indicate that he shared the assessments of some more supportive critics who pointed out that German television had not found a recipe for interesting, visually and emotionally compelling historical documentaries, which avoided discursive overload and had true mainstream appeal.[35] In the realm of television fiction *Holocaust*, *Heimat*, and many other, less famous television plays had shown how the general audience could be integrated into the important task of collective remembrance.[36] But factual, documentary television had never followed suit and a closer look at the aesthetics of Knopp's early programs explains this shortcoming. Despite all his efforts Knopp still produced illustrated history lectures. The voice-over commentaries, delivered in terse, fairly monotone voices dominated the productions. The footage of historical sites and eyewitness accounts remained static. The interviewees delivered long-winded, staged testimony that occasionally exposed their shameful past conduct and dubious rationalizations for the few experts in front of the screen, but had little appeal for the uninitiated.[37] When Knopp himself appeared on the screen, which was increasingly the case, he sometimes came across as an arrogant lecturer talking down to his audience, or worse, like a student in an exam.[38] As a result, the Nazi newsreels remained the most exciting, dynamic component of the programs.

The situation began to change slowly in the late 1980s as the Knopp productions picked up speed and displayed more visual complexity. After these modest innovations, some reviewers quickly complained about hectic storylines and visual overloads.[39] These reactions reflected the increasing impatience among intellectuals with the lack of analytical depth in Knopp's programs and were hardly representative for the opinion of the general audience. But it is very likely that the viewers and television administrators of the 1980s were also not yet ready for the radical aesthetics and reinterpretations of German history that Knopp was aiming for. The viewers' familiarity with fast-paced, commercial television and the administrators' fear of competition were preconditions for the development and successful reception of Knopp's later works. In 1988 this familiarity and fear did not yet exist because privately owned networks, introduced in 1984, had not yet reached sizable audiences and the administrators in the powerful public television stations had not yet realized the full extent of the coming threat. By the early 1990s, however, when Knopp achieved his aesthetic and audience breakthrough, the viewers were familiar with the pace and style of commercial television and the administrators had felt the pressure of competition. Both groups could now appreciate Knopp's attempt to emulate and compete with that new style of television. Consequently, only the transformation of the West German television landscape into a dual system of commercial and public networks created the cultural and political basis for the radicalization of German memory after unification.[40]

Knopp's early programs already featured some of the components of his later successes. Already in the early 1980s Knopp added machine gun sounds to the silent footage of mass executions, used segments of feature films, and staged historical events (all of which the critics dutifully objected to).[41] But the programs still lacked the *Gesamtkunstwerk* effect based on the elegant integration of image and sound and, most important, speed and scale. For instance, Knopp had yet to realize that eyewitness testimony, which helps to create an aura of authenticity, is best accelerated by "cutting the interviewee to pieces," – by using only small sound bites at a time that correspond exactly to the parallel moving images. All these innovations were gradually introduced as Knopp took on his most dramatic subject matter, World War II and Hitler and his henchmen, who had already once before been the subject of a sustained, polished and very successful media campaign.

Knopp used the many historical anniversaries of 1989 to delineate a vague outline of his goals as a documentary filmmaker.[42] But his public commitment to suspenseful, biographically structured programs has very little to say about his concrete media strategies and certainly does not capture the interesting aesthetic innovations that were developed in the ZDF in the coming years. In addition, the first sequels of Knopp's long World War II epic, *Die Saat des Krieges*, broadcast in the same year, still reflects conventional historiographical ambition and, as a consequence, is not very compelling as a visual document.[43] The first part reconstructs in great detail the diplomatic intrigues before and during the Munich treaty. The viewer is quickly lost in a maze of names and locations that are strung together by a complicated, long-winded commentary with few visual highlights. The included visual gimmicks do not change that experience – in fact, they remain gimmicks precisely because they appear so out of place. We see blurry figures behind glass doors engaged in hectic negotiations in Czech that are conveniently summarized for us by the voice-over comment. We see a ghost-like, faceless Hitler planning military mischief, and we observe an unintentionally comic Guido Knopp in front of the historic conference hotel pretending that Chamberlain and Hitler are just behind those walls and could walk out any second. Stretching his talents as an actor Knopp showed considerable commitment to the cause of filmmaking but little ingenuity as a filmmaker.[44]

That changed when the production of *Der verdammte Krieg* began in 1991 and the attack on the Soviet Union was jointly reenacted by the ZDF and Gostelcradio in Moscow.[45] Providing most of the funds, the German station was the dominant force of the production and the final cut was determined in Mainz, not in Moscow.[46] Nevertheless, the public relations officers of the ZDF emphasized the themes of partnership and reconciliation and announced the project with great pathos and hyperbole. The series, they said, deals with "the biggest battle in world history . . . which stood for many decades like an ocean of blood and tears between Russians and Germans."[47] But now, after fifty years, the pioneering collaboration would bring the one, indivisible truth and the message of peace and reconciliation to the viewers "between Aachen and Görlitz, between Brest and Wladiwostok."[48] The geographical ambition and pride, vaguely reminiscent of Hitler's obsession with colonial empires in the East, illustrates the uneasy combination of pacifist intentions and militaristic jargon characteristic for the whole series.[49] As the language slips its peaceful moorings and begins to celebrate the Sixth Army that "accomplishes its handiwork with deadly precision," the images enact an epic struggle that makes it difficult for the German viewers not to root for "their team", which faces extraordinary obstacles in the depth of the Russian steppe.[50]

Befitting such an exceptional competition the coverage begins with profiles of the cranky team leaders, Hitler and Stalin, and analyses of the line-up. The subsequent clashing of the titans is cast in the simple, compelling, and balanced aesthetics of a sports event as the German men advance swiftly on the screen, preferably from left to right, and are met by equally determined Soviet troops, including Cossacks on horseback flying from right to left. In the "brutal, dirty war on both sides" the men serve with great courage and suffer from the inhumane conditions and the destructive orders of their dictators and generals, as the selected eyewitnesses confirm repeatedly.[51] In some respects the Germans are more brutal, but their exceptionally vicious crimes are perpetrated against bystanders of the war and therefore not of much concern for the filmmakers (or, presumably, their audience).[52] In the meantime, like cheerleaders, the women eagerly support the war efforts in the armament industries at home. Finally, as with all good sports events, the competition is decided by chance. An untimely uprising in Yugoslavia, the early onset of winter with mud and snow, betrayal by spies, and the repeated irrational decisions of the Führer seal the fate of the German team. For the German viewers this approach sets in motion a string of attractive counterfactuals: what if the attack had been earlier, the winter later, or the Führer brighter? These questions and their answers, clearly implied by the films, expose the not so hidden emotional point of gravity of the whole undertaking.[53] The "we" in "we would have won" is right below the attractive visual surface and even more powerful because that affirmative "we" in relation to World War II has no place in the official culture of the Federal Republic. Occasionally, that "we" even sneaks in through the back door, for instance when Knopp turns to his Russian counterpart with the great line "All the sacrifices did not count for our dictator. What about yours?"[54]

The intellectual content of the series amounts to little more than above ironic summary but this simplistic emplotment is delivered with an exceptional wealth of finely tuned images. The subject matter and the international cooperation suggest the overall binary plot structure of the series, made possible by stunning visual material, especially from the Soviet archives. Rare color footage of the war reduces the distance between past and present and draws the viewers into the events. Engaging eyewitness testimony, by survivors who enjoy returning to their sites of memory, celebrates the courage and resilience of the average soldier. Dynamic black and white battle scenes attest to the awesome scale of the war, and the propaganda shots of the dictators remind the viewer, like the contemporaries, who was pulling the strings. The images and the contrasting rhythmic editing drive the narrative, set up the epic competition, and define the emotional stakes.

For the first time in Knopp's career as a television maker the language of the script, however revealing it may be, became subservient to a very attractive, transgressive visual text. Knopp and his associates might not even have been aware of their accomplishments (which made it easier for them to continue to attach simple, politically correct messages to much more ambivalent, provocative productions) but the aesthetics that came into existence when they reworked the intrinsically dramatic events of World War II with access to great material and within the context of an international collaboration produced a documentary paradigm that was the appropriate German answer to *Holocaust* precisely because it provided a much more honest reflection of German collective memory. It was also a fitting answer because *Der verdammte Krieg*, like *Holocaust* before, came into existence in a commercially charged environment, which encouraged television makers to take political risks and test the limits of historical taste. Few intellectual observers clearly perceived the change and even fewer were able to put them into language. Focusing on the explicit political and historical messages of the production they took issue with the tiresome political correctness, the overemphasis on questions of military strategy, and the fast, suspense-driven plot structure.[55] Occasionally, the critics went even further and argued that *Der verdammte Krieg* simply reinforced the visual and discursive codes of Nazi propaganda, resurrected the pathos of the front experience, and obliterated the question of German guilt.[56] But they often missed the real subject and achievements of the films, which have nothing to do with historical analysis, least of all historiographical analysis, and deal instead with honor, fate, myth, heroism, and, most important, repressed German military pride. As a sophisticated collage *Der verdammte Krieg* does not double Nazi aesthetics and propaganda. Rather, Knopp and Co. translate the topics of Nazi discourse into the visual and political languages of the late twentieth century and present a highly ambivalent, suspenseful film that is driven by its own internal contradictions, especially between its explicit political message and its aesthetic revisionism. This makes for good entertainment for today's audiences precisely because the programs are not direct reflections of Nazism but fragmented and fractured visions of the past that offer audiences the exceptional pleasure of remaining within the political consensus of the German democratic mainstream while playfully exploring the perspectives of the former perpetrators in a collective setting.

The ratings of *Der verdammte Krieg* look solid but unspectacular until one takes into consideration the rapidly changing television landscape in Germany in the 1990s. The first six episodes in June 1991 reached an average of 4.2 million viewers, the second installment of five episodes in January 1993, focusing on Stalingrad, was watched by 4.6 million, and the final six episodes of March/April 1995, covering the events until the end of the war, still attracted 3.8 million viewers.[57] Considering that the ZDF's overall market shares dropped from 25.4 to 14.7 per cent during the same period as result of commercial competition, the ratings represent an extraordinary success.[58]

The ratings indicate that many audience members considered *Der verdammte Krieg* the most interesting or the least objectionable program available at that point in time, but the viewers' involvement in the story on the screen could still fall anywhere within the wide spectrum between curious indifference and intense participation.[59] However, there are good reasons to assume that the latter is more likely than the former because an unusually large number of consumers of Knopp TV tend to engage in an active process of communication with the station during and after the broadcast of the shows through mail, telephone, and recently also e-mail. The number of letters and phone calls is very small in relation to the total audience. Their content is hardly representative, but viewers of Knopp documentaries are more likely to contact the station than viewers of other programs on the topic of Nazism.[60]

In response to *Der verdammte Krieg* the ZDF received a number of anti-Semitic and anti-Russian phone calls that have accompanied many programs on the subject matter.[61] In addition, and more to the point, the reactions to *Der verdammte Krieg* indicate that the audience appreciated the liberating, revisionist implications of its aesthetics and perceived and suggested remedies for the obvious contradiction between the visual language and the voiceover commentaries. For this purpose many viewers picked up the phone or wrote letters recommending that Knopp look into the theory that Barbarossa was a pre-emptive war. The repeated references to this standard myth of revisionist, nationalistic circles in thirty out of a total of eighty letters indicate that the authors expected sympathy for these ideas among the television makers and that, in their eyes, an explicit acknowledgement of these themes would bring the commentary in line with the show's appealing aesthetics.[62] The viewers' interests and interpretations also became embarrassingly obvious during the final television discussion as some callers were permitted to pose their question live on the air. Instead of joining in the celebration of reconciliation they bickered with the experts in the studio about the precise number of victims on the eastern front and insisted on the defensive nature of the campaign.[63] Knopp certainly did not create these attitudes but, intentionally or inadvertently, he invited the *post factum* identification with the perspective of the German military that is reflected in these reactions from the audience.

Taking the risk of producing expensive, high-profile, international documentary mini-series, rarely tried before, had paid off handsomely for the station and Knopp in times of tough competition with private networks. In a culture saturated with memory products in the form of memorials, museum exhibits, popular history books, newspaper coverage, and anniversary programs, Knopp made his mark at a moment when the public stations were generally losing ground as they could no longer afford the expensive investment in "Vergangenheitsbewältigung" that ARD and ZDF had pursued in the 1960s and especially the 1980s.[64] Having taken the decisive step of developing real documentary television history (as opposed to what we might call distant learning history lessons) Knopp could now apply and fine-tune the recipe with other, related subjects. The first target, already the implicit center of so many earlier programs, was Hitler himself. In 1989, commenting on Hitler's 100th birthday, Knopp had still argued that the private life of the Führer was trivial and that any concentration on Hitler's personal life smacked of personality cult. Consequently, the ZDF would not waste any airtime on the criminal.[65] Given the many ZDF documentaries that had featured Hitler this was already an astonishing statement in 1989, but by 1995, in light of new production and commercial opportunities, Knopp had clearly reversed his opinion. His new six part series *Hitler: Eine Bilanz* dedicated 45 prime-time minutes to Hitler's private life followed by in depth coverage of his propaganda accomplishments, his foreign and interior policies, his military leadership, and his career as a mass murderer.[66]

Knopp pursued ambitious goals with the new series. In his assessment, Germans were held hostage by their history, which handicapped them in a number of ways, for instance, by preventing them from supporting highly gifted students, discussing euthanasia in a calm fashion, and embracing genetic engineering without inhibitions. Knopp wanted to liberate Germans from this burden by confronting Hitler's legacy directly because, in his opinion, nobody needed to be afraid of the Führer five decades after his death and "the best weapon against Hitler-nostalgia is Hitler himself."[67] But even in the carefully edited text, which Knopp published to mark the media event *Hitler: Eine Bilanz*, the burden of the past becomes synonymous with nostalgia for the Führer and fear turns into fascination. As a result, Knopp defined the purpose of his historicization campaign with peculiar ambivalence: "When we can say without inhibitions: Beethoven and Goethe were Germans, but Hitler was too – then we are on the right path."[68]

*Der verdammte Krieg* was structured as an epic contest between two dictators and their countries and that structure provided an excellent visual rhythm to the series. Agency was limited to the two leaders and the war itself, which emerged as a faceless, powerful force in its own right. For the new Hitler documentaries Knopp and his associates invented a less obvious but similarly compelling visual structure that repeated and radicalized their interpretation of the phenomenon of Hitler. The usual collage of eyewitness accounts, propaganda footage, and play scenes was divided into semantic units through Hitler close-ups and Hitler quotes each accompanied by loud, high-pitched, monotonous sounds. Firmly established in the center of the programs, Hitler represented the only real historical agent since all other people either deferred to his authority or responded to his challenges. Each of the six sequels of *Hitler: Eine Bilanz*, as well as many subsequent ZDF documentaries, followed the same blueprint; they presented in endless variations the one-sided, uneven relationships between Hitler and his people, Hitler and his henchmen, Hitler and his generals, and Hitler and his foreign opponents. The programs thus simply depicted what Knopp had believed all along and what he expressed very succinctly before the broadcast: "Without Hitler the Third Reich would have disappeared like a bad dream."[69]

*Hitler: Eine Bilanz* became a stunning ratings success. Although all but one of the six parts were aired after 10 pm the series still reached an average of five million viewers, which corresponded to 11 per cent of all television households and 22 per cent of all television viewers at the time of broadcast.[70] As before, the audience engaged very actively with the series. In over 800 phone calls, especially during the obligatory final television discussion, the viewers expressed a wide range of complaints.[71] In addition to some anti-Semitic and anti-Turkish slurs, the audience objected to the program's anti-German tendencies, the abuse of Wagner's music, and the selection of eyewitnesses.[72] But viewers were most irate about the fact that they were unable to reach the station during the final discussion and could not intervene in the debate.[73] The ZDF had arranged for a special phone number and permitted a few lucky audience members to pose their questions live on the air, but apparently neither the station nor the phone company was prepared for such a high volume of calls.

In contrast to the audience the critics seemed unprepared for the media event, *Hitler*. Some reviewers magnanimously welcomed the use of cutting-edge digital technology and admitted that programs on Hitler may be entertaining, that they invariably admonished the lack of historical context and explanation and dutifully yet helplessly pointed out that the demonization of Hitler obliterated German guilt.[74] These observations, neither new nor inaccurate, failed to grasp the series' specific achievement. After acknowledging, even valorizing the suffering and achievements of the German military and civilians during and after the war, Knopp had finally resurrected the contemporary perception of Hitler himself and translated that image into the visual language of the late twentieth century.[75] The series captured the awe-inspiring combination of power and performance not by way of an explanation (for instance through Weber's concept of charismatic leadership) but by way of a reinactment, a simulation: a stylized, seamless, empathetic, emotionally compelling ride without distance or irony, only the flimsy safety belt of an anti-anti-Nazi discourse that adds to the thrill because it underscores the pretense that the ride is really dangerous.

After all these successes, the station's administrators authorized more docu-series on such diverse topics as the history of espionage, the Vatican, turning points in twentieth century German history, and especially the Third Reich.[76] Not a year has gone by without another prominent Knopp product and another opportunity for Hitler to enthrall his people from his (nonexistent) grave. To serve that purpose more effectively Knopp's unit for contemporary history was elevated in the ZDF administrative hierarchy and, one of the biggest achievements, the programs from the Knopp factory were for the first time scheduled in prime-time starting in 1997.[77] All this generosity is easily explained. Ratings and PR-interests figure prominently in the making of the Knopp phenomenon but revenue played the decisive role. Since ZDF Enterprises, the commercial subsidiary of the public station ZDF, has been very successful in selling the series in foreign markets, in some cases to more than forty countries, the fairly small subdivision of contemporary history, with a full-time editorial staff of nine associates, is one of the ZDF's premier cash cows.[78] In addition, Knopp's rise to national prominence reflects the German networks' explicit strategy of creating and relying on a few television stars to define their public image and safeguard their market shares in the dual system. Since the public stations have long lost the bidding war for German television stars like Thomas Gottschalk and Harald Schmidt they have to contend themselves with turning lesser stars like Guido Knopp into brand name products.[79] In the process, Knopp himself has become a multi-media event. His superiors came to love him as much as his editors at Bertelsmann because the many books that have accompanied the many series, boosted by free advertisement on the ZDF screen, have regularly been ranked on Germany's nonfiction bestseller lists.[80] As long as these strategies work, as long as Knopp manages to sell his products all over the globe and remains an affordable and popular public television star, no German viewer will have to be without the next Knopp.

After *Hitler: Eine Bilanz* Knopp delivered another blockbuster with *Hitlers Helfer*. The first six episodes, aired in January and February 1997, dealt with Hess, Himmler, Goebbels, Göring, Speer, and Dönitz.[81] Provided with prime-time opportunities Knopp pulled out all the stops. *Hitlers Helfer* and the subsequent *Hitlers Krieger*, which presented biographies of Hitler's top generals, were exceptionally well-crafted programs.[82] The cut was even faster, the images more seductive, and the score more dramatic. As Knopp made very clear in an interview before the broadcast, prime time is no place to be analytical or offer background information: "We have to appeal to the audience directly and visually."[83] The first six episodes of *Hitlers Helfer* attracted almost seven million viewers every night and have remained Knopp's most successful television programs to date.[84]

The show on Rommel, the first sequel of *Hitlers Krieger*, illustrates how specific assessments and interpretations can be expressed through cutting techniques that seem to create an innocent, pluralistic collage of diverging points of view.[85] About one third through the documentary Rommel's military exploits in Northern Africa become the subject of an invented dialogue between a range of eyewitnesses who have never seen each other face to face but who have been elegantly pitched against each other on the cutting tables of the ZDF. Having been informed by the voice-over that Rommel's troops took more prisoners but also sustained more casualties than any other units and that he had therefore been criticized as a *karrieresüchtiger Hasardeur* by his superiors, the viewer confronts the first eyewitness, a German veteran, who confirms Rommel's reckless and selfish behavior as a commander.[86] Without any further elaboration, the next eyewitness, another German veteran of the Africa campaign, contradicts vehemently maintaining that Rommel always put the well-being and safety of his troops first. At this point of impasse in the imagined dialogue Knopp introduces testimony of superior credibility. A jovial British veteran attests that Rommel treated his own troops as well as his opponents with honor and integrity and that he was one hell of a general. This statement clinches the case. If even his former enemies confirm the general's moral rectitude, the jealous superiors and disgruntled inferiors must be mistaken or worse, intentionally lying. The film includes further snippets of critical testimony by Jewish survivors (so identified by captions) who feared about Palestine and considered all soldiers in Hitler's services to be criminals.[87] The viewer might forgive this "subjective," "special interest" testimony in particular since they learn that Rommel had shown *Rückgrat* in the negotiations with his superiors, and was deeply disturbed by illicit news about the "Final Solution." Sadly, a former assistant informs us, Rommel never again showed the enthusiasm and drive that he displayed in Northern Africa although he tried his best when the Allies landed in Normandy. In conclusion, the documentary stages and mourns the suicide of a German military genius in sepia colors and permits his son, Manfred Rommel, the former mayor of Stuttgart, to ponder if he himself is a better human being than his father was and if he would not have done the same.[88] An idol reborn.

A number of reviewers perceived *Hitlers Helfer* as Knopp's answer to Daniel Goldhagen.[89] While it is very likely that Knopp seized the opportunity and rode on the coattails of a media event that he had helped put on stage, it is also clear that the momentum generated by the success of *Hitler: Eine Bilanz* would have brought him to Hitlers henchmen with or without Goldhagen.[90] In order for his stories to work Knopp needed a clear biographical focus and a factual or imagined connection to Hitler. Therefore, his search for new subject matter made him realize that Germans other than Hitler shared responsibility for the catastrophe of Nazism, but in contrast to Goldhagen he resisted the radical move of indicting the whole German people because that interpretation went against his perception of German history, might have alienated his audience, and, most important, did not fit the conceptual and aesthetic framework that had proven so successful. For all these reasons the project *Hitlers Volk* that Knopp has contemplated for some years has not yet materialized.[91]

Many programs of the series *Hitlers Helfer* and *Hitlers Krieger* turned out to be the single most successful program of the evening in all of Germany, which is an exceptional accomplishment for a historical television documentary. In an age of rapidly diversifying television offerings and fragmented audiences Knopp documentaries provided a common reference point for many viewers.[92] This phenomenon was part of a larger trend that Knopp might have helped create but that went far beyond the confines of the ZDF's division of contemporary history on the Lerchenberg in Mainz. After a decade of cheap television fiction that followed the introduction of commercial television, German viewers turned to nonfiction and especially historical nonfiction in the mid-1990s.[93] TV executives were pleasantly surprised by this development, because even a well made documentary costs about a 60 per cent less than the average TV play.[94] As before, Knopp proved to be at the right place at the right time. For many years he had developed the new type of infotainment that the ZDF could now produce very quickly to satisfy and profit from the surprising audience demand.[95] Therefore, after years in a niche market Knopp received unprecedented airtime and broadcast opportunities in prime time.

As is often the case, the historians and self-proclaimed intellectuals among the journalists came out in full force as the show was already winding down. They only reacted after the second installment of *Hitlers Helfer* was aired in April and May 1998 perhaps because these programs featured Mengele and Eichmann and the feuilleton was not willing to have the Holocaust debased on public television. The *Süddeutsche Zeitung* objected that Knopp's programs were just too much fun to watch (too much *Spaßkompatibilität*) and even the *FAZ*, certainly positively inclined towards Knopp, complained about "the enthusiasm for evil" that allegedly emanated from Knopp's work.[96] None of the critiques was particularly original, reviewers had noted the same reservations for several years, but the Medienforum Köln in June 1998 offered a rare showdown between the historians of the ZDF and their professorial colleagues. Historian Ulrich Herbert emerged as the most outspoken critic when he claimed that the ZDF produced "Nazi-Kitsch" and that the adaptation of the visual language of the Third Reich had turned the ZDF from a champion of education and enlightenment into a protagonist of Nazi aesthetics.[97] Not all historians shared this point of view. Knopp and his associates found important defenders including Simon Wiesenthal, who had been a frequent visitor to the ZDF screen, and Eberhard Jäckel, who had offered professional advice for many of Knopp's programs.[98]

Considering this prehistory, the new Holocaust program of 2000, designed as another important highlight in Knopp's long career, was anticipated with much trepidation. Knopp had already made a number of excellent documentaries on the history of the "Final Solution," for instance in the early 1990s,[99] but the concerns even intensified when the ZDF released the title of the new series. Called *Holokaust* instead of *Holocaust* the show's more German sounding name was intended to signal the television makers' and their audience's acceptance of the "Final Solution" as an extremely negative, yet central element of modern German history. But this play with letters was easily misunderstood as a cheap PR gag, or worse, an appropriation of the "Final Solution" as a German event over which German intellectuals claimed interpretive sovereignty.[100]

In the end, the actual broadcast of *Holokaust* in 2000 proved anticlimactic because the series turned out to be one of the best productions about the "Final Solution" ever to be aired by German television.[101] Knopp's staff was again exceptionally successful in tracking down new footage and eyewitnesses. But unlike in earlier productions the ZDF's division for contemporary history refrained from any fictitious simulations of Holocaust history, kept the musical score within the narrow limits delineated by *Schindler's List*, and contributed a very modest, at times even elliptic commentary. Through exceptionally diligent research the ZDF staff managed to put some of the best-known Holocaust footage into context and relate the famous images to precise testimony by survivors, bystanders, and even perpetrators. In contrast to earlier programs the eyewitnesses could develop their point of view at some length and thus the survivors, not Hitler and his henchmen, represented the clear, undisputed focus of the program.[102] If anything, Knopp and his colleagues could be faulted for being too subdued in their interpretation of the genocide of European Jewry. They often merely presented the events rather than explained them and thus indirectly subscribed to the notion of the Holocaust's incomprehensibility that is championed by some of the program's senior historical advisers.[103] The unusual restraint exhibited by the ZDF team on this occasion highlights the exceptional status of the Holocaust in German memory but it might also explain the show's disappointing ratings. The series only reached average market shares of 8.1 per cent and less than three million viewers in contrast to the 21 per cent market shares and almost seven million viewers that *Hitlers Helfer* had attained in the same programming spot at 8:15 pm in 1997.[104] The viewers stayed away from *Holokaust* because even in the year 2000 a German television program on the "Final Solution" is not likely to offer the kind of transgressive pleasures that *Hitler* and *Hitlers Helfer* had provided. Nobody, not even Guido Knopp, is likely to use the theme of the Holocaust to create an ambivalent exploration of Nazi aesthetics and Nazi power.

In 1998, after the broadcast of *Hitlers Krieger* one reviewer prematurely counted his blessings when he remarked "what good luck that Hitler was not successful with women, otherwise Knopp would present us with *Hitlers Frauen*."[105] In the meantime, that has already happened; the ZDF aired *Hitlers Frauen* in April and May 2001, one year after the broadcast of *Hitlers Kinder*. The former consisted of an ill-matched string of TV biographies of Eva Braun, Magda Goebbels, Winifred Wagner, Zarah Leander, and, most incongruently, Marlene Dietrich, and the latter presented another lamentation of the loss of a whole generation to Hitler's and Goebbel's seductive powers.[106] In addition, Knopp had his associates revisit World War II on a global scale in *Der Jahrhundertkrieg*, produced together with the History Channel, [107] and reached one of implicit destinations of his whole television career when he remembered the suffering of the German refugees and expellees in *Die große Flucht*.[108] At this stage of the evolution of German memory such one-sided mourning about German suffering hardly raises any eyebrows. After Martin Walser's indictment of Germany's self-critical memory industry in 1998[109] and after Grass' recovery of his childhood trauma in *Im Krebsgang* in 2002,[110] Knopp finds himself in the company of esteemed fellow travelers who are not known for their high regard of popular taste and the dictates of the marketplace. But Knopp faces another problem: he is simply running out of suitable topics and is losing his audience.[111] Throughout his career Knopp has experimented with subject matters other than Nazism. But his programs on the history of the Federal Republic, the power of the popes, and the biggest political scandals and espionage cases of the twentieth century have never had the same impact as Hitler and the Third Reich. Only Nazism provided Knopp with an opportunity to be a taboo breaker, to present to his viewers an appealing combination of fascist and post-modern aesthetics for the alleged purpose of political education. No other topics offered such interesting, suspenseful inconsistencies for Knopp and his audience. Therefore, until his retirement in 2011, Knopp will likely remain the butt of many jokes about his exceptional "historischen Durchhaltewillen" and the upcoming release of *Hitlers Hunde*.[112] Even in this respect Knopp has been an involuntary trendsetter. It has only been a few years that German comedians dare to make fun of Hitler and include the Third Reich in their comedy routines.[113] At least this Hitler wave, unlike its precursor of 1977, has been entertaining *and* educational.[114] To a large extent that is Guido Knopp's achievement and legacy.

At first sight Knopp's vision of Nazism represents a perfect illustration for Susan Sontag's 1980 critique of the culture of "fascinating fascism" and Saul Friedlander's contemporaneous concerns about the combustible mixture of kitsch and death in postwar representations of Nazism.[115] But Sontag's and Friedlander's moralistic indictments of the historical culture of the 1970s implicitly claim to have understood the social and political dynamisms of Nazi culture. Their criticism is based on the conviction that the texts they analysed – including films, photographs, and novels – duplicate Nazi culture in essential respects and therefore also duplicate the political risks inherent in Nazi culture. From our perspective many of these concerns and the underlying political certainties and connections appear problematic. On a technical and formal level many of the strategies of representation invented or perfected in the Third Reich have been employed by the postwar culture industry without any obvious fascist political repercussions. In addition, in their concern for elite culture Sontag and Friedlander failed to acknowledge that many of the texts in question had limited mass appeal and therefore bore few political risks. However, even if the moral/political gesture of their interventions might be less compelling today, some of their insights help us understand the specificity of Knopp's innovation, whose own perceptions of Nazism were very likely decisively influenced by the visual culture of the 1970s and its representations of the Third Reich.

Like the texts that Sontag and Friedlander analysed Knopp's document-aries express a thinly veiled fascination with violence, subjugation, and death, and lack intellectual self-reflexivity. Knopp is the antithesis of a filmmaker who would invite his viewers to contemplate the specific gaps and biases in his vision of Nazism or intentionally complicate his interpretations of the past to the point of interpretive instability. In this sense, because of his subject matter and his aesthetic approach, Knopp appeals to what Sontag called the fascist desires within us, and what Friedlander identified as the attractive combination of harmony and power, which characterized Nazism as well as its postwar reflections.[116] Knopp's specific, daring innovation consists of crafting documentaries in the most important medium of communication that explore the official limits of historical taste by inviting the viewers' temporary identification with the Nazi perpetrators. As an ingenious mixture of historical porno-graphy and historical education Knopp TV invites the viewers to join the historical actors and eyewitnesses, adore the Führer, and fight the battle on the eastern front. The visual stream – especially the simulations which have no other function – creates a slick projective surface, which allows the audience to become Nazi, while that pleasure is at the same time rendered illegal and even more interesting through the superficial yet efficient commentary, which directly contradicts the visual language. In the past the pornographic pleasure of becoming Nazi was primarily the result of the contradiction between particular subcultural representations of Nazism and the official memory culture of the Federal Republic.[117] Now, for the first time, the contradictory messages are assembled within one seemingly endless stream of documentaries for generations of Germans who might not have internalized the representational taboos and can only experience and appreciate the pleasures of transgression if they receive the rules as well as their violations in the same media package.

At this stage of the evolution of German collective memory the seductive contradictions of Knopp television can only be produced in documentaries and not television fiction. It would still be impossible to have Nazis as heroes in conventional television plays where discursive and visual levels create a harmonious narrative universe. Only the fractious, multi-dimensional surface of this new type of documentary, tolerated as a result of the visual illiteracy of critics and supervisors, creates the indeterminate imaginary spaces that program makers call anti-Nazi education but that many consumers might use to play Nazis. Also, only the documentaries can still lay claim to an authenticity that is never achieved in fiction. Here, in a specific environment the viewers produce "authentic" German memories and playfully retain the roles of perpetrators that have been so carefully edited out of all German historical culture until recently.

On one occasion, the production of a successful documentary marking the fiftieth anniversary of the Olympic Games of 1936, Knopp had reason to look closely at one the best, visually most compelling and complex propaganda films ever produced, Leni Riefenstahl's *Olympia*.[118] Knopp's film, which contains extensive quotes from *Olympia*, gives no indication that he was aware of the interesting parallels between his own and Riefenstahl's efforts, but it is more than likely that Knopp realized the attractive structure of the Nazi footage in his repeated search for suitable material. Like Riefenstahl, he tried to tell dramatic factual stories of competition, triumph, and defeat and use all the visual means at his disposal to make these stories attractive to the largest possible audience without highlighting the biases and construction principles of said stories. In addition, as in the case of Riefenstahl, Knopp's specific innovations were developed at the cutting table. Despite these parallels it would be anachronistic to call Knopp a fascist because he operates in a completely different historical context with very different political objectives in mind. But the visual language he developed to reach his objectives has more in common with visual language of Nazi culture than with visual structures of modern documentary classics like Resnais' *Night and Fog*, Ophüls' *The Sorrow and the Pity*, Syberberg's *Hitler, a Film from Germany,* or Lanzman's *Shoah*.[119] Or, put differently, main stream television, as a means of communication and political tool has more in common with the films of Goebbels than above self-reflexive auteur documentaries, even if one of the auteurs in question (i.e. Syberberg) entertains peculiar, perhaps even reactionary opinions.[120] That explains why so many postwar German filmmakers have tried to avoid and undercut the conventions of mainstream visual culture, especially but not only in their representations of German history.[121]

Like many media events of our time Knopp television is the result of a careful adaptation and manipulation of the audience's taste for commercial purposes.[122] Knopp shares this pursuit of the consumer with many past and present media experts, including Goebbels.[123] Like the former propaganda minister and many postwar television makers, Knopp mixes entertainment with the politically correct messages of the day. But, unlike Goebbels, he faces a more sophisticated audience – or so we hope. The viewers might enjoy the titillating fiction of Hitler's limitless power and the tragedy of the rise and fall of his political genius in the course of their evening entertainment. However, on the morning after, their political identities and decisions are probably as dangerous or as harmless as they were before their visit to Knopp's Hitlerland.

Since the majority of Knopp viewers are over 50 years of age it is likely that they enjoy a new perspective on a historical topic that has created lots of discussion in their lifetime and that some of them have still experienced themselves.[124] The programs allow them to revisit, reorganize, and reinvent their own memories, but they are not likely to change their current political identities. For this segment of the audience the consumption of Knopp's documentaries might even have some exceptionally positive effects. As veteran consumers of the West German media they have experienced the revolution of mainstream historical representations in the 1980s as public television brought a wide range of programs into the German living rooms that remembered the Holocaust and created sympathy for the survivors.[125] At that stage, despite all the efforts of moral and cultural reparations, German mainstream culture had very little to say about the perpetrators and bystanders of the "Final Solution." It was only after Goldhagen, the exhibition *Crimes of the German Wehrmacht*, and Knopp television that we can look back at a sustained interest in the perpetrators, the most challenging legacy of the Holocaust. Considering these different layers in the media consumption of older generations of West Germans, it is very possible that the audience's temporary identification with the perspective of the Nazi leaders and soldiers – in light of earlier identification with the survivors of the Holocaust – might lead to more self-critical interpretations of Nazism than Knopp's at times infuriatingly one-sided, apologetic representations indicate.

Ironically, however, the effects of Knopp television might not be as productive or harmless for the minority of youthful viewers, who Knopp is particularly proud to count among his audience, but who have not experienced the hitherto most self-critical phase of German collective memory in the 1980s.[126] Unless they have encountered more self-reflexive approaches to the burden of the past in schools and families, which is unlikely at least for a substantial part of unified Germany, they might not have at their disposal information and interpretations that help them counterbalance Knopp's rather one-sided celebration of Nazi power.

For lack of interesting political and aesthetic alternatives they might not as easily as their older compatriots return from their temporary identification with the ordinary soldiers and the political elite of the Third Reich.

This thought experiment reveals that Knopp television without counterweight remains a frightening idea and that the real challenge for German television makers has not yet been met. It should be possible to craft attractive mainstream representations of Nazi history that invite identification with the perpetrators and bystanders of the "Final Solution" but also, within the same program, offer equally attractive and suspenseful critical perspectives on their decisions and actions. These opposing perspectives have to be developed discursively and visually (and not just discursively as in the case of Knopp television) in order to create tensions and ruptures in the process of identification that cause at least a minimum of unease and reflection. In addition, and this is the real challenge, all of this would have to be accomplished without undermining the purpose of entertainment, which is the primary condition for mainstream appeal. Very few popular representations of Nazi history released in the German context have ever come close to this theoretical ideal, with the possible exception of *Holocaust*. After all, *Holocaust* offered the families Weiss *and* Dorf as possible objects of projection and provided a suspenseful, entertaining as well as moderately contradictory perspective on the "Final Solution."[127]

This challenge will very likely not be tackled by Knopp, who appears as a fairly naïve executor of a new historical paradigm of representation. Knopp has taken advantage of the political and aesthetic opportunities that the commercialization of German television and German unification offered to people in his position but that very few have used as efficiently and successfully. He established historical pornography as a new documentary genre when Germany's public television networks tried desperately to thwart off competition from commercial networks, which had broken all rules of good taste since their introduction in the mid 1980s, for instance through the screening of real pornography.

# Notes

1. Lutz Kinkel, "Viele Taten, wenig Täter: Die Wehrmacht als Sujet neuerer Dokumentationsserien des öffentlich-rechtlichen Rundfunks," in Michael Greven and Oliver von Wrochem (eds), *Der Krieg in der*

*Nachkriegszeit: Der Zweite Weltkrieg in Politik und Gesellschaft der Bundesrepublik*, Opladen, 2000, pp. 113–30.

2. The Knopp-aesthetics are exemplified in the 1995 ZDF documentary mini-series *Hitler: Eine Bilanz*; see the six sequels *HEB I: Der Privatmann*, ZDF, 9 November 1995; *HEB II: Der Verführer*, ZDF, 12 November 1995; *HEB III: Der Erpresser*, ZDF, 19 November 1995; *HEB IV: Der Diktator*, ZDF, 26 November 1995; *HEB V: Der Kriegsherr*, ZDF, 3 December 1995; *HEB VI: Der Verbrecher*, ZDF, 10 December 1995. See also the excellent review by Barbara Sichtermann, "Auf den Effekt kalkuliert," *Die Welt*, 23 November 1995; and "Kritisch gesehen," *Stuttgarter Zeitung*, 21 November 1995.

3. The soundtrack of *Hitler: Eine Bilanz* has been effectively criticized by Joachim Westhoff, "TV-Kritik," *Westfälische Rundschau*, 11 November 1995; and Karin Hanig, "Am Mythos nur gekrazt," *Sächsische Zeitung*, 13 December 1995.

4. *Mein Kampf* (Erwin Leiser, Minerva; Sweden, 1959); *Hitler – Eine Karriere* (Christian Herrendoerfer and Joachim Fest, Interart; Germany, 1976/77).

5. Prior to Knopp's Hitler programs, the ZDF had only aired three programs specifically about Hitler in the 31 years between 1963 and 1993, if we exclude Chaplin's *The Great Dictator* (*Der große Diktator*, ZDF, 24 June 1979). The programs in question are the docu-drama *Wie er es wurde: Ein junger Mann aus dem Innviertel – Adolf Hitler*, ZDF, 30 November 1973; a public reading of *Mein Kampf* by the actor Qualtinger, *Helmut Qualtinger liest: Adolf Hitler: "Mein Kampf,"* ZDF, 27 August 1974; and the US TV play *Der Führerbunker*, ZDF, 8 November 1981.

6. It has to be emphasized from the outset that it is difficult to determine the question of authorship in any traditional sense for many of the programs discussed below. In contrast to auteur documentaries by filmmakers like Leiser and Fest, the programs of the ZDF division for contemporary history depend more on teamwork, as is the rule in television. Guido Knopp certainly screens all productions quite carefully and the ZDF's PR experts present him as the mastermind of the new discourse of history, but it is impossible to determine from the outside who in the team actually developed the radical editing strategies in the 1990s. The cutters not the scriptwriters, are the real authors of these films.

7. See Peter Zimmermann's very helpful survey "Geschichte von Dokumentarfilm und Reportage von der Adenauer-Ära bis zur Gegenwart," in Peter Ludes et al. (eds), *Geschichte des Fernsehens in der Bundesrepublik Deutschland III: Informations- und Dokumentarsendungen*, Munich, 1994, pp. 213–324, especially pp. 288–91.

8. *Die deutsche Einheit: Hoffnung, Alptraum, Illusion?*, ZDF, 27 May 1979.

9. For the impact of *Holocaust* in Germany see for instance Peter Märtesheimer and Ivo Frenzel (eds), *Im Kreuzfeuer: Der Fernsehfilm Holocaust: Eine Nation ist betroffen*, Frankfurt, 1979.

10. Uwe Magnus, "*Holocaust* in der Bundesrepublik: Zentrale Ergebnisse der Begleituntersuchungen aus der Sicht der Rundfunkanstalten," *Rundfunk und Fernsehen* 28 (1980), 534–42.

11. *Narben: Danzig – oder: Wie Menschen Geschichte erleiden I : Menschen am Kreuzweg*, ZDF, 3 May 1981; *Narben: Danzig – oder: Wie Menschen Geschichte erleiden II : Treibjagd*, ZDF, 7 May 1981; *Narben: Danzig – oder: Wie Menschen Geschichte erleiden III : Stadt im Sturm*, ZDF, 17 May 1981. *Narben* was specifically designed to bring emotionally compelling *Alltagsgeschichte* to the screen in order to implement the lessons of *Holocaust* (Detlev Sprickmann, "Im Mittelpunkt der Zeitgeschichte steht der Mensch," *ZDF Jahrbuch 1979*, pp. 101–6). Sprickmann anticipated additional international coproductions about the history of the Nazi era in the spirit of reconciliation, but he thought primarily about British, French, and US television stations not Soviet/Russian TV which became Knopp's partner of choice in the 1990s.

12. Internal memo of director general of the ZDF, Karl-Günther von Hase to the head of the section for society and politics, Detlev Sprickmann dated 28 March 1980; and internal memorandum of Detlev Sprickmann to the deputy editor in chief, Volker von Hagen dated 27 February 1980.

13. Teleskopie Gesellschaft für Fernsehzuschauerforschung (ed.), *Telejour: Einschalt- und Sendeverhalten zu den Sendungen von ARD und ZDF: 18. Woche 1981*, Bonn, 1981, p. 8; Teleskopie (ed.), *Telejour: 19. Woche*, Bonn, 1981, p. 4; Teleskopie (ed.), *Telejour: 20. Woche 1981*, Bonn, 1981, p. 8.

14. Armin Biergann, "*Narben*: Holprig und zu betulich," *Kölnische Rundschau*, 19 May 1981; "Kritisch gesehen: *Narben*," *Stuttgarter Zeitung*, 19 May 1981; and "Nicht schön aber notwendig," *Main-Echo*, 19 May 1981.

15. Guido Knopp's internal application ("Vorlage zur Stoffzulassung") to develop the concept for a roundtable discussion after the broadcast of *Narben* dated 10 October 1980.

16. *Narben: Was steht noch zwischen Polen und Deutschen?*, ZDF, 17 May 1981. Von Hase had "suggested" including a moderate expellee who would be acceptable to the expellee organizations in the Federal Republic, see von Hase's notes on the permission to develop concept (*Zulassungsbescheid*) dated 29 October 1980.

17. Minutes of the ZDF telephone staff (*Protokoll des Telefondienstes*) of 17 May 1981.

18. "Ein sehr ehrenwerter Versuch," *Westdeutsche Allgemeine Zeitung*, 19 May 1981; Sigrid Schniederken, "Authentizität will gewagt sein," *Funk-Korrespondenz*, 20 May 1981.

19. Officially Detlev Sprickmann remained in control of the subdivision for contemporary history, which he had led since it was formed in 1978. But in April 1981 Knopp became his temporary replacement because Sprickmann was transferred to Tokyo for three years. Subsequently, the unit for contemporary history was officially disbanded in 1982 but reemerged in 1984, now with Knopp officially at the helm. See *ZDF Jahrbuch 1978*, p. 244; *ZDF Jahrbuch 1980*, pp. 38, 270; *ZDF Jahrbuch 1984*, p. 48; *ZDF Jahrbuch 1985*, pp. 8, 315.

20. *"Der Deutschen Mai:" Hambach heute – Jubelfeier oder Auftrag?*, ZDF, 23 May 1982; *Keine Angst vor Kernkraft?*, ZDF, 29 November 1982. Under the series title *Fragen der Zeit*, the ZDF broadcast between 35 and 50 interviews with scholars and scientists each year. The series was replaced in 1984 by the more historically oriented series *Damals: Vor vierzig Jahren*. Before Knopp became a media star these low-profile programs, broadcast on Sunday and Saturday afternoon in front of small audiences, were the bread and butter of his work at the ZDF.

21. *Warum habt Ihr Hitler nicht verhindert?*, ZDF, 23 January 1983; and *Warum habt Ihr Hitler widerstanden?*, ZDF, 18 July 1984; see also the review of Thomas Thieringer, "Bombenerfolg," *Süddeutsche Zeitung*, 25 January 1983.

22. *Der Verführer: Anmerkungen zu Goebbels*, ZDF, 29 November 1987.

23. Sigrid Schniederken, "Übereilige 'Fertigstellung'," *FUNK-Korrespondenz*, 11 December 1987; Sybille Simon-Zülch, "Alle gleich honorig," *epd: Kirche und Rundfunk*, 5 December 1987; and Ulrich Rose, "Regelgerecht flach," *Badische Zeitung*, 1 December 1987.

24. Uwe Walter, "Fernsehen kritisch: Warum habt Ihr Hitler nicht verhindert?" *Stuttgarter Nachrichten*, 25 January 1983.

25. Hans Janke. "Räsonables Resümee," *epd: Kirche und Rundfunk*, 2 February 1983; and Walter, "Warum habt Ihr Hitler nicht verhindert?".

26. *Keine Zeit für Tränen: Frauen zwischen Tod und Trümmern*, ZDF, 30 November, 1986.

27. For contemporary scholarly debates about "Alltagsgeschichte" see for instance Institut für Zeitgeschichte (ed.), *Alltagsgeschichte der NS-Zeit: Neue Perspektiven oder Trivialisierung*, München, 1984. For an excellent review of *Keine Zeit für Tränen* see Hans Messias, "Unstatthafter

Blick auf deutsche Vergangenheit," *Funk-Korrespondenz*, 5 December 1986.

28. Between 1981 and 1988 Knopp produced 10 documentaries about the Nazi past which were broadcast after 10 p.m. and reached an average of 12 per cent of television households. While nonfiction programs about other topics, for instance animal shows, were often more successful, Knopp's ratings compare favorably to the audience sizes of other historical documentaries aired in similar time slots. In addition to Knopp's programs, the ZDF broadcast twenty-seven other documentaries about different aspects of the Nazi past during the same years; they only reached an average of 9 per cent of television households.

29. Representative for this repeated charge Lutz Hachmeister, "So und so," *epd: Kirche und Rundfunk*, 11 October 1986, a review of *Das Urteil von Nürnberg*, ZDF, 28 September 1986.

30. For a survey of the politics of memory of the Kohl administration see Siobhan Kattago, *Ambiguous Memory: The Nazi Past and German National Identity*, Westport, 2001, especially pp. 48–57.

31. The anniversary of the constitution was remembered in the following Knopp productions: *So entstand die Bundesrepublik I: Kalter Krieg um Deutschland*, ZDF, 7 May 1989; *SedB II: Provisorisch, aber gründlich*, ZDF, 8 May 1989; *Ein Grund zum Feiern? 40 Jahre Bundesrepublik*, ZDF, 23 May 1989. Unification became the subject of a six part series in 1990: *Die deutsche Einheit I: Teilung auf Befehl*, ZDF, 15 July 1990; *DdE II: Ungenutzte Chancen*, ZDF, 17 July 1990; *DdE III: Getrennte Wege*, ZDF, 22 July 1990; *DdE IV: Kleine Schritte*, ZDF, 23 December 1990; *DdE V: Zwei Staaten – Eine Nation*, ZDF, 26 December 1990; and *DdE VI: Der Weg nach Deutschland*, ZDF, 30 December 1990.

32. *ZDF-Jahrbuch 1990*, p. 315.

33. An average of less than three million West German viewers were interested in *So entstand die Bundesrepublik* and *Die deutsche Einheit*, *ZDF-Jahrbuch 1990*, p. 299; and *ZDF-Jahrbuch 1989*, p. 287.

34. See for instance the great review by Momos (= Walter Jens) of the fiftieth anniversary coverage of 20 July 1944 in ARD and ZDF, "Schmierentheater," *Die Zeit*, 26 July 1984.

35. A particularly insightful review of Knopp's *"Was soll aus Deutschland werden:" Die Konferenz von Potsdam*, ZDF, 28 July 1985, pointed out this deficit, but also applauded Knopp for trying to avoid the dry discourse of historians and political scientists and developing instead a visual language for television history, "Kritisch gesehen: Potsdamer Konferenz," *Stuttgarter Zeitung*, 30 July 1985. For Knopp's programmatic statements see below note 41.

36. For the impact of *Holocaust* on West German Television programming see Knut Hickethier, *Geschichte des Deutschen Fernsehens*, Stuttgart, 1998, p. 355f.; and Michael Geisler, "The Disposal of Memory: Fascism and the Holocaust on West German Television," in Bruce Murray and Christopher Wickham (eds), *Framing the Past: The Historiography of German Cinema and Television*, Carbondale, 1992, pp. 220–60. Edgar Reitz's eleven-part television mini-series *Heimat*, which was broadcast by the ARD between 16 September and 24 October 1984, represented a conscious German response to *Holocaust* and helped define the genre of *Alltagsgeschichte* on television, see Anton Kaes, *From Hitler to Heimat: The Return of History as Film*, Cambridge, 1989, pp. 161–92.

37. That applies in particular to the productions *Warum habt Ihr Hitler nicht verhindert?*; *Warum habt Ihr Hitler widerstanden*; *Was soll aus Deutschland werden*; and *Ich wurde von Deutschen versteckt*, ZDF, 20 July 1983.

38. See for instance the review of *Die Mauer*, ZDF, 12 and 13 August 1986 by Heinrich von Nussbaum, "Mediengedenktag," *epd: Kirche und Rundfunk*, 20 August 1986; and Hachmeister, "So und so." As Knopp's visibility increased on the screen he was also criticized for his allegedly narcissistic tendency of casting himself in front of the camera, see for instance Dietrich Leder, "Die Zehnminuten-Geschichts-Terrine," *FUNK-Korrespondenz*, 25 July 1991; Leder reviewed the first sequels of Knopp's series *Bilder, die Geschichte machten*, which presented famous photos and their historical context in short, ten minute features. Begun in 1991 the series was continued in 1992 and 1994 with ten episodes each year.

39. The reactions to Knopp's *Als die Synagogen brannten . . .: Novemberprogrom '38 – Hitlers Reichskristallnacht*, ZDF, 8 November 1988, illustrate this response; Eberhard Fehre, "Zeitzeugen," *Westdeutsche Zeitung*, 11 November 1988; Barbara Sichtermann, "Angst und Scherben," *Die Zeit*, 18 November 1988; and Stefan Pieroth, "Effekthascherei," *Rheinpfalz*, 10 November 1988.

40. On the transformation of German television after the introduction of commercial networks see Dietrich Schwarzkopf (ed.), *Rundfunkpolitik in Deutschland: Wettbewerb und Öffentlichkeit*, 2 vols, Munich, 1999.

41. Sound was added in *Warum habt Ihr Hitler widerstanden* and scenic reconstructions figured prominently in *Die Mauer* and *Als die Synagogen brannten*.

42. Guido Knopp, "Zwischen Krieg und Frieden: Zeitgeschichte im ZDF 1989," *ZDF-Jahrbuch 1989*, pp. 80–84; see also Knopp, "Geschichte im Fernsehen: Perspektiven der Praxis," in Guido Knopp and Siegfried Quandt (eds), *Geschichte im Fernsehen: Ein Handbuch*,

Darmstadt, 1988, pp. 1–9; and Knopp, "Zeitgeschichte im ZDF," in Jürgen Wilke (ed.), *Massenmedien und Zeitgeschichte*, Konstanz, 1999, pp. 309–16.

43. *Die Saat des Krieges I: Der erkaufte Frieden*, ZDF, 20 August 1989; and *Die Saat des Krieges II: Der erzwungene Krieg*, ZDF, 24 August 1989.

44. Some reviewers shared this assessment, see for instance "Wozu die Schauspielerei," *Hannoversche Allgemeine Zeitung*, 26 August 1989; and especially Patrick Bahners, "Der kostümierte Diktator," *Frankfurter Allgemeine Zeitung*, 26 August 1989.

45. The first six episodes of 1991: *Der verdammte Krieg: Das Unternehmen Barbarossa I: Der Wahn vom Lebensraum*, ZDF, 16 June 1991; *DvK: DUB II: Der Überfall*, ZDF, 17 June 1991; *DvK: DUB III: Die Illusion des Sieges*, ZDF, 18 June 1991; *DvK: DUB IV: Der Kampf um Leningrad*, ZDF, 19 June 1991; *DvK: DUB V: Den Kreml im Visier*, ZDF, 21 June 1991; and *DvK: DUB VI: Der Anfang vom Ende*, ZDF, 23 June 1991; see also the live discussion: *Nach fünfzig Jahren: Deutsche und Russen diskutieren*, ZDF, 23 June 1991. The second installment of five episodes broadcast in 1993: *Der verdammte Krieg: Entscheidung Stalingrad I: Tödliche Weisung*, ZDF, 1 January 1993; *DvK: ES II: Haß wider Haß*, ZDF, 20 January 1993; *DvK: ES III: Leningrad will leben*, ZDF, 21 January 1993; *DvK: ES IV: Die Falle schnappt zu*, ZDF, 22 January 1993; *DvK: ES V: Das Ende an der Wolga*, ZDF, 24 January 1993. The last installment of six episodes in 1995: *Der verdammte Krieg: Bis zum bitteren Ende I: Der Feuersturm*, ZDF, 5 March 1995; *DvK: BzbE II: Verbrannte Erde*, ZDF, 12 March 1995; *DvK: BzbE III: "Die Russen kommen!,"* ZDF, 19 March 1995; *DvK: BzbE IV: Der Zusammenbruch*, ZDF, 26 March 1995; *DvK: BzbE V: Die Schlacht um Berlin*, ZDF, 2 April 1995; and *DvK: BzbE VI: Triumph und Tragödie*, ZDF, 9 April 1995.

46. Heiko Strech, "Blitz und Donner," *Tages-Anzeiger*, 19 June 1991.

47. *ZDF Pressedienst* 26/1991, Anmerkungen XIII; see also the elaborate pamphlet which the ZDF distributed to the Press: ZDF (ed.), *Der verdammte Krieg: Das Unternehmenn Barbarossa*, Mainz, 1991.

48. *ZDF Pressedienst* 26/1991, Anmerkungen XIII. Although the ZDF PR office emphasized the allegedly single, indivisible historical truth represented in the production, the partners in Mainz and Moscow could not agree on an identical voice-over commentary for the broadcast in Germany and in the Soviet Union, see Peter Carstens, "Auf geistigen Feldhernhügeln." *Frankfurter Allgemeine Zeitung*, 20 June 1991.

49. In fact, the pride of broadcasting over such a large territory recalls the famous Nazi radio Christmas program of 1942 that featured live

coverage from many far-away places of the extended front, including Stalingrad.

50. The quote is from the voice-over commentary of the second installment of *Der verdamte Krieg: Entscheidung Stalingrad*, see Jan Ross, "Gemeinsam zu den Gräbern," *Frankfurter Allgemeine Zeitung*,

51. Quote from the voice-over commentary at the end of *Der verdammte Krieg: Entscheidung Stalingrad I: Tödliche Weisung*, 19 January 1993.

52. Carstens, "Auf geistigen Feldherrnhügeln;" Ulrich von Sanden, "Geschichte als Völkerverständigung," *Stuttgarter Nachrichten*, 18 June 1991.

53. Very perceptive on this point Bettina Schulte, "Barbarischer Feldzug," *Badische Zeitung*, 20 June 1991; Tilmann Gangloff, "Gedankenloses Kriegsspiel," *Mannheimer Morgen*, 25 June 1991; and Günter Jekubzik, "Wie 'Risiko'," *Aachener Volkszeitung*, 25 June 1991.

54. Quote from Knopp's closing remarks in *Der verdammte Krieg: Das Unternehmen Barbarossa V: Den Kreml im Visier*.

55. See for example Hans Bachmüller, "Auflösung eines Feindbildes," *epd. Kirche und Rundfunk*, 3 July 1991, Dieter Malmecke, "Der verdammte Krieg," *Das Parlament*, 12 July 1991; "Die offizielle Geschichte," *Südkurier*, 18 June 1991; and "Rückblick auf Sendungen der Woche," *Neue Züricher Zeitung*, 1 February 1993.

56. See especially Martina Wengierek, "Sorgfältige Spurensuche," *Kieler Nachrichten*, 19 January 1993; Christian Hörburger, "Der verdammte Krieg," *Tagespiegel*, 19 January 1993; Ralf Rummel, "Zeichen der Versöhnung," *Bremer Nachrichten*, 18 January 1993; and Ross, "Gemeinsam zu den Gräbern."

57. *ZDF Jahrbuch 1991*, p. 323; *ZDF Jahrbuch 1993*, p. 339; and *ZDF Jahrbuch 1995*, p. 342.

58. *ZDF Jahrbuch 1993*, p. 202; *ZDF Jahrbuch 1995*, p. 199.

59. For the interpretations of ratings see James Webster et al., *Ratings Analysis: The Theory and Practice of Audience Research*, Mahwah, 2000.

60. The minutes of the ZDF telephone staff indicate that the fifty documentaries and television discussions that Knopp produced between 1981 and 1993 received an average of thirty-five calls despite the fact that the programs were often aired after 10 pm. During the same years even the ZDF's prime programs on the topic of Nazism received only an average of twenty-four calls per broadcast.

61. See for example the minutes of the ZDF telephone staff (*Protokoll des Telefondienstes*) of 16, 17, 18, 19, 21, and 23 June 1991.

62. The ZDF subdivision for contact with viewers (Referat Zuschauerpost- und Telefonredaktion) compiles a weekly report about the quantity and

most important trends in the feedback from the audience, see the reports for the weeks 20 June through 26 June 1991 and 27 June through 3 July 1991 dated 28 June and 5 July 1991.

63. Bettina Schulte, "Friedensgeste," *Badische Zeitung*, 25 June 1991; "Nach fünfzig Jahren," *Mannheimer Morgen*, 25 June 1991; and "Nach fünfzig Jahren," *Abendzeitung*, 25 June 1991.

64. On the memory culture of the 1990s see Harold Marcuse, *Legacies of Dachau: The Uses and Abuses of a Concentration Camp, 1933–2001*, Cambridge, 2001, pp. 372–406. The quantitative development of the broadcast of contemporary history in the Federal Republic from the 1960s to the 1990s is documented in Wulf Kansteiner, "Nazis, Viewers, and Statistics: Television History, Televisions Audience Research, and Collective Memory in West Germany," *Journal of Contemporary History* (forthcoming).

65. Knopp, "Zwischen Krieg und Frieden," p. 80.

66. *Hitler: Eine Bilanz I: Der Privatmann*, ZDF, 9 November 1995; *HEB II: Der Verführer*, ZDF, 12 November 1995; *HEB III: Der Erpresser*, ZDF, 19 November 1995; *HEB IV: Der Diktator*, ZDF, 26 November 1995; *HEB V: Der Kriegsherr*, ZDF, 3 December 1995; *HEB IV: Der Verbrecher*, ZDF, 10 December 1995.

67. Guido Knopp, "Keine Angst vor Hitler? – 50 Jahre danach," *ZDF Jahrbuch 1995*, pp. 88–90, 88.

68. Knopp, "Keine Angst vor Hitler?," p. 90.

69. Knopp, "Zwischen Krieg und Frieden," p. 81; see also *ZDF Pressedienst* (1997), 66.

70. *ZDF Jahrbuch 1995*, 342.

71. Heinz Braun, "Im direkten Kontakt mit dem Zuschauer," *ZDF Jahrbuch 1995*, pp. 204–6.

72. Minutes of the ZDF telephone staff of 9, 19, 26 November and 3 December 1995.

73. The television discussion *Hitler heute* (ZDF, 10 December 1995), which was broadcast live after the last sequel of *Hitler: Eine Bilanz* from 22:56 p.m. to 23:57 p.m., produced 462 phone calls to the station. These calls were received in addition to the calls to the special phone number which the ZDF had leased to screen and process questions from viewers, see minutes of the ZDF telephone staff of 10 December 1995.

74. "Hitler und kein Ende," *Stuttgarter Zeitung*, 11 November 1995; Joachim Westhoff, "TV-Kritik," *Westfälische Rundschau*, 11 November 1995; Barbara Sichtermann, "Auf den Effekt kalkuliert," *Die Welt*, 23 November 1995; Rolf Potthoff, "Ein Hitler-Portrait mit Bildern wie Blendwerk," *Westdeutsche Allgemeine Zeitung*, 1 December 1995; and

Karin Hanig, "Am Mythos nur gekratzt," *Sächsische Zeitung*, 13 December 1995. It is also remarkable that *Hitler: Eine Bilanz* received significantly fewer reviews than Knopp's earlier programs. Apparently, as Knopp was celebrating his most successful series up to that point and clearly moving audiences, the critics were losing interest.

75. This strategy of representation is reminiscent of Philipp Jenninger's botched speech in German parliament in November 1988 as his empathetic attempt to explore the popularity of Hitler with the German people cost him his job as the president of that parliament, see Astrid Linn, *". . . noch heute ein Faszinosum . . .:" Philipp Jenninger zum 9. November 1938 und die Folgen*, Münster, 1990; and Fritz Wolf, "Der eine und der andere General," *epd medien*, 4 November 1998.

76. With the exception of some of the sequels the following series did not deal with the Nazi past: *Top-Spione*, six sequels, ZDF, between 6 November and 11 December 1994; *Skandal: Die großen Affären*, four sequels, ZDF, between 16 June and 7 July 1996; *Vatikan: Die Macht der Papste*, five sequels, ZDF, between 30 October and 26 November 1997; and *Kanzler*, six sequels, ZDF, between 6 April and 11 May 1999. *Unser Jahrhundert: Deutsche Schicksalstage*, three sequels, ZDF, between 19 May and 2 June 1998, continued with a second installment of 12 sequels in 1999, featured a number of programs on NS history.

77. *ZDF Jahrbuch 1996*, p. 61, and pp. 276–7.

78. The global reach of the ZDF historians has been proudly advertised on many occasions, see for example *ZDF Pressedienst* (1997), 66. For the relative size of the subdivision of contemporary history see *ZDF Jahrbuch 1998*, pp. 269–73.

79. Dieter Stolte, "Vom Markt zur Marke: Marktstrategien für das öffentlich-rechtliche Porgamm der Zukunft," *ZDF Jahrbuch 1995*, pp. 45–50; and Dieter Schwarzenau, "Marken markieren: Anmerkungen zur Pressearbeit in einem verschärften Wettbewerb," *ZDF Jahrbuch 1995*, pp. 195–7. For the rise of the star system in German television see Hickethier, *Geschichte des deutschen Fernsehens*, p. 530.

80. Knopp already published a book for the first documentary he produced with the ZDF, *Warum habt Ihr Hitler nicht verhindert* (Frankfurt, 1983), but the business really took off with *Der verdammte Krieg* and Knopp's collaboration with Bertelsmann: *Der verdammte Krieg: Das Unternehmen Barbarossa*, Gütersloh, 1991; *Entscheidung Stalingrad*, Gütersloh, 1993; and *Das Ende 1945*, Gütersloh, 1995. Ever since each new series of the ZDF's divisions of contemporary history has been accompanied by a volume that is based on the research undertaken in preparation for the programs, written by the members of Knopp's staff or

a professional writer (for instance Rudolf Gültner in the case of the three volumes for *Der verdammte Krieg*), and marketed under Knopp's name.

81. *Hitlers Helfer I: Der Stellvertreter – Rudolf Hess*, ZDF, 14 January 1997; *HH II: Der Vollstrecker – Heinrich Himmler*, ZDF, 21 January 1997; *HH III: Der Brandstifter – Josef Goebbels*, ZDF, 28 January 1997; *HH IV: Der Zweite Mann – Hermann Göring*, ZDF, 4 February 1997; *HH V: Der Architekt – Albert Speer*, ZDF, 18 February 1997; *HH VI: Der Nachfolger – Karl Dönitz*, ZDF, 25 February 1997; and *Hitlers Helfer – Die Diskussion*, ZDF, 25 February 1997. The second installment of six more sequels followed in 1998: *Hitlers Helfer: Täter und Vollstrecker I: Eichmann – Der Vernichter*, ZDF, 7 April 1998; *HH: TV II: Ribbentrop – Der Handlanger*, ZDF, 14 April 1998; *HH: TV III: Freisler – Der Hinrichter*, ZDF, 21 April 1998; *HH: TV IV: Bormann – Der Schattenmann*, ZDF, 28 April 1998; *HH: TV V: Schirach – Der Hitlerjunge*, ZDF, 5 May 1998; *HH: TV VI: Mengele – Der Todesarzt*, ZDF, 12 May 1998.

82. *Hitlers Krieger I: Rommel – Das Idol*, ZDF, 13 October 1998; *HK II: Manstein – Der Stratege*, ZDF, 27 October 1998; *HK III: Paulus – Der Gefangene*, ZDF, 3 November 1998; *HK IV: Udet – Der Flieger*, ZDF, 10 November 1998; *HK V: Canaris – Der Verschwörer*, 17 November 1998; *HK VI: Keitel – Der Gehilfe*, ZDF, 24 November 1998; and *Hitlers Krieger – Die Diskussion*, ZDF, 24 November 1998; see also Kinkel, "Viele Taten, wenig Täter."

83. "Von Hess bis Goebbels: Sechsteiler über die wichtigsten Nazi-Schergen," *Hamburger Abendblatt*, 14 January 1997.

84. The precise figure of 6.85 million viewers on average corresponded to an excellent market share of 21.1 per cent, *ZDF Jahrbuch 1997*, p. 349. The single most successful program was the show on Goebbels that attracted an unprecedented 7.38 million viewers, corresponding to a 22.6 per cent market share, see GfK-Fernsehforschung (ed.), *ZDF Einschaltquoten für Dienstag, 28. Januar 1997*.

85. *Hitlers Krieger I: Rommel – Das Idol*.

86. Ibid.

87. One of the Jewish eyewitnesses was Inge Deutschkron, who survived the Third Reich in hiding and published and lectured about her experience, see Deutschkron, *Ich trug den gelben Stern*, Munich, 1985.

88. *Hitlers Krieger I: Rommel – Das Idol*.

89. Marius Meller, "Hitlers willige Helfer," *Stuttgarter Zeitung*, 16 January 1997; Ralf Schlüter, "Gespenstisch," *Berliner Zeitung*, 16 January 1997; and Fritz Wolf, "Zur Metaphysik ist es nicht weit," *epd medien*, 5 February 1997.

90. Knopp moderated one of the TV discussions with Daniel Gold-hagen, see *Hitlers willige Helfer? Die Deutschen und der Holocaust*, ZDF, 8 September 1996.

91. Thomas Gehringer, "Der totale Knopp: Geschichte satt bis 2000," *Tagesspiegel*, 25 October 1997; see also Knopp, "Zeitgeschichte im ZDF," p. 313.

92. For the changes in television programming in the 1990s see especially Hickethier, *Geschichte des deutschen Fernsehens*, pp. 517–43.

93. Peter Arens, "Dokus in voller Fahrt: Über die wundersame Rennaissance des IQ-Fernsehens," *ZDF Jahrbuch 1997*, pp. 92–4.

94. Ibid., p. 92.

95. Explicitly referring to *Hitlers Helfer* Oswald Ring attested to "the drastically improved competitiveness of modernized information television," Ring, "Beratung und Orientierung sind gefragt," *ZDF Jahrbuch 1996*, pp. 65–8.

96. See Klaus Naumann's excellent summary and analysis of the debate in Naumann, "Der totale Knopp: Der Erfinder des 'ZDF-Docutainments' Guido Knopp gibt der Geschichte dramaturgische Nachhilfe," *Die Woche*, 15 May 1998.

97. Thomas Gehringer, "'NS-Kitsch:' Fernsehen und Zeitgeschichte. Eine Auseinandersetzung," *Tagesspiegel*, 16 June 1998; see also Hans-Jürgen Krug, "Geschichte, Fernsehen, Geschichtsfernsehen: Wie das Medium Fernsehen sich der Historie bedient," *Frankfurter Rundschau*, 22 August 1998.

98. Rudolf Grimm, "Aufklärung braucht Reichweite: Historiker und Publizisten zwiespältig im Urteil über die ZDF-Reihe *Hitlers Helfer*," *Tagesspiegel*, 12 May 1998; see also Ulrike Langer, "Historische Aufklärung darf kein Privileg sein," *Frankfurter Rundschau*, 17 June 1998; and Guido Knopp, "Aufklärung braucht Reichweite," *ZDF Jahrbuch 1999*, pp. 68–9.

99. *Der Holocaust-Beschluß: 50 Jahre nach der Wannsee-Konferenz*, ZDF, 19 January 1992; *Kinder des Feuers: Die Zwillinge von Auschwitz*, 15 March 1992; and *Die Wahrheit über Auschwitz*, 22 January 1995.

100. The ZDF had adopted the title *Holokaust* upon the suggestion of Eberhard Jäckel, who was also a consultant during the production of the series. Before making the decision the station had sought the advice of other academics, for instance Walter Jens, who came to the surprising conclusion that "one should use the term "Holokaust" for the fact that millions were turned to ashes because the term is precise and offers additional insight through aesthetic alienation," see Edo Reents, "Zur rechten Zeit," *Süddeutsche Zeitung* 13 October 2000; see also Alexander

Kissler, "Vom Zeugen zum Täter," *Frankfurter Allgemeine Zeitung* 17 October 2000; and especially Henryk Broder's entertaining comments about the choice of terminology "Kopyright auf Holokaust: Die ZDF-Schreibung für "Holocaust" steht für den deutschen Sündenstolz," *Tagesspiegel* 18 October 2000.

101. *Holokaust I: Menschenjagd*, ZDF, 17 October 2000; *Holokaust II: Entscheidung*, 24 October 2000; *Holokaust III: Getto*, ZDF, 31 October 2000; *Holokaust IV: Mordfabrik*, ZDF, 7 November 2000; *Holokaust V: Widerstand*, ZDF, 14 November 2000; *Holokaust VI: Befreiung*, ZDF, 21 November 2000.

102. See the positive reviews by Kirsten Decker, "Ganz verbrennen: Nach *Holocaust*, nach *Shoah*: Wie das ZDF den Mord an den Juden dokumentiert," *Tagesspiegel* 14 October 2000; Paul Meyer, "Aufklärung zur rechten Zeit," *Die Woche* 20 October 2000; and especially Norbert Frei, "Mäßige Zuschauerzahlen, enttäuschende Resonanz: Warum die ZDF-Reihe *Holokaust* gut war, aber kein Erfolg," *Süddeutsche Zeitung* 21 November 2000; and compare to "Ästhetisierte Vernichtung," *tageszeitung* 17 October 2000.

103. See for example Jürgen Tremper, "Vor allem beschrieben und zu wenig hinterfragt," *Nordkurier* 18 November 2000; and "*Holokaust*: Wenig Erklärungen für das Morden," *Neue Züricher Zeitung*, 4/5 November 2000.

104. Frei, "Mäßige Zuschauerzahlen."

105. Matthias Arning, "Eindimensional," *Frankfurter Rundschau*, 15 October 1998.

106. *Hitlers Frauen*, 5 sequels, ZDF, 25 April and 2, 23, 30 May and 13 June 2001; *Hitlers Kinder I: Verführung*, ZDF, 14 March 2001; *Hitlers Kinder II: Hingabe*, ZDF, 21 March 2001; *Hitlers Kinder III: Zucht*, ZDF, 28 March 2001; *Hitlers Kinder IV: Einsatz*, ZDF, 4 April 2001; and *Hitlers Kinder V: Opferung*, ZDF, 14 April 2001, 5 sequels, ZDF, 14, 21, 28 March 2001.

107. The first of 21 sequels of *Der Jahrhundertkrieg* was broadcast in January 2002, see Reinhard Lüke, "Schiffe versenken: Guido Knopps Mammutreihe 'Der Jahrhundertkrieg'," *Frankfurter Rundschau*, 10 January 2002.

108. *Die große Flucht I: Der große Treck, Kampf um Ostpreußen*, ZDF, 20 November 2001; *DgF II: Der Untergang der Gustloff*, ZDF, 27 November 2001; *DgF III: Die Festung Breslau*, ZDF, 4 December 2001; *DgF IV: Die Stunde der Frauen: Überleben in Pommern*, ZDF, 11 December 2001; and *DgF V: Die verlorene Heimat*, ZDF, 18 December 2001.

109. The Walser-Bubis debate is documented in Frank Schirrmacher (ed.), *Die Walser-Bubis-Debatte: Eine Dokumentation*, Frankfurt, 1999.

110. Günter Grass, *Im Krebsgang*, Göttingen, 2002; see also "Eine Katastrophe, aber kein Verbrechen," *Stern*, 14 February 2002; and Thomas Schmidt, "Ostdeutscher Totentanz," *Die Zeit*, 14 February 2002.

111. On the decreasing audiences for Knopp's programs see the graph "Schwindendes Interesse: Dokumentationen im ZDF über die Hitler-Zeit," *Der Spiegel*, 3 April 2000; and the graph "Marktanteile der ZDF-Reihen," *Der Spiegel*, 20 November 2000. One notable exception was the program on Eva Braun which reached a market share of 19 per cent in April 2001, see "Hitlers Frauen beliebt," *Der Spiegel*, 30 April 2001.

112. Tom Peukert, "Warten auf Hitlers Hunde," *Tagesspiegel*, 11 February 2000; see also Oliver Maria Schmitt, "Der Fluch der Verknoppung," *Tageszeitung*, 16 March 2000.

113. Tina Angerer, "Hitler – ein Witz? Der Nazi-Diktator als Comedy-Figur hat Konjunktur im deutschen Fernsehen," *Tagespiegel*, 29 January 2000.

114. Anneliese Mannzmann, *Hitlerwelle und historische Fakten*, Königstein, 1979.

115. Susan Sontag, *Im Zeichen des Saturns*, München, 1981; Saul Friedlander, *Reflections of Nazism*, New York, 1984.

116. Sontag, *Im Zeichen des Saturns*, p. 117; and Friedlander, *Reflections of Nazism*, p. 33.

117. That applies, for instance, to the first Hitler wave of 1977, see Mannzmann, *Hitlerwelle*.

118. *Olympia*, Leni Riefenstahl; Olympia-Film, Germany, 1936–38; Knopp's production was *Der schöne Schein: Olympia "36*, ZDF, 27 July, 1986.

119. *Nuit et Brouillard*, Alain Resnais; Como/Argos, France, 1955; *Le Chagrin et la Pitie*, Marcel Ophüls; Rencontre/SSR/NDR, Switzerland/Germany, 1969; *Hitler, ein Film aus Deutschland*, Hans-Jürgen Syberberg; TMS/Solaris/WDR/INA/BBC, Germany/France/England, 1976–7; *Shoah*, Claude Lanzmann; Les Films Aleph/Historia Films, France, 1974–1985.

120. Hans Jürgen Syberberg, *Vom Unglück und Glück der Kunst in Deutschland nach dem lezten Kriege*, Munich, 1990.

121. Eike Wenzel, *Gedächnisraum Film: Die Arbeit an der deutschen Geschichte in Filmen seit den sechziger Jahren*, Stuttgart, 2000.

122. See the succinct, exceptionally insightful remarks of Stefan Bauer, "Geschichte auf Hochglanz," *Gong*, 23 January, 1997.

123.  For the politics of culture and the political effects of the Nazi film industry see Eric Rentschler, *The Ministry of Illusion: Nazi Cinema and its Afterlife*, Cambridge, 1996, especially pp. 215–223.

124.  Knopp, "Zeitgeschichte im ZDF," p. 311.

125.  Wulf Kansteiner, "Ein Volkermord ohne Täter? Die Darstellung der 'Endlösung' in den Sendungen des Zweiten Deutschen Fernsehens," *Tel Aviver Jahrbuch für Deutsche Geschichte 2003*, pp. 253–86.

126.  Knopp, "Zeitgeschichte im ZDF," p. 311.

127.  See the exceptionally insightful text of Barbara Sichtermann, "Das Tabu," *Die Zeit*, 11 November 1988.

# 20
# Between Media History and the History of Social Communication

*Volker Depkat*

The "Third Reich", World War II and the Holocaust have been motion picture events right from the start. The Nazis made widespread use of the medium film as a propaganda tool that was supposed to stabilize their regime and to interpret their social and political utopias to their audiences. World War II was a propaganda war on all sides with each side drawing heavily on film to legitimize its goals, keep up its own morale and demoralize its enemy. With the end of World War II, the Holocaust came to the German and international public as moving imagery showing haunting montages of the unimaginable concentration camp horrors. Films have been a very powerful means to communicate Nazi crimes ever since the 1940s when the Allies used filmed material in their attempts to denazify and re-educate the Germans, and both Doherty and Kansteiner stress the exceptional force of motion pictures in documenting and dramatizing the "Third Reich", National Socialism and the Holocaust. Films – and not texts or other sources historians use – have shaped the knowledge of and the notions about the history of the twentieth century in general and that of the "Third Reich" in particular. Outside of academia, cinema and television communicated the Nazi past of Germany to a mass audience; these media shaped the pictures in our heads about the "Third Reich", World War II and the Holocaust that we carry around with us.

Doherty's and Kansteiner's papers confront us with two very different approaches to representations of the Nazi past in films. Doherty's main impetus is to define the genre Holocaust cinema, to classify its various types, and to suggest frames of analysis that could guide a historical inquiry into the documentaries and dramas representing the extermination of the Jews in moving imagery. Doherty draws a clear line between documentary and fictional forms of Holocaust cinema, and then goes on to subdivide each major category into a number of subtypes. In the end, he sketches out four frames of analysis that organize a perspective on the material and structure the examination of it. According to Doherty,

Holocaust cinema can be analysed from an aesthetic, a historical, a technological and a cultural angle. Thus the general aim of his paper is quite clear; it is about defining and classifying the material, showing ways of dealing with it and pointing out some methodological pitfalls in the terrain of Holocaust cinema. This lets his contribution appear as a preparatory exercise on the way to analysing concrete films about the Holocaust; we do not learn too much about its representation in moving imagery as such. Kansteiner, however, does just that.

Kansteiner's paper deals with the phenomenon of Guido Knopp and the new visual aesthetics he invented to show Germany's Nazi past on television. Kansteiner identifies Knopp's television documentaries on the "Third Reich", World War II and the Holocaust as truly visual texts that create a new language of history, a language adequate to the thoroughly commercialized television landscape that developed in Germany after 1984. Kansteiner shows convincingly how Knopp, who started out as a rather conventional television historian producing illustrated history lectures in the late 1970s, developed into the radical visual innovator who relegated discourse to a secondary position by making it subservient to a very attractive, transgressing and fast moving visual text, which was able to attract a mass audience at prime time. Kansteiner sees a causal link between the development of a dual system of commercial and public television networks in Germany and Knopp's new forms of visually representing the Nazi past on the screen.

Both papers, as different as they are, can be linked by the problem of genre and also by the conditions, possibilities and restrictions of the medium of film. They are both contributions to media history in its broadest sense. They both ask how a specific medium deals with a certain aspect of the past, and how the specific dynamisms of the medium condition and shape the way in which this past reality is represented. However, as Jörg Requate has pointed out quite rightly, there is no autonomous media history driven solely by technical and commercial factors. We should rather describe the development of the media, their subjects and their aesthetics, in their interdependence with ongoing processes of social change.[1] Taking this into consideration, the historical question really is not so much the one of how the Nazi past, or any other past for that matter, is represented in a medium; rather, the question that has to be answered then is, when and why does a historical topic become a topic in a medium like film, when and why does a genre like Holocaust cinema emerge – or vanish – in a society in the first place, and what does this tell us about the society? The following comment will elaborate on these problems in two respects. First, it addresses the question of how

374

historians should study the media without leaving it at a media history. Second, it will deal with the problem of assessing the functions of historical subjects in a commercialized mass media landscape.

## Media History or History of Social Communication?

Media history should not be written as an isolated history of the media – as a history of those technological means by which human beings in the course of time have distributed news, conserved knowledge, arranged entertainment, and shaped opinions. Media history should not fulfill itself in a history of sign systems, communication technologies, forms, and contents of the various media, their makers and their audiences, their place and function in the overall media system. This is not to say that it is unimportant to know all these things, however, what I miss in the two papers on visual representations of the "Third Reich' on television and in cinema, is the connection between social history and media history. I am not thinking about a social history of the media that analyses the social profile of the journalists and filmmakers and that of their audiences. What I have in mind is social history as communications history. In such an analytical framework, one would have to analyse the historical development of the media in their relevance for, their functions in, and their effects on processes of social communication.

What is a history of social communication? Briefly, it is the history of those communicative practices and situations through which societies and social groups produce, sustain, reproduce, or transform their order. Social communication is about legitimacy and meaning, about identity and memory, about hierarchy and power in a society. When you look at it that way, communication becomes the basic category of society as such, as Jürgen Habermas or Niklas Luhmann have argued, although in two fundamentally different approaches.[2] At the heart of a history of social communication lies the idea that society happens as communication, that social reality emerges from communicative interaction, that society is the sum of its members' communication.[3] Social communication takes place in institutionally, socially, and regionally differentiated spheres, and it manifests itself as a concrete social practice structured by power and hierarchy and the technologies of communication. These spheres, situations and practices of social communication can be identified and described in terms of change over time. This, however, means identifying not only the who, the what and the how of communication, but also the when and why – the concrete historical moment in which a subject becomes a subject in the processes of social communication. Geared to the problem of communicating the Nazi past on television and in cinemas, this would mean analysing National Socialism and particularly the Holocaust in its relevance for mass media based social self-descriptions in the postwar and post-Cold War societies of the twentieth century.[4] Seen from this perspective, communicating the Nazi past on television and in the cinema touches on questions of self-conceptions, national identities and political cultures in the "worlds after 1945" respectively the "worlds after 1989/90". It is this aspect that I miss in the papers by Doherty and Kansteiner.

Ever since the end of World War II, Germans, as all other nations, have lived in the shadow of the Nazi past, and the debates about the "Third Reich", World War II and the Holocaust have been central factors shaping the processes of social communication in both German states right from their inception.[5] In the Federal Republic of Germany as well as in the German Democratic Republic the experience of National Socialism was central for the formulation of post-totalitarian or post-fascist world views, and the collective memory of the Nazi past in the two Germanies split up along the lines of the political antagonism of the Cold War. Both the Federal Republic of Germany and the German Democratic Republic were eager to differentiate themselves from each other not only by taking sides in the Cold War but also through the specific way in which they dissociated themselves from the Nazi past.[6] The uses that East and West Germans made of the Nazi past were always intended to create historical legitimacy, moral integrity, and political orientation for the two new states and societies. The following remarks will concentrate on the developments in the Federal Republic of Germany because scholars have only just begun to inquire into the ways in which the Nazi past was integrated into collective memories in the German Democratic Republic. We know a lot more about the developments in West Germany.

Literally from the end of World War II on there was a more-or-less continuous flow of films on the Nazi past in German cinemas and on television. Even in the 1950s, a decade that has been identified by Hermann Lübbe as a period of relative silence on the Nazi past, the "Third Reich", World War II and the Holocaust were omnipresent as subtexts of the processes of social communication through which West Germans defined their place in the "world after Hitler".[7] Yet, there can hardly be a doubt that most Germans in the early Federal Republic refused to accept the "Third Reich" and particularly the Holocaust as an integral part of their own historical identity. Students of the subject have spoken of *Erinnerungsverweigerung* (the refusal to remember) and *Schuldabwehr* (the denial of guilt) to characterize the way in which West Germans dealt with the Nazi past in the 1950s and early 1960s.[8] In those days, the television and film industry helped Germans to escape from their problematic and guilt laden past.[9] By producing sentimental films in idealized regional settings (*Heimatfilme*) or war movies that portrayed noble and heroic German soldiers as seduced victims of the Nazi regime, the movies of the Adenauer era served their audience's longing for an innocent Germany. Although there were films like Wolfgang Staudte's (1906–84) *Die Mörder sind unter uns* (1946) and *Rosen für den Staatsanwalt* (1959), which attempted to unearth the brown roots of West Germany's society and expose its hypocritical ways of dealing with the Nazi past, the general impression from today's perspective is that the reappraisal of the Nazi past was "half-hearted", that there was an "inability to mourn", and that there apparently was only little awareness of the healing, liberating, and forward looking power of dealing with the Nazi past openly and truthfully in the Adenauer era.[10] However, Lübbe has argued – and I think he really has a point there – that this relative silence on the immediate past was a necessary condition for the transformation of the post-fascist West German society into a democratic one. According to Lübbe, it was just this communicative concealment of the Nazi past that contributed to West Germany's reconstruction and the stabilization of its democracy in the early days of the Federal Republic.[11]

Then, from the late 1950s on, things began to shift. The trials against firing squads in Ulm in 1958 and Adolf Eichmann (1906–62) in 1961, which gained wide public attention, ended the period of half-heartedness and ushered in a new concern with the Nazi past that went along with an intensified prosecution of the perpetrators. In the late 1960s, the student movement forced West German society to deal with National Socialism and the crimes committed by the generation of their parents during the "Third Reich" on a broad scale.[12] These highly moral debates demanded that Germans thought of themselves not only as victims of National Socialism but also as active participants in the totalitarian system. This led to a substantial transformation of the political culture in West Germany. Now the crimes of the "Third Reich" began to enter mainstream historical consciousness. Again television and cinema went along with this trend in history and identity politics. As they largely had helped Germans to escape from the past in the 1950s and early 1960s, they now forced them to deal with the crimes of the "Third Reich" and accept them as an integral part of their historical identity in a post-totalitarian, democratic world. It appears to me that television and cinema then even began to take the lead in keeping the past alive and transforming attitudes towards the Nazi past.

It was a television series – the 1978 *Holocaust* docu-drama – that ended a long period of silence on the extermination of the European Jews in Germany.[13] It was this television program that introduced the term "Holocaust" as a universal referent for the destruction of Europe's Jewry, and television historian Guido Knopp went one step further yet when he decided to spell the word "Holocaust" not with a "c" but with a "k" – German spelling as if it were a German word. Since Germans committed the Holocaust, Knopp argued, it indicates a dissociation from this historical fact when one denotes it with a word in the English spelling. By introducing the German spelling of the word "Holokaust", Knopp intended to force the Germans to embrace this historical event as an integral part of their history and historical identity.[14] I know that many historians have differing opinions about this, but seen against the backdrop of the early Federal Republic, Knopp's decision to spell the word Holocaust with a "k" is a remarkable step – and that he does so on television in front of a mass audience is even more remarkable.

Having sketched out some thoughts on the relevance of the "Third Reich" and the Holocaust for social self-descriptions in West Germany after 1945, let me now turn to American theatre. In the Federal Republic, the Nazi past in general and the Holocaust in particular were important factors in shaping social discourses, either as a subject openly addressed or as subtext of many other discussions about a wide variety of topics. In the German arena, this is not too surprising – it is the land of the perpetrators, and the development of the debates about the Nazi past over the years has to be seen as a move toward a higher degree of moral and political hygiene. But why did the Holocaust move to the center of public debates and collective memories in the United States as well? Why was the *Holocaust* series an American production? Why this television- and cinema-fueled burst of attention for the "Third Reich" in the 1990s, why this "Americanization of the Holocaust"? Is it really just because the Americans cannot bear the fact that the most dramatic event in the twentieth century happened outside of the United States, as Doherty seems to suggest? I think this is a very weak explanation that hardly does justice to the problems involved. In my view, there is a lot more to the process of "Americanizing the Holocaust" as soon as we start to analyse it in terms of identity struggles and identity politics within the American society. It cannot be sufficiently explained with the inner dynamisms of the medium film, its technological possibilities and the constraints of the market; it is not a question of the tropes and patterns of Holocaust cinema or of the postmodern aesthetics of television documentary. This has to be explained in the broader framework of a history of social communication.

## Television and Cinema between Memory and History

The recent debates about collective memories center on the opposition between history and memory. Scholars as different as Maurice Halbwachs and Jan Assmann, Arnold Esch and Pierre Nora have argued that memory has to do with identity, while history has to do with the scholarly reconstruction of past realities as they actually were.[15] Whereas memory is always the memory of a specific group whose inner cohesion is sustained among other things by a commonly shared memory, historiography is identity neutral and aims at complexity, differentiation, and scholarly explanations of historical developments in terms of cause and effect. While memory is about the uses of the past as such and as an instrument for identity politics, historiography, due to its scholarly interests, has the effect of destroying identity patterns resting in particular notions of the past and images of history. Where do we place television and cinema in this tension between history and memory? Two points seem to be worth considering in this context; first, the question of films as sources and the very possibility of depicting the past in moving imagery; second, the question of how to relate cinema and television as popular culture media to what is happening in academia.

Films in general are highly problematic sources because they suggest a direct and authentic access to past realities.[16] The very power of the moving images tends to numb their viewers critical capacities. While you are hardly inclined to believe everything that is written, you are most willing to believe everything you see – historians not excepted. Doherty is clear on this point, when he defines film as a high definition medium that thrives on verisimilitude, the quality of being lifelike. It is just this suggestion of verisimilitude that makes films and photos highly problematic sources; they have never been a more reliable reflection of past realities than any of the other materials we historians use as sources – and the German controversy about the exhibition on Wehrmacht crimes that relies solely on photographs has shown this quite clearly.[17] In this context, the dangers that grow out of the computer revolution can hardly be overestimated, as both Doherty and Kansteiner point out. Modern technologies have outpaced the ability of the audience to differentiate between fact and fiction, between authentic documentary and later artistic re-enactment. Nowadays, film technology can change the rules of the historical game.

However, can you depict the past in moving imagery at all? It is not only the Holocaust that is beyond persuasive cinematic depiction, all historical subjects are. The past in its full complexity and ambiguity is past, and all historiography is but a re-enactment of past realities in the historian's mind. These intellectual re-enactments of bygone times are necessarily incomplete and problematic, because the sources only open up certain perspectives on the past; they never give us the whole picture. Scholarly explanations of past ages tend to be highly complex and, more importantly, highly abstract. Although history is about people and life, our books tend to be about the general and the abstract, about ideal types, about anonymous structures and processes, not about the individual and the concrete. Most of the things we, as historians, do can hardly be visualized in their full complexity. Cinema and television, however, center on life-likeness. They need a story, they need concrete individuals and need to focus on specific events. Historians tend to cultivate the behavior of detached observers of the past with which they claim to deal *sine ira et studio*; cinema and television, however, want to draw their audience into the subject, they want to arouse emotions and create some form of consternation. The question about communicating the past on television and in the cinema then really is: what is stronger, the impulse of the medium to inform and enlighten about the past as it really was, or the willingness to shape collective memory as a means of identity politics? Are cinema and television not really more about producing certain images of the past that the audiences can identify with or dissociate themselves from than about inquiring into the full complexity of bygone times? Historians should remain aware that the academic debates and the mass media each fulfill different functions in the social communications of a society. Television and cinema should not be mistaken for a history classroom at the university – and vice versa.

In this context, I argue that academic historians who criticize Knopp for not being in tune with the recent scholarship on Hitler somehow miss the point. Historiographically speaking, his documentary on Hitler and the historical explanations he gives are a relapse into the 1950s, a period that cultivated an essentially personalized view on the "Third Reich", according to which a small band of criminals lead by the demonic Adolf Hitler managed to seduce the German people.[18] Knopp basically ignores the academic discussions of the 1960s, 1970s and 1980s about the ambivalent character of the "Third Reich" as a regime between totalitarian norm and polycratic reality or those on the role of Hitler as weak or strong dictator.[19] He also refuses to relate his documentaries to the most recent developments in the historiography of the "Third Reich" – explorations into the German people's willingness to participate in the dialectics of seduction and to act as Hitler's "willing executioners".[20] Most importantly, and for scholars most disturbingly, Knopp does not even indicate that there is a scholarly debate about these things. Rather, he presents an authoritative visual master narrative on the "Third Reich" that suggests certainty and unambiguity where there actually is controversy. This has earned him much severe criticism from professional historians, and from a scholarly point of view rightly so. However, what his critics fail to acknowledge is that Knopp is not at all interested in these academic questions but very much interested in identity and memory politics. His documentaries are about healing the wounds of the past, about reconciliation between former combatants and enemies, about life stories and emotions hitherto suppressed. The enormous response of the audience to Knopp's documentaries only underlines this – his documentaries are really events of social communication through which German society tries to reach an understanding about its past and its historical identity in a collective discussion effort. His documentaries on the Nazi past are meant to be contributions to the present orientation of the Germans in the world. In this context, I can imagine worse forms of dealing with the Nazi past than trying to strengthen a democratic and pro-Western consensus in a postwar and post-Cold War Germany by putting Hitler and the "Third Reich" on television.

Another point seems worth mentioning in context with the phenomenon of Guido Knopp. In a radically changed, largely Americanized television landscape, full of fun and music videos, talk and game shows, soccer and *real* pornography, Knopp at least manages to put the Nazi past on the screen. He at least communicates history to a mass audience in Germany, and even the otherwise critical Kansteiner has to admit that Knopp has invented a new form of "interesting, visually and emotionally compelling documentaries" that actually reaches a large number of people. Now, you can argue that it is bad history that Knopp does, that his interpretation of Hitler and the "Third Reich" is flawed, biased and outdated – and I willingly go along with that – but at least *there is history on the screen* where otherwise there would probably be yet another game show. Knopp keeps the past alive on television, and who knows how many people in the audience might take Knopp's documentaries as an inspiration to study the subject on their own a little further. This, however, is the most important question that needs to be answered by media and communications historians: who is the audience, and *how does it relate* to the things on television and in the movies?

# Notes

1. Jörg Requate, "Öffentlichkeit und Medien als Gegenstände histor-ischer Analyse," *Geschichte und Gesellschaft* 25 (1999), 15.

2. Jürgen Habermas, *Theorie des kommunikativen Handelns*, 2 vols., Frankfurt a. M., 1981; Jürgen Habermas, *Strukturwandel der Öffentlich-keit: Untersuchungen zu einer Kategorie der bürgerlichen Gesellschaft. Mit einem Vorwort zur Neuauflage 1990*, Frankfurt a. M., 1990; Niklas Luhmann, "Evolution und Geschichte," in Niklas Luhmann, *Sozio-logische Aufklärung*, Opladen, 1975, vol. 2 pp. 150–69; Niklas Luhmann, *Gesellschaftstruktur und Semantik: Studien zur Wissenssoziologie der modernen Gesellschaft*, 4 vols, Frankfurt a. M., 1980–95; Niklas Luh-mann, "Geschichte als Prozeß und die Theorie sozio-kultureller Evolu-tion," in Niklas Luhmann, *Soziologische Aufklärung*, Opladen, 1981, vol. 3, pp. 178–97; Niklas Luhmann, "Veränderungen im System gesellschaft-licher Kommunikation und die Massenmedien," in Niklas Luhmann, *Soziologische Aufklärung*, Opladen, 1981, vol. 3, pp. 309–20; Niklas Luhmann, *Soziale Systeme: Grundriß einer allgemeinen Theorie*, Frank-furt a. M., 1984; Niklas Luhmann, "Wie ist Bewußtsein an Kommuni-kation beteiligt?" in Niklas Luhmann, *Soziologische Aufklärung*, Opladen, 1995, vol. 6, pp. 37–54; Niklas Luhmann, "Was ist Kommunikation?" in Niklas Luhmann, *Soziologische Aufklärung*, Opladen, 1995, vol. 6, pp. 113–24; Niklas Luhmann, *Die neuzeitlichen Wissenschaften und die Phänomenologie*, Vienna, 1996; Niklas Luhmann, *Die Gesellschaft der Gesellschaft*, Frankfurt a. M., 1997. For a detailed comparison of the two approaches to communication see: Volker Depkat, "Kommunikations-geschichte zwischen Mediengeschichte und der Geschichte sozialer Kommunikation," in Karl-Heinz Spieß (ed.), *Medien der Kommunikation im Mittelalter*, Stuttgart, 2003, pp. 9–48.

3. Nolte has exemplified this in his study on the history of German notions of social order in the twentieth century. Paul Nolte, *Die Ordnung der deutschen Gesellschaft: Selbstentwurf und Selbstbeschreibung im 20. Jahrhundert*, Munich, 2000.

4. For the concept of social self-description see: Luhmann, *Die Gesellschaft der Gesellschaft*, 866–1149.

5. Although there is a highly controversial scholarly debate about how to judge the efforts of West German society to come to grips with its Nazi past, one cannot really deny that the "Third Reich" and its consequences were a central theme in the Federal Republic from its foundation onwards. The discussions took place on different levels, had different forms and varying degrees of intensity and publicity to be sure, but there can hardly

be a doubt that the "unmasterable past" of the "Third Reich" was omnipresent in the social discourses of the West German society. Charles S. Maier, *The Unmasterable Past: History, Holocaust, and German National Identity*, Cambridge MA, 1988; Jeffrey Herf, *Divided Memory: The Nazi Past in the Two Germanys*, Cambridge MA, 1997; Hermann Lübbe, "Der Nationalsozialismus im deutschen Nachkriegsbewußtsein," *Historische Zeitschrift* 236 (1983), 579–99; Norbert Frei and Sybille Steinbacher (eds), *Beschweigen und Bekennen: Die deutsche Nachkriegsgesellschaft und der Holocaust*, Göttingen, 2001; Nicolas Berg, "Lesarten des Judenmords," in Ulrich Herbert (ed.), *Wandlungsprozesse in Westdeutschland: Belastung, Integration, Liberalisierung 1945–1980*, Göttingen, 2002, pp. 91–139; Jan Friedmann and Jörg Später, "Britische und deutsche Kollektivschuld-Debatte," in Ulrich Herbert (ed.), *Wandlungsprozesse in Westdeutschland*, 53–90. In the 1980s, the so called "Historikerstreit" gained widespread public attention. Matthias Peter and Hans-Jürgen Schröder, *Einführung in das Studium der Zeitgeschichte*, Paderborn et al., 1994, pp. 84–97; Reinhard Kühnl (ed.), *Vergangenheit, die nicht vergeht: Die "Historiker-Debatte". Darstellung, Dokumentation, Kritik*, Cologne, 1987; Reinhard Kühnl (ed.), *"Historikerstreit": Die Dokumentation der Kontroverse um die Einzigartigkeit der nationalsozialistischen Judenvernichtung*, Munich, 1987.

6. Herf, *Divided Memory*.

7. Lübbe, "Der Nationalsozialismus im deutschen Nachkriegsbewußtsein," p. 585. For the debates of the 1950s and early 1960s: Wilfried Loth and Bernd A. Rusinek, (eds), *Verwandlungspolitik. NS-Eliten in der westdeutschen Nachkriegsgesellschaft*, Frankfurt a. M., 1998; Norbert Frei, *Vergangenheitspolitik: Die Anfänge der Bundesrepublik und die NS-Vergangenheit*, Munich, 1996; Gotthard Jasper, "Wiedergutmachung und Westintegration. Die halbherzige justizielle Aufarbeitung der NS-Vergangenheit in der frühen Bundesrepublik," in Ludolf Herbst (ed.), *Westdeutschland 1945–1955: Unterwerfung, Kontrolle, Integration*, Munich, 1986, pp. 183–202; Hermann Graml, "Die verdrängte Auseinandersetzung mit dem Nationalsozialismus," in Martin Broszat (ed.), *Zäsuren nach 1945: Essays zur Periodisierung der deutschen Nachkriegsgeschichte*, Munich, 1990, pp. 169–83; Detlef Garbe, "Äußerliche Abkehr, Erinnerungsverweigerung und "Vergangenheitsbewältigung": Der Umgang mit dem Nationalsozialismus in der Frühen Bundesrepublik," in Axel Schildt and Arnold Sywottek (eds), *Modernisierung im Wiederaufbau: Die westdeutsche Gesellschaft der 50er Jahre*, Bonn, 1993, pp. 693–716; Hartmut Berghoff, "Zwischen Verdrängung und Aufarbeitung: Die bundesdeutsche Gesellschaft und ihre nationalsozial-

istische Vergangenheit in den Fünfziger Jahren," *Geschichte in Wissenschaft und Unterricht* 49 (1998), 96–114; Manfred Kittel, *Die Legende von der "Zweiten Schuld": Vergangenheitsbewältigung in der Ära Adenauer*, Frankfurt a. M., 1993; Peter Reichel, "Zwischen Dämonisierung und Verharmlosung: Das NS-Bild und seine politische Funktion in den 50er Jahren. Eine Skizze," in Schildt and Sywottek (eds), *Modernisierung im Wiederaufbau*, pp. 679–92.

8. Garbe, "Äußerliche Abkehr," 693, 699.

9. Irmgard Wilharm, "Filmwirtschaft, Filmpolitik und der "Publikumsgeschmack" im Westdeutschland der Nachkriegszeit," *Geschichte und Gesellschaft* 28 (2002), 267–90; Wilharm, "Krieg in deutschen Nachkriegsspielfilmen," in Gottfried Niedhart im Auftrag des Arbeitskreises für historische Friedensforschung (ed.) *Lernen aus dem Krieg? Deutsche Nachkriegszeiten 1918–1945. Beiträge zur historischen Friedensforschung*, Munich, 1992, pp. 281–99; Bernd Hey, "Zwischen Vergangenheitsbewältigung und heiler Welt: Nachkriegsdeutsche Befindlichkeiten in deutschen Spielfilmen," *Geschichte in Wissenschaft und Unterricht* 52 (2001), 229–37; Peter Gleber, "Zwischen Gestern und Morgen: Film und Kino im Nachkriegsjahrzehnt," in Franz-Josef Heyen and Anton M. Keim (eds), *Auf der Suche nach neuer Identität: Kultur in Rheinland-Pfalz im Nachkriegsjahrzehnt*, Mainz, 1996, pp. 451–520; Anton Kaes, *Deutschlandbilder: Die Wiederkehr der Geschichte als Film*, Munich, 1987; Peter Pleyer, *Deutscher Nachkriegsfilm*, Münster, 1965; Ursula Bessen, *Trümmer und Träume: Nachkriegszeit und fünfziger Jahre auf Zelluloid. Deutsche Spielfilme als Zeugnisse ihrer Zeit: Eine Dokumentation*, Bochum, 1989.

10. The notion of a "half-hearted" reappraisal was elaborated on by: Jasper, "Wiedergutmachung und Westintegration," 1986. The phrase "inability to mourn" was coined by: Alexander and Margarethe Mitscherlich, *Die Unfähigkeit zu trauern*, Munich 1967.

11. Lübbe, "Der Nationalsozialismus im deutschen Nachkriegsbewußtsein," p. 585.

12. Jasper, "Wiedergutmachung und Westintegration," pp. 200–2; Lübbe, "Der Nationalsozialismus im deutschen Nachkriegsbewußtsein," pp. 582f., 592; Rudolf Morsey, *Die Bundesrepublik Deutschland*, Munich, 2000, pp. 89–91; Jan Friedmann and Jörg Später, "Britische und deutsche Kollektivschuld-Debatte," pp. 87–9.

13. Matthias Weiß, "Sinnliche Erinnerung. Die Filme "Holocaust" und "Schindlers Liste" in der bundesdeutschen Vergegenwärtigung der NS-Zeit," in Norbert Frei and Sybille Steinbacher (eds), *Beschweigen und Bekennen: Die deutsche Nachkriegsgesellschaft und der Holocaust*, Göttingen, 2001, pp. 1–102.

14. Guido Knopp, *Holokaust*, Munich, 2001, pp. 20–2.

15. Maurice Halbwachs, *Les cadres sociaux de la mémoire*, Paris, 1925; Maurice Halbwachs, *La mémoire collective*, Paris, 1950; Jan Assmann, *Das kulturelle Gedächtnis: Schrift, Erinnerung und politische Identität in frühen Hochkulturen*, Munich, 1999; Pierre Nora, *Les lieux de mémoire* 3 vols, Paris, 1984–1992; Pierre Nora, *Zwischen Geschichte und Gedächtnis*, Berlin, 1990; Arnold Esch, *Zeitalter und Menschenalter: Der Historiker und die Erfahrung vergangener Gegenwart*, Munich, 1994.

16. For a critique of films as sources: Ernst Opgenoorth, *Einführung in das Studium der neueren Geschichte*, Paderborn et al., 1997, pp. 109–14.

17. Hamburger Institut für Sozialforschung (ed.), *Verbrechen der Wehrmacht: Dimensionen des Vernichtungskrieges 1941–1944. Ausstellungskatalog*, Hamburg, 2002; Hannes Heer and Klaus Naumann (eds), *Vernichtungskrieg: Verbrechen der Wehrmacht 1941–1944*, Hamburg, 1995; Hamburger Institut für Sozialforschung (ed.), *Eine Ausstellung und ihre Folgen: Zur Rezeption der Ausstellung "Vernichtungskrieg: Verbrechen der Wehrmacht 1941 bis 1944"*, Hamburg, 1999; Stefan Balkenohl, *Die Kontroverse um die Ausstellung "Vernichtungskrieg: Verbrechen der Wehrmacht 1941 bis 1944" in Münster· Eine qualitative Auswertung der Reaktionen*, Münster, 2000.

18. For an overview over the development of the scholarly debates cf. Klaus Hildebrand, *Das Dritte Reich*, Munich, 1995, pp. 135–55.

19. A good summary of these problems: Michael Ruck, "Führerabsolutismus und polykratisches Herrschaftsgefüge: Verfassungsstrukturen des NS-Staates," in Karl Dietrich Bracher et. al. (eds), *Deutschland 1933–1945: Neue Studien zur nationalsozialistischen Herrschaft*, Düsseldorf, 1992, pp. 32–56; Hildebrand, *Das Dritte Reich*, pp. 178–88.

20. It was not really Goldhagen's infamous book that started the scholarly discussion, although one might gain this impression from the wide and highly controversial discussion of his work in newspapers, journals and on television. Cf. Christopher Browning, *Ordinary Men: Reserve Police Battalion 101 and the Final Solution in Poland*, New York, 1992; Daniel Jonah Goldhagen, *Hitler's Willing Executioners: Ordinary Germans and the Holocaust*, New York, 1996.

# 21
# "Vergangenheitsbewältigung": Mastering the "Holokaust" in, through and with Film

## Olaf Kistenmacher and Regina Mühlhäuser

Wulf Kansteiner and Thomas Doherty discuss film productions about National Socialism and the Final Solution. Kansteiner examines the historical documentaries produced by Guido Knopp, and investigates the history of their success between 1978 and 2001 – during a period of time when the German television landscape changed from being comprised of a few state owned stations only to a commercialized production system with more and more privately owned networks. Doherty, on the other hand, defines a genre called "Holocaust film", and establishes a variety of subcategories by cataloguing themes and styles of exemplary documentaries and dramas.

Both contributions appear to contain parallels to Walter Benjamin's very prominent essay *The Work of Art in the Age of Mechanical Reproduction*, which was first published in French in 1936.[1] While Kansteiner explicitly refers to Benjamin's essay with the title of his paper, *The Radicalization of German Collective Memory in the Age of its Commercial Reproduction*, Doherty attempts to understand the specifics of the historic event that we are used to calling the "Holocaust" by analysing how its uniqueness (speaking in Benjamin's terms: its "Aura") is modified in the course of mass media film production. Both authors, Kansteiner as well as Doherty, try to explain the drastic changes in the interpretation of World War II and the Final Solution primarily in terms of technological progress and the aesthetic development of the medium film.

At first sight their approach does seem to correspond to Benjamin's account in *The Work of Art*, however, in their focus on technological and aesthetic developments, neither Kansteiner nor Doherty pay detailed attention to the historical and political changes of society. In this respect their contributions significantly differ from Benjamin's approach: in his analysis of pieces of art in the nineteenth and twentieth centuries, Benjamin claims that aesthetic and cultural changes are not primarily due to technological progress, but rather to the interplay between the development of technology and modern society – mutual interdependencies between technological, historical, cultural and political changes. Benjamin's approach thus implies the necessity to view media, social and political history as inseparable spheres.[2] Consequently, his aesthetic investigation in *The Work of Art* turns out to be an intrinsically political analysis of a society that gradually moves to fascism.

Starting from Benjamin's methodological approach, the following commentary attempts to examine Kansteiner's and Doherty's analyses through the lens of the historical and political development of the past twenty years by addressing the following questions: Is the rapid technical development and its introduction in film the *main* factor that caused a shift in collective memory about National Socialism and the Final Solution, or is the changing representation of the Holocaust in film "only" a manifestation of broader changes of and in society? In which respect do film and television "create history"? Can their producers be seen as agents of history? And how is film production connected to social and political development after the end of the Cold War? In order to shed light on these questions, the following commentary will avert the focus from film as text, and shift towards a perspective of contemporary German history – on *Vergangenheitspolitik* (politics of/with the past) and *Erinnerungspolitik* (politics of/with remembrance).[3] Along the way different debates on historiography, positionality, and the uniqueness of the Final Solution will be addressed.

# I. Technical Mediation and Historiography

Since the second half of the 1990s, historical documentary programs are frequently shown on German television during prime time evening hours. The vast majority of these programs address the history of National Socialism. Ten years earlier, this presence of the German past in mass media had been unthinkable. The credits for the introduction of a mass-compatible type of documentary are generally awarded to Guido Knopp. According to Kansteiner, the success of Knopp's historical documentaries

> is the result of a complicated interaction between market forces, the evolution of modern communication technologies, and the generational dynamisms of German historical culture. But at the heart of the Knopp phenomenon are the radical visual aesthetics of a new type of historical documentary . . .[4]

The development of these new "radical visual aesthetics" is said to be primarily due to the technical craftsmanship of Knopp and his production team – computer morphing, graphic imaging, digital editing techniques, special sound effects, and so forth. The deployment of special effects, however, is generally met with ambivalence. On the one hand, it is seen as the main reason for Knopp's "box office success"; on the other hand it is often regarded as problematic for its lack of appropriate seriousness: in the majority of cases, critics say, a rational historical narrative is abandoned in favor of thrilling excitement and emotional blackmailing.[5] Doherty detects the same ambivalence regarding "technological breakthroughs": "The rule of motion picture technology holds that if the FX means exist to achieve an effect, filmmakers will deploy them. In short, if Forrest Gump can appear in newsreel footage from the Kennedy administration, he can also pop up at Bergen-Belsen."[6]

If Forrest Gump "pops up at Bergen-Belsen" a variety of moral and political debates about the appropriate treatment of the history of the Final Solution, about "Holocaust-comedies", and so forth, will be at stake. The crucial question is, however, what happens when "technological breakthroughs" blur the distinction between "the apparently real and the obviously fabricated":

> When the technology of photofabrication, in videotape and cinema no less than the still picture, outpaces the ability of the spectator to detect it [the technical apparatus in use], the integrity and veracity of any moving image, perhaps the whole notion of documentary cinema, is called into question . . . Once unimpeachable testimony of the reality of the Holocaust – 35 mm photography being the template of truth – film is now an infinitely malleable medium, no more a reliable reflection of reality than any other pictorial expression.[7]

The blending of historical film material with recordings from the present is clearly not set out to visualize different layers of time. Rather past and present become indistinct by the means of optic assimilation. Doherty stresses that this fairly new technical and aesthetic tendency will indeed change the representation and perception of the historic event itself. At the same time, however, Doherty suggests that "archival originals", filmed during National Socialism and at the end of the war, used to be "the template of truth", "a reliable reflection of reality". He thus implies that, in comparison to today, spectators used to be able to perceive the technical conditions and the process of film production. Furthermore, by detecting, understanding and "subtracting" the production process, spectators could grasp an idea of the real, the authentic historic events.

This understanding of photographic images as authentic evidence to prove a historic event, does not take into account that the visual material in question is first and foremost a product of National Socialist propaganda. The newsreel footage from *Wochenschau*, and so forth, which shows images of the war or the ghettos, exhibits a filmed event, which film-makers and censors, employed by the propaganda department of the NSDAP, wanted the spectators to see.[8] As in this example, filmed images always constitute a certain narrative of a given historical moment; they will never present an objective historical truth. The historical facts cannot be grasped prior to interpretation; they can only be understood – in a sense of discourse, ideology, and so forth – in a mediated way. Film as well as historiography has to be understood as one way of producing a narrative about "the past", as Kansteiner has pointed out during the conference discussion.

In the process of production and representation of a historical narrative, the testimonies of eyewitnesses play a crucial role. Likewise, personal narratives have gained a more and more important role in film production. In this context, Doherty detects "two recurrent documentary characters": "the unimpeachable eyewitness" – either the warrior or the victim – and "the star witness" – "a natural character actor . . . whose articulate testimony . . . dominates the screen space."[9] Furthermore, Doherty points out that "human memory recalling traumatic events from over half a century ago" is a difficult and conflicting process.[10] Events will be suppressed, forgotten, and changed over time.

The historian Ulrike Jureit has conducted an interdisciplinary analysis of the narratives of concentration camp survivors. In her study she gives different examples of how eyewitness testimonies can help to determine historical facts. She points out, however, that methodologically an eyewitness testimony cannot be used to prove an event.[11] In fact, it is the historiographical analysis that takes into account how an event is reported under certain historical and political circumstances, and how the past is constructed in the present. Thus the historiographical analysis of eyewit-ness testimonies can provide important insights into individual and collective processes of coming to terms with the past. Furthermore, it allows an understanding of the personal, political and cultural conditions for the construction of historical narratives.

In filmic representations, however, eyewitness testimonies will usually be introduced without exposing the specificities of the material.[12] Guido Knopp's documentaries are a perfect example for the exploitation of eyewitness testimonies. As Kansteiner has pointed out, Knopp's docu-mentaries present only very short extracts of personal narratives to illustrate and prove his interpretation and filmic dramatization of a certain event. The eyewitnesses seem to be staged to guarantee a truthful and accurate depiction of the historic events. Correspondingly, Doherty criticizes most documentaries for their way of setting the eyewitness into scene:

> Clearly too many eyewitnesses featured in archival documentaries have told their stories more than once; some speak with the pacing and eloquence of the practiced raconteur. Yet the apparatus of cinematic grammar invariably baths eyewitnesses in an aura of credence and respect – though, sometimes, surely, they do not deserve it.[13]

Doherty, however, does not stop at criticizing filmmakers for introducing the eyewitness as an unimpeachable moral instance. In addition he displays a certain resentment when he claims that not all eyewitnesses deserve respect and when he accuses Eli Wiesel of not having lived up to his own dictum, that Auschwitz could only be met by silence.

The question on how historic events are constituted by means of their interpretation leads to the question of how the concept "Holocaust" came into being in Western civilization. We suggest that what is called "Holocaust" is not the event itself, but the combination of different meanings resulting from various discourses since 1945. Against this background, the following section will outline a number of dominating images and ideas of German "learning from the past" which we believe to be essential to locate and, for that matter, understand "Holocaust-films" in general, and specifically Knopp's television series.

## II. German Discourses on Germany's Past

German *Vergangenheitsbewältigung* (mastering of the past) has not followed a straight path, neither in the two German states before 1990 nor after "reunification" until today. From the present point of view, however, one can identify a number of stages that have paved the way of today's national self-understanding. To illuminate this development, the following section will mark some of the crucial stages from the 1980s onwards by highlighting statements made in the *Parliament of the Federal Republic of Germany* (Deutscher Bundestag). State-politics only serve as an example: The analysis of historical, political, and literary debates of the past decade would show many of the same ideas,[14] – the Historikerstreit of 1985–6, the discussion about Daniel Jonah Goldhagen's *Hitler's Willing*

*Executioners* of 1996,[15] the reactions following the exhibition *War of Extermination. Crimes of the German Wehrmacht 1941–1944*, the dispute around the building of a Holocaust memorial in Germany's capital city of Berlin,[16] the *Entschädigungsdebatte*,[17] the scandals around Norman Finkelstein's publication *Holocaust Industry*,[18] and so forth. Furthermore, it would be interesting to analyse how these various public debates are interwoven with the aspects of this discourse in private lives.[19]

By starting our line of reasoning in the 1980s we do not imply that there were no "earlier confrontations with the past", as was suggested by a conference participant, rather, we detect the beginning of a shift in German *Vergangenheitspolitik* around that time: instead of suppression and denial of Auschwitz as a cipher for the German past, one can observe a confession, reinterpretation, and appropriation of the Final Solution. As Christine Achinger has pointed out:

> The way in which Germany's crimes are remembered seems to give rise to tendencies to distance and generalize them, to turn them into an event altogether disconnected from history, a kind of fate that has befallen victims and perpetrators alike, as Germany's catastrophic tragic flaw invokes both nemesis and reconciliation.[20]

These changes in dominant attitudes towards the crimes of the "Third Reich" play an important role in the formation of a new national identity.[21]

On 8 May 1985, in his famous speech on the fortieth anniversary of the end of World War II, West German President Richard von Weizsäcker expressed his view that Germany has atoned for the National Socialist crimes during World War II by the division of the country: "The dreadful result of sin always is separation".[22] Weizsäcker then cited a Jewish tradition – "Forgetting prolongs exile, and the secret of redemption [sic!] is remembrance"[23] – to paraphrase a strategy for the treatment of the National Socialist past. The implication of using a Jewish saying, and thus the voice of the victims of the Final Solution in the perpetrator's country is telling: the silenced victims are appropriated "in order to give Germany a mandate for new self-empowerment."[24]

Consequently, the "reunification" of 1989 was seen as *Erlösung* (redemption). With the so-called "end of the post-war period,"[25] *Normalisierung* (normalization) has been one of the major goals of national and international policies. This is exemplified by the strong political emphasis on the return of Germany as a military power on the stage of international politics.[26] As German chancellor Gerhard Schröder has stated during the NATO attacks on Serbia in 1998, Germany needs to attain "the self-confidence of an adult nation which does not have to feel superior or inferior to anyone."[27]

Whereas in the early 1990s, intellectuals like Dan Diner worried that "the calling back to life of the [German] nation-state will only be possible at the expense of the memory about the NS-regime and its crimes,"[28] the official policies of dealing with the German past today are not simply about forgetting or denying. Political statements rather focus on an active integration of National Socialist crimes in national memory. Thus, it becomes possible to be proud of the German *Vergangenheitspolitik* as a national success. At the same time, this strategy of active integration of the past paves the way for the belief that Germany has a special responsibility to enforce Human Rights all over the world. During the Cold War era it was argued that the German states should not participate in international military missions "because of Auschwitz". This, however, has changed in the 1990s: since 1995, the political discussions concentrated on the argument that Germany had a specific *obligation* to intervene in Yugoslavia – "because of Auschwitz".[29]

This is illustrated when, on the occasion of the first German Holocaust Remembrance Day on 27 January 1996, President Roman Herzog suggested the existence of a present German obligation "to prevent a repetition [of Auschwitz], regardless where and in which form it appears." According to his line of reasoning, the German people "had to learn to a greater extent than others [sic!] that the completely unbelievable can happen despite of everything."[30] Here, as in many other political statements of the past years, the driving force behind the Holocaust is blurred as "das Böse".[31] The Evil – according to Herzog – exists "despite of everything", "everything" being progress in terms of civilization, Human Rights Conventions, and so forth. Behind this idea of "Evil" the actual perpetrators disappear: The party that organized the extermination, the personnel who guaranteed the smooth operation of the concentration camps, and the people who denounced and let the trains roll. Auschwitz appears as "fate, and Hitler as its incarnation";[32] the Germans were only the tools of this Evil.

# III. Personification

In this context, Guido Knopp obviously plays an important role. He gives this Evil a face: the face of Hitler.[33] In his article, Kansteiner hints at a possible connection between Knopp's 1991 series *Der verdammte Krieg* (*The Damned War*) about the German attack on the Soviet Union and the so called "Walser-Bubis-Debatte" of 1998: In his acceptance-speech for the *Friedenspreis des deutschen Buchhandels* (Peace Prize of the German Publishing Houses), Walser lamented that as a German one would constantly be reminded of Auschwitz. Germans would be oppressed by the so-called "Moral-Keule" (moral-bat). Furthermore, he encouraged Germans to feel self-confident and strong as Germans, and to free themselves from the bad conscience resulting from Auschwitz.[34] In this logic, Germans appear primarily as victims, abused and deceived not only by *Hitler*, *Hitler's Helpers* and *Hitler's Warriors* (titles of three of Knopp's documentary series, 1995, 1997 and 1998), but also by the Allied forces and the New World Order. Walser, however, did not explicitly mention this bold implication.

Neither does Knopp explicitly verbalize Germany's retrospective victimization. However, a rather similar notion appears on the visual level. Kansteiner is aware of this when he observes the sports-team atmosphere of Knopp's *Der verdammte Krieg*: "That 'we' in we would have won' is right below the attractive surface and even more powerful because that affirmative 'we' in relation to World War II has no place in the official culture of the Federal Republic."[35]

The "we" Kansteiner analyses is a symbol, an expression of a rising new German self-confidence – seven years before the "Walser-Bubis-Debatte" and one year before a racist mob made the homes of Vietnamese immigrants in Rostock-Lichtenhagen the center of their racially motivated riots for several days. Generally there had been a striking increase of neo-fascist, extremist riots after 1989 – Mölln, Solingen, Hattingen, Krefeld, Lübeck, and so forth.[36] This is the situation in which Knopp produces his six-part series *Hitler: Eine Bilanz* in 1995. Only six years earlier Knopp had argued, that the private life of the "Führer" would be trivial and that any exclusive focus on Hitler would indicate a secret personality cult. By 1995, however, he seems to have undergone a change of opinion. In the booklet of the home video version of his 1995 television production, Knopp states:

Like no other politician Hitler was able to play with the masses. In the role of the demagogic agitator, he showed his most prominent traits of character. His mastery of manipulation of the masses, led him on the path of power . . . If we understand what he stood for, we will be immune against similar and other temptations to call for a strong leader (*einen starken Mann*) in times of crisis.[37]

Knopp's change of opinion between 1989 and 1995 is not unusual. Many others who accused the generation of the perpetrators and the followers of National Socialism in the 1960s and 1970s underwent the same change of perspective. The most prominent example is the current German Minister of Foreign Affairs, Joseph Fischer. Empathizing with the perpetrators, the so-called "dialogue between the generations" dominates German discourses on the National Socialist past today. This is also exemplified by the vast number of diaries on National Socialism published during the past five years: Through the eyes of the innocent German they offer us a view of a completely normal everyday-life during the time of the Final Solution.

Kansteiner has analysed this narrative strategy in Knopp's document-aries very precisely. He cites one episode from Knopp's series *Hitler's Warriors* as an example. According to Kansteiner, the empathy with the perpetrators becomes unquestionably evident in the episode about "desert fox" Erwin Rommel: "In the conclusion, the documentary stages and mourns the suicide of a German military genius in sepia colors and permits his son, Manfred Rommel, to ponder if he himself is a better human being than his father and if he would not have done the same. An idol is reborn."[38]

Manfred Rommel's self-identifying empathy for his father exemplifies the above mentioned "dialogue between the generations". Against this background, the crucial question is: why does Knopp focus on the person of Hitler, his helpers and his warriors, on *Hitler's Children* (2000) and *Hitler's Women* (2001) from the middle of the 1990s onwards? Kansteiner ascribes this shift in focus to Knopp's "desire to attract the masses", and the new technological possibilities to do so. This is, of course, one motivation for Knopp's new personality cult, but it does not take into account the preconditions and effects of the discourse. In addition, it is essential to put the development of German *Vergangenheitspolitik* and *Erinnerungspolitik* into a context, to fully understand the preconditions and the effects of what Kansteiner calls "the Knopp phenomenon". Summarizing, Kansteiner shows pointedly that Knopp's docudramas "personalize" National Socialism. Kansteiner himself, however, personal-izes the shift in German collective memory in quite a parallel way by proclaiming a "Knopp phenomenon".

## IV. The Germanization of the Holocaust

It has become clear that we believe that it is necessary to integrate the social and political situation in the analyses of "Holocaust-film". Conse-quently, we do not agree with Kansteiner's account, that the voice-over commentaries in Knopp's documentaries are politically correct while the visual level works in a much more ambivalent and provocative way: from an American point of view this might be correct – although the idea of political correctness would have to be discussed first – but in the German context the implications will be different.[39] In order to shed light on the importance of the difference of perspective, the following section will turn the focus on the title of Knopp's 2000 series, *Holokaust*.

The phrase *Holocaust* is used in Germany to describe the extermination of the European Jews during World War II. It is an American phrase, which was first introduced to the German public by the television series *Holocaust: Die Geschichte der Familie Weiss* in 1979. In the German title of his six-part television series *Holokaust*, Guido Knopp spells the term with a "k" instead of a "c". This goes back to an idea of the historian Eberhard Jäckel, and was widely agreed upon by linguists and historians. But what difference does Guido Knopp make when he tries to Germanize the term Holocaust by writing it with a "k"? He adopts the perspective of United States Americans:

> The crime originated from German soil. The murder of the European Jews belongs to German history. To designate this murder with an English expression equals a distancing. When we really want to confront our historical responsibility for this crime, then the spelling Holokaust [with "k" instead of "c"] is a symbolic act of appropriation of our own history."[40]

In Germany, one prefers to talk about the extermination of the European Jews in the language of the United States Americans.[41] We – that is not the perpetrators anymore,[42] we – that is the liberators (in the English translation, the title of the same series is, tellingly enough, *Hitler's Holocaust*). And that is the perspective from which Guido Knopp can say: "We Germans who were born after the war are not to be blamed [*verantwortlich*] for the Holokaust. But we are even more responsible [*verantwortlich*] for remembering. To be responsible means to confront ourselves with our own history."[43]

What it means to be confronted "with our own history" becomes clear when one looks more closely at Knopp's six part series about the history of the Final Solution. Compared to earlier ZDF productions *Holokaust* is a thoroughly researched and carefully commentated historical documentary, which presents previously unknown film material, puts many of the historical sources into a context, and is critical against the strategies of self-defense of the perpetrators.[44] However, *Holokaust* follows a straight, highly superficial plot without contradictions or inconsistencies.

On the whole, the series relates the story of a loss of humanity, a loss that has been experienced by victims and perpetrators alike. As the historian Hanno Loewy puts it:

> Holokaust . . . is supposed to tell a tragic story – or at least as "tragic" as a horror-movie allows: stories of involved, "unguilty-guilty" human beings, stricken by fate, enticed or traumatized by a demon who had transformed humans into subhuman creatures. The classic tragedy as prototype: a story which makes a claim for a "higher" point of view, from where the "romance" of survival might appear as an American trivialty.[45]

Thus, in Knopp's documentaries Germans appear not only as tools, but also as victims of the Evil. The voice-over commentaries might be ambivalent in their "political correctness", but they do not oppose the impact of the pictorial material.[46]

# V. Singularity and Antisemitism

In order to understand how the Final Solution is mediated and modified in the course of mass media film production it is not only necessary to examine technological, cultural, and political developments. In addition, one needs to grasp an idea of the specificity and singularity of the historical subject in question. Doherty takes up this essential need for historical awareness when he outlines two main concepts explaining the ultimate causes of the "Holocaust": The first concept explains the Final Solution as a result of two thousand years of Antisemitism. On the contrary, the second line of reasoning argues that modern bureaucracy and capitalism have been the crucial factors in organizing the extermination of the European Jews.

Doherty himself supports the latter line of reasoning when he enumerates various historical genocides and then cites Richard Rubenstein's point of view about the Final Solution being a product of "the mainstream of Western culture". In addition, Doherty's investigation of "Holocaust film" is based on the assumption that "the sheer quantity and exceptional force of film footage makes the Holocaust singular among genocides."[47]

From our point of view, however, the question about the singularity of the Final Solution needs to be examined more thoroughly. The first disturbing fact is that it was absolutely senseless – from any moral, religious or economic point of view. Furthermore, as Moishe Postone has pointed out, the extermination of the European Jews did not help the

Germans to win the war. Quite on the contrary, the deportations of Jews during the last years of the war often occupied the railway tracks, which otherwise could have been used to transport German troops.

> The extermination of the Jews was not a means to another end. They were not exterminated for military reasons, or in order to violently acquire land (as was the case with the American Indians and the Tasmanians), or in order to wipe out those segments of the population around whom resistance most easily crystallize so that the rest could be exploited as helots (as was Nazis policy towards the Poles and Russians), or for any other "extrinsic" goal. *The extermination of the Jews not only was to have been total, but was its own goal – extermination in order to exterminate – a goal which acquired absolute priority.*[48]

To question the specificity and uniqueness of the Final Solution thus raises the following questions: why the Jews? Why did the German National Socialists murder Jews regardless of age, gender, nationality, religious practices, and so forth?[49] What is Antisemitism?[50] For what reasons did Antisemitism become a racist ideology, thus making ordinary people to mass murderers?[51] And what about the years after the war? Did Germans feel sorry for what they had done? Did they look for a way to deal with their crimes and to compensate the victims? Of course one does not need to answer all of these questions before one can examine Knopp's documentaries or "Holocaust films" in general. However, they have to be asked over and over again to retain the specificity and uniqueness of the historic subject.

In the course of this commentary, we have demonstrated that the German attempts to comprehend the Final Solution generally resulted in an inadequate appropriation of the past. The perspectives of the victims and the liberators have been annexed in order to master the disturbances and uncertainties that derive from the Final Solution.[52] An analysis that, like Benjamin's, wants to be understood as political practice, needs to endure these disturbances and uncertainties, it needs to endure the "Aura" of the historic event in the present. From Benjamin's work we can learn to approach the meaning of something in a tentative way in order to retain its "Aura".[53]

# Notes

1. The first German version was published in 1955 by Theodor W. Adorno. Our reading of the text is based on the last of three versions,

Walter Benjamin, "Das Kunstwerk im Zeitalter seiner technischen Reproduzierbarkeit (Dritte Fassung)", in Walter Benjamin, *Gesammelte Schriften*, ed. by Rolf Tiedemann and Hermann Schweppenhäuser, 7 vols, Frankfurt a. M., 1991, vol. 1, part 2, pp. 471–508.

2. What is more, Benjamin explicitly states that his analysis and his terminology are meant to be useless for any "fascist" understanding of art. In a sense his writings should thus be read as a political, "anti-fascist" practice.

3. In the limited dimension of this article we will solely focus on a German perspective.

4. Wulf Kansteiner, "The Radicalization of German Collective Memory in the Age of its Commercial Reproduction," in this volume.

5. In February 2001, the ZDF started an exemplary new Knopp production. The weekly series is titled *History: So spannend ist Geschichte* (*History: This is How Exciting/Thrilling History Is*) and can be characterized as an infotainment magazine that presents short journalistic feature films about various historic events.

6. Thomas Doherty, "The Holocaust on Screen: Speculations on an American Motion Picture Genre," in this volume.

7. Ibid.

8. Judith Keilbach, „Fernsehbilder der Geschichte: Anmerkungen zur Darstellung des Nationalsozialismus in den Geschichtsdokumentationen des ZDF," *1999: Zeitschrift für Sozialgeschichte des 20. und 21. Jahrhunderts* 17 (2002), 102–13, 104f.

9. Doherty, "The Holocaust on Screen."

10. Ibid.

11. Ulrike Jureit, *"Erinnerungsmuster": Zur Methodik lebensgeschichtlicher Interviews mit Überlebenden der Konzentrations- und Vernichtungslager*, Hamburg, 1999, p. 389ff.; Sabine Moller et al., *"Opa war kein Nazi": Nationalsozialismus und Holocaust im Familiengedächtnis*, Frankfurt a. M., 2002.

12. An exception is Claude Lanzman's film *Shoa* which expounds the specificities of dealing with narratives of eyewitnesses and the construction of history.

13. Doherty, "The Holocaust on Screen."

14. For parallels see Christine Achinger, "'Das Geheimnis der Erlösung heisst Erinnerung?' The German deployment in Kosovo as fight against the past," in Ronit Lentin (ed.), *Representing the Shoah for the 21st Century*, Oxford and New York, 2003.

15. Rainer Erb and Johannes Heil (eds), *Geschichtswissenschaft und Öffentlichkeit: Der Streit um Daniel J. Goldhagen*, Frankfurt a. M., 1998.

16. Michael Jeismann (ed.), *Mahnmal Mitte: Eine Kontroverse*, Cologne, 1999; Michael S. Cullen (ed.), *Das Holocaust-Mahnmal: Dokumentation einer Debatte*, Zurich, 1999.

17. Ulrike Winkler (ed.), *Stiften gehen: NS-Zwangsarbeit und Entschädigungsdebatte*, Cologne, 2000; Lars Rensmann, "Entschädigungspolitik, Erinnerungsabwehr und Motive des sekundären Antisemitismus," in Rolf Surmann (ed.), *Das Finkelstein-Alibi: "Holocaust-Industrie" und Tätergesellschaft*, Cologne, 2001, pp. 126–53.

18. Rolf Surmann, "Der jüdische Kronzeuge: Die Reaktion auf Finkelsteins Pamphlet als Ausdruck eines zeitgeschichtlichen Paradigmenwechsels," in Rolf Surmann (ed.), *Das Finkelstein-Alibi: "Holocaust-Industrie" und Tätergesellschaft*, Cologne, 2001, pp. 104–25.

19. Moller et al., *"Opa war kein Nazi"*.

20. Achinger, "Das Geheimnis der Erlösung heisst Erinnerung?"

21. Hanno Loewy has spoken about the "undertow of a desired identity formation: The Holocaust as a theme for the representation of the German nation, as proof of completed purgation, the Holocaust and its remembrance as a cathartic act of purification" (Hanno Loewy, "Ein kurzer, verschämter, paradoxer Augenblick des Eingeständnisses: Deutsche Identitäten vor und nach dem Holocaust," *Frankfurter Rundschau*, 7 October 2000, p. 9.)

22. Richard von Weizsäcker, "Originaltext der Ansprache 'Zum 40. Jahrestages der Beendigung des Krieges in Europa und der NS-Gewaltherrschaft 1985'," in Ulrich Gill and Winfried Steffani (eds), *Eine Rede und ihre Wirkung: Die Rede des Bundespräsidenten Richard von Weizsäcker vom 8. Mai 1985*, Berlin, 1987, p. 179.

23. Richard von Weizsäcker, "Originaltext der Ansprache", 180. This statement is attributed to the Jewish mystic Baal Shem Tov, which is inscribed in Yad Vashem in Israel.

24. Achinger, "Das Geheimnis der Erlösung heisst Erinnerung?"; see also Torsten Michaelsen, *Das Volkstrauerjahr 1995*, radio documentary, Freies Sender Kombinat, Hamburg (first broadcast on 8 May 1996); Ole Frahm, Olaf Kistenmacher and Regina Mühlhäuser (eds.), *Der Vernichtung, der Befreiung gedenken*, Hamburg, 2004 (forthcoming). The German desire to identify with the victims of the Final Solution can be traced back to the end of World War II: see among others Elizabeth Heineman, "The Hour of Women: Memories of German "Crisis Years" and Western German Identity," *The American Historical Review* 101 (1996), 354–95; Robert G. Moeller, "Deutsche Opfer, Opfer der Deutschen: Kriegsgefangene, Vertriebene, NS-Verfolgte. Opferausgleich als Identitätspolitik," in Klaus Naumann (ed.), *Nachkrieg in Deutschland*,

Hamburg, 2001, pp. 29–58; Regina Mühlhäuser, "Vergewaltigungen in Deutschland 1945: Nationaler Opferdiskurs und individuelles Erinnern betroffener Frauen," in Klaus Naumann (ed.), *Nachkrieg in Deutschland*, pp. 384–408. In addition, the continuing existence of this identification has been analyzed in the recent debate about the national Holocaust memorial in Berlin: Rafael Seligmann, "Genug bemitleidet: Gegen ein deutsches Holocaust-Memorial," *Der Spiegel*, 16 January 1995, 84; Eike Geisel, *Triumph des guten Willens: Gute Nazis und selbsternannte Opfer. Die Nationalisierung der Erinnerung*, Berlin, 1998, p. 57.

25. An expression mainly coined by former chancellor Helmut Kohl, "Das Ende der Nachkriegszeit," *Die Welt*, 7 May 1990, 7.

26. Achinger, "Das Geheimnis der Erlösung heisst Erinnerung?"; Andrei S. Markovits and Simon Reich, *The German Predicament: Memory and Power in the New Europe*, Ithaca and London, 1997, p. 137ff.; Tjark Kunstreich, *Ein deutscher Krieg: Über die Befreiung der Deutschen von Auschwitz*, Freiburg, 1999, p. 41ff.

27. Gerhard Schröder, Regierungserklärung, 10 November 1998.

28. Dan Diner, *Kreisläufe: Nationalsozialismus und Gedächtnis*, Berlin, 1995, p. 23; see also Wolfgang Wippermann, *Wessen Schuld? Vom Historikerstreit zur Goldhagen-Kontroverse*, Berlin, 1997, p. 126; Edgar Wolfrum, "Geschichtspolitik in der Bundesrepublik Deutschland 1949–1989: Phasen und Kontroversen," in Petra Bock and Edgar Wolfrum (eds), *Umkämpfte Vergangenheit: Geschichtsbilder, Erinnerung und Vergangenheitspolitik im internationalen Vergleich*, Göttingen, 1999, p. 74.

29. Achinger, "Das Geheimnis der Erlösung heisst Erinnerung?"; Joachim Rohloff, "Kriegsverwendungsfähig: Zwei Möglichkeiten, Auschwitz zu benutzen, um es zu erledigen," in Wolfgang Schneider (ed.), *Wir kneten ein KZ: Aufsätze über Deutschlands Standortvorteil bei der Bewältigung der Vergangenheit*, Hamburg, 2000, pp. 54–70; Kunstreich, *Ein deutscher Krieg*, p. 45f.

30. Roman Herzog, "Aus der Erinnerung immer wieder lebendige Zukunft werden lassen: Ansprache des Bundespräsidenten zum Holocaust-Gedenktag am 27. Januar 1996," http://www.bundes praesident.de/frameset/index.jsp (consulted March 2003); for the political exploitation of "Auschwitz" see Markovits and Reich, *The German Predicament*, p. 145ff.

31. The Evil – a religious figure that Saul Friedländer has analysed some years ago: Saul Friedländer, "Writing the History of the Shoa[h]: Some Major Dilemmas," in Horst Walter Blanke (ed.), *Dimensionen der Historik: Geschichtstheorie, Wissenschaftsgeschichte und Geschichtskultur heute*, Cologne, 1998, p. 407f.

32. Loewy, "Bei Vollmond: Holocaust. Genretheoretische Bemerkungen zu einer Dokumentation des ZDF," *1999: Zeitschrift für Sozialgeschichte des 20. und 21. Jahrhunderts* 17 (2002), 114–27.

33. This kind of personification can be seen as a general phenomenon: a fact that is illustrated when Knopp's documentary *Hitler: Eine Bilanz* is sold to more than fifty different countries – see Karsten Linne, "Hitler als Quotenbringer: Guido Knopps mediale Erfolge," *1999: Zeitschrift für Sozialgeschichte des 20. und 21. Jahrhunderts* 17 (2002), 96. In the German context, however, the desire for personification is interwoven with the desire for a disposal of the Nazi past.

34. Martin Walser, "Die Banalität des Guten: Erfahrungen beim Verfassen einer Sonntagsrede," *Frankfurter Allgemeine Zeitung*, 12 October 1998, p. 15; for a thorough analysis see Achinger, "Das Geheimnis der Erlösung heisst Erinnerung?"; Jan-Holger Kirsch, "Identität durch Normalität: Der Konflikt um Martin Walsers Friedenspreisrede," *Leviathan: Zeitschrift für Sozialwissenschaften* 27 (1999), 309–54; Moshe Zuckermann, *Gedenken und Kulturindustrie: Ein Essay zur neuen deutschen Normalität*, Berlin and Bodenheim, 1999, pp. 9–32.

35. Kansteiner, "The Radicalization of German Collective Memory."

36. Alex Demirovic, "Rechtsextremismus in der Bundesrepublik," in Institut für Sozialforschung (ed.), *Rechtsextremismus und Fremdenfeindlichkeit: Studien zur aktuellen Entwicklung*, Frankfurt a. M. and New York, 1994, pp. 29–57; Autonome L.U.P.U.S. Gruppe, *Lichterketten und andere Irrlichter: Texte gegen finstere Zeiten*, Berlin and Amsterdam, 1994, pp. 16–36.

37. Guido Knopp, *Hitler: Eine Bilanz,* (Video) 1995.

38. Kansteiner, "The Radicalization of German Collective Memory."

39. The question of perspective and positionality can also be applied to the Anti-Americanism which shows in Thomas Doherty's paper. In the present German political context his position will call on a completely different political perspective than in the United States.

40. Guido Knopp, *Holokaust: Der Mord an den Juden*, Munich, 2000, p. 22. One could argue that writing Holocaust with a "c" comes from Latin in the first place and does not derive from "US-American cultural imperialism". Spelling the term with a "k", on the other hand, means to go back to its Greek roots: Giorgio Agamben, *Remnants of Auschwitz: The Witness and the Archive*, New York, 1999, p. 28.

41. Detlev Claussen, *Grenzen der Aufklärung: Die gesellschaftliche Genese des modernen Antisemitismus*, Frankfurt a. M., 1994, p. 14.

42. See also Ole Frahm, "Vom Holocaust zu Holokaust: Guido Knopps Aneignung der Vernichtung der europäischen Juden," *1999: Zeitschrift für Sozialgeschichte des 20. und 21. Jahrhunderts* 17 (2002), 128–38.

43. Knopp, *Holokaust*, p. 20.

44. For two years historians researched in more than fifty archives and hundreds of interviews were conducted – with survivors, perpetrators, bystanders and spectators.

45. Loewy, "Bei Vollmond," p. 125f.

46. This telling ambivalence can also be observed in Knopp's series on Stalingrad which has been televised in 2003, sixty years after the events. Whereas many references are made towards the German perpetratorship, almost every part of the series ends with an idea of all parties being victims first and foremost.

47. Doherty, "The Holocaust on Screen."

48. Moishe Postone, "Anti-Semitism and National Socialism: Notes on the German Reactions to 'Holocaust'," *New German Critique* 19 (1980), 97–115 (italics by Postone).

49. Daniel Jonah Goldhagen, *Hitler's Willing Executioners: Ordinary Germans and the Holocaust*, New York, 1996.

50. Thomas Haury, *Antisemitismus von links: Kommunistische Ideologie, Nationalismus und Antizionismus in der frühen DDR*, Hamburg, 2002, 25–159; Saul Friedländer, *Nazi Germany and the Jews: The Years of Persecution, 1933–1939*, New York, 1997; Goldhagen, *Hitler's Willing Executioners*, pp. 27–128.

51. Friedländer, *Nazi Germany and the Jews*.

52. The appropriation of the Final Solution for specific political interest is not an exclusively German problem: Ronit Lentin, *Israel and the Daughters of the Shoah: Re-occupying the Territories of Silence*, Oxford and New York, 2000, p. 117ff.

53. Thanks to Michaela Hampf and Norbert Finzsch, Else and Justus Jonas!

# Selective Bibliography

*Norbert Finzsch*

This bibliography contains books or monographs arranged according to the sequence of the session during the conference. We did not include articles in newspapers or scholarly journals in order to keep the bibliography concise and the titles easily retrievable. In some cases we had to include older titles, but we tried to achieve a selection that was both representative and up to date. In order to shorten the bibliography we abstained from a topical arrangement within each chapter but gave the keywords of each entry at the bottom of the title.

## Part I

Abbey, Merrill R. Communication in Pulpit and Parish. Philadelphia: Westminster Press. 1973.
*Keywords:* Communication – Religious Aspects – Christianity/Preaching
Ackva, Friedhelm, Martin Brecht, and Klaus Deppermann. Der Pietismus im achtzehnten Jahrhundert. Göttingen: Vandenhoeck & Ruprecht. 1995.
*Keywords:* Pietism – History – 18th Century/Protestantism – History
Albaugh, Gaylord P. History and Annotated Bibliography of American Religious Periodicals and Newspapers Established from 1730 through 1830. Worcester MA: American Antiquarian Society. 1994.
*Keywords:* Religious Newspapers and Periodicals – United States – History/Religious Newspapers and Periodicals – United States – Bibliography
Alexander, John K. The Selling of the Constitutional Convention: A History of News Coverage. Madison WI: Madison House. 1990.
*Keywords:* United States. Constitutional Convention (1787) – Public Opinion/Public Opinion – United States – History – 18th Century/Press and Politics – United States – History – 18th Century/United States – Politics and Government – 1783–1789

Bailyn, Bernard, and John B. Hench. The Press and the American Revolution. Worcester MA: American Antiquarian Society. 1980.
*Keywords:* Press – United States – History – 18th Century/Printing – United States – History – 18th Century/United States – History – Revolution, 1775–1783

Beermann, Matthias. Zeitung zwischen Profit und Politik: Der *Courier du Bas-Rhin*, 1767–1810: Eine Fallstudie zur politischen Tagespublizistik im Europa des späten 18. Jahrhunderts. Leipzig: Leipziger Universitätsverlag. 1996.
*Keywords:* Courier du Bas-Rhin – History/Press and Politics – Germany – Kleve (North Rhine-Westphalia) – History/Kleve (North Rhine-Westphalia, Germany) – Newspapers – History – 18th Century

Berg, Johannes van den, and Martin Brecht. Der Pietismus vom siebzehnten bis zum frühen achtzehnten Jahrhundert. Göttingen: Vandenhoeck & Ruprecht. 1993.
*Keywords:* Pietism – History – 17th Century/Pietism – History – 18th Century/Protestantism – History

Bond, Donovan H. , and W. R McLeod. Newsletters to Newspapers: Eighteenth-Century Journalism: Papers Presented at a Bicentennial Symposium, at West Virginia University, Morgantown, West Virginia, 31 March–2 April 1976. West Virginia University. School of Journalism. Morgantown, WV: School of Journalism, West Virginia University. 1977.
*Keywords:* Press – United States – History – 18th Century/Press – Great Britain – History – 18th Century

Boning, Holger, and Emmy Moepps. Deutsche Presse: Biobibliographische Handbücher zur Geschichte der deutschsprachigen periodischen Presse von den Anfängen bis 1815. Stuttgart-Bad Cannstatt: Frommann-Holzboog. 1996.
*Keywords:* Press – Germany – History – Bio-Bibliography/German Newspapers – Bibliography/German Newspapers – History – Bio-Bibliography/German Periodicals – Bibliography/German Periodicals – History Bio-Bibliography

Borst, Otto. Buch und Presse in Esslingen am Neckar: Studien zur städtischen Geistes- und Sozialgeschichte von der Frührenaissance bis zur Gegenwart. Esslingen: Stadtarchiv Esslingen. 1975.
*Keywords:* Book Industries and Trade – Germany (West) – Esslingen am Neckar – History/Press – Germany (West) – History/Private Libraries – Germany (West) –

Bradley, Patricia. Slavery, Propaganda, and the American Revolution. Jackson MS: University Press of Mississippi. 1998.

*Keywords:* Press and Propaganda – United States – History – 18th Century/Antislavery Movements – United States – History – 18th Century/Slavery – United States – History – 18th Century/United States – History – Revolution, 1775–1783 – Propaganda/United States – History – Revolution, 1775–1783 – Afro-Americans

Brecht, Martin, and Klaus Deppermann. Geschichte des Pietismus. Göttingen: Vandenhoeck & Ruprecht. 1993.
*Keywords:* Protestantism – History/Pietism – History – 17th Century/ Pietism – History – 18th Century

Brown, Richard D. Knowledge is Power: The Diffusion of Information in Early America, 1700–1865. New York: Oxford University Press. 1989
*Keywords:* Communication – United States – History/United States – Civilization/United States – Civilization

Brown, Walt. John Adams and the American Press: Politics and Journalism at the Birth of the Republic. Jefferson NC: McFarland & Co. 1995.
*Keywords:* Adams, John, 1735–1826 – Relations with Journalists/Press and Politics – United States – History – 18th Century/United States – Politics and Government – 1797–1801

Bryant, M. Darrol. Jonathan Edwards' Grammar of Time, Self, and Society: A Critique of the Heimert Thesis. Lewiston NY: E. Mellen Press. 1993.
*Keywords:* Heimert, Alan Religion and the American Mind/Edwards, Jonathan, 1703–1758/Great Awakening/Religious Thought – United States – 18th Century/Theology, Doctrinal – United States – History – 18th Century/United States – Church History – to 1775/United States – Intellectual Life – 18th Century

Buechner, Frederick. Telling the Truth: the Gospel as Tragedy, Comedy, and Fairy Tale. San Francisco: Harper & Row. 1977.
*Keywords:* Preaching/Communication – Religious Aspects – Christianity

Bumsted, J. M. (comp.). The Great Awakening; the Beginnings of Evangelical Pietism in America. Waltham MA: Blaisdell Publishing Co. 1970.
*Keywords:* Great Awakening

Bumsted, J. M, and John Edward Van de Wetering. What must I Do to be Saved? The Great Awakening in Colonial America. Hinsdale IL: Dryden Press. 1976.
*Keywords:* Great Awakening

Bushman, Richard L. The Great Awakening: Documents on the Revival of Religion, 1740–1745. Chapel Hill NC: Published for the Institute of Early American History and Culture by the University of North Carolina Press. 1989.
*Keywords:* Great Awakening

Coalter, Milton J. Gilbert Tennent, Son of Thunder: a Case Study of Continental Pietism's Impact on the First Great Awakening in the Middle Colonies. New York: Greenwood Press. 1986.
*Keywords:* Tennent, Gilbert, 1703–1764/Presbyterian Church – United States – Clergy – Biography/Great Awakening/Pietism – Influence/ Middle Atlantic States – Religious Life and Customs

Cornehl, Peter, Hans Eckehard Bahr, and Hans-Rudolf Müller-Schwefe. Gottesdienst und Öffentlichkeit. Zur Theorie und Didaktik neuer Kommunikation. (Hans-Rudolf Müller-Schwefe zum 60. Geburtstag.) Hamburg: Furche-Verlag. 1970.
*Keywords:* Public Worship/Preaching/Communication – Religious Aspects – Christianity

Demeter, Richard L. Primer, Presses, and Composing Sticks: Women Printers of the Colonial Period. Hicksville NY: Exposition Press. 1979.
*Keywords:* Women Printers – United States – Biography/Printing – United States – History – 17th Century/Printing – United States – History – 18th Century/United States – History – Colonial Period, 1600–1775

Depkat, Volker. Amerikabilder in politischen Diskursen: Deutsche Zeitschriften von 1789 bis 1830. Stuttgart: Klett-Cotta. 1998.
*Keywords:* Press and Politics – Germany – History/Discourse Analysis – Political Aspects – Germany/Democracy – Germany – History/ German Periodicals – History/Public Opinion – Germany – History/ United States – Foreign Public Opinion, German

Deppermann, Andreas. Johann Jakob Schutz und die Anfänge des Pietismus. Tübingen: Mohr Siebeck. 2002.
*Keywords:* Schutz, Johann Jakob, 1640–1690/Pietism – Germany – History

Doherty, John J. The Communication of the C[h]ristian Message in a Secularized Society: A Study of the Pastoral Theological Consequences of the Writings of Harvey Cox, John A. T. Robinson and Johannes Metz: With Special Concern for the Area of the Sermon. Freiburg Universiy. 1975.
*Keywords*: Preaching/Communication – Religious Aspects – Christianity

Dyer, Alan. A Biography of James Parker, Colonial Printer. Troy NY: Whitston Pub. Co. 1982.
*Keywords:* Parker, James, 1714–1770/Printers – United States – Biography/Printing – United States – History – 18th Century

Egertson, Paul Wennes. Sacramental Rhetoric: The Relation of Preaching to Persuasion in American Lutheran Homiletics. Dissertation, School of Theology at Claremont CA. 1976.

*Keywords*: Preaching/Communication – Religious Aspects – Christianity/Lutheran Church

Fiering, Norman, Susan L. Newbury, and Julie Greer Johnson. Printing and Publishing in the Colonial Era of the United States: A Supplement to the Book in the Americas (1988) with a Checklist of the Items in that Catalogue. John Carter Brown Library. Providence RI: John Carter Brown Library. 1990.

*Keywords:* John Carter Brown Library – Exhibitions/Printing – United States – History – 18th Century – Exhibitions/Publishers and Publishing – United States – History – 17th Century – Exhibitions/Publishers and Publishing – United States – History – 18th Century – Exhibitions/ Books – United States – History – 17th–18th Centuries – Exhibitions/ Printing – United States – History – 17th Century – Exhibitions/Early Printed Books – United States – Bibliography – Exhibitions/United States – Imprints – Exhibitions

Fischer, Heinz Dietrich. Deutsche Kommunikationskontrolle des 15. bis 20. Jahrhunderts. München, New York: K. G. Saur. 1982.

*Keywords:* Mass Media – Law and Legislation – Germany (West) – History/Press Law – Germany (West) History

——. Handbuch der politischen Presse in Deutschland, 1480–1980: Synopse rechtlicher, struktureller und wirtschaftlicher Grundlagen der Tendenzpublizistik im Kommunikationsfeld. Düsseldorf: Droste. 1981.

*Keywords:* Press and Politics – Germany – History

Foster, Mary Catherine. Hampshire County, Massachusetts, 1729–1754: A Covenant Society in Transition. Dissertation, University of Michigan. Ann Arbor MI. 1972.

*Keywords.* Puritans – Massachusetts/Great Awakening/Church and State – Massachusetts/Hampshire County (Mass.) – History

Freiberger, Maria. Die Anfänge Der Zeitung in München (Bis zur Entstehung der periodischen Presse 1627/32). München: Stadtarchiv München. 1962.

*Keywords:* Press – Germany Munich – History

Freund, Hilger. Die Bücher- und Pressezensur im Kurfürstentum Mainz von 1486–1797. Karlsruhe: C. F. Müller. 1971.

*Keywords:* Censorship – Germany – Mainz (Rhineland-Palatinate) – History/Press Law – Germany – Mainz (Rhineland-Palatinate) – History

Gawthrop, Richard L. Pietism and the Making of Eighteenth-Century Prussia. Cambridge, New York: Cambridge University Press. 1993.

*Keywords:* Pietism – Germany – Prussia – History – 18th Century/ Prussia (Germany) – History – 1640–1740/Prussia (Germany) – History – 1740–1789/Prussia (Germany) – Church History

Gierl, Martin. Pietismus und Aufklärung: Theologische Polemik und die Kommunikationsreform der Wissenschaft am Ende des 17. Jahrhunderts. Göttingen: Vandenhoeck & Ruprecht. 1997.
*Keywords:* Pietism – Germany – History/Enlightenment – Germany

Goen, C. C. Revivalism and Separatism in New England, 1740–1800: Strict Congregationalists and Separate Baptists in the Great Awakening. The Frank S. and Elizabeth D. Brewer Prize Essay of the American Society of Church History. Middletown CT, Scranton PA: Wesleyan University Press. Distributed by Harper & Row. 1987.
*Keywords:* Great Awakening/Dissenters, Religious – New England – History – 18th Century/Congregational Churches – New England – History – 18th Century/Baptists – New England – History – 18th Century/New England – Church History

Gray, Elma E. Elma Edith, and Leslie Robb Gray. Wilderness Christians; the Moravian Mission to the Delaware Indians. New York: Russell & Russell. 1973.
*Keywords:* Moravian Church – Missions/Delaware Indians – Missions

Greene, Jack P. , and William Gerald McLoughlin. Preachers and Politicians: Two Essays on the Origins of the American Revolution. American Antiquarian Society. Worcester MA: American Antiquarian Society. 1977.
*Keywords:* Great Awakening/United States – History – Revolution, 1775–1783 – Causes/United States – History – Revolution, 1775–1783 – Religious Aspects

Hall, Timothy D. Contested Boundaries: Itinerancy and the Reshaping of the Colonial American Religious World. Durham NC: Duke University Press. 1994.
*Keywords:* Great Awakening/Itinerancy (Church Polity) – History of Doctrines – 18th Century/Circuit Riders – United States – History – 18th Century

Hamilton, John Taylor. A History of the Missions of the Moravian Church during the Eighteenth and Nineteenth Centuries. Bethlehem PA: Times. 1990.
*Keywords:* Moravian Church – Missions

Harlan, David. The Clergy and the Great Awakening in New England. Ann Arbor MI: UMI Research Press. 1980.
*Keywords:* Great Awakening/Clergy – New England – Attitudes/New England – Church History

Harlan, David Craig. The Clergy and the Great Awakening in New England. Dissertation, University of California, Irvine CA. 1979.

*Select Bibliography*

*Keywords*: Clergy – New England/Great Awakening/New England – Church History
Heaton, Dale L. Improving Pulpit Communication: an Experimental Approach in a Congregational Setting. Dissertation, San Francisco Theological Seminary, San Anselmo CA. 1977.
*Keywords*: Preaching/Communication – Religious Aspects – Christianity
Herrlitz, Hans-Georg, and Horst Kern. Anfänge Göttinger Sozialwissenschaft: Methoden, Inhalte und soziale Prozesse im 18. und 19. Jahrhundert. Göttingen: Vandenhoeck & Ruprecht. 1987.
*Keywords:* Schlözer, August Ludwig von, 1735–1809/Universität Göttingen – Curricula – History – 18th Century/Universität Göttingen – Curricula – History – 19th Century/Universität Göttingen – Faculty – Biography/Social Sciences – Study and Teaching (Higher) – /Social Sciences – Study and Teaching (Higher) – Germany – Göttingen – History – 19th Century/Press – Germany – Göttingen – History – 18th Century
Hilkert, Mary Catherine. Towards a Theology of Proclamation: Edward Schillebeeckx's Hermeneutics of Tradition As a Foundation for a Theology of Proclamation. Dissertation, Catholic University of America, Washington DC. 1984.
*Keywords:* Schillebeeckx, Edward, 1914/Preaching/Tradition (Theology) – History of Doctrines – Catholic Church/Communication – Religious Aspects – Christianity
Hilton, Allen R. The Dumb Speak: Early Christian Illiteracy and Pagan Criticism. Dissertation, Yale University, Ann Arbor MI. 1997.
*Keywords*: Bible. New Testament Acts – Criticism, Interpretation – Communication – Religious Aspects – Christianity – History/Church History – Primitive and Early Church 30–600/Literacy – History
Jaeger, Roland. Goldener Bär, silberner Bär: Drucker und Literaten in Leipzig. Festvortrag zur 96. Jahresversammlung der Gesellschaft der Bibliophilen e. V. am 18. Juni 1995 in Leipzig. München: Gesellschaft der Bibliophilen. 1995.
*Keywords:* Breitkopf Family/Book Industries and Trade – Germany – Leipzig – History – 18th Century/Printing – Germany – Leipzig – History – 18th Century/Publishers and Publishing – Germany – Leipzig – History – 18th Century/Leipzig (Germany) – Intellectual Life
Jestadt, Franz-Ulrich. Erfurter Drucke um 1800: Die Politisierung des Erfurter Buchwesens in der Aufklärung und zur Zeit der Französischen Revolution. Eine Titelblatt-Dokumentation. Erfurt: Ulenspiegel-Verlag. 2000.

411

*Keywords:* Printing – Germany – Erfurt – History – 18th Century/ Enlightenment – Germany/Erfurt (Germany) – Imprints/France – History – 1789–1815

Johnsen, Leigh Dana. Toward Pluralism: Society and Religion in Middleborough, Massachusetts, 1741–1807. Dissertation, University of California at Riverside CA. 1984.
*Keywords:* California. University, Riverside. Dept. Of History – Dissertations/Religious Pluralism – Massachusetts – Middleborough (Town)/Protestant Churches – Massachusetts – Middleborough (Town)/ Christianity – Massachusetts – Middleborough (Town)/Great Awakening – Massachusetts – Middleborough (Town)/Baptists – Massachusetts – Middleborough (Town)/Congregational Churches – Massachusetts – Middleborough (Town)/Massachusetts – Church History/Middleborough (MA: Town) – Church History/Dissertations, Academic – History

Kampendonk, Gustav. Die Geschichte des Krefelder Zeitungswesens von den Anfängen bis 1814: Ein Beitrag zur Presse- und Kulturgeschichte des Niederrheins. Dissertation, Universität Leipzig. 1933.
*Keywords:* Press – Germany – Krefeld – History

Knight, Carol Lynn H. The American Colonial Press and the Townshend Crisis, 1766–1770: a Study in Political Imagery. Lewiston NY: E. Mellen Press. 1990.
*Keywords:* Townshend, Charles, 1725–1767/Press and Politics – United States – History – 18th Century/Great Britain – Colonies – America – Economic Policy/United States – History – Revolution, 1775–1783 – Economic Aspects/United States – Politics and Government – 1775–1783

Koszyk, Kurt. Vorläufer der Massenpresse. Ökonomie und Publizistik zwischen Reformation und Französischer Revolution. Öffentliche Kommunikation im Zeitalter des Feudalismus. München: W. Goldmann. 1972.
*Keywords:* Press – Germany – History/Journalism – Social Aspects

Kraft, Thomas. Pietismus und Methodismus: Sozialethik und Reformprogramme von August Hermann Francke (1663–1727) und John Wesley (1703–1791) im Vergleich. Stuttgart: Medienwerk der evangelisch-methodistischen Kirche GmbH. 2001.
*Keywords:* Francke, August Hermann, 1663–1727/Wesley, John, 1703–1791/Pietism/Methodism

Krebs, Roland, Jean Moes, and Pierre-André Bois. Les Lettres Françaises dans les Revues Allemandes du XVIIIe Siècle. Bern, New York: P. Lang. 1997.

*Keywords:* French Literature – 18th Century – History and Criticism – Congresses/Press – Germany – History – Congresses/German Periodicals – History – 18th Century – Congresses

Lacey, Barbara E. Women and the Great Awakening in Connecticut. Dissertation, Clark University, Ann Arbor, MI. 1985.
*Keywords:* Great Awakening/Women and Religion/Connecticut – History – Colonial Period, Ca. 1600–1775

Lambert, Frank. Inventing the "Great Awakening". Princeton, NJ: Princeton University Press. 1999.
*Keywords:* Great Awakening/Revivals – New England – History – 18th Century/Revivals – New Jersey – History – 18th Century

——. Pedlar in Divinity: George Whitefield and the Transatlantic Revivals, 1737–1770. Princeton, NJ: Princeton University Press. 1994.
*Keywords:* Whitefield, George, 1714–1770/Evangelists – Biography/ Revivals – Great Britain – History – 18th Century/Great Awakening/ Evangelical Revival/Preaching – History – 18th Century/Revivals – North America – History – 18th Century

Larson, Barbara Ann. Prologue to Revolution: the War Sermons of the Reverend Samuel Davies: A Rhetorical Study. Milwaukee WI: The Speech Communication Association. 1978.
*Keywords:* Davies, Samuel, 1723–1761/Presbyterian Church – Sermons/ Sermons, American/Great Awakening/Preaching – History – 18th Century/Preaching – Virginia/United States – History – French and Indian War, 1755–1763 – Sermons

Lause, Mark A. Some Degree of Power: From Hired Hand to Union Craftsman in the Preindustrial American Printing Trades, 1778–1815. Fayetteville AR: University of Arkansas Press. 1991.
*Keywords:* Printing Industry – Employees – Labor Unions – United States – History/Printing Industry – United States – History – 18th Century/Printing Industry – United States – History – 19th Century/ Printers – United States – Directories

Lehmann, Hartmut, Manfred Jakubowski-Tiessen, and Otto Ulbricht. Religion und Religiosität in der Neuzeit: Historische Beiträge. Göttingen: Vandenhoeck & Ruprecht. 1996.
*Keywords:* Pietism – Germany – History/Pietism – South Australia – History/Germany – Church History/South Australia – Church History

Lehmann, Hartmut, Hans-Jürgen Schrader, and Heinz Schilling. Jansenismus, Quietismus, Pietismus. Historische Kommission zur Erforschung des Pietismus (Germany). Göttingen: Vandenhoeck & Ruprecht. 2002.
*Keywords:* Pietism/Jansenists/Quietism/Religious Thought – 17th

Century/Religious Thought – 18th Century/Europe – Religion – 17th Century/Europe – Religion – 18th Century

Lerg, Winfried B. Deutschsprachige Kolonialpublizistik am Vorabend der Amerikanischen Revolution: Fünf Beiträge zur Funktion deutscher Drucker und ihrer Periodika. Münster: LIT. 1999.
*Keywords:* German-American Newspapers – History/Press – United States – History – 18th Century/Printers – United States – 18th Century Biography

Lindemann, Margot. Deutsche Presse bis 1815. Berlin: Colloquium Verlag. 1969.
*Keywords:* Press – Germany – History

Lindhardt, Jan. Martin Luther: Knowledge and Mediation in the Renaissance. Lewiston: E. Mellen Press. 1986.
*Keywords:* Luther, Martin, 1483–1546 – Contributions in Christian Doctrine of Man/Luther, Martin, 1483–1546 – Contributions in Christian Doctrine of Communication/Man (Christian Theology) – History of Doctrines – 16th Century/Communication – Religious Aspects – Christianity – History of Doctrines – 16th Century/Renaissance

Lodge, Martin Ellsworth. The Great Awakening in the Middle Colonies. Dissertation, UC Berkeley CA. 1980.
*Keywords*: Great Awakening/United States – Church History – to 1775

Mason, J. C. S. The Moravian Church and the Missionary Awakening in England, 1760–1800. Woodbridge, Suffolk and Rochester NY: Royal Historical Society, Boydell Press. 2001.
*Keywords:* Moravian Church – Missions – History – 18th Century/ Moravian Church – England – History – 18th Century/Missions, English – History – 18th Century

Mehnert, Gottfried. Evangelische Presse: Geschichte und Erscheinungsbild von der Reformation bis zur Gegenwart. Bielefeld: Luther-Verlag. 1983.
*Keywords:* Press, Protestant – Germany – History

Mollney, Ulrike. Norddeutsche Presse um 1800: Zeitschriften und Zeitungen in Flensburg, Braunschweig, Hannover und Schaumburg-Lippe im Zeitalter der Französischen Revolution. Bielefeld: Verlag für Regionalgeschichte. 1996.
*Keywords:* German Periodicals – Germany, Northern – History – 18th Century/German Periodicals – Germany, Northern – History – 19th Century/Press and Politics – Germany – Germany, Northern – History – 18th Century/Press and Politics – Germany – Germany, Northern – History – 19th Century

Select Bibliography

Morz, Stefan. Vom Westboten zur Rheinpfalz: Die Geschichte der Presse im Raum Ludwigshafen von den Anfängen bis zur Gegenwart. Ludwigshafen: Stadtarchiv Ludwigshafen am Rhein. 1994.
*Keywords:* Press – Germany – Ludwigshafen Am Rhein Region – History/Ludwigshafen Am Rhein Region (Germany) – History

Nichols, J. Randall. The Restoring Word: Preaching As Pastoral Communication. San Francisco: Harper & Row. 1987.
*Keywords:* Preaching/Communication – Religious Aspects – Christianity

Nissenbaum, Stephen, (comp.). The Great Awakening at Yale College. Belmont CA: Wadsworth Pub. Co. 1972.
*Keywords:* Yale University – History – Sources/Great Awakening – History – Sources

Nobles, Gregory H. Divisions Throughout the Whole: Politics and Society in Hampshire County, Massachusetts, 1740–1775. Cambridge, New York: Cambridge University Press. 1983.
*Keywords:* Great Awakening/Hampshire County (MA) – Politics and Government/Hampshire County (MA) – Social Conditions/Massachusetts – Politics and Government – to 1775 – Case Studies/Hampshire County (MA) – Church History

Nolle, Albert. Geschichte Des Zeitungswesens in Hohenzollern von seinen ersten Anfängen bis zum Jahre 1850. Dissertation, Ludwig-Maximilians Universität zu München. 1935.
*Keywords*: Press – Germany – Hohenzollern – History – 19th Century

Pasley, Jeffrey L. "The Tyranny of Printers": Newspaper Politics in the Early American Republic. Charlottesville, VA: University Press of Virginia. 2001.
*Keywords:* Journalism – United States – History – 18th Century/Journalism – United States – History – 19th Century/Press and Politics – United States – History – 18th Century/Press and Politics – United States – History – 19th Century

Peterson, Mark A. The Price of Redemption: The Spiritual Economy of Puritan New England. Stanford CA: Stanford University Press. 1997.
*Keywords:* Third Church (Boston, MA) – History/Westfield Church (MA) – History/Spirituality – Puritans – History/Economics – Religious Aspects – Puritans – History of Doctrines/Puritans – Massachusetts – History/Great Awakening/Massachusetts – Church History – 17th Century/Boston (MA) – Church History/Westfield (MA) – Church History/Massachusetts – Church History – 18th Century

Prange, Carsten. Die Zeitungen und Zeitschriften des 17. Jahrhunderts in Hamburg und Altona: Ein Beitrag zur Publizistik der Frühaufklärung. Hamburg: Christians. 1978.
*Keywords:* Press – Germany – Hamburg – History – 17th Century

415

Rawlyk, George A. The Canada Fire: Radical Evangelicalism in British North America, 1775–1812. Kingston ON: McGill-Queen's University Press. 1994.
*Keywords:* Evangelical Revival – Canada/Great Awakening

Paisey, David. Deutsche Buchdrucker, Buchhändler und Verleger, 1701–1750. Wiesbaden: O. Harrassowitz. 1988.
*Keywords:* Book Industries and Trade – Germany – History – 18th Century/Booksellers and Bookselling – Germany – Registers/Publishers and Publishing – Germany – Registers/Printing – Germany – History – 18th Century/Printers – Germany – Registers

Reese, William S. The Printers' First Fruits: An Exhibition of American Imprints, 1640–1742, from the Collections of the American Antiquarian Society. American Antiquarian Society. Worcester, MA: The Society. 1989.
*Keywords:* American Antiquarian Society – Exhibitions/Printing – United States – History – 17th Century – Exhibitions/Printing – United States – History – 18th Century – Exhibitions/Early Printed Books – United States – Bibliography – Exhibitions/United States – Imprints – Exhibitions

Reid, Clyde H. The Empty Pulpit: A Study in Preaching as Communication. New York: Harper & Row. 1967.
*Keywords:* Preaching/Communication – Religious Aspects – Christianity

Reid-Maroney, Nina. Philadelphia's Enlightenment, 1740–1800: Kingdom of Christ, Empire of Reason. Westport CT: Greenwood Press. 2001.
*Keywords:* Great Awakening/Enlightenment – Philadelphia/Religion and Science – Philadelphia – History – 18th Century/United States – Church History – 18th Century

Roeder, Corinna. Frühe Kölner Wochenzeitungen: Die Unternehmen der Offizinen Mertzenich und Kempen 1620 bis 1685. Köln: Greven. 1998.
*Keywords:* Press – Germany – Cologne – History – 17th Century/ Cologne (Germany) – History

Rosenfeld, Richard N, and William Duane. American Aurora: A Democratic-Republican Returns. The Suppressed History of Our Nation's Beginnings and the Heroic Newspaper That Tried to Report It. New York: St. Martin's Press. 1997.
*Keywords:* Aurora General Advertiser/Press and Politics – United States – History – 18th Century/United States – Politics and Government – 1775–1783/United States – Politics and Government – 1783–1809/ United States – Politics and Government – to 1775

Rutman, Darrett Bruce, (comp.). The Great Awakening; Event and Exegesis. New York: Wiley. 1970.
*Keywords:* Great Awakening – Addresses, Essays, Lectures

Schlesinger, Arthur Meier. Prelude to Independence: The Newspaper War on Britain, 1764–1776. Westport, CT: Greenwood Press. 1979.
*Keywords:* Press – United States – History – 18th Century/United States – History – Revolution, 1775–1783 – Causes

Schulz, Gunther. Geschäft mit Wort und Meinung: Medienunternehmer seit dem 18. Jahrhundert: Büdinger Forschungen zur Sozialgeschichte 1996 und 1997. Büdinger Vorträge (34th: 1996), and Büdinger Vorträge (35th: 1997). München: H. Boldt. 1999.
*Keywords:* Mass Media – Germany – History Congresses/Capitalists and Financiers – Germany – History Congresses/Capitalism and Mass Media – Germany – History Congresses/Publishers and Publishing – Germany – History Congresses/Press – Germany – History Congresses

Schulz, William F. Transforming Words: Six Essays on Preaching. Boston: Skinner House Books. 1996.
*Keywords:* Preaching/Pastoral Theology – Unitarian Universalist Churches/Communication – Religious Aspects – Christianity

Schwarz, Reinhard, and Sabine Ullmann Samuel Urlsperger (1685–1772): Augsburger Pietismus zwischen Außenwirkungen und Binnenwelt Berlin: Akademie Verlag. 1996.
*Keywords:* Urlsperger, Samuel, 1685–1772 – Congresses/Pietism – Germany – Augsburg – Congresses/Augsburg (Germany) – Religious Life and Customs – Congresses

Silver, Rollo Gabriel. The American Printer, 1787–1825. Charlottesville VA: Published for the Bibliographical Society of the University of Virginia [by] the University Press of Virginia. 1967.
*Keywords:* Printing – United States – History – 19th Century/Printing – United States – History – 18th Century/Early Printed Books – United States – 18th Century/United States – Imprints – History

Sloan, W. David William David, and Julie Hedgepeth Williams. The Early American Press, 1690–1783. Westport CT: Greenwood Press. 1994.
*Keywords:* Press – United States – History – 18th Century

Stearns, Monroe. The Great Awakening, 1720–1760; Religious Revival Rouses Americans' Sense of Individual Liberties. New York: Watts. 1970.
*Keywords:* Great Awakening/Great Awakening/United States – History – Colonial Period, 1600–1775

Steele, Ian Kenneth. The English Atlantic, 1675–1740: An Exploration of Communication and Community. New York: Oxford University Press. 1986

*Keywords*: Communication and traffic – North America – History/ Communication and traffic – West Indies, British – History/Great Britain – Colonies – America – Commerce

Stewart, Gordon T. Documents Relating to the Great Awakening in Nova Scotia, 1760–1791. Champlain Society. Toronto: The Champlain Society. 1982.
*Keywords:* Revivals – Nova Scotia – History – 18th Century – Sources/ Nova Scotia – Church History – 18th Century – Sources

Sweet, Leonard I. Communication and Change in American Religious History. Grand Rapids, MI: Eerdmans. 1993.
*Keywords:* Communication – Religious Aspects – Christianity – History/United States – Church History

Tagg, James. Benjamin Franklin Bache and the Philadelphia Aurora. Philadelphia: University of Pennsylvania Press. 1991.
*Keywords:* Bache, Benjamin Franklin, 1769–1798/Washington, George, 1732–1799 – Relations With Journalists/Bache's Philadelphia Aurora/Press and Politics – United States – History – 18th Century/ Journalists – United States – Biography/United States – Politics and Government – 1789–1797

Taylor, Barbara Brown. When God Is Silent. Cambridge MA: Cowley Publications. 1998.
*Keywords:* Preaching/Hidden God/Communication – Religious Aspects – Christianity

Tracy, Joseph. The Great Awakening: A History of the Revival of Religion in the Time of Edwards and Whitefield. Boston: Tappan & Dennet. 1990.
*Keywords:* Great Awakening/Revivals – United States/United States – Church History

Wallmann, Johannes, and Udo Strater. Halle und Osteuropa: Zur europäischen Ausstrahlung des Hallischen Pietismus. Internationales Kolloquium "Halle und Osteuropa" (1994: Franckesche Stiftungen). Halle, Tübingen: Verlag der Franckeschen Stiftungen. M. Niemeyer. 1998.
*Keywords:* Pietism – Germany – Halle an Der Saale – Congresses/Halle an Der Saale (Germany) – Religious Life and Customs – Congresses/ Europe, Eastern – Religious Life and Customs – Congresses

Warner, Michael. The Letters of the Republic: Publication and the Public Sphere in Eighteenth-Century America. Cambridge MA: Harvard University Press. 1990.
*Keywords:* Publishers and Publishing – United States – History – 18th Century/Literature and Society – United States – History – 18th Century/Literature Publishing – United States – History – 18th Century/

Books and Reading – United States – History – 18th Century/Printing – United States – History – 18th Century/Popular Culture – United States – History – 18th Century/Politics and Literature – United States – History – 18th Century/American Literature – 1783–1850 – History and Criticism/Public Opinion – United States – History – 18th Century

Wessel, Carola. Delaware-Indianer und Herrnhuter Missionare im Upper Ohio Valley, 1772–1781. Tübingen: Niemeyer. 1999.
*Keywords:* Moravian Church – Missions/Delaware Indians – Missions – History – 18th Century/Moravians – Missions – North America – History – 18th Century/Indians of North America – Missions – History – 18th Century/Indians of North America – Missions – Ohio River Valley – History – 18th Century

Westerkamp, Marilyn J. Triumph of the Laity: Scots-Irish Piety and the Great Awakening, 1625–1760. New York: Oxford University Press. 1988.
*Keywords:* Revivals – Middle Atlantic States – History – 17th Century/ Revivals – Middle Atlantic States – History – 18th Century/Great Awakening/Scots Irish – Middle Atlantic States – History – 17th Century/Scots Irish – Middle Atlantic States – History – 18th Century/ Presbyterian Church – Middle Atlantic States – History – 17th Century/ Presbyterian Church – Middle Atlantic States – History – 18th Century/ Middle Atlantic States – Church History/Middle Atlantic States – History – Colonial Period, 1600–1775

Williams, Julie Hedgepeth. The Significance of the Printed Word in Early America: Colonists' Thoughts on the Role of the Press. Westport CT: Greenwood Press. 1999.
*Keywords:* Books and Reading – United States – History – 17th Century/Books and Reading – United States – History – 18th Century/ Press – United States – History – 17th Century/Press – United States – History – 18th Century/Book Industries and Trade – United States – History – 17th Century/Book Industries and Trade – United States – History – 18th Century

Wilson, Renate. Pious Traders in Medicine: German Pharmaceutical Networks in Eighteenth-Century North America. University Park PA: Pennsylvania State University Press. 2000.
*Keywords:* Medicine – United States – History – 18th Century/Medicine – Germany – History – 18th Century/Pietists – United States – History – 18th Century/Pietists – Germany – History – 18th Century/ Pharmacy – United States – History – 18th Century/Missionaries, Medical – United States – History – 18th Century

Select Bibliography

Zimmermann, Walter. Entwicklungsgeschichte des Nürnberger "Friedens-und Kriegskuriers" (Nürnberger Kurier) von seinen ersten Anfängen bis zum Übergang an den "Fränkischen Kurier" 1663–1865. Ein Beitrag zur Geschichte des deutschen Zeitungswesens. Dissertation, Friedrich-Alexander Universität Erlangen, 1930.
*Keywords*: Friedens- Und Kriegskurier (Nürnberger Kurier)/Fränkischer Kurier/Press – Germany – Nuremberg – History

# Part II

AT & T Bell Laboratories, and American Telephone & Telegraph Company. A History of Engineering and Science in the Bell System: Transmission Technology (1925–1975). AT & T Bell Laboratories, and American Telephone & Telegraph Company. Indianapolis, IN: AT&T Bell Laboratories. 1985.
*Keywords:* Telephone – History
Ault, Phillip H. Wires West. New York: Dodd, Mead. 1974.
*Keywords:* Telegraph – West (U. S. ) – History/West (U. S. ) – History
Basse, Dieter. Wolff's Telegraphisches Bureau 1849 bis 1933: Agenturpublizistik zwischen Politik und Wirtschaft. München, New York: K. G. Saur. 1991.
*Keywords:* Wolf's Telegraphisches Bureau – History/Telegraph – Germany – History/German Newspapers – History
Bates, David Homer. Lincoln in the Telegraph Office: Recollections of the United States Military Telegraph Corps During the Civil War. Lincoln, NE: University of Nebraska Lincoln. 1995.
*Keywords:* Lincoln, Abraham, 1809–1865/United States. Military Telegraph Corps/Military Telegraph – United States – History – 19th Century/United States – History – Civil War, 1861–1865 – Communications
Beauchamp, K. G. History of Telegraphy. Institution of Electrical Engineers. London: Institution of Electrical Engineers. 2001.
*Keywords:* Telegraph – History
Blake, George G. George Gascoigne. History of Radio Telegraphy and Telephony. New York: Arno Press. 1974.
*Keywords:* Telegraph, Wireless – History/Telephone, Wireless – History
Blanz, Robert C., Robert K. Timothy, and Walter K. Koch. Mountain Bell: Seventy-Five Years of Growth and Change. Newcomen Society of the

United States. New York: Newcomen Society of the United States. 1986.
*Keywords:* Mountain States Telephone and Telegraph Company – History/Telephone – United States – History

Blondheim, Menahem. News Over the Wires: The Telegraph and the Flow of Public Information in America, 1844–1897. Cambridge MA: Harvard University Press. 1994.
*Keywords:* Journalism – United States – History – 19th Century/ Newspaper Publishing – United States – History – 19th Century/ Telegraph – United States – History – 19th Century

Bonel, A. Auguste. Histoire de la Telegraphie: Déscription des Principaux Appareils Aeriens et Eléctriques. Paris, Caen: Ballay et Conchon. Buhour. 1978.
*Keywords:* Telegraph – History

Briggs, Charles F. Charles Frederick, and Augustus Maverick. The Story of the Telegraph, and a History of the Great Atlantic Cable: A Complete Record of the Inception, Progress, and Final Success of that Undertaking, a General History of Land and Oceanic Telegraphs, Descriptions of Telegraphic Apparatus, and Biographical Sketches of the Principal Persons Connected With the Great Work. New York: Rudd & Carleton. 1970.
*Keywords.* Telegraph – History/Cables, Submarine – Atlantic

Brunel, Marc Isambard Sir, and J. Frederic Daniell. As the Electric Telegraph Has Recently Attracted a Considerable Share of Public Attention, Our Friends, Messrs. Cooke and Wheatstone, Have Been Put to Some Inconvenience, by a Misunderstanding Which Has Prevailed Respecting Their Relative Positions in Connexion [sic] with the Invention. London: W. Lewis and Son, printers. 1980.
*Keywords:* Telegraph – History

Coates, Vary T, and Bernard S. Finn. A Retrospective Technology Assessment: Submarine Telegraphy: The Transatlantic Cable of 1866. Program of Policy Studies in Science and Technology. San Francisco, CA: San Francisco Press. 1979.
*Keywords:* Cables, Submarine – Atlantic – History

Coe, Lewis. The Telegraph: a History of Morse's Invention and Its Predecessors in the United States. Jefferson NC: McFarland. 1993.
*Keywords:* Morse, Samuel Finley Breese, 1791–1872/Telegraph – United States – History/Inventors – United States – Biography

Coll, Steve. The Deal of the Century: The Breakup of AT&T. New York: Atheneum. 1986.

*Keywords:* American Telephone and Telegraph Company – Reorganization – History/Telephone Companies – United States – History
Deloraine, E. M. When Telecom and ITT Were Young. New York: Lehigh Books. 1976.
*Keywords:* International Telephone and Telegraph Corporation – History
Dickerson, E. N. Edward Nicoll. Joseph Henry and the Magnetic Telegraph: An Address Delivered at Princeton College, June 16, 1885. New York: C. Scribner's Sons. 1970.
*Keywords:* Henry, Joseph, 1799–1878/Telegraph – History
Downey, Gregory John. Telegraph Messenger Boys: Labor, Technology, and Geography, 1850–1950. New York: Routledge. 2002.
*Keywords:* Messengers – United States – History/Telegraph – United States – Employees – History
Dwyer, John B. To Wire the World: Perry M. Collins and the North Pacific Telegraph Expedition. Westport CT: Praeger. 2001.
*Keywords:* Collins, Perry Mcdonough, 1813–1900/Telegraph – Russia – Siberia – History – 19th Century/Telegraph – North America – History – 19th Century
Epstein, Samuel M. Behind the Telephone Debates – 4: a Conceptual Framework for Pre- and Post-Divestiture Telecommunications Industry Revenue Requirements. Cambridge, Mass: Harvard University, Center for Information Policy Research. 1985.
*Keywords:* American Telephone and Telegraph Company – Reorganization – History/Telephone Systems/Telecommunication
Fagen, M. D. A History of Engineering and Science in the Bell System: The Early Years (1875–1925). Bell Telephone Laboratories, Inc. [New York]: Bell Telephone Laboratories. 1975.
*Keywords:* American Telephone and Telegraph Company – History/ Telephone – United States – History/Telecommunication – United States – History
Fahie, J. J. John Joseph. A History of Electric Telegraphy to the Year 1837. New York: Arno Press. 1974.
*Keywords:* Telegraph – History
——. A History of Wireless Telegraphy, 1838–1899: Including Some Bare-Wire Proposals for Subaqueous Telegraphs. New York, London, Edinburgh: Dodd, Mead. W. Blackwood and Sons. 1973.
*Keywords:* Telegraph, Wireless – History
Feldenkirchen, Wilfried. Werner von Siemens: Erfinder und internationaler Unternehmer. München: Piper. 1996.

Select Bibliography

*Keywords:* Technology – Germany – History/Technology – Germany
– History – Sources
Standage, Tom. The Victorian Internet: The Remarkable Story of the
Telegraph and the Nineteenth Century's On-Line Pioneers. New York:
Walker and Co. 1998.
*Keywords:* Telegraph – History
Stummvoll, Josef. Technikgeschichte und Schrifttum: Kurze Einführung
in die Probleme der Geschichte der Technik und bibliographische Doku-
mentation der Fachliteratur. Wien: Österreichisches Institut für Biblio-
theksforschung, Dokumentations- und Informationswesen. 1975.
*Keywords:* Science – Documentation/Technology – Documentation
Taylor, William B. William Bower. An Historical Sketch of Henry's
Contribution to the Electro-Magnetic Telegraph: With an Account of the
Origin and Development of Prof. Morse's Invention. Washington, DC:
Government Printing Office. 1970.
*Keywords:* Henry, Joseph, 1797–1878/Telegraph – History
Temin, Peter, and Louis Galambos. The Fall of the Bell System: A Study
in Prices and Politics. Cambridge, New York: Cambridge University
Press. 1987.
*Keywords:* American Telephone and Telegraph Company – Reorgani-
zation – History/Telephone Companies – United States – History
Thompson, Robert Luther. Wiring a Continent; The History of the
Telegraph Industry in the United States, 1832–1866. New York: Arno
Press. 1972.
*Keywords:* Telegraph – United States – History
Tosiello, Rosario Joseph. The Birth and Early Years of the Bell Telephone
System, 1876–1880. New York: Arno Press. 1979.
*Keywords:* American Telephone and Telegraph Company – History
Townsend, John Wilson, and Samuel Woodson Price. The Life of James
Francis Leonard: the First Practical Sound-Reader of the Morse
Alphabet. Filson Club, Louisville, KY. Louisville, KY: J. P. Morton &
Co., printers to the Filson Club. 1993.
*Keywords:* Leonard, James Francis, 1834–1862/Crockett, Joseph,
1742–1829/Telegraph – History/Kentucky – Biography
Vail, Alfred. The American Electro Magnetic Telegraph: With the Reports
of Congress, and a Description of All Telegraphs Known, Employing
Electricity or Galvanism. Philadelphia: Lea & Blanchard. 1972.
*Keywords:* Telegraph – History
——. Eyewitness to Early American Telegraphy. New York: Arno Press.
1974.
*Keywords:* Telegraph – United States – History

Wasserman, Neil H. From Invention to Innovation: Long-Distance Telephone Transmission at the Turn of the Century. Baltimore: Johns Hopkins University Press. 1985.
*Keywords:* American Telephone and Telegraph Company – History/ Telephone – United States – History
Weinhaus, Carol L, and Anthony G Oettinger. Behind the Telephone Debates. Norwood, N. J: Ablex Pub. Corporation. 1988.
*Keywords:* American Telephone and Telegraph Company – Reorganization – History/Telephone Companies – United States – History
Wiesner, Lothar. Telegraph and Data Transmission Over Shortwave Radio Links: Fundamental Principles and Networks. [Berlin, München], London: Siemens-Aktiengesellschaft, [Abt. Verl. ]. Heyden. 1979.
*Keywords:* Radioteletype/Data Transmission Systems/Shortwave Radio
Wilke, Jürgen, (ed. ). Telegraphenbüros und Nachrichtenagenturen in Deutschland: Untersuchungen zu ihrer Geschichte bis 1949. München, New York: K. G. Saur. 1991.

# Part III

Anderson, Jack, and James Boyd. Confessions of a Muckraker: The Inside Story of Life in Washington during the Truman, Eisenhower, Kennedy and Johnson Years. New York: Random House. 1979.
*Keywords:* Anderson, Jack, 1922/Pearson, Drew, 1897–1969/Journalists – United States – Biography
Applegate, Edd. Journalistic Advocates and Muckrakers: Three Centuries of Crusading Writers. Jefferson, NC: McFarland. 1997.
*Keywords:* Journalism – United States – History/Journalists – United States – Biography
Becker, Klaus-Bert. Die Muckrakers und der Sozialismus: Eine Untersuchung zum politischen Bewusstsein in der *Progressive Era*. Bern, Frankfurt/M: Herbert Lang. Peter Lang. 1974.
*Keywords:* Social Reformers – United States/Socialism – United States
Bohrmann, Hans. Strukturwandel der deutschen Studentenpresse: Studentenpolitik und Studentenzeitschriften 1848–1974. München: Verlag Dokumentation. 1975.
*Keywords:* College Students – Germany – Political Activity/Student Newspapers and Periodicals – Germany – History

Brady, Kathleen. Ida Tarbell: Portrait of a Muckraker. New York: Seaview/ Putnam. 1984.
*Keywords:* Tarbell, Ida Minerva, 1857–1944/Journalists – United States – Biography

Brasch, Walter M. Forerunners of Revolution: Muckrakers and the American Social Conscience. Lanham, MD: University Press of America. 1990.
*Keywords:* Social Problems/Social Reformers – United States/United States – Social Conditions – 20th Century

Citizen Muckraking: How to Investigate and Right Wrongs in Your Community. Center for Public Integrity. Monroe, ME: Common Courage Media. 2000.
*Keywords:* Whistle Blowing – United States/Political Corruption – United States/Corporations – United States – Corrupt Practices/ Investigations

Chalmers, David Mark. The Social and Political Ideas of the Muckrakers. Freeport, NY: Books for Libraries Press. 1964.
*Keywords:* Journalism – Social Aspects/Journalism – Political Aspects

Cook, Fred J. The Muckrakers: Crusading Journalists Who Changed America. Garden City, NY: Doubleday. 1972.
*Keywords:* Journalism – Social Aspects/Journalism – Political Aspects – United States/Journalists – United States – Biography

[Deutsche Presseforschung]. Presse und Geschichte II: Neue Beitrage zur historischen Kommunikationsforschung. München, New York: K. G. Saur. 1987.
*Keywords:* Journalism – Germany – History – Congresses/German Newspapers – History – Congresses

Doerfert, Carsten. Das Archiv des Öffentlichen Rechts, 1885–1918: Zur Geschichte einer Wissenschaft und ihrer Zeitschrift. Berlin: Duncker & Humblot. 1993.
*Keywords:* Archiv des Öffentlichen Rechts/Journalism, Legal – Germany – History

Downie, Leonard. The New Muckrakers. Washington: New Republic Book Co. 1976.
*Keywords:* Reporters and Reporting

Doyle, Arthur T. Front Benches and Back Rooms: A Story of Corruption, Muckraking, Raw Partisanship and Intrigue in New Brunswick. Toronto: Green Tree. 1976.

Ettema, James S, and Theodore Lewis Glasser. Custodians of Conscience: Investigative Journalism and Public Virtue. New York: Columbia University Press. 1998.

*Keywords:* Investigative Reporting/Journalism – Objectivity/Journalists – Interviews

Filler, Louis. Appointment at Armageddon: Muckraking and Progressivism in the American Tradition. Westport CN: Greenwood Press. 1976.
*Keywords:* Progressivism (United States Politics)/United States – Politics and Government – 1865–1933/United States – Social Conditions – 1865–1918

———. The Muckrakers. Stanford CA: Stanford University Press. 1993.
*Keywords:* Social Problems/Social Reformers – United States/United States – Social Conditions – 20th Century

———. Muckraking and Progressivism in the American Tradition. New Brunswick NJ: Transaction Publishers. 1996.
*Keywords:* Progressivism (United States Politics)/United States – Politics and Government – 1865–1933/United States – Social Conditions – 1865–1918

———. Progressivism and Muckraking. New York: R. R. Bowker Co. 1976.
*Keywords:* Social Reformers – United States – Bibliography/Social Problems – Bibliography/Progressivism (United States Politics)/United States – Social Conditions – Bibliography

Fisher, Richard Bernard. The Last Muckraker: The Social Orientation of the Thought of Upton Sinclair. Dissertation Yale University, Ann Arbor, MI. 1985
*Keywords:* Sinclair, Upton, 1878–1968

Fitzpatrick, Ellen F, Lincoln Steffens, Ida M. Tarbell, and Ray Stannard Baker. Muckraking: Three Landmark Articles. Boston: Bedford Books of St. Martin's Press. 1994.
*Keywords:* Press and Politics – United States/Investigative Reporting – United States

Frölich, Jürgen C. Die Berliner "Volks-Zeitung" 1853 bis 1867: Preußischer Linksliberalismus zwischen Reaktion und Revolution von Oben. Frankfurt am Main, New York: P. Lang. 1990.
*Keywords:* Berliner Volks-Zeitung – History/Liberalism – Germany – History – 19th Century/Journalism – Germany – History – 19th Century/Prussia (Germany) – Politics and Government – 1815–1870/ Germany – Politics and Government – 1848–1870

Frome, Michael. Greenspeak: Fifty Years of Environmental Muckraking and Advocacy. Knoxville, TN: University of Tennessee Press. 2002.
*Keywords:* Environmentalism/Conservation of Natural Resources/ Environmental Protection

Grenier, Judson. The Origins and Nature of Progressive Muckraking. Dissertation UCLA, Los Angeles. 1965

*Keywords:* Political Corruption – United States/Journalists – United States/Progressivism (United States Politics)/United States – Social Conditions/Dissertations, Academic – History

Habermas, Jürgen. The Structural Transformation of the Public Sphere: An Inquiry into a Category of Bourgeois Society. Cambridge: Polity Press. 1992

*Keywords:* Communication – Social aspects/Public opinion/Social history/Middle class/Political sociology/Newspapers

——. Strukturwandel der Öffentlichkeit: Untersuchungen zu einer Kategorie der bürgerlichen Gesellschaft. Frankfurt am Main: Suhrkamp. 1990

*Keywords:* Sociology – Methodology/Social structure/Middle class/ Political sociology/Newspapers

Harry, M. The Muckraker's Manual: Handbook for Investigative Reporters. Port Townsend, WA: Loompanics Unlimited. 1984.

*Keywords:* Investigative Reporting

Hornung, Alfred. Narrative Struktur und Textsortendifferenzierung: Die Texte des Muckraking Movement (1902–1912). Stuttgart: Metzler. 1978.

*Keywords:* Discourse Analysis/Narration (Rhetoric)/Structuralism (Literary Analysis)/United States – Social Conditions – 1865–1918

Jensen, Carl. Stories That Changed America: Muckrakers of the 20th Century. New York, London: Seven Stories. Turnaround. 2002.

*Keywords:* Journalists – United States – Biography/Investigative Reporting – United States/Investigative Reporting – Social Aspects – United States/Investigative Reporting – Political Aspects – United States

Kochersberger, Robert C. More Than a Muckraker: Ida Tarbell's Lifetime in Journalism. Knoxville TN: University of Tennessee Press. 1994.

*Keywords:* Tarbell, Ida M. (Ida Minerva), 1857–1944/Women Journalists – United States – Biography

Korling, Martha. Die literarische Arbeit der Zeitschrift *Hochland* von 1903 bis 1933: Untersuchungen über die Verwirklichung eines publizistischen Programms. Dissertation, Freie Universität. Berlin. 1958

*Keywords:* Muth, Karl/Hochland/German Literature – 20th Century – Periodicals/Journalism – Germany – History – 20th Century/German Periodicals – History – 20th Century

Lerg, Winfried B, Michael Schmolke, Universität Münster, and Institut für Publizistik. Massenpresse und Volkszeitung: Zwei Beiträge zur Pressegeschichte des 19. Jahrhunderts. Assen: Van Gorcum. 1968

*Keywords:* Press – History/Press – Germany – History

431

Lindley, Daniel. Ambrose Bierce Takes on the Railroad: The Journalist as Muckraker and Cynic. Westport CT: Praeger. 1999.
*Keywords:* Bierce, Ambrose, 1842–1914? – Knowledge – Journalism/ Railroads – Political Aspects – California – History/Journalism – California – San Francisco – History/Journalists – United States – Biography/Authors, American – 19th Century – Biography

Marx, Gary T. (comp.) Muckraking Sociology: Research as Social Criticism. New Brunswick NJ: Transaction Books; distributed by Dutton [New York]. 1972.
*Keywords:* United States – Social Conditions – 1960–1980

Miraldi, Robert. Charles Edward Russell: "Chief of the Muckrakers". Columbia, SC: Association for Education in Journalism and Mass Communication. 1995.
*Keywords:* Russell, Charles Edward, 1860–1941/Journalists – United States – Biography/Investigative Reporting – United States – History – 20th Century

———. The Muckrakers: Evangelical Crusaders. Westport CT: Praeger. 2000.
*Keywords:* Journalists – United States – Biography/Journalism – Social Aspects – United States – History – 20th Century/Investigative Reporting – United States – History – 20th Century

———. Muckraking and Objectivity: Journalism's Colliding Traditions. New York: Greenwood Press. 1990.
*Keywords:* Journalistic Ethics – United States/Journalism – United States – Political Aspects/Journalism – Objectivity – United States

———. Objectivity and the New Muckraking: John L. Hess and the Nursing Home Scandal. Columbia SC: Association for Education in Journalism and Mass Communication. 1989.
*Keywords:* Journalism – Objectivity/Social Problems – United States/ Nursing Homes – United States

Mitford, Jessica. The Making of a Muckraker. London: M. Joseph. 1979.
*Keywords:* Mitford, Jessica, 1917/Journalists – United States – Correspondence/Journalism – Social Aspects – United States – History – 20th Century

———. Poison Penmanship: The Gentle Art of Muckraking. New York: Farrar, Straus and Giroux. 1988.
*Keywords:* Journalism – Muckraking /Journalism – Social Aspects – United States – History – 20th Century

Muelder, Hermann R. Hermann Richard. Missionaries and Muckrakers: The First Hundred Years of Knox College. Urbana IL: University of Illinois Press. 1984.

*Keywords:* Knox College, Galesburg IL – History/Journalism – Social Aspects – United States – History – 20th Century

Nickel, Gunther. Die Schaubühne – die Weltbühne: Siegfried Jacobsohns Wochenschrift und ihr ästhetisches Programm. Opladen: Westdeutscher Verlag. 1996.
*Keywords:* Jacobsohn, Siegfried, 1881–1926/Journalism – Germany – History – 20th Century/Criticism – Germany – History – 20th Century/ Germany – Intellectual Life – 20th Century

Ollman, Bertell, and Jonathan Birnbaum. The United States Constitution: 200 Years of Anti-Federalist, Abolitionist, Feminist, Muckraking, Progressive, and Especially Socialist Criticism. United States. New York: New York University Press. 1990.
*Keywords:* Constitutional History – United States – Journalism

Regier, Cornelius C. The Era of the Muckrakers. Peter Smith. 1957
*Keywords:* Political Corruption/Journalism – United States/United States – Politics and Government – 20th Century

Requate, Jörg. Journalismus als Beruf: Entstehung und Entwicklung des Journalistenberufs im 19. Jahrhundert: Deutschland im internationalen Vergleich. Göttingen: Vandenhoeck & Ruprecht. 1995.
*Keywords:* Journalism – Germany – History – 19th Century/Journalism – History – 19th Century

Serrin, Judith, and William Serrin. Muckraking! The Journalism That Changed America. New York: New Press. 2002.
*Keywords:* Social Problems – United States – History – 20th Century/ Journalism – Social Aspects – United States/United States – Social Conditions – 20th Century

Shapiro, Herbert (comp.) The Muckrakers and American Society. Boston: D. C. Heath. 1968.
*Keywords:* United States – Social Conditions/Journalism – Social Aspects – United States – History – 20th Century

Smith, John Kares. The Muckraking Movement and Its Legacies. Speech Communication Association. 1984.
*Keywords:* Exposition (Rhetoric)/Public Relations/Journalism – Social Aspects – United States – History – 20th Century

——. Poisoned Penmanship: The American Art of Muckraking. 1983.
*Keywords:* Exposition (Rhetoric)/Political Corruption in Literature

——. Upton Sinclair and the Dead Hand Series: The Case of the Muckraker As Jeremiah. Eastern Communication Association. 1983.
*Keywords:* Sinclair, Upton, 1878–1968/Exposition (Rhetoric)/Political Corruption in Literature

Barfield, Ray E. Listening to Radio, 1920–1950. Westport CT: Praeger. 1996.
*Keywords:* Radio Broadcasting – United States – History/Radio Programs – United States – History

Barnouw, Erik. The Golden Web: a History of Broadcasting in the United States, 1933 to 1953. New York: Oxford University Press. 1968.
*Keywords:* Radio Broadcasting – United States – History/Television Broadcasting – United States – History

———. A History of Broadcasting in the United States. New York: Oxford University Press. 1966.
*Keywords:* Broadcasting – United States – History

———. A Tower in Babel: A History of Broadcasting in the United States, to 1933. New York: Oxford University Press. 1966.
*Keywords:* Radio Broadcasting – United States – History/Television Broadcasting – United States – History

Bausch, Hans. Rundfunkpolitik nach 1945. München: Deutscher Taschenbuch Verlag. 1980.
*Keywords:* Radio Broadcasting Policy – Germany – History/Broadcasting Policy – Germany – History

Bensman, Marvin R. The Beginning of Broadcast Regulation in the Twentieth Century. Jefferson NC: McFarland & Co. 2000.
*Keywords:* Broadcasting – Law and Legislation – United States – History

Bergreen, Laurence. Look Now, Pay Later: The Rise of Network Broadcasting. Garden City NY: Doubleday. 1980.
*Keywords:* Broadcasting – United States – History

Bierbach, Wolf. Rundfunk zwischen Kommerz und Politik: Der Westdeutsche Rundfunk in der Weimarer Zeit. Frankfurt am Main, New York: P. Lang. 1986.
*Keywords:* Westdeutscher Rundfunk – History/Radio Broadcasting – Germany – History/Germany – Politics and Government – 1918–1933

Blakely, Robert J. To Serve the Public Interest: Educational Broadcasting in the United States. Syracuse, NY: Syracuse University Press. 1979.
*Keywords:* Educational Broadcasting – United States – History

Bliss, Edward. Now the News: the Story of Broadcast Journalism. New York: Columbia University Press. 1991.
*Keywords:* Broadcast Journalism – United States – History/Broadcasting – United States – History/Radio Broadcasting – United States/Television Broadcasting – United States/Cable Television – United States/Electronic News Gathering – United States

Boll, Friedhelm, Beatrix Bouvier, Dieter Dowe, Patrick von zur Mühlen, Hans Pelger, and Michael Schneider, eds. Archiv für Sozialgeschichte: Medienkommunikation und Massenkommunikation in Deutschland. Bonn, Braunschweig: Verlag J. H. W. Dietz Nachfahren. 2001.

Braun, Alfred. Achtung, Achtung, Hier Ist Berlin! Aus der Geschichte des Deutschen Rundfunks in Berlin 1923–1932. Berlin: Haude & Spener. 1968.
*Keywords:* Radio Broadcasting – Germany – Berlin – History

Brown, Robert J. Robert John. Manipulating the Ether: the Power of Broadcast Radio in Thirties America. Jefferson NC: McFarland & Co. 1998.
*Keywords:* Roosevelt, Franklin D. (Franklin Delano), 1882–1945/War of the Worlds (Radio Program)/Radio Broadcasting – United States – History/Radio Broadcasting – United States – Social Aspects/Radio in Politics/Radio Journalism

Bruehl, Thomas Leo. A Descriptive History of the Frederic W. Ziv Company, Its Syndicated Broadcast Activities, and Its Transition to Television. Dissertation UCLA. Los Angeles CA 1972.
*Keywords*: Ziv, Frederic W/Frederic W. Ziv Company – History/Radio Broadcasting – United States – History/Television Broadcasting – United States – History/Dissertations, Academic – UCLA – Theater Arts

Camporesi, Valeria. Mass Culture and National Traditions: the B. B. C. and American Broadcasting, 1922–1954. Fucecchio: European Press Academic Publishing. 2001.

Cantor, Louis. Wheelin' on Beale: How WDIA-Memphis Became the Nation's First All-Black Radio Station and Created the Sound That Changed America. New York: Pharos Books. 1992.
*Keywords:* WDIA (Radio Station: Memphis TN) – History/Radio Broadcasting – United States – History/Afro-Americans in Radio Broadcasting/Afro-American Radio Stations

Columbia Broadcasting System, Inc. (ed.). Serious Music on the Columbia Broadcasting System: a Survey of Series, Soloists and Special Performances From 1927 Through 1938. New York: Columbia Broadcasting System. 1939.
*Keywords:* Radio and Music/Radio Programs, Musical/Radio Broadcasting – United States – History

Corwin, Norman Lewis, and Douglas Bell. Years of the Electric Ear: Norman Corwin. Metuchen NJ: Directors Guild of America. Scarecrow Press. 1994.
*Keywords:* Corwin, Norman Lewis, 1910/Radio Broadcasting – United States – History/Radio Producers and Directors – United States – Interviews

Cox, Jim. Say Goodnight, Gracie: the Last Years of Network Radio. Jefferson NC: McFarland & Co. 2002.
*Keywords:* Radio Broadcasting – United States – History

Craig, Douglas B. Fireside Politics: Radio and Political Culture in the United States, 1920–1940. Baltimore MD: Johns Hopkins University Press. 2000.
*Keywords:* Radio Broadcasting – United States – History/Radio Broadcasting – Political Aspects – United States – History/Radio Broadcasting Policy – United States – History/Radio in Politics – United States – History

Dahl, Peter P. Arbeitersender und Volksempfänger: Proletarische Radio-Bewegung und Bürgerlicher Rundfunk bis 1945. Frankfurt am Main: Syndikat. 1978.
*Keywords:* Radio Broadcasting – Germany – History/Radio in Politics – Germany – History/Socialism – Germany/Working Class – Germany/Radio in Propaganda – Germany

Deutsches Rundfunkarchiv (ed.). "Hier Spricht Berlin –": Der Neubeginn des Rundfunks in Berlin 1945. Potsdam: Verlag für Berlin-Brandenburg. 1995.
*Keywords:* Radio Broadcasting – Germany – Berlin – History

Diller, Ansgar. Rundfunkpolitik im Dritten Reich. München: Deutscher Taschenbuch Verlag. 1980.
*Keywords:* Radio Broadcasting Policy – Germany – History/Broadcasting Policy – Germany – History

Diller, Ansgar, and Wolfgang Mühl-Benninghaus. Berichterstattung über den Nürnberger Prozess gegen die Hauptkriegsverbrecher 1945/46: Edition und Dokumentation Ausgewählter Rundfunkquellen. Deutsches Rundfunkarchiv. Potsdam: Verlag für Berlin-Brandenburg. 1998.
*Keywords:* Nuremberg Trial of Major German War Criminals, Nuremberg, Germany, 1945–1946 – Press Coverage – Germany Sources/Radio Broadcasting – Germany

Donahue, Hugh Carter. The Battle to Control Broadcast News: Who Owns the First Amendment? Cambridge MA: MIT Press. 1989.
*Keywords:* Equal Time Rule (Broadcasting) – United States – History/Fairness Doctrine (Broadcasting) – United States – History

Douglas, George H. The Early Days of Radio Broadcasting. Jefferson, NC: McFarland. 1987.
*Keywords:* Radio Broadcasting – United States – History/Radio Programs – United States – History/Radio Supplies Industry – United States – History

Douglas, Susan J. Susan Jeanne. Listening in: Radio and the American Imagination: From Amos 'n' Andy and Edward R. Murrow to Wolfman Jack and Howard Stern. New York, N.Y: Times Books. 1999.
*Keywords:* Radio Broadcasting – United States – History/Radio Programs – United States – History/Radio Broadcasting – Social Aspects – United States

Douglas, Susan Jeanne. Inventing American Broadcasting, 1899–1922. Baltimore MA: Johns Hopkins University Press. 1989.
*Keywords:* Radio Broadcasting – United States – History/Radio – United States – History

Duncan, James H. American Radio, Tenth Anniversary Issue, 1976–1986: a Prose and Statistical History. Kalamazoo MI: Duncan's American Radio. 1986.
*Keywords:* Radio Broadcasting – United States – History/Radio Broadcasting – United States – Statistics/Radio Stations – United States – Statistics

Ely, Melvin Patrick. The Adventures of Amos 'n' Andy: A Social History of an American Phenomenon. New York, Toronto, New York: Free Press. Maxwell Macmillan Canada. Maxwell Macmillan International. 1991.
*Keywords:* Amos 'n' Andy (Radio Program)/Amos 'n' Andy (Television Program)/Broadcasting – Social Aspects – United States/Popular Culture – United States/Afro-Americans in Television Broadcasting/Afro-Americans on Television/United States – Race Relations/United States – Social Conditions

Engelman, Ralph. Public Radio and Television in America: a Political History. Thousand Oaks CA: Sage Publications. 1996.
*Keywords:* Public Broadcasting – Political Aspects – United States – History/Radio Broadcasting – Political Aspects – United States – History/Television Broadcasting – Political Aspects – United States – History

Erenberg, Lewis A. Steppin' Out: New York Nightlife and the Transformation of American Culture, 1890–1930. Chicago: University of Chicago Press. 1984.
*Keywords:* Popular Culture – New York (State) – New York/Music-Halls (Variety-Theaters, Cabarets, etc.) – New York/Restaurants /New York (NY) – Social Life and Customs

——. Swingin' the Dream: Big Band Jazz and the Rebirth of American Culture. Chicago: The University of Chicago Press. 1998.
*Keywords:* Big Band Music – History and Criticism/Jazz – History and Criticism/Popular Culture – United States

Erenberg, Lewis A., and Susan E. Hirsch. The War in American Culture: Society and Consciousness During World War II. Chicago: University of Chicago Press. 1996.
*Keywords:* World War, 1939–1945 – Social Aspects – United States/ United States – Civilization – 1918–1945

Estermann, Monika, and Edgar Lersch. Buch, Buchhandel und Rundfunk 1945–1949. Wiesbaden: Harrassowitz. 1997.
*Keywords:* Publishers and Publishing – Germany – History – 20th Century – Congresses/Radio and Literature – Germany – History – 20th Century – Congresses/German Literature – 20th Century – History and Criticism – Congresses

——. Buch, Buchhandel und Rundfunk 1950–1960. Deutsches Literaturarchiv (Germany). Wiesbaden: Harrassowitz. 1999.
*Keywords:* Publishers and Publishing – Germany – History – 20th Century – Congresses/Radio and Literature – Germany – History – 20th Century – Congresses/German Literature – 20th Century – History and Criticism – Congresses

Fasse, Norbert. Vom Adelsarchiv zur NS-Propaganda: Der symptomatische Lebenslauf des Reichsrundfunkintendanten Heinrich Glasmeier (1892–1945). Bielefeld: Verlag für Regionalgeschichte. 2001.
*Keywords:* Glasmeier, Heinrich, B. 1892/Radio Broadcasting – Germany – History – 20th Century/Radio in Propaganda/National Socialism/Nazis – Biography

Flamm, Leo. Westfalen und der Westdeutsche Rundfunk: Eine rundfunkhistorische Studie zur Regionalisierung. Köln: Kohlhammer. Grote. 1993.
*Keywords:* Westdeutscher Rundfunk – History/Radio Broadcasting – Germany – North Rhine-Westphalia – History/Radio Broadcasting – Social Aspects – Germany – North Rhine-Westphalia – History/ Regionalism – Germany – History

Fohrbeck, Karla, and Andreas Johannes Wiesand. Der WDR als Kultur- und Wirtschaftsfaktor. Köln: Kohlhammer. Grote. 1989.
*Keywords:* Westdeutscher Rundfunk – History/Radio Broadcasting – Germany (West) – History

Fornatale, Peter, and Joshua E. Mills. Radio in the Television Age. Woodstock NY: Overlook Press. 1980.
*Keywords:* Radio Broadcasting – United States – History

Foust, James C. Big Voices of the Air: the Battle Over Clear Channel Radio. Ames IO: Iowa State University Press. 2000.
*Keywords:* Radio Frequency Allocation – United States – History – 20th Century/Radio Broadcasting Policy – United States – History – 20th Century

scholarly debate about these things. Rather, he presents an authoritative visual master narrative on the "Third Reich" that suggests certainty and unambiguity where there actually is controversy. This has earned him much severe criticism from professional historians, and from a scholarly point of view rightly so. However, what his critics fail to acknowledge is that Knopp is not at all interested in these academic questions but very much interested in identity and memory politics. His documentaries are about healing the wounds of the past, about reconciliation between former combatants and enemies, about life stories and emotions hitherto suppressed. The enormous response of the audience to Knopp's documentaries only underlines this – his documentaries are really events of social communication through which German society tries to reach an understanding about its past and its historical identity in a collective discussion effort. His documentaries on the Nazi past are meant to be contributions to the present orientation of the Germans in the world. In this context, I can imagine worse forms of dealing with the Nazi past than trying to strengthen a democratic and pro-Western consensus in a postwar and post-Cold War Germany by putting Hitler and the "Third Reich" on television.

Another point seems worth mentioning in context with the phenomenon of Guido Knopp. In a radically changed, largely Americanized television landscape, full of fun and music videos, talk and game shows, soccer and *real* pornography, Knopp at least manages to put the Nazi past on the screen. He at least communicates history to a mass audience in Germany, and even the otherwise critical Kansteiner has to admit that Knopp has invented a new form of "interesting, visually and emotionally compelling documentaries" that actually reaches a large number of people. Now, you can argue that it is bad history that Knopp does, that his interpretation of Hitler and the "Third Reich" is flawed, biased and outdated – and I willingly go along with that – but at least *there is history on the screen* where otherwise there would probably be yet another game show. Knopp keeps the past alive on television, and who knows how many people in the audience might take Knopp's documentaries as an inspiration to study the subject on their own a little further. This, however, is the most important question that needs to be answered by media and communications historians: who is the audience, and *how does it relate* to the things on television and in the movies?

# Notes

1. Jörg Requate, "Öffentlichkeit und Medien als Gegenstände histor-
ischer Analyse," *Geschichte und Gesellschaft* 25 (1999), 15.
2. Jürgen Habermas, *Theorie des kommunikativen Handelns*, 2 vols.,
Frankfurt a. M., 1981; Jürgen Habermas, *Strukturwandel der Öffentlichkeit: Untersuchungen zu einer Kategorie der bürgerlichen Gesellschaft.
Mit einem Vorwort zur Neuauflage 1990*, Frankfurt a. M., 1990; Niklas
Luhmann, "Evolution und Geschichte," in Niklas Luhmann, *Soziologische Aufklärung*, Opladen, 1975, vol. 2 pp. 150–69; Niklas Luhmann,
*Gesellschaftstruktur und Semantik: Studien zur Wissenssoziologie der
modernen Gesellschaft*, 4 vols, Frankfurt a. M., 1980–95; Niklas Luhmann, "Geschichte als Prozeß und die Theorie sozio-kultureller Evolution," in Niklas Luhmann, *Soziologische Aufklärung*, Opladen, 1981, vol.
3, pp. 178–97; Niklas Luhmann, "Veränderungen im System gesellschaftlicher Kommunikation und die Massenmedien," in Niklas Luhmann,
*Soziologische Aufklärung*, Opladen, 1981, vol. 3, pp. 309–20; Niklas
Luhmann, *Soziale Systeme: Grundriß einer allgemeinen Theorie*, Frankfurt a. M., 1984; Niklas Luhmann, "Wie ist Bewußtsein an Kommunikation beteiligt?" in Niklas Luhmann, *Soziologische Aufklärung*, Opladen,
1995, vol. 6, pp. 37–54; Niklas Luhmann, "Was ist Kommunikation?" in
Niklas Luhmann, *Soziologische Aufklärung*, Opladen, 1995, vol. 6, pp.
113–24; Niklas Luhmann, *Die neuzeitlichen Wissenschaften und die
Phänomenologie*, Vienna, 1996; Niklas Luhmann, *Die Gesellschaft der
Gesellschaft*, Frankfurt a. M., 1997. For a detailed comparison of the two
approaches to communication see: Volker Depkat, "Kommunikationsgeschichte zwischen Mediengeschichte und der Geschichte sozialer
Kommunikation," in Karl-Heinz Spieß (ed.), *Medien der Kommunikation
im Mittelalter*, Stuttgart, 2003, pp. 9–48.
3. Nolte has exemplified this in his study on the history of German
notions of social order in the twentieth century. Paul Nolte, *Die Ordnung
der deutschen Gesellschaft: Selbstentwurf und Selbstbeschreibung im 20.
Jahrhundert*, Munich, 2000.
4. For the concept of social self-description see: Luhmann, *Die
Gesellschaft der Gesellschaft*, 866–1149.
5. Although there is a highly controversial scholarly debate about how
to judge the efforts of West German society to come to grips with its Nazi
past, one cannot really deny that the "Third Reich" and its consequences
were a central theme in the Federal Republic from its foundation onwards.
The discussions took place on different levels, had different forms and
varying degrees of intensity and publicity to be sure, but there can hardly

Fromhold, Martina. Hermann Kasack und der Rundfunk der Weimarer Republik: Ein Beitrag zur Geschichte des Wechselverhältnisses zwischen Literatur und Rundfunk. Aachen: Alano, Rader Publikationen. 1990.
*Keywords:* Kasack, Hermann, 1896–1966 – Appreciation – Germany/ Radio Broadcasting – Germany – History – 20th Century

Führer, Karl Christian. Wirtschaftsgeschichte des Rundfunks in der Weimarer Republik. Potsdam: Verlag für Berlin-Brandenburg. 1997.
*Keywords:* Radio Broadcasting – Germany – History/Germany – Economic Conditions – 1918–1945

Galle, Petra, and Axel Schuster. Archiv- und Sammlungsgut des RIAS Berlin: Ein Findbuch zum Bestand im Deutschen Rundfunkarchiv. Potsdam: Verlag für Berlin-Brandenburg. 2000.
*Keywords:* Rundfunk Im Amerikanischen Sektor (Berlin, Germany) Archives Catalogs/Deutsches Rundfunkarchiv – Catalogs/Radio Broadcasting – Germany – Berlin – History – Archival Resources Catalogs

Gillum, Marion, and Jorg Wyrschowy. Politische Musik in der Zeit des Nationalsozialismus: Ein Verzeichnis der Tondokumente (1933–1945). Deutsches Rundfunkarchiv. Potsdam: Verlag für Berlin-Brandenburg. 2000.
*Keywords:* Deutsches Rundfunkarchiv – Catalogs/Political Ballads and Songs – Germany – 20th Century – Discography Catalogs/National Music – Germany – 20th Century – Discography Catalogs/World War, 1939–1945 – Europe – Songs and Music – Discography Catalogs/ Radio Programs, Musical – Germany – Discography Catalogs

Glassgen, Heinz. Katholische Kirche und Rundfunk in der Bundesrepublik Deutschland, 1945–1963. Berlin: V. Spiess. 1983.
*Keywords:* Catholic Church – Germany (West) – History – 20th Century/Radio in Religion – Catholic Church – History/Radio in Religion – Germany (West) – History/Germany (West) – Church History

Godfrey, Donald G, and Frederic A Leigh. Historical Dictionary of American Radio. Westport CT. Greenwood Press. 1998.
*Keywords:* Radio Broadcasting – United States – History – Dictionaries/Radio – United States – History – Dictionaries

Greguletz, Alexander, (ed.). Inventar der Manuskriptbestände des Berliner Rundfunks (1945–1950). Deutsches Rundfunkarchiv. Potsdam: Verlag für Berlin-Brandenburg. 1999.
*Keywords:* Berliner Rundfunk/Radio Scripts – Bibliography – Catalogs

Groth, Peter. Hörspiele und Hörspieltheorien sozialkritischer Schriftsteller in der Weimarer Republik: Studien zum Verhältnis von Rundfunk und Literatur. Berlin: Spiess. 1980.

*Keywords:* Authors, German – 20th Century – Political and Social Views/German Drama – 20th Century – History and Criticism/Radio Plays – History and Criticism

Haaf, Oskar. Beim Gongschlag – München: Olzog. 1983.
*Keywords:* Haaf, Oskar, 1905/Radio Broadcasters – Germany – Biography/Radio Broadcasting – Germany – History

Halder, Winfrid. Exilrufe nach Deutschland: Die Rundfunkreden von Thomas Mann, Paul Tillich und Johannes R. Becher 1940–1945. Analyse, Wirkung, Bedeutung. Münster: LIT. 2002.
*Keywords:* Mann, Thomas, 1875–1955/Tillich, Paul, 1886–1965/ Becher, Johannes Robert, 1891–1958/World War, 1939–1945 – Propaganda/Radio Broadcasting – United States – History – 20th Century

Halper, Donna L. Radio Music Directing. Boston: Focal Press. 1991.
*Keywords:* Radio Programs, Musical – Planning/Radio Music Directors/ Radio – Production and Direction/Radio Broadcasting – United States – History

Hamm, Margot, Bettina Hasselbring, and Michael Henker. Der Ton, das Bild: Die Bayern und ihr Rundfunk 1924–1949–1999: Begleitbuch zur Ausstellung des Hauses der Bayerischen Geschichte und des Bayer-ischen Rundfunks: 13. April bis 4. Juli 1999, Funkhaus, München: 22. Juli bis 17. Oktober 1999, Museum für Post und Kommunikation, Nürnberg. Augsburg: Haus der Bayerischen Geschichte. 1999.
*Keywords:* Munich. Bayerischer Rundfunk – History Exhibitions/ Munich. Bayerisches Fernsehen – History Exhibitions/Radio Broadcast-ing – Germany – Bavaria – History Exhibitions/Television Broad-casting – Germany – Bavaria – History Exhibitions

Hampf, Michaela. Freies Radio in den USA: Die Pacifica-Foundation, 1946–1965. Münster: LIT. 2000.
*Keywords:* Pacifica Foundation – History/Pacifica Radio – History/ Public Radio – United States – History/Radio Broadcasting – United States – History

Hilliard, Robert L., and Michael C. Keith. The Broadcast Century: A Biography of American Broadcasting. Boston: Focal Press. 1992.
*Keywords:* Broadcasting – United States – History/Broadcasting – United States – Biography

——. The Broadcast Century and Beyond: A Biography of American Broadcasting. Boston: Focal Press. 2001.
*Keywords:* Broadcasting – United States – History/Broadcasting – United States – Biography

Hilmes, Michele. Hollywood and Broadcasting: From Radio to Cable. Urbana, IL: University of Illinois Press. 1990.
*Keywords:* Broadcasting – United States – History/Motion Picture Industry – California – Los Angeles – Influence/Motion Picture Studios – California – Los Angeles – Influence/Hollywood (Los Angeles, CA) – History
——. Only Connect: a Cultural History of Broadcasting in the United States. Belmont CA: Wadsworth/Thomson Learning. 2002.
*Keywords:* Broadcasting – United States – History – 20th Century/ United States – Social Life and Customs – 20th Century
——. Radio Voices: American Broadcasting, 1922–1952. Minneapolis MN: University of Minnesota Press. 1997.
*Keywords:* Radio Broadcasting – United States – History
Hilmes, Michele, and Jason Loviglio. Radio Reader: Essays in the Cultural History of Radio. New York: Routledge. 2002.
*Keywords:* Radio Broadcasting – History
Horten, Gerd. Radio Goes to War: The Cultural Politics of Propaganda During World War II. Berkeley CA: University of California Press. 2002.
*Keywords:* Radio Broadcasting – Political Aspects – United States/ Radio in Propaganda – United States – History – 20th Century/Radio Broadcasting – United States – History – 20th Century
Huff, W. A. Kelly. Regulating the Future: Broadcasting Technology and Governmental Control. Westport CT: Greenwood Press. 2001.
*Keywords:* Broadcasting – United States – History – 20th Century/ Broadcasting – Political Aspects – United States – 20th Century
Jarvik, Laurence Ariel, and David Horowitz. Public Broadcasting and the Public Trust. Center for the Study of Popular Culture. Los Angeles CA: Center for the Study of Popular Culture. 1995.
*Keywords:* Public Broadcasting – United States – History/Television Broadcasting – United States – History/Radio Broadcasting – United States – History
Jenter, Steffen. Alfred Braun – Radiopionier und Reporter in Berlin. Deutsches Rundfunkarchiv. Potsdam: Verlag tur Berlin-Brandenburg. 1998.
*Keywords:* Braun, Alfred, 1888–1978/Radio Journalists – Germany – Biography
Jung, Donald J. The Federal Communications Commission, the Broadcast Industry, and the Fairness Doctrine, 1981–1987. Lanham MD: University Press of America. 1996.
*Keywords:* United States. Federal Communications Commission – History/Fairness Doctrine (Broadcasting) – United States – History

Kapfer, Herbert, Christoph Lindenmeyer, and Katarina Agathos. Vom Sendespiel zur Medienkunst: Die Geschichte des Hörspiels im Bayerischen Rundfunk: Das Gesamtverzeichnis der Hörspielproduktion des Bayerischen Rundfunks, 1949–1999. München. Bayerischer Rundfunk. München: Belleville. 1999.
*Keywords:* Radio Programs – Germany Catalogs/Radio Plays, German Catalogs/Bayerischer Rundfunk

Keith, Michael C. Sounds in the Dark: All-Night Radio in American Life. Ames, IO: Iowa State University Press. 2001.
*Keywords:* Radio Broadcasting – United States – History/Radio Broadcasters – United States Interviews/Talk Shows – United States

——. Talking Radio: An Oral History of American Radio in the Television Age. Armonk NY: M. E. Sharpe. 2000.
*Keywords:* Radio Broadcasting – United States – History

——. Voices in the Purple Haze: Underground Radio and the Sixties. Westport CT: Praeger. 1997.
*Keywords:* Alternative Radio Broadcasting – United States – History – 20th Century/Subculture – United States – History – 20th Century/United States – Social Conditions – 1960–1980

Kisseloff, Jeff. The Box: An Oral History of Television, 1920–1961. New York: Viking. 1995.
*Keywords:* Television Broadcasting – United States – History/Television Producers and Directors – United States – Interviews/Television Actors and Actresses – United States – Interviews/Television Personalities – United States – Interviews

Kleinsteuber, Hans-Jürgen, Denis McQuail, and Karen Siune. Electronic Media and Politics in Western Europe: Euromedia Research Group Handbook of National Systems. Euromedia Research Group. Frankfurt, New York: Campus Verlag. 1986.
*Keywords:* Mass Media Policy – Europe/Mass Media – Political Aspects – Europe/Radio Broadcasting – Europe/Television Broadcasting – Europe

Kohler, Wolfram, and Klaus Berg. Der NDR zwischen Programm und Politik: Beiträge zu seiner Geschichte. Hannover: Schlüter. 1991.
*Keywords:* Norddeutscher Rundfunk – History/Radio Broadcasting – Germany, Northern – History

Krugler, David F. The Voice of America and the Domestic Propaganda Battles, 1945–1953. Columbia MO: University of Missouri Press. 2000.
*Keywords:* Voice of America (Organization) – History/International Broadcasting – United States – History

Kutsch, Arnulf. Rundfunkwissenschaft im Dritten Reich: Geschichte des Instituts für Rundfunkwissenschaft der Universität Freiburg. München, New York: K. G. Saur. 1985.
*Keywords:* History/Radio Broadcasting – Germany – Study and Teaching (Higher) – Germany – History

Lacey, Kate. Feminine Frequencies: Gender, German Radio, and the Public Sphere, 1923–1945. Ann Arbor, MI: University of Michigan Press. 1996.
*Keywords:* Broadcasting – Germany – Employees/Mass Media and Women – Germany/Women in the Mass Media Industry – Germany/ Radio Broadcasting – Germany – History

Lasar, Matthew. Pacifica Radio the Rise of an Alternative Network. Philadelphia: Temple University Press. 2000
*Keywords*: Alternative radio broadcasting – United States

Lenk, Carsten. Die Erscheinung des Rundfunks: Einführung und Nutzung eines neuen Mediums 1923–1932. Opladen: Westdeutscher Verlag. 1997.
*Keywords:* Radio Broadcasting – Germany – History/Popular Culture – Germany – History – 20th Century

Leonhard, Joachim-Felix. Programmgeschichte des Hörfunks in der Weimarer Republik. München: Deutscher Taschenbuch Verlag. 1997.
*Keywords:* Radio Broadcasting – Germany – History

Lerg, Winfried B. Die Entstehung des Rundfunks in Deutschland: Herkunft und Entwicklung eines publizistischen Mittels. Frankfurt am Main: J. Knecht. 1970.
*Keywords:* Radio Broadcasting – Germany – History

———. Rundfunkpolitik in der Weimarer Republik. München: Deutscher Taschenbuch Verlag. 1980.
*Keywords:* Radio Broadcasting Policy – Germany – History/Broadcasting Policy – Germany – History

Lieberman, Philip A. Radio's Morning Show Personalities: Early Hour Broadcasters and Deejays From the 1920s to the 1990s. Jefferson NC: McFarland & Co. 1996.
*Keywords:* Radio Broadcasters – United States – Biography/Disc Jockeys – United States – Biography/Radio Broadcasting – United States – History

Low, Bernd. Hörspiel, 1945–1949: Eine Dokumentation. Deutsches Rundfunkarchiv. Potsdam: Verlag für Berlin-Brandenburg. 1997.
*Keywords:* Radio Programs – Germany Catalogs/Radio Plays, German Catalogs

Lucae, Gustav. 40 Jahre Rundfunkwirtschaft in Deutschland, 1923–1963: Unter besonderer Berücksichtigung der Funkindustrie und des "Verband der Funkindustrie (VDFI)", der jetzigen "Interessengemeinschaft für

Rundfunkschutzrechte (IGR)". Düsseldorf: Eigenverlag der "IGR". 1963.
*Keywords:* Verband Der Funkindustrie (Germany)/Interessenge-meinschaft Fur Rundfunkschutzrechte (Germany)/Radio Broadcasting – Germany – History/Radio Broadcasting – Germany (West) – History/ Television Broadcasting – Germany (West) – History

Maatje, Christian. Verkaufte Luft: Die Kommerzialisierung des Rund-funks. Hörfunkwerbung in Deutschland (1923–1936). Verlag für Berlin-Brandenburg. 2000.
*Keywords:* Radio Advertising – Germany – 20th Century

MacDonald, J. Fred. Don't Touch That Dial! Radio Programming in American Life, 1920–1960. Chicago: Nelson-Hall. 1979.
*Keywords:* Radio Broadcasting – United States – History/Popular Culture – United States

Maltin, Leonard. The Great American Broadcast: A Celebration of Radio's Golden Age. New York: Dutton. 1997.
*Keywords:* Radio Broadcasting – United States – History

Marssolek, Inge, and Adelheid von Saldern. Radiozeiten: Herrschaft, Alltag, Gesellschaft (1924–1960). Deutsches Rundfunkarchiv. Pots-dam: Verlag für Berlin-Brandenburg. 1999.
*Keywords:* Radio Broadcasting – Germany – History Congresses

Marssolek, Inge, Adelheid von Saldern, and Daniela Munkel. Radio im Nationalsozialismus: Zwischen Lenkung und Ablenkung. Tübingen: Edition Diskord. 1998.
*Keywords:* Radio Broadcasting – Germany – History/Radio in Propa-ganda – Germany/Radio Broadcasting – Social Aspects – Germany – History

McChesney, Robert Waterman. The Battle for America's Ears and Minds: the Debate Over the Control and Structure of American Radio Broad-casting, 1930–1935. Dissertation, University of Washington. Ann Arbor MI. 1989.
*Keywords*: Radio Broadcasting – United States – History/Radio in Politics – United States – History/Radio Broadcasting Policy – United States – History

——. Telecommunications, Mass Media, and Democracy: The Battle for the Control of U.S. Broadcasting, 1928–1935. New York: Oxford University Press. 1993.
*Keywords:* Radio Broadcasting Policy – United States – History

McMahon, Morgan E. A Flick of the Switch, 1930–1950. Palos Verdes Peninsula CA: Vintage Radio. 1975.

*Keywords:* Radio – History/Radio – Equipment and Supplies – Collectors and Collecting/Radio Broadcasting – United States – History

Mendelsohn, John. German Radio Intelligence and the *Soldatensender*. New York: Garland. 1989.
*Keywords:* United States. Office of Strategic Services – History – Sources/World War, 1939–1945 – Secret Service – Germany – Sources/ World War, 1939–1945 – Cryptography – History – Sources/Military Intelligence – History – 20th Century – Sources/Radio Broadcasting – Germany – History – Sources

Meyer, Andreas. Kriminalhörspiele, 1924–1994: Eine Dokumentation. Deutsches Rundfunkarchiv. Potsdam: Verlag für Berlin-Brandenburg. 1998.
*Keywords:* Detective and Mystery Radio Programs – Germany Catalogs/ Radio Plays, German Catalogs

Mitchell, Curtis. Cavalcade of Broadcasting. Chicago: Follett Pub. Co. 1970.
*Keywords:* Broadcasting – United States – History

Mott, Robert L. Radio Sound Effects: Who Did It, and How, in the Era of Live Broadcasting. Jefferson NC: McFarland. 1993.
*Keywords:* Radio Broadcasting – United States – History/Radio Broadcasting – Sound Effects – Anecdotes

Naber, Hermann, Helga Gutsche, and Marita Gleiss. Dichtung und Rundfunk – 1929: Ein Dokument der Stiftung Archiv der Akademie der Künste. Akademie der Künste (Berlin, Germany). Stiftung Archiv. Berlin: Stiftung Archiv der Akademie der Künste. 2000.
*Keywords:* Radio Broadcasting – Germany – History Congresses/Radio Broadcasting – Germany – History – Sources/Radio and Literature

Nachman, Gerald. Raised on Radio: In Quest of the Lone Ranger, Jack Benny. New York: Pantheon Books. 1998.
*Keywords:* Radio Broadcasting – United States History

O'Connell, Mary C. Connections: Reflections on Sixty Years of Broadcasting. New York: National Broadcasting Corporation. 1986.
*Keywords:* National Broadcasting Company, Inc/Broadcasting – United States – History

Paper, Lewis J. Empire: William S. Paley and the Making of CBS. New York: St. Martin's Press. 1987.
*Keywords:* Paley, William S. (William Samuel), 1901/Cbs Inc – Biography/Broadcasting – United States – History/Broadcasters – United States – Biography

Pegler, Westbrook. George Spelvin, American; and Fireside Chats. New York: Scribner. 1942.

Penka, Thomas. "Geistzerstäuber" Rundfunk: Sozialgeschichte des Südfunkprogramms in der Weimarer Republik. Deutsches Rundfunkarchiv. Potsdam: Verlag für Berlin-Brandenburg. 1999.
*Keywords:* Süddeutscher Rundfunk/Radio Broadcasting – Political Aspects – Germany – History/Radio Broadcasting – Social Aspects – Germany – History/Radio Programs – Germany – History/Germany – History – 1918–1933

Pohle, Heinz. Der Rundfunk als Instrument der Politik. Hamburg: Verlag Hans Bredow-Institut. 1955.
*Keywords:* Radio Broadcasting – Germany – History/Radio in Propaganda/Germany – Politics and Government. – 1918–1933/Germany – Politics and Government – 1933–1945

Poteet, G. Howard. Radio! Dayton OH: Pflaum Publications. 1975.
*Keywords:* Radio Broadcasting – United States – History

Projektgruppe Programmgeschichte. Zur Programmgeschichte des Weimarer Rundfunks. Frankfurt am Main: Deutsches Rundfunkarchiv, Historisches Archiv der ARD. 1986.
*Keywords:* Radio Programs – Germany – History and Criticism/Radio Broadcasting – Germany – History

Pulitzer, Joseph, and Michael E. Pulitzer. Pulitzer Publishing Company: Newspapers and Broadcasting in the Public Interest. New York: Newcomen Society of the United States. 1988.
*Keywords:* Pulitzer, Joseph, 1847–1911/Pulitzer, Joseph, 1885–1955/ Pulitzer Publishing Company/St. Louis Post-Dispatch

Pusateri, C. Joseph. Enterprise in Radio: WWL and the Business of Broadcasting in America. Washington, DC: University Press of America. 1980.
*Keywords:* WWL (Radio Station: New Orleans, LA ) – History/Radio Broadcasting – United States – History

Reichardt, Ernst Hartmut. Grundzüge Der Rundfunkpolitik in Deutschland: Ein Deutsches Syndrom? Vergleichende Analyse der Entwicklung deutscher Rundfunkpolitik an Hand von Einführungssituationen neuer Medien (1920–1980). Frankfurt am Main: Haag & Herchen. 1984.
*Keywords:* Radio Broadcasting Policy – Germany (West) – History/ Radio Broadcasting Policy – Germany – History

Riedel, Heide. Lieber Rundfunk – 75 Jahre Hörergeschichte(n). Berlin: Vistas. 1999.
*Keywords:* Radio Broadcasting – Germany – History

Rimmele, Lilian-Dorette. Der Rundfunk in Norddeutschland 1933–1945: Ein Beitrag zur nationalsozialistischen Organisations-, Personal- und Kulturpolitik. Hamburg: H. Lüdke. 1977.
*Keywords:* Radio Broadcasting Policy – Germany, Northern – History

Rindfleisch, Hans. Technik im Rundfunk: Ein Stück deutscher Rundfunk-geschichte von den Anfängen bis zum Beginn der Achtziger Jahre. Norderstedt: Mensing. 1985.
*Keywords:* Radio Broadcasting – Germany – History/Television Broadcasting – Germany – History
Roller, Walter. Tondokumente zur Kultur- und Zeitgeschichte 1933–1935: Ein Verzeichnis. Potsdam: Verlag für Berlin-Brandenburg. 2000.
*Keywords:* Deutsches Rundfunkarchiv – Catalogs/Sound Recordings – Germany – Catalogs/Germany – History – 1933–1945 Discography
Roosevelt, Franklin Franklin Delano, Kenneth Yeilding, and Paul Howard Carlson. Ah, That Voice: The Fireside Chats of Franklin Delano Roosevelt. Presidential Museum. Odessa, TX: John Ben Shepperd, Jr. Library of the Presidents, Presidential Museum. 1974.
*Keywords:* United States – Politics and Government – 1933–1945/ United States – Economic Policy – 1933–1945
Rosen, Philip T. The Modern Stentors: Radio Broadcasters and the Federal Government, 1920–1934. Westport CT: Greenwood Press. 1980.
*Keywords:* Radio Broadcasting – United States – History/Radio Broadcasting Policy – United States – History
Saldern, Adelheid von, Inge Marssolek, Daniela Munkel, Monika Pater, and Uta C. Schmidt. Radio in der DDR der Fünfziger Jahre: Zwischen Lenkung und Ablenkung. Tübingen: Diskord. 1998.
*Keywords:* Radio Broadcasting – Germany (East) – History/Germany (East) – History
Savage, Barbara Dianne. Broadcasting Freedom: Radio, War, and the Politics of Race, 1938–1948. Chapel Hill, NC: University of North Carolina Press. 1999.
*Keywords:* Radio Broadcasting – Social Aspects – United States – History – 20th Century/Radio Programs – United States – History – 20th Century/World War, 1939–1945 – United States/Afro-Americans – Civil Rights – History – 20th Century/Afro-Americans in Radio Broadcasting – History – 20th Century/United States – Race Relations
Schechter, Danny. News Dissector: Passions, Pieces, and Polemics, 1960–2000. New York: Akashic. 2001.
*Keywords:* Schechter, Danny/Counterculture – United States – History – 20th Century/Alternative Radio Broadcasting – United States – History – 20th Century
Schildt, Axel. Moderne Zeiten Freizeit, Massenmedien und "Zeitgeist" in der Bundesrepublik der 50er Jahre. Hamburg: Christians. 1995
*Keywords*: Germany (West) – Social life and customs/Germany (West) – Social conditions

Schiller-Lerg, Sabine. Walter Benjamin und der Rundfunk: Programmarbeit zwischen Theorie und Praxis. München, New York: K. G. Saur. 1984.
*Keywords:* Benjamin, Walter, 1892–1940 – Knowledge – Communication/Benjamin, Walter, 1892–1940/Authors, German – 20th Century – Biography/Journalists – Germany – Biography/Radio Journalism – Germany – History

Schneider, Christof. Nationalsozialismus als Thema im Programm des Nordwestdeutschen Rundfunks (1945–1948). Potsdam: Verlag für Berlin-Brandenburg. 1999.
*Keywords:* Nordwestdeutscher Rundfunk/National Socialism/Radio Programs – Germany

Schneider, Irmela. Radio-Kultur in der Weimarer Republik: Eine Dokumentation: Mit einer Einleitung. Tübingen: G. Narr. 1984.
*Keywords:* Radio Broadcasting – Germany – History/Radio Plays – History and Criticism

Schütte, Wolfgang. Die Westdeutsche Funkstunde: Frühgeschichte des WDR in Dokumenten. Köln, Berlin: Grote. 1973.
*Keywords:* Westdeutscher Rundfunk/Radio Broadcasting – Germany (West) – History

Schwoch, James. The American Radio Industry and Its Latin American Activities, 1900–1939. Urbana IL: University of Illinois Press. 1990.
*Keywords:* Radio Broadcasting – Economic Aspects – Latin America – History/Capitalism – Latin America – History/Capitalism – United States – History/Radio-Broadcasting – Economic Aspects – United States – History

Settel, Irving. A Pictorial History of Radio. New York: Grosset & Dunlap. 1967.
*Keywords:* Radio Broadcasting – United States – History

Sies, Luther F. Encyclopedia of American Radio, 1920–1960. Jefferson NC: McFarland. 2000.
*Keywords:* Radio Broadcasting – United States Encyclopedias

Slate, Sam J, and Joe Cook. It Sounds Impossible. New York: Macmillan. 1963.
*Keywords:* Radio Broadcasting – United States – History

Slotten, Hugh Richard. Radio and Television Regulation: Broadcast Technology in the United States, 1920–1960. Baltimore, MD: Johns Hopkins University Press. 2000.
*Keywords:* Broadcasting Policy – United States – History – 20th Century Broadcasting – United States – History – 20th Century

Smith, Curt. Voices of the Game: the First Full-Scale Overview of Baseball Broadcasting, 1921 to the Present. South Bend IN: Diamond Communications. 1987.
*Keywords:* Radio Broadcasting of Sports – United States – History/ Television Broadcasting of Sports – United States – History/Baseball – United States – History

Smulyan, Susan. Selling Radio: The Commercialization of American Broadcasting, 1920–1934. Washington DC: Smithsonian Institution Press. 1994.
*Keywords:* Radio-Broadcasting – Economic Aspects – United States – History/Radio Advertising – United States – History/Corporate Sponsorship – United States – History

Sobel, Robert. RCA. New York: Stein & Day/Publishers. 1986.
*Keywords:* Sarnoff, David, 1891–1971/Radio Corporation of America – History/Electronic Industries – United States – History/Broadcasting – United States – History

Soppe, August. Der Streit um das Hörspiel 1924/25: Entstehungsbedingungen eines Genres. Berlin: Spiess. 1978.
*Keywords:* Radio Broadcasting – Germany – History/Radio Plays – Germany

Stapper, Michael. Unterhaltungsmusik im Rundfunk der Weimarer Republik. Tutzing: H. Schneider. 2001.
*Keywords:* Radio and Music – Germany/Radio Music – Germany – History and Criticism/Popular Music – Germany – 1921–1930 – History and Criticism/Music – Germany – 20th Century – History and Criticism

Stein, Reiner. Vom Fernsehen und Radio der DDR zur ARD: Die Entwicklung und Neuordnung des Rundfunkwesens in den neuen Bundesländern. Marburg. Tectum. 2000.
*Keywords:* Broadcasting – Germany (East) – History

Steininger, Rolf. Deutschlandfunk: Die Vorgeschichte einer Rundfunkanstalt, 1949–1961. Ein Beitrag zur Innenpolitik der Bundesrepublik Deutschland. Berlin: V. Spiess. 1977.
*Keywords:* Deutschlandfunk – History/Radio Broadcasting – Germany (West) – History

Sterling, Christopher H., and John M. Kittross. Stay Tuned: A Concise History of American Broadcasting. Belmont CA: Wadsworth. 1990.
*Keywords:* Broadcasting – United States – History

——. Stay Tuned: a History of American Broadcasting. Mahwah NJ: Lawrence Erlbaum Associates. 2002.
*Keywords:* Broadcasting – United States – History

Streeter, Thomas. Selling the Air: A Critique of the Policy of Commercial Broadcasting in the United States. Chicago: University of Chicago Press. 1996.
*Keywords:* Broadcasting Policy – United States/Broadcasting – Law and Legislation – United States/Broadcasting – United States – History
Stuhlmann, Andreas. Radio-Kultur und Hör-Kunst: Zwischen Avantgarde und Popularkultur, 1923–2001. Würzburg: Königshausen und Neumann. 2001.
*Keywords*: Radio/Broadcasting/Germany/United States/History
Tichy, Roland, and Sylvia Dietl. Deutschland einig Rundfunkland? Eine Dokumentation zur Wiedervereinigung des deutschen Rundfunksystems 1989–1991. München: R. Fischer. 2000.
*Keywords:* Broadcasting – Germany – History
Tillich, Paul, Ronald H Stone, and Matthew Lon Weaver. Against the Third Reich: Paul Tillich's Wartime Addresses to Nazi Germany. Louisville KY: Westminster John Knox Press. 1998.
*Keywords:* Tillich, Paul, 1886–1965/Radio Broadcasting – United States – History – 20th Century/World War, 1939–1945 – Propaganda/ Propaganda, American/Jews – Persecutions – Germany/Radio Addresses, Debates, etc. – United States – History – 20th Century/ National Socialism/Propaganda, Anti-German – United States – History – 20th Century/Anti-Nazi Movement – United States
Tischler, Carola. Inventar der Quellen zum deutschsprachigen Rundfunk in der Sowjetunion (1929–1945): Bestände in deutschen und ausländischen Archiven und Bibliotheken. Deutsches Rundfunkarchiv. Potsdam: Verlag für Berlin-Brandenburg. 1997.
*Keywords:* International Broadcasting – Archival Resources/Radio Broadcasting – Germany – Archival Resources/Radio Broadcasting – Soviet Union – Archival Resources
United States. Federal Communications Commission. The Historical Evolution of the Commercial Network Broadcast System. Washington DC: The Commission. 1979.
*Keywords:* Broadcasting – United States – History
Viehoff, Reinhold. Literaturkritik im Rundfunk: Eine empirische Untersuchung von Sendereihen des Westdeutschen Rundfunks/Köln 1971–1973. Tübingen: Niemeyer. 1981.
*Keywords:* Book Review Radio Programs – Germany (West) – History and Criticism
Wagner, Hans-Ulrich. "Der gute Wille, etwas Neues zu schaffen": Das Hörspielprogramm in Deutschland von 1945 bis 1949. Potsdam: Verlag für Berlin-Brandenburg. 1997.

*Keywords:* Radio Plays, German – History and Criticism/Radio Programs – Germany – History and Criticism/Radio Broadcasting – Political Aspects – Germany/Radio Broadcasting – Germany – History
——. Gunter Eich und der Rundfunk: Essay und Dokumentation. Deutsches Rundfunkarchiv. Potsdam: Verlag für Berlin-Brandenburg. 1999.
*Keywords:* Eich, Gunter, 1907–1972 – Criticism and Interpretation/ Radio and Literature – Germany
——. Rückkehr in die Fremde? Remigranten und Rundfunk in Deutschland 1945–1955. Eine Dokumentation zu einem Thema der deutschen Nachkriegsgeschichte; Begleitbuch zur gleichnamigen Ausstellung. Arbeitskreis Selbständiger Kultur-Institute (Germany). Berlin: Vistas. 2000.
*Keywords:* Radio Broadcasting – Germany – History – 20th Century – Exhibitions/Return Migration – Germany – History – 20th Century – Exhibitions/Germany – History – 1945–1955 – Exhibitions
Walker, Jesse. Rebels on the Air: an Alternative History of Radio in America. New York: New York University Press. 2001.
*Keywords:* Radio Broadcasting – United States – History/Radio Broadcasting Policy – United States/Amateur Radio Stations – United States
Ward, Mark. Air of Salvation: The Story of Christian Broadcasting. Grand Rapids, MI: Baker Books. 1994.
*Keywords:* Religious Broadcasting – United States – History/Religious Broadcasting – Christianity – History
Wilke, Jürgen. Mediengeschichte der Bundesrepublik Deutschland. Köln: Böhlau. 1999.
*Keywords:* Broadcasting – Germany (West) – History/Communication – Political Aspects – Germany (West) – History/Mass Media – Germany (West) – History/Telecommunication – Germany (West) – History
Winter, William. Voice From America: a Broadcaster's Diary, 1941–1944. Pasig, Metro Manila, Philippines: Anvil. 1994.
*Keywords:* Winter, William/World War, 1939–1945 – Communications/ World War, 1939–1945 – Propaganda/World War, 1939–1945 – Asia/ Propaganda, American/Radio Broadcasting – United States – History – 20th Century/Radio Broadcasters – United States – Biography

Select Bibliography

# Part V

Ahren, Yizhak. Das Lehrstück "Holocaust": Zur Wirkungspsychologie eines Medienereignisses. Opladen: Westdeutscher Verlag. 1982.
*Keywords:* Holocaust (Television Program) – Public Opinion/Holocaust, Jewish (1939–1945) – Public Opinion/Public Opinion – Germany, West

Ahren, Yizhak, Stig Hornshoj-Moller, and Christoph B Melchers. Der Ewige Jude: Wie Goebbels hetzte. Untersuchungen zum nationalsozialistischen Propagandafilm. Aachen: Alano. 1990.
*Keywords:* Ewige Jude (Motion Picture)/Antisemitism in Motion Pictures/Antisemitism – Germany/Motion Pictures – Germany – History

Arbeitsgruppe "Cinematographie des Holocaust". Die Vergangenheit in der Gegenwart: Konfrontationen mit den Folgen des Holocaust im Deutschen Nachkriegsfilm. Tagung (1999: Frankfurt am Main, Germany), and Deutsches Filminstitut, DIF. München: Edition Text + Kritik. 2001.
*Keywords:* Holocaust, Jewish (1939–1945), in Motion Pictures Congresses/Motion Pictures – Germany Congresses/Holocaust, Jewish (1939–1945) – Germany – Influence Congresses

Avisar, Ilan. The Aesthetics and Politics of the Holocaust Film. Dissertation Indiana University. Ann Arbor MI. 1986.
*Keywords:* Holocaust, Jewish (1939–1945), in Motion Pictures

——. Screening the Holocaust: Cinema's Images of the Unimaginable. Bloomington: Indiana University Press. 1988.
*Keywords:* Holocaust, Jewish (1939–1945), in Motion Pictures

Barthel, Manfred. So war es wirklich: Der deutsche Nachkriegsfilm. München: Herbig. 1986.
*Keywords:* Motion Pictures – Germany (West) – History

Bartov, Omer. Murder in Our Midst: The Holocaust, Industrial Killing, and Representation. New York: Oxford University Press. 1996.
*Keywords:* Holocaust, Jewish (1939–1945) – Historiography/Holocaust, Jewish (1939–1945), in Motion Pictures/Holocaust, Jewish (1939–1945) – Museums/Genocide/Industrial Killing

Bauer, Barbara, and Waltraud Strickhausen. "Für ein Kind war das anders": Traumatische Erfahrungen jüdischer Kinder und Jugendlicher im Nationalsozialistischen Deutschland. Berlin: Metropol. 1999.
*Keywords:* Jewish Children – Germany/Jewish Children in the Holocaust/Holocaust, Jewish (1939–1945), in Art/Holocaust, Jewish (1939–1945), in Literature/Holocaust, Jewish (1939–1945), in Motion Pictures

454

Bernard-Donals, Michael F, and Richard R Glejzer. Between Witness and Testimony: The Holocaust and the Limits of Representaion. Albany: State University of New York Press. 2001.
*Keywords:* Holocaust, Jewish (1939–1945) – Personal Narratives – History and Criticism/Holocaust, Jewish (1939–1945) – Influence/ Holocaust, Jewish (1939–1945) – Psychological Aspects/Holocaust, Jewish (1939–1945), in Literature/Holocaust, Jewish (1939–1945), in Motion Pictures

Bessen, Ursula. Trümmer und Träume: Nachkriegszeit und Fünfziger Jahre auf Zelluloid. Deutsche Spielfilme als Zeugnisse ihrer Zeit. Eine Dokumentation. Bochum: Studienverlag Dr N. Brockmeyer. 1989.
*Keywords:* Motion Pictures – Germany (West) – History/Motion Pictures – Germany – Bochum – History

Bliersbach, Gerhard. So grün war die Heide: Der deutsche Nachkriegsfilm in neuer Sicht. Weinheim: Beltz. 1985.
*Keywords:* Motion Pictures – Germany (West) – History

Bongartz, Barbara. Von Caligari zu Hitler, von Hitler zu Dr. Mabuse? Eine psychologische Geschichte des deutschen Films von 1946 bis 1960. Münster: MakS Publikationen. 1992.
*Keywords:* Motion Pictures – Germany History/Motion Pictures – Germany – Psychological Aspects/National Characteristics, German, in Motion Pictures

Bunk, Willi. Zeitgeschichte im Film: Arbeitsheft zur Schulfernsehreihe des SFB "Fragen an die Deutsche Geschichte". Berlin: Colloquium Verlag. 1974.
*Keywords:* Television and History/Germany – History – 20th Century – Outlines, Syllabi, etc./Germany – History – 20th Century – Motion Pictures

Classen, Christoph. Bilder der Vergangenheit: Die Zeit des National-sozialismus im Fernsehen der Bundesrepublik Deutschland 1955–1965 Köln: Böhlau. 1999.
*Keywords:* Television Programs Germany (West) – History/Television – Germany (West) – History/National Socialism – Historiography/ Holocaust, Jewish (1939–1945) – Historiography/Germany (West) – Intellectual Life

Cole, Tim. Images of the Holocaust: the Myth of the "Shoah Business". London: Duckworth. 1999.
*Keywords:* Holocaust Memorials/Holocaust, Jewish (1939–1945) – Influence/Holocaust, Jewish (1939–1945) – Public Opinion/Holocaust, Jewish (1939–1945) – Psychological Aspects/Holocaust, Jewish (1939–1945) – in Mass Media – History

Daly, Peter M. Building History: The Shoah in Art, Memory, and Myth. New York: P. Lang. 2001.
*Keywords:* Holocaust, Jewish (1939–1945) – Influence – Congresses/ Holocaust, Jewish (1939–1945), in Motion Pictures Congresses/ Holocaust, Jewish (1939–1945) – Study and Teaching Congresses/ Kristallnacht, 1938

Doneson, Judith E. The Holocaust in American Film. Syracuse NY: Syracuse University Press. 2002.
*Keywords:* Holocaust, Jewish (1939–1945), in Motion Pictures/ Antisemitism in Motion Pictures/Jews in Motion Pictures/Motion Pictures – United States

Fensch, Thomas. Oskar Schindler and his List: the Man, the Book, the Film, the Holocaust and its Survivors. Forest Dale VT: Paul S. Eriksson. 1995.
*Keywords:* Schindler, Oskar, 1908–1974/Keneally, Thomas Schindler's List/Schindler, Oskar, 1908–1974 – in Literature/Spielberg, Steven, 1947/Schindler's List (Motion Picture)/Righteous Gentiles in the Holocaust – Poland – Krakow – Biography/Holocaust, Jewish (1939–1945), in Literature/Holocaust, Jewish (1939–1945), in Motion Pictures/Holocaust Survivors

Flanzbaum, Hilene. The Americanization of the Holocaust. Baltimore MD: Johns Hopkins University Press. 1999.
*Keywords:* Holocaust, Jewish (1939–1945) – Foreign Public Opinion, American/Holocaust, Jewish (1939–1945) – Moral and Ethical Aspects – United States/Holocaust, Jewish (1939–1945), in Literature/Holocaust, Jewish (1939–1945), in Motion Pictures/Public Opinion – United States

Fohrmann, Jürgen, Klaus L. Berghahn, and Helmut J. Schneider. Kulturelle Repräsentationen des "Holocaust" in Deutschland und den Vereinigten Staaten. New York: P. Lang. 2002.
*Keywords:* Schindler's List (Motion Picture)/Holocaust, Jewish (1939–1945), in Motion Pictures Congresses/Holocaust, Jewish (1939–1945), in Literature – Congresses

Gundelsheimer, Erwin, Frank Ostermann, Heino Mass, Friedrich Knilli, and Siegfried Zielinski. Betrifft, "Holocaust": Zuschauer schreiben an den WDR: Ein Projektbericht. Westdeutscher Rundfunk, and Technische Universität Berlin. Berlin: V. Spiess. 1983.
*Keywords:* Holocaust (Television Program)/Holocaust, Jewish (1939–1945) – Public Opinion/Public Opinion – Germany, West/Television Programs – Germany (West) – Rating

Heinzlmeier, Adolf. Nachkriegsfilm und Nazifilm: Anmerkungen zu einem deutschen Thema. Frankfurt am Main: Frankfurter Bund für Volksbildung GmbH. 1988.
*Keywords:* Motion Pictures – Germany – History/Motion Pictures – Germany – Plots, Themes, etc./National Socialism and Motion Pictures

Heller, Heinz-B., and Peter Zimmermann. Bilderwelten, Weltbilder: Dokumentarfilm und Fernsehen. Marburg: Hitzeroth. 1990.
*Keywords:* Documentary Films – Germany (West) – History and Criticism – Congresses/Documentary Television Programs – Germany (West) – History – Congresses

Hickethier, Knut, and Peter Hoff. Geschichte des deutschen Fernsehens. Stuttgart: Verlag J. B. Metzler. 1998.
*Keywords:* Television Broadcasting – Germany – History/Television – Germany – History

Insdorf, Annette. L'Holocauste à L'Ecran. [Paris]: Cerf. 1985.
*Keywords:* Holocaust, Jewish (1939–1945), in Motion Pictures

——. Indelible Shadows: Film and the Holocaust. Cambridge, New York: Cambridge University Press. 1989.
*Keywords:* Holocaust, Jewish (1939–1945), in Motion Pictures

Johnson, Mary, and Margot Stern Strom. Facing History and Ourselves: Elements of Time. Facing History and Ourselves National Foundation. Brookline, Mass: Facing History and Ourselves. 1989.
*Keywords:* Holocaust, Jewish (1939–1945) – Study and Teaching/Holocaust, Jewish (1939–1945), in Motion Pictures

Joos, Rudolf, Isolde I. Mozer, and Richard Stang. Deutsche Geschichte ab 1945: Zwischen Vergangenheitsbewältigung und utopischen Entwürfen: Filmanalytische Materialien. Gemeinschaftswerk der Evangelischen Publizistik (Germany). Frankfurt am Main: Gemeinschaftswerk der Evangelischen Publizistik. 1990.
*Keywords:* Motion Pictures and History/Historical Films – Germany – History and Criticism/Motion Pictures – Germany – History

Kaes, Anton. Deutschlandbilder: Die Wiederkehr der Geschichte als Film. München: Edition Text + Kritik. 1987.

——. From Hitler to Heimat: The Return of History as Film. Harvard University Press. 1989.
*Keywords:* Motion Pictures – Germany (West) – History/Motion Picture Producers and Directors – Germany (West)/Motion Picture Plays – History and Criticism/Motion Pictures and History

Kansteiner, Wulf. Television and the Historization of National Socialism in the Federal Republic of Germany: The Programs of the Zweite Deutsche Fernsehen Between 1963 and 1993. UCLA. 1997

*Select Bibliography*

*Keywords:* Zweites Deutsches Fernsehen/Television and History –
Germany (West)/National Socialism/Television Programs – Germany
(West)/Dissertations, Academic – UCLA – History
Karpf, Ernst, Doron Kiesel, and Karsten Visarius. "Getürkte Bilder": Zur
Inszenierung von Fremden im Film. Marburg: Schuren. 1995.
*Keywords:* Aliens in Motion Pictures/Motion Pictures – Germany –
History
Kluge, Alexander, and Alf Brustellin. Bestandsaufnahme, Utopie Film:
Zwanzig Jahre neuer deutscher Film/Mitte 1983. Frankfurt am Main:
Zweitausendeins. 1983.
*Keywords:* Motion Pictures – Germany (West) – History
Knilli, Friedrich, and Siegfried Zielinski. Holocaust zur Unterhaltung:
Anatomie eines Internationalen Bestsellers: Fakten, Fotos, Forschungs-
reportagen. Berlin: Verlag für Ausbildung und Studium. 1982.
*Keywords:* Holocaust (Television Program)
Knopp, Guido, and Siegfried Quandt. Geschichte im Fernsehen: Ein
Handbuch. Darmstadt: Wissenschaftliche Buchgesellschaft. 1988.
*Keywords:* Historical Television Programs – Germany (West)/Televi-
sion Broadcasting – Germany (West)/Television and History
Koch, Gertrud. Die Einstellung ist die Einstellung: Visuelle Konstruk-
tionen des Judentums. Frankfurt am Main: Suhrkamp. 1992.
*Keywords:* Jews in Motion Pictures/Holocaust, Jewish (1939–1945), in
Motion Pictures/Yiddish Films – History and Criticism
Krah, Hans. Geschichte(n): NS-Film, NS-Spuren heute. Kiel: Ludwig.
1999.
*Keywords:* National Socialism and Motion Pictures/Motion Pictures –
Germany – History
Kramer, Sven. Auschwitz im Widerstreit: Zur Darstellung der Shoah in
Film, Philosophie und Literatur. Wiesbaden: Deutscher Universitäts-
Verlag. 1999.
*Keywords:* Levi, Primo – Criticism and Interpretation/Holocaust,
Jewish (1939–1945), in Motion Pictures/Holocaust, Jewish (1939–
1945) – Influence
Krankenhagen, Stefan. Auschwitz Darstellen: Ästhetische Positionen
zwischen Adorno, Spielberg und Walser. Köln: Böhlau. 2001.
*Keywords:* Adorno, Theodor W., 1903–1969/Walser, Martin, 1927/
Auschwitz (Concentration Camp)/Holocaust, Jewish (1939–1945), in
Literature/Holocaust, Jewish (1939–1945), in Motion Pictures
Kraus, Petra. Deutschland Im Herbst: Terrorismus Im Film. Münchner
Filmzentrum: Münchner Filmzentrum. 1997.

## Select Bibliography

*Keywords:* Deutschland Im Herbst (Motion Picture)/Motion Pictures –
Germany – History/Terrorism – Germany – Drama
Kurowski, Ulrich, and Thomas Brandlmeier. Nicht mehr fliehen: Das
Kino der Ära Adenauer. [München]: Münchner Filmzentrum. 1981.
*Keywords:* Motion Pictures – Germany (West) – History/Motion
Pictures – Germany (West) – Reviews
Lewis, Stephen, and Aron Appelfeld. Art Out of Agony: The Holocaust
Theme in Literature, Sculpture and Film. Montreal, New York: CBC
Enterprises/les Enterprises Radio-Canada. 1984.
*Keywords:* Holocaust, Jewish (1939–1945), in Literature/Holocaust,
Jewish (1939–1945), in Art/Holocaust, Jewish (1939–1945), in Motion
Pictures
Lichtenstein, Heiner, and Michael Schmid-Ospach. Holocaust: Briefe an
den WDR. Westdeutscher Rundfunk. Wuppertal: P. Hammer. 1982.
*Keywords:* Holocaust (Television Program) – Public Opinion/Holo-
caust, Jewish (1939–1945) – Public Opinion/Public Opinion – Germ-
any, West
Loshitzky, Yosefa. Spielberg's Holocaust: Critical Perspectives on
Schindler's List. Bloomington: Indiana University Press. 1997.
*Keywords:* Schindler's List (Motion Picture)/Holocaust, Jewish (1939–
1945), in Motion Pictures
Lowy, Vincent. L'Histoire Infilmable: Les Camps d'Extermination Nazis
à L'Ecran. Paris: Harmattan. 2001.
*Keywords:* Holocaust, Jewish (1939–1945), in Motion Pictures
Mintz, Alan L. Popular Culture and the Shaping of Holocaust Memory in
America. Seattle WA: University of Washington Press. 2001.
*Keywords:* Judgment at Nuremberg (Motion Picture)/Pawnbroker
(Motion Picture)/Schindler's List (Motion Picture)/Holocaust, Jewish
(1939–1945) – Foreign Public Opinion, American/Holocaust, Jewish
(1939–1945) – Influence/Holocaust, Jewish (1939–1945) – Histori-
ography/Holocaust, Jewish (1939–1945), in Motion Pictures/Jews –
United States – Attitudes/Public Opinion – United States
Munz-Koenen, Ingeborg. Fernsehdramatik: Experimente, Methoden,
Tendenzen: Ihre Entwicklung in den Sechziger Jahren. Berlin: Akademie-
Verlag. 1974.
*Keywords:* Television Plays, German – Germany (East) – History and
Criticism
Murray, Bruce Arthur, and Chris Wickham. Framing the Past: The
Historiography of German Cinema and Television. Carbondale IL:
Southern Illinois University Press. 1992.

*Keywords:* Motion Pictures – Germany – History/Historical Films – Germany – History and Criticism/Motion Pictures in Historiography/ Television Broadcasting – Germany – History/Television and History

Pflaum, Hans Günther, and Heinz Müller. Film in der BRD. Berlin: Henschelverlag. 1990.
*Keywords:* Motion Pictures – Germany (West)/Motion Pictures – Germany (West) – Biography

Pleyer, Peter. Deutscher Nachkriegsfilm 1946–1948. Münster: Fahle. 1965.
*Keywords:* Motion Pictures – Germany – History

Rabinbach, Anson, and Jack David Zipes. Germans and Jews Since the Holocaust: The Changing Situation in West Germany. New York: Holmes & Meier. 1986.
*Keywords:* Holocaust (Television Program)/Jews – Germany (West)/ Holocaust, Jewish (1939–1945) – Public Opinion/Public Opinion – Germany, West/Antisemitism – Germany/Germany (West) – Ethnic Relations

Santner, Eric L. Stranded Objects: Mourning, Memory, and Film in Postwar Germany. Ithaca NY: Cornell University Press. 1990.
*Keywords:* Reitz, Edgar – Criticism and Interpretation/Syberberg, Hans Jurgen, 1935- – Criticism and Interpretation/Motion Pictures – Germany (West) – History/Motion Pictures – Social Aspects – Germany (West)/World War, 1939–1945 – Motion Pictures and the War/ Holocaust, Jewish (1939–1945), in Motion Pictures/Germany – History – 1945–1955

Scherpe, Klaus R., and Manuel Koppen. Bilder des Holocaust: Literatur, Film, Bildende Kunst. Köln: Böhlau. 1997.
*Keywords:* German Literature – 20th Century – History and Criticism/ Holocaust, Jewish (1939–1945), in Literature/Holocaust, Jewish (1939–1945), in Motion Pictures/Holocaust, Jewish (1939–1945), in Art

Seidl, Claudius. Der Deutsche Film Der Fünfziger Jahre. München: W. Heyne. 1987.
*Keywords:* Motion Pictures – Germany – History

Siedler, Joachim. "Holocaust": Die Fernsehserie in Der Deutschen Presse: Eine Inhalts- Und Verlaufsanalyse Am Beispiel Ausgewählter Printmedien. Münster: LIT. 1984.
*Keywords:* Holocaust (Television Program)/Holocaust, Jewish (1939– 1945) – Public Opinion/Press – Germany (West)/Public Opinion – Germany, West

Spieker, Markus. Hollywood unterm Hakenkreuz: Der amerikanische Spielfilm im Dritten Reich. Trier: Wissenschaftlicher Verlag. 1999.
*Keywords:* Motion Pictures, American – Germany – History

Steinmetz, Rudiger, and Helfried Spitra. Dokumentarfilm als "Zeichen der Zeit": Vom Ansehen der Wirklichkeit im Fernsehen. München: Olschläger. 1989.
*Keywords:* Documentary Television Programs – Germany (West) – History – Congresses

Thiele, Martina. Publizistische Kontroversen über den Holocaust im Film. Münster: Lit. 2001.
*Keywords:* Holocaust, Jewish (1939–1945), in Motion Pictures/Film Criticism – Germany

Trimborn, Jürgen. Fernsehen der Neunziger: Die deutsche Fernsehlandschaft seit der Etablierung des Privatfernsehens. Köln: Teiresias. 1999.
*Keywords:* Television – Germany – History – 20th Century/Television Programs – Germany – History

Weiss, Christoph. "Der Gute Deutsche": Dokumente zur Diskussion um Steven Spielbergs "Schindlers Liste" in Deutschland. St. Ingbert: Röhrig. 1995.
*Keywords:* Schindler's List (Motion Picture)/Holocaust, Jewish (1939–1945), in Motion Pictures/Motion Pictures – Germany – Reviews

Wenzel, Eike. Gedächtnisraum Film: Die Arbeit an der deutschen Geschichte in Filmen seit den 60er Jahren. Stuttgart: Metzler. 2000
*Keywords:* Motion Pictures – Germany – History/Germany – in Motion Pictures

Westermann, Barbel. Nationale Identität im Spielfilm der Fünfziger Jahre. Frankfurt am Main, New York: Peter Lang. 1990.
*Keywords:* National Characteristics, German, in Motion Pictures – History/Motion Pictures – Germany – Plots, Themes, etc. – History

Wiebel, Martin. Deutschland auf der Mattscheibe: Die Geschichte der Bundesrepublik im Fernsehspiel. Frankfurt am Main: Verlag der Autoren. 1999.
*Keywords:* Television Broadcasting – Germany – History/Television Programs – Germany – History

Zielinski, Siegfried. Audiovisionen: Kino und Fernsehen als Zwischenspiele in der Geschichte. Reinbek bei Hamburg: Rowohlt. 1989.
*Keywords:* Television – History/Television – Germany – History/Motion Pictures – History/Television – Forecasting

———. Audiovisions: Cinema and Television as Entr'actes in History. Amsterdam: Amsterdam University Press. 1999.
*Keywords:* Television – History/Television – Germany – History/Motion Pictures – History/Television – Forecasting

# Index of Names

# Index of Names

# Index of Places

## Index of Places